SELECTED TOUR COMMENTRIES
FOR CHINA'S FAMOUS TOURIST ATTRACTIONS

中國著名旅遊景區

導遊詞 >>精選

← 王浪 主編

英漢對照

（大中原地區）

>>1部書 >>2種語言 >>3個地區

>>18個省、市、自治區及特別行政區

>> 81個著名景觀點

崧燁文化

目錄

前言

　　人們常說：「一個出色的導遊帶來一次成功的旅遊活動」，「江山美不美，全憑導遊一張嘴」。實踐也表明，一個地方導遊素質、能力水平的高低和導遊服務質量的好壞，會直接影響到該區域旅遊業的總體形象和可持續發展。高質量的導遊服務亦需要高質量的導遊人才，高質量的導遊人才的培養則需要高質量的導遊圖書。而市面上的導遊外語用書基本都是針對某個具體省份的，針對全中國旅遊景區（點）編寫的參考書尚不多見。正是基於這樣的宗旨，我們編寫了《中國著名旅遊景區導遊詞精選》（英漢對照）一書，以滿足旅行社經營管理人員、導遊人員及外國朋友希望瞭解全中國旅遊景區（點）訊息的需要。

　　本書以中國地理區域為依據，將全書劃分為華北地區、華東地區、中南地區三個部分（另一本《中國著名旅遊景區導遊詞精選：英漢對照（邊陲地區）》收錄有西南地區、西北地區、東北地區以及港澳台地區四個部分）。每個地區又以省（直轄市、自治區和特別行政區）為單位具體介紹其區域範圍內的景區景點。本書所選景區（點）以綜合知名度較高的景區（點），作為本書的主要收錄內容。

　　本書對每個區域的介紹主要包含以下三項內容，即，本省（市、自治區）簡介、知名旅遊城市簡介和精選景區（點）導遊詞。各篇導遊詞內容豐富生動，融故事、神話、歷史和景點介紹為一體，並特別注重語言的口語化和親和力。為方便讀者使用本書，所有導遊詞均採用英漢對照形式。本書希望能最大程度地向讀者呈現中國豐富多樣的旅遊資源以及這些旅遊資源所積澱的民族特色文化，為推動國際間的跨文化傳播、弘揚中華民族的優秀文化，稍盡綿薄之力。

　　本書集中國著名旅遊景區（點）導遊詞於一冊，南北西東，包羅萬象，希望能為中國的旅遊文化傳播添磚加瓦。同時，也因為本書收錄內容涉及面較寬，而各區域景區（點）資源尚處於不斷組合變化之中，某些景區（點）訊息難免與最新的情況有所出入，敬望廣大讀者在使用過程中予以建議和反饋，以便使本書內容修訂再版時更加完善成熟。

王浪

Part I North China 華北地區

☆Beijing Municipality（北京市）

☆Tianjin Municipality（天津市）

☆Shanxi Province（山西省）

☆Hebei Province（河北省）

☆Inner Mongolian Autonomous Region（內蒙古自治區）

Beijing Municipality北京市

A Glimpse of the Municipality （本市簡介）

Beijing is China's capital and political center. It is also one of China's leading cultural and economic centers, as well as a major transportation hub and magnet for tourism and international exchange. These characteristics combine to give the city an international cosmopolitan flavor.

Beijing is located at 39° 56´ north latitude and 116° 20´ east longitude.It is bordered by Taihang Mountain to the west and Yanshan Mountain in the north.The Bohai Sea lies to the east, while North China Plain lies south of the city. Beijing thus serves as a pivot, connecting the northeast, the northwest and the central plain in China. Its geographical shape resembles a bay, which is how it got its ancient name, "Beijing Bay". The city consists of 16 districts and 2 counties and was China's first self-governing municipality to come directly under central government authority.

Tourism Resource

People started living in Beijing 70,000 years ago. It was then called Jicheng and was located in the Yan kingdom, which was one of the seven powerful ducal states during the so-called War States period, which lasted from 475 to 221 B.C. in Chinese history. The city was renamed, Youzhou in Tang Dynasty, Dadu in Yuan Dynasty, and then Dijing in the Ming and Qing dynasties. Modern Beijing has experienced nearly ten successive dynasties, giving the city historical and cultural sites. These include the world's largest imperial palace—the Forbidden City, the largest temple—the Temple of Heaven, the rarely seen royal garden—the Summer Palace, the Great Wall of China—one of the eight wonders of the world, the world's largest ancient tomb group—the Thirteen Ming Tombs, and the Zhoukoudian Peking Man Site, all of which have been listed by UNESCO as world cultural heritage.

Beijing also has some very famous religious buildings. These include the Tanzhe Monastery, which is the biggest and the best among the ancient architectural examples. The Cattle Street Mosque has the longest history among all of Beijing's many mosques, while the Yonghe Palace is the city's biggest Tibetan Buddhist temple. The Dajue Temple is Beijing's biggest Xishan Temple—there are some 300 such temples in the city—and the White Cloud Taoist Temple, built by imperial order, was once the most influential Taoist temple in the capital. The Jietai Monastery was built in Liao Dynasty architectural style and the Hongluo Temple is known as the "No.1 temple in the northern part of Beijing". Of course Beijing also boasts the grand and imposing Tian'anmen Square, the North Sea Royal Garden, beautiful Fragrant Hill Park, the Purple Bamboo Park(Zizhuyuan Park), Yuyuantan Park, and other major scenic spots. These places are not religious buildings, but are among the city's best and most interesting places to visit.

In Beijing you can see and experience not only the ancient China's majesty, grandeur, and ups and downs throughout history, but also the busy downtown of contemporary Beijing, with all of its hustle and bustle and modern-day conveniences. When you set your foot in Beijing, you can feel the bustling atmosphere right away. With the 29th Olympic Games in 2008, Beijing once again demonstrated her enchanting charisma to the whole world.

Peking Cuisine and Local Snacks

Beijing dishes are cooked in various ways of tasty and inviting cooking methods, such as baking, bursting, burning, stewing, and swilling.Beijing's local specialties have a history of more than 600 years and include over 300 dishes, like Han Chinese and Hui specialty snacks, special food prepared for the emperor, and the like. All Beijing restaurants have a team of professional chefs. There are also French, American, Italian, and Russian restaurants, as well as Japanese, Korean, Vietnamese, Indonesian, and Thai cuisine. If you want to save your time and money, you can eat delicious snacks in the small stores on the street. Such places always have lots of Beijing's buns, dumplings, noodles and home-style dishes for sale. The local dishes and snacks include roast meat, Wang Zhihe fermented bean curd, Beijing grilled duck, swilled mutton, all fish dinner, Crystal Palace pudding, shredded pork head in soy sauce, Haihong shark's fins, jellied bean curd, spicy hare meat, and the like.

Attraction Recommendation

Tian'anmen Square lies in the center of Beijing. It is rectangular in shape and is 500 meters wide from east to west and 880 meters long from north to south and can accommodate up to hundreds of thousands of people. As the largest square in the world, it attracts everyone who visits Beijing and thousands of tourists and residents come here to see raising and lowering of the national flag ceremony and to take pictures of it and the square.

The Forbidden City served as the royal palace of the Ming and Qing dynasties, and

24 emperors once lived there over a period of 500 years. Constructed from 1406 to 1420, covering an area of 720,000 square meters, it is the largest and best preserved ancient palace in the world.

The Great Wall is one of the seven architectural wonders of the world.It streches 6,350 kilometers from the Yalu River in the east to the Jiayu Pass in the far west.Some of the Great Wall's most famous sec-tions, such as Badaling, Jinshanling, Mutianyu and Simatai, are located in the Beijing area.

Constructed in 1750, the Summer Palace was originally the abode and imperial garden of the Qing emperors, but was destroyed in 1860 by British and French troops during the Second Opium War. In 1888 Empress Dowager built a new Summer Palace, using money that had been budgeted for the Chinese Navy. The new Summer Palace consists of Mt.Wanshou, Kunming Lake and imperial chambers and it is one of the most famous four palaces. Its gardens represent a high point in Chinese gardening art and are famous not just in China, but overseas as well.

The Temple of Heaven was where the Qing emperors offered sacrifices to Heaven and prayed for good harvests. It was built in 1420, the 18th year of the Yongle's Reign of the Ming Dynasty.and it is the largest ancient temple complex in both China and the entire world.

北京，中華人民共和國的首都，全國政治、文化、交通、旅遊和國際交往的中心，位於北緯39°56´，東經116°20´，西擁太行、北枕燕山，東臨渤海，南面華北大平原，是連接中國東北、西北和中原的樞紐，由於形似「海灣」，故自古就有「北京灣」之稱。全市由16個區和2個縣組成，為中國四大直轄市之首。

旅遊資源

70萬年前，北京人在這裡繁衍生息，然後延續至燕之薊城，又從燕之薊城到唐之幽州，再從元之大都至明清之帝京。如今的北京歷經數十個朝代的經營，擁有眾多輝煌的帝都景觀和豐厚濃郁的文化底蘊，世界最大的皇宮故宮、中國最大的祭天神廟天壇、世所罕見的皇家園林頤和園、世界八大奇蹟之一的長城、北京最大的古墓群明十三陵和周口店北京猿人遺址都已被聯合國教科文組織列入世界文化遺產。

此外，北京的宗教建築也是赫赫有名。潭柘寺是北京古建築中最精美、最大的，牛街禮拜寺是北京地區歷史最悠久的清真寺，雍和宮是北京地區最大的一座藏傳佛教寺院，大覺寺是「西山三百寺之巨剎」，白雲觀曾是道教全真派的宮觀，戒台寺是一座具有遼代建築風格的寺廟，紅螺寺是「京北第一古剎」…… 當然，還有氣勢非凡的天安門、皇家花園北海、景色秀麗的香山公園、竹林遍地的紫竹院、環境幽雅的玉淵潭等。這些雖非宗教建築，但也都極具北京特色。

來到北京，看到的、感受到的不僅是古老帝都的雄偉莊嚴、厚重滄桑，還有現代大都市的時尚繁華、高速便捷。濃重的現代化氣息在剛踏進北京城時就已撲面而來了，伴隨著2008年第29屆奧運會的舉行，北京再一次將它迷人的魅力展現在全世界人面前。

風味美食

京菜擅長烤、爆、燒、燜、涮，聽起來豪爽，吃起來痛快。北京風味小吃有600多年的歷史，包括漢民風味小吃、回民風味小吃和宮廷風味小吃等300多種。北京的各大飯店歷來是名廚薈萃，還有正宗的法式、美式、意式、俄式餐廳和日本料理、韓國燒烤以及越南、印度尼西亞、泰國風味的菜館。若為了省時實惠，還可以光顧街頭小店，這裡不乏具有北京特色的包子、餃子、麵條及家常炒菜，當然，環境就不如大餐館講究了。當地小吃還有：烤肉、王致和臭豆腐、北京烤鴨、宮廷御膳「老唐烤雞」、天福號醬肘子、涮羊肉、火鍋、全魚宴、水晶門釘、醬豬頭肉、海紅魚唇、豆腐腦兒、五香野兔等。

主要推薦景點

天安門廣場　位於城區中心，東西寬500米，南北長880米，可容納幾十萬人舉行盛大集會、遊行，是世界上最大的廣場。這裡是中外遊客必遊的勝地，每天都有大量遊人來這裡遊覽、攝影和參觀早、晚的升、降旗儀式。

故宮博物院　　原為明清兩代的皇宮，共有24個皇帝在此居住，統治中國近500年。故宮建於1406～1420年。占地72　萬平方米，是世界上現存規模最大，最完整的古代宮殿建築群。

長城是　世界古代七大建築奇蹟之一，它東起鴨綠江，西至嘉峪關，全長6350千米。北京地區有八達嶺長城和金山嶺長城、慕田峪長城和司馬台長城等。

頤和園　　原為清代皇帝的行宮和御苑。始建於1750年，1860年被英法聯軍所毀。1888年，慈禧太后挪用海軍經費重建，改稱頤和園。它主要由萬壽山、昆明湖和宮廷區組成，為中國四大名園之一，在中外園藝藝術上有極高的地位。

天壇　原為明、清帝王祭天祈谷之處，始建於明永樂十八年（公元1420 年），是中國現存最大的古代壇廟建築群。

Tian'anmen Square and Rostrum （天安門廣場及城樓）

Ladies and gentlemen,

Good morning! Welcome to Beijing. I am very glad to be your tour guide today. First of all, I'd like to take this opportunity to introduce myself to you all. (Introduce yourself to the guests.) Well, if you have any problems or special interests, please don't hesitate to let me know.I will do my best to make your visit as pleasant as possible. We are now going to pay a visit to the world famous Tian'anmen Square and Rostrum. Please follow me!

Monument to the People's Heroes

Please look ahead! In the center of the Tian'anmen Square is the Monument to the People's Heroes. It symbolizes the people's commemoration of revolutionary martyrs.It has demonstrated the heroic struggles of the Chinese people against enemies at home and abroad and reminds them of the source of today's happy life.

The Monument to the People's Heroes was built to commemorate heroes who have sacrificed their lives in the revolutionary struggles since 1840. The Monument faces the Tian'anmen Gate. The front of the obelisk bears the inscription "People's heroes are immortal" in the late Chairman Mao Zedong's handwriting. On the back side, the inscription was composed by the late Chairman Mao and handwritten by the late Premier Zhou Enlai.It reads, "Eternal glory to the people's heroes who laid down their lives in the people's war of liberation and the people's revolution over the past 3 years! Eternal glory to the people's heroes who laid down their lives in the people's liberation war and people's revolution over the past 30 years! Eternal glory to the people's heroes who laid down their lives in the struggles against enemies at home and abroad to strive for the national independence and people's liberty and happiness since 1840."

On September 30, 1949, the first session of the General Assembly of the Chinese People's Political Consultative Conference adopted the resolution to build a monument to the people's heroes who sacrificed their lives for the country on Beijing's Tian'anmen Square in the capital. At 6 p.m. of that same day, all delegates attending the meeting took part in the foundation ceremony of the Monument. The late Chairman Mao laid the foundation for the Monument himself. Construction began in 1952 and was completed on May 1, 1958.

The body of the Monument is built with 413

Recommendations regarding the Monuments design were sought from architectural and art circles all across China. The final design plan was been reviewed several times before being approved, so it can be seen as the fruit of collective wisdom. The Monument covers an area of 3,100 square meters. It is 37.94 meters high, or 4.07 meters higher than the Tiananmen Gat e.The base is composed of double platforMs.The lower part takes the shape of flowering crabapple and is surrounded by white marble railings and staircases. The base is 61.54 meters long from north to south, and 50.44 meters wide from east to west. The tablet stone is supported by a base decorated with 8 huge bas-reliefs engraved on white marble. The bas-reliefs have demonstrated the revolutionary history in the past 100 plus years. Starting from the east in historical sequence are "Destruction of Opium in Humen", "Jintian Uprising", "May 4th Movement", "May 30th Movement", "Nanchang Uprising", "Wuchang Uprising", "Anti-Japanese Guerrilla War", and "Triumphant Crossing of the Yangtze River". On both sides of the "Triumphant Crossing of the Yangtze River" are two pieces of decorative bas-reliefs, "Supporting the Front-line" and "Welcoming the People's Liberation Army". The bas-relief is 2 meters high, 2 to 6.4 meters wide and 40.68 meters long. There are more than 170 heroic figures depitcted in different postures and expressions. The upper level is surrounded by 8 pieces of flower patterns decorated with chrysanthemums, lotuses, and lilies, symbolizing peoples memory and respect for the revolutionary martyrs noble qualit y.The two sides of the tablet stone are decorated with designs of five stars, pine and cypress trees, and flags. The top of the Monument is designed in traditional style.Its design, handwriting, bas-reliefs and decorative patterns all boast distinctive themes, strict and simple structures, excellent engravings and vivid figures.It is a master piece which took highly skilled sculptors and craftsmen 5 year to complete.It has praised as reflecting the historic achievements made by the peoples heroes and will forever inspire our people to march forward. pieces of different-sized granite stones in 32 layers. The stone in the center is 14.7 meters long, 2.9 meters wide and 1 meter thick.It weighs 60 tons. This huge piece of granite stone was transported to Beijing from Qingdao in Shandong Province, where it was quarried.Another 17,000 pieces of stones in different sizes were used in the building of the Monument. The stones are clear and bright in colors which make the Monument look solemn and elegant. The stones are mostly from Fangshan in Beijing and Tai'an in Shandong Province.

The Monument stands in the center of the Tian'anmen Square. It is not only eulogizes the great and everlasting achievements of the people's heroes, but also is a great and lasting artistic and architectural treasure.

The Monument is a place where people's heroes are memorized and where people are inspired to work hard. On January 8th, 1976, the late Premier Zhou Enlai passed away. On April 5th, thousands and thousands of people gathered in front of the Monument voluntarily to mourn over the death of Premier Zhou Enlai, which gave rise to the "April 5thMovement" denouncing the "Gang of Four".

Now, everyday thousands and thousands of people come here to pay respect to the people's heroes. People come here for commemorative activities to show their respect for and memory of the revolutionary martyrs. A lot of foreign state leaders have come here to present floral wreaths while they are visiting China.

A Bird's-eye View of the Tian'anmen Square from the Rostrum

[On the Rostrum] Now we are on the Tian'anmen Rostrum, an ideal place to get a bird's-eye view of Tian'anmen Square.Located in the center of Beijing proper and first built in 1417, Tian'anmen Square was originally named Cheng-tianmen(Gate of Heavenly Succession), which means being endowed with power from the heaven and succumbing to Providence. The Gate was burned down by Li Zicheng's peasant uprising at the end of Ming Dynasty.The Gate was renamed Tian'anmen(Gate of Heavenly Peace) after being renovated in 1651. The Rostrum is 33.7 meters high. There are nine bays from east to west and five bays from north to south.The figures "nine" and "five" were to reflect the highly-exalted status of the Emperor. In the Ming and Qing dynasties, the Gate was the place where the Emperor promulgated imperial edicts. Now please look down. Below the Rostrum is the Golden Water River, spanned by five exquisite marble bridges; hence the name Golden Water Bridges. Guarded by elegant columns, the Rostrum is an exquisite piece of architecture.

Please look ahead.This is the world-famous Tian'anmen Square. The Square is 880 meters long from north to south and 500 meters wide from east to west, with an area of 400,000 square meters(40 hectares). It is currently the largest square in the world and can accommodate hundreds of thousands of people.

Northernmost in the Square and also the place where we are presently standing is the magnificent Tian'anmen Rostrum. In the north of the Square flies the National Flag of the People's Republic of China. The Monument to the People's Heroes stands in the center of the Square. South of the Monument is the solemn Chairman Mao Memorial Hall. The southernmost part of the square has the splendid Arrow Gate(Zhengyangmen Gate). All these grand buildings are on the central axis. The Great Hall of the People flanks Tian'anmen Square on the west, while on the east stands the National Museum of China. The modern and ancient buildings constitute a grand panorama, making Tian'anmen a world-famous landmark.

Tian'anmen Square was a forbidden area in the Ming and Qing dynasties. There used to be a gate called the Gate of Great Ming at the present site of the Chairman Mao Memorial Hall. In the Qing Dynasty, it was renamed the Gate of Great Qing and after the 1911 Revolution, the name was changed to Zhonghua Gate(the Gate of China).There also used to be a Left Chang'an Gate on the east and Right Chang'an Gate on the west sides of the Tian'anmen Square.All of these gates were linked by high walls, giving the square a T shape.At that time the Square was very small, with an area of only 11 hectares. In Qing Emperor Qianlong's time, three gates were added outside the east and west Chang'an Gate. No passage or admittance by the ordinary people was permitted. The Beijing residents at the time had to make a detour by walking from south of the Qing Gate or north of the Di'anmen Gate in order to go from west to east or the other way round. The Thousand Pace Corridor with 144 bays altogether ran alongside both sides of Tian'anmen Square. On the two sides of the Thousand Pace Corridor were the central government offices at that time, where the highest rulers of the feudal system exercised their power.

Tian'anmen Square witnessed great changes in the Chinese history testifying to the revolution and victory of the Chinese people's struggles against imperialism, colonialism. On May 4th, 1919, the May 4thMovement broke out, which had an epoch-making significance in the Chinese history and fired the first shot against imperialism, feudalism in China's New Democratic Revolution. The Incident on May 30, 1925 in Shanghai incited the fury of the Chinese people against imperialism. The patriotic people in Beijing convened at Tian'anmen Square to express their sympathy, making it the center stage of antiimperialism demonstration. On March 18, 1926, some people gathered on Tian'anmen Square to protest against the invasion of Japanese warship in China. After demonstrating on the street, this crowd of people were ruthlessly gunned down by the warlord government, leading this event to be called the famous March 18thIncident. On December 9, 1935, a group of patriotic students convened on Tian'anmen Square to protest against the Japanese imperialism.After the convention, they demons-trated in the street, and their movement came to be known as the famous December 9th Movement. On May 20, 1947, some student with progressive ideas gathered on Tian'anmen Square in a demonstration against the reactionary rulers for making civil strife. After the gathering, they staged an anti-hunger, anti-civil war demonstration.On October 1th, 1949, Chairman Mao Zedong solemnly declared to the world on Tian'anmen Rostrum, "The founding of People's Republic of China. And the Chinese people have now stood up ever since." The Central People's Government was declared simultaneously to have been founded. In the meantime, Chairman Mao Zedong himself raised the first Five-Star Red Flag. On January 8th, 1976, Premier Zhou Enlai passed away. The "Gang of Four" sought to prevent crowds of people mourning Zhou's death from gathering at Tian'anmen Square. From January 8 to the Qingming Festival, the whole Square became a meeting and battlefield of denouncing the crimes of the "Gang of Four" . On April 5th, the "Gang of Four" put down the struggle of crowds on Tian'anmen Square, which incited even more vigorous resistance of the people and marking yet another heroic chapter of Chinese history.

In the 1987 vote for the sixteen most scenic spots in Beijing, Tian'anmen Square, on account of its special location, rich historic background and high prestige, topped the list with the highest number of votes(286, 404) and hence was given First View of Beijing status.

Now you have fifteen minutes of free time.You can take photos, or continue to visit the Square.Then we'll meet at here.

各位朋友，大家好！

歡迎大家來北京參觀遊覽！很高興能成為大家這次旅行的導遊。首先讓我來簡單的自我介紹一下（自我介紹）。好的！如果您有什麼問題或者要求的話，請告訴我，我會盡我最大的努力使您有一個舒適愉快的旅程。今天我們將要參觀的是聞名世界的天安門廣場和城樓。請隨我來！

人民英雄紀念碑

朋友們，請向前看！在天安門廣場的中心，聳立著一座人民英雄紀念碑。它像徵著全國人民對革命先烈的懷念，表現了中華民族反抗外來侵略、推翻反動統治、爭取自由和平的英勇鬥爭史，並向後人表明我們今天的生活來之不易。

人民英雄紀念碑是為了紀念1840年以來犧牲的人民英雄而興建的。碑的正面向著天安門，刻有毛澤東主席題寫的「人民英雄永垂不朽」8　個鎏金大字。碑的背面，是毛澤東主席撰文、周恩來總理書寫的碑文：「三年以來，在人民解放戰爭和人民革命中犧牲的人民英雄們永垂不朽！三十年以來，在人民解放戰爭和人民革命中犧牲的人民英雄們永垂不朽！由此上溯到一千八百四十年，從那時起，為了反對內外敵人，爭取民族獨立和人民自由幸福，在歷次鬥爭中犧牲的人民英雄們永垂不朽！」

1949年9　月30　日，中國人民政治協商會議第一屆全體會議通過了在首都天安門廣場建立一座為國犧牲的人民英雄紀念碑的決議。當天下午6點鐘，出席會議的全體代表在天安門廣場舉行了奠基典禮。毛澤東主席親自為紀念碑奠基。1952　年正式開工興建，1958年5月1日竣工揭幕。

　　紀念碑的造型設計曾向全國的建築界、美術界、文藝界等各界人士徵求意見，經過了多次討論和反覆修改，可以説是集體智慧的結晶。紀念碑占地3100　平方米，碑高37.94　米，比天安門還高出4.07米。碑的基座是雙重月台，最下面的一層是海棠形。四周有漢白玉石欄杆，四面均有台階。碑座南北長61.54米，東西寬50.44米，再上去是兩層須彌座承托著碑身。下面一層較大的須彌座四周，裝飾著8幅漢白玉石刻制的大浮雕。浮雕以鮮明的形象，極其概括地表現了100多年來驚天動地的革命歷史。從東面按著歷史的順序排列為「虎門銷煙」、「金田起義」、「武昌起義」、「五四運動」、「五卅運動」、「南昌起義」、「抗日遊擊戰爭」和「勝利渡長江」；在正面一幅「勝利渡長江」的兩側，還有「支援前線」和「歡迎人民解放軍」兩幅裝飾性浮雕。浮雕高2米，寬2米至6.4米，總長度為40.68米，共雕刻了170多個性格、神態各異、接近真人大小的英雄人物形象。再上面一層須彌座的四周，雕刻著中國人民喜愛的菊花、荷花、百合花等花卉織成的8個花卉圖案，表示對革命先烈們高風亮節、堅貞不屈的高貴品質的懷念和崇敬。碑身的兩側，刻著由五星、松柏和旗幟等組成的裝飾花紋。最上端是採用民族傳統的盝頂作為碑頂。紀念碑的造型、題字、浮雕和裝飾花紋等，主題思想鮮明，構造嚴謹樸素，雕刻技藝精湛，人物形象逼真，是中國優秀雕塑藝術家和高級工匠們用5年時間創作出來的精品。它歌頌了人民英雄不可磨滅的歷史功勛，永遠激勵著人們奮發前進！

　　紀念碑的碑身是由大小不同的413　塊花崗石砌成的。碑心石長14.7　米，寬2.9米，厚1米，重約60噸。這塊巨型花崗石是從山東青島浮山開採後運抵北京的。紀念碑雖用了17000多塊大小不同的石料，但色澤光潤，調配適當，使紀念碑更顯得莊重精美。這些石料大都來自北京房山和山東泰安。

　　紀念碑在寬闊的天安門廣場中心拔地而起，彰顯出它的英雄氣魄。它表彰了人民英雄的光輝業績和千古不朽的功勛，是一個具有高度完美藝術價值的建築珍品。

　　紀念碑是人們寄託哀思，發憤圖強的精神支柱。1976年1月8日周恩來總理逝世。4月5日，幾十萬人自發來到人民英雄紀念碑前悼念周總理，爆發了聲討「四人幫」的「四五運動」。

現在，每天都有數以萬計的旅遊者前來瞻仰人民英雄紀念碑。人們經常在這裡舉行紀念活動，表示對革命先烈的敬仰和懷念。許多來訪的外國領導人，也到人民英雄紀念碑前敬獻花圈。

從城樓俯瞰天安門廣場

〔在天安門城樓上〕我們現在所在的地方是天安門城樓，是觀賞天安門廣場景色的絕好地點。天安門位於北京市城區的中心，始建於明永樂十五年（公元1417年），原名承天門，取名「承天啟運，受命於天」之意。明朝末年，李自成率農民起義軍進入北京，在被清兵逐出城門時，承天門毀於戰火。1651年改建後更名為天安門。城樓高33.7米，東西為9間，南北進深5間，暗合「九五」，以示帝王尊嚴。明清時天安門是皇帝舉行「金鳳頒詔」的地方。請各位往下看，城樓下是金水河，河上有五座雕琢精美的漢白玉石橋，因而被稱為金水橋。城樓前兩對雄健的石獅和挺秀的華表相配合，使天安門成為一座完美的建築藝術傑作。

請大家向前方看，前面是舉世聞名的天安門廣場。廣場南北長880米，東西寬500米，面積44萬平方米，可容納幾十萬人集會，是目前世界上面積最大的廣場。

廣場的最北面，是我們現在所在的地方——金碧輝煌的天安門城樓。在廣場的北沿，高高飄揚著中華人民共和國國旗。人民英雄紀念碑聳立在廣場中央。紀念碑的南面是莊嚴肅穆的毛主席紀念堂，最南端是四壁生輝、光彩耀人的正陽門。這些宏大的建築，從北到南在一條中軸線上。西側的人民大會堂和東側的中國國家博物館相襯托，這些古今建築精品交相輝映構成一幅氣勢磅 、宏偉壯觀的畫卷。這裡已成為世界著名的參觀遊覽勝地。

明清時代的天安門廣場是一塊禁地。南面有大明門，清朝改稱為大清門，辛亥革命後叫中華門，就是現在毛主席紀念堂的位置。東面有長安左門，西面有長安右門。各門之間用高大的圍牆連接，使天安門廣場呈「T」字形，當時的廣場很小，只有11萬平方米（11公頃）左右。清朝乾隆時，又在東西長安門外加築「三座門」，嚴禁行人過往，老百姓絕對不準入內。當時住在北京的人，從東城到西城，或從西城到東城都要從大清門以南或地安門以北繞行。廣場的兩側，建有東西千步廊，共有朝房144 間。千步廊兩旁分布著當時的中央衙門，是封建統治階級的最高權力者實施封建統治的場所。

歷盡滄桑的天安門廣場，可以說是中國人民反帝、反封建革命鬥爭取得勝利的歷史見證。1919年5月4日，在北京爆發了在中國歷史上具有劃時代意義的「五四」運動，打響了反帝、反封建的新民主主義革命第一炮。1925年，上海發生「五卅慘案」，激起了中國人民的反帝風暴。北京的愛國群眾在天安門廣場集會聲援，這裡變成了反帝示威活動的中心。1926 年3 月18 日，中國人民反對日艦侵入中國，在天安門廣場舉行大會，會後遊行示威的群眾慘遭軍閥政府的槍殺，造成震撼全國的「三‧一八」慘案。1935年12月9日，北京愛國學生在天安門廣場集會反對日本帝國主義，會後舉行了聲勢浩大的遊行示威活動，這就是著名的「一二‧九運動」。1947年5月20日，北京進步學生在天安門廣場集會，向反動統治者示威，反對國民黨製造內亂，會後舉行了反饑餓、反內戰大遊行。1949年10月1日，毛澤東主席在天安門城樓上莊嚴地向全世界宣告：「中華人民共和國成立了，中國人民從此站起來了！」同時宣布中央人民政府成立，並親自升起了第一面五星紅旗。1976 年1月8日周恩來總理與世長辭，人民群眾到天文門廣場舉行悼念活動，受到「四人幫」的阻撓和破壞。從1 月8 日至清明節前，整個廣場變成悼念周總理的會場和聲討「四人幫」的戰場。4月5日，「四人幫」在天安門廣場對人民群眾血腥鎮壓，激起了人民更強烈地反抗。在這裡又譜寫了可歌可泣的歷史篇章。

天安門廣場由於位置特殊，歷史內涵豐富，知名度高，在1987年北京十六景評選中，以286 404最高票名列榜首，成為北京第一景。

現在開始15分鐘的自由活動，大家可以照照相，也可以繼續參觀天安門廣場，15分鐘後在原地集合。

Palace Museum (The Forbidden City) （故宮博物院／紫禁城）

Ladies and gentlemen,

The grand architectural complex in front of us is the Imperial Palace Museum. Located in the center of Beijing proper, the Palace Museum, also called the Forbidden City or the Purple Forbidden City, served as the imperial palaces of the Ming and Qing dynasties. It is the largest and the most consummate example of a palatial complex still in existence not only in China, but in the rest of the world as well. It mainly embodies the superb tradition and unique styles of the Chinese ancient architecture and has a crucial standing in the history of world architecture.

During feudal times, admittance or access to the imperial residence by ordinary people was not permitted. The whole complex was encircled by high walls and was heavily guarded. Only the royal family of emperors, concubines and imperial posterity were able to live inside, hence the name the Purple Forbidden City. Why is it called the Purple Forbidden City? There are many answers to this question, but no general agreement exists about them. However, there exist three popular explanations. One is that the color purple means the advent of the purple cloud from the east. The purple cloud, which is an auspicious cloud, symbolizes the Emperor. Another is that the mythical Providence lived in the Purple Palace; therefore the imperial palace was also called the Purple Forbidden City. The third is that the Purple Forbidden City derives its name from the imaginary Purple Tiny Celestial Wall. Ancient Chinese astronomers believed that stars were divided into three celestial walls, 28 major constell-ations and other minor constellations. The three celestial walls include the Universal Tiny Celestial Wall, the Purple Tiny Celestial Wall and the Celestial Wall of the Market. The Purple Tiny Celestial Wall is located in the center of the three celestial walls and represents the constellation of the Providence. There is an old saying that goes that the son of Heaven, Emperor, sits in the middle and officials are distributed in the whole country.

The Palace Museum was first built in 1406 in the Ming Dynasty and completed after 15 years of work. It now has a history over 600 years. The design and layout of the whole palatial complex embody the "exalted dignity" of the feudal emperors and the strict feudal hierarchy. Covering an area of over 720,000 square meters, the Palace Museum has more than 9,900 rooms, pavilions and chambers and about 150,000 square meters of construction area. It is encircled with 10-meter high wall, which itself is surrounded by a 52-meter wide moat. The moat is also called Tongzi Moat(Most of Tube). The Palace Museum is about 960 meters long from north to south and 760 meters wide from east to west. On each of the four corners of the Forbidden City stands a watchtower whose structure is both fantastic and harmonious in appearance. A gate is located on each side of the palatial complex. The south gate is the Wumen(the Meridian Gate), north gate is called the Shenwumen (the Gate of Military Prowess), east gate, the Donghuamen, and west gate, the Xihuamen. Built on such a large area and integrated with miscellaneous architectural styles, such a large architectural complex does not create a disorderly image. On the contrary, it produces a feeling of structural compactness, splendid color and a regular layout. This is attributed to the construction style's emphasis on the distinct axis, which is about 8 kilometers long and is wisely connected with the layout of the whole Beijing city. The imperial residence takes up about one third of the total length of the axis.

The layout of the Palace Museum is divided into the "Outer Halls" and the "Inner Courts". The part from the Meridian Gate to the Gate of Heavenly Purity contains the Outer Halls. With the Hall of Supreme Harmony, the Hall of Complete Harmony and the Hall of Preserving Harmony as its center, Outer Halls are flanked on two sides by two sets of symmetric Wenhuadian and Wuyingdian. The Outer Halls are magnificent in appearance. The three halls stand on the same T-shaped marble terraces. There are three terraces and they are altogether 8 meters high. Each of the terraces is encircled by marble balustrades carved with designs. There are three "Imperial Roads" with stone carvings on the three terraces. The Hall of Supreme Harmony, also known as Throne Hall is the largest building in the Palace Museum, and also the largest and the most splendid ancient wooden architectural structure in China. Inside the Gate of Heavenly Purity is the Inner Court, which is also symmetric in its layout. The central part of the Palace of Heavenly Purity, Hall of Union and Peace, and Palace of Earthly Tranquility were the places where the feudal emperors lived and attended daily affairs. The six palaces on the east and west sides were the living quarters for concubines, and the five chambers on the two sides were for the imperial posterity. Three gardens for the Emperor's entertainment are located inside the Inner Court: the Imperial Garden, the Cining Garden and the Qianlong Garden. The inner Golden River winds its way along from the west side of the Inner Court through the Wuyingdian, Gate of the Supreme Harmony, and Wenhuadian to the outside of the Forbidden City. The river is spanned by a white marble bridge. The two sides of the river are protected by winding marble balustrades in various shapes, like a jade band. Most of the buildings in the Palace Museum are roofed with yellow glazed tiles and look splendid, solemn and graceful in the sunshine.

Apart from the emphasis on the axis, various methods are applied to stress the characteristics of each set of buildings, like the placement of the terraces, shape of the roofs, number of decorative animals and mythical creatures, and the concoction of color and design. In this way, not only the main buildings are made more exalted and spectacular, but the hierarchy differences among the various buildings are also displayed. The construction of the Palace Museum involved 100,000 famous artisans and one million ordinary workers from across the whole country. The building materials were from various parts of China. Therefore, the construction was really a large-scale one. Legend has it that the Forbidden City has 9,999 and a half rooms, while the imperial palace in Heaven has 10,000 rooMs.The Emperor on the earth claimed himself "the Son of Heaven", and dared not own the same number of rooms as did Providence. So there is a difference of a half room. Then where is the half room? It refers to the small room on the west side of Wenyuan Pavilion. In fact, the Forbidden City has more than 9,000 rooMs.The so-called half room does not exist at all. The room on the west side of Wenyuan Pavilion, although small in size and with space only enough for a staircase, is still a complete room.

The building in front of us is called the Meridian Gate. It is the main gate of the Forbidden City, popularly known as the Five-Phoenix Tower. On the 15 th of January on China's lunar calendar in the Ming Dynasty, lanterns would be put up and the Emperor would favor his officials with grand feasts. Spring pancakes were handed out on the Day of the Beginning of Spring, cold cakes on Dragon Boat Day(May 5 th on the Chinese lunar calendar) and glutinous rice cake on the Double Ninth Festival (9 th day of the 9 th lunar month). On the first day of the 10 th lunar month, the next year's almanac was promulgated. In ancient times, any official who offended the Emperor and was condemned to be punished would be brought to the outside of the Meridian Gate and beaten with sticks.

The Hall of Supreme Harmony and the Courtyard in front of It

[After going through the Gate of Supreme Harmony] Ladies and gentlemen, the Hall in front of us is called the Hall of Supreme Harmony, also popularly called the Throne Hall. It is the largest hall in the Forbidden City. With a construction area of 2,377 square meters, the double-eaved hall which ranks the highest among palaces, is the largest among the three halls in the Outer Halls. The Hall of Supreme Harmony was built on a T-shaped three tired terrace. The marble terrace with stone carvings is over 10 meters high, with 21 steps in the bottom part and 9 steps in the middle and upper parts respectively.

In the center of the Hall, there is a 2-meter high platform, upon which is placed the wooden throne carved with nine dragons. In the rear of the platform, there is a gold painted screen, and in the front, there is an imperial desk. On the two sides are decorations of an elephant, crane, unicorns, and other real and mythical creatures. The elephant is carrying a vase in which grains are stored, which signifies peace and bumper harvests. Unicorns are imaginary animals in ancient Chinese mythology. They are said to be able to travel 18,000 kilometers a day and can speak every language in the country. They only come to escort the aboveboard emperor with books.

There are altogether 72 pillars supporting the whole palace. Six of them are carved with dragon designs and gilded with gold encircling the throne. On top of the six pillars is a caisson ceiling with a Xuanyuan Mirror hanging in the middle. The Xuanyuan Mirror is said to be created by Emperor Xuanyuan (also known as Emperor Huangdi) in ancient times. The Emperor had this mirror hung here in order to show that he was the legitimate emperor. The mirror was placed just over the throne. However, the mirror now is not right over the throne. It is said that Yuan Shikai was afraid that the mirror might drop and injure him and so he had it moved a little bit to the present site. There is also another historic story about the throne. In 1916, on his coronation, Yuan Shikai had the original throne moved away and replaced by a big western chair with his empire's emblem designed by himself. After 1949 an older throne resembling the one seen in pictures was found in a junk warehouse. Experts examined this throne, declared it to be the real one, so it was put on display.

The twenty-four emperors of the Ming and Qing dynasties ascended the throne and promulgated the imperial edicts here. The emperors held grand ceremonies and received obeisance from officials and generals on the new year's day, winter solstice, Emperor's birthday, conferring on empresses, dispatch of generals, issuing the order from the throne ball, and bestowing favors.

[On the terrace of the Hall of Supreme Harmony] This is an incense burner used to burn sandalwood during grand ceremonies. There are altogether 18 incense burners, representing the 18 provinces of the Qing Dynasty. Four bronze vats are placed on the two sides outside the hall, which represent territorial integrity and were once used to store water to prevent fire. Placed on the east and west sides of the terrace are a bronze crane and a tortoise, the emblems of longevity. The thing made of bronze is called a Jialiang. It was the standard of measurement indicating that the Emperor treated everything fairly and knew everybody's conduct clearly. Opposite it is the stone-made sundial, a time clock in ancient times. It symbolized that the Emperor had the standards of time and measurement that was just and aboveboard in judging men and affairs.

The courtyard below is the courtyard of the Hall of Supreme Harmony. It is 30,000 square meters in area. There are neither trees nor grass on the spacious and tranquil courtyard, making it appear overwhelmingly solemn. In the center is the imperial road flanked by the brick-paved roads on two sides. The bricks were laid seven layers lengthwise and eight layers crosswise, making up fifteen layers in all to prevent people from tunneling their way into the palace. Why was the courtyard built so large? It was to make people sense the grandeur and solemnity of the Hall of Supreme Harmony. Looking upwards from below, visitors can see the brilliant yellow tiles under the blue sky and the white stone terrace which looks perfectly splendid and luxurious. On grand occasions, candles were lit on the enamel crane plates inside the Hall, sandalwood was burned in the incense pavilions and burners, pine twigs were burned in the bronze vats, tortoises and cranes on the terrace, musical bands queued on the two corridors in front of the Hall, and the guards of honor lined from the terrace all the way to Tian'anmen Gate. Columns of incense spread in and out of the hall and it was extremely quiet. When the Emperor ascended the throne, music was played, drums were beaten, and civil officials and military officers kneeled down in the courtyard according to their rank, wishing the Emperor longevity and paying their respect to his supremacy and dignity.

Puyi, the last emperor of the Qing Dynasty, ascended the throne in 1908 at the age of three. His father, Prince Regent Zaifeng, carried him to the throne. When the grand ceremony began and music was played up, the little Emperor was scared and cried for going home. Zaifeng was very worried and soothed the little Emperor: "Don't cry, don't cry and it will soon finish." Coincidently, three years later the rule of the Qing Dynasty collapsed, and more than 2,000-year-old feudal system ended.

OK, Now you have 10 minutes free time. We will meet below the terrace 10 minutes later.

From Hall of Mental Cultivation to Imperial Garden

After visiting the three big palaces of the Palace Museum, I will take you from the Hall of Mental Cultivation to the Imperial Garden. This is the Hall of Mental Cultivation. It is located south of the Six West Palaces, which are on the western side of the Palace Museum. Next to the Hall of Supreme Harmony, it was the most important place in the Palace Museum during the Qing Dynasty. The two Chinese characters "養心" (p　ny　n: y　n　x　n), meaning "mental cultivation" were adopted from the teaching of Meng Zi (Mencius). They emphasize exercising selfcontrol so as to cultivate the traditional feudal ideology. The hall was built in the Ming Dynasty. A military office was constructed outside the hall.

Before Emperor Kangxi, the emperors took the Palace of Heavenly Purity as their residence. Emperor Yongzheng moved his residence here when he came to the throne. And the state affairs were also conducted here. In the center of the Hall, there is a throne and an imperial desk. This was a place where the emperor received officials. The east hall was known as the place of "ruling the state behind the screen" . After 1861, Empress Dowager Cixi usurped the power and put two thrones here. The child emperor sat in front while Empress Dowager Cixi sat behind. There was a screen between them. When officials reported to the child emperor, she gave the order and made the decision behind the screen. The present display is original and dates back to when the two Empress Dowagers ruled the state behind the screen during the childhood of Emperor Guangxu. In 1912 Empress Dowager Longyu announced here the imperial edict of giving up the throne. Emperor Puyi who gave up his throne and continued to live here for another 13 years due to preferential treatment rendered to him. In 1924, he was driven out of the Palace Museum by General Feng Yuxiang.

There was an imperial bed, sitting bed, throne, long red sandalwood desk and wardrobe in the central room of the back hall of the Hall of Mental Cultivation. It was the residence for 8 emperors from Yongzheng to Xuantong in the Qing Dynasty. The rooms in the east and west courtyards of the back hall were the waiting rooms for concubines. Three emperors of the Qing Dynasty Shunzhi, Qianlong and Tongzhi all passed away here.

Now, we are going to visit the inner court, the Hall of Heavenly Purity, the Hall of Union and the Palace of Earthly Tranquility. Then, we will visit the Imperial Garden. The inner court was the residential and living quarters for the Emperor and his family. The Palace of Heavenly Purity was the main hall of the inner court. It was built during the Yongle Emperor's reign. The throne was placed in the center of the Palace and there were rooms on two sides. There was a board hung above the throne which was inscribed with "being open and aboveboard" handwritten by Emperor Shunzhi. It was a secret place for the Emperor to store and hide imperial edicts. The old Emperor wrote down the name of his successor in advance. One copy was kept by himself, the other was sealed in a box which was hidden behind the board. When the old Emperor passed away, the officials in charge would open the box together. The name of the successor would be announced officially after verification. Emperors Qianlong, Jiaqing, Daoguang and Xianfeng all climbed up the 9-dragon throne according to this system.

The Palace of Heavenly Purity was the residence of the Emperor where he lived and conducted the day-to-day affairs in the Ming and Qing dynasties. After Emperor Yongzheng in the Qing Dynasty, the residence of the Emperor was moved to the Palace of Mental Cultivation. Family banquets were held here on New Year's day, the Lantern, Dragon Boat, Longevity and Mid-Autumn Festivals, as well as the Winter Solstice. In the Qing Dynasty, this was an audience hall for the Emperor to receive foreign envoys.

[In the Hall of Union] The Hall of Union is located between the Palace of Heavenly Purity and the Palace of Earthly Tranquility. It symbolized the union of the heaven and the earth. The hall was built in 1420 and rebuilt in 1798. It is square and is three rooms wide and three rooms deep. The top of the Hall is covered with yellow glazed tiles. It is smaller than the Hall of Supreme Harmony. A board inscribed with "Let things take their own course" handwritten by Emperor Kangxi is hung in the Hall. The throne is placed in the hall. There are 4 screens behind the throne. The "Hall of Union" handwritten by Emperor Qianlong was inscribed on the screens. The hall has a caisson ceiling. Ceremonies conferring titles on the empress or celebrating her birthday took place in this Hall.

[In the Palace of Earthly Tranquility] The Palace of Earthly Tranquility was the empress's residence in the Ming Dynasty. It was turned into a place for worship and the Emperor's wedding ceremony in the early Qing Dynasty. It is behind the Hall of Union. When it was rebuilt in the Qing Dynasty, the central door was opened in a room on the east according to the custom of Manchu national minority. The design of the windows was also changed. The west room was changed into a ring-like Kang(a beatable brick bed) with south, west, and north-facing sides. All of these features have made this palace different from the architectural style of the other palaces. In the Qing Dynasty, religious services were held here everyday. The Emperor and empresses would personally attend important worship-ping occasions. The east room was the Emperor's bridal chamber.

[On the way to the Imperial Garden] The Imperial Garden is at the back of the Palace of Earthly Tranquility on the central axis. This garden is compactly laid out, famous for its architecture and has the imperial court's distinctive style. The trees, rockeries and flower beds are well fitted in the garden. The garden is mostly surrounded by buildings and is small in size. It covers an area of 12,000 square meters. Due to its compact and delicate design, it not only has clear levels, but also the imperial court's strong atmosphere. While most of the buildings in the Garden are symmetrical, visitors can still find differences with respect to design and decoration. The courtyard of the Qin'an Hall is separated by the trees, which gives visitors a good visual effect and a sense of quietness.

The Qin'an(Imperial Peace) Hall is located in the central north part of this area and it is the main building of the Imperial Garden. The other halls and rooms are located symmetrically on the east and west. The Qin'an Hall's base is made of marble and the ceiling is flat. The God Zhenwu believed by Taoism is worshipped here. At the beginning of spring, summer, autumn and winter, the Emperor would worship at this place. Emperor Jiajing of the Ming Dynasty believed in Taoism and often came here to do religious worship. There are a couple of cypress trees in front of the hall which are already 400 years old. They have the same trunk but different roots. There are 10 couples of pine and cypress trees in the garden.

The Yanhui Pavilion is located in northwest of the Qin'an Hall. There is a green hill in the northeast part of this area. It is 14 meters high and consists of a pile of differently shaped Taihu stones in Wuxi, Jiangsu Province. There is a couple of engraved stone dragon heads from which water gushes out. The water spurts as high as 10 meters and more. What a magnificent scene! The twisting path at the foot of the hill leads to the top of it. The Pavilion of Royal Scenery is on the top of the hill. On the Double Ninth Festival(9 th day of the 9 th lunar month), the Emperor accompanied by his concubines would climb up the hill to enjoy the scenery both within and outside the Forbidden City.

The West Qiongyuan Gate and the East Qiongyuan Gate located at southwest and southeast of the Garden lead to the Six Western Palaces and Six Eastern Palaces respectively. The Shunzhenmen Gate in the north is composed of three glazed doors standing side by side at the north palace wall. The gate was usually closed and was opened only when emperors, empresses and concubines came in and went out. Today, we will go through the gate like emperors and empresses and leave the Forbidden City by the Shenwumen Gate. We will gather on the coach. Thank you!

　　各位朋友：大家眼前的雄偉建築就是故宮博物院。故宮位於北京市中心，是明清兩朝的皇宮，又稱「紫禁城」，是中國現存規模最大，最完整的宮殿建築群，也是世界上最大的宮殿群。它集中體現了中國古代建築藝術的優秀傳統和獨特風格，在建築史上具有十分重要的地位。

封建社會皇帝居住的宮殿是不許人民進入或靠近的，所以皇宮被一道高大的城牆環繞起來，戒備森嚴，只有皇帝、皇后、妃子和皇太子等皇族嫡親才能住在裡面，所以叫「禁城」。但是，為什麼叫「紫禁城」呢？普遍流傳的説法有三種：一種説法認為，「紫禁城」的「紫」字和「紫氣東來」的「紫」字是一個意思，以祥瑞雲氣象徵皇帝。第二種説法認為，傳説中的「天帝」住在天上的「紫宮」，因此便把皇宮也稱為紫禁城。第三種説法認為，「紫禁城」借喻紫微星垣而來。中國古代天文學家曾把天上的恆星分為三垣、二十八宿和其他星座。三垣包括太微垣、紫微垣和天市垣。紫微星垣在三垣的中央，是代表天帝的星座。

故宮從明永樂四年（公元1406　年）開始修建，用了15年的時間才基本建成，到今天已有600多年的歷史。整個宮殿的設計和布局都表現了封建君主的「尊嚴」和封建等級制度的森嚴。故宮占地72萬多平方米，有宮殿樓閣的9900多間，建築面積約15萬平方米。四周圍有高10多米的城牆，牆外是52米寬的護城河，俗稱筒子河。城南北長約960米，東西寬約760米，四角各有一座結構奇異、和諧美觀的角樓。城四周各設一門，南面的正門是午門，北門叫神武門，東門叫東華門，西門叫西華門。在這麼大的面積上，建造一組規模如此宏大、集各種建築手法之大成的建築群，不但沒有表現得紛繁雜亂，反而給人以結構嚴謹、色彩輝煌和布局規整的感覺，主要是建造中突出了一條極為明顯的中軸線。這條中軸線和整座北京城有機地結為一體，總長度約8 千米，在皇家禁苑內的部分，約占三分之一。

故宮建築布局分為「外朝」與「內廷」兩大部分。由午門到乾清門之間的部分為「外朝」，以太和、中和、保和三大殿為中心，東西兩側有文華、武英二組宮殿，左右對稱，形成「外朝」雄偉壯觀的格局。大殿前後排列在一個龐大的「工」字形漢白玉石台基上。台基高8　米，分為三層，每層有漢白玉石刻欄杆圍繞，臺中間有三座石階，石基的中央由巨石鋪成「御路」，上刻海水、江崖、蟠龍、升龍，托以流雲。太和殿俗稱金鑾殿，是故宮最高大的一座建築物，也是國內最高大、最壯麗的古代木構建築。乾清門以內為「內廷」，建築布局也是左右對稱。中部為乾清宮、交泰殿、坤寧宮，是封建皇帝居住和日常處理政務的地方。兩側的東、西六宮是嬪妃的住所，東、西五所是皇子的住所。「內廷」還有為皇室遊玩的三處花園：砌花園、慈寧花園、乾隆花園。內金水河沿「內廷」西邊蜿蜒繞過武英殿、太和門、文華殿流出宮外，河上有白玉石橋，沿河兩岸有曲折多姿的漢白玉雕欄，形似玉帶。故宮建築絕大部分以黃琉璃瓦為頂，在陽光下金碧輝煌，莊嚴美觀。

故宮中的建築除了突出中軸線外，還運用各種手法，使城中各組建築均具特色。如殿基的處理，殿頂的形式、吻獸和垂脊獸的數目，彩繪圖案的規制等。這樣，不僅使主要建築更顯得高大、壯觀，而且還表現了宮中建築的等級差別。故宮在施工中共徵集了全國的能工巧匠10萬多名，民夫100萬人。所用的建築材料來自全國各地。由此也可以看出當時工程之浩大。民間傳說故宮有房九千九百九十九間半，並說天上的皇宮一共有房一萬間，地上的皇帝自稱「天子」，不敢與其同數，所以就少了半間。這半間房又在哪兒呢？有人說是指文淵閣西頭那一小間。實際上紫禁城有房九千餘間，所謂的這半間是根本不存在的。文淵閣兩頭一間，面積雖然很小，僅能容納一個樓梯，但它仍是一整間。

我們眼前的建築叫午門，它是紫禁城的正門，俗稱五鳳樓。明代正月十五，午門懸燈賜宴百官。皇帝在立春日賜春餅，端午日賜涼糕，重陽日賜花糕。在農曆十月初一，頒發次年曆書。以前凡有大臣惹怒皇帝而被批「逆鱗」者，也都被帶到午門外受廷杖。

太和殿及殿前廣場

〔經過太和門之後〕前面的大殿叫人和殿，俗稱金鑾殿，是故宮內最大的宮殿。建築面積2377平方米，重檐廡殿頂，是殿宇中的最高等級，為外朝三大殿中最大的一座。太和殿建在三層重疊的「工」字形須彌座上。該座由漢白玉雕成，離地10餘米，下層台階21級，中、上層各9級。

殿的中央擺放著雕有九條龍的楠木寶座。後面有金漆圍屏，前面有御案，左右有對稱的寶象、角端、仙鶴、香筒等陳列。象馱寶瓶，內裝五穀，象徵太平有象，五穀豐登。角端是中國古代神話傳說中的一種神獸，可「日行一萬八千里」，通曉四方語言，只有明君駕臨，它才捧書而至、護駕身旁。

殿內共有72根大主柱，支撐其全部重量，其中6根雕龍金柱，瀝粉貼金，圍繞在寶座周圍。6柱當中，上為盤龍金鳳藻井，正中懸垂一球形軒轅鏡。相傳軒轅鏡是中國遠古時代軒轅氏——黃帝所造。後代皇帝高掛此鏡，以示自己是正統皇帝。鏡下正好對著寶座，現在的軒轅鏡並未正對寶座，據說是袁世凱怕大圓球掉下來把他砸死，故將寶座向後挪到現在的位置。關於龍椅，還有段歷史故事。中華民國五年（公元1916年）袁世凱登基時，把原來的寶座搬走了，換了一把西式高背大椅，上飾他自己設計的帝國徽號。新中國成立後，有人刻意尋找那把龍椅，根據過去的一張照片，在破家具庫找到了一把破椅，經專家鑒定，此椅即是皇帝寶座，後經修復展出。

明清兩朝曾有24個皇帝在此登基，宣布即位詔書。元旦、冬至、皇帝生日、冊立皇后、派將出征、金殿傳臚以及賜安等，皇帝都要在這裡舉行儀式，接受文武百官朝賀。

〔在太和殿的石台上〕這是銅香爐，是皇帝舉行典禮時焚燒檀香用的。這裡一共有18座，代表清朝18個省。殿外左右安放4只銅缸，象徵「金甌無缺」，作為儲水防火之用。台基東西兩側各有一只銅製仙鶴和烏龜，是長壽的象徵。這個由銅鑄做成的器具叫嘉量，嘉量是當時測重量的衡器，表示皇帝公平處事，誰半斤，誰八兩，心裡自然有數。對面還有一個石頭做成的東西叫做日晷，是古代的測時儀。皇帝的意思是：量和時的基準都在自己手裡。

下邊的廣場是太和殿廣場，廣場面積達3萬平方米。整個廣場無一草一木，空曠寧靜，給人以森嚴肅穆的感覺。正中為御路，左右是海墁磚地，地面鋪的磚橫七豎八，共15層，以防有人挖地道進入皇宮。為什麼要建這麼大的廣場呢？這是為了讓人們感覺到太和殿的雄偉壯觀。站在下面向前望去：藍天之下，黃瓦生輝。再加上下面白色的石台，給人以豪華絢麗之感。舉行大典時，殿內的　琅仙鶴盤上點蠟燭，香亭、香爐燒檀香，露台上的銅爐、龜、鶴燃松柏枝，殿前兩側廊下排列樂隊。從露台至天安門，排列著各種儀仗，殿內外香煙繚繞，全場鴉雀無聲。皇帝登上寶座時，鼓樂齊鳴，文武大臣按品級跪伏在廣場，仰望著雲中樓閣齊呼萬歲，以顯示皇帝無上權威與尊嚴。

清朝末代皇帝溥儀1908年年底登基時，年僅3歲，由他父親攝政王載灃把他抱扶於寶座上。當大典開始時，突然鼓樂齊鳴，嚇得小皇帝哭鬧不止，嚷著要回家去。載灃急得滿頭大汗，只好哄著小皇帝說：「別哭，別哭，快完了，快完了！」說來也巧，3年後清朝就滅亡了，從而結束了中國2000多年的封建統治。

好，現在開始10分鐘的自由活動，10分鐘後在石階下集合。

養心殿至御花園

參觀過故宮三大殿後，我將陪同大家遊覽養心殿至御花園各處。現在，各位看到的就是養心殿。它位於故宮內西路西六宮南端，與內東路的齋宮、奉先殿相對稱。在清宮中，除太和殿外，此處便是最重要的地方。養心殿的「養心」二字是借用孟子說的「存其心，養其性，以事天」一語，意在涵養天性，培養傳統的封建觀念。這座宮殿建於明朝，為工字形建築，前後殿相連，廊廡環抱，門外設有辦事機構——軍機處。

康熙以前，皇帝以乾清宮為寢殿，雍正以後，皇帝以此殿為寢宮，並在這裡處理日常政務。正殿設寶座、御案，是皇帝召見大臣、官員的地方。西暖閣是皇帝批閱奏摺、處理重要文件的地方。東暖閣就是「垂簾聽政」處。1861年以後，慈禧篡權，就在這裡設兩重寶座。年幼的皇帝坐在前面，慈禧坐在後面，當中隔一塊紗簾，大臣向皇帝奏事，由她在後邊發話，做出決定。現在的陳設是光緒皇帝幼年兩宮太后垂簾聽政時的原狀。1912年清朝隆裕皇太后就在此處宣布退位詔書，宣布退位的皇帝溥儀，根據優待條件，仍在這裡居住達13年之久，1924年11月5日才被馮玉祥驅逐出故宮。

養心殿後殿正間，設有龍床、坐炕、寶座、紫檀木雕長案和雲龍大立櫃等，是清代8位皇帝的寢宮，居住過從雍正開始到宣統為止的8位清帝。後殿東西兩小院的排房，是后妃們聽候皇帝召喚的休息室。清朝順治、乾隆、同治三位皇帝，均死在這裡。

好，現在我們去內廷，也就是乾清宮、交泰殿、坤寧宮，然後去御花園。乾清門以北為**內**廷，是帝后生活和居住的地方。乾清宮是**內**廷正殿，建於明永樂年間，飛金走彩，雍容華貴。殿正中設有寶座，兩頭有暖閣，寶座上方懸「正大光明」匾額一塊，為順治皇帝御筆，是雍正之後秘密儲藏詔書的地方。老皇帝事先寫好繼承人的名字，一份帶在身邊，另一份封在匣**內**置於「正大光明」匾後。當皇帝駕崩後，便由顧命大臣共同打開建儲匣，經核實後宣布皇位的繼承人。乾隆、嘉慶、道光、咸豐四帝，均是按此制度登上九龍寶座的。

乾清宮是明清兩代皇帝的寢宮及平時處理政事的地方。清代雍正以後，寢宮遷往養心殿。此殿每年元旦、元宵、端午、中秋、冬至、萬壽等節，按例舉行家宴。晚清時期，亦在此殿召見外國使臣。

〔在交泰殿〕交泰殿位於乾清宮與坤寧宮之間，象徵著天地交合、平安康泰。交泰殿始建於1420年，重建於1798年。殿平面呈方形，面寬進深均為3間，黃琉璃瓦四角攢尖鎏金寶頂，小於中和殿，殿**內**高懸康熙御筆「無為」二字。殿中設有寶座，寶座後有4扇屏風，上有乾隆御筆「交泰殿銘」。殿頂**內**正中為藻井。該殿是皇后每逢大典及生日受賀的地方。

〔在坤寧宮〕坤寧宮原為明代皇后住的正宮，清初改為祭神和皇帝結婚的場所，位於交泰殿之後，是後三殿之末。清代重修時，按照滿族的習慣，將正門開在偏東的一間，並將菱花格窗改為直條格窗，殿西部的西暖閣改為南、西、北三面的環形大炕，使此殿有別於其他宮殿的建築風格。清代每日在兩暖閣進行朝祭、夕祭；大祭之日皇帝皇后親自參加。東部的東暖閣是皇帝大婚時的洞房。

〔出坤寧門到御花園〕御花園在坤寧門後面，位於中軸線上，這是一處布局緊湊，以建築取勝，具有宮廷色彩的遊覽和休憩園地。園**內**古木參天，名花奇石點綴其間，大部分建築環繞四周。此園面積不算大，僅有12000 多平方米，但由於構思精細、安排得當，所以既層次清楚，又不失宮廷氣魄。園中建築多為對稱，但在造型、裝飾上又有變化，中間的欽安殿院落與樹木竹林相隔，產生了良好的視覺效果和幽深的感覺。

御花園正中北面的欽安殿是園中的主體建築，其餘殿宇軒齋對稱分置於東西兩側。欽安殿殿基是以漢白玉石為材的須彌座，殿頂平坦，周圍四脊環繞。殿內供奉道教真武大帝，每年立春、立夏、立秋、立冬四節，皇帝都要到此拈香行禮。明嘉靖皇帝信奉道教，常於此做道場。殿前有一棵連理柏，已有400多年歷史，是同幹異根的柏樹。園內一共有10多棵連理樹，多由松、柏培育而成。

欽安殿西北有延暉閣，東北有堆秀山。山高14米，是用各種形狀的太湖石堆成的。山前一對噴水的石刻龍頭，噴水高達10多米，景象十分壯觀。山下小路曲折盤旋通向山頂。頂上有一個亭子叫御景亭，每年九月初九重陽節，皇帝都要攜帶一群后妃登上堆秀山，眺望皇宮內外景色。

御花園西南、東南的「瓊苑西門」、「瓊苑東門」，分別通往西六宮和東六宮。北面的順貞門是北宮牆並列的三座琉璃門，平時關閉，僅在帝后妃嬪出入時開啟。今天我們要當一次皇帝、皇后，經過琉璃門，從神武門出故宮，到旅遊車上集合。謝謝大家！

Badaling Great Wall （八達嶺長城）

Ladies and gentlemen,

[On the coach] The Great Wall is the symbol of the Chinese nation. Chinese people are proud of the Great Wall. It is the largest military defense project in the world and is listed as one of the seven ancient architectural wonders of the world. Parts of the Great Wall were first built during the Warring States Period. The walls constructed in the Qing Dynasty have a history of 2, 300 years. The walls built in the Ming Dynasty have a history of more than 600 years. The current Great Wall section in Beijing was built in the Ming Dynasty. Having seen hundreds years of hardships and witnessed the changes of dynasties, the Great Wall is still standing upright in China.

The Great Wall is well known at home and abroad for its long history, extraordinary length, massive construction and superb architecture. It is one of the most famous tourist destinations. It is said that you are not a real man if you do not climb up the Great Wall. Many foreign state leaders, high ranking officials, and millions of Chinese and foreign tourists visiting Beijing come to the Great Wall and enjoy and experience its magnificence for themselves. According to the report of the American astronauts, the Great Wall of China and the Grand Dyke of the Netherlands are the only manmade objects that they could see on the moon. The Great Wall is a real wonder in the world.

[The coach passing through the Guan'gou Valley] Our coach is now at a place called Guan'gou. It is a 15-kilometer long valley. The entrance in the south is the Nankou Town; the exit in the north is Badaling. Juyongguan Pass is in the central section of Guan'gou. There are flourishing trees and flowers on the two sides of the hills. Visitors can have a good view if they climb up the hill;therefore, the Juyongguan Pass was one of the eight scenic spots of Yanjing (today's Beijing) in the Jin Dynasty. A stone tablet was set up in the reign of Emperor Qianlong. It is said that there were 72 scenic spots in Guan'gou. Some of the spots are related to the story of Family Yang, such as the statue of Yang Wulang, the stake where Yang Liulang tied his horse and the platform where Mu Guiying called the muster roll of officers and assigned them tasks. The scenic spots also include the Cloud Platform, an important unit under state preservation of cultural relics, as well as the Wangjing Stone and the place where Maitreya listened to music.

Outside of the north gate of Juyongguan Pass lie the relics where military exercises were reviewed. Nine kilometers away from the north of Juyongguan Pass is the Qinglong Railway Station. The Museum of Zhan Tianyou, a famous Chinese engineer and his mausoleum are just located in the northeast of the station. He made outstanding contributions to the design and building of Jing Zhang (Beijing-Zhangjiakou) Railway. At that time, foreigners could not believe that the railway could be built at this place. Zhan Tianyou made the survey and designed the railway by himself. The Jing Zhang (

Beijing-Zhangjiakou) Railway passed through Nankou with a slope of 3.3%. Zhan Tianyou introduced the method of digging a tunnel, and designed the track in the shape of "人" (a Chinese character meaning man). In less than 4 years, the Jing Zhang Railway was completed and opened to traffic, two years ahead of schedule. To memorialize his achievements, Zhan Tianyou's bronze statue was set up by the Qinglong Station. Later on his mausoleum was also built here.

[Arriving at the Badaling Great Wall] Now, we have arrived at Badaling section of the Great Wall. Please get off the coach. The Badaling Great Wall is located in Yanqing County north of Beijing. In this section, the terrain goes up and down and features high mountains and dangerous peaks. It is 70 kilometers away from the city of Beijing. This was the north gate of the ancient Beijing city. The Badaling Great Wall was built between the two magnificent and precipitous mountains. It almost seems as if one man could hold back an army of 1,0000 while defending this spot. Since ancient times, Badaling has been an important military and civilian communications hub. It leads to Beijing in the south, Yanqing in the north, Miyun and Xinglong in the east, and Huailai, Zhangjiakou, Xuanhua and Datong in the west. The roads going every direction all start here. This is what Badaling means in Chinese. The area outside the town gate was built in 1505 in the Ming Dynasty. A board inscribed with the words "External Town of Juyong" was hung on the East Town Gate, while another inscribed with the words "Key to North Gate" was hung on the West Town Gate. The town occupied an area of more than 5, 000 square meters and served as a military garrison. Now, it is a place for tourists to rest and go shopping.

Five Ming Dynasty cannons are on display at the entrance to Badaling. The biggest one has a 2.85 meter-long barrel and a 105 millimeters caliber. It was built in 1638, the 11thyear of Chongzhen's reign and is named the "General Weiwu" .

There are two peaks in this section of the Great Wall. They are normally referred to as the northern peak and the southern peak. The highest point is 1,000 meters above the sea level. The Great Wall in this section is very representative. The base of the Wall was built up with granite stones. Each piece weighs more than 500 kilograMs.The upper level of the Wall was built with bricks filled with crushed stones and packed dirt clods. The top was built with square bricks, The Great Wall is 8.5 meters high (the average height is 7.8 meters). It is 6.5 meters thick at the bottom and 5.7 meters thick on the top. Five horsemen could ride abreast. There are short walls on both sides of the Great Wall called the Wall of Yu; the external part is also called the crenellated wall and it is 11.7 meters high. There are crenels on the wall served as a lookout on patrol duty. There are holes under the crenel for arrow shooting. The internal side of the wall of Yu is 1 meter high. In the inner part of the wall, there are gates, which were built at certain intervals. There are also stone staircases within each gate leading to the top of the wall.

A platform higher than the Great Wall and which protrudes from it was built on the wall at intervals of 300 to 500 meters. There were two kinds of platforMs.One was like a two-story fortress, 7 meters higher than the Wall. It was also wider than the Wall. This type was called resisting building. On the upper level, one could both watch and shoot at attacking enemy troops. The lower part could be used to house defending troops, provide them a resting place, and to store their weapons. Another kind of platform, which is a little higher than the Wall, is called fighting platform or wall platform. It was used for patrol or attacking. These platforms were all built at the corner or precipitous places to form a shape of a horn. Shooting could be done in different directions, which had made it a comprehensive and complete defense network.

Beacon towers were built along the Wall at high places or commanding points. When enemies were sighted, smoke was set off at daytime and bonfires were lit at night. When the other beacon towers sighted the smoke and bonfire, they would also immediately set off the smoke and light bonfires. All the beacon towers would do the same one by one, so that the message would be transmitted to the headquarters as soon as possible. This was one ancient means of communication.

Viewed from the top of the wall, it winds into the distance like an immense dragon whose head and tail are invisible. Looking west, you can see the Guanting Reservoir shining in Huailai Basin. Looking south in fine weather, you can see the city of Beijing and its innumerable buildings. Looking north, you can find threadlike roads snaking through the valleys and gradually disappearing in the mountains. What a magnificent and spectacular landscape!

The Great Wall has a history of more than 2,000 years. It had been restored and reinforced during many successive dynasties. The current one was mostly built in the Ming Dynasty. What was the purpose of building the Great Wall? It was for holding back invading nomadic tribes coming down from the north. If you build a wall 3 feet thick and 15 feet high with the bricks and stones used in the building of the Great Wall, the wall would surround the earth for one circle. How was such a great project built? The Great Wall was all built on precipitous hills and desolate deserts. Construction was very difficult. Apart from transporting stones and bricks by donkeys and other animals, all the rest work had relied on manpower. Our people gave full play to their wisdom, invented ingenious construction skills and finally overcame great difficulties. The Great Wall is an illustration of the diligent, courageous and firm spirit of the Chinese people and nation. The Great Wall of China is the longest defense wall in the current world.

This is the end of our visit to the Great Wall. Please get on the coach, and go to the next scenic spot. Thank you!

女士們、先生們：你們好！

〔在旅遊車上〕萬里長城是中華民族的象徵，中國人的驕傲。它蜿蜒曲折橫貫於中國北部，全長6350多千米，是世界上規模最大的軍事防禦工程，被列為世界七大建築奇蹟之一。中國遠在春秋戰國時期就開始修築長城，至今已有2700多年的歷史，明代修築的長城，至今也有600多年的歷史了。現在保存的北京段長城是明代修築的，它經歷了千百年的風霜雨雪，目睹了無數朝代更迭和人間滄桑，依然屹立在世界的東方。

中國長城以其歷史悠久、連綿不絕、工程浩大和工藝高超四大特點而聞名中外，成為舉世著稱的旅遊勝地之一。不到長城非好漢，許多訪華來京的外國元首、高級官員，以及其他無數中外旅行者幾乎都要親臨長城遊覽一番，以飽覽萬里長城的宏偉雄姿。據美國登月宇航員報告，他們在月球上憑肉眼遙望地球，就能看到中國的萬里長城和荷蘭的圍海大堤，可見長城真的是天下奇觀啊！

〔旅遊車進入關溝後〕我們的車已經到了關溝。所謂關溝，是一條15公里長的山谷。南端入口處是南口鎮，北端出口處，即是八達嶺。居庸關位於關溝中段，兩側重巒層疊，過去樹木茂盛，山花野草鋪蓋山坡，登高眺望，遍山碧波翠浪，因此，早在金代，「居庸疊翠」已成為燕京八景之一，清乾隆時也刻石立碑。關溝過去有72景之説，其中有不少是和楊家將的傳説有關，如五郎像、楊六郎拴馬椿、穆桂英點將台等。此外還有全國重點文物保護單位雲台，以及望京石、彌勒聽琴等景點。

居庸關北門外，有閱武場遺址。距關北9 公里處，是青龍橋火車站。中國著名的工程師詹天佑紀念館和墓園就在站的東北側。他為設計、修築京張鐵路做出了傑出的貢獻。當時外國人認為無法在這裡修築鐵路，詹天佑卻親自進行勘測、設計。京張鐵路由南口進入後，坡度為千分之三十三，詹天佑採用開隧洞，設「人」字軌等辦法，用時不到四年，提前兩年修通了京張鐵路。人們為了紀念他的功績，在青龍橋火車站建了他的銅像，以後又修建了他的墓園。

〔到達八達嶺長城〕八達嶺長城到了，請各位跟好隊伍下車！八達嶺長城在北京北部延慶縣境內。這一帶山巒起伏、多險峰峻嶺，離北京市區70多公里。此地為古京城的北大門，八達嶺城關築於兩山之間，十分雄險，大有「一人當關，萬夫莫開」之勢。自古以來，八達嶺便是交通要道和軍事重地，南通北京，北達延慶，東達密雲、興隆，西往懷來、張家口、宣化、大同等地。路從此分，四通八達，故名八達嶺。城關建於明弘治十八年（公元1505年），東面城門上的匾額為「居庸外鎮」，西面城門上為「北門鎖鑰」，城內面積僅有5000多平方米，過去是駐軍的地方，現在是遊人休息和購物的場所。

在八達嶺登城處，陳列著5門明代大砲，其中最大的一門筒長2.85米，口徑105毫米，崇禎十一年（公元1638年）鑄造，名叫「威武大將軍」。

八達嶺長城有兩處高峰，一般稱為北高峰和南高峰，最高點海拔約為1000米。這一帶的長城，很有代表性，城牆的基部用花崗岩條石築成，每塊重達千斤以上，其上部砌大城磚，當中填碎石、土塊，頂部鋪方磚。城牆高8.5米（平均高度為7.8米），下寬為6.5米，上寬是5.7米，可以五馬並行，人可十行並進。城上兩旁有矮牆，名叫宇城，外側的牆又叫堞牆，高11.7 米，上面有堆口，是巡邏、放哨時瞭望用的，堆口下面有射擊孔，是射箭用的。內側宇牆，高1 米。在城牆內側，每隔一段距離有券門，門內有石階可以登城。

城上每隔300～500 米，有一處高於城牆，並凸出於牆身的城台。城台有兩種類型，一種是雙層城堡式的，高於城牆7米，也寬於城牆。這種式樣的叫做敵樓，上層可以瞭望、射擊，下層可以住人、休息或存放武器。另一種略高於城牆的平台，叫做戰台或牆台，是巡邏放哨或攻戰用的。這類城台都建在拐角或險要的地方，互為犄角，可交叉射擊，構成一套完整的防禦工事。

沿長城全線內外的高處或變通要道的高山頂上，設置許多零散的墩台或碉堡。其中有的作為煙墩，又叫烽火台。如發現敵情，白天燃煙，夜間舉火，遠處的墩台發現煙火，也立即點燃煙火，逐個相傳，能較快地傳到指揮機關。這是古代通信聯絡方式之一。

站在長城的峰頂上，極目遠望，群巒聳立，連綿不絕，長城從遠方雲嵐深處奔騰而來，又朝天際蜿蜒而去，不見首尾。西望懷來盆地，官廳水庫閃閃發光；南眺北京，天氣晴好時，可看到樓海無盡；北邊山谷中，公路如線，逐漸消失在群山之中。真是山河壯麗，氣象萬千。

長城已有兩千多年的歷史，歷代都曾修建。現存長城，大部分是明朝修建的。

為什麼要修長城呢？當時是為了防禦北方遊牧民族的侵擾。有人曾對長城做過粗略計算，如果把長城的磚石用來修築一條1米寬、5米高的城牆，那麼可以環繞地球一週。如此浩大的工程，是怎樣修建起來的呢？萬里長城全部是在陡斜的山坡峽谷間和荒涼的沙漠地區建造的，施工相當艱難。除運磚可以使用毛驢等牲畜外，其餘全部勞動都得靠人力。中國古代人民發揮自己的聰明才智，創造了巧妙的施工方法，克服了巨大困難。長城可以說是中華民族勤勞、勇敢、堅韌不拔精神的體現。

好的，八達嶺長城今天就遊覽到此，請諸位上車，參觀下一個景點。

Summer Palace （頤和園）

Ladies and Gentlemen,

Good morning! Now we are at the Summer Palace. Welcome here and I sincerely hope that all of you will have a good time here.

Long Corridor and Marble Boat

This is the famous Long Corridor. You can see that there are hundreds of buildings on the Longevity Hill. However, they are in a very good order. Why? One of the main reasons is that the Long Corridor has connected the hill with the water, linking all the buildings together and making them into a complete whole.

The Long Corridor was built in 1750 during the reign of Emperor Qianlong. It was destroyed in 1860 and rebuilt during Emperor Guangxu's reign. In the building of Chinese palaces, the corridor is a subordinate building which links up all the major buildings. It is also a place for taking a rest which protects people from wind, rain or sunshine. The corridor in front of Longevity Hill is 728 meters long. If you take the space between two pillars as one room, there are 273 rooms along the corridor. It is famous for its unique architectural style and colorful paintings. It is called the Long

Corridor. It has already been listed into the Guinness Book of Records as the longest corridor in the world. You can imagine what a landscape and how pleasant it is when you take a walk along the corridor during the rain with the green hill in the north and blue water in the south.

With the Hall of Dispersing Clouds as the center, the corridor winds its way from the Gate of Inviting Moon in the east to the Shizhang Pavilion in the west. When you walk into the corridor from the Gate of Inviting Moon, you will see at once a corridor without end. In some sections, it is very straight, while in others, it winds and twists. There are four pavilions along the Corridor which symbolize spring, summer, autumn and winter. There is an opened veranda in the eastern and western part of the corridor respectively. The base and body of the corridor goes up and down following the terrain of the southern foot of the Longevity Hill. Four octagonal pavilions are the connecting points of the high and low terrain as well as at changes of direction. Because of its unique design and utilization of the scenery along the two sides to divert people's attention, you can hardly feel the ups and downs and its twisting trend. The Long Corridor is really a magnificent masterpiece in the ancient Chinese palaces and gardens.

This is the Marble Boat. Built in 1755, the whole boat was made of marble stone. It is 36 meters long. Emperor Qianlong had very clear intentions when he ordered this boat to be built. He adopted the words used by Prime Minister Wei Zheng of the Tang Dynasty when he told the Tang Dynasty Emperor to work hard. The words read "water can carry the boat and the boat can also be overturned by water." The building of the boat symbolized at the same time that the reign of Emperor Qianlong was as stable as the Marble Boat and it could never be overturned no matter how strong the wind and waves were. However, the corrupt rule of the Qing Dynasty could not exist as long as the Marble Boat. This was the only "boat" left after the Northern Navy was defeated. It never moved.

The cabin of the Marble Boat was first built in the Chinese style. After it was burned in 1860, it was rebuilt in Western style in 1893. In 1903, one floor of western style and wooden structure was added by Empress Dowager Cixi with windows glassed in five colors. Big mirrors were placed both downstairs and upstairs which could reflect ripples on the lake surface. If visitors sit in front of the mirror, you would feel like floating on the lake. Hence the Empress Dowager Cixi very much liked to sit there to drink tea and enjoy the scenery.

There are four dragon heads in the body of the boat stretching outward. When it rains, the water on top of the cabin would fall into the dragon mouth through the four-cornered hollow pillar. Architects call this kind of drainage design an internal drainage in architecture.

This was originally a platform where captive animals were set free in the Yuan Dynasty. After it was changed into the shape of a boat, on April 8th each year in lunar calendar, Emperor Qianlong would accompany his mother to set captive animals free here.

Garden of Harmonious Interest

Ladies and gentlemen, we are now going to visit the next place, the Garden of Harmonious Interest. The Garden of Harmonious Interest is located in the northeastern part of the Summer Palace at the foot of the east side of the back hill. Built in 1751, it was originally called the Garden of Huishan. It is not only a garden within the Summer Place, but also takes in all the beauty and uniqueness of the gardens in southern China. Therefore, it is called the Real Garden of Harmonious Interest.

When Emperor Qianlong toured south China for the first time in 1751, he visited the Jichang Garden in the city of Wuxi. His grandfather Emperor Kangxi also paid a visit there during his trip to the south. The name of the Jichang Garden was autographed by his grandfather. Emperor Qianlong liked the Garden very much. He asked somebody to make a painting of it and bring it back to Beijing. He had an identical garden built in the Summer Palace and named it the Garden of Huishan. Emperor Qianlong wrote a poem which read "One pavilion one road, one step one scene. The scene changes with step moves. Uniqueness and interests are found every-where. " The Garden was rebuilt in 1811 and the name was changed into the Garden of Harmonious Interest. It was burned down by the British and French Allied Forces in 1860 and rebuilt in 1893.

There are altogether 13 pavilions, terraces and rooms connected by 100 verandas and 5 bridges in different designs. In the center of the garden lies a pond skirted by a ring of halls and pavilions. In the northwest part of the garden, there is a mountain spring falling down in the shade of bamboo grove. The spring is formed by the water in the back lake, which falls down because of the natural terrain. This special scene has revitalized the scenery of gardens in south China. The main building in the garden is the Hall of Hanyuan, which was built with sandalwood. It was the place for Empress Dowager Cixi to relax when she was going sightseeing and angling in the Garden. She usually took a nap here in the hall after she enjoyed a performance at the Grand Stage. There is a stone bridge at southeast corner. It is the famous "Know-the-Fish Bridge" . The bridge is quite low and close to the water surface. It is an ideal place for people to enjoy fish and go angling.

Some people believe that there are eight interests in the Garden of Harmonious Interest. They are interest of seasons, interest of water, interest of bridges, interest of books, interest of building, interest of paintings, interest of verandas, and interest of imitation.

The interest of seasons refers to the garden's different scenes during different seasons. In spring breezes blowing over willows create ripples on the lake's surface. In summer lotus flowers bloom and their fragrance is wafted through the garden. In autumn the blowing willows are reflected in water. And in winter snow covers the pavilions and verandas like a thin silk cloth.

The interest of water refers to the water from a mountain spring that pours into the lotus pond. The source of the spring comes from the east end of Kunming Lake's back end. The main reason the garden is built on such a low terrain is to create this mountain spring, so as to form a drop of 1 to 2 meters between the water surface of the garden and water surface of the lake. With the 1 to 2 meters water drop and the piling-up of mountain stones, it is divided into 9 levels which make the water sound like playing a musical instrument. This is why visitors can find a huge stone lying by the spring on which there are three engraved words "Jade Zither Gorge".

The interest of bridges refers to the garden's five bridges which were designed in different styles. Some of the bridges are connected with the road on one end and with the veranda on the other end. Some face the water on one end and lean against the veranda on the other end. The most famous bridge is the "Know-the-Fish Bridge". It was told that there were two ancient philosophers of different schools Zhuang Zi and Hui Zi who were one day watching the fish together. Zhuang Zi said: "The fish are swimming happily". Then, Hui Zi said: "You are not fish, how do you know that they are happy?" Zhuang Zi replied: "You are not me, how do you know that I do not know the fish are happy?" In those years, Empress Dowager Cixi liked angling in the Garden of Harmonious Interest. The pavilion on the water was the place for her to go angling. It is said that when Empress Dowager Cixi went angling here, in order to please her, the eunuch would dive into the water with fish alive. When she put down the hook, the eunuch would hang the fish onto the hook. Therefore, her fishing rod could never be empty.

The interest of books refers to the calligraphy in the Garden.

The interest of building refers to the building in the Garden. If visitors look at the building's interior, they will see that it has two stories. If visitors look at it from outside, it has only one story.

The interest of paintings refers to the colored paintings of Su style in the verandas of the Garden. And the beauty of the paintings could match that of the Long Corridor. There are more than 100 paintings on the buildings of the Garden. There are paintings of mountains and rivers as well as paintings of figures.

The interest of verandas refers to the four pavilions along the pond which have been linked up as a whole by the twisted corridor. The buildings, pavilions and verandas are linked up together by the twisted corridor. Compared with the Long Corridor, it is also very charming and interesting.

The interest of imitation refers to the Garden of Harmonious Interest is a garden within the garden of the Summer Palace. It was built in a very unique style as it imitated the Jichang Private Garden. In addition to being magnificent and dignified, it is very peaceful and elegant.

This is the end of our visit to the Garden of Harmonious Interest. Thank you for your cooperation.

各位遊客大家好！

現在我們所在的地方就是頤和園。歡迎大家來頤和園遊玩，我真誠地希望您在這裡玩得開心。

長廊和石舫

我們現在看到的就是著名的長廊。不知大家注意到沒有，在北側的萬壽山上有一百多處建築，但卻無雜亂之感。為什麼呢？其中一個主要原因是因有長廊這條綵帶，既銜接了山水，又把各處建築物有機地串聯起來，構成了一個整體。

長廊始建於乾隆十五年，也就是1750 年，1860年被毀，光緒時重建。在中國的庭園建築中，走廊是聯繫各主要建築物的一種附屬建築，有擋風雨蔽日晒和裝飾的作用。由於萬壽山前的這條走廊特別長，有728米，如果把兩根柱子之間的一塊地方稱為一間的話，這條走廊共有273間。因此人們都稱之為「長廊」。長廊已列入「金氏世界紀錄大全」，稱為世界最長的長廊。大家可以想像，北為青山，南為綠水，細雨霏霏之時，遊走於長廊之間該多麼愜意呀。

長廊以排雲殿為中心。向東、西延伸，東起邀月門，西止石丈亭。當人們走進長廊東端的邀月門就進入了一個一眼看不到盡頭的走廊。有的地段直得像一條線，有時又曲折回轉，宛如畫境。從東往西，其間點綴著留佳、寄瀾、秋水、滑邇四個亭子，象徵春、夏、秋、冬四季。長廊的東西兩部，各有一座臨水敞軒，它們是對鷗舫和魚藻軒。長廊的地基和廊身隨萬壽山南麓的地勢高低起伏，四座八角亭是高低和變向的連接點。由於處理巧妙，利用左右的借景而轉移了人們的視線。所以遊長廊時並不感覺到地勢不平、走向曲折。長廊不愧是中國古典園林建築中的藝術傑作。

〔在石舫〕現在大家看到的這個大船就是石舫，公元1755年建，船體全部用大理石製作，通長36米。乾隆對建造這座石舫是有用意的。他引用唐朝魏徵告誡唐太宗「水能載舟，亦能覆舟」的典故，勉勵自己勵精圖治，同時也像徵他的統治像石舫一樣堅固，任憑風吹浪打，而無覆舟之虞。但是清王朝的腐朽統治不可能與這石舫共存。這也是北洋水師作戰失利後留下的唯一一條「船」，一條不動的船。

石舫原有中式艙樓，1860 年被燒燬後，又於光緒十九年（公元1893 年）改建成洋式艙樓，並在船體兩側加上兩個機輪。取「河清海晏」之意，名清晏舫。1903年，慈禧又加蓋了一層洋式層樓（木質結構），窗上嵌著五色琉璃，上下樓各有大鏡子一塊，可以反射湖裡的波紋，坐在鏡子前面有在湖中飄蕩之感。慈禧時常在上邊飲茶作樂，觀賞湖山景色。

石舫船體上有四個龍頭突出在外，下雨時，艙樓頂部的雨水透過四角空心栓流進龍口吐出水來，這種排水設計在建築上稱內排水。

此處原是明代圓靜寺的放生台，乾隆時改為船形後，每年四月初八浴佛日，乾隆皇帝陪其生母孝聖皇太后在此放生。

諧趣園（園中園）

朋友們，現在我們去參觀下一個景點——諧趣園。諧趣園在頤和園東北端，後山東側山腳之下，建於乾隆十六年（公元1751 年），原名惠山園。諧趣園是頤和園的園中之園，它內涵了江南園林的全部秀美特色，故又被稱為「諧趣真園」。

乾隆皇帝1751 年第一次下江南時，曾到無錫寄暢園遊覽。乾隆的祖父康熙皇帝南巡時，也曾去那裡遊覽過，並且用御筆題寫了「寄暢園」三字。乾隆非常喜歡這所庭園，就命人繪了圖樣帶回北京，在清漪園（頤和園前身）照樣仿建，並命名為惠山園。根據乾隆詩序：「一亭一徑、一步一景、景隨步移、步步皆奇趣」，嘉慶十六年（公元1811年）該園重修，改名諧趣園。咸豐十年（公元1860 年）該園被英法聯軍燒燬，光緒十八年（公元1892年）重建。

諧趣園內共有亭、台、堂、榭13處，並用百間遊廊和5座形式不同的橋相溝通。園中所有建築都圍繞中間的水池展開，循廊前進，一步一景。

園內西北角的玉琴峽，利用天然地勢形成的落差，引來後湖之水，造就一道山泉，瀉出於綠竹之間。這種小橋流水的景緻，再現了江南園林的特色。園內主體建築涵遠堂，所用木材全部是檀香木，是慈禧太后在諧趣園內的便殿，供她遊覽、釣魚時休息之用。慈禧在大戲台看戲後，就在此午睡。東南角有一座石橋，橋頭石舫上寫著「知魚橋」，最負盛名。橋面低平近水，是觀魚、垂釣的好地方。

諧趣園的特色有人概括為八趣，即時趣、水趣、橋趣、書趣、樓趣、畫趣、廊趣、仿趣。

時趣是指諧趣園在四季中的不同景色。春天，微風吹柳，水波粼粼；夏天，荷花開放，滿園飄香；秋天，水榭楊柳，倒映水中；冬天，雪蓋廊亭，銀裝素裹。

水趣是因為有山泉注入荷池，這道山泉的水源，來自昆明湖的後湖東端。諧趣園取如此低窪的地勢，主要就是為了形成這道山泉，使諧趣園的水面與湖的水面形成一二米的落差，而在一二米的落差中，又運用山石的堆疊，分成九個層次，使川流不息的水聲高低揚抑，猶如琴韻，所以橫臥在泉邊的一塊巨石上，刻有「玉琴峽」三個字，是為水趣。

橋趣是因為園中有橋五座，風格各異，有的一端連路一端連廊，有的一側臨水一側靠廊，有的一側有橋欄望柱，而一側蕩然水上……其中最著名的為「知魚橋」。橋名取《秋水‧濠上》中莊子和惠子相互辯論的故事。相傳這兩位不同哲學學派的代表人物，在水邊共同觀魚。莊子説：「魚兒在水中游得很快樂。」惠子説：「你不是魚，怎麼知道魚快樂。」莊子反問説：「你不是我，怎麼知道我不知道魚快樂？」當年，慈禧喜歡在諧趣園中釣魚。凌駕在水上的綠水榭，便是慈禧最愛下鉤之處，傳説，每逢她來這裡釣魚，太監為了討她的歡喜，便帶著活魚先行潛入水中，慈禧一下鉤，太監便將魚掛在釣上，於是她總是提竿不空。

書趣是因為園中書法墨寶隨處可見。

樓趣是指園內西部有一座矚新樓，這座樓從園內側看是兩層，若從外側看，卻只有一層。

畫趣是因為園中遊廊的蘇式彩畫可與長廊媲美。園內建築上有百餘幅繪畫，有山水畫和人物畫等。

廊趣是因曲折的走廊將沿池的四座名亭連為一體，樓堂亭榭以曲廊相連，三步一回，五步一折，與長廊相比，另有情趣。

仿趣是因為諧趣園是頤和園的園中之園，應是典型的皇家園林。但該園的造園手法別具一格，仿造的是寄暢園私家園林，在金碧輝煌、端莊肅穆中，獨顯其靜雅清幽。

今天諧趣園就遊覽到此，謝謝大家。

Temple of Heaven （天壇）

Ladies and gentlemen:Today, we are going to visit the Temple of Heaven. First I would like to give you general information about the Temple of Heaven and its functions throughout history.

The Temple of Heaven, located in southeast Beijing, was the place where Ming and Qing emperors worshipped heaven and prayed for bumper harvests. It is now the largest temple group of its kind in China. Ancient Chinese Emperors believed that heaven dominated the world, and they themselves were the sons of heaven to rule the world. The Temple of Heaven is the outcome of the combination of political power and religious authority. It creates an appearance of mystery and fantasy for the purpose of maintaining the emperor's rule.

The Temple of Heaven was built in 1420, and has a history of more than 500 years. It covers an area of 273 hectares, smaller than the Summer Palace and nearly four times as large as the Forbidden City. It is in the shape of "回", and divided into the inner altar and the outer altar, separated by walls. The outer wall is as long as 6,414 meters. As first, the temple only had the western gate, plus the main gate for the emperor to come to worship. The eastern, southern and northern gates were opened later. The inner wall is as long as 3,292 meters and has four gates in the four directions. The northern inner and outer walls are higher and semicircular; while the southern ones are lower and rectangular. This coincides with the ancient Chinese belief that the heaven is circular and the earth is square.

The main buildings of the Temple of Heaven are concentrated within the inner altar. There is the Circular Mound Altar in the south and the Hall of Prayer for Good Harvests (Qiniandian) in the north. The northern and southern altars are joined by a 360-meter-long, 28-meter-wide and 2.5-meter-high raised passage, known as "the Red Stair Way Bridge". The whole compound fully displays the superb architectural art of the ancient Chinese people.

In the early years of the Ming Dynasty, both the earth and the heaven were worshipped here. In 1530, the Fangze Altar (the Temple of Earth) was built in the northern suburbs; only the heaven was worshipped here.

The Emperor attached great importance to worshipping the heaven, and would come to the Temple of Heaven twice a year to personally worship it. The first time was on the 15thof the first lunar month when the Emperor would come to Qiniandian to pray for bumper harvests. The second time was on the Winter Solstice. The Emperor would come to the Circular Mound Altar to report the bumper harvests and expressed his thanks and respect to the heaven for answering his prayers.

While ordinary people were not admitted to the Temple of Heaven's forbidden area, this part of the complex was overrun by foreign troops during Old China's troubled later history. In 1860, the Anglo French Allied Forces sacked and looted the Temple of Heaven after they entered Beijing. In 1900, the Eight Allied Forces turned the Temple of Heaven into their imperialist barracks and headquarters. In 1916 Yuan Shikai, the arch usurper of state power, sought to make himself emperor and performed the last farce of worshipping the heaven here.

After the founding of New China, the Temple of Heaven returned to the people, and has now become an important tourist attraction under special protection. Much renovation has been done to preserve the original buildings and trees and grass has been planted, and play areas for children have been added. Now it has taken on a completely new look. The imperial temple has now become a special tourist park in the city of Beijing.

OK. So much for the introduction to the general information and function of the Temple of Heaven. Now we are going to visit the Red Stairway Bridge and the Circular

Mound Altar.

The Red Stairway Bridge and Circular Mound Altar

Ladies and Gentlemen, just now I told you some general information regarding the Temple of Heaven and its function. Now we are on the way to the Red Stairway Bridge and the Circular Mound Altar. We'll move to the Circular Mound Altar first, and then we'll go to the Red Stairway Bridge.

[On the Circular Mound Altar] The Circular Mound Altar is located in the south of the Temple of Heaven and is also known as the Altar of Worshipping Heaven. Built in 1530 and expanded in 1749, it has a history of over 400 years. The three-tier circular altar protected by balustrades of marble stone is 5 meters high. The altar is encircled by two walls. The inner wall is circular and the outer one is square, which represents the belief that the heaven is round and the earth is square. Looking from above, the Circular Mound Altar looks like a three-dimensional target in a shooting range. In the Ming and Qing dynasties, the Emperor held grand ceremonies worshipping the heaven on Winter Solstice here each year.

There are many interesting stories about the architecture of the Circular Mound Altar. It is a building designed with a geometric theory by the ancient Chinese laboring people. Geometric theory was not only applied in its outer appearance, but also in its structure. All of the mathematical calculations about the building materials were very accurate. It is really amazing for tourists both at home and abroad.

There are three terraces on the Circular Mound Altar, and on each terrace there are nine steps. Each terrace is protected by marble balustrades with carvings. The number of balustrades is all multiples of nine:the upper terrace is 72, the middle one is 108 and the lower one is 180. At the same time, the number of bricks paved on each terrace is also nine or the multiples of nine. The central stone on the upper terrace is a whole marble stone, and from its outwards, there is nine bricks on the first circle, 18 on the second circle, and 81 on the ninth circle; and 90 on the tenth circle of the middle terrace, and 162 on the 18thcircle of the middle terrace; and 171 on the 19thcircle of the lower terrace, and 243 on the 27thcircle of the lower terrace. All together there are 378 "nines", which means 3402. At the same time, the diameter for the upper terrace is nine zhang (1*9), the diameter for the middle terrace is 15 zhang (3*5), and the diameter for the lower terrace is 21(3*7). The combination of the three is 45(5*9), which is not only a multiple of nine, but also the figure of nine and five carries the meaning of dignity.

Then why are nine or the multiples of nine used in the design of the Temple of Heaven? There are many reasons for this. One is that legend has it that God of Heaven lived in the Ninth Heaven, and the number nine or the multiples of nine represent the Ninth Heaven. meaning the supremacy of the heaven. Another saying is that in ancient China, odd numbers were regarded as numbers of Yang(male), and even number were regarded as number of Yin (female). The heaven is Yang and the earth is Yin. The Temple of Heaven was used to worship the heaven, therefore only the number of Yang could be used in its construction. The figure of nine is the largest figure of Yang, and is regarded as the most auspicious number. It is a superstitious belief, but it also shows that the artisans at that time had superb mathematical knowledge and calculation skills.

[In the center of the upper terrace of the Circular Mound Altar] This is a round marble, located in the center of Circular Mound Altar, and it is the most interesting place. When you stand on this stone and speak softly, your voice sounds quite loud to yourself, and also echoes somewhat. However, people outward the second or the third circle have no such feelings. Why not have a try? This is also an acoustic phenomenon, because the ground of the altar is very smooth, and when the sound wave is transmitted to the marble stones of the same distance, it can be reflected immediately. According to the test of acousticians, it takes only 0.07 second for the sound wave to transmit and reflect. Therefore, the speaker can not distinguish the original sound and its echo. The echo is very strong for people speaking at the central stone. The feudal rulers attributed this phenomenon to the people's devotion and loyalty to them.

Now please look around. The stones of the same shape and size are laid without any crevices. From Qianlong's time till today, the surface has experienced more than 200 years, and it is still smooth and without any crevices, or dents.

[North of the Circular Mound Altar] This is a circular wall with only one gate in the south for people to enter or leave. Inside of it are the Imperial Vault of Heaven, Triple Sound Stones, and Echo Wall. They were not designed from the point of view of acoustics, but when the park was open to the public, visitors found fantastic phenomenon which is in accord with acoustic theory. We shall visit the Triple Sound Stones, Imperial Vault of Heaven and Echo Wall one after another.

[On the stairs leading to the Imperial Vault of Heaven] This road is paved from the north to the south with three stones, popularly known as the Triple Sound Stones. Standing on the first stone and speaking, the visitor can hear one echo; standing on the second and third stones and speaking, the visitor can hear two echoes and three echoes respectively. This is because the third stone is located in the center of the Echo Wall; a sound wave can be reflected back from the wall. Because the distances from the three stones to the wall are different, the numbers of echoes made on different stones are different. Feudal rulers also added mysterious color to the phenomenon.

[In the Imperial Vault of Heaven] This circular hall, crowned by a gilded dome which is supported by a complicated span-work, is roofed with blue glazed tiles and stands on the white marble terrace, like a gigantic open umbrella. The hall was built in 1530 and has a history of more than 400 years. It is 19.5 meters high. The diameter at the bottom is 15.6 meters. The whole hall is supported by 8 pillars without beams on the ceiling. The ceilings are just piles of sets of brackets on top of the columns supporting the beams with roof eaves withdrawing one by one making up a beautiful vault roof. This structure is not only delicate in structure inside, but also beautiful in outer appearance. There are paintings inside, with green as the main color, and the dragon as the main design. This unique architecture is very rare, and has a high value of architectural art. In the very center of this structure is a throne upon which lies the tablet of God of Heaven. The stone desk in front of the throne is the place where the tablets of ancestors of the Emperor are placed. The tablets of the Gods of the Sun, Moon, Stars, Wind, Cloud, Rain and Thunder are stored in the east and west subordinate halls outside the Imperial Vault.

The famous Echo Wall is the wall of the Imperial Vault Hall. If two visitors standing on the east and west respectively speak to the wall in the direction of north, the outcome is like making a phone call. You may have a try. What accounts for this very interesting phenomenon? This is also an example of the application of acoustics in the architecture. The reason is that the wall is cornered with overflowing tiles which prevent the sound waves from disappearing, so the sound waves are echoed and transmitted along it.

[On the Red Stairway Bridge] Also called the Haiman Walk, the Red Stairway Bridge is a stone passage from the north to the south. It is 360 meters long and 28 meters wide. The whole bridge is raised from the south to the north gradually. The south end is one meter high, and the north end is three meters high. The road is designed in such a way in order to symbolize that the Emperor is ascending step by step to heaven. It also means that there is a long distance between the earth and the heaven.

The stairways of ancient palaces were mostly painted red. If this is a straight walk, then why is it called a bridge? There is a tunnel from east to west, and this walk is just the flyover, therefore it is called a bridge.

There is a tunnel underneath the walk, called the Gate of Livestock. On the day of worshipping, livestock were brought across the tunnel with music playing. This gate is also called the Pass of Ghost. Nobody dared approach the gate at an ordinary time. On the east side of the middle of the Red Stairway Bridge is a platform where the Emperor changed clothes before he went to the Hall of Prayer for Good Harvests to worship.

OK, we finish our tour to the Red Stairway Bridge and the Circular Mound Altar. Keep closer to us and we'll continue to visit the Hall of Prayer for Good Harvests.

Hall of Prayer for Good Harvests

Ladies and gentlemen, this is the splendid Hall of Prayer for Good Harvests, the place where Ming and Qing emperors prayed for good harvests. It is a lofty cone-shaped structure with triple eaves, and the top is crowned by a gilded ball. The hall is the main building in the Temple of Heaven and is regarded as its landmark, and it is also a world-renowned building.

The Hall of Prayer for Good Harvests was built in 1420 and was originally named Daqi Hall and was rectangular in shape. In 1545, it was made a three-tier circular hall and renamed Hall of Daxiang. The original colors for the glaze tiles were blue for the upper tier, yellow for the middle tier and green for the lower tier. The three colors represented three social strata. The blue is the color for the heaven, the yellow is the color for the Emperor, and the green is the color for officials and people. In 1715 the hall was renamed and given its present name. The three colors were changed to the blue color only, symbolizing the blue heaven. In 1889, the hall was destroyed in a thunderstorm and was rebuilt the following year.

The Hall of Prayer for Good Harvests was built in a triple tiered stone terrace which is 6 meters high and covers an area of 5,900 square meters. The hall is 38 meters high, and the diameter at the base is 24 meters. The three tiered roofs are all covered with blue glazed tiles. The whole structure shrinks as it goes up in height, and at the top is a gilded ball. Thus the hall is overwhelming and towering.

The Hall of Prayer for Good Harvests is also known as a beamless hall. There are neither beams nor nails supporting the hall. Only 28 massive pillars support the hall and a number of bars, laths, joints and rafters connect each part. This is really a wonder in the Chinese classical wooden structure. Former US Secretary of State, Dr.Kissenger, was amazed at the structure of the hall. As you know, Dr.Kissenger once studied architecture knew a lot about it.

The hall is a wooden structure with 28 pillars supporting it. The pillars and ceilings are beautifully decorated. On the facade of the hall is a screen with various dragon designs. In front of the screen is the throne for worshipping the God of Heaven.

The Hall of Prayer for Good Harvests was designed according to the principle of "worshipping the Gods in the heaven". The hall is round, meaning the heaven is round; the tiles are blue, which symbolizes the blue sky. The numbers of pillars inside are supposed to be erected according to astronomy. The four central pillars represent the four seasons of spring, summer, autumn and winter. The 12 pillars in the middle symbolize the 12 months of a year. The outer 12 pillars stand for the divisions in a day. The number of pillars in the middle and outside combined represents the 24 solar terMs.The number of all pillars together which is 28, represents the 28 constellations. Together with the 8 smaller pillars on the top, the number is 36, representing the 36 Big Dipper. The pillar under the dome symbolizes the whole empire under one ruler. Another interesting story is about the dragon-phoenix stone. On the central stone of the ground is carved a walking dragon and a flying phoenix. It is said that at first there was only a phoenix carved on the stone and the dragon was carved in the ceiling. With time passing by, the dragon and the phoenix got inspirations and the dragon always flew down to play with the phoenix. It so happened that once the Emperor was worshipping the heaven and was kneeling down, and so the dragon and the phoenix were pressed inside the stone. Therefore, it got the name of dragon-and-phoenix stone.

In front of the Hall of Prayer for Good Harvests are subordinate halls for storing the tablets of Gods of the Sun, Moon, Stars, Wind, Rain, Clouds and Thunder. North of the Hall of Prayer for Good Harvests is the Hall of Imperial Zenith, known as the Heavenly Storeroom, the place where the tablets of God of Heaven and ancestors of the Emperor were stored. The inscriptions of the horizontal tablet on the Hall of Imperial Zenith were handwritten by Emperor Jiajing. There are splendid paintings inside the hall.

The Hall of Prayer for Good Harvests is a beautiful picture looking from afar. On the white terrace rests a grand hall with red wall and blue roof, and with towering ancient trees surrounding it, it is extremely spectacular. No wonder people describe it as a heavenly palace.

OK. We finished our tour in the Temple of Heaven today. Please follow the group and proceed to the bus.

各位朋友大家好！現在我們將要遊覽的是天壇。首先，我來講一講天壇概況。

天壇位於北京城區的東南部，原是明、清兩代皇帝祭天、祈谷的聖地，為中國現存最大的一處壇廟建築。在中國古代，封建帝王把「天」看做萬物之主宰，皇帝則是「天」的兒子，自稱「天子」，「受命於天」而統治人間。天壇便是這種政權與神權相結合的產物，給人以神秘奇幻之感，目的是維護其封建統治。

天壇建於明朝永樂十八年（公元1420年），距今已有500多年的歷史。占地273萬平方米，略小於頤和園，相當於故宮面積的近4倍。整個建築布局呈「回」字形，分為內外壇兩大部分，各有壇牆相圍。外壇牆總長6414 米。原來僅設西門，為天壇的正門，是當年皇帝前來天壇祭祀時進出的大門。東、南、北各門都是後來開闢的。內壇牆長 3292米，分別設有東、南、西、北四大「天門」。內外壇北面的圍牆高大，均為半圓形；南邊的圍牆較低而呈方形。這種北圓南方的建築形式，象徵中國古代「天圓地方」的宇宙觀。

天壇的主體建築均集中於內壇，南有圜丘壇，北有祈年殿。南北兩壇之間由一條長360米，寬28米和高2.5米的「海墁」大道——「丹陛橋」相聯結，組成了一個完整、壯觀的建築群體，充分體現了中國古代人民高超的建築藝術水平。

明代初年，祭天地都在此處舉行，名為天地壇。嘉靖九年（公元1530　年），在城北另建方澤壇（地壇），實行天地分祭，從此這裡專門用於祭天，成為名副其實的天壇。

歷代封建皇帝對祭天活動都極為重視，每年要兩次親臨天壇祭天。第一次是在農曆正月十五，至祈年殿舉行祈穀禮，求「皇天上帝」保佑五穀豐登，為百穀祈求膏澤。第二次是在冬至，到圜丘壇稟告五穀業已豐收，感謝天地的保佑之恩。此外，如逢乾旱少雨，則在圜丘壇臨時舉辦「常等禮」或「大禮」等求雨祭祀活動。每次祭天典禮都非常隆重，以表示對天帝的虔誠與尊崇。

在封建社會，天壇這塊神聖不可觸犯的禁地，一般人不能隨便進入，但在內憂外患的舊中國，天壇也難逃蹂躪之災。如清朝咸豐十年（公元1860年），英法聯軍攻入北京後，闖入天壇進行搶掠洗劫。光緒二十六年（公元1900　年），八國聯軍入侵北京，這裡成了帝國主義列強的兵營與司令部。1916年，竊國大盜袁世凱為當皇帝製造輿論，曾在天壇演出了最後一場祭天鬧劇。

中國新政權成立後，天壇回到了人民手中，並被列為全國重點文物保護單位之一。政府對天壇進行了大規模維修，不但保留了古建築群體的雄姿，而且還植樹種草，美化環境，並增添文化娛樂設施，開闢了兒童遊藝場，使其面貌煥然一新。原來的皇家壇廟，變成了一處北京市區富有特色的旅遊公園。

好！天壇概況就介紹到此，下面我們將參觀遊覽丹陛橋和圜丘壇。

丹陛橋和圜丘壇

遊客朋友們，剛才向各位介紹了天壇的概況，現在我們來參觀遊覽丹陛橋和圜丘壇。我們先參觀圜丘壇，然後遊覽丹陛橋。

〔在圜丘壇〕圜丘壇位於天壇南部，俗稱祭天壇，建於明嘉靖九年（公元1530年），清乾隆十四年（公元1749 年）擴建，距今已有200 多年的歷史。圜丘壇由白石雕欄圍護，通高5 米，潔白如玉，極其美麗壯觀。它嵌放在裡圓外方的兩重圍牆裡，形成一幅既精巧又完整的幾何圖案。從上空看圜丘壇就像一座立體的靶環，「裡圓外方」表示「天圓地方」。明清兩代，每年冬至日皇帝的隆重祭天禮儀，就在此壇舉行。

圜丘壇在建築形式上，有著許多神奇有趣的說法。這是中國古代人民巧妙運用幾何學原理設計的一座傑出建築。這一建築不但造型上像幾何圖形，整個結構上也是對幾何圖形的巧妙運用，各項建築材料的數學計算均極其精確，深為中外廣大遊人讚嘆與稱奇。

圜丘壇共分三層，每層四面各有台階九級。每層周圍都設有精雕細刻的白玉欄杆。欄杆的數字均為9的倍數，即上層72根、中層108根、下層180根。同時，各層鋪設的扇面形石板，也是九或九的倍數。如最上層的中心是一塊圓形大理石（稱做天心石或太極石），從中心石向外，第一環為9塊，第二環18塊，到第九環81塊；中層從第十環的90塊至十八環的162塊；下層從十九環的171 塊至二十七環的243塊，三層共 378 個「9」、為3402塊。

同時，上層直徑為9 丈（取一九），中層直徑為15丈（取三五），下層直徑為21 丈（取三七），合起來45丈，不但是九的倍數，並且有九五之尊的含義。

為什麼要用九或九的倍數來設計建造祭壇呢？原因之一是，據神話傳說，皇天上帝是住在九重天裡，用九或九的倍數來像徵九重天，以表示天體的至高與至大。原因之二是，中國古代把單數（奇數）看做陽數，而將雙數（偶數）視為陰數。天為陽、地為陰。天壇是用來祭天的，只能用陽數進行建築。而「九」又被視為「極陽數」，這是最吉祥的數字。除了封建迷信的因素外，這種設計規制，反映出當時工匠們高超的數學知識和計算才能，實在令人嘆服。

〔在圜丘壇上層中間位置〕這是一塊圓心石，在圜丘壇上層中心位置，這塊圓心石是遊人最感興趣的奇妙處之一。當你站在圓心石上輕聲說話時，自己聽起來聲音很宏大，有共鳴回音之感，但站在第二、三環及以外的人，則無此感覺。各位不妨試一試。這是為什麼呢？原來，這也是一種聲學現象：由於壇面十分光潔平滑，聲波傳到周圍等距離的石欄板後，能夠迅速地被反射回來。據聲學家測驗，從發音到聲波再回到圓心石的時間，總共僅有0.07秒鐘。說話者根本無法分清它的原音和回音，所以站在圓心石的人聽起來，其共鳴性回音就特別響亮。封建統治者把這種聲學現象說成是「上天垂象」，是天下萬民對於朝廷的無限歸心與一致響應，同時還賦予「億兆景從石」的美名。

各位向四周看一看，這些石板的形狀相同，大小一致，而安裝起來又都驚人地嚴絲合縫。從乾隆時代至今天，經歷200多年的風風雨雨，台面依然平整如鏡，接縫依然嚴密無隙，更沒有下沉和上翹等現象。人們看到這樣精巧優美的建築，無不欽佩古代工匠們絕妙的設計和高超的工藝水平。

〔圓丘壇北〕各位，這是一道圓形圍牆，只有正南方一門可出入。門內有圓殿皇穹宇及著名的三音石、回音壁等。這組建築雖非從聲學的角度進行設計，但開放為公園後，逐漸發現了這些符合聲學原理的奇特現象。下面我們依次觀賞三音石、皇穹宇和回音壁。

〔在皇穹宇台階前〕這裡是一條從北向南由三塊石板鋪成的甬道，俗稱三音石。站在階前第一塊石板上發出聲音，可以聽到一次回聲，站在第二、三塊石板上發出聲音分別可聽到二次和三次回聲。這是因為這三塊石板處於回音壁的中心部位，聲波從圓壁反射回來，又由於三塊石板到圓壁的距離各有不同，所以聽到回聲的次數也就不同了。但封建統治者把此聲學反射現象也蒙上神秘的色彩，說此為「人間喁語」、「天聞若雷」之故，是皇天上帝給予回聲的結果。這些石板還有一個尊稱，叫做「天聞若雷石」。

〔在皇穹宇〕這是一座單層圓形殿宇，攢尖鎏金寶頂，覆蓋藍色琉璃瓦，豎立於白石須彌座上，宛如一把張開的巨傘，極為端莊秀麗。該殿建於1530年，距今已有400多年歷史。殿高19.5米，底部直徑15.6米，磚木結構。整個殿宇用8根簷柱支撐，頂無橫樑，由眾多斗栱層層上疊，天花板層層收縮，組成美麗的穹隆圓頂式的藻井。這種多層斗栱結構，不但使殿內奇巧壯觀，也使建築外形更加優美。殿內有描金和瀝粉貼金彩畫，以青綠為基調，以金龍為主要圖案，輝煌華麗，非同一般。這一建築形式獨具一格，極為罕見，具有很高的藝術價值，是中國寶貴的文化遺產。

殿內正中的石台寶座，是放置皇天上帝神牌的地方。寶座前左右的石台，是放置皇帝歷代祖先牌位之處。殿外的東西配殿，為供奉日月星辰和雲雨風雷諸神牌位之所。

著名的回音壁就是皇穹宇的圍牆。如果兩個人一東一西均對牆朝北低聲說話，就好像打電話一樣，極其奇妙有趣。各位可以試一試。為什麼會有這種奇妙的現象呢？這也是聲學原理在建築上的巧妙運用。因為圍牆是圓形的，且又磨磚對縫，地面十分光潔；再加上圍牆頂部蓋有檐瓦，聲波不易散失，便沿著圍牆連續反射傳遞了。

〔在丹陛橋〕丹陛橋也稱海墁大道，這是一條南北走向的石砌台基之道。全長360米，寬28米，整個橋體由南向北逐漸升高，南端高約1米，北端高3米左右。如此設計建造，一則像徵皇帝步步升高，寓升天之意；二則表示從人間到天上，有遙遠的路程。

「丹」者，紅也，「陛」，原指宮殿前的台階。古時宮殿前的台階多以紅色塗飾，故稱「丹陛」。這明明是一條筆直坦蕩的大道，為何又稱「橋」呢？原來道路下有一個東西走向的券洞，與上面的大道正好形成立體交叉，故稱為橋。

橋下這個東西走向的券洞叫進牲門，從犧牲所到宰牲亭要通過此門。祭前，由所牧（即所長）帶所軍，用黃絨繩將「牲」捆好，用木盆盛活角，擊鼓奏樂穿門而過。此門俗稱鬼門關，平時無人敢走進此門。丹陛橋中部東側為一座凸字形平台，這是皇帝往祈年殿行祀谷禮時，更換冕服的地方。

各位，丹陛橋和圜丘壇就參觀遊覽到此，請跟好隊伍，我們繼續前進，去參觀祈年殿。

祈年殿

女士們、先生們，這就是巍峨壯麗的祈年殿，是明清兩代皇帝祈禱五穀豐登的地方。它是一座鎏金寶頂、藍瓦紅柱、金碧彩繪三層重檐的圓形大殿，是天壇最突出的一座建築，被視為天壇的標誌，也是中外馳名的建築物。

祈年殿建於明永樂十八年（公元1420年），初名叫大祀殿，呈長方形。明嘉靖二十四年（公元1545年），改成三重檐圓殿，改名為大享殿。當時三重檐的琉璃瓦是三種顏色，上藍、中黃、下綠，相傳這三色代表三個等級。藍代表天色，黃是皇帝的代表色，綠是一般臣庶顏色。清乾隆十六年（公元1751年）重修該殿，把三重檐改成一色藍琉璃瓦，以象徵藍天。清光緒十五年（公元1889 年），該殿毀於雷火，次年依原樣重建。

祈年殿採用上屋下壇的構造形式，建在高約6米、占地5900平方米的三層白石雕欄環抱的圓台之上，殿高38米，底部直徑24米。三層殿頂均覆以深藍色的琉璃瓦，呈放射形。整個建築由台基的最下一層逐漸向上收縮，直至鎏金寶頂，給人一種拔地而起、高聳雲天的感覺，象徵殿宇隱入天際，與天相接。

祈年殿俗稱無樑殿，整座建築不用大樑及鐵釘，完全依靠28根擎天柱及眾多的枋、枕、桷、閂支撐和榫接起來。這是抬樑式木造構架建築中的傑出典範，具有極高的研究價值，為中國古典木構建築中的一大奇觀。美國前國務卿季辛吉博士對此曾讚歎不止，大家知道季辛吉博士是學過建築的。

大殿全部採用木結構，28根大柱支撐著整個殿頂的重量。古鏡式的柱礎，海水寶相花的柱身，瀝粉堆金，分外壯觀。3層殿脊以鋪鎏金斗栱作支撐，卯榫交叉，獨具匠心。殿內梁枋大木和天花板，均採用龍鳳和璽彩畫，裝飾精美，金碧輝煌。藻井內有木雕龍鳳圖案，相對地面中心，有塊平面圓形大理石，上面有自然形成的龍鳳花紋，上下映襯，別具情趣。殿內正面艾葉膏石須彌座上，是漆金浮雕雲龍的屏風，頂部透雕騰龍，屏前放著祭祀皇天上帝用的寶座。

祈年殿是按照「敬天禮神」的思想設計的，殿為圓形，象徵天圓。瓦用藍色，象徵著藍天。殿內柱子的數目，據說是按照天象建立起來的。中間的4根通天柱，象徵春夏秋冬四季。中層的12根金柱，象徵1年的12個月。外層的12根檐柱，象徵一天中子丑寅卯等12個時辰。中外層相加24根，象徵24個節氣。3　　層相加共28根，象徵周天二十八星宿。再加柱頂8根童柱，象徵三十六天罡。寶頂下的雷公柱，象徵著皇帝的「一統天下」。更有趣的是關於龍鳳石的傳說：殿內地面中心的大理石表面上的墨色紋理頗像一條行龍和一只飛鳳。龍紋色深，角、須、爪、尾俱全。鳳紋色淺，嘴、眼、羽毛隱約可辨，粗具鳳形，俗名叫龍鳳呈祥石。傳說這塊石上原來只有鳳紋，而殿頂藻井內只有雕龍，年長日久，龍鳳有了靈感，金龍常常飛下來觀鳳。不料有一次正趕上皇帝來祭天，在石上跪著行禮，把金龍玉鳳全部壓到圓石裡面去了。從此，這塊石頭就變成了龍鳳石。豐富的想像和美麗的傳說，為這座古老的祭壇增添了幾分神秘色彩。

在祈年殿前兩側，有供奉日月星辰、風雲雷雨諸神位的配殿。祈年殿北面是皇乾殿，古稱天庫，是儲藏皇天上帝和皇帝祖先神牌的大殿。匾額上「皇乾殿」三個大字為嘉靖御筆。殿內金碧輝煌。東門外有長廊、神庫、神廚、宰牲亭、七塋石等。

站在遠處眺望祈年殿，猶如一幅絢麗的圖案。潔白的壇台上托起一座藍色琉璃瓦頂的大殿，四周古柏環抱，殿上白雲繚繞，寶頂燦爛。再襯以對比性的建築，顯得特別端莊富麗，畫面和諧，情趣高尚。難怪有人讚譽它：白玉高壇紫翠重，不是天宮似天宮。

好，天壇的參觀遊覽到此結束，請大家跟好隊伍，上車去遊覽下一個景點。

Tianjin Municipality天津市

Touring Tianjin （天津之旅）

Good morning, ladies and gentlemen. Welcome to Tianjin. Now, I would like to give you a brief introduction to Tianjin.

Tianjin, also called "Jin" for short. Tianjin is one of the four municipalities in China. Its name means "the place where the emperor crossed the river". In recent years, Tianjin has received more and more attention from tourists both at home and abroad due to its numerous tourism attractions and rich history.

Located at the western shore of Pacific Ocean and in the center of Bohai-Rim, backed by the vast area of north China and facing north-east Asia, Tianjin, is an important hub for connections to more than ten provinces and cities in northern China. Tianjin is only 120 kilometers away from Beijing. With the Haihe River, one of the five largest rivers in China, crossing from north to south, Tianjin has long been renowned as "Sea Inlet of Nine Rivers" and "Communications Center of River and Sea". Tianjin has a total area of more than 11, 800 square kilometers, with 153 kilometers coastline and its land boundary is over 1, 100 kilometers long.

Tianjian has a semi-humid continental monsoon climate of warm-temperate zone with four distinct seasons and adequate sunshine. It has cold winters and hot summers while spring and autumn are short and pleasant. The annual average temperature stands at around 12℃. In general, January is the coldest month and July is the hottest. The average frost free season lasts about 200 days; and annual average rainfall is about 600 millimeters.

Tianjin has developed a well-organized tourism program, which takes the Haihe River as the axial line, downtown area as the main attraction, and Jixian County and Binhai New Area as its new tourist spots. Various tourist spots have been developed, such as tour via water route, tour to the former residence of the celebrities, famous street travelling, outing to Yuyang, Xiqing folk custom travelling and tour to Binhai New Area. In addition, a series of large tourism events are also held on annual basis, like Folk Custom Temple Fair (during Spring Festival), Peach Blossom Cultural and

Travel Festival on the Great Canal (in March), Huang-yaguan Great Wall International Marathon Event (in May), European Charm Festival (in June), Tianjin-Tanggu Sea Travel (in July), Tianjin Mazu Cultural and Travel Festival (in September), Yuyang Autumn Travel Festival, Gulou International Folk Custom Travel Festival (in October), Haihe River Travel Festival and International College Students Dragon Boat Competition.

Tianjin has four world-known folk arts including "Zhang's Art of Clay", "Yangliuqing Spring Festival Paintings", "Wei's Kites" (which won the Golden Prize in World's Panama Exposition in 1914) and "Liu's Brick Sculpture". In addition, Tianjin's folk arts are also renowned for its Tianjin paper cutting, lanterns, velvet silk flowers and various international and domestic award-winning carpets and tapestries.

Tianjin also has a variety of traditional style foods, in which, "Three Unique Foods of Tianjin" are comprised of Goubuli's Stuffed Buns, Guifaxiang Fried Dough Twists and Ear-Hole Fried Cake. Other special foods include:Zhang's Peanuts, Cao' Meat, Lu's Fried Cake, Bai's Dumplings, Zhilanzhai Sweetened Rice Flour, Dafulai's crispy rice with vegetables and Stone Door Steamed Stuffed Buns.

Renowned as the "Ferry of the Emperor" and seated on the seashore with a landscape of mountains and lakes, Tianjin has rich tourism attractions and enjoys the fame as "the epitome of modern China". It has many famous scenic spots, including Panshan Mountain in Jixian County, known as the "Back Yard Garden" of Tianjin and Beijing, due to its famous mountains, quiet forests, clean water, impregnable passes and old temples. Other attractions are Folk Custom Residences like the famous house in Jinmen, Shi Family Mansion; the former Residence of Huo Yuanjia, the famous martial art master, the Tianjin Mazu Temple, one of the three largest Mazu temples in China, and Yangliuqing Spring Festival Paintings Museum. And the city has the former residences of many famous Chinese historical figures such as Sun Yat-sen, Zhang

Xueliang, Liang Qichao, Pu Yi (the last emperor), 7 presidents and 5 prime ministers of the late Qing Dynasty and the early Republic of China, as well as the place where the US President Herbert Hoover stayed during a visit made to China before he became President. Finally, Tianjin contains many other historical buildings with architectural styles from different countries on the five main roads and downtown area near the Haihe River, making the city known as the "exposition center of world architectures". Tianjin's oceanfront includes not only the harbor, but also beaches, forts, a retired aircraft carrier, Haimen Old Temple, Imported Goods Market, Haihe Beach Park, wetlands and lakes, such as Qilihai Lake in Ninghe County, Tuanbowa Lake in Jinghai County, and Dongli Lake in the Dongli District.

Well, my friends, so much for my brief introduction to Tianjin, any questions are welcomed! Thank you for your support and cooperation.

各位朋友大家好！歡迎大家來天津旅遊！下面我把天津的基本情況給大家簡單介紹一下。

天津簡稱津，是中國四個直轄市之一，它的名字的意思是天子渡河的地方。近年來，由於豐富的旅遊資源及悠久的歷史，天津市受國內外越來越多的關注。

天津地處太平洋西岸環渤海經濟圈的中心，背靠中國北方的廣大腹地，面向東北亞，是中國北方十幾省、市、區對外交往的重要通道，與中國首都北京相距120千米。中國五大流域之一的海河流域縱貫全境，素有「九河下稍」和「河海要衝」之稱。天津地域總面積1.18萬平方千米，海岸線長153千米，陸界長1100多千米。

天津屬暖溫帶半濕潤大陸季風型氣候，四季分明，日照充分。氣候的主要特徵是：季風顯著，溫差較大。年平均氣溫在12℃左右，最冷一般在1月，最熱一般在7月。平均無霜期為200天左右，年平均降水量在600毫米左右。

天津旅遊業已形成了以海河為軸線、以市區為主體、以薊縣和濱海新區為兩翼的旅遊景觀開發格局，推出了水路風光遊、名人故居遊、名街休閒遊、漁陽山野遊、西青民俗遊、濱海風情遊等諸多精品旅遊線路。天津每年都要舉辦一系列大型旅遊活動，如：春節期間的民俗旅遊廟會，3月份的運河桃花文化旅游節，5月份的黃崖關長城國際馬拉松旅遊活動、6月份的歐陸風情節，7月份的津沽旅遊海會，9月份的天津媽祖文化旅遊節、漁陽金秋旅遊節，10月份的鼓樓國際民俗風情旅遊節，海河旅遊節暨國際大學生龍舟賽等。

天津有馳名天下的四大民間藝術：「泥人張」彩塑藝術、人工彩繪的「楊柳青年畫」、1914　年獲巴拿馬國際博覽會金獎的「魏記風箏」、以「刻磚劉」為代表的建築裝飾磚雕。此外，衛派天津剪紙、天津燈籠、天津絨絹花以及在國際和國內多次獲獎的天津地毯、掛毯等，都是近現代天津民間藝術的代表。

天津傳統風味食品也是多種多樣的，有「津門三絕」的狗不理包子、十八街（桂發祥）麻花、耳朵眼炸糕。還有張記果仁、曹記驢肉、陸記燙麵炸糕、白記水餃、芝蘭齋糕乾、大福來鍋巴菜、石頭門檻素包等。

天津以「天子渡口」而得名，這裡山海共存，河湖相伴，具有豐富的旅遊資源，享有「近代中國看天津」的美譽。比較著名的風景名勝有：薊縣盤山是集名山、幽林、秀水、雄關、古剎於一地的京津「後花園」和綠色觀光休閒渡假旅遊勝地。民俗故居有津門名宅石家大院、精武元祖霍元甲故居、中國三大媽祖廟之一天津媽祖廟、中國三大年畫之一楊柳青年畫館等。名人寓所有孫中山、張學良、梁啟超以及末代皇帝溥儀、清末民初的七大總統、五位總理和前美國總統胡佛等國內外名人寓所數十處。天津具有「萬國建設築博覽館」之稱，在「五大道」及海河市中心附近留有風格各異的大量世界各國歷史風貌建築。濱海風光有海灘、海港、炮台、航母、海門古剎、海河外灘公園、洋貨市場等。濕地湖泊有寧河縣七里海、靜海縣團泊窪、東麗區東麗湖等。

朋友們，我的講解就先到這裡，如果大家有什麼問題的話，歡迎提問！非常感謝大家對我的支持與合作！

Shanxi Province山西省

A Glimpse of the Province （本省簡介）

Shanxi Province is located along the middle reaches of the Yellow River and sits on the eastern of the Loess Plateau. It has complex terrain and diverse landforms, surrounded by mountains and rivers. Shanxi has a moderate climate with four distinct seasons. The province's gorgeous scenery reflects nature's exquisite handwork. Shanxi is one of the birthplaces of Chinese national civilization and its history is glorious and well-established, so it has long been called China's Ancient Art Museum and Literary Capital. Some seventy per cent of China's existing national ancient architecture is located here. Thus one popular saying in the tourism industry goes as follows: "To know the recent ten years'development of China, you can see Shenzhen; To know the recent one hundred years' development of China, you can see Shanghai; To know the recent one thousand years' development of China, you can see Beijing; To know the recent three thousand years'development of China, you can see Shaanxi; To know the recent five thousand years' development of China, you can see Shanxi. " The beautiful natural scenery, ancient civilization, revolutionary historical sites and contemporary monuments and achievements together provide Shanxi with an abundance of colorful tourist attractions and resources.

Shanxi is one of Chinese civilization's birth-places. Its one-character abbreviation is Jin, after the state of Jin that existed here during the Spring and Autumn Period. The local tourist attractions are very rich. This fact was due to the multitudinous cultural heritage left behind by the centuries-old history plus the complex terrain and landforms, and the natural scenery formed by the rivers and mountains. Shanxi has the most extant historic buildings in China, among which fifty are under state protection and four hundred are under provincial protection. The temples of Mt.Wutai, which is one of the four Buddhism holy lands, had aggregated the essence of a millennium all together. Among them, China's most ancient wooden construction—South Buddhist Temple, Buddha Light Temple and Xiant-ong Temple, which used many kinds of construction techniques from the Northern Wei Dynasty to Qing Dynasty and the Dagoba of Pagoda

Yard are the most famous. The precipitous and picturesque Mount Hengshan is one of the five holy mountains in China. Midway up its slope is the Xuankong (Overhanging) Monastery, a rare alpine complex built in the late Northern Wei, with many halls and chambers hanging on the rock face of a sheer cliff. Jin Ci Temple of Taiyuan, which gathered many styles of ancient buildings, is a tourist paradise. Pingyao Ancient City, one of the three China extant ancient cities, has been listed as a world cultural heritage site. The Ruicheng Yongle Palace is a highly representative Yuan Dynasty architectural style Taoist temple; the murals on the inner wall are one of China's art treasures. Yongji Pujiu Temple is the birth place of Romance of the West Chamber, which is also called The Story of Yingying. The Xiezhou Temple of Guanyu is the biggest military temple in China, while the Yungang Grottoes is one of the three biggest Buddhism grottoes in the country. They are imposing and finely carved. Built in Song Dynasty, Wooden Tower in Ying County is the tallest ancient wooden construction and stands 67.31 meters high. The Qiao Family's Living Quarter in Qi County, which has been made well-known by Zhang Yimou's film, "Raise the Red Lantern", plus the Qu Family's Living Quarter in Qi County, Wang Family's Living Quarter in Lingshi and Sanduo Hall in Taigu together form the Shanxi Jinzhong's yard folk custom culture. Famous mountains and big rivers can be found throughout Shanxi Province. The natural landscape is exquisite and the scenic resources are rich. As a state-level scenic spot, North Mountain Hengshan is one of the Five Famous Mountains in China. Mount Mian has been the summer resort since old times. It has the pleasant weather. The famous minister Jiezitui of Jin State was burned to death with his mother just on this mountain. North Mt.Wudang, Mt.Kongling and Mt.Guancen and so on also have their unique characteristics. Hukou Waterfall of the Yellow River, which is the statelevel scenic spot, is the second biggest waterfall of our nation behind Huangguoshu Waterfall. Pangquangou, Mt.Luya, Mt.Li, the Mang River and many other nature reserves exist in Shanxi. The scenery there is beautiful and quite varied, with ancient plants and rare animals. One example of these rare animals, enjoying state level protection, is the Brown Eared-Pheasant.

Shanxi is the veteran revolutionary base. The revolution movement ruins and the revolutionary cultural relics are spread throughout the entire province. There are famous former sites of the Eighth Route Army, such as its headquarter, Licheng Huangyadong Ordnance Factory, Wenshui Liu Hulan Memorial Hall, and the like.

Characteristic Products

The Fen liquor and the bamboo-green tea are Shanxi's most famous special local products. Others include the old aged vinegar of Qingxu, Wutai Mountain Tai mushrooms, Datong day lily buds, Mt.Heng Radix Astragali, Jishan jujube, Pinglu Lily, Puzhou green persimmon, Yuanqu kiwi fruit, Qingxu grapes, Shangdang Ginseng, Jincheng large Chinese hawthorn, Dai county hot pepper, Qinzhou Millet and Jinci rice, Hongtong soft-shelled turtle, Yuncheng Yellow River carp, Gaoping silk, and Pingyao wood engraved lunar new year's painting and Tuiguang lacquer of Pingyao.

Local Flavor Cuisine

Shanxi cuisine can be divided into three schools. They are schools of southern Shanxi, northern Shanxi and central Shanxi. Cuisine from southern Shanxi is best known for seafood with a light taste. Cuisine from northern Shanxi makes heavy use of flavorful cooking oils. And central Shanxi food is salty, rather sour and sugary. This kind of cooked food has crisply rotten, fragrant tender, heavy color and taste characteristics. The flour food of Shanxi is especially famous for being delicious and refreshing, thereby making a lasting impression on those who eat it. The most famous local flavor snacks of Shanxi include smoked bacon, boiled chitterlings with pork, saut ed fried pork, stewed pork with the salt soaked cabbage, stir-fried Huha Mutton, Tounao, sliced noodles, Boyu—a kind of flour food made in fish shape, Mao'erduo—a kind of flour food made in catear shape, Kaolaolao, Wenxi Pancake and so on.

Attractions Recommendation

Datong Yungang Grottoes, Mount Wutai, Memorial Temple of Jin, Pingyao Ancient

City, Qiao Family's Living Quarter, Hukou Waterfall, Mt.Hengshan, Xinghua Village and Taihang Memorial Hall of the Eighth Route Army.

　　山西省位於黃河中游，黃土高原的東部。山西丘陵縱橫，山環水繞，地形複雜，地貌多樣，氣候適中，四季分明，大自然神工鬼斧般地造就了一處處絢麗多彩的景色。山西又是中華民族文明的發祥地之一，歷史悠久，源遠流長，素有「中國古代藝術博物館」、「文獻之邦」的美稱，保留有中國70%的地面古代建築，旅遊界有這樣一句話，說：「十年中國看深圳，百年中國看上海，千年中國看北京，三千年中國看陝西，五千年中國看山西。」自然美景、歷史文明、革命史蹟和新時期建設成就，共同構成了山西得天獨厚、古今兼備、多姿多彩的旅遊資源。

　　山西是中華文明發祥地之一，春秋時為晉國，故簡稱晉。悠久的歷史留下眾多的文化遺產，加上複雜的地形地貌、河流山川形成的自然景觀，旅遊資源十分豐富。山西現存的古建築居中國之首，列為國家級重點保護單位的有50處，省級的也有400多處。四大佛教聖地之一的五台山，寺廟群集千年之萃。其中，以中國現存最古的木構建築南禪寺，集北魏至清代多種建築為一體的佛光寺及顯通寺，塔院舍利塔最為有名。建於北魏的恆山懸空寺懸於懸崖峭壁之上，以驚險奇特著稱。太原的晉祠是形式多樣的古建築薈萃的遊覽勝地。平遙古城是中國現存三座古城之一，被列入世界文化遺產名錄。芮城永樂宮是典型的元代道觀建築群，宮內壁畫是中國繪畫藝術的珍品。永濟普救寺是《西廂記》、《鶯鶯傳》故事的發生地。解州關帝廟是中國規模最大的武廟。雲岡石窟是中國三大佛教石窟之一，氣勢雄偉，雕刻精細。應縣木塔建於宋代，高67.31米，是中國古代最高的木構建築。因拍攝電影《大紅燈籠高高掛》而聞名的祁縣喬家大院，與祁縣渠家大院、靈石王家大院、太谷三多堂共同組成山西晉中大院民俗文化系列景點。山西名山大川遍布，自然風光資源豐富優美。北嶽恆山是五嶽之一，國家級風景名勝區；綿山氣候宜人，自古就是避暑勝地，晉國名臣介子推攜母被燒死於此山；北武當山、靈空山、管涔山等也各有特點；黃河壺口瀑布是僅次於黃果樹瀑布的中國第二大瀑布，國家級風景名勝區。山西還建有龐泉溝、蘆芽山、歷山、莽河等自然保護區，風景秀麗。

　　山西是老革命根據地，革命活動遺址和革命文物遍布全省，著名的有八路軍總部舊址、黎城黃崖洞八路軍兵工廠、文水劉胡蘭紀念館等。

特色產品

山西特產以汾酒、竹葉青最為有名。此外還有清徐老陳醋、五台山「台蘑」、大同黃花、恆山黃芪、稷山板棗、平陸百合、蒲州青柿、垣曲奇異果、清徐葡萄、上黨「黨參」、晉城紅果、代縣辣椒、沁州小米、晉祠大米、洪洞甲魚、運城黃河鯉魚、高平絲綢、平陽木版年畫、平遙推光漆具等。

風味美食

山西菜點分為南、北、中三派。南路菜品以海味為最，口味偏清淡。北路菜餚講究重油重色。中路菜以鹹味為主，酸甜為輔，菜餚具有酥爛、香嫩、重色、重味的特點。山西麵食尤其著名，滑利爽口，餘味悠長。山西著名的風味菜點有：燻豬肉、釀粉腸、過油肉、喇嘛肉、炒蝴哈羊肉、頭腦、刀削麵、撥魚、貓耳朵、　面栲栳、聞喜餅等。

推薦景點

大同雲岡石窟、五台山、晉祠、平遙古城、喬家大院、壺口瀑布、恆山、杏花村和八路軍太行紀念館等。

Mt.Hengshan　（恆山）

Ladies and gentlemen,

Today I'll take you to visit a peak known as "the second highest mountain in China", which is one of the five most famous mountains in China. Mt.Hengshan together with Mt.Taishan, Mt.Huashan, Mt.Songshan and Mt.Hengshan are called the Five Mountains, is well-known throughout the world. Mt.Hengshan is the watershed of the Sanggan River and the Hutuo River. It is said that there are 108 peaks in Mt.Hengshan, stretching 250 kilometers from east to west. The Xuanwu peak, which is the main peak of Mt.Hengshan, is in the South of Huiyuan County and is 2016. 8 meters high. The whole Mt.Hengshan is of magnificent spectacle and is known as "the second highest mountain in China"; it is only second to Mt.Taishan among the Five Mountains.

Mt.Hengshan is also called Mt.Damao and Mt.Changshan. According to historical records, as early as 4,000 years ago, Mt.Hengshan was conferred a title of "Beiyue" by King Shun. In the Qin Dynasty, Mt.Hengshan was highly praised as "the second mountain in the world". In the Northern Wei Dynasty, Emperor Touba reached the summit of Mt.Hengshan to personally worship it. In the Ming and Qing Dynasties, emperors sent chancelleries to offer a sacrifice to Heaven at Mt.Hengshan.

In the early years of Western Han Dynasty, temples were built in Mt.Hengshan, which are now more than 2,000 years old. The main temple, the Flying Stone Grottoes, was built in the Northern Wei and was rebuilt in the Tang, Jin, and Yuan Dynasties. Unfortunately, the majority of them have been destroyed, and now few are left. According to legend, Mt.Hengshan has long served as an important Taoist venue. One of the Eight Immortals, Zhang Guolao, was said to have practiced Taoism at Mt.Hengshan.

Big Character Bay

Going down from the dam, crossing the Mt.Hengshan tunnel, walking about 2 kilometers, and then turning to the southeast along the mountain road, you'll see the Decree Stopped Ridge. According to historical records, in the northern terrain of Decree Stopped Ridge, there were 2 buildings, which were the Zhenwu Temple and Wangyue Tower. It is said that from the Wangyue Tower, you could see the summit of Mt.Hengshan, with its extremely dangerous rocks and the red walls lined in green trees. Unfortunately Wangyue Tower collapsed in the early days after China's Liberation. The Zhenwu Temple was destroyed during decade-long chaos of China's culture revolution. Just one stone tablet remains here now, but the first half has weathered off and only the lower part remains in the ruins. Go along the winding trails to the west and a cliff like a large knife will come into sight. The two Chinese characters "恆宗" (pinyin: héng zōng) on the cliff are more than 20 meters high, looking like a tremendous character tablet hanging on the cliff. So the gulf next to the cliff is called "Big Character Bay". There are four ancient pines in front of the Big Character Bay, which are named "four officials". The roots of these four ancient pines hang in and firmly seize the rock. Exactly when people started calling them "officials" has been remaining unknown, but their vigorous height and straight appearance add great charm to the Big Character Bay.

As you walk along the Big Character Bay from the north, the mountain is high and steep. It is really dangerous to climb. The danger and magnificence of the mountain path quickly become apparent. After climbing the mountain for a while, you have to gasp for breath. When you look up, you'll see the trails are more rugged. It seems that the mountain path is the only way to the height of the clouds, and it is just like a ladder stretching towards the heaven, so it is the "Buyun Road" in Chinese. This means that as you climb step by step up along the Buyun Road, you will find that the misty clouds surround your body and the entire scene appears like a fairyland.

Tiger Drafts

After climbing the Buyun Stairs, you'll see the high cliff on the right and deep valleys on the left. There are three Chinese characters "虎風口" (pinyin: hǔ fēng kǒu; literally means "Tiger Drafts") on a huge stone. You can feel strong wind here. Standing on the Tiger Drafts, with the breeze drying your wet clothes, enjoying the ancient pines on the slopes, makes for a quite pleasant experience. Some of the pine trees are like umbrellas standing on the side of Bird Road; some like kiosks standing near springs. It is absolutely lifelike and varied.

In the past, Mt.Hengshan had abundant wildlife. As a result of the war and manmade calamities, the forest resources were greatly damaged and the natural ecology was not balanced. Very little remains of the original lush green forest is left. Most of the mountain streams have dried up; animal species, which were active in the midst of the forest, have been greatly reduced. Many other kinds of creatures are extremely rare; even the wind whistle, due to the declining number of trees, is less and less seen.

Sheshen Cliff

Leave the Tiger Drafts and continue to climb on the mountain from the north; you'll come to Guolao Ridge. A succession of natural green stones contribute to the curved path, which is like an artificial laying trace. Many nature-made small marks look like the footprints traced by a donkey. According to the legend, this is the road along which Zhang Guolao had ridden a small donkey to Heaven in Mt.Hengshan. The legends are not real; Zhang Guolao of course will not appear again. The mountain path is really difficult; visitors can not help but slip a few steps back. In the east of the Guolao Ridge, there is a quite dangerous peak facing the west. The ancient pine trees are indeed magnificent and are another one of Mt.Hengshan's attractions. The cliff is known as the "Sheshen Cliff" and its magnificent scenery reflects the extremely dangerous peak at the time of sunset.

Flying Stone Grottoes

Leaving the Sheshen Cliff, go on to the north for six or seven hundreds meters and turn to the southeast and across the layers of rock steps, and you'll see the other buildings, which are mainly the palaces and dressing tables. The palaces and dressing tables were constructed on a huge natural fallen rock in the middle of the gully. It is surrounded by the walls, but it is like the door opening towards the north. In the middle, is a spacious courtyard, which is about 200 square meters. According to historical records, a stone suddenly fell down before King Shun while he was hunting here. It is said that the piece of huge stone broke off from these grottoes. This is the imprint that a huge rock flying out of the caves has left, so it is called "Flying Stone Grottoes". The palace is built under the cliff in the east of the grotto. The "History of Hengshan" records that the palace was built in Northern Wei Dynasty (435 A.D.); it was then repeatedly rebuilt after the building was damaged. The present building remaining here was rebuilt in 1368. To the south of the palace, there is a cave, called "Huanyuan Cave", which is linked to the distant East Sea by legend. When approaching the entrance to the cave, you will feel the blowing cold wind. To the north of the palace, you can see a temple and a clay statue. The statue is a woman who was in charge of land at Mt.Hengshan. The Flying Stone Grottoes's walls bear many inscriptions written by visitors throughout history praising Mt.Hengshan's magnificent scenery. A bridge was once built to connect Flying Stone Grottoes. Unfortunately, the flying bridge collapsed, and the deep gully now can not be crossed. Look toward the south, behind the wall of the palace and you will see the "Eagle Wing Rock", which resembles an eagle spreading the wings and about to fly.

Walk down the stairs of the palace and turn left along the mountain. Below the trail in the middle of a saddle lie two Taoism temples. And along the side of the hill, there are a number of unexplored deep caves. In the past, there was a ladder for visitors to climb into the holes. However, these ladders decayed over a long period of time, so now visitors can look down into the caves and sigh. Seen from a distance, the temples seem to be embedded in the cliff. There is a small cave near the temple on the mountainside. Whenever the rain is coming, the clouds will stream continuously out from the cave, which is one of the wonders of Mt.Hengshan.

Beiyue Temple

Beiyue Temple was built approximately in 1501 and is Mt.Hengshan's most magnificent temple. It is located on Mt.Hengshan's summit. It is large-scale, well-structured, with a unique style.

Walk along the paths in the Zhizi Valley and after a little while, you will see the entrance to the Temple. Go into the entrance, you'll see the stairs with 103 steps, but it is rumored that these steps are uncountable. Each step is about 60 centimeters high and 25 centimeters wide, making the steep ladder more dangerous. When visitors climb to the middle of the step ladder, they will feel dizzy. On both sides of the stairs, there had been the Halls of Dragon and Tiger. Unfortunately, they are now almost collapsed.

Climbing up along the steep stairs, we enter the yard of the main hall. The hall has a horizontal tablet with the characters "貞元之殿", from which hang two long couplets. The couplets are mainly written in praise of the grand vision, but also pay homage to feudal rulers. These inscriptions are valuable material to study the history and heritage of Mt.Hengshan. The "History of Hengshan" records that during 27thyear of Ming Emperor Wanli's reign (1599), Buddhist scriptures were presented at the Mt.Hengshan Temple, which were originally stored in four large cabinets in the palace. It is really a pity that they were completely lost. There is also an authentic map of Mt.Hengshan carved in a monument, which is an extremely valuable heritage.

Tianfeng Peak

There are two paths leading to the peak. The east road is about one kilometer, but is rough and difficult. The west road is about 2 kilometers, but the road is flat. There are no trees on Tianfeng Peak, but clusters of wild flowers and weeds. As you climb up the peak, you'll feel cool and pleasant. Looking around, you will enjoy views of beautiful landscapes: the Sanggan River running eastward, the Great Wall winding constantly, and magnificent Mt.Guanshan with mist veil and white cloud around the hills, you will enjoy the miraculous scene, with thoughts flooding in your mind.

Well, everyone, so much for our tour today. I hope you will enjoy yourselves very much! Goodbye!

　　遊客朋友們大家好！今天我將帶領大家遊覽的是有「天下第二山」之稱的中國五嶽名山之一——北嶽恆山。北嶽恆山與東嶽泰山，西嶽華山，南嶽衡山，中嶽嵩山並稱五嶽，齊名天下。恆山是桑乾河與滹沱河的分水嶺，號稱108峰，東西綿延250千米。恆山主峰玄武峰，在渾源縣城南，海拔2016.8米。恆山氣勢磅　　，蔚為壯觀，有「天下第二山」之稱，在五嶽中，僅次於泰山。

　　恆山又稱常山、大茂山，亦名太恆山、元岳、紫岳、恆宗，被譽為「人天北柱」、「絕塞名山」。據史書記載，早在4000　年前，舜帝巡狩四方，北至恆山看到這裡山勢險峻，奇峰壁立，遂封恆山為「北嶽」。到秦始皇時，封天下十二名山，恆山被推崇為天下第二山。秦始皇曾到恆山觀光，漢武帝也曾來這裡祭祀。北魏時，太武帝拓跋燾親自登臨恆山天峰頂。到宋代，宋帝頂禮遙祝。明、清兩代帝王，則派使臣赴恆山祭祀。

　　恆山在西漢初就建有寺廟，迄今已有兩千多年的歷史。飛石窟內的主廟，始建於北魏，唐、金、元三代重修。明、清時，建築林立，規模宏大，祠宇樓台，聳峙巍峨。可惜多數已遭到破壞，現已所剩無幾。恆山作為道教的活動場所由來已久。據傳，中國傳說中八仙之一的張果老，就是在恆山隱居潛修的。

大字灣

　　走下水庫大壩，穿過恆山隧洞，再行約2千米，然後順著山路往東南方向一拐，就到了「停旨嶺」。過去封建皇帝派遣祭祀北嶽的使者，到這裡必須下馬，與前來迎旨的恆山道人一同步行上山，到北嶽廟祭祀。「停旨嶺」因此而得名。據史書記載，在停旨嶺北面地勢突起的高阜處，曾建有真武廟和望岳樓兩處建築，年代已無據可考。望岳樓，取登樓望岳之意。據説在望岳樓上憑欄而望，可見奇峰插天，危岩萬狀，飛泉噴玉，老松百態，紅牆襯綠，古廟藏蔭，北嶽恆山雄偉磅　之勢盡收眼底。可惜望岳樓已在解放初期倒塌，真武廟也在十年動亂中被毀。這裡現在僅留御碑一座，而且上半部已風化斷落，只剩下半截立於廢墟之上。過真武廟，再順著彎彎曲曲的山徑西轉，一座刀劈斧削似的聳天峭岩出現在人們的眼前。峭壁的中腰像經過鬼斧神工一般，岩石光平如鏡，上面刻著「恆宗」兩個大字。兩字總高20多米，字體雄渾，遒勁有力，遠遠看去，就像一塊巨大無比的字匾，懸掛在頂天立地的石壁之上，氣宇軒昂，引人入勝。峭岩旁邊的山灣因此而被人稱做「大字灣」。在大字灣前面的石樑上，豎立著四株形態奇特的唐代古松，名曰「四大夫」。這四株古松，根部懸於石外，緊緊抓住岩石，傲然迎風而立，經千年而不衰。它們是什麼朝代被封為「大夫」的已經不得而知，但那蒼勁挺拔的雄姿，卻給大字灣的宏偉景緻增色不少。

從大字灣繼續北上，山勢更加險峻。懸石如飛，斷崖欲墜，溝壑深邃，山道陡立，恆山地險山雄之勢，在這裡便展現出來。遊人攀登這樣的山路，用不多久，便會氣喘吁吁，熱汗淋淋，當你正要坐下來喘息一下的時候，抬頭一望，前面的山徑更加崎嶇難行。只見山間小道刻石為階，一直通往雲霧迷漫的高處，簡直像一條通天的階梯，這就是「步雲路」。從步雲路拾級而上，步步登高，白紗一樣的輕雲薄霧就在身邊繚繞，猶如神山仙境，不禁使人如醉如痴，飄飄欲仙。

虎風口

登完步雲石階，峰迴路轉，右為高入雲天的陡壁，左為不見溝底的深壑，巨石上刻有「虎風口」三個大字。一到此處，只覺狂風驟起，聲如虎嘯，令人不寒而慄。站在虎風口，一面讓颯颯涼風吹乾汗水浸濕的衣衫，一面極目遠望，觀賞山坡上的古松，也頗有趣味。一株株蒼勁的古松，有的倒掛絕壁之上；有的直立丹崖石罅之中；有的像一把翠傘，停在鳥道之側；有的似一座角亭，坐落山泉之旁。真是維妙維肖，千姿百態。

過去恆山森林遍布，泉溪縱橫，野生動物資源十分豐富；由於歷代戰爭的摧殘和人為的洗劫，恆山地區的自然生態失去平衡，森林資源遭到極大的破壞。原來茂密蔥蘢的森林，只剩下稀疏的樹木；縱橫山間的淙淙溪流，大多也已乾涸；活躍在林間泉邊的動物種類也因此大大減少，虎、豹一類猛獸早已絕跡，其他許多種禽獸也極為罕見；就連那虎口驚心動魄的風嘯聲，也因樹木的減少，大大失去了當年的氣勢。

華北地區

捨身崖

離開虎風口繼續向北攀緣而上，便到了「果老嶺」，嶺上的彎彎小路，都是由一塊接一塊的青石天然接連而成，好似人工鋪設一般。在其中一塊很大的青石上，有許多自然形成的小石坑，極似人的足跡和毛驢的蹄印。據傳說，「八仙過海，各顯神通」的八仙之一張果老曾經倒騎著一頭小毛驢從恆山上天。傳說既非真事，張果老當然也不會重來，但那青石鋪就的崎嶇山道確實不太好走，遊人到此，也不免滑上幾跤。就在這果老嶺的東側，一座萬仞險峰面西而立，直插雲端。翹首而望，看那古松摩雲，危崖欲傾，確實雄偉壯觀。這就是恆山另一處勝景「捨身崖」。每當日落之時，此處「餘暉返照千山色，滿峪參差入畫中」，瑰麗的晚霞映著詭奇萬狀的險峰怪石，奇光異景，色彩繽紛，令人讚嘆不已。

飛石窟

離開捨身崖，向北再走六七百米，轉而東南，跨過層層石階，便看到以寢宮、梳妝台為主的另一組建築群。寢宮、梳妝台等，建在一個巨大的天然崩石凹壑之中。東南西三面環壁，北面豁開若門，中間空地約200平方米，如同一座寬敞的庭院。據史書記載，舜巡狩來到北嶽時，忽有一石飛墜帝前。據說，那塊巨石，就是從這裡飛出的。這石窟便是巨石飛出後留下的印跡，因此命名為「飛石窟」。寢宮，建在飛石窟內東側的石壁之下。殿堂重檐歇造，結構窈窕，原來為古北嶽廟。據《恆山志》記載，寢宮建於北魏太武帝太延元年（公元435年），後經多次毀建。現在留下的建築，是明洪武年間（公元1368年）復建的。明弘治十四年（公元1501年）擴修時改古北嶽廟為寢宮。寢宮南側耳殿內有一洞穴，名叫「還元洞」，其深莫測，傳說與遙遠的東海相通。一走近洞口，便覺冷風颼颼，寒氣逼人。寢宮北面，緊貼石壁建有殿台一間，內塑一夫人泥像。據說這就是恆山掌管土地的女神后土夫人之廟。飛石窟內的三面石壁上，留著歷代遊人的許多款題刻石，內容大多是詠贊恆山壯美之景的。這裡曾建有飛橋連通兩崖，渡橋而過可直達恆山山門。可惜飛橋不知在什麼時候早已坍塌，深澗已無法跨越。向南而望，緊貼著寢宮背後山牆的是「鷹翅岩」，其形如雄鷹展翅，躍躍欲飛。

走下寢宮前面的石階向左轉，沿著蜿蜒遠去的山間小徑前行不遠，就到了夕陽岩的背後。在山崖的斷壁中腰，鑿石依山，建有「得一庵」和「閻道祠」兩座小小的廟宇。閻道祠內，立有一座道人的泥塑，據說這就是在恆山修煉成仙的閻道真身煉丹的遺蹟。另外，在山壁的高處，還有一個不知有多深的山洞，名曰「紫芝洞」。洞口原架有一副木梯，供遊人攀登進洞。因時間太久，木梯早已朽壞，人們只能在下面望洞興嘆。這一組小小的建築群，上載峭峰，下臨絕地，從遠處相望，只見紅牆若染，綠瓦泛翠，廟宇玲瓏剔透，如鑲如嵌卻也別有一番情趣。

在離后土夫人廟不遠的山腰上，還有一個小山洞，無徑可通，名為「出雲洞」。每當陰雨即將來臨之時，便有縷縷白雲從洞中飄出，為恆山奇景之一。

北嶽廟

北嶽廟大約建於公元1501　年，是恆山氣勢最恢宏的一座寺廟。北嶽廟位於恆山頂端，規模很大，建築獨具特色。

從紫芝峪沿著古松蔭罩、花草指路的盤山小徑而行，走不多時，就看到了朝殿的山門。山門為單檐歇山屋宇式建築，朱門銅釘，綠瓦紅牆，氣勢壯觀。門內佇立著體態高大魁梧的恆山之神泥塑。跨進山門，便是著名的「陡若天梯」的石階。石階踏跺共有103級，但卻傳言難以數清。每級石台高約60釐米，寬約25　釐米。因腳踏面向前傾斜40度，所以使得階梯更加險陡。遊人爬至中腰，便覺膽寒，不敢直立。石階的兩邊，東西相對，疊石台為基，建有龍虎二殿，取青龍、白虎之意。可惜現已瀕於毀壞。

膽顫心驚地爬上「天梯」，便進了朝殿大院。朝殿當中楹額上懸掛著一塊大匾，上題「貞元之殿」四字。對聯的文義主要是讚揚北嶽恆山的宏偉氣魄，但其中也有歌頌當時的封建統治者之意。朝殿的前廊下，置放著清代御祭恆山文碑20余通，這些碑文都是研究恆山歷史及文物的寶貴資料。據《恆山志》記載，明萬曆二十七年（公元1599年）曾贈送恆山廟大藏經1584種，原來儲存在四只大經櫥內，藏於寢宮。民國初年完全遺失，不知去向，實在可惜。朝殿廊前，還有一座恆山真跡圖碑，即恆山全景圖碑，是一件有保存價值的文物。

天峰嶺

從朝殿出來，恆山主峰天峰嶺已在眼前。由此攀登峰頂，有東西兩條小徑。東路約有1千米，但岩石參差，小路曲折，坎坷難行，從恆山後背上山者多走此路。西路約有2千米，但山路比較平緩。步出朝殿山門，從東路上天峰嶺，漫山遍野灌木叢生，綠草如茵。沿著彎曲崎嶇的羊腸小道奮力攀登，用不多時，就可登上峰頂。天峰嶺上沒有樹木，只有叢生的野花雜草。一上峰頂，頓覺山風驟起，涼爽宜人。舉目四望，豁然開闊，大好河山盡收眼底。只見那萬峰由南而來，桑乾河東流而去，長城透迤不斷，關山雄姿百態。此刻，山間白雲繚繞，薄霧縹緲，山川之色朦朦朧朧，似隱似現，更顯得壯麗神奇，使人不禁心曠神怡，浮想聯翩。

各位朋友，今天我們的行程就到這裡。希望恆山的山山水水永遠留給您美好的回憶！再見！

Mt.Wutai （五台山）

Ladies and gentlemen,

Welcome to Mt.Wutai. First, I'll briefly introduce Mt.Wutai to you.

Mt.Wutai is one of the four most famous Buddhist Temples in China. It is located in northeast Xinzhou District in Shanxi Province and most of its scenic spots are located in the Huaitai Town of Wutai County, while some small parts are in Fanshi, Dai County and Fuping County in Hebei Province. Mt.Wutai is famous for the five peaks and the eternally running Qinshui River. The essence of Mt.Wutai is the Buddhist temples.

Mt.Wutai is the vivid summary of the common characteristics of the five peaks. The five peaks of the mountains are tall platforms, so it is called Mt.Wutai（ "Wu" in Mandarin means "5", while tai is "platform"）. Mt.Wutai is more than 2,700 meters above the sea level and the north summit is 3,058 meters high, making it the highest peak in Northern China. Hence it is known as the "Roof of North China". Shanxi Province is located on the Loess Plateau, so most of it is dry, but Mt.Wutai is an exception. Here the trees are tall, weather is cool, and the ground is covered with vegetation. Because it has beautiful and spectacular scenery, Mt.Wutai is a well-known summer tourist attraction. Though it lies in a deep valley, transportation to it is very convenient.

Mt.Wutai is famous mainly because it is the holy land for Buddhists. How did Mt.Wutai become the Buddhist holy land? During the Eastern Han Dynasty (68 A.D.), two Indian monks preached Buddhism in China. When they came to Mt.Wutai, they saw that its mountain topography was almost identical to the place where the Sakyamuni Buddha meditated and worshipped. After they returned to Luoyang, they asked the

華北地區

emperor of Han to build a monastery in Mt.Wutai and the Temple was then constructed. The temple was the Xiantong Temple's predecessor, which is as famous as the White Horse Temple in Luoyang, one of China's earliest Buddhist temples, so Mt.Wutai has become the Buddhist holy land. During the Northern and Southern Dynasties, Mt.Wutai had more than 200 temples, and during the Tang Dynasty, this number grew to 360. These temples housed more than 3,000 Buddhist monks and nuns. However, during Tang Emperor Wuzong's reign and Zhou Emperor Shizong's reign practically all of Mt.Wutai's Buddhist Temples were destroyed. During the Song, Yuan, Ming and Qing dynasties, the temples were gradually rebuilt. During the Ming Dynasty, Mt.Wutai had nearly 104 temples. Kangxi, Qianlong and Jiaqing, the three early Qing Dynasty Emperors, attached great importance to Mt.Wutai and constantly made heavy investments in temple construction there. By the late Qing Dynasty, Mt.Wutai had a total of 122 temples and more than 1,000 Buddhist monks and nuns.

Mt.Wutai now just has a little more than 50 temples. But among the four most famous Buddhist temples, Mt.Wutai is still the most popular tourist attraction. Mt.Wutai's Tang, Song, Liao, Jin, Yuan, Ming and Qing Dynasty Buddhist temples have grand architecture marked by rigor and continuity. It is a wonderful place to study and appreciate the ancient Chinese architecture from the Tang Dynasty onward. In addition, the inscriptions of Buddhist sculptures are highly skilled and diversified in form, such as clay, brass and jade carvings, making Mt.Wutai the best place to appreciate the evolution of Buddhist sculpture art.

The small town in front of us is called Dongye town, and about 10 kilometers in the northwest of the town is our first tour destination—Nanchan Temple.

Nanchan Temple

Here we are. Before climbing Mt.Wutai from the south, we'll first visit this ancient temple, which is the most valuable heritage in Mt.Wutai, because Nanchan Temple has the oldest existing wooden structure—the Large Buddhist Hall. You may know, Shanxi Province's many still existing old buildings make it known as China's outdoor museum and the best place in the country to study older architecture. Most ancient architecture of Shanxi Province is concentrated at Mt.Wutai, and the Nanchan Temple is one of the mountain's most ancient buildings.

Nanchan Temple is located on one side of the Galaxy River, near a small village in Wutai County. The temple faces the south, with both the front and the back facing a ridge. Lush forests, clear streams, and red walls surround the temple. Nanchan Temple has stood in this beautiful environment for 1,200 years. The temple is not big, with a total area of over 3,000 square meters, and is 60 meters long from north to south, 51 meters in width. It has two courtyards, six halls.

The Large Buddha Hall is the main building in the temple, which has three rooms outside and one room inside, supported by 12 wooden pillars. The walls are not loaded. Their main purpose is to protect the building from storms and separate inside and outside of the hall. This is a typical Tang Dynasty architectural style. According to the inscriptions on the beams, we can see that this temple was reconstructed in 782 A.D., has existed for above 1,200 years, and it is the elder brother of all the existing wooden structure buildings in China. This is the reason why Nanchan Temple is famous world-wide. The statues are from the Tang Dynasty. In the center is the Sakyamuni Buddha, while the Samantabhadra and Bodhisattva are on both sides of the hall; the rest of the statues and disciples are other kings, which create a good solemn Buddhist community and harmonious atmosphere. They are vivid, artistic masterpieces, and their styles and colors are the same as Dunhuang Mogao Grottoes. There are 70 brick statues surrounding the Buddhist altar, which rank among the Tang Dynasty's most valuable artistic treasures. Indeed, when you are in Nanchan Temple, it is like entering an art hall of Tang Dynasty and you may wonder how the building and its treasures could be so well preserved. We can find the answer in three ways. The first factor is the mountain's high terrain and dry climate, which are conducive to preserving such relics.

The second factor is its geographical location. Nanchan Temple is far away from Taihuai Town, where most temples concentrate and because it was not very noticeable, the temple was able to escape from the mass destruction and robbery in the aftermath of the Tang Dynasty's collapse. The last factor is the diligence of the local population in ensuring that the temple was protected and maintained. For these reasons the 1,000-year-old Nanchan Temple is well preserved. After the Liberation, the Chinese local and national governments have paid special attention to the ancient temple, listing it as a key national culture relic unit and allocating special funds for its maintenance. As a result, Nanchan Temple has been well protected. Now our tour to Nanchan Temple is over, I'll take you to enjoy another famous Tang Dynasty architectural masterpiece, the Foguang Temple.

Foguang Temple

This is the Foguang Temple. Known as the "Gem of China", it has a long history and grand scale. It is surrounded by mountains to the east, south and north, but opens out to the west. Numerous pine trees standing around the Foguang Temple give its immediate environment a green complexion and elegant appearance. The Foguang Temple has many Northern Wei Dynasty relics and inscriptions, which are relatively rare now. When talking about the artistic value and historical value of the temple, we must mention its discoverer—Liang Sicheng, who was an architecture expert and son of the modern thinker, Liang Qichao. In the summer of 1937, Liang Sicheng and four other professors excitedly went to the Mt.Wutai. They had been to Dunhuang before and among its many bright and colorful murals, one caught their attention: on the pictures, there were ancient temples and many visitors, and a tower not seen before.

In the Foguang Temple, Professor Liang Si-cheng found this tower, which was the same as the one on the paintings. After 1,400 years, the tower still existed! It is an historic relics of the Northern Wei Dynasty. It is not only ancient architectural treasure, but also the monument of the culture exchange between China and India. Liang's discovery far exceeded his expectations: in addition to the "ancient tower", the Foguang Temple also turned out to be an ancient treasure house. Since its discovery, the Foguang Temple has been seen as belonging not just to China, but to the entire world as well. Some foreign scholars have publicly called it the "Asian Temple".

Foguang Temple was built during the Northern Wei Dynasty and was destroyed later. The main hall of Foguang Temple we see now was built in the Tang Dynasty. Because it is located on the high ground in the east, it is called East Basilica. The Buddha altar is in the Foguang Temple's center and above it, there are three Buddha and Bodhisattva and other 35 Buddha statues. This is a standard Tang Dynasty arrangement and is similar to the statue placement in Gansu Province's Dunhuang Grottoes. There are also Bodhisattvas squatting on the tall rosette. This kind of statue is also rare in China —the only other places it can be found is at the Dunhuang Grottoes in Gansu and Huayan Temple in Datong.

This is my entire introduction. Thanks for your cooperation. I do hope my introduction is helpful and enjoyable. I wish you have a pleasant journey.

女士們、先生們：

歡迎大家來中國四大佛教名山之首的五台山旅遊觀光。首先，我向大家介紹一下五台山概況。

五台山是第一批國家級風景名勝區，位於山西省忻州地區東北部，風景區絕大部分坐落在以台懷鎮為中心的五台縣境內，有小部分跨繁峙、代縣和河北阜平。五台山的壯美風景在於它的東西南北中五座高峰和奔流不息的清水河。五台山的名勝精華則是它那眾多佛教寺廟。

五台山這一名稱是對五座山峰的共同特點的形象概括。東西南北中五座高峰的山巔都是高大的緩坡平台，所以叫五台山。五台的海拔高度多在2700米以上，最高的北台海拔達到3058米，為華北第一高峰，素有「華北屋脊」之稱。地處黃土高原的山西，絕大部分地區乾旱少雨，而五台山則是個例外。這裡山高林深，氣候涼爽，降雨較多，植被覆蓋率很高，風光秀麗，景色壯觀，有清涼山之稱，是旅遊避暑的勝地。五台山雖然山高谷深，但對外交通比較方便。

五台山主要是以佛教聖地而名揚天下的。那麼五台山是如何成為佛教聖地的呢？東漢明帝永平十一年（公元68年），印度兩位高僧攝摩騰、竺法蘭在中國傳播佛教。他們來到五台山，見五座台頂拱圍台懷腹地，其山形地貌與釋迦牟尼佛的修行地靈鷲山幾乎相同，返回洛陽後就奏請漢明帝去五台山修建寺院。明帝準奏頒旨，在五台山修建了大孚靈鷲寺，即今天顯通寺的前身，成為與洛陽白馬寺齊名的中國最早的佛寺之一，五台山也就成為佛教聖地。從此五台山的佛寺越來越多，香火日盛一日。到南北朝時，五台山已有寺廟200多處，唐代更達到360多處，有僧尼3000餘人。但由於唐武宗、周世宗兩次大規模滅法，佛寺幾乎全部被毀。宋、元、明、清，五台山的佛寺逐漸得到恢復和發展，明朝時寺廟已近104處。清朝的康熙、乾隆、嘉慶諸帝均對五台山佛寺極為重視，不斷投入巨資予以修建，到清末，五台山共有寺廟122處，僧尼1000多人。

五台山現有寺廟50餘座，儘管與歷史上不能相比，但在四大佛教名山中仍然是寺廟最為集中，香火最為旺盛的。而且五台山的佛寺，唐、宋、遼、金、元、明、清各代以及民國均有遺存，建築宏偉，式樣繁多，精細嚴整，手法典型，連續性強，本身就是一部唐代以來中國建築史，是研究和欣賞中國古建築的難得場所。另外，寺內佛教造像手法多樣，技藝高超，泥塑、木雕、銅鑄、玉雕應有盡有，是欣賞中國佛教造像藝術發展演變的最佳場所。

前面這個小城叫東冶，東冶鎮西北10餘裡便是我們這次五台之行的第一個遊覽點——南禪寺。

南禪寺

南禪寺到了。我們從南路上五台山，首先遊覽這座古剎。南禪寺內有中國現存最古老的木結構建築——大佛殿。大家可能知道，山西素有地上文物博物館的美譽，現存古建築，其數量之多、價值之高都居中國之首。山西的古建築以五台山地區最為集中，而五台山的古建築又以南禪寺最為古老。

南禪寺位於五台縣陽白鄉李家村附近小銀河一側的河岸土崖上，廟宇坐北朝南，迎面和背面各有一道山樑，寺旁渠水環繞，林木繁茂，紅牆綠樹，碧水青山，極為幽靜。南禪寺就是在如此美麗的環境中已經存在了1200　多年。寺院並不大，占地約3000多平方米，南北長60米，東西寬51米，分兩個院落，共有殿堂六座。

大佛殿為寺院主體建築，面寬和進深都是三間，而內裡卻是一大間，是單檐歇山頂建築，共用十二根巨柱支撐殿頂，牆身並不負重，只起間隔內外和防禦風雨侵襲的作用。四周檐柱柱頭微微內傾，四個角柱稍高，使得層層伸出的斗栱翹起。這樣，大殿既穩固又俏麗，是典型的唐代建築風格。據大殿橫樑上題記可知，此殿重建於唐德宗建中三年（公元782年），距今已有1200多年，是中國現存所有木構古建築的老大哥。這也是南禪寺海內外聞名的主要原因。殿內的塑像都是唐代作品，以釋迦牟尼佛為中心，兩旁是文殊、普賢二位菩薩，其餘為大弟子阿難和迦葉及護法天王等群像，主次分明，錯落有致，營造出佛界肅穆而和諧的良好氛圍。其風格與敦煌莫高窟彩塑如出一轍。佛壇四周嵌有磚雕70幅，是唐代磚面浮雕藝術傑作，同樣頗具藝術價值。置身大佛殿內，猶如進入一座唐代藝術殿堂，不論建築，還是塑像、磚雕均是稀世國寶。

走出大佛殿，大家可能會產生這樣的疑問，這樣一座唐代建築為何能夠完好地保存下來？答案應有三方面：從地勢和氣候上說，這裡高而背風，較為乾燥，有利於木構建築物的完好保存；從所處地理位置上講，南禪寺遠離寺廟最集中的台懷鬧區，藏於偏僻山鄉之中，不太引人注意，所以能夠躲過唐代以後歷次大規模滅法和刀兵之劫；最後還要歸功於當地人民群眾的精心保護，免去了可能發生的其他人為破壞。正是這幾個方面的原因，使南禪寺這座千年古剎得以保存。新中國成立後，國家對古剎極為珍視，把它列為中國重點文物保護單位，撥專款進行維護，進而使南禪寺得到了更好的保護。

我們的南禪寺之行暫且到此，下面我帶大家去欣賞與南禪寺齊名的另一處唐代古建築——佛光寺。

佛光寺

　　這就是在佛剎中被譽為「中華瑰寶」的佛光寺，它是一座歷史悠久、規模宏偉的佛教寺院。佛光寺東、南、北三面環山，只有西向開闊，寺因山勢而建，坐東朝西，整個寺區松柏蒼翠，殿宇巍峨，環境清雅；寺院布局疏朗，排列有序。寺內有北魏以來的建築和許多文物古蹟，這在中國都是比較少見的。講到它的藝術價值和歷史價值我們不能不提起它的發現者——中國古建築專家梁思成（近代思想家梁啟超之子）先生。

　　1937年的夏天，梁思成先生等四位教授，興沖沖地來到五台山，在這之前，他們曾去了敦煌，在絢麗多彩的眾多壁畫中，有一幅五台山圖，特別引起他們的注意，畫面上古剎林立，遊人不絕，還有一座不曾見到過的寶塔……

　　在佛光寺，梁思成教授找到了這座塔，與畫上的一模一樣，1400　年的風風雨雨，依然健在！它是北魏遺物，雙層六角，上實下空，繩紋切磚，有印度的束蓮柱。它不僅是中國古建築的珍品，也是中國和印度古代文化交流的紀念碑。大大出乎梁思成所料的，就是除了這「祖師塔」，整個佛光寺都是一個古代藝術的新大陸。佛光寺不只是屬於中國，也屬於世界，有的外國學者公開稱呼佛光寺為「亞洲佛光」。

　　佛光寺始建於北魏，後來被毀。現在的佛光寺正殿為唐代所建。因其在寺內東部的制高點上，是佛光寺的大雄寶殿，故名東大殿。在五台山是首屈一指的。大殿正中的大佛壇上面有三佛和菩薩脅侍等像三十五尊。佛壇的正中間是降魔釋迦像，左邊是彌勒佛，右邊是阿彌陀佛。這是唐代中葉以後菩薩塑像的特性，與甘肅敦煌的塑像同出一範。

　　另外，供養菩薩均為一足蹲一足跪在高聳的蓮座上。這種塑像除了甘肅敦煌石窟和山西大同華嚴寺以外，在國內還不多見。

佛壇的左梢間又有普賢菩薩騎像，兩個菩薩服侍，獠蠻牽著象，普賢像前有起陀和一個童子像。佛壇的右梢間是文殊菩薩騎獅像，拂林牽著獅子，兩個菩薩脅侍。這和通常文殊居左，普賢居右的配置是不相同的。

我的介紹到此就結束了，謝謝您的合作，我希望我的介紹能夠給大家帶來收穫和樂趣。祝您一路平安，身體健康！

Pingyao Ancient City （平遙古城）

Hello, everyone. We are now arriving at Pingyao, one of China's most famous historic cities. The towering wall of bricks on the right of us are among the four ancient city walls and moats still in a complete state of preservation in our country. On December 3,1997, UNESCO's Worldwide Heritage Committee declared that the ancient cities of Lijiang in Yunnan Province and Pingyao in Shanxi Province, as well as the classical gardens in Suzhou, jiangsu Province to be World Heritage sites.

Pingyao has a long history. It is written that during the West Zhou Dynasty the Emperor Zhouxuan dispatched warriors to fight against Sayou and set up the city of Jingling in order to resist the aggressive northern nomads. This city was built on the site of the Jingling Village; about 7 kilometers to the northeast of the Pingyao County today, and the two characters Jing and Ling have been used as the name of the place till today. This can be seen as the beginning of Pingyao, and Jingling is what Pingyao was at that time. From then on it has already had a history stretching back about 2,800 years.

There is no clear historical record of the time when Pingyao was built. About at North Wei Dynasty Emperor Taiwu changed the county Pingtao to Pingyao to avoid the word "Tao" in his name "Tuo Ba Tao", and named Pingyao as the new official county. The city was then built. During its long history, the city saw great prosperity but was destroyed many times in the war. The city wall we see now was formed by rebuilding the old one to higher and thicker size during the third year of Ming Emperor Hongwu's reign. The city wall was rebuilt and repaired several times through the Ming and Qing dynasties; however, its style has stayed the same.

There are many ancient buildings maintained in Pingyao, such as Wenmiao Temple Palace, Qingxu Palace, City Building, Temple of Chenghuang, and Play Platform of Wumiao. Even the streets and ordinary residential buildings are built according to Ming and Qing architectural style. Walking around the streets we can see all kinds of antique mansion doors, courts, exquisitely-made ancient architectural decorations, and even the stones that people had to get off horses.

Pingyao not only has a long history, but also has been the birthplace of many famous people. These include old historical figures like the famous Jin Dynasty historian, Sun Cheng, who wrote truthfully in spite of the threat that he and his entire family would be executed and Sunkang, who was famous for reading by the light of snow. More recent famous figures include scholars like Hou Wailu, former director of the Historic Research Institute of Chinese Academy of Sciences; Hou Jieyi, former vice director of China's Language Research Institute; and Wang Yao, former director of Chinese Literature Research Institute. Finally, a number of famous artists hail from this city, such as the painter Li Gou and the singer, Guo Lanying. So Pingyao certainly deserves to be regarded as a famous historic and cultural city.

Now we are on the Huiji Bridge, made of stone and with nine arches. It was built during Emperor Kangxi's reign of Qing Dynasty and rebuilt during Emperor Tongzhi's reign. The eminent calligrapher and art theorist Fu Shan once wrote on it for commemoration of its building during Qing Dynasty. Though this bridge is small and doesn't have a long history, its molding is graceful. Unlike most other stone bridges, its flat surface ensures the convenience for cars and horses. And strangely enough, yet another bridge was built below it. Due to the absence of historical records, people didn't know about this bridge until August 1977, when a storm caused serious flooding and washed away much of the river's sand bed and banks. The flood revealed that the Huiji Bridge was built on the surface of the old bridge. It certainly makes sense to use the old bridge as the solid base of the new one, saving not only money and labor but also time. It also makes the Huiji Bridge one of the most interesting bridges in the world.

Please follow me to visit on the city wall.

Here is the Xia Dong Gate. As you can see, the twelve-meter-high city wall is very grand. A moat surrounded the city in the past and a drawbridge hung beside the city's gate, providing a solid defense during the infrequent outbreaks of war.

Now we are entering the Weng city at Xia Dong Gate which was built to defend the city wall. Its size is small and it's surrounded by high walls. Even if the enemy soldiers managed to fight their way into Weng city, only few could crowd into this small space and they would be immediately surrounded. Some Weng city's gates are not directly opposite the city gate; they are instead built on a left or right turn. This arrangement's purpose was to make it harder for the enemy soldiers to go directly from the city gate through Weng City and into Pingyao itself. This design underscores the practical experience gained by ancient Pingyao's inhabitants over long periods of war and conflict.

Look, there is an exquisitely built court. What's it used for? This is a small temple for Emperor Guan. Emperor Guan is the saint of force. It's a unique creation of Pingyao people to build a temple for Emperor Guan within Weng City. Please follow me into the city and visit on the city wall.

Now we are on the city wall. The city buildings before were destroyed in the war. The table built on the city wall is said to be the place where Yin Jifu conducted wars. Please follow me to have a look at the construction of the city.

As we see, on both sides of the city wall there is a short wall named Daughter Wall, why? The following written explanation appears in The Ways of Building compiled during the Song Dynasty: It refers to humbleness. The wall is to the city what a woman is to a man. It means the city wall is high and solid, just like a strong man; the daughter wall is short and weak, just like a delicate woman. There's a story prevailing in some places: In the beginning there was no daughter wall. Once, when an old man was forced to work, his only little granddaughter living with him together accompanied him to the city everyday, and sat nearby and watched him work. One day a tired laborer walked perilously close to the edge of the city wall. The little girl was afraid that he would fall off, so she pushed him inward forcefully, and because she pushed so hard, the laborer was rescued, while she was thrown to the death. In order to commemorate her, workers built the short wall, and named it Daughter Wall. This is really a moving story, but also illustrates the function of protecting of Daughter Wall. Look! The Daughter Wall's two sides are different. On the outward Daughter Wall were built concaves with small holes for watching and shooting, which were defense features used in time of war.

As we notice, every other section of the city wall has a part stretching out, which is called a platform for bending the knees toward the floor. What's it used for? It's used to defend the city wall. As we know, one main weapon in ancient wars was the bow and arrow. They can be launched either from the above or from the below. Therefore the soldiers on the city wall dare not to stretch out. This makes the city wall's base a hard place to defend. With the platform the disadvantage can be made up. The defending force becomes greatly intensified by forming a strong three-dimensional shooting net. On every platform is set up a building against enemy for watching and shooting.

Besides these characteristics, which can be seen in the walls of all ancient Chinese cities, Pingyao's wall has something unique.

This unique feature is thick cultural colors Pingyao's inhabitants dubbed on to the city's wall. They built the Star Building in the southeastern spot of the city wall symbolizing cultural star in the sky. According to statistics, there are 3,000 platforms and 72 buildings against enemy, all of which symbol the 3,000 disciples and 72 saints of Confucius, the saint of art.

The ancient city of Pingyao looks like a turtle, and has always been called the city of turtle. It is said to symbolize immortality, in the same way the fairy turtle and water signify long life. There are six city gates all around the city. The south gate is like the head, and faces south, same as the outside gate of Weng City, thereby allowing the turtle head to extend forward and back freely. The north gate is like a tail. The outside gate of Weng City faces east like the tail of turtle throwing eastward. The two gates in both eastern and western sides are like the feet of the turtle. The three outside gates of Weng City face south, as if the turtle is crawling by bending and stretching its legs in turn. Only the outside gate of Weng City at the Xia Dong Gate, which we just passed, faces east. It's said that fear of the turtle escaping led people to use a shapeless rope to tie the turtle's left behind foot to the tower 10 kilometers to the east of the city. Its leg has been pulled straight. Outside the south gate there's a well on each side. The two wells are said to be the pair of bright eyes of the fairy turtle. In the center of the city, in the position of the turtle a city building is set up, which is the building clearly higher than others. On the two slopes of the top of the city building are spelled the characters of "happy" and "longevity", made of yellow and blue and separated encaustic tiles. It fully represents the ancient city's unique cultural atmosphere and expresses the good wishes of Pingyao people. It can be seen as adding the finishing touch to the turtle city's construction design.

Pingyao has many cultural relics. On city's southwest corner, lie the Chenghuang Temple and Temple of Wealth, which are built with glossy stones. From nearby we can see the grand scene of the building angle towing, the paint colorings.

The conspicuous modern building nearby is the teaching building of Pingyao

Middle School. The grand hall of Wenmiao Temple is just at campus, but we can't see it clearly from here. To maintain the ancient atmosphere, generally it's forbidden to build in the old city. But Pingyao's inhabitants went out of their way to set up a teaching building for the school so as to illustrate the value they place on educating children. They were not disappointed. The Pingyao Middle School is a key provincial middle school in Shanxi Province and has compiled an excellent record and assumed leading role in the province's educational system.

So much for my explanation of the Pingyao ancient city, you can visit it freely now.

各位遊客，大家好！

中國歷史文化名城平遙古城就要到了，右前方那高聳的磚牆就是中國現存較為完整的四座古城池之一——平遙古城。1997 年12 月3 日，聯合國教科文組織世界遺產委員會通過決議，將中國雲南省麗江古城、山西省平遙古城和江蘇省蘇州古典園林列入世界文化遺產名錄。現在大家可以觀賞一下古城的遠景和比較完整的外觀。

平遙古城歷史悠久。據載：西周時期周宣王為抵禦北方遊牧民族的侵擾，曾派兵北伐薩猶，並修建了京陵城。京陵城就建在今平遙縣城東北約7千米的京陵村，京陵二字作為地名一直沿用至今。這可以説是平遙建城的開端，也是現在平遙城的前身。這樣計算的話，平遙古城至今已有2800 多年的歷史了。

現在這座平遙城始建於何時，歷史上沒有明確記載。大約在北魏太武帝拓跋燕時，為避名諱，將原來的平陶縣改為平遙縣，並把縣址從別處遷到這裡。建城時間應該是在這以後。在漫長的歷史歲月中，這裡曾有過它的繁華，也曾多次遭受戰火的破壞。我們現在看到的這座城牆，是明代洪武三年（公元1370年）把原來的土城牆加高加厚加磚擴建而成的，明清以來雖曾數次維修，但風格未變。

平遙城內古建築保存很多，像文廟大成殿、清虛觀、市樓、城隍廟、武廟戲台等。就是街道民居，也基本保存明清時代風貌。漫步街頭，你會看到各種古色古香的院門、院鋪、精雕細刻的古建築裝飾，甚至還能看到門前的接馬石椿、下馬石等，一派古城風貌。

平遙不僅歷史悠久，而且名人輩出。敢於不顧「滿門抄斬」的恐嚇、秉筆直書的著名晉代史學家孫盛、以「映雪讀書」流傳千古的孫康等古代名人，當代已故中科院歷史研究所所長侯外廬、已故語言研究所副所長侯稽一、已故中國文學研究會會長王　、著名畫家李苟、著名歌唱家郭蘭英等都出生在這片古老的土地上。平遙古城不愧為歷史文化名城。

我們現在正行駛在惠濟橋上，惠濟橋是一座九拱石橋，修建於清代康熙年間，同治年間重建。清代名宿傅山先生曾親筆為它寫碑記。這座橋規模不算大，歷史也不算很長，但造型優美，橋面平坦，沒有像一般石橋那樣高高隆起，便於車馬行走。而且更有一個奇處，就是這座橋下還有一座橋。下面的橋不見文字記載，人們原來也不知道。1977年8月，一場暴雨造成特大洪災，滾滾洪水帶走了不少淤積多年的河沙。水退後，人們驚奇地發現，原來惠濟橋疊架在舊橋的橋面上，形成橋上橋的奇觀。利用舊橋做新橋的牢固基礎，既節省財力、人力，又省時間，多聰明的構思呀！這在造橋史上也是一個奇蹟。

請大家隨我上城牆參觀。〔帶遊客進「下東門」〕

這裡就是平遙古城的「下東門」。大家看這高達12米的城牆多麼雄偉壯觀。城外還有護城河，城門處架有吊橋，在古代戰亂的日子裡，這的確是一道難以踰越的防線。

我們現在所在的地方是下東門甕城，它是為保衛城門而設立的。城門是城牆上的薄弱環節，有了甕城，就大大增強了城池的防衛手段。這裡地方很小，四周為高牆圍護，即便敵人攻入甕城也只能進來少數人，而且立即陷入包圍之中，成為甕中之鱉。有的甕城門並不是開在城門對面，而是拐個彎開在旁邊，更可防止衝入的敵兵一鼓作氣衝到城門下，透過拐彎來挫動敵兵銳氣。這些設計思想都是古人在長期實戰經驗中總結出來的。

大家看，甕城裡還有一個建造講究而小巧的院落，這是幹什麼的呢？原來這是一座小關帝廟。關帝是武聖人，把關廟修進甕城裡，確是平遙人的獨特創造。請大家隨我進城，上城牆參觀。

現在我們已經在城牆上了，這裡本來還有城樓，但在戰爭中毀掉了。這座建在城牆上的台，傳說就是尹吉甫的點將台。請大家隨我觀賞一下古城的建構。〔帶遊客向南慢步，邊走邊說，約走2～3個墩台即可停下〕

我們看城牆上兩邊各有一道矮牆，叫女兒牆，為什麼叫女兒牆呢？宋代官府編寫的《營造法式》上有個書面解釋：「言其卑小。比之於城，若女子與丈夫也。」意思是說城牆高大厚實，像偉丈夫；女牆單薄短小，像弱女子。民間有的地方卻流傳著這樣的故事：早先城上並沒有女兒牆，有一次一個老人被拉來做工，和他相依為命的小孫女也天天隨他來到城上，坐在旁邊觀看。一天，一位累極了的民工昏昏沉沉中竟走到城牆邊上，小女孩怕他掉下城去，用力向裡推他，不料因用力過大，民工雖得救了，小女孩卻摔死了。為了紀念她，工匠們在城上修起了矮牆，並把它叫做女兒牆。這實在是個感人的故事，但確實說明了女兒牆的保護性功能。我們看：兩邊的女兒牆並不一樣，向外的女兒牆上還修築了堆口，堆口還留著供瞭望和射擊使用的小孔，這當然是為了實戰的需要。

大家都注意到了，城牆每隔一段，就有一個向外突出的部分，這叫做墩台，它是幹什麼用的呢？對！它是保衛城牆的。我們知道，古代攻守城池的主要武器是弓箭和彎機，上面既可射下去，下面也可射上來，因此守城的士兵輕易不敢探出身去。這樣，城牆腳下反而成了防禦的死角。有了墩台，就可以彌補這個不足，從三面組成一個強大的立體射擊網，城防力量大大加強。在每個墩台上，還修有一座敵樓，上面有孔，也是為觀察和射擊用的。

平遙古城除了具備這些共性特點外，還有自己獨特的地方。

城牆本是戰爭的產物，平遙人卻偏偏喜歡給它抹上一層濃濃的文化色彩，把象徵文化星宿的魁星樓修在了城牆東南角上（指形狀獨特的魁星樓）。據統計，古城上共有3000 個堆口、72 座敵樓，那是象徵著文聖人孔夫子的 3000 弟子 72賢人。

　　平遙古城形似烏龜，歷來有龜城之稱。據說是取神龜壽水長存之意。全城六座城門，南門似頭，城門和甕城外門都向南，任龜首自由伸縮，北門似尾，甕城外門折而東向，好像龜尾東甩，東西各二門似龜腳。三座甕城外門拐向南開，好像神龜正緩緩伸腿屈肢向前爬行，只有咱們剛才進來的下東門甕城外門不向南拐而向東開，傳說是怕神龜爬向別處，所以用一根無形的繩索把左後腳牢牢地拴在城東10千米的麓台塔上，把這條腿都拉直了。在南門外左右各有一口井，人們說那就是神龜的一對明亮的眼睛。在市中心，也就是龜心的位置，還修有一座市樓，就是我們看到的那座高踞眾屋之上的樓，在市樓樓頂兩坡上，還用黃、藍兩色琉璃瓦拼出喜字和壽字，它充分體現了古城獨特的文化氛圍，表達了平遙人民良好的願望，這也可以說是龜城城建構思的點睛之作了。

　　平遙城內文物眾多，西南方向那一片覆蓋琉璃的建築，就是城隍廟、財神廟建築群，近處觀看，可以見到它瞻角高桃、群昂飛動、油漆彩繪的壯麗景色。在它附近很顯眼的那座現代大樓是平遙中學教學樓。文廟大成殿就在校園內，從這裡看不清楚。為保護原來的風貌，古城中一般是不準建樓的，平遙人卻為學校破例修了一座教學樓，足見其對教育的重視。平遙中學也不負眾望，一直以優異的成績保持著這所省級重點中學在省內的領先地位。

　　平遙古城的講解就到這裡，現在大家可以自由參觀。

Qiao Family Compound （喬家大院）

My dear friend,

Before we start visiting the major scenic spots, I'd like to give you a brief introduction to the Qiao family compound.

The Qiao family compound is located in the center of Qiaojiapu Village in Qi County. It is a group of grand buildings and structures. From a bird's eye view, the arrangement of the compound's buildings resembles the Chinese character "喜" symbolizing good luck and happiness. The whole compound covers an area of 8,724 square meters. It is divided into six big yards, including 20 small yards, and 313 houses. Shaped like a castle, the compound faces streets on the three sides. Around the compound are closed brick walls, more than 10 meters high. Daughter walls and observation posts are built on and around the walls. These are both solid and dignified. Its exquisite distribution and subtle art fully represent the unique style of Qing Dynasty Chinese residential houses and palaces. Due to its unique appearance and history, the compound can be seen as an unmatched architectural art treasure and has been praised by experts and scholars as "one precious stone of northern civilian construc-tion." No wonder that people say after a visit "The Qiao Family Compound to civilian houses is what the Imperial Palace is to royal compounds".

An 80-metre-straight road made of stone at the gate of the inside compound divides the six yards into two rows in the south and north. On both sides of the road are slopes for protection. The Qiao Family Memorial Temple lies at the compound's west end facing the far gate. The compound is composed of four fundamental buildings and a total of six gate buildings, buildings for time, and pavilions for looking over the area. On the top of buildings in different yards are ways connecting one another for patrol and safety and tidiness; when viewing these from the inside, we feel their magnificence and orderliness. It represents the living style of the Chinese northern feudal families. The severe layout, exquisite construction, and standardization with variation, all combine to give the compound both an overall beauty and magnificent variety. Even the over 140 rooftop chimneys differ from one another. The platforms, pavilions, painted beams and all of the decorations display the compound's exquisite designs and the skill that went into building it.

The compound was first built in the 20thyear of the Qing Emperor Qianlong's reign

(1756 A.D.). After first being built, it was then enlarged twice and repaired once. It was first rebuilt during the Tongzhi Period of Qing Dynasty, and this job was presided over by Qiao Zhiyong. The compound was then rebuilt again during the middle and late Guangxu Period; on this occasion, Qiao Jingyi and Qiao Zuiyan directed the work. The final repair work was done after the first decade of the Chinese Republic and was separately completed by Qiao Yingxia and Qiao Yingkui. Thus nearly two centuries elapsed between construction of the compound's first buildings to its more modern structures. Though the time span is large, the compound appears to be uniform in style, since the late rebuilding and repair work was based on the original designs.

In line with traditional naming practices, the compound's three northern yards are called, in east to west order, the Old Yard, Northwestern Yard and Study Yard. The three southern yards are called in order the Southeastern Yard, the Southwestern Yard and the New Yard. The names of the six yards in south and north represent the building order for all of the Qiao Family Compound's yards.

During the Qing Dynasty's Qianlong Period, part of Qiaojipu Village's crossing stood on the compound's present location. After dividing up family property with his two elder brothers, Qiao Quanmei bought several sites in the northeastern corner of the crossing and began to construct buildings. The fundamental building was made of bricks and tiles with solid roof. It has windows but no doors, with many floors inside. It's main features are thick walls, small windows and firm construc-tion. Five yards are located inside the building and three are located outside of it. To the east of the fundamental building was the former yard, which became the supporting yard after the compound was repaired. The second door in the supporting yard was changed into a study place, which was the first yard of the compound and was also known as the Old Yard. It was said that there was a memorial temple and two Chinese scholar trees with strange shape in front of the temple called "the divine tree" by the compound's residents. After getting the right to use this land, the Qiao family first planned to move the temple without trees. Later Qiao Quanmei dreamed the God Jingjia told him: "If the trees are moved alive, the temple will flourish; if you want to get a good result, you must move the trees and temple together. Four or five steps eastward is just the place where trees can be moved to remain alive. If you move the temple without trees, the trees will become dead and people won't get rich..." Soon after the trees become quite weak, Qiao Guanmei was afraid of offending the God, so he moved the trees as the dream referred. The trees really revived and flourished as before. It was like "the true God appeared". So another memorial temple was built in front of the supporting yard, which still exists today. At the same time there was a large brick land temple between the fundamental and supporting yards, carved with stone hills, deer eating mythic fungus. The layout of this area emphasizes luckiness, or metaphors with the meaning of "being lucky all the time". Thus the temple's wall had pine trees and six pairs of deer close to each other, symbolizing "being lucky and happy".

When Qiao Zhiyong took charge of the family, he continued to built for his family's fame. He bought a large building site beside the lane west to the Old Yard, and built another yard with floors inside, also with five court inside and three outside. The two buildings face each other. The fundamental buildings were designed with a roof shaped like a hanging hill with shining pillars. The doors are high, and at the angles on the roof are the wood-carved paintings. Onward are galleries and corridors. Going onto the corridors we can see brick-carved handrails in front, and the paint of one hundred grape babies in the middle. Standing on the gallery, we can see the entire yard. Since the southern and northern yards are arranged in a row, with a lane in between them, and the two buildings are both outstanding, the style is called "double silver ingot," which was used as money in feudal China.

After completing the building, Qiao Zhiyong set up two square yards with five houses in row and line, facing two buildings over the street. Four yards were situated in the four corners of the crossing, and these ensure the later layout of being connected into a whole.

During the middle and late Guangxu Period, local governmental authority declined and the area became less safe and more chaotic. To make the compound more secure, Jingyi and Jingyan of the Qiao Family bought the use rights for the streets and spent considerable money and overcame many problems in doing this. After this, Qiao family blocked up the lane and changed it into a supporting yard with a northwestern yard and a southwestern one. In east they blocked up the street and built a gate. In west they built a memorial temple. In north outside the two yards, they rebuilt two stretching yards with two new gates without corridors. By building bars between the stretching yards and turning arching gate's surface into a bridge, they connected the southern and northern yards together to form a compound like a castle.

In the beginning years of the old Republic of China, the Qiao Family's living houses were not large enough to accommodate the family's larger size, so they bought more land and extended westward. After the 10thyear of the old Republic of China, Qiao Yingxia and Qiao Yingkui built new yards close to the southwestern yard, with a layout similar to the southeastern yard. But the windows were decorated with large cases of glasses in western style. The light could go through windows easily. With clear changes to the style, carvings on the walls facing gates in the yard were quite subtle. At the same time Qiao Yingxia designed and rebuilt the northwestern yard. He blocked up the corridors of the outside yard connecting with the old yard, and changed them into a guest hall, together with the former cooking house. He also built a bath room beside the guest hall and a toilet in western style. All this adds an exotic romantic feeling to the compound.

During the War Against Japanese Aggression, the entire Qiao Family fled the compound, leaving just a few servants behind. But throughout all of this Qiao Family Compound has remained a splendid example of northern residential palace construction.

In brief, the Compound of Qiao Family is not only a treasure house of architecture, but also a palace of local history and culture. So touring the Compound of Qiao Family is worth your money and time from all aspects.

親愛的朋友們，大家好！

在遊覽主要景點之前，我先給大家簡單介紹一下喬家大院的基本情況。

喬家大院位於祁縣喬家堡村正中。這是一座雄偉壯觀的建築群體，從高空俯視院落布局，酷似一個像徵大吉大利的雙「喜」字。整個大院占地8724平方米，建築面積3870平方米。分六個大院，內套20個小院，313 間房屋。大院形如城堡，三面臨街，四周全是封閉式磚牆，高三丈有餘，上邊有掩身女兒牆和瞭望探口，既安全牢固，又顯得威嚴氣派。其設計之精巧，工藝之精細，充分體現了中國清代民居建築的獨特風格，具有相當高的觀賞、科學研究價值，確實是一座無與倫比的藝術寶庫，被專家學者恰如其分地讚美為「北方民居建築的一顆明珠。」難怪有人參觀後感慨地説：「皇家有故宮，民宅有喬家。」

進入喬家院大門是一條長80米筆直的石鋪甬道，把六個大院分為南北兩排，甬道兩側靠牆有護坡。西盡頭處是喬家祠堂，與大門遙相對應。大院有主樓四座，門樓、更樓、眺閣六座。各院房頂上有走道相通，用於巡更護院。縱觀全院，從外面看，威嚴高大，整齊端莊；進院裡看，富麗堂皇，井然有序，顯示了中國北方封建大家庭的居住格調。整個大院布局嚴謹，建築考究，規範而有變化，不但有整體美感，在局部建築上也各有特色，即使是房頂上的140餘個煙囱也都各不相同。全院亭台樓閣，雕樑畫棟，堆金立粉，完全顯示了中國古代高超的建築藝術水平，確實是不可多得的藝術珍品。

喬家大院始建於清乾隆二十年（公元 1756年），以後有兩次擴建，一次增修。第一次擴建約在清同治年間，由喬致庸主持，第二次擴建為光緒中、晚期，由喬景儀、喬景儼經手；最後一次增修是在民國十年後，由喬映霞、喬映奎分別完成。從始建到最後建成現在的格局，中間經過了近兩個世紀。雖然時間跨度很大，但後來的擴建和增修都能按原先的構思進行，使整個大院風格一致，渾然一體。

喬家大院依照傳統的叫法，北面三個大院，從東往西依次叫老院、西北院、書房院。南面三個大院依次為東南院、西南院、新院。南北六個大院的稱謂，表現了喬家大院中各個院落的建築順序。

　　清乾隆年間，現喬家大院坐落的地方，一部分正好是喬家堡村的大街與小巷交叉的十字口。喬全美和他的兩個兄長分家後，買下了十字口東北角的幾處宅地，起建樓房。主樓為硬山頂磚瓦房，磚木結構，有窗櫺而無門戶，在室內築樓梯上樓。特點是牆壁厚，窗戶小，堅實牢固，為裡五外三院。主樓的東面是原先的宅院，也進行了翻修，作為偏院。還把偏院中的二進門改建為書塾，這是喬家大院最早的院落，也就是老院。傳說偏院外原來有個五道祠，祠前有兩株槐樹，長得離奇古怪，人們稱為「神樹」。喬家取得這塊地皮的使用權後，原打算移廟不移樹。後來喬全美在夜間做了一夢，夢見金甲神對他說：「樹移活，祠移富，若要兩相宜，祠樹一齊移。往東四五步，便是樹活處。如果移祠不移樹，樹死人不富……」沒有多久，此樹便奄奄一息。喬全美恐怕得罪了神靈，便照夢中指示的地方，把樹移了過去，樹真的復活了，而且枝葉繁茂如初。這好像是「真神顯靈」，真有其神，於是又在側院前修了個五道祠，直至今天依然存在。同時主院與側院間有一大型磚雕土地祠，雕有石山及口銜靈芝的鹿等。土地祠各有四個磚雕獅子和一柄如意，隱喻「四時如意」。祠壁上還有梧桐和松樹，六對鹿雙雙合在一起，喻意「六合通順」。

　　喬致庸當家後，為光大門庭，繼續大興土木。他在老院西側隔小巷置買了一大片宅基地，又蓋了一座樓房院，也是裡五外三，形成兩樓對峙，主樓為懸山頂露明柱結構。通天櫺門，門樓的卡口是南極星騎鹿和百子圖木雕。上有陽台走廊。走廊前沿有磚雕扶欄，正中為葡萄百子圖。站在陽台上可觀全院。由於兩樓院隔小巷並列，且南北樓翹起，故叫做「雙元寶」式。

　　明樓竣工後，喬致庸又在與兩樓隔街相望的地方建築了兩個橫五豎五的四合鬥院，使四座院落正好位於街巷交叉的四角，奠定了後來連成一體的格局。

　　光緒中晚期，地方治安不穩，喬家的景儀、景儼為了保護自身的安危，費了不少周折，花了很多銀兩，買下了當時街巷的占用權。喬家取得占用權後，把巷口堵了，小巷建成西北院和西南院的側院；東面堵了街口，修建了大門；西面建了祠堂；北面兩樓院外又擴建成兩個外跨院，新建兩個燕廊大門。跨院間有柵欄通過，並以拱形大門頂為過橋，把南北院互相連接起來，形成城堡式的建築群。

民國初年，喬家人口增多，住房顯得不足，因而又購買地皮，向西擴張延伸。民國十年後，喬映霞、喬映奎又在緊靠西南院建起新院，格局和東南院相似。但窗戶全部刻上大格玻璃，西洋式裝飾，採光效果也很好，顯然在式樣上有了改觀，就是院內迎門掩壁雕刻也十分細緻。與此同時，西北院也由喬映霞設計改建，把和老院相通的外院之敞廊堵塞，連同原來的灶房，改建為客廳。還在客廳旁建了浴室，修了「洋茅廁」，增添了異國風情。

日軍侵占時期，喬家外逃，剩下空院一處，只留部分家人看護。延續至今，喬家大院成了北方民居中一顆光彩奪目的明珠。

總之，喬家大院既是建築藝術的寶庫，也是民俗學的殿堂。步入其間，既會得到美的享受，又會使人增長許多知識。因此，喬家大院一遊，從藝術、科學、文化、趣味每個方面，都會使您感到，不虛此行。

Hebei Province河北省

A Glimpse of the Province （本省簡介）

Hebei province has a long history and its abbreviation is "Ji". During the Spring and Autumn Period, northern Hebei Province was part of the Yan State, while southern Hebei Province was part of the Zhao State. It thus got the nickname "Yanzhao Area". It has been called Hebei since 1928.

It is located in the North China Plain, on the north bank of the Yellow River—the word Hebei means "north of the river" in China—and west of Bohai Bay. The exact location is from 113.04 degrees to 119.53 degrees longitude in the east, and from 36.01 degrees to 42.37 degrees latitude in the north. It covers an area of 187,700 square kilo-meters, with Taihang Mountain located to the west and Yanshan Mountain located to the north. The north part of Yanshan Mountain is referred to as the Zhangbei Plateau, while much of the rest of the province is called Hebei Plain. Hebei Province's highest point is a mountain named Small Wutai, which is 2,870 meters in elevation. Nearly half the province, or 43% of the plain area is no more than 100 meters high.

Hebei's weather is moderate, and it has a monsoon season. The four seasons have the following distinct characteristics. Winters are cold and have limited snow and other percipitation. Summers are hot and much of Hebei's rainfall occurs during this season. Spring is windy, autumns are cool, and both seasons are relatively short. The average temperature ranges from-27℃ to 2℃ in January and from 18 to 27 in July. The annual precipitation ranges from 350 to 750 millimeters.

Hebei is administratively divided into 11 cities, 109 counties, and 6 autonomous counties. The capi-tal city is Shijiazhuang. The 11 cities are Shijia-zhuang, Zhangjiakou, Chengde, Tangshan, Baoding, Langfang, Qinhuangdao, Hengshui, Cangzhou, Xing-tai, Handan. There are many ethnic nationalities, including the Uygur, Manchurian, Mongolian, and Korean national minorities.

Getting into and out of Hebei is very easy. Most airlines regularly fly from Hebei's capital to other major Chinese cities, like Beijing, Guangzhou, Nanjing, Shanghai, Changsha and Chongqing. The rail links running in and out of Hebei are also good, and the seasonal trains like Beijing—Chengde, Beijing—Qinhuangdao bring many tourists from other parts of our county to the province's famous tourist cities.

Tourism Resources

There are many famous scenic spots and relics in Hebei Province. The cities of Chengde and Baoding have been listed as historical and cultural Chinese cities. Many parts of the Great Wall are in Hebei Province, as is the famous "First Pass Under the

Heaven". There are many world famous scenic spots and religious relics, such as the largest imperial garden—the Mountain Resort and the Eight Outer Temples, the splendid Eastern and Western Qing Tombs, the Han tomb complex which lies in Mancheng County and is famous for the gold thread jade clothes, Zhaozhou Bridge, Longxing Temple (the big Buddha Temple) and the Iron Lion. Many famous Hebei places have been inscribed in the World Heritage List. These include the Zhaozhou Bridge (1991), Mountain Resort and the Outlying Temples (1994), and the Eastern Qing Tombs (2000). And the Iron Lion has been listed as a "Top in China" tourist attraction. With respect to natural scenery, Qinhuangdao and Beidaihe are famous for their seashores, and the Mulan Hunting Land is famous for the vast grassland. Recent years have seen the emergence of a new resort—Yesanpo, or the Three Natural Hillsides—which is famous for its natural scenery and designated as a "China Famous Scenic spot."

Local Snacks

Jizhou sesame cake in Jizhou and salty donkey meat, Chaigoubao bacon, Baoding baked wheaten cake and Islamic braised chicken, Xinglong blood sausage, Zhangjiakou dried mushrooms, Baiyangdian preserved eggs, and Tangshan fried dough twist with honey.

Local Specialties

Hebei's agriculture is advanced, and other industries like fishing, iron and steel, and porcelain are all very important. There are many local specialties, such as Zhao County pears, Xinglong County haw, Shenzhou peaches, Xuanhua grapes, "Hunting land" mushrooms, chestnuts east of Beijing, and the like. You can also get many special souvenirs in Hebei Province, such as Chengde wood sculptures, Tangshan porcelain, Qinhuangdao shell sculptures, Hengshui sniff pots, Quyang stone sculptures, and the like.

Local Culture

Bangzi is Heibei's main local opera. In addition, tourists can enjoy Dagu, which is a versified story sung to the accompaniment of a small drum and other instruments, in Xihe and Laoting, as well Wuqiao's world famous acrobatic show.

Tourist City

Shijiazhuang is the capital city of Hebei province, and also the political, economic and cultural center of the province. Xibaipo is the famous site of revolutionary education. In May 1948, under the leadership of Mao Zedong, the Party's Central Committee and the headquarters of the Chinese People's Liberation Army moved into this village. This made it the last rural command center prior to the decisive battles between the Communist Party and the Kuomintang. In 1991 Zhu Muzhi, who was Minister of the Information Office of the State Council at that time, wrote this inscription for Xibaipo: "The destiny of China was determined in this village." "New China set off from here" is a famous sentence written by writer Yan Tao, and it speaks of Xibaipo's significance in Chinese history.

Chengde City is located in the north part of Hebei Province. It was known as "the second political center in Qing Dynasty" and is one of China's most important historical and cultural cities. It boasts the world famous Mountain Resort and the Eight Outer Temples within its urban area, while "the Mulan hunting land" is located in the north part of Chengde city. The latter landmark was where Qing Emperors went hunting; however, today it is mainly a nice place for ordinary Chengde residents to escape from the heat during the summer.

Qinhuangdao is famous for its beautiful beaches. The famous scenic spots include the beach tourist landscape, which is located at Beidaihe, and the pass landscape, which is located by Shanhaiguan.

Recommended Tour Routes

1.The tour of culture and historic sites—famous garden, temples, mausoleums and ancient buildings.

Chengde—the Eastern Qing Mausoleum (Zunhua county)—Qinhuangdao—the Western Qing Mausoleum (Yi County).

2.The tour for leisure—grassland, beach.

Chengde—Mulan Hunting Land—Beidaihe.

3.The tour of experiencing the Great Wall.

Qinhuangdao—Beidaihe—Ji county (the boundary of Hebei and Tianjin)—the Great Wall Under the Water (Panjiakou in Chengde)—Jinshanling Great Wall.

4.The tour of studying "the Red Culture of China".

Shijiazhuang—Xibaipo—Baoding.

河北省簡稱「冀」，在春秋時期，它的北部屬於燕國，南部屬趙國，因此被稱為「燕趙大地」，自1928年改稱河北。

河北省坐落在華北平原，黃河以北，渤海以西，具體的地理位置為東經113°04´至119°53´，北緯36°1´至42°37´，面積為18.77萬平方千米，西部是太行山脈，北部為燕山山脈，燕山山脈北部被稱為張北高原，其他部分被稱為河北平原，河北的最高點被稱為小五台，海拔2870米，平原部分有43%的面積海拔高度均不足100米。

河北屬季風性氣候，四季分明，冬季寒冷，微量降雪，夏季炎熱，降水量充足，春季多風且短暫，秋季涼爽，年降水量350～750毫米。

從行政角度劃分，河北為11 個市，109 個縣，6個自治縣。省會為石家莊，其他十個市分別為張家口、承德、唐山、保定、廊坊、秦皇島、衡水、滄州、邢台、邯鄲。河北有很多少數民族，如維吾爾族、滿族、蒙古族、朝鮮族等。

河北的交通比較發達。航空線將省會石家莊同北京、廣州、南京、上海、長沙、重慶和中國其他各大城市連接起來。鐵路線也很發達，季節性旅遊列車把來自中國各地的旅遊者帶到了河北省的著名旅遊城市。

旅遊資源

河北省有許多著名的文物古蹟，承德市與保定市被列為中國的歷史文化名城，長城的大部分均位於河北省境內，著名的天下第一關也位於此，這裡還有許多舉世聞名的旅遊景點和宗教古蹟，如著名的皇家園林避暑山莊和外八廟、雄偉壯麗的清東西陵，滿城漢墓和金縷玉衣、趙州橋、隆興寺（大佛寺）和鐵獅子。在這些著名的景點中，趙州橋於1991年被列入世界文化遺產、避暑山莊及其周圍廟宇於1994年被列入世界文化遺產、清東陵於2000年被列入世界文化遺產名錄、滄州鐵獅子被列入「中國之最」。自然資源方面，秦皇島和北戴河以海濱著名，木蘭圍場以其廣袤的草原而聞名。近年來湧現出的新興景觀野三坡以其特殊的自然景觀被列為中國著名景點。

風味美食

河北的風味美食有：冀州燒餅、晉州鹹驢肉、柴溝堡燻肉、保定清真煮雞、興隆血腸、張家口口蘑、保定火燒、白洋澱松花蛋、唐山蜂蜜麻花等。

地方特產

河北省的農業比較發達，其他產業如漁業、鋼鐵和製瓷業也都非常重要，土特產品很豐富，如趙縣的雪花梨、深州的桃、宣化的葡萄、圍場的蘑菇、京東的板栗、興隆的山楂等。在河北省，也可以買到很多有特色的紀念品，如承德的木雕、唐山的瓷器、秦皇島的貝雕、衡水的鼻煙壺、曲陽的石雕等。

地方文藝

河北梆子為主要地方戲，此外還有西河大鼓、樂亭大鼓等，吳橋雜技也是舉國聞名。

主要旅遊城市

石家莊是河北省的省會，也是全省的政治、經濟和文化中心。西柏坡是著名的革命教育基地，1948年5月，毛澤東同志率領中共中央、中國人民解放軍總部移駐這裡，使這個普通的山村成為「解放全中國的最後一個農村指揮所」，成為中國共產黨領導中國人民和人民解放軍與國民黨進行戰略大決戰，創建新中國的指揮中心。「中國命運定於此村」，這是1991年時任中共中央對外宣傳辦公室主任的朱穆之同志的題詞。「新中國從這裡走來」是作家閻濤的一句名言，可見西柏坡在中國歷史上至關重要的作用。

承德市位於河北省的北部，在清朝的時候被稱為第二個政治中心，是中國歷史文化名城之一，市區內有舉世聞名的避暑山莊及外八廟，市區北部的木蘭圍場是清朝皇帝行圍涉獵的場所，也是現今避暑的好去處。

秦皇島以其優美的海濱風光而聞名，著名的旅遊勝地有以北戴河為中心的海濱旅遊風景區，以山海關為中心的關城風景區等。

推薦旅遊路線

1.文化古蹟遊—名園、寺廟、陵寢及古建築

承德—清東陵（河北省遵化縣）—秦皇島—清西陵（河北省易縣）。

2.休閒之旅—草原、海濱

承德—木蘭圍場—北戴河。

3.感受長城之旅

秦皇島—北戴河—薊縣（天津與河北交界處）—水下長城（承德潘家口）—金山嶺長城。

4.紅色之旅

石家莊—西柏坡—保定。

Chengde Mountain Resort （承德避暑山莊）

Ladies and Gentlemen,

Welcome to the Chengde Mountain Resort. The Mountain Resort is located in northern Chengde city and is the largest imperial garden in China.

The Mountain Resort is the symbol of the Qing Dynasty's so-called "Kangqian Heyday". As the founders of the Mountain Resort, the Kangxi and Qianlong Emperors had travelled to Southern China six times and enjoyed its beautiful scenery. Thus when the Mountain Resort was built, it incorporated the best craftsmanship of the garden construction and the scenery of both Northern and Southern China, making the resort a miniature of the Middle Kingdom. In 1994, Unesco listed the Mountain Resort and its Outlying Temples "World Cultural Heritage" sites.

Work on the Mountain Resort began in 1703 and was finished 89 years later, in 1792. When the Mountain Resort was completed, every Qing Emperor would come here to escape the summer heat. Since many state affairs were then dealt with at this location, the Mountain Resort also became known as the Qing Dynasty's second political center. The Mountain Resort covers an area of 5.64 square kilometers, making it twice as large as the Summer Palace and eight times bigger than Beihai Park. The wall around the Mountain Resort is 10 kilometers long. Inside the Mountain Resort, there are 120 scenic spots, and the most famous ones are "the 72 scenic spots named by Emperor Kangxi and Qianlong". Of these scenic spots, Emperor Kangxi named 36 scenic spots with four Chinese characters, and Emperor Qianlong named the rest only with three characters. Because Emperor Kangxi was the grandfather of Emperor Qianlong, and Emperor Qianlong did so in order to show his respect to his grandfather. The Mountain Resort consists of four parts: the palace, lake, plain and mountain districts. While the Mountain Resort named after "the mountain", its most beautiful scenery is located in the lake district, which was inspired by the landscape of Southern China.

Here is the famous Mountain Resort.

Lizheng Gate

The gate in front of us is called Lizheng Gate, which is the first view of the 36 beautiful sceneries named by Emperor Qianlong and the first entrance to the main palace. In ancient China, all palace entrances southwards are called Lizheng Gate or Zhengyang Gate to symbolize the legitimacy and almightiness of the emperor. A horizontal tablet on which five national languages were carved hangs above the gate: from the right to the left are Mongolian, Uygur, Chinese, Tibetan and Manchu. It symbolizes that China is a multinational country. The two lions in front of the gate are the symbol of the emperor's power and majesty.

The Picture of the Mulan Hunting

Now we are at the palace area's front yard. Here you can see the Mulan Hunting Land painting, which was painted by a Qing Dynasty artist, depicting a scene of an imperial hunt.

The Mulan Hunting Land is situated about 150 kilometers northwest of Chengde city. In the Qing Dynasty, Emperors led the Eight-Banner Troops to the imperial hunting land for shooting every summer. This area had lots of wild animals, including tigers, deer, leopards, bears, wolves, wild boars, and the like. In order to ensure that these wild animals were not over-hunted, the area was divided into 72 enclosed fields, and the hunting was limited to 10 fields or so for each time. When the troops arrived at the Mulan Hunting Land, they encamped in the forest and selected a place with luxuriant grass for hunting. They then built a stand for the Emperor and enclosed wild animals. In the early morning, the soldiers got up very early and wore the clothes made of deer skin and blew the wooden whistles to imitate the sound of female deer to attract the deer or other wild animals. In the picture, we can see the Qing Emperor wearing the red robe, riding his warhorse with bow and an arrow in his hands shooting the deer. The Emperor shot first, then the soldiers followed him shooting. The scene was magnificent and spectacular. Finally the emperor would inspect the troops and award the soldiers according to the numbers of animals they killed. Afterwards a big celebration, including a barbecue and a campfire party would be held.

In fact, the real purpose of hunting was closely related to the political situation. From the 16thto the 17thcentury, Tsarist Russia frequently harassed and invaded the Chinese northern frontiers. At the same time, one of the northern border minorities in the northern border staged frequent rebellions, while a few upper chiefs of the Mongolian tribes collaborated with Tsarist Russia with the aim of splitting China apart. In addition, the fighting abilities of the Qing Dynasty armies gradually weakened due to long periods of peace and inexperience at fighting battles. Emperor Kangxi was very worried about this situation, so he made a decision to lead his Eight-Banner Troops during the Mulan hunts. In this way, he could train his soldiers, strengthen ties with the Mongolian race and the other minorities, against the invasion of the Tsarist Russia and consolidate China. Along the 360-kilometer-long road from Beijing to the Mulan Hunting Land, more than twenty temporary palaces were built. Chengde city was located at an important place connecting Beijing and the Hunting Land. The scenery here was beautiful and the climate was suitable, so Emperor Kangxi decided to have the largest imperial garden built here and that was the Mountain Resort. Every summer the Qing Emperors came here to spend a holiday and lived for six months. They arrived in May and went to the imperial hunting ground to hunt for a month, then returned to Beijing in late autumn.

The Main Palace District

The Mountain Resort's palace district consists of four parts: the Main Palace, Songhe Zhai (the Palace of the Pine and Crane), Wan He Song Feng (Ten Thousand Ravines and Pine Soughing) and the East Palace. The Main Palace's important structures were all built along the north-south axis, while the east and west annex halls were arranged symmetrically and nine courtyards were built. Why were nine courtyards built here? According to the traditional Chinese philosophy, the odd numbers are one, three, five, seven and nine which belonged to Yang (positive) and stand for the active and independent character. The even numbers are two, four, six, eight and ten which belonged to Yin (negative) and stand for gentle, passive and dependent character. "Nine" was the biggest in the odd number that stands for the highest rank. "Five" is in the middle of the odd number that stands for righteousness, "Nine and Five" implies that the emperor was both supreme and righteous. In ancient China, the emperors used the "Nine and Five" to indicate their supremacy, honesty, justice and selflessness. This kind of layout also reflected the ruling thought of the emperor who lived in the "Ninth Heaven". In the Qing Dynasty, four emperors once lived here. During that time, they handled the state affairs, held big ceremonies, received the nobles, the princes, the chiefs of minorities and the foreign envoys, signed important treaties with some foreign countries and carried on many other political activities.

The Hall of Simplicity and Sincerity

The main hall in the Main Palace is named the Hall of Simplicity and Sincerity; it is also called Nanmu Hall. Nanmu is a kind of cedar wood. In rainy seasons, it gives off a light and refreshing fragrance. The name of the hall was given by Emperor Kangxi, who was inspired by the following quote from Zhu Geliang's book, "Simplicity can help one clear his ambition, and calm mind can make great foresight." We can see the emperor's yellow throne placed on a sandalwood platform in center of the hall. In the Qing Dynasty, "Yellow" was the special color used only by the imperial family and Buddhist temples; everyone else was prohibited from using this color. A sandalwood screen, with 163 vivid figures carved on it showing men at work ploughing and women weaving, stands behind the emperor's throne. In the east and west side walls stand the book shelves in which Collection of Ancient and Contemporary Books were originally stored. These books are now in Beijing. On the ceiling, the windows and the doors, you can find the patterns of the swastika, peach and bat. In ancient China, the "swastika" symbolized the sun and good luck, the "peach" represented longevity, while the pronunciation of "bat" is "Fu" in Chinese which is similar to the word for "happiness." In this hall, the emperors handled state affairs, presided over grand ceremonies, received nobles, princes, chiefs of minorities, and the foreign envoys, just as he did in the Forbidden City's "Hall of Supreme Harmony."

The Hall of Refreshing Mist and Waves and the West Chamber

The hall in front of us is called "the Hall of Refreshing Mist and Waves". It is a place where the emperor met his mother, brothers and sisters. The far west room is a bedroom, it is also called the "West Chamber". Here we can see the emperor's "Dragon Bed". Emperors Kangxi, Qianlong, Jiaqing, Xianfeng once slept in this room. In 1860, the British-French allied troops invaded Beijing, Emperor Xianfeng sought refuge here and died in this room. The adjoining house in the west is "the West Compound" where Dowager Cixi once lived. The house is quite near to the emperor's bedroom and it is said that while crossing the side door, Cixi once went stealthily to the back of the emperor's bedroom, and eavesdropped the conversation of Emperor Xianfeng and his ministers. He said that it was possible that she would make troubles and disturbances to the court. As expected, after Emperor Xianfeng died, she controlled China for nearly half a century. Two years after she died, the Qing Dynasty,

China's last feudal dynasty, collapsed.

The Lake District

We come to the lake district along with the winding stairs in the rockery of Wan He Song Feng. The islands and islets are scattered freely, so as to resemble the beautiful seaside scenery in the south of China. In the Qing Dynasty, Emperor Kangxi and Qianlong often went to Southern China and were greatly taken by it's lovely landscape. When Emperor Kangxi decided to have the Mountain Resort built in Chengde, he intended to have it mirror the landscape and seascape he had fallen in love with in Southern China. Thus much of the lake districts imitates Southern China. One example is the "Lion Grove," which was modeled after a garden in Suzhou, Jiangsu Province. The "Zigzag Embankment" and Water Center Pavilion resemble similar structures in Hang-zhou's famous West Lake. The "Golden Hill Tower" replicated "God's Pagoda" in Zhenjiang, Jiangsu Province, while the "Tower of Misty Rain" copied the same building of the south lake in Jiaxing, Zhejiang Province.

After visiting the Mountain Resort, you must be impressed by its magnificent and beautiful landscape as well as the rich culture and history. I sincerely hope that the sightseeing of the Mountain Resort can give you a nice experience and good memory!

女士們、先生們：

歡迎大家來承德避暑山莊觀光遊覽。避暑山莊位於承德市區北部，是中國現存最大的皇家園林。

避暑山莊是清代康乾盛世的象徵。作為山莊締造者的康熙、乾隆都曾六下江南，遍歷天下景物之美，因此在修建避暑山莊的時候博采眾家之長，融中國南北園林的風格為一體，整個避暑山莊就是祖國錦繡河山的縮影。1994年，避暑山莊及其周圍寺廟群被聯合國教科文組織列入世界文化遺產名錄。

避暑山莊興建於1703年，於1792年竣工，歷時89年，自山莊修建後，清朝歷代的皇帝都要到此避暑，期間的國家大事也要在此處理，因此避暑山莊也被稱為清朝的第二個政治中心。山莊占地5.64平方千米，是北京頤和園的兩倍，北海公園的8倍，僅環繞山莊的宮牆就有10千米長。山莊裡共有景點120多個，最著名的就是「康乾七十二景」，其中康熙皇帝以四字題名36景，乾隆皇帝以三字題名36景。康熙皇帝是乾隆皇帝的祖父，為了表示對祖父的尊崇，乾隆皇帝僅以三字題名景點。整個山莊由四部分組成，即宮殿區、湖區、平原區和山區。山莊以「山」命名，而其勝趣卻在水。在湖區我們可以欣賞到仿照江南美景而修建的景點。

這裡就是著名的避暑山莊了。

麗正門

我們面前的這座門就叫「麗正門」，它是乾隆36景中的第一景，也是山莊的第一個入口，在古代中國，所有面朝南的宮殿門都叫「麗正門」或「正陽門」，象徵著皇帝的至高無上。大家可以清晰地看到在門的上方懸掛著一幅橫匾，上面從右到左依次刻著5種民族語言：蒙語、維吾爾語、漢語、藏語和滿族語。這象徵著中國是統一的多民族國家。門前的這兩個石獅子是皇帝權力和尊嚴的象徵。

木蘭秋獮圖

現在我們來到正宮區的第一個院落。在東配殿裡你能看到由清代藝術家繪製的木蘭秋獮圖，圖上描繪了皇家打獵時的場景。

木蘭圍場位於承德市西北部約150千米處。在清代，皇帝每年夏季都要率領他的八旗部隊到木蘭圍場去行圍打獵。當時那裡有很多的野生動物，如老虎、鹿、豹子、熊、狼和野豬等。為了保證野生動物的繁殖，木蘭圍場共分為72個圍，每次射獵被限定在10個圍左右。部隊到達那裡之後，士兵們在森林中紮下營盤，選擇獵場，然後為皇帝搭起看台，進行圍獵。第二天清晨，士兵們早起，穿上用鹿皮縫製的衣服，吹響木製的長哨來模仿母鹿求偶的聲音，以此來吸引鹿群和其他野生動物。在歷史上我們可以看見皇帝穿著紅袍，騎著戰馬，搭弓引箭，先行射獵，士兵們緊隨皇帝進行圍獵，場面極其宏偉壯觀。最後，皇帝要根據將士們所獵獲動物的數量來論功行賞，然後舉行大型的慶祝活動，進行野餐和篝火晚會。

打獵的真正目的是和當時的政治形勢有關。因為在16～17　世紀，沙皇俄國經常侵擾中國的北部邊疆。同時，北方邊境的少數民族也不斷發生叛亂，一些蒙古部落上層的少數首領與沙俄相勾結進行分裂祖國的叛亂活動，此外由於很長一段時間沒有大的戰事，軍隊和士兵的戰鬥力下降。看到這一嚴峻的形勢，康熙皇帝非常憂慮，於是決定率領他的八旗軍隊到木蘭圍場去打獵。這樣，可以訓練八旗士兵，加強同蒙古族和其他少數民族的聯繫，抵禦沙俄進犯，鞏固北方邊疆，達到「習武綏遠」的目的。從北京到木蘭圍場大約有360多千米，沿著這條路建起了二十幾座行宮，承德處於連接北京和木蘭圍場的重要的地理位置，且景色秀美，氣候宜人。於是，康熙皇帝決定在承德興建最大的皇家園林避暑山莊。每年夏季皇帝都要到這裡來住上半年左右的時間，他們五月份來，去圍場打獵需要用一個月左右的時間，秋季返回京城。

正宮區

避暑山莊的宮殿區由正宮、松鶴齋、萬壑松風和東宮四組建築所組成。在正宮區，主體建築位於南北走向的中軸線上，東西配殿對稱而置，建造了九進院落。為什麼這裡要建造九進院落呢？原因是根據中國古代傳統哲學，一、三、五、七、九為陽數，代表陽剛和積極獨立的性格，二、四、六、八、十為陰數，代表陰柔和消極依附的性格。「九」是陽數的最高數，代表最高等級。「五」是陽數的最中位，代表中正。「九五」含有「至尊中正」的意思。中國古代帝王以「九五之尊」自喻，標榜自己「至尊中正，剛正無私」。這種建築布局也反映出天子身居九重的思想。清代共有四位皇帝在這裡居住。皇帝在居住期間要處理政治、軍事事務，舉行重大的慶典活動，接見少數民族的王公貴族、首領和外國使節，並與一些國家簽訂重要的條約，進行各種政治活動。

澹泊敬誠殿

宮殿區的正殿名為「澹泊敬誠殿」，也叫「楠木殿」。在雨季，楠木散發出陣陣幽香，沁人心脾。「澹泊敬誠」由康熙皇帝命名，他引用了諸葛亮在《誡子書》中的一句話：「非澹泊無以明志，非寧靜無以致遠。」在大殿內，可以看見放置在紫檀平台正中的黃色的寶座。在清代，「黃色」這種特殊的顏色專用於皇家和佛教寺廟，其他人是不允許使用的。御用寶座的後面樹立著紫檀屏風，上面刻有163個栩栩如生的人物，描繪了男耕女織的勞動場景。北面牆上的東西兩端擺放著書架，原存有《古今圖書集成》，此套書現存於北京。在木製的天花板和門窗的表面刻有萬字符、壽桃和蝙蝠等圖案。在古代中國，萬字符代表太陽和吉祥，壽桃代表長壽，蝙蝠則取其「福」字的諧音，代表幸福。在這裡，皇帝處理朝政，主持重大的慶典活動，接見王公貴族、少數民族的首領和外國使節，相當於北京故宮的「太和殿」。

煙波致爽殿與西暖閣

我們面前的這座殿稱為「煙波致爽殿」，是皇帝和嬪妃居住的地方。皇帝在這裡會見他的母后和兄弟姐妹。西面這間是臥室稱為「西暖閣」，在這裡能看到皇帝的龍床，康熙、乾隆、嘉慶和咸豐都曾在此床上住過。1860　年，英法聯軍攻占北京，咸豐來避暑山莊避難，第二年就病逝在這個房間。西面的配房叫「西所」，是慈禧曾經住的屋子，這間房離皇帝的房間最近。據說穿過這個側門，慈禧曾經偷偷溜到皇帝臥室的後面，偷聽咸豐和大臣的談話。咸豐和各大臣所擔心的慈禧會干擾朝政這一憂慮在咸豐駕崩後成為事實。慈禧統治了清朝近半個世紀。在她死後的第三年中國封建社會最後一個朝代清朝滅亡了。

湖區

沿著萬壑松風彎曲陡峭的假山蹬道，我們來到湖區，這裡洲島錯落，風景秀麗，我們可以領略到江南水鄉的美景。在清朝，康熙和乾隆皇帝多次下江南去巡視，他們被那裡優美的風景所吸引。當康熙皇帝決定在承德興建避暑山莊時，就打算把所有的美景集中在一園來建造。所以，在這裡我們可以看到許多江南的美麗景色。如仿照蘇州獅子林建造的文園獅子林，仿照杭州西湖蘇堤修建的芝境雲堤，仿照江蘇鎮江金山寺修建的金山寺，仿照杭州西湖湖心亭修建的水心榭，仿照嘉興南湖煙雨樓建造的煙雨樓等。

參觀完避暑山莊，您一定會被山莊的宏偉秀麗和它豐富的歷史文化內涵所感動。我真誠的希望，此次避暑山莊的遊覽能給您留下美好的經歷和回憶。

Beidaihe Beach （北戴河海濱）

China has a long coastline whose total length is 18,000 kilometers, and abundant beach resorts exist all along it. Among these beach resorts, the following four are particularly well-known: Beidaihe in Qinhuangdao, Hebei Province; Golden Pebble Beach in Dalian, Liaoning Province; Huiquanwan in Qingdao, Shandong Province; and The End of the Earth in Sanya, Hainan Province. Today we'll pay a visit to Beidaihe.

Beidaihe is one of the districts of Qinhuangdao city and is about 300 kilometers east of Beijing. The city covers an area of 70.3 square kilometers and has a population of 60,000. It is located on Bohai Bay, so the climate here is relatively comfortable. With a damp monsoon climate, it has four distinct seasons, neither too hot in summer nor too cold in winter. There are only 7 days annually when the temperature is over 30 degrees centigrade. During the summer the cool sea breezes keep the average temperature 3-5 degrees lower than that of Beijing, while during the winter, with the air current from the Bohai Bay, temperatures seldom go below-12℃. Bei-daihe is famous for bird-watching and is China's first protection area for migrating birds. Some 405 different kinds of birds, or nearly 40% of all of China's existing bird species, can be seen here. Birds are superb connoisseurs of the natural environment, so their habitats also make good places for humans to vacation during holidays. Moreover, Beidaihe is one of nine famous sunrise watching spots in China. This is why Beidaihe Beach is so famous both at home and abroad. While it is suitable for all year round visits, the best time to travel to here is from May to October.

The long coastline to its south has soft sand and seawater of moderate salinity, making it an excellent place to sunbathe and swim. Many modern holiday villages and public bathing places have been established, where you can taste local snacks and delicious seafood, or ride in a speedboat. If you want to get away from the masses, a stroll on the pebbled sand will bring you close to nature.

In the central area of the scenic spot is a famous attraction called Tiger Rock Park. This rock formation is composed of several huge rocks protruding from the sea like crouching tigers. Standing on the rocks, one can feel the sea breeze pushing against your face, the waves beating the rocks, and the vast sea will make you feel refreshed and energetic. This is also a good spot for photography.

The Eagle Rock in the east is one of the most popular attractions of Beidaihe. It is a separate rock with the unique shape of an eagle perched upon it. Groups of wild doves once dwelled in the rock caves there, so it is also known as "the Dove Nest". The Yingjiao Pavilion on the top of the peak is the best place to watch the sunrise.

Not just the beach, the beautiful environment around Beidaihe offers verdant mountains and lush vegetation. Lianfeng Mountain, whose base touches the beach, has two peaks covered by abundant green pines and cypresses. Lush vegetation, strange grottoes, secluded paths and winding bridges cover the mountain and make it unique and appealing. Looking down from Seaside Pavilion at the top of the hill, one can see the misty sea in all its majesty and feel carefree and joyous.

Beidaihe Beach is currently attracting more and more attention from around the world with more than 4 million people traveling here every year, I sincerely hope that you will enjoy your stay here.

中國有著漫長的海岸線，全長共有1.8 萬千米，人們在沿岸興建了大量的海濱避暑勝地。在眾多的海濱避暑勝地中，下面的四處較之其他地方更具盛名，分別是：河北秦皇島的北戴河、遼寧大連的金石灘、山東青島的匯泉灣及海南三亞的天涯海角。今天我們就到北戴河一遊。

北戴河是河北省秦皇島市的一個區，位於北京以東300 千米，總面積70.3 平方千米，人口6　萬。北戴河坐落在渤海灣，氣候非常宜人，受潮濕的季風氣候影響，有鮮明的四季，夏無酷暑，冬無嚴寒，一年當中氣溫超過30℃的天數只有7天，夏季的平均氣溫要比北京低3℃ ～5℃，海風拂面，更覺涼風習習。受來自渤海灣的氣流的影響，冬季的最低氣溫很少低於-12℃。北戴河是著名的觀鳥地，是中國的第一個候鳥保護區，在這裡我們可以看到405種鳥，占中國現存鳥類的40%。鳥類是最權威的自然環境鑒定師，所以人類選擇鳥類棲息的地方去渡假是最明智的選擇。

北戴河南部漫長的海岸線上沙質柔軟，海水鹽度適中，因此這裡是進行日光浴和游泳的最佳地點。在這裡修建了很多現代化的渡假村和公共浴場，您可以品嚐風味小吃和海鮮，可以駕駛快艇出遊。如果您想遠離喧囂，可以在布滿小鵝卵石的沙灘上漫步，親近大自然。

在景區的中部是著名的景點「老虎石公園」。它是由很多從海裡突出來的狀似群虎的礁石組成。站在礁石上，海風拂面，海浪擊打著礁石，浩瀚的大海會讓您感覺疲勞頓消，精力充沛。這裡也是最佳的攝影地。

東部的鷹角岩也是北戴河的著名景觀之一。它是一塊獨立的岩石，彷彿一只形狀獨特的老鷹蹲在上面，過去成群的野鴿子在礁石上面的岩洞裡安家，所以這裡也被稱為「鴿子窩」。位於礁石頂端的鷹角岩是觀日出的最佳地點。

北戴河不僅僅是海灘美，它周圍優美的環境使得群山疊翠，植被蔥鬱。北戴河背靠的聯峰山有兩座山峰，均被鬱鬱蔥蔥的松柏所覆蓋。蔥鬱的植被、奇特的岩洞、隱蔽的山間小徑和蜿蜒的小橋遍布山中，使其獨具魅力。從山頂的望海亭往下望，您可以看到水霧繚繞的壯麗的大海，頓覺心曠神怡。

現在，北戴河海濱得到了越來越多的關注，每年有400多萬遊客來這裡旅遊。我真心地希望您能夠在此度過一個愉快的假期。

The Western Qing Mausoleum （清西陵）

The Western Qing Mausoleum is one of the two imperial mausoleums of the Qing Dynasty (1644-1911). It lies at the foot of Yongning Mountain, about 15 kilometers west of Yi County, Hebei Province and 120 kilometers west of the Capital Beijing. It is also a close neighbor to the twisting and bewitching Yishui River in the south, as well as the Zijingguan Pass (a Hebei Province Great Wall section) in the west. It covers an area of about 800 square kilometers with a perimeter of 100 kilometers. The whole area is surrounded by more than 20 thousand pines, which are ancient but healthy. With its enthralling scenery, high cultural values, delicate craft work and unique designs, UNESCO listed the Western Qing Mausoleum as World Cultural Heritage Site in 2000.

Construction of the Western Qing Mausoleum began in 1730, the eighth year of Emperor Yong-zheng's reign, and was finally finished 186 years later, in 1915. It contains fourteen royal mausoleums where a total of 76 members of the royal household are buried. These people include four Qing Dynasty Emperors and their empresses, imperial concubines, princes and princesses, as well as other royal household members. The architecture fully displays the old feudal society's strict ranking system. The emperors' mausoleums are the largest among the whole group, which are successively followed by those of the empresses, concubines and lesser individuals. There are over a thousand rooms in the palaces and over hundred ancient stone buildings and carvings sprinkled around this area. All these structures are majestic, rich in sculptural artifacts, reflecting the pageantry of that time. In particular, the tops of the emperors and empress' mausoleums are covered by yellow glazed tiles while those of other mausoleums are green. All the mausoleums have their own characteristics that reveal the ancient Chinese people's high level of technique and wisdom.

The Tai Mausoleum for Emperor Yongzheng, who reigned from 1723-1735, is the largest, earliest and the most complete one and is located at the center of the Western

Qing Mausoleum. It is said that the mausoleum was originally positioned in the Eastern Qing Mausoleum, but Emperor Yongzheng thought that location was geologically unsuitable and instead chose the present site, which he saw as an "eternal and auspicious kingdom". At the entrance stands a Large Red Gate and three very gorgeous stone archways, which together form a "Four Harmony Yard" (it is called Siheyuan in Chinese and is a traditional residential place with houses around a courtyard), and set this mausoleum apart from all others in China.

Not far to the west of the Tai Mausoleum is the Chang Mausoleum for Emperor Jiaqing. It was completed in 1803, or the eighth year of Jiaqing's reign, even though Jiaqing was not buried there until March 1821. The two mausoleums are nearly identical in terms of the number of buildings and style of architecture. The rear square rampart of the Chang mausoleum stands higher than that of the Tai mausoleum. The floor in the Hall of Eminent Favor was paved with bright piebald stones elaborately decorated with natural purple patterns, which were then called "Full of Gems in the Palace". Another wonder is the Echoing Stone and Echoing Wall in the Western Chang Mausoleum, which was built for Emperor Jiaqing's Empress. This Echoing Wall is similar to the Echoing Wall in the Temple of Heaven in Beijing.

Mu Mausoleum is for Emperor Daoguang (reigned 1821-1850). The scale is not as large as the other two mausoleums, but its buildings are no less ostentatious and enchanting. The whole of the Hall of Eminent Favor is built out of Nanmu, a kind of very fragrant and valuable timber from trees grown on Yunnan and Guizhou Plateau, and the ceiling and the windows are all decorated with many vigorous dragons, which toss their heads and appear to be flying through the clouds and waves. Hence the famous saying, "Ten thousand dragons collect together to spray their fragrance".

The Chong Mausoleum for Emperor Guangxu is five kilometers of the southeast of Tai Mausoleum. Built in 1909, it is the last imperial tomb to be constructed, even though its occupant was not the last emperor of China. The construction of Guangxu's mausoleum was begun posthumously and remained unfinished when the Qing Dynasty fell in 1911. Funds given to the former Qing imperial household by the Republican government enabled it to be completed in 1915. Though the Chong Mausoleum is relatively small and has no stele pavilion and stone sculptures, the entire structure is nevertheless quite dignified. The Hall of Eminent Favor was made of precious mesua ferrea, which won it the name of "Bronze Beam and Iron Pillar". The elaborate drainage system still continues to work well right up to this present day.

清西陵是清朝帝王兩大陵寢之一，位於河北省易縣城西15千米處的永寧山下，離北京120多千米。這裡南傍蜿蜒流淌的易水河，西臨紫荊關，面積達800餘平方千米，周界約100千米，整座陵區被兩萬餘棵參天古松所環繞。由於這裡景色迷人，具有較高的文化內涵，工藝精美，設計獨特，聯合國教科文組織於2000年將其列入世界文化遺產。

清西陵始建於清雍正八年（公元1730年），並於1915年竣工，歷時186年。西陵共有皇家陵寢14座，總計埋葬4位皇帝及皇后、皇妃、阿哥、公主及其他皇室成員。建築充分體現了當時封建社會嚴格的等級制度。在所有的陵寢中，皇帝的陵寢規模最大，以下依次是皇后、妃嬪和其他皇室成員。1000多間宮殿及100多座石雕和石製建築散布其間，所有建築均規模宏大，雕刻技藝精湛，富麗堂皇。特別值得一提的是，皇帝及皇后的陵寢均採用黃色琉璃瓦蓋頂，而其他人的園寢則使用綠色的琉璃瓦。每座陵寢各具特色，反應了中國古代勞動人民高超的技藝和智慧。

泰陵是為雍正皇帝（公元1723～1735年在位）建造的，是清西陵的中心，規模最大，建築最早，體系最完整。據說，這座陵寢最初是在清東陵選址的，但雍正皇帝認為所選之處地質不太合適，因此將它遷到了現在的地址，他認為這才是他的「萬年吉地」。陵區的入口是大紅門和三座巍峨高大的琉璃牌坊，二者構成了一座「四合院」，這在中國是獨一無二的。

昌陵是嘉慶皇帝的陵墓，位於泰陵西側不遠處，於嘉慶八年（公元1803年）建成，直到1821年嘉慶皇帝才入葬昌陵。這兩座陵墓建築形式大同小異，規模並列，昌陵後部的寶城比泰陵還要高大。隆恩殿裡，用光彩耀目的豆瓣石砌墁，上面飾有天然雅緻的紫色花紋，素有「滿堂寶石」之稱。另外一個絕妙之處是嘉慶皇帝的皇后陵昌西陵的回音石、回音壁，可與北京天壇的回音壁相媲美。

慕陵是為道光皇帝（公元1821～1850年在位）修建的。雖然其規模較之前兩座陵墓稍小，但其建築卻毫不遜色。整座隆恩殿全部用金絲楠木（一種產於雲貴高原的珍稀木材，能散發香味）製成，天花板及門窗上雕刻有威龍聚首，騰雲駕霧的花紋，有「萬龍聚首，龍口噴香」之稱。

光緒皇帝的崇陵，位於泰陵東南5千米處。雖然內部埋葬的不是中國的末代皇帝，但它卻是中國帝陵中的最後一座，建於1909　年。光緒陵於光緒駕崩後方始修建，直到1911　年清朝滅亡時尚未完工。1915年，共和政府撥款給前清王室，崇陵才得以竣工。雖然崇陵規模較小，沒有碑樓和石像生等建築，但整座建築卻依然威嚴。隆恩殿中的木料，均採用異常珍貴的鐵力木，被譽為「銅梁鐵柱」。其優良的排水系統至今仍然完好。

The Eastern Qing Mausoleum （清東陵）

The Eastern Qing Mausoleum is in Zunhua County, Tangshan City, 125 kilometers east of Beijing, 30 kilometers northwest of Zunhua County, 150 kilometers away from Tianjin. It covers an area of 2,500 square kilometers, and UNESCO inscribed it in the World Heritage List in 2000.

The Qing Dynasty was China's last feudal dynasty of China. It ruled the country for 268 years, from 1644 to 1911, and had 10 emperors altogether. These emperors lived in the Forbidden City and enjoyed the most luxurious life while they were alive and naturally expected to live this way in the afterlife following their deaths. So, except the last Emperor Puyi, 9 of the Qing emperors had their mausoleums built in Zunhua and Yi counties respectively. These two sites are the Eastern Qing and Western Qing MausoleuMs.Three other mausoleums also exist. They are the Fu mausoleum and Zhao mausoleums, which are located in Shenyang, Liaoning Province, and the Yong mausoleum in Hebei's Xinbin County. Although these mausoleums have their own particular features, the Eastern Qing Mausoleum is the most splendid and complete.

In 1663 Emperor Shunzhi was buried here. Following his death, the Qing Dynasty spent vast sums of money and mobilized immense labor forces in building such structures. Altogether 161 persons were buried here, including 5 emperors, 15 empresses, 136 concubines, 3 princes, and 2 princesses. It is the most complete and largest imperial mausoleum built in China.

In the Qing Dynasty, the Eastern Qing Mau-soleum was divided into two parts, the "Houlong" (inner city) and the "Qianquan" (outer city). The length from north to south is 125 kilometers, and the width from east to west is 20 kilometers. The inner city is the place where the auspiciousness originated, so the emperor's bodies were buried here, while the outer city is where the mausoleum's buildings are located. The mausoleum is surrounded by mountains with rivers flowing through from the east and the west, and the middle part for the main buildings is a plain. According to the "Geomantic omen", this kind of arrangement of buildings, especially for mausoleum, is most auspicious. The ancient Chinese believed that the body must be buried in a place where mountains and rivers were around, as it reflects the traditional Chinese philosophy that "human beings exist in harmony with nature」.

Xiao Mausoleum for Emperor Shunzhi is located at the center of the Eastern Qing Mausoleum, with Jing mausoleum for Emperor Kangxi and Hui mausoleum for Emperor Tongzhi to its east, and the Yu mausoleum for Emperor Qianlong and Ding mausoleum for Emperor Xianfeng to its west. There are also nine mausoleums for four Empresses and five concubines. The geomantic wall around these mausoleums is 20 kilometers long and more than 400 buildings exist within it.

Among these magnificent tombs, the most splendid one is the Yu mausoleum for

Emperor Qianlong.

Emperor Qianlong, the fourth emperor after the Qing government entered the Great Wall, became an emperor at the age of 25 and ruled China for 60 years. He then gave the throne to his son and died during the third year of his son's reign at the age of 89. No other Chinese Emperor lived this long. Work on the Yu mausoleum began during the 8thyear of Emperor Qianlong's reign (1743), and was completed 57 years later. This marked the Qing Dynasty's high point and since its revenues were strong, the Yu mausoleum was more luxurious than any of the other mausoleuMs.Its most splendid area was the Underground Palace. The mausoleum's materials included Nanmu wood and fir from the Yunnan and Guizhou plateau, stones from Beijing, wall bricks from Shandong Province, and golden bricks were made in Jiangsu Province. Even the earth for the mausoleum was specially selected.

The approach to the Yu Mausoleum is a long road known as the Sacred Way, which is connected to the Main Sacred Way of Emperor Shunzhi's mausoleum. A stele tower stands in front of it, inside which are two 6-meter-high monuments carved in both Han and Manchu. Further north, the road is lined with gigantic stone statues of animals and figures; there are eight pairs of stone statues, including horses, Chinese unicorns, elephants, camels, lions, suannis (mythical animal), civil and military officials. This mausoleum is on a grander scale and of higher artistic quality than most imperial mausoleums and cost 90 tons of silver.

The Underground Palace of Emperor Qianlong's mausoleum is the most luxurious and most representative one among the Eastern Qing Mausoleum. It is 54 meters in depth, covers an area of 372 square meters, and consists of 9 chambers, all of which are rectangular in shape. In this way, the shape of the Underground Palace looks like a Chinese character "zhu" (master). There are four double-leaf doors inside and each door leaf has a 1.5-meter-high statue of Buddha holding different Buddhist articles. These articles were designed to eliminate monsters and ghosts and protect the body inside the Underground Palace. On the wall behind the door, there are patterns of the "eight treasures" to symbolize that this is a propitious place.

In the first chamber, statues of the Four Heavenly Guardians are carved on both sides of the wall. According to the Buddhist scripture, the Four Heavenly Guardians are in charge of the four directions of the human world; however, they are now also the emperor's living place, which makes it very easy for us to see that the emperor exercised supreme power when he was alive.

Emperor Qianlong's coffin and burial chamber lie in the underground palace's innermost recess. It was placed over a well that never runs dry. Coffins of two empresses and three concubines were on both sides, but only four coffins are here now, and all the jewels and other treasures buried with them were stolen. Only their bodies were left undisturbed. Inside each coffin there is another small coffin, and the body is kept inside the inner coffin. Three Buddhist flowers with 24 petals are carved on the chamber's ceiling. The middle parts of these flowers consist of statues of Buddha and Sanskrit script, the walls are carved with Buddhist scriptures in Tibetan and Sanskrit, and there are altogether 29,464 Tibetan and 647 Sanskrit letters. The Underground Palace is both a treasure of the stone carvings and a solemn underground Buddhist hall.

清東陵位於北京以東125 千米處的唐山市遵化境內，在遵化西北30千米處，距離天津150千米。占地2500平方千米，於2000年被世界教科文組織列入世界文化遺產。

清朝是中國最後一個封建王朝，統治中國長達268年，其間經歷了10位皇帝。這些皇帝生前在紫禁城享受極盡奢華的生活，希望死後繼續享受。因此，除末代皇帝溥儀外，其他的9位皇帝分別在河北的遵化和易縣修建了陵寢，即清東陵和清西陵。此外，清朝還有三處墓群，分別是位於瀋陽的福陵、昭陵和位於新賓的永陵。雖然這些陵墓群各有特色，各具千秋，但規模最宏大、體系最完整的就要數遵化境內的清東陵了。

　　自從1663年順治帝埋葬於此之後，清政府花費了大量的人力和物力來建造他們的福地。這裡共葬有5位皇帝、15位皇后、136位妃嬪、3位阿哥、2位公主，總計161人，它是中國現存規模最大、保存最完整的皇家陵墓群。

　　清王朝統治時期，東陵分「後龍」和「前圈」兩部分，整座陵區南北長125千米，東西寬20千米。「後龍」為「風水來龍」之地，「前圈」是陵寢分布的地方。陵寢四周群山環繞，中間野闊寬平，東西各有一灣碧水緩緩流淌，根據風水學，這樣的位置，尤其對於陵寢而言，是不可多得的福地。中國古人認為，人應該被埋葬在青山綠水環繞的地方，而這裡正符合這一要求。

　　清東陵的陵區以順治的孝陵為中心，東側有康熙帝的景陵，同治帝的惠陵，西側有乾隆帝的裕陵，咸豐帝的定陵，此外還有四座皇后陵和五座妃嬪的園寢，由一道長達20千米的風水牆將400多座建築圍攏起來。

　　在這些宏大的陵寢當中，最宏偉的要數乾隆皇帝的裕陵了。

　　乾隆皇帝是清朝入關後的第四帝，25歲即位，在位60年，而後禪位給他的兒子，又做了3年的太上皇，89歲壽終正寢。他是中國歷史上壽命最長的皇帝。裕陵的修建始於乾隆八年（公元1744年），歷時57年，當時正值清朝鼎盛時期，財力雄厚，所以裕陵的修建極盡奢華，尤以地宮為最。建陵時遍選天下美料。陵寢木料選自雲貴高原的楠木、杉木，石料采自北京，牆磚燒自山東，金磚制於江蘇，就連建陵時使用的土也是精挑細選的。

　　通往裕陵的神道與順治孝陵的主神道相連。陵前有一座碑樓，內置兩個六米高，以滿漢兩種文字書寫的墓碑。碑亭以北，位於神道兩側有八對石像生，文臣武將、馬、麒麟、象、駱駝、獬犰、獅子。這座陵寢較之其他皇家陵寢，規模宏大，有很高的藝術價值，耗費白銀90噸。

　　裕陵的地宮在清陵中最豪華、最有代表性。地宮進深54米，面積372平方米，由九道墓券組成，均為長方形，使地宮平面構成「主」字形。石門四道，每扇石門上都刻有一尊1.5米高的菩薩像，她們手裡都拿著一種法器，據說可以驅除妖魔鬼怪，保護地宮裡的亡靈。石門後面的牆上，雕有「八寶」圖案，象徵著吉祥如意。

在第一道的門洞券裡，兩側的牆上雕刻有四大天王像。佛經當中說，四大天王分別掌管著人類世界的四方天，但在地宮中卻為皇帝看守宮門，由此不難看出，皇帝生前追求一種至高無上的權力。乾隆皇帝的棺槨位於地宮的最裡面，它被放置在一口永不枯竭的井上面，兩位皇后和三位妃嬪的棺槨位於兩側，但目前只餘四具棺槨，棺中的寶物已經喪失殆盡，只餘他們的屍骨。棺槨分內外兩層，屍骨被置於內側。墓券的券頂雕有三朵大佛花，外層有24個花瓣，花心由梵文和佛像組成，所有的牆面上都刻有梵文、藏文的經咒，藏文29464字，梵文647字。這座地宮不僅是一座石雕藝術的寶庫，也是一座莊嚴肅穆的地下佛堂。

Inner Mongolian Autonomous Region內蒙古自治區

A Glimpse of the Autonomous Region （本自治區簡介）

The Inner Mongolian Autonomous Region (or Inner Mongolia for short) is located at China's northern frontier. It is bordered by Heilongjiang, Jilin and Liaoning provinces in the east, while Hebei, Shanxi, Shaanxi, Ningxia, and Gansu provinces are along its southern and western boundaries, and Russia and Mongolia lie to its north. Inner Mongolia's borders altogether stretch for some 4,221 kilometers. It is China's first autonomous region and was established on May 1,1947. With a total area of 1.8 square kilometers, it is the third largest Chinese autonomous region after the Xinjiang and Tibetan Autonomous regions. Inner Mongolia is divided into twelve leagues and cities and another 101 subdivided banners, counties, districts and townships. A total of 49 nationalities live here. Hohhot is the capital of Inner Mongolia.

Rainfall in Inner Mongolia is scarce and unpredictable and temperatures can change abruptly. The province generally has hot and short summers and long and bitterly cold winters, giving it a typical mid-temperate monsoon climate. However, it is not quite accurate to say that all of Inner Mongolia, due to its great length, is characterized by one kind of climate pattern. The province stretches from North East to Western China. Thus many people say that parts of Inner Mongolia can experience all four seasons in a single day, as the climate gradually changes from a temperate monsoon climate in the east to a continental monsoon climate in the west.

The different climatic conditions make Inner Mongolia's natural scenery diverse and unique. For example, from the Hulun Buir Grassland in eastern Inner Mongolia to the Wulanchab and Wulate grasslands and northern Yinshan Mountains, winter lasts for almost half, a year. Snow and ice covers the ground during this long period. Average winter temperatures can drop to minus 28℃. However, there is little noticeable difference between spring, summer, and autumn weather. The climate in May to September is mild and cool, making these months the best time to travel on the grasslands. At the same time, however, from the Alxa desert to the Badain Jaran Desert west to the Yinshan Mountains, the climate is very dry. Heavy winds blow from the middle of April to the end of May, while the summers are scorching hot and winters are very cold. Autumn, which lasts from mid-August to the end of September, is the best time to tour this area.

Tourism Resources

Relying on its rich unique tourism resources and advantageous geographical position, Inner Mongolia has developed series of tourism products focusing on its grasslands and the unique and interesting ethnic, customs and lifestyles that go with it. These two features, along with the province's forests, deserts, cultural and historic sites, and rivers and lakes are the main highlights of Inner Mongolian tours. Inner Mongolia's northern border also gives the province unique tourist sites, for example, the province boasts the important border towns of Manzhouli and Erlianhot.

Natural Resources: Inner Mongolia is world-famous for its vast grasslands, which cover a total area of 880,000 square kilometers and are among China's four largest grasslands. Due to its special climate and geography, the eastern part of the region contains the Greater Khingan Mountains'dense green primeval forest, while its western part has the golden-colored Kubuqi, Maowusu, Ulan Buh, Tengger, and Badain Jaran Deserts. Over 1,000 rivers and rivulets criss-cross Inner Mongolia and over 1,000 big and small lakes such as the Lake Hulun, Lake Buir, Dalinor Lake, Daihai, Hasuhai, Wuliangsuhai can be found throughout its vast, beautiful and wide-open spaces. Other scenic wonders include the magnificent stone forest in Hexigten Banner in the Xing'an Mountains, the eternal diversifolious poplars, numerous hot and mineral springs, rare species of flora and fauna, and wintertime snow, ice, and soft frost in the mountains. These features serve as the basis for many unique tourist experiences, including grassland and desert expeditions, hiking in the forest, lakeside leisure, visits to health spas, observing rare flora and fauna, and skiing. The winter Nadam Fair and the Grassland Carnival have many participants and attract large numbers of visitors. Triple A rated natural scenic spots include the Hulun Buir Grassland, Erdos Shizhenyuan Tourist Area, and Hailaer National Forest Park. Mongolia also has numerous 4-A rated natural scenic attractions such as the Dalad Banner Sand Gorge, Chifeng Asihatu Stone Forest, Daqing Gully Nature Reserve, and Gegentala Grassland.

Historical Relics and Ethnic Customs: Chinese civilization has three origins: the Yangtze and Yellow Rivers and northwestern grasslands. Historical relics and sites from the Paleozoic Era to the early activities of mankind, from the nomadic ethnic tribes in North China to the formation of the Mongolian nationality, from the collapse of Yuan Dynasty to the founding of New China have been found all over Inner Mongolia. The Dayao, Salawusu, and Hongshan cultures provide evidence of early human civilization in Inner Mongolia. And the Wang Zhaojun Tomb, Gaxian Cave, Heichengzi site of the ancient Western Xia Dynasty capital, historical Liao Dynasty sites and ruins, Genghis Khan Mausoleum, Lamaseries and the Great Wall chart the development of this civilization and interaction between different northern ethnic minorities during this process. Minority Mongolians live in compact communities, much like their descendants during the reign of Genghis Khan. This way of life greatly interests tourists, so various

Mongolian culture tours now exist. These include visits to historical and cultural sites, Mongolian clothing and jewelry shows, ethnic performing arts, Mongolian cuisine, horsemanship displays, wrestl-ing, archery, herding, Mongolian weddings, festival celebrations, religious rites, Nadam fair, and stays in Mongolian yurts. We also have cultural tours showcasing the unique lifestyles of the Ewenki, Orogen, and Daur national minorities.

Finally tourists can also visit modern livestock farms, ecological demonstration zones, modern dairy companies, woolen mills, coal mines, power plants, iron and steel works, weapons testing, and a launching site for China's space program.

Local Snacks

Finger Mutton: Big slices of boiled lamb which you cut into smaller slices with a knife and eat with your hands. Mongolian people believe that rare meat has more flavor and is nutritious, so guests are given the most tender slices as a gesture of hospitality. In old Mongolian tradition, only nobles were entitled to eat such meat.

Whole Lamb Banquet: A whole lamb is first stuffed with seasonings before being roasted in a stove and is then served to the guests on a wooden platter.

Barbecued sheep back; stir-fried rice; the Fish Banquet: Local fish and prawns are cooked in more than a 100 different ways.

Local Special Products

World famous Erdos cashmere wool; Xiaofei-yang mutton (rinsed mutton); Mongolian Milk products; Wuchuan oats and wheat; Dongsheng buckwheat; and healthy wild vegetables.

Local Culture

Mongolian music and Mongolian dances are renowned not only in China but throughout the world. Other notable Mongolian performance art includes the grand singing and dancing dramas Erdos Wedding, Barhu Wedding, and Ancient Majesty of the Holy Ground.

Major Tourism Cities

Hohhot: Hohhot means "blue city" in Mongolian and is located in middle Inner Mongolia. It has been recognized as a famous Chinese historical and cultural city. Hohhot has a long history and many historical sites and relics. Major tours based in the city include the Dayao Culture site, Tuchengzi ancient town, White Pagoda, Great Wall in Qingshuihe County, Five Pagoda Temple, and Heshuokejin Princess Residence, all of which are under state protection. Other natural scenic spots include the Hasuhai Resort, Hadamen National Forest Park, and One-Hundred-Pavilion Ecological Park in Holinger County. Hohhot is an Inner Mongolian tourism hub connecting Inner Mongolia with Beijing, Hebei, Shanxi, Shanxi and Gansu. And visitors can easily travel to other Inner Mongolian destinations from the city. And in 2003 Hohhot was designated a "China Excellent Tour City".

Baotou: Baotou means "the haunt of deer" in Mongolian and is located in mid-west Inner Mongolia. Its major historical sites and cultural relics include the Qin State Great Wall in Guyang County, Aolunsumu ancient town, and Wudang and Meidai Lamaseries, all of which are under state protection. Jiufengshan Nature Reserve, North Weaponary Town, and Baotou Frescos Gallery are also major tourist attractions. Baotou is Inner Mongolia's manufacturing center and an important Chinese industrial city; in 2000 it was designated a "China Excellent Tour City".

Erdos City: Called the "palace of yurts" in Mongolian, Erdos is located in southwestern Inner Mongolia and has a long history and abundant tourist attractions. These include historical relics, Mongolian ethnic customs, desert ecology, Yellow River valley scenery, hot springs, and rare wildlife. Some historical sites, notably the Genghis Khan Mausoleum, and Arzhai Grotto have been listed as national important historical relics under the state protection. Some spots, such as Tourist Area of Resonant Sand Gorge, Shizhenyuan Tourist Area, Engebei Eco-tourist Area, are known worldwide. Tourists sites with unique features, like the Erdos Cultural Tourism Resort and Jiuchenggong, showcase authentic Mongolian custoMs.The world-famous and jubilant singing and dancing drama, Erdos Wedding, is well worth watching.

Hulun Buir City: Named after the sister lakes Hulun and Buir, it is situated in northeastern China, west of Heilongjiang and bordered on the northwest by Russia and on the southwest by Mongolia. It is Inner Mongolia's best grasslands and folk customs tourist destination. Several major minorities, including the Mongolian, Ewenki, Oroqen, Daur, and Russian ethnic groups live in compact communities displaying their special ways of life. Visitors from all over the world are attracted by the area's natural beauty and ethnic custoMs.Major tour destinations include the Hulun Buir Grassland, Jinzhanghan and Xishan National Forest Parks, Hulun Lake, Sino-Russian Mutually Beneficial Trade Market, China's North Gate, Phoenix Mountain, Gaxian Cave, and Heishantou ancient town.

Four Major Tour Routes in Inner Mongolia

1.Hohhot—Baotou—Mongolian Culture in Dongsheng City—grassland—Kubuqi desert.

Major tour spots along this route include Gegentala Grassland, Wang Zhaojun Tomb, Wudang Lamasery, Resonant Sand Gulf, Genghis Khan Mausoleum, Engebei Eco-area, Shizhenyuan (world rare animal species reserve).

2.Hulun Buir City—Xing'an Meng.

This tour features grasslands, forests, ice and snow, and the trade market on the

Sino-Russian and Sino-Mongolian border. The main scenic spots are the Hulun Buir Grassland, Greater Xing'an Mountains Forest, Arshan area's ice and snow scenery, Erguna River, and border city of Manzhouli.

3.Xilinhaote—Chifeng.

This tour showcases grasslands, Mongolian and Liao Dynasty culture, as well as geographical wonders such as hot springs. Major tourist spots include the Xilin Gol Grassland, Chinese northern ethnic national minorities' nomadic culture, Yuan Dynasty Yuanshangdu ruins, Liao Dynasty historical sites, Asihatu stone forest, and hot springs.

4.Alashan Meng.

This tour covers the Alashan Meng (one of 12 prefecture-level divisions of Inner Mon-golia). Its highlights include Lamaism religion, Juyan cultural ruins, the Dongfeng Space City, and Moon Lake desert scenery.

內蒙古自治區位於中國的北部邊疆，簡稱內蒙古，東部與黑龍江、吉林、遼寧接壤，中部與河北交界，西部與山西、陝西、寧夏、甘肅毗鄰，在北面隔著長達4221千米的漫長國境線與蒙古國和俄羅斯相望。內蒙古，是中國建立最早的一個民族自治區，也是中國繼新疆、西藏之後的第三大自治區，總面積118.3萬平方千米，轄有12個盟市和101個旗縣市區，居住著49個民族。

內蒙古屬於典型的中溫帶季風氣候，降水量少而不均，寒暑變化顯著，冬季漫長而寒冷，夏季溫熱而短暫。由於地域跨度大，地形狹長，自東北向西南傾斜，橫跨中國的東北、華北、西北「三北」，各地氣候不盡相同。有一種關於內蒙古氣候的說法：「一天四季」，就是描繪內蒙古氣候從東部溫帶季風氣候向西部大陸氣候過渡的特徵。

這樣的氣候造就了自然風景的多樣性與奇特。從東端呼倫貝爾草原至陰山以北的烏蘭察布草原和烏拉特草原，冬季冰天雪地，歷時半年之久，平均氣溫在零下

28℃左右。夏、春、秋幾乎相連，5　　～9月氣候涼爽宜人，是旅遊草原的最佳季節。從陰山以西阿拉善沙漠高原至巴丹吉林沙漠是沙漠氣候區，這個區域每到春日（4月中至5月底）多風暴，降雨較少，但日照充足，夏天炎熱，冬季奇寒。最佳的旅遊季節是秋季（8月初至9月底），氣候溫和，最是涉足沙漠的好時間。呼和浩特是內蒙古自治區的首府城市。

旅遊資源

依託獨特優越的地緣位置，內蒙古具有以草原風光和民族風情為主題的系列旅遊資源。草原、古蹟、民俗、森林、沙漠、河流湖泊「六大奇觀」構成內蒙古獨特的旅遊勝景。自東向西綿延4200千米的邊境線，是開展對俄羅斯、蒙古國邊境旅遊的有利條件，其中滿洲里、二連浩特是重要的出入境口岸城市。

自然風光：內蒙古以遼闊的草原聞名世界，88萬平方千米的草原雄居中國四大草原之首。特殊的地理位置和氣候條件鑄造了內蒙古獨特多彩的自然景觀，從東部到西部依次呈現綠色茫茫、金色點點的風景特色。茂密的大興安嶺原始森林將自治區東部撒滿綠色，浩瀚的毛烏素、庫布齊、烏蘭布和、騰格里、巴丹吉林等沙漠則為西部覆蓋金色。在內蒙古大地上，黃河、額爾古納河、嫩江、西遼河等1000多條河流縱橫交錯，呼倫湖、貝爾湖、達裡諾爾、岱海、哈素海、烏梁素海等1000多個湖泊點綴其中，還有那興安山地雄偉的石林、沙海中不朽的胡楊、眾多的溫泉礦泉、珍貴的野生動植物、漫山遍野的冰雪樹掛成為旅遊奇觀。依託豐富的自然資源，內蒙古已開發出草原觀光、沙漠探險、森林渡假、河湖休閒、溫泉健身、野生動植物觀賞、滑雪等多樣性旅遊產品。冬季那達慕，草原上的狂歡節，更是讓人流連忘返。著名的旅遊景點有呼倫貝爾大草原、呼倫湖、鄂爾多斯世珍園、響沙灣、赤峰阿斯哈圖石林景區、大青溝自然保護區、格根塔拉草原旅遊中心、海拉爾國家森林公園等。

文物、民俗、文化景觀：中華文明的起源除長江、黃河之外，還應該有草原，草原文化是華夏文明的發祥地之一，到處可見的文物古蹟可以佐證。從古生物時代到人類的早期活動，從中國北方遊牧民族部落繁衍生息到蒙古族的形成，從元王朝的崩潰到新中國的成立，都留下了寶貴的遺蹟。大窯文化、沙拉烏蘇文化、紅山文化、夏家店文化、鄂爾多斯青銅器文化，以及遍布銀山山脈和阿拉善一帶的岩畫，反映了人類早期在內蒙古的活動。大型恐龍、猛 象化石的發現使內蒙古在中國古生物學上占有重要一席。昭君墓、嘎仙洞、黑城子、遼遺蹟、成吉思汗陵、喇嘛教寺廟、歷代長城等充分反映了北方少數民族的發展歷史和各民族交往的歷史。書寫過輝煌歷史的蒙古族人民創造了燦爛的歷史文化。成吉思汗後代的生活、生產方式，具有較強的旅遊吸引力。依託深厚的文化積澱和獨特的民族風情，內蒙古已開發了以參觀文物古蹟為主的文化之旅和以體驗民族風情為主的風味飲食、歌舞服飾、騎乘馬術、射箭摔跤、遊牧曠野、婚禮表演、節日慶典、宗教祭祀、相聚那達慕、走進牧民家、住宿蒙古包以及反映鄂溫克、鄂倫春、達斡爾等民族生產生活的風情之旅。

今日的現代化牧場、生態建設示範區、乳品紡織、煤田電廠、兵器鋼鐵、航空技等也被開發為工農牧業和科技旅遊項目。

地方風味

手把肉、全羊宴、羊背子、炒米、全魚宴。

地方特產

羊絨、小肥羊、奶製品、武川產 麥、東勝產蕎麥、各種保健功效的山野菜。

地方文藝

蒙古族歌舞是世界文化藝術寶庫中的燦爛明珠。大型歌舞劇有《鄂爾多斯婚禮》、《巴爾虎婚禮》、《聖地古韻》等。

主要旅遊城市

呼和浩特：蒙古語意為「青色的城」，位於內蒙古中部的歷史文化名城。旅遊以歷史文化古蹟為主，主要景點有大窯文化、土城子古城、白塔、清水河長城、五塔寺、和碩恪靖公主、希拉穆仁大草原、哈素海旅遊渡假村、哈達門國家森林公園、烏素圖旅遊開發區、府，這些均是重點文物保護單位。主要民俗和自然旅遊景觀有：葛根塔拉大草原南山生態百亭園等。呼和浩特是內蒙古旅遊的中心，連接北京、河北、山西、陝西、寧夏、甘肅和蒙古國，交通便利，旅遊設施齊全。

包頭市：包頭蒙古語意為「有鹿」，位於內蒙古中西部，離呼和浩特150多千米。境內擁有眾多歷史文化古蹟，主要的有：受國家重點文物保護的固陽縣秦長城、敖倫蘇木古城、五當召、美岱召；自然旅遊景點有九峰山自然保護區和北方兵器工業城。岩畫館達到了世界一流的水平。包頭稀土資源居世界首位，是內蒙古最大的工業城市，也是中國重要的工業基地。

鄂爾多斯市：鄂爾多斯的蒙古語意思是「宮帳群」，位於內蒙古的西南部，具有悠久的歷史和豐富的歷史文物古蹟，旅遊資源豐富，主要以文物古蹟、民族風情、大漠生態、黃河峽谷、草原溫泉和珍稀動植物為主。成吉思汗陵等是國家重點文物保護單位，響沙灣、世珍園、沙漠綠洲恩格貝生態示範區、七星湖等名揚中外。鄂爾多斯文化渡假村、九城宮等系列景點真實地再現了鄂爾多斯蒙古族人民的民風習俗。大型歌舞劇《鄂爾多斯婚禮》氣勢恢弘、規模壯觀，體現當地蒙古族熱情豪放、能歌善舞、歡快奔騰的精神面貌。

呼倫貝爾市：得名於呼倫和貝爾兩湖，位於中國東北部，東與黑龍江毗鄰，西北和西南分別與俄羅斯和蒙古國交界，是內蒙古草原旅遊的最佳目的地。那裡草原遼闊，風光秀麗，民俗風情濃厚，蒙古族、鄂溫克族、鄂倫春族、達斡爾族、俄羅斯等少數民族居住集中，是草原觀光、體驗蒙古族民俗文化的理想目的地。著名景點有享譽中外的呼倫貝爾大草原、金帳汗、西山國家森林公園、呼倫湖、中俄互市貿易區、國門、鳳凰山、五泉山和嘎仙洞遺址、黑山頭城址等古蹟。

主要旅遊路線

1.呼和浩特—包頭—東勝蒙古族文化—草原—沙漠觀光旅遊線。

這條線路上主要景區景觀有：格根塔拉草原、昭君墓、五當召、響沙灣、成吉思汗陵、恩格貝、世珍園等。

2.呼倫貝爾—興安盟草原、森林、冰雪、邊貿旅遊線路。

這條線路上的主要景區景觀有：呼倫貝爾草原、大興安嶺森林、阿爾山冰雪、額爾古納界河、邊城滿洲裡等。

3.錫林浩特—赤峰草原、蒙古族文化、遼文化、地質奇觀、溫泉渡假旅遊。

4.阿拉善宗教朝聖、居延文化、航天科普、沙漠觀光旅遊。

這條線路上的主要旅遊景區景觀有：喇嘛教寺廟、居延文化遺址、東風航天城、月亮湖沙漠景區等。

Genghis Khan Mausoleum （成吉思汗陵）

Ladies and gentlemen,

Welcome to the beautiful land of Inner Mongolia! First of all, I'd like to invite you to visit the famous Genghis Khan Mausoleum. When you come near the Mausoleum by bus, you will see three brightly yellow round roofs over there. That is where the Genghis Khan Mausoleum is!

Genghis Khan Mausoleum is located in Erdos's Ejin Horo Banner, which is 65 kilometers away from the municipal capital city Erdos and 185 kilometers south of Baotou. It is one of the world's most important mausoleums and has great historical significance. In 1982 it was designated as an key national historic relic under state protection.

Genghis Khan Mausoleum consists of three big Mongolian-yurt-shaped mansions and two long corridors connecting them. The mansions have pure white walls, vermilion doors, and roofs covered by colored glazed tiles. A tall red wall surrounds the buildings. This color scheme emphasizes the Mausoleum's grandness and inviolability. Darhut people, a local Mongolian group very loyal to Genghis Khan and who treat Khan as their God, have been in charge of guarding the mausoleum and have offered sacrifices to the Khan for more than 300 years.

The mausoleum is divided into six parts: the main, east, west, and rear halls, and the east and west corridors. The main hall, standing between the east and west halls, has an octagonal shape and is over 20 meters high. The roof has a concave quaquversal shape, like that of Mongolian yurt, with double-layered eaves. The two side halls are inequilaterally octagonal with the same style of roof as the main hall but with a single-layered eave. All the three roofs are covered with yellow glazed tiles and the eaves with blue glazed tiles. The colored roofs and eaves together with all the white walls and vermilion doors make the Mausoleum look grand and splendid!

The main hall is the Genghis Khan Commemorative Hall. Standing in the middle is a five-meter-tall statue of Genghis Khan, who appears powerful and dignified wearing his wartime clothes, sitting against an arch background wall, with his two eyes staring into the distance. On the background wall, there is a map of the Khan's "Four Great States" territory, showing his remarkable military successes achieved over 700 years ago when he led on his warriors on a campaign conquest covering central China, mid-Asia, and Eastern Europe. In the bedchamber behind the front part of the main hall, are four Mongolian yurt-shaped mausoleums, which are covered with huge pieces of orange damask. Six coffins are inside these halls: one is for Genghis Khan and another three are for his three wives. Along the two sides of these four coffins are another two coffins which are for the Khan's two younger brothers. In front of the coffins are displayed three huge "Suledings", which are said to be the iron spearheads on the war flag the Khan used when going out to battle. Finally three saddles and other possessions left by Khan after his death are also on display here.

Both the west and east halls are 23 meters high. In the east hall lay Khan's fourth son Tuolei's (father of Kublai Khan) and his wife's coffins, while in the west hall nine flags are displayed symbolizing his nine high-rank warriors as well as their weapons and other iteMs.

In the east and west corridors there are large-format paintings on the walls, which in the west corridor depict major events of Genghis Khan, such as his birth date, the perils he encountered, his march from the west to the east, unification of the Mongolian tribes, conquests, and the like.

On every lunar month—March 21st, May 15th, August 12thand October 3rd—great memorial ceremonies are held in the Mausoleum. At such times every year, large numbers of pilgrims come here, even if the journey is long and hard, to display their full loyalty and respect to Genghis Khan's memory by sacrificing clean white Hadas (a piece of silk used as gifts by Mongolians to show their respect and warm welcome), fat sheep, milk-colored fresh ghee, and mellow mare's milk. They also burn incense while making these sacrifices.

女士們，先生們：

歡迎來到美麗的**內**蒙古大草原！首先，我想邀請您去參觀著名的成吉思汗陵。我們的遊覽車到陵附近時，你們會看到三個明黃色的圓形屋頂。那兒就是成吉思汗陵所在地。

成吉思汗陵位於鄂爾多斯市伊金霍洛旗境**內**，距市政府所在地65公里，包頭市南185公里處，是國**內**外有重要影響的帝王陵，1982年被列為中國重點文物保護單位。

成吉思汗陵由三座鑲嵌著彩色琉璃瓦的蒙古包殿堂建築和與之相連的廊房組成，由達爾扈特人守護和祭祀，距今已有300多年的歷史。四周圍護著紅色高牆，白亮的牆壁、朱紅的門窗、輝煌奪目的金黃色琉璃寶頂，使這座帝陵顯得特別莊嚴。

　　陵園分為正殿、東殿、西殿、寢宮、東廊、西廊六個部分。正殿平面呈八角形，重檐蒙古包式穹廬頂，高達20餘米；東西兩殿為不等邊八角形單檐蒙古包式穹廬頂，穹頂外面為黃色琉璃瓦，房檐均覆以藍色琉璃瓦。三座大殿的房檐屋頂與白色牆壁和朱紅門窗相輝映，構成了絢麗奪目的建築外貌。整個陵園的造型，猶如展翅欲飛的雄鷹，具有濃郁的蒙古民族獨特的藝術風格。

　　陵園的正殿為成吉思汗紀念堂，正中有5米高的成吉思汗塑像。他戎裝端坐，雙眼遠望，神態威嚴。塑像後的弧形背景是「四大汗國」的疆圖，象徵著700多年前成吉思汗統帥大軍南進中原，西進中亞和歐洲的顯赫戰績。紀念堂後的寢宮安放著4個蒙古包式的大靈包，上面覆蓋著巨大的橘紅色緞子，這就是成吉思汗和他的三位夫人的靈柩，兩旁還安放著成吉思汗兩個胞弟的靈柩。靈柩前陳列著3個巨大的「蘇勒錠」，相傳這「蘇勒錠」就是成吉思汗出徵用的大旗上端的鐵矛頭。此外還陳列著他生前使用過的三個馬鞍及其他紀念物品。

　　東西殿高23米。東殿安放著成吉思汗的四子拖雷（元世祖忽必烈之父）及其夫人的靈柩。西殿則供奉著象徵其九員大將的九面旗幟和當時他們使用過的武器和其他物品。

　　在正殿的東西兩廊有大型壁畫。西廊的壁畫主要描繪成吉思汗出生、遇險、西征、東征、統一蒙古各部等重大事件。

　　在每年的農曆三月二十一、五月十五、八月十二和十月初三，要在此舉行四次隆重的祭奠活動。每當祭奠之日，眾多虔誠的拜謁者不辭辛苦地長途跋涉而來，向這位偉人獻上潔白的哈達、明亮的蠟燭、芬芳的香燭、肥壯的整羊、乳黃的酥油、醇香的馬奶酒等祭品，追憶他的雄才大略，表達對他的無限敬仰與緬懷之情。

Hulun Buir Grassland （呼倫貝爾大草原）

The famous historian Jian Bozan wrote in his book, A Probe into Inner Mongolian History, "Hulun Buir is the best rangeland of Inner Mongolia now, and it has been the best grassland since ancient times...It has been called 『cradle of Chinese northern nomadic people'...If we compare Inner Mongolia as a history stage, then the Hulun Buir Grassland is its background". Today, the Hulun Buir Grassland still remains charming and appealing!

Situated west of the Greater Khingan Mountains between the 115° 31′ -121° 10′ eastern longitude and 47° 20′ -50° 13′ northern latitude, the Hulun Buir Grassland covers an area of about 100,000 square kilometers. Natural grassland accounts for 80% of this area. It is one of the few primeval and unpolluted grasslands left in the world. Winters here are long and bitterly cold with lots of ice and snow, while summers can be both very hot and comfortably cool. At this time of the year, the grass is green and lush and clear streams flow through it. The summer is the best season to visit the Hulun Buir Grassland.

Hulun Buir is famous for its abundance in natural scenery, which not only includes the grassland, but forests, rivers, and lakes as well. It is also a place where visitors can appreciate the unique customs and culture of the Ewenki, Orogen, Daur, and Russian ethnic national minorities. Major tourist scenic spots and cultural sites are the Huhnor Grassland, Xishan National Forest Park, Hulun Lake, Sino-Russian Mutual Trade Market, and the Phoenix Mountain. Here we'll just visit the Huhnor and Baiyanhada Grasslands and Hulun Lake, as they are representative of the Hulun Buir Grassland's scenery.

Huhnor Grassland

The Huhnor Grassland Tourist Area lies in the interior of old Barhu Grassland in northwestern Hulun Buir city. It is 50 kilometers from Hailar and 110 kilometers from Manzhouli city. It got its current name because it is near the Huhnor (blue lake in Mongolian) Lake. The grassland remains one of China's last pristine natural grasslands.

Embellished with the lake and rivulets, the beautiful verdant grassland of the area can be seen in miniatures at the Hulun Buir Grassland.

Now we are at the Huhnor Lake. The lake covers an area of 12 square kilometers. To its northeast, the Morigele River, which is famous for being "the first zigzag river in the world", meanders through the endless grassland and rills before converging with the Hailar River to the south. As you look around here, you will see an endless open expense of green grass. This peaceful scenery will relax your mind and body. The area boasts more than 500 species of wildlife. Vast green grass, the lake's clear water, and the blue sky with white clouds combine to form a unique and beautiful picture.

Aside from the gorgeous scenery, Barhu-Mongolian customs also draw visitors from all over the world to this grassland. Barhu, originally a name for a Mongolian nomadic area, later became the name of the Mongolian. Here the local inhabitants have maintained their unique nomadic way of life and carry on the customs and culture associated with it. It can thus be said that the Huhnor grassland is the cradle of the Mongolian nomadic people.

Tourists here can experience what it is like to live in a Mongolian yurt and enjoy local Mongolian delicacies. Tourists will also be entertained by a welcoming ceremony given by mounted horseman, grassland sightseeing, herding in the wilderness, visiting herdsmen's households, sacrifice offering to Aobao (heaps of sand, stone or earth spread out as road markers), horse racing, saddling, and lassoing, wrestling, archery, the Nadam fair, and bonfires and performance art.

Hulun Lake

Hulun Lake—Hulun means "otter" in Mongolian—is also called Dalai Lake or Hulun Pond. It is located in the middle of the Hulun Buir Grassland and is China's fifth largest freshwater lake. It has abundant fish and fowl. The lake is shaped like an irregular quadrate, is 93 kilometers long and has an average width of 32 kilometers with a perimeter totaling 447 kilometers, making its total area 2, 339 square kilometers. The water's average depth is 5. 75 meters and it is clear and pristine.

The Hulun Lake is one of China's few remaining pristine and unpolluted freshwater lakes. Here tourists can truly appreciate nature, the grassland, and see the wildlife. The area around the lake is warm but not hot during summer, and lake's waters are refreshing and cool, making it an ideal summer destination. Tourists can enjoy the lake's sunrises and mirages on Ou Island, and the waves lapping against its shore. Lots of birds dwell in the nearby reed marshes. And tourists can also inspect the nearby stone stakes and enjoy views of the surrounding tiger- and elephant-like mountains. Summer tourist activities include boating, fishing, sunbathing on the sand beaches, swimming, and fish banquets, while ice fishing is done during the winter.

The Baiyanhada Grassland

The Baiyanhada Tourist Area ("Rich Mountain" in Mongolian) is located in the Chenbarhu Banner, in the middle of the Hulun Buir Grassland 60 kilometers away from Hailar city. The Grassland covers an area of 1.5 square kilometers.

The Baiyanhada Grassland has piclu-resque scenery and it is a perfect placc for touring the grassland and appreciating its natural scenery. The Hailar River flows quietly through the area and its banks are lined with lush shrubs, which are reflected in its clear blue waters. The sky is also blue, with white clouds, and herds of cattle and sheep wander about. Rare species of flora and fauna enhance the area's appeal. In summer lots of swans, geese, and pheasants fly leisurely in the sky, while in winter foxes, hares and roe deer are seen on the grassland.

This wildlife supplies the people living in the Mongolian yurts with lots of fresh meat throughout the year. Tourists can watch boke-wrestling ("Boke", with the meaning of "strong and healthy" in the Mongolian Language, is a kind of wresting practised only by the Inner Mongolians and is popular among people living on the grasslands.), wool shearing, milking cows, Barhu Wedding (a traditional Mongolian wedding ceremony), Mongolian clothing shows and song and dance performances. You can also see equestrian performances, including horse riding and lassoing, as well talks and presentations dealing with Mongolian horsemanship. Other activities are offering sacrifices to Aobao, fishing, sliding on the grass, along with skiing and horse-drawn sleigh rides in winter. Tourists can also experience first-hand what it is like living in a herdsman's household, learning daily Mongolian activities such as herding animals, milking cows, and boiling milk tea.

Dear distinguished guests, after the tour of the grassland I believe you must have a general idea of what the Mongolian grasslands look like and how the Mongolian people live here. I believe the grassland and its people enjoyed your visit as much as you did and look forward to your next one.

Ladies and gentlemen, I hope to have another chance to meet you again on this very land, Erdos and Hulun Buir Grassland! Thank you!

正如著名歷史學家翦伯贊在《內蒙古訪古》中所說：「呼倫貝爾不僅現在是內蒙一個最好的牧場，自古以來就是最好的草原。……歷來被稱做是『北方遊牧民族的搖籃』。……假如內蒙古是遊牧民族的歷史舞台，那麼呼倫貝爾草原就是這個歷史舞台的後台。」如今的呼倫貝爾草原依然迷人、依然令人神往！

呼倫貝爾大草原位於大興安嶺西側，其地理坐標為東經115°31´～121°10´，北緯47°20´～50°13´，面積約10萬平方公里，其中天然草場面積曾經占80.1%，她是至今仍保持原始性的少數草原之一。這片舉世聞名的大草原是全球難得的最後「綠色淨土」之一。這裡屬於溫帶季風氣候，冬季嚴寒漫長，冰天雪地；夏季溫熱涼爽，碧草連天，湖藍水秀，是令遊人嚮往的草原旅遊勝地。

呼倫貝爾以美麗富饒的大草原著稱，森林、河流、湖泊、冰雪等自然資源豐富，境內鄂溫克、鄂倫春、達斡爾、蒙古、俄羅斯等各族人民和睦相處，富有濃厚的民族風情。主要旅遊景點有：呼和諾爾草原旅遊區、西山國家森林區、呼倫湖、中俄互市貿易市場以及鳳凰山莊等。

呼和諾爾草原旅遊區

呼和諾爾草原旅遊區，位於呼倫貝爾市西北部古老的巴爾虎草原中心地帶，距海拉爾50公里，距滿洲裡市110 公里。它是中國目前少數未受任何工業汙染和農業開發的天然優良草原之一。區內綠草如茵，湖泊河流點綴其中，水草肥美，景色秀麗，可謂呼倫貝爾草原的縮影。因坐落於呼和淖爾（蒙語意為青色的湖）湖畔而得名。

呼和諾爾湖面積12 公里，有「天下第一曲水」美譽的莫日格勒河從呼和諾爾湖東北方流入湖中，湖水又向南注入海拉爾河，湖的四周是一望無際的大草原，500多種野生動植物生長活動於這片土地。獨特的自然環境與豐富的野生動植物資源共同構成了一幅別具一格的自然畫卷，使這裡成為草原生態自然觀光的理想之地。

與此富饒美麗的自然旅遊資源相映生輝的是當地濃郁的巴爾虎蒙古族風情。巴爾虎，原是蒙古人的一個遊牧地區的名字，後來蒙古人便被稱為「巴爾虎」了。巴爾虎蒙古族人民世世代代生活在這裡，他們以自己獨特的生活、生產方式、民俗禮儀向來自遠方的客人講述著巴爾虎蒙古族的歷史與文化，展示著天人合一、自然富足、豪放快樂的生活，展示這裡作為北方遊牧民族成長搖籃之風采。

旅遊區能提供蒙古包住宿、民族風味餐飲，有馬隊迎賓、草原觀光、遊牧旅遊、訪牧戶、祭敖包、賽馬、馴馬、套馬、摔跤（博克）、射箭、篝火晚會、文藝演出、那達慕、遊湖垂釣等活動項目。是觀賞呼倫貝爾大草原的最佳去處。

呼倫湖

呼倫湖又稱「達賚湖」、「呼倫池」，位於呼倫貝爾草原腹中，湖形呈不規則長方形，湖長93 公里，平均寬度32 公里，平均水深5.75 米，周長447 公里，湖水面積2339平方公里，像一顆碩大而晶瑩的明珠鑲嵌在呼倫貝爾草原腹部。

呼倫湖是中國較大的淡水湖中唯一未受汙染的湖泊，保持了原始的自然風貌，是遊客認識自然、享受自然、保護自然的最佳旅遊景區，更是開展草原湖泊生態觀光、觀賞各種野生動植物的旅遊勝地，湖區氣候溫涼，亦是避暑佳境。呼倫湖最為迷人的觀光項目有：水上日出、湖田蜃樓、石椿戀馬、玉灘淘浪、虎嘯呼倫、象山望月、蘆蕩棲鳥、歐島聽琴，這是呼倫湖上遠近聞名的「八景」。湖面泛舟、湖中戲水、岸邊垂釣、沙灘日光浴、桌上全魚宴和冬季冰上捕魚等項目更是令人嚮往。在呼倫湖區遊覽，還可以乘坐遊艇觀賞湖光景色，讓鬧市的喧囂和忙亂都散落在這靜靜的湖中。

白彥哈達草原旅遊區

「白彥哈達」蒙古語意為富饒的山，位於呼倫貝爾陳巴爾虎旗境內，著名的呼倫貝爾大草原腹地，巴爾虎草原深處，距海拉爾市60 公里，景區占地1.5平方公里。

海拉爾河蜿蜒流過景區，兩岸樹影婆娑，優美的灌木樹林倒映在水中，與河畔、一望無際的草原，藍天白雲，潔白的蒙古包和成群的牛羊構成一幅美麗和諧的畫面，真是美不勝收，令人心曠神怡。豐富的野生動植物資源，為白彥哈達草原帶來色彩與生氣。夏季天鵝、大雁等在空中悠然地飛翔，冬季狐貍、野兔、　子等出沒在林間。在白彥哈達草原遊覽區不同季節可以享受異樣的景色風光。

這裡有多功能的蒙古包，可用於會議、就餐。遊客可以觀看摔跤（也有音譯為「博克」）、剪羊毛、擠奶、巴爾虎婚禮、蒙古族服飾、民族歌舞表演。該景區還設有騎馬俱樂部，遊客可以騎馬、參加馬文化講座，觀看賽馬、賽車、套馬等表演。除此之外，景區還有祭敖包、釣魚、滑草、冬季滑雪、乘坐馬拉雪橇等活動。遊客還可以到牧民家體驗牧民生活，嘗試學習蒙古語生活用語、擠奶、煮奶茶、製作奶製品等蒙古族生活生產方式。

Part II East China華東地區

☆Shanghai Municipality（上海市）

☆Zhejiang Province（浙江省）

☆Jiangsu Province（江蘇省）

☆Shandong Province（山東省）

☆Jiangxi Province（江西省）

☆Fujian Province（福建省）

☆Anhui Province（安徽省）

華東地區

Shanghai Municipality上海市

A Glimpse of the Municipality（本市簡介）

Shanghai, located on the middle part of East China coast, is the gateway to the Yangtze River Delta and a major transportation and communications hub, as well as a center for international exchange. The municipality covers an area of 6, 341. 5 square kilometers. Its registered population numbers 13. 5 million; another 6 million unregistered people live here. The city stands on the Yangtze River Delta's flat land and is crisscrossed with waterways. One of these, the Huangpu River, divides Shanghai into its eastern and western halves. While the east half makes up the city's center and encompasses much of its proud history, the newly built up west half is rapidly developing and has become Shanghai's new hot spot.

The weather in Shanghai is mild and humid with four distinct seasons. The rainy season falls between spring and summer when there are often sudden showers.

Shanghai occupies an important position in China's contemporary history. In the early 1920s, Dr.Sun Yat-sen, forefather of China's Democratic Revolution, lived in Shanghai to carry out his democratic revolutionary program. In July of 1921 the Communist Party of China held its First National Congress in Shanghai, formally declaring the founding of the Party.

Tourism Resources

Shanghai is a must on any agenda during a tour of China. Visitors to Shanghai are not only dazzled by the modern metropolis, but also able to immerse themselves in the unique Shanghai culture, a combination of Chinese and Western elements. In the heart of this commercial center visitors will find elegant buildings, glittering shops and malls, the imposing riverside Bund, and fascinating museuMs.Shanghai bustles by day and lives life to the full by night in some of China's best night spots. As an international metropolis, Shanghai presents different pictures for visitors with different purposes. It is known as the leading shopping capital of China, a paradise for leisure and pleasure for tourists, a dazzling world of entertainments for arts and music lovers, and an exhibition of international architecture.

Historical and contemporary scenic spots: Yuyuan Garden, the Bund, the Oriental Pearl TV Tower, and Jinmao Tower.

New and exciting tourist attractions: Magnetic Levitated Train, Bund Sightseeing Tunnel, Shanghai Oriental Arts Center, Shanghai Ocean Aquarium and Shanghai Xintiandi.

Cultural Tour: Shanghai Grand Theatre, Shanghai Museum, Shanghai Urban Planning Exhibition Hall, Shanghai Art Museum, and Shanghai Library.

"International Architecture Exhibition" : Shanghai's architecture is a fascinating tourist attraction. It shows how styles have changed with the course of modern history. Classical European, Asian and Chinese architectural styles exist side by side. The city is literally known as "International Architecture Exhibition" . Walking by the riverside of the Bund, you will see different kinds of Western-style architecture. Most of them are adorned with clock towers and turrets, marble pillars and wrought-iron entrances, each representing a distinctively indivi-dual appearance. The buildings which remain are of scientific, historic and cultural value.

Paradise for Shoppers

There are numerous shops in the flourishing commercial district running alongside the Nanjing and Huaihai roads. The area is an ideal setting in which to shop and learn about Shanghai folklore. Here people can find the most stylish clothing, the latest electronic goods, and the best of arts and crafts. The name of the city is synonymous with excellence, elegance, and the best quality.

Local Culture

Integrating the Chinese with the Western, synthesizing Northern and Southern China, Shanghai culture embodies a character expressing the trend of the times radiating far and wide to every corner of the country. Various cultural activities are held in Shanghai such as the Shanghai International Arts Festival, Shanghai International Film Festival, and Shanghai Tourism Festival. Hu opera, Burlesque in local dialect and Jinshan Farmer's painting are popular among local people.

10 Sightseeing Routes in Shanghai

Shanghai Sightseeing Bus Center is a self-help tourist center especially set by Shanghai Municipal Tourism Commission to assist individual Chinese and foreign tourists in undertaking tours of the city. The center has set up branch offices and

華東地區

departure yards at Shanghai Stadium, Hongkou Football Field, Yangpu Stadium, Circus City in Zhabei District, and under the Nanpu Bridge in Huangpu District.

雄居於中國東海岸中部的上海是長江三角洲的門戶，也是中國交通運輸和國際貿易交易的重要樞紐。上海市總面積為6341.5 平方公里，人口為1350多萬，流動人口有600多萬。由於上海地處長江三角洲沖積平原，小溪和渠道縱橫交錯。黃浦江是上海的天然隔離帶，把上海分割成了東、西兩部分。浦西是上海的中心，也曾經是上海的驕傲，而浦東的開發越來越吸引全球的目光，已成為世人矚目的焦點。

上海四季分明，氣候溫和濕潤，春夏之交常伴有陣雨。

上海在中國現代史上占有十分重要的地位。孫中山先生是中國民主革命的先驅，1920 年代早期他生活在上海，開展民主革命運動。1921年7月，中國共產黨在上海召開了第一次中國代表大會，大會選舉了領導人並通過了第一個黨綱，正式宣布了中國共產黨的成立。

旅遊資源

上海是海外遊客到中國旅遊的必到之地。在這個商業中心，遊客們可以欣賞到千姿百態的建築群，雄偉壯麗的外灘，燈火輝煌的商店和極富魅力的博物館。上海白天喧囂繁忙，到了晚上，人們在夜生活場所盡情享受。作為一座國際大都市，上海可以為不同的旅遊者呈現出不同的畫面。它既是中國主要的購物城市，又是休閒旅遊者的天堂。

主要歷史文化景點：豫園、外灘、東方明珠電視塔、金茂大廈。

主要新興旅遊點：磁懸浮、外灘觀光隧道、上海東方藝術中心、上海水族館、上海新天地。

文化之旅：上海大劇院、上海博物館、上海城市規劃展示館、上海圖書館。

「萬國建築博覽會」

上海的建築群吸引著眾多遊客，它向人們展示了上海建築風格在現當代史中的變化。歐洲古典風格、亞洲風格和中國風格的建築鱗次櫛比。不同的殖民者來到中國，依照本國的風格設計他們的辦公樓宇和住宅。上海也因此被譽為「萬國建築博覽會」。漫步外灘，你會看到各種各樣的西式建築，其中大多數都裝點有鐘塔、角樓、大理石柱和精緻的鐵門。這些建築風格迥異，各領風騷，具有藝術、歷史和文化價值。

購物者的天堂

上海還是一個購物天堂。南京路、淮海路等商業街上的店鋪數不勝數。這裡是感受上海鄉土特色的好地方。在這裡，人們能看到最流行的服飾、最新型的電子產品以及最好的藝術品、手工藝品。上海，這個城市名字就代表著超群、富麗堂皇和一流質量。在上海購物就是一次愉快的體驗。

當地文化

中西貫通、南北兼容的海派文化適應時代潮流，輻射到大江南北。上海每年舉辦國際藝術節，國際電影節和旅遊節。滬劇、滑稽戲和金山農民畫深受上海市民喜愛。

10條旅遊線路

為了方便市民和海外旅遊者自助旅行，上海市旅遊事業委員會設立了上海旅遊集散中心。該中心在上海體育館、虹口足球場、楊浦體育館、閘北馬戲城和南浦大橋停車場設發車點。

Zhujiajiao Ancient Town （朱家角）

Located in Qingpu District in the southwestern suburbs of the city, Zhujiajiao

華東地區

Ancient Town covers an area of 4.7 square kilometers in the shape of a fan filled with a landscape of lakes and hills. Of the tens of thousands of tourists, who have visited there, some call it Shanghai's Venice and everyone regards it as a bright pearl inlaid in the bank of Dianshan Lake.

Famous for its traditional scenes of riverside town in south of Yangtze River, Zhujiajiao Ancient Town was already a renowned country fair as early as 1,700 years ago. During the Ming Dynasty Emperor Wanli's reign, the town attracted lots of merchants and became very prosperous. One thousand Ming and Qing Dynasty houses and buildings still stand, and 36 stone bridges retain their ancient designs. Various rivers and ports crisscross in the town and its nine big streets stretch out along the river bank.

Zhujiajiao's ancient Fangsheng Bridge(Setting-Fish-Free Bridge) is the best among all its stone bridges. It is 72 meters long, 5. 8 meters wide, with 5 openings spanning the Caogang River like a rainbow. This bridge was built in 1571 and rebuilt in 1814. The bridge has a stone tablet named the Dragon Gate Stone. Eight lifelike coiling dragons encircling a shining pearl are carved on to the stone. Four stone lions on top of the bridge greet visitors with smiles.

Ming-Qing Street and Town God Temple are the most fascinating sights featuring the unique style. Of them, the local 26 lanes are worth mentioning. Zhujiajiao is better known for its ancient, quiet, strange, and deep lanes than any other ancient town in southern China. It is very interesting when traveling in the alleys to feel a sense of confusion. Walking along the zigzag pavement at narrow and small lanes, you will feel as if you were inside a simple and elegant water-and-ink painting. You can learn from them the interesting layout of Northern China's hutongs, while experiencing the quietness of small lanes in southern China.

Another fascinating point is that the town has been home to many famous Chinese people, numerous Ming and Qing architectural landmarks, stone paths for boat pullers, and teahouses. If you are a careful observer, you can find various carvings and sculptures on stones, some of which look like sword, some look like strange animals, and some are carved into "Ruyi", indicating luck and happiness.

The teahouse is the best place to relax after a long walk. These teahouses include luxury teahouses close to the Setting-Fish-Free Bridge, teahouses with a long history, as well ones located on a boat. Visitors can savor Zhujiajiao's unique water scenery while sipping a cup of tea. However, the highlight of any visit to Zhujiajiao is a boat trip on the river. Only by sailing on the quiet river, listening to the rhythmical sounds of rowing, can the visitor feel that he or she is really part of the city.

Zhujiajiao features beautiful water, small boats, ancient arched stone bridges, and fascinating streets paved with stones and elegant gardens. People can only truly appreciate its charm and beauty by visiting here themselves.

華東地區

古老的江南水鎮朱家角坐落在上海的東南角的青浦區，占地4.7平方公里。在這片扇形地域裡星羅棋布地分布著許多湖泊和小山。許許多多到過這裡的遊客，無不稱它為上海的威尼斯，澱山湖畔的一顆明珠。

朱家角古鎮以其優美的水鎮景色聞名於江南。早在1700年前，這裡早已有遠近聞名的集市貿易。在明朝萬曆年間，商人們雲集於此，使其成為一座繁榮的城鎮。一千座明清時期的房屋依然保存完好，36座石橋古韻猶存。這裡有許許多多河流小巷縱橫交錯，九條主要街道則建在河堤上。

這裡的放生橋是上海現存石橋中最好的一座，它長72米，寬5.8米，有五個橋孔，如一道彩虹橫跨漕港河。此橋建於1571 年，1814 年重建。在橋上有一塊碑叫「龍門石」，鐫盤龍八條，環繞明珠，形象逼真。橋頂四只迎客石獅，憨態可掬。

明清街和鎮上的神廟是最具特色且引人入勝的景點，其中值得一提的是當地的26 條小巷。朱家角的古弄幽巷以古、奇、深、靜，聞名遐邇，一般江南其他古鎮上是不能相比的。穿弄走巷，如入迷魂陣。漫步在曲曲彎彎的小巷中，你彷彿置身於一幅水墨畫中。更為有趣的是，在這裡，你既可以感受到北方的胡同文化，又可以體驗到南方裡弄的氛圍。朱家角的「古巷旅遊」深受國內外遊客的喜愛。

朱家角是許多名人的故鄉，這裡保存著許多明清時的建築、碼頭、縴夫道以及許多茶館。如果你善於觀察，可以發現許多形狀各異的石雕，有的鑿成寶劍，有的刻成怪獸，還有的琢成含有吉祥之意的「如意」。

漫步朱家角，最佳的休息之處就是茶樓。這裡既有近「放生橋」的豪華型茶樓，也有年代久遠古老的茶樓，更有遊船茶館。品名茶，看水景，煞是優哉游哉，不亦樂乎？不用説，大家只有去乘輕舟遊覽，才能真正不虛此行。只有乘上咿呀小舟，臨聽富有節奏感的划水聲，你才能有「船在水上行，人在畫中遊」的感覺。

在朱家角，你既可以看到碧水輕舟、拱形石橋，又可以領略到古弄幽巷和迷人奇特的園林。不臨其境，難言其妙。

Oriental Pearl TV Tower （東方明珠電視塔）

Pudong's rapid economic development and striking new architecture have made it Shanghai's new hot spot. When visiting Shanghai, tourists will inevitably be introduced to the 468-meter-high Oriental Peal TV Tower which is the highest in Asia and third highest in the world. It has become Shanghai's landmark. The designer's inspiration was derived from a line written by Bai Juyi, a prominent Tang Dynasty Poet. The line goes, "The rhythmical music sounds like pearls of various sizes dropping onto the emerald plate."

The Oriental Pearl TV Tower consists of three big columns which are 9 meters in diameter, the space module, the upper sphere, the lower sphere, five small spheres, tower base, and the square. The designers magically set the eleven beautiful spheres of various sizes up from the green grassland to the blue sky with two giant spheres shining like a pair of rubies. The tower has a double-decked elevator which can hold 50 people at a time and can run at a speed of 7 meters per second. The tower is equipped with three-dimensional lighting fixtures, which make the whole tower very colorful and beautiful.

Shanghai Historical Museum in the Oriental Pearl TV Tower displays the city's modern development. The exhibition is divided into several parts, such as "a state within a state" on Chinese land, municipal construction for the development of the city, the increasing modernization of the city's economy, the atmosphere provided by modern culture, the coexistence of the old and new social life, and the city's changing political arena. Supple-mented by advanced audio-visual equipment, over a thousand items of precious cultural relics, archives, literature and historical pictures are vividly displayed.

It takes 40 seconds by elevator to reach the upper sphere, 263 meters above ground with a diameter of 45 meters which is actually a spherical observation deck. It is an ideal place for having a bird's-eye-view of the city. On the 271-meter level are 20 karaoke private rooMs.Through the glass panes of the revolving restaurant which can accommodate 1,600 diners, visitors can see a panoramic view of Shanghai. Down below, the Huangpu River flows past like a jade ribbon. The Nanpu and Yangpu bridges look like two rainbows flying across the river and Pudong Park resembles an exquisite emerald plate.

華東地區

隨著經濟和城市建設的快速發展，浦東新區已成為上海的熱點地區。每當遊客遊覽上海時，一定會被介紹去參觀468 米高的電視塔。人們習慣叫它東方明珠，它是上海人心中的標誌性建築。設計者的靈感源自於唐代一位傑出的詩人白居易的詩句——大珠小珠落玉盤。

東方明珠電視塔由三個巨大的直徑為9 米的支柱，太空艙上球體、下球體，5個小球體，塔基和廣場組成。設計者巧妙地把11個大小各異的精美球體從綠地一直安插到藍天，而兩個大球猶如紅寶石般閃閃發光。在電視塔裡有一架雙層電梯，每秒速度達到7米。電視塔配備了三維立體的燈光設備，使整座塔五彩繽紛，美麗異常。

東方明珠電視塔**內**的上海歷史博物館展示了近代上海城市發展的歷史。整個展覽分幾個部分，比如日漸現代化的城市經濟，開風氣之先的近代文化，新舊並存的社會生活，風韻蕩漾的政治舞台。借助於較為先進的視聽設備，博物館生動地展示了 1000 餘件珍貴文物、檔案文獻和歷史圖片。

乘電梯到直徑45米，離地263米高的上球體需要40秒。上球體實際上是一個觀景平台。這是一個俯瞰整個城市面貌的理想之地。在271 米的高度是20間卡拉 OK 包房。透過能容納1600 名用餐者的旋轉餐廳的窗格玻璃，遊客們能看到上海的全景。正下方，黃浦江蜿蜒流過，宛如一條玉帶。南浦、洋浦兩座大橋橫跨其上，彷彿是兩條彎彎的彩虹，而浦江公園儼然是一個精緻的翡翠玉盤。

The Bund （外灘）

The Bund is Shanghai's tourist calling card and has been seen as the main symbol of the city. The newly-renovated Bund lies along the Huangpu River's west bank between the Waibaidu and Nanpu Bridges. Now we have come to the wide embankment which offers ample room for strolling and is used by locals for morning exercises and evening gatherings. Over fifty buildings lining the shoreline of the Huangpu River present us a living exhibition of Gothic, Baroque, Art-Deco, Roman, Classic Revival and Renaissance architectural styles, as well as combinations of Chinese and Western styles. In the evening colorful lights illuminate the bridges across the river and buildings along both banks to create a shimmering image, giving Shanghai its reputation as the Pearl of the Orient.

The Bund has always closely linked with the development of Shanghai so we sometimes call it a condensation of the city's recent history. Now let's look at the other side of the river. It is called Lujiazui Finance and Trade Zone and we can clearly see the Oriental Pearl TV Tower and several dozens of high-rises. But before early 1990s, what we could see were a few old buildings. The scenic Huangpu River is the birthplace of the city. Cruise boats meander northward along the waterway to the intriguing "three layer waters" at the Wusong Mouth, the confluence of the Huangpu and Yangtze Rivers. On a clear night, gazing from the boat, you can see the stately row of buildings and the splendid skyline on both sides of the river.

外灘是上海的亮點，也是上海的象徵。經過改造的新外灘北起外白渡橋、南至南浦橋下。現在，我們已來到了寬敞的外灘。這兒也是上海市民早上鍛鍊，晚上納涼的地方。沿岸的50多座大樓猶如給我們呈現了一場萬國建築展，既有哥德式、巴洛克式、裝飾藝術派、羅馬式，也有歐洲文藝復興時代建築風格和中西合璧的建築風格。每當夜幕降臨時，各色各樣的綵燈照亮了橫跨浦江的大橋和兩岸的主要建築，變幻出無數絢麗的圖像，使夜幕下的上海真正成為東方之珠。

外灘與上海的發展密切相關，可以説它見證了上海近代歷史。請大家看看浦江的對岸，對面是陸家嘴金融貿易區，我們可以清楚地看到東方明珠電視塔、金茂大廈和數十幢高樓。但在1990年代初，對岸只是幾幢破舊的大樓。風景如畫的黃浦江孕育了上海。游輪沿金色的水陸向北漫遊至吳淞口奇妙的「三夾水」，這裡就是黃浦江與長江的交匯處。在晴朗的夜晚，從船上遠望，你會看到一排宏偉的外灘建築群和變幻無窮的色彩。

Yuyuan Garden （豫園）

As an outstanding representative of the classical architectural style, Yuyuan Garden is known as the "top beauty in southeast China". This classical garden, integrating the gardening art and Ming and Qing architectural styles with magnificent chambers and halls, beautiful rockeries and ponds, luxuriant trees and plants, is notable for its grace and peace and can strike visitors as being both large and small. The garden was owned by a high-ranking official named Pan Yunduan, a native of Shanghai who once took

華東地區

office in Sichuan Province. Pan had the garden built from 1559 to 1577 in order to both please his father and for his own enjoyment.

As time went by, the garden had changed hands several times and was once left wild and deserted until 1760, when a few rich businessmen purchased the site collectively and rebuilt the pavilions and chambers in the hope of restoring its former glory. During the early 18th century, the garden was made the offices of trade guild office for soy-bean, sugar, and cloth trading. It suffered great damage during the Opium War and Taiping Revolution.

Fortunately, the major parts of the garden were still standing at the time of Shanghai's liberation in 1949. From 1956 on, the Chinese government allocated substantial funds to restore its elegance.

There are altogether 48 scenic points, with five dragon walls separating the gardens into six different scenic sections, each having its own special attraction.

Before entering the garden, we can see a beautiful lotus pond with a nine-zigzag bridge and a pavilion-like tea-house, which is a favorite place for elderly people and tourists to enjoy chatting with each other over a cup of tea. Please allow me to make clear that the whole area is called the City God Temple, which consists of the temple itself, bazaar and temple fair area, and the East and West Gardens. Another name of Yuyuan Garden is West Garden while the Inner Garden inside the Yuyuan Garden is actually the East Garden.

As soon as we step into the garden, we can see the Three-Corn-Ear Hall in the central part of the park. It was erected in the reign of the Emperor Qianlong of the Qing Dynasty. Chinese farmers firmly believed that three ears on the stalk were a sign of good harvest. So the name of Three-Corn-Ear expresses the best wishes of farmers and grain traders for a bumper harvest.

Close to it is the Yangshan Hall (Hall for Viewing the Big Rockery), a construction of the style of a waterside pavilion. A corridor with railings winds its way around the back of the hall. Leaning against the railings, we can have a full view of the big Rockery which resembles a real mountain range with towering peaks and precipitous cliffs.

Big Rockery, an artificial rockery hill, was piled up with approximately two thousand tons of rocks carried from Wukang area in Zhejiang Province. This majestic looking rockery, verdant with luxuriant old trees, presents a view of steep cliffs, hidden winding paths and labyrinth caves, giving the viewer a sense of retreat from the hustle and bustle of the city. It is the most original in style among all the Ming rockeries so far preserved south of the Yangtze River. On top of its highest peak, 12 meters in height, stands a pavilion by the name of Viewing Surfs for visitors to take a break.

There are beautiful scenes east of the Big Rockery, namely, the Happy Fish Waterside Pavilion erected beside a creek flowing eastward. The creek, partitioned in the middle by a decorated wall and its water flowing through an arched door at the lower part of the wall, looks deeper and longer than itself as if there is no end.

Further eastward, there is the Double Corridor partitioned in the middle by a wall with latticed windows of various shapes, through which travelers may view scenes on both sides. One side of the corridor presents travelers with chambers and a stoneboat. The other side offers visitors the views of creeks, rocks, trees and flowers. Walking along the corridor is just like entering a Chinese painting.

The magnificent Spring Hall was once used as the headquarter of the Small Sword Society, which staged an armed uprising that was supported by transportation workers and craftsmen, as well as suburban peasants who were too poor to pay heavy land rent. As one of the historical sites with revolutionary significance in our country, the Spring Hall displays weapons, sun-or-moon-shaped coins, and notices used or issued by the

華東地區

Small Sword Society. Visitors can also enjoy a traditional Chinese painting, "Appreciating the Sword", done by the famous Qing Dynasty painter Ren Bonian. The name of the hall came from one of the lines written by the famous Song Dynasty poet Su Dongpo.

In the eastern part of the Yuyuan Garden is the Scenes Gathering Tower, wherefrom one can catch sight of all the beautiful scenery of the garden. Close to it is the Nine-Lion Study, a pavilion tucked away amidst ancient trees. Next to the Liushang Pavilion is a three-cornered stone bridge.

Walking across the bridge, travelers will find themselves in a world of "jade". To the east of the garden, there is a huge piece of exquisite jade-like stone, which is said to be a legacy of the Song Dynasty. This stone is 3.3 meters high. As one of the three famous stones south of the Yangtze River, this piece features a wrinkled surface and 72 holes eroded by water. It is also said that if incense is burned underneath, smoke will float out of each hole, drifting away with the wind, and when water is poured from the top of the stone, it will trickle out through the holes.

The Jade Magnificence Hall was used as the study of Pan Yunduan. It is said that he used to come here to enjoy the exquisite jade stone for some time before he sat down to write in the hall. Visitors can see the things on display, such as writing brushes, ink stone and ancient books.

To the west of the Jade Magnificence Hall is the Moon Tower, the upper part of a two-storied structure built by a pond in 1883. As evening falls, the bright moon reflects from the pond. Travelers can enjoy either the beautiful lotus or the moon in the pond. On the eaves of the hall, there are many Chinese characters for longevity carved out of wood, hence the name "Hundred Longevity Map".

To the south of the Exquisite Jade Stone are the Screen wall and the Coiling

Dragon Bridge, both of which are Ming style structures. The screen wall was a symbol of rank in ancient times. According to the Western Zhou system of rites, only royal palaces, noblemen's mansions and religious temples could have a screen wall. Apart from keeping passers-by from peeping into the courtyard, the screen wall could also be used by the visitors, who would get off from the carriage and, standing behind the wall, tidy up his dress before going in.

Located in the southeastern corner of the garden, the Inner Garden is actually "a garden within a garden". Originally it was inside the City God Temple. Built in 1709, the 48thyear of the Qing Emperor Kangxi's reign, it used to serve as a temple garden called the "Spiritual Garden".

The inner garden, though covering only an area of 1, 300 square meters, appears spacious and zigzag due to the designer's ingenuity. The halls, chambers, pavilions, towers, pond, rockeries and hills all are artistically arranged to fit into the space. The crenate walls and corridors are skillfully laid out so as to make the small garden highly enchanting. In front of the Hall for Watching Billows stands a rockery with various shapes respectively resembling a demon, lion, leopard, deer, monkey, and elephant head. A variety of old trees, such as the podocarpus, Chinese little leaf box, and wisteria tower over the top of the rockery. Shrouded in verdure is a double-story building named the Towering Emerald Pavilion.

In the east lies the Nine-dragon Pond, which is given this name because the pond is dragon-shaped, with four dragons carved on the sides. These dragons and their reflections on the water altogether make up nine dragons.

The five dragon walls winding concentrically around the garden have impressively fluid lines. Before leaving the Yuyuan Garden, visitors can find a sleeping dragon, the last of the five ones in the whole garden. It is carved out of clay, while the scales of the other four dragons are made of tiles. In China the dragon, an imaginary animal, is

華東地區

the principal motif for decorative designs on the buildings, clothing, and other daily use articles in imperial palaces.

作為古典建築風格的傑出代表，豫園被譽為江南一絕。這座古典園林集明清時代建築風格與園林藝術之大成，富麗堂皇的樓榭、美麗的假山和池塘及茂盛的樹木植被融為一體，展示了其高雅、寧靜、精緻的特質，美輪美奐。此園面積雖小，給人的印象卻是庭院深深。

豫園是歷史上一位高官潘允端的私家花園。園主潘允端是上海人，曾任四川布政史。為了取悅父親同時也為了自己享樂，他修建了這座花園。

隨著歲月的流逝，豫園幾易其主，甚至曾一度荒廢，成為棄園。直至1760年，一些商賈集資買下了這座曾經風光一時的花園。為了重現其昔日的風采，他們重建了亭台樓榭，更名為「西園」。18世紀初，豫園又成了當時進行豆類、食糖和布匹交易的貿易行會的公所。後來，在鴉片戰爭和太平天國起義期間，豫園又屢遭破壞。

值得慶幸的是，豫園的主體部分直到1949　年上海解放時依然保存完整。自1956 年以來，上海市政府屢次撥出專款全面整修豫園，重現它古樸典雅的風韻。

豫園內有48 處景點，五堆龍牆將其分成六個主要景區，各有千秋。

尚未踏入豫園，遊人們便會看到一個美麗的荷花池。荷花池上有一座九曲橋和一間類似小亭子的茶館，那是老人們和遊客們品茗聊天的最佳去處。

這裡的整個區域被稱為城隍廟，它是由廟宇、商場、廟會的場所及東、西兩個園林組成。豫園也叫西園，而其內園叫做東園。

一進入豫園，我們就可以看到壯觀的「三穗堂」坐落在豫園的中央。它始建於清乾隆年間。人們普遍認為三穗是豐收的象徵，取名為「三穗堂」正寄託了人們對豐收的美好願望。

「三穗堂」的旁邊是一座臨水亭榭風格的「仰山堂」，廳堂的後面是蜿蜒的帶有護欄的遊廊。臨欄而望，大假山一覽無遺。置身其中，便如來到了高聳陡峭的萬山叢中。

大假山由採於浙江武康縣的大約2000　噸石頭人工堆砌而成。假山氣勢雄偉，古樹鬱鬱蔥蔥，集峭壁、曲徑和迷宮般的山洞於一體，使觀賞者產生了遠離都市喧囂，回歸自然的感覺。它是江南地區現存的明代假山中風格最為正宗的一座。高達12米的假山頂矗立著「望江亭」，供遊客休息。

大假山東側是美景佳處「魚樂榭」，旁邊是一條東流的小溪。花牆把小溪分成兩個部分，溪水從牆下部的拱門中流過，更顯得其深遠，彷彿沒有盡頭。

再往東走是「兩宜軒」。這是一條復廊，中部被嵌有格窗的牆隔開。透過這些窗戶，遊客們可以欣賞兩邊的景色。一面是亭台樓榭和石舫，一面是清溪巨石、紅花綠樹。徜徉其中，猶如步入了一幅中國山水畫。

華麗的「點春堂」曾是清末小刀會的總壇。小刀會發動了一場由運輸工人、工匠和繳不上地租的貧農參加的武裝起義。作為中國具有革命歷史意義的景點之一，「點春堂」裡陳列著武器、日月形的硬幣以及小刀會曾發布的文告。遊客們還可以欣賞到曾參加過起義的清代著名畫家任伯年所作的《觀劍圖》。「點春堂」得名於宋代大詩人蘇東坡的詩句。

豫園東面是「會景樓」，從那兒可以一覽園中美景。緊挨著的是「九獅軒」，一座隱沒於古樹之間的樓閣。「流殤亭」旁是三曲石橋。

走過石橋，遊客們會發現自己已置身於「翡翠世界」之中。豫園的東側一角，有一塊巨大的玉玲瓏，據說是宋代的遺物。相傳宋徽宗醉心於收集奇石，此玉正是進獻的供品之一。他派人到各地搜尋玉石，並千里迢迢的送到開封御花園。而這塊玉玲瓏在途中遭遇暴風雨，同船一併沉入黃浦江。再後來，潘允端僱船伕潛入水底去尋找。他們用鐵鏈穿孔，才把它拖到岸上。玉玲瓏高達3.3　米，造型優美。作為江南三大名石之一，更有其獨到之處。整塊玉石表面褶皺，造型纖細，色澤透明，並有72個因水侵蝕而成的小孔。據說，從下面燒一炷香，上面會孔孔冒煙；從上面澆一盆水，下面會洞洞流泉。

「玉華堂」是潘允端的書齋。據說他在揮毫潑墨之前，總要到這兒玩賞一番玉玲瓏。遊客們在這兒可以看到展示的潘允端曾用過的毛筆、硯台和古籍。

「玉華堂」西面是建於1883年的「得月樓」。它是建在池塘邊上的兩層建築。每當夜幕降臨，皎潔的月光灑在池塘中，遊客們可以欣賞到美麗的蓮花和荷塘月色。屋簷上有許多木刻的壽字，由此得名「百壽廊」。

玉玲瓏以南是照壁和「環龍橋」，都承襲了明代的建築風格。在古代，照壁是地位的象徵。根據西周的禮儀，只有皇家宮殿、貴族邸宅和宗祠廟宇才可以修建此牆。照壁可以防止外人偷窺，登門拜訪者下轎後，在進門之前，還可以在此牆後整衣束冠。牆上刻有四個大字「寰中大快」，意為「普天同慶」。

豫園的東南角是堪稱「園中園」的內園。它原先在城隍廟內，內園於清康熙四十八年（公元1710年）建成。當時作為寺廟花園，名曰「廟園」。

雖然內園占地僅約1300　　平方米，但由於設計者獨具匠心，這裡顯得開闊清幽，堂、宇、樓、塔、池、石、山，無一不恰到好處地安排其間。鋸齒牆和遊廊也巧妙地安置於園中，使小小的花園頗具風采。「觀濤樓」前屹立著一座假山，山石形態迥異，如惡魔、獅子、豹、鹿、猴和象頭。假山上有各種古樹，如羅漢松，中國小葉黃楊和紫藤等。掩映於綠叢中的是一幢兩層建築「聳翠亭」。

「九龍池」位於其東部。池塘以龍為造型，四邊各雕有一條龍，加上水中的倒影，共九條龍，以此得名。

五堵龍牆在園中蜿蜒，其流暢的線條給人以深刻的印象。在豫園的出口處，有人們會看到一條沉睡的龍，這是園內五條龍中的最後一條。其他四條龍的鱗片由瓷磚製成，只有這一條是由黏土雕刻而成。在中國的皇宮中，龍這種虛構的動物是建築、衣飾乃至日用品的標誌圖樣。

Zhejiang Province浙江省

A Glimpse of the Province （本省簡介）

Zhejiang is located in the southern part of the Yangtze River Delta on the southeast coast of China. It faces the East China Sea on the east and neighbors Fujian on the south. Its extensive hinterland shares borders with Jiangxi and Anhui on the west and Shanghai and Jiangsu on the north. Zhejiang has an area of 101, 800 square kilometers, of which 70. 4%are hills and mountains. It is therefore said that "Zhejiang is 70% hills, 10% water and 20%plains". The land slopes from the southwest to the northeast with its major rivers flowing eastward into the East China Sea.

Zhejiang has a subtropical and monsoon type climate with four distinct seasons, and plentiful sunshine. It has an average annual temperature of 16℃-19℃, 230-270 frost-free days and an average annual rainfall of 1, 000-1, 900 millimeters.

Tourism Resources

Zhejiang Province has a long history and brilliant culture, with charming natural scenery, places of historical and cultural interest, and many other tourist attraction. It has been named "the land of fish and rice, the place of silk and tea, the town of cultural and historical relics, and the tourist destination. " The whole province has 16 national level scenic areas, including Hangzhou's West Lake, Qiandao Lake, Putuo Mountain, and the like, 37 provincial level scenic areas, including Dongqian and Nanbei Lakes, as well as 38 AAA grade scenic areas/spots, including Hangzhou's Song Dynasty Town and Shaoxing Keyan. It also boasts 73 cultural relics under national government protection and 279 cultural relics enjoying provincial governmental protection. The province has 78 national and provincial forest parks, and 8 national and 8 provincial natural preservation zones. Zhejiang boasts 5 national historic and cultural cities, 12 provincial historic and cultural cities, and 16 of China's excellent tourist

華東地區

cities. Moreover, the province has 4 national museums dealing with tea, silk, Southern Song Dynasty's imperial kiln and the Chinese traditional medicine as well as a large number of provincial level museuMs. "Lyric Land, Scenic Zhejiang" is the tourism theme for the province, which has its unique charm and characteristics, integrating nature and culture, beautiful scenery with rich historic figures and cultural heritage.

Local Snacks

Zhejiang cuisine consists of Hangzhou, Shao-xing and Ningbo style dishes and is one of China's eight main cooking styles. Dongpo Pork and West Lake Vinegar Fish are two typical Zhejiang dishes that are famous in China. Zhejiang also has many kinds of local snacks, such as Wushan Fried Biscuit, Jinhua Ham, and the like.

Local Culture

Zhejiang has a rich variety of operas. Local operas such as the Yue, Kun, Shao, and Wu Opera are thriving, as are the province's puppet shows. With its fresh and polished artistic style, the Yue Opera has ascended to a distinct position and become one of the major forms of Chinese opera.

Special Local Products

Notable local products include Zhejiang Silk, West Lake Dragon Well Tea, Changhua Chicken Blood Stones, Qingtian Stones and Qingtian stone carvings, Wenzhou Oranges, Fenghua Peaches, Tangxi Loquats, Silk Umbrellas, West Lake Fans and Boxwood Carvings.

Attraction Recommendation

West Lake is well-known for its beautiful scenery, multitude of historical sites, brilliant cultural relics, and profusion of native products. Qiandao Lake attracts visitors with its green wonderland. Xitang is an old town with thousands of years of history, located in Jiaxing County. Putuo Mountain has been called one of China's four famous Buddhist Mountains and has also long been reputed to be the Sea-Heaven Buddha Kingdom. Other places worth seeing in Zhejiang include the Lingyin Temple, Song Dynasty City, Chinese Tea Museum, General Yue Fei's Temple, South Tai Lake, Nanxun Ancient Town, Shuanglong Cave, Hengdian Movies City, Fenghua Xikou Xuedou Mountain, Mount Yandang, Nanxi River.

Tourism City

Hangzhou, Ningbo and Shaoxing have been designated first-rank "China Excellent Tourist Cities".

浙江省位於中國東南沿海長江三角洲南部，東瀕東海，南依福建，西接江西、安徽，北靠上海和江蘇。面積10.18萬平方公里，其中70.4%是山地丘陵，所以浙江又有「七分山，一分水，兩分平原」之説。浙江省地勢西南高東北低，境內主要河流由西往東流入東海。

浙江地處亞熱帶季風氣候區，四季分明，日照充足。年均氣溫16℃　～19℃，全年無霜期230～270天，年降水量1000～1900毫米。

旅遊資源

浙江有著悠久的歷史，燦爛的文化。獨特的自然風光、歷史遺蹟、文化遺產和豐富的旅遊資源吸引著無數國內外遊客來到浙江。浙江享有「魚米之鄉」、「絲綢之鄉」、「茶葉之鄉」、「歷史文化名城」、「最佳旅遊目的地」等多項美譽。浙江省擁有16個國家級風景名勝區，其中著名的有杭州西湖、千島湖、普陀山；37個省級風景名勝區，包括東錢湖、南北湖。3A級國家旅遊區有38個，包括杭州宋城、紹興柯岩。浙江省有73　處國家歷史文物保護單位，279處省級歷史文物保護單位，78個國家和省級森林公園，8個國家自然保護區和8　　個省級自然保護區。除此之外，浙江省有5　個國家歷史文化名城，12個省級歷史文化名城，16個中國優秀旅遊城市。浙江省還擁有4　個有關茶葉、絲綢、南宋官窯和中藥的國家博物館。「詩畫江南，山水浙江」是浙江的旅遊形象口號，這一口號全面展示了浙江省獨一無二的旅遊特色，整合了浙江自然和人文旅遊資源，把眾多的歷史人物、豐富的文化遺產、優美的自然風光融於一體，帶給大家一個無限驚喜的浙江！

風味美食

浙菜以杭州菜、紹興菜、寧波菜為主。東坡肉、西湖醋魚是浙菜的典型代表，名揚中外。浙江的風味小吃品種極多，吳山酥油餅、金華火腿久負盛名。

地方文藝

浙江地方戲劇豐富多彩，百花齊放。代表劇種有越劇、崑曲、紹劇、婺劇和木偶戲。其中越劇以其精緻清新的藝術表現形式贏得極高的藝術地位，是中國戲劇的傑出代表之一。

地方特產

浙江地方特產有浙江絲綢、西湖龍井、昌化雞血石、晴田葉蠟石。浙江名果有溫州蜜橘、奉化水蜜桃、塘棲枇杷等。著名手工藝品有杭州織錦、西湖扇子、綢傘、青田石刻、黃陽木雕等。

主要推薦景點

杭州西湖以其優美宜人的風景、豐富多彩的歷史文化遺蹟和久負盛名的地方特產享譽海內外。千島湖則是一個綠意盎然的神奇之地。嘉興西塘古鎮已有千年歷史。海天佛國——普陀山為中國四大佛教聖地之一。除此之外，靈隱寺、杭州宋城、中國茶博物館、岳飛廟、南太湖、南潯古鎮、雙龍洞、橫店影視城、奉化溪口雪竇山、雁蕩山、楠溪江等，都值得一去。

主要旅遊城市

杭州、寧波、紹興是中國首批「優秀旅遊城市」。

Hangzhou City （杭州之旅）

Ladies and Gentlemen,

Before you visit Hangzhou, you might have heard of the saying "In the sky, the best is heaven; on the earth, the best are Suzhou and Hangzhou." It means Hangzhou and Suzhou are as beautiful as Heaven. Why has Hangzhou been described as heaven on the earth? Follow me, you will find the answer.

Hangzhou is situated along the southeastern coast of China, on the lower reaches of Qiantang River, a famous national tourist city with a rich culture and long history. It is the capital city of Zhejiang Province and is also the Southern Yangtze Delta's political and cultural center, as well as its economic hub.

Hangzhou is one of the cradles for Chinese civilization. The city was founded 2,200 years ago during the Qin Dynasty and one of the seven ancient capitals of China. But the city wall was not constructed until Sui Dynasty(591 A.D.). It was the capital of the Wu Yue Kingdom for more than 200 years, during the Five Dynasties and Ten Kingdoms Period.

The oldest Buddhist temple in the city is believed to be Lingyin Si. Like most of the other landmarks in this city, it has gone through numerous cycles of destruction and reconstruction. The contemporary building was finished in 1910.

Hangzhou was the capital and political, economic and cultural center of the Southern Song Dynasty with a population of over 1. 5 million. During that period, the city was the gravity center of Chinese civilization as what used to be considered the "Central China" in the north was controlled by the Jin ethnic minority. Numerous

華東地區

philosophers, politi-cians, and writers, including some of the most celebrated poets in Chinese history such as Su Shi, Lu You, and Xin Qiji came here to live and die.

West Lake is an artificial, not natural lake, and is largely surrounded by mountains. In 1089, Su Shi constructed a 2. 8-kilometer-long dike across the lake, which Qing Emperor Qianlong considered particularly attractive in the early morning of the spring time. Yue-Wang Miao near the West Lake was originally constructed in 1221 in memory of General Yue Fei, who lost his life during the fight against Jin.

The city used to be a port until the middle Ming Dynasty when its harbor was slowly silted up by sediments. It is still the southern most port on the Grand Canal.

The temperature of Hangzhou is pleasant. It enjoys distinct seasons, mild and humid weather with the annual average temperature of 16. 2°C, over 230 frost-free days every year, and an average annual precipitation of 1, 321 millimeters. Its northwest and southwest areas belong to the Zhongshan highland of Zhejiang Province. The highland's highest point, Qingliang Peak, is 1787 meters high and is located along the boarder between Zhejiang and Anhui Province. Its northeast and southeast areas are on the North Zhejiang Plain with rivers densely distributed.

Hangzhou boasts a highly developed economy. It is always ranked second among all provincial capitals and in the top ten among all Chinese big-middle cities in China with respect to level of economic development. Hangzhou's industries have traditionally been textiles, silk and machinery, but electronics and other light industries are developing, especially since the start of the 1992 economic opening policy. Tea is produced on the outskirts of town at Longjing(Dragon's Well). It is the only remaining place where tea is still baked by hand and this tea is said to be the best green tea in China.

As a famous scenic city in China, Hangzhou attracts more than 20 million domestic and foreign tourists every year. As the famous Italian traveler Marco Polo described "the finest and most splendid city in the world". Hangzhou is waiting for you!

Ladies and gentlemen, I hope thc Hangzhou city has left you a wonderful impression. Thank you. Goodbye and good luck!

各位遊客朋友們：

來杭州之前，您一定聽説過「上有天堂，下有蘇杭」這句名言吧？它的意思就是説蘇州和杭州就像天堂一樣美麗。為什麼人們把杭州描述得像天堂一樣美呢？跟我一起來，大家就能找到答案了。

杭州坐落在中國東南海岸線上，位於錢塘江下游，是一座有著悠久歷史和深厚文化底蘊的歷史文化名城。杭州是浙江省的省會，同時也是長江三角洲地區的政治、經濟和文化中心之一。

杭州是中華文明的搖籃之一，早在2200　年前的秦朝就有杭州城。杭州是中國七大古都之一，但是其城牆直到隋朝（公元591　年）才建造起來。五代十國時，杭州曾作為吳越國的都城長達 200餘年。

杭州城裡最古老的寺廟當屬靈隱寺了，像其他眾多城市的標誌性建築一樣，靈隱寺也經歷了無數次的被毀和重修，目前我們所能看到的靈隱寺是1910年重建的。

早在南宋時期，杭州作為其都城，人口就已經達到150萬，是南宋政治、經濟、文化的中心。因為當時北方中原被少數民族政權——金朝所統治，杭州理所當然成為中華文明的中心。中國歷史上許多文人政客都曾在這裡留下過生活的足跡，其中有我們大家所熟悉的著名詩人蘇軾、陸游、辛棄疾。

杭州西湖是一個群山環抱的人工湖。1089年，蘇軾在西湖上修建了一條長2.8公里的大堤，清朝的乾隆皇帝認為其在春天的清晨最具有吸引力，「蘇堤春曉」便由此而來。接近西湖的岳王廟是1221年為紀念抗金將領岳飛而修建的。

杭州歷史上曾是一個繁忙的港口城市，直到明朝中葉，杭州灣慢慢地被一些沉積物給填積。現在它仍然是京杭大運河南部的一個重要港口城市。

杭州的氣候舒適宜人，四季分明、天氣溫和、空氣濕潤，全年的平均氣溫為16.2℃，無霜凍期超過230天，年均降水量1321毫米。其西北和西南地區屬於浙江省的高原地區，地處浙江和安徽之間的清涼山頂為最高點，海拔有1787　多米。東北和東南地區則屬於浙北平原河流分布密集區。

杭州的經濟發展水平很高，它的經濟實力連續幾年在省會城市中排名第二，經濟總體實力在中國的大中型城市中也名列前十。杭州的工業以傳統的紡織業、絲綢、機械製造業等為主，自從1992　年開放型經濟大門打開以來，杭州的電子和其他輕工業正處於飛速發展中。杭州茶葉的生產製作仍主要以市郊的龍井地區為主，這是唯一一個保留著傳統手工烤茶的茶葉生產基地，龍井茶製作工藝非常的精細考究，不愧是全中國最好的綠茶。

作為中國著名的旅遊城市，杭州每年吸引著200多萬人次國內外遊客。正如著名的義大利旅行家馬可波羅所説，杭州是「世界上最精彩的城市」。杭州等著你！

希望杭州的旅行能給大家留下美好的印象，謝謝大家！

West Lake （西湖）

Ladies and Gentlemen,

You might have heard that the famous Italian traveler Marco Polo was so impressed by the beauty of Hangzhou that he described it as "the most fascinating city in the world, where one feels as if he was in paradise". There is a similar saying in Chinese, which goes, "As there is paradise in heaven, so there are Suzhou and Hangzhou on earth". Hangzhou is famous primarily for its picturesque West Lake. Since the lake is beautiful all the year round, Su Dongpo, a celebrated poet of the Song Dynasty, compared it to a beauty "who is equally becoming, whether in light or heavy makeup". The Hangzhou residents, however, comment on the lake in their own words, "the west lake looks more delightful on rainy days than on clear days, and it is at its best during the night."

My friends, now I'm going to take you to visit the West Lake from Yuemiao port. Before we start sailing, I would like to give a brief introduction to the West Lake. West Lake is situated in the west of Hangzhou City with mountains surrounding on three sides. The lake is about 15 kilometers in circumference, it is 3.2 kilometers from north to south, and 2.8 kilometers from west to east, and covers a water area of 5.68 square kilometers. It is 1.55 meters in average depth. The deepest place measures 2.8 meters. The shallowest part is around 1 meter. The quantities of its water are around 8.5 million to 8.7 million cubic meters. The Su Dyke and Bai Dyke separate the lake into several small lakes, such as the Outer Lake, the North Li, West Li, Yue and Little South Lakes. West Lake has lots of beautiful scenic spots. In ancient time it was once known for its best ten famous sights：Spring Dawn at Su Dyke（蘇堤春曉）, Lotus Stirred by Breeze in Quyuan Garden（曲院風荷）, Autumn Moon Over the Calm Lake（平湖秋月）, Melting Snow Scene on the Broken Bridge（斷橋殘雪）, Viewing Fish at Flower Pond（花港觀魚）, Evening Bell Ringing at Nanping Hill（南屏晚鐘）, Double Peaks Kissing the Sky（雙峰插雲）, Leifeng Pagoda Silhouette against the Sunset（雷峰夕照）, Three Pools Mirroring the Moon（三潭印月）, and Orioles Singing in the Willows（柳浪聞鶯）. Within the 60-square-kilometer area centered around West Lake, there are more than 40 scenic spots and more than 30 protected sites of historical value. On November 8th, 1982, West Lake was listed among the first key scenic resorts. In 1985, the West Lake took the third place during the national competition among beautiful scenic resorts.

The West Lake is rich in beautiful legends. Once upon a time, there lived an immortal boy and an immortal girl in the heaven. The boy was named Yu Long (Jade

華東地區

Dragon) and the girl, Jin Feng(Gold Phoenix). They found a white jade on the island by the Milky Way. They polished the jade for many years until the jade changed into a shining pearl. Wherever it shined, the trees turned green and the flowers bloomed. Later the news was spread in the heaven, and the Queen Mother sent soldiers to rob them of the pearl. Yu Long and Jin Feng fought with Queen Mother and the pearl fell down from the hand of the Queen Mother to earth and became the West Lake. Yu Long and Jin Feng were punished and changed to two mountains, Yulong Mountain and Fenghuang Mountain. They therefore have been here protecting the West Lake from time immemorial.

The water of the lake is clear. Just now, someone asks why it is so clear? I will give you the answer from the very beginning of story about the Lake. Some 12,000 years ago, the lake was a shallow bay connecting the Qiantang River. Wu and Baoshi (Precious Stone) mountains were located to the north and south and formed the capes of the bay. Later the mud and stone brought by the tide piled up and separated the bay and the Qiantang River. The original lake was formed during the Western Han Dynasty. and it grew into its present size during the Sui Dynasty. After five large-scale construction efforts led by Bai Juyi, Qian Liu, Su Dongpo, Yang Mengying and Ruan Yuan, it was finally transformed from a natural lake into a beautiful half-closed lake.

Historically West Lake had different names in different dynasties. In the Han Dynasty it was called Wulin Water, and Golden Ox and Mingsheng Lakes. Shihan and Qiantang Lakes and some other names were used during the Tang Dynasty. In the Northern Song Dynasty, the governor of Hangzhou, Su Dongpo, wrote a poem to describe the beauty of the West Lake. He compared it to Xi Shi, one of the four most famous ancient beauties in Chinese history. So the West Lake has another name "Xizi Lake".

As a famous tourism resort, West Lake has been a favorite spot for many well-known and influential people to visit. The late Chairman Mao made 40 trips here and once for seven months. Mao always praised the lake and considered it as his second home. According to the people who had worked with him, Chairman Mao thought that one of Su Dongpo's poems called "Drinking on the lake with sun and then rain" best described West Lake's beauty. Chairman Mao had written a lot of poems but none of them about the lake. The lake was loved not only by Chinese great persons but also by China's foreign friends such as the American ex-president, Richard Nixon, who visited here twice. He said that Beijing is the capital of China, but Hangzhou is the heart of China, and promised to return. He also brought to Hangzhou a redwood tree as a gift from his home state of California.

Now we are moving from west to east. The scene here is called Gu Hill. It is connected to the Xileng Bridge over to its west and the Bai Embankment on its east. It is 35 meters high and covers 200 thousand square meters. It has been popular since the Tang and Song dynasties; indeed, during the Qing Dynasty Emperor Kangxi took this place as his interim palace. You may ask that if Gu Hill is the biggest island in the lake, then why is it called Gu Hill(Lone Hill)? Well, due to its beauty, the emperors of different dynasties reserved this place solely for them. So it is called Gu Hill(Lone Hill). The Hill was formed by the explosion of a volcano and is really a peninsula. So the local interesting saying goes like this, "the Lone Mountain is not lonely, the Broken Bridge is not broken and the Long Bridge is not long. "

Please look ahead and you will see West Lake's truly fantastic sights. The Xileng Bridge is located to the west of the Gu Hill. The Xileng Bridge, together with the Broken Bridge and the Long Bridge, are bridges of love.

Passing by the Xileng Bridge we will see a white marble statue of a lady in the back of the Gu Hill. You see, her left hand is in the waist and a sword in her right hand. Her eyes are staring ahead. Who is she? She is Ms.Qiu Jin, the great women liberation pioneer, who has lost life in activities against the Qing Dynasty. The statue is 2.7 meters tall and its base is 2 meters tall. In front of the stele, there are four Chinese characters which mean "heroine" written by Mr.Sun Yat-sen. West Lake has become known not only for beautiful sights, but also because of tombs of many national heroes, both ancient ones like Yue Fei, Yu Qian and Zhang Cangshui, as well as contemporary revolutionaries like Ms.Qiu Jin, Xu Xilin, and Tao Chengzhang. Their noble deeds and spirits will always encourage later generations.

We are heading slowly to the east. Now you can see the white wall and the famous Xileng Press is located inside this wall. On the right of the press, stands a building that combines Chinese and the Western architectural styles. It is the restaurant called Louwailou and its name is taken from a poem. It was built in 1848 and many famous people such as Sun Yat-sen and Lu Xun dined there. In 1952 this restaurant started to receive foreigners such as the Prince of Cambodia. Premier Zhou dined here with state guests on nine separate occasions. The restaurant's most famous dish is West Lake vinegar fish and it uses West Lake's grass carp. The fish must be left in the clear fresh water for about two days before cooking to eliminate its muddy smell. The well-done fish is tender and delicious and tastes somewhat like crab; it is Hangzhou's signature dish.

Now our boat is heading to Zhongshan Park. We can see the front gate of Gu Hill. Gu Hill is not only known for its beautiful landscape but also for its rich historical heritage. Beside the Zhongshan Park, we can see lots of new buildings. They are the Zhejiang Province Museum and it houses more than 1,700 Hemudu cultural relics, which date back 7,000 years. The ancient building at the back of the museum is the Wenlan Pavilion which was the Qing Dynasty's imperial library. It is one of the seven famous libraries built for storing "The Si Ku Quan Shu" (Complete Library in the Four Branches of Literature).

There is a double-eaved pavilion called the "Ping Hu Qiu Yue" by the lake. It is built during Qing Emperor Kangxi's reign. This place marks the start of the Bai Dike and also is one of the three famous places where you can enjoy the sight of the moon in Hangzhou. Throughout history Hangzhou people could go to one of the three isles, the lake embankment or Phoenix Mountain to enjoy the moon.

Now here is the Bai Dyke. Both sides of the dyke are lined with different trees. Especially during the spring, when the dyke is green and red all over, tourists may have the feeling of being in a fairyland. The Bai Dyke's original name is Bai Sha Dyke and its popularity dates back more than 1,000 years ago to the Tang Dynasty. However, this dyke was not the one Bai Juyi had ordered to be built. People called it Bai Dyke just to memorialize him. The Su Dyke was built by Su Dongpo, and it and the Bai Dyke are like two satin belts in the lake. In the middle of the Bai Dyke, there is a bridge called Shigong Bridge whose original name is Wooden Bridge or Hanbi Bridge. At the end of the Bai Dyke is the ring bridge. It is the famous Duanqiao Bridge, also known as the "Broken Bridge." The one kilometre long Bai Dyke ends at the Duanqiao Bridge.

Duanqiao Bridge, literally "Broken Bridge", was so named in Tang Dynasty. In the Song Dynasty, it was called Baoyou Bridge, while in the Yuan Dynasty, it was called Duanjia Bridge. It was an old stone arch bridge covered with bryophyte. Despite being just a common stone arch in appearance, it is West Lake's most famous bridge because it is connected with the love story of the White Snake.

You may ask a question that why it is called Broken Bridge since it is not broken. Let me explain it to you. The bridge is facing the mountain and has the city behind it. It also is the connecting point between the North Li Lake and the Outer Lake. It is the best place to enjoy snow in winter. When the sun comes out after snowing the snow on the south side will melt while the other side is still covered with snow. Looked at from afar, the bridge is like a broken bridge. Besides, the bridge is the end of the Bai Dyke. In Chinese "duan" also means "ending". Now you've got why the bridge is so named.

Ladies and gentlemen, please look at the mountain behind the Broken Bridge, it is Baoshi(Precious Stone) Mountain. The Baoshi Mountain is 78 meters high. Precious

華東地區

stones can be actually found in this mountain. Some stones are like diamonds shining under the sunlight. That is why the mountain is called Baoshi(Precious Stone) Mountain. There is a tower on the top of the mountain and its name is Baoshu Tower. This tower was built in the North Song Dynasty and was rebuilt in 1933. It is 45.3 meters tall and made from bricks. It is the most beautiful tower in Hangzhou and its surrounding areas and is often compared to a beautiful girl. Another tower named Leifeng used to be located to its south. People used to liken Leifeng to an old monk while saying that Baoshu resembled a beautiful young girl. They have different styles resulting in different charMs.But unfortunately the Leifeng Tower collapsed long ago.

So much for the lakeside scenery, now lets go to the three isles on the lake.

First, we will visit the biggest island on the lake—Santanyinyue. It is also called Xiaoyingzhou. It is actually a park on the lake. Other islands are spread around it. It covers an area of 70 thousand square meters and 60% of this area is water. The isle is shaped like a square. The island is surrounded by many flowers, including water lilies and small lotuses. One of these flowers, West Lakes water shield, has become known for being rich in protein, vitamin C and ferrous element. It can be eaten fresh with sugar. West Lakes water shield soup is also famous.

The Huxin Pavilion is located in the middle of the lake and it is West Lake's biggest pavilion. Finished in 1552, it is also the earliest island built in West Lake and has a history of over 440 years. Emperor Qianlong once came here and praised it for its boundless beauty.

In the northwest of the Huxin Pavilion, there is a small island called Ruangongdun. It is the lake's smallest island and covers just 5, 561 square meters. It was built in 1800. Ruan Yuan, the official of Zhejiang Province in the Qing Dynasty directed its construction. It was created when people moved mud to the location from a flood protection project. It is a good place to go fishing and walk about at night, when the West Lake is even more beautiful.

After visiting the three isles, we are heading for the Su Dyke. It is across the lake from the north to the south and it is 2.8 kilometers long. There are 6 stone arch bridges in the dyke. The Su Dyke always reminds us of Su Dongpo, a very well known poet and scholar in the Song Dynasty. He had made great contribution to the local people through his great efforts to control West Lake. The Su Dyke was built under his leadership when he was the local official. The Su Dongpo Memorial Museum was built in order to commemorate him. People always describe the West Lake and Switzerland's Lake Geneva as the twin pearls of the east and west.

The West Lake is the famous scene which has been visited by many presidents from different countries. Mr.Sun Yat-sen said that West Lake's scenery was unique in the world. No other lakes could be compared with it. The lake in Geneva is too big to have a full view while the West Lake is neither too big nor too small. So the West Lake is the pearl of Hangzhou, the pearl of the East and the pearl of the world.

Well, everyone, so much for our tour today. I hope you will enjoy yourselves very much! Goodbye!

遊客朋友們，大家好！

大家可能聽說過義大利著名的旅行家馬可波羅，他曾經被西湖的美景深深地打動，他說：「這是世界上最迷人的城市，就好像置身於天堂一般。」中國也流傳著一句同樣的話，「上有天堂，下有蘇杭」，而杭州最具吸引力的景點就是風景如畫的西湖了。西湖四季如春，宋朝著名的詩人蘇東坡曾把西湖比作美人，稱讚她：「淡妝濃抹總相宜」。杭州本地的居民用自己的語言描述它：「西湖的雨天比晴天美，而最美的時候是在晚上」。

朋友們，下面就隨我一起從岳廟碼頭乘船去遊覽西湖。在船啟動之前，我先來介紹一下西湖的概況：西湖位於杭州城西，三面環山，東面瀕臨市區，南北長約3.2

公里，東西寬約2.8公里，繞湖一週近15公里。湖面約5.68　平方公里，包括湖中島嶼為6.3平方公里，平均水深1.55　米，最深處在2.8　米左右，最淺處不足1米，蓄水量在850萬～870萬立方米之間。蘇堤和白堤將湖面分成外湖、北里湖、西里湖、岳湖和小南湖5　個部分。西湖處處有勝景，歷史上除有「錢塘十景」、「西湖十八景」之外，最著名的是「西湖十景」：蘇堤春曉、曲院風荷、平湖秋月、斷橋殘雪、花港觀魚、南屏晚鐘、雙峰插雲、雷峰夕照、三潭印月、柳浪聞鶯。「春夏秋冬花，晚雲夕月柳」，道出了無論春夏秋冬，無論明晦晨昏，西湖勝景時時處處都有特色。在以西湖為中心的60平方公里的園林風景區內，分布著主要風景名勝有40多處，重點文物古蹟有30　多處。概括起來西湖風景主要以一湖、二峰、三泉、四寺、五山、六園、七洞、八墓、九溪、十景為勝。1982年11月8日，中國國務院將西湖列為第一批國家重點風景名勝之一。1985年，在「中國十大風景名勝」評選中，西湖被評為第三。

西湖這麼美，當然孕育著許多奇妙動人的傳說。相傳在很久以前，天上有玉龍和金鳳在銀河邊的仙島上找到了一塊白玉，他們一起打磨了很多年，白玉就變成了一顆光芒四射的明珠，這顆寶珠的珠光照到哪裡，哪裡的樹木就常青，百花就盛開。後來消息傳到天宮，王母娘娘就派天兵天將前來把明珠搶走。玉龍和金鳳趕去索珠，遭到王母拒絕。於是他們就開始你爭我奪地搶起明珠來。後來，王母被掀翻在地，她兩手一鬆，明珠就掉落到了人間，變成了晶瑩清澈的西湖，玉龍和金鳳也隨之降落，變成了玉龍山（玉皇山）和鳳凰山，永遠守護在西湖之濱。

剛才有的朋友問西湖的水為什麼這樣清澈純淨？這就要從西湖的成因講起。西湖在1.2　萬年以前還是與錢塘江相通的淺海灣，聳峙在西湖南北的吳山和寶石山，是環抱這個海灣的兩個岬角。後來由於潮水的衝擊導致泥沙淤塞，把海灣和錢塘江分隔開來。到了西漢時期西湖的湖形已基本固定，西湖真正固定下來是在隋朝，地質學上把這種由淺海灣演變而成的湖泊叫潟湖。此後西湖承受山泉活水的沖刷，再經歷過由白居易、蘇東坡、楊孟瑛、阮元等發動的五次大規模的人工疏濬治理，終於從一個自然湖泊變成為風光秀麗的半封閉的淺水風景湖泊。

歷史上西湖有很多名稱。漢朝時稱為武林水、金牛湖、明聖湖；唐朝時稱石函湖、錢塘湖。此外還有高士湖、賢者湖、上湖、龍川、錢源等稱呼。蘇東坡做杭州地方官時，寫了一首讚美西湖的詩：「水光瀲灩晴方好，山色空濛雨亦奇，欲把西湖比西子，淡妝濃抹總相宜。」詩人別出心裁的把西湖比作中國古代美女西施，於是，西湖又多了個「西子湖」的雅稱。

許多中外名人對西湖情有獨鍾。毛澤東一生中共40次來杭州，最長的一次整整住了7個月之久，他把杭州當做「第二個家」。毛澤東常常稱讚西湖秀美，但他生前從未正式發表過描寫西湖的詩詞。中國偉人喜歡西湖，國際友人對西湖更是流連忘返。美國前總統尼克森兩次來杭州，他讚歎道：「北京是中國的首都，而杭州是這個國家的心臟，我還要再來。」尼克森還把家鄉加州出產的紅杉樹送給了杭州。

我們的船已緩緩啟動了。現在船正在自西向東行駛，各位看到的是孤山一帶的景色。孤山西接西泠橋，東連白堤，景色唐宋年間就已聞名，南宋理宗曾在此興建規模宏大的西太乙宮，把大半座孤山劃為御花園。清朝康熙皇帝又在此建造行宮，雍正皇帝改行宮為聖因寺，與當時的靈隱寺、淨慈寺、照慶寺並稱「西湖四大叢林」。或許有的朋友要問：孤山既是西湖中最大的島嶼，為什麼要取名「孤山」呢？這是因為歷史上此山風景特別優美，一直被稱為孤家寡人的皇帝所占有，所以被稱為「孤山」。從地質學上講，孤山是由火山噴出的流紋岩組成的，整個島是和陸地連在一起的，所以「孤山不孤，斷橋不斷，長橋不長」被稱為西湖三絕。

大家再看前方那座環洞石拱橋，地處孤山西面，名叫西泠橋。它和斷橋、長橋並稱為西湖古代的三大情橋。

過了西泠橋，孤山後麓的綠樹叢中有尊漢白玉塑像，只見這位女英雄左手叉腰，右手按劍，目光炯炯，昂首注視前方，似在探求著革命的真理。她是誰呢？她就是中國婦女解放運動的先驅，為推翻清王朝，爭取民族獨立而壯烈犧牲的「鑑湖女俠」秋瑾。這尊塑像高2.7米，墓座高2米，正面碑石上刻有孫中山手書「巾幗英雄」4個大字。秋瑾烈士的塑像，給了我們一種啟示：西湖的聞名，不僅僅是占了山水之勝，它更因眾多的歷史人物而倍增光彩。在西湖風景區內，被譽為「湖上三傑」的岳飛、于謙、張蒼水，還有與秋瑾一起為振興中華而獻身的近代民主革命先烈徐錫麟、陶成章等，都安葬在西子湖畔。

我們的船繼續徐徐往東行駛，各位看到前面的一道粉牆，那裡便是著名的西泠印社。印社右側那幢中西合璧的建築，就是百年老店樓外樓。樓外樓創建於1848年，店名取自南宋詩人林升「山外青山樓外樓」名句。樓外樓得天時、地利、人和之便，曾經接待過許多中外名人。樓外樓的當家名菜自然要數西湖醋魚了，它是選用西湖中在規定範圍內養殖的草魚，先在清水中餓一兩天，除去泥土味，然後烹製而成的。成菜後的西湖醋魚色澤紅亮，肉質鮮嫩，酸甜可口，略帶蟹味，是杭州最有代表性的風味名菜。

現在船已駛向中山公園，孤山的正門就在這裡。「山不在高，有仙則名」，孤山既是一座風景名山，又是一座文化名山。孤山的地位在西湖景區中之所以這麼重要，是因為它蘊藏著豐富的歷史、文化內涵，景區內有著名的「西湖天下景」，這些景點等上岸後我們將前往參觀。

中山公園旁的這一組建築是「浙江省博物館」，裡面陳列著上至7000　年前的河姆渡文化，下到近現代的文物展品1700餘件。博物館後面的古建築是清代的皇家藏書樓文瀾閣，它是中國為珍藏《四庫全書》而修建的七大書閣之一。

請看前面那座凸出湖面的水泥平台的重檐亭子，這座建於清代康熙年間的建築，名叫平湖秋月。它是白堤的起點，也是杭州的三大賞月勝地之一。歷史上杭州人中秋賞月有三大去處：湖中首推三島之一的三潭印月，山上應是鳳凰山坡的月岩景點，至於岸邊，就數這月白風清、水天共碧的平湖秋月了！

現在各位看到前面這條「間株楊柳間株桃」的遊覽長堤就是白堤。當我們的船駛到這裡，西湖最秀麗的風光就呈現在大家面前了。瞧！堤上兩邊各有一行楊柳、碧桃，特別是在春天，柳枝泛綠、桃樹嫣紅，一片桃紅柳綠的景色，遊人到此如臨仙境。白堤原名「白沙堤」，早在1000多年前的唐朝，就以風光旖旎而著稱。它雖與白居易主持修築的白堤不在一個方位，但杭州人民為緬懷這位對杭州作出傑出貢獻的「老市長」，仍把它命名為白堤。它與蘇東坡主持建造的蘇堤猶如湖中的兩條錦帶，絢麗多姿，交相輝映。大家再看，白堤中間的這座橋叫錦帶橋，以前是座木橋，名為「涵碧橋」，如今更名為石拱橋。

在白堤的盡頭便是斷橋，全長1公里的白堤就由此而「斷」。斷橋的名字最早取於唐代，宋代稱寶祐橋，元代又叫段家知，以前是座苔蘚斑斑的古老石橋。我們現在看到的這座橋雖然是座很普通的石拱橋，但它的名字卻和《白蛇傳》的故事聯繫在一起，因而成了西湖中最出名的一座橋。

講到這裡，我看到有的朋友已經在仔細觀察，或許你們馬上會問：這座橋根本沒有斷，為什麼要取名「斷橋」呢？這個問題就讓我來解答吧。斷橋是著名的西湖十景之一，所處的位置背城面山，處於北里湖和外湖的分水點，視野開闊，是冬天觀賞西湖雪景最好的地方。每當瑞雪初晴，橋的陽面已經冰消雪化，而橋的陰面卻還是白雪皚皚，遠遠望去，橋身似斷非斷，「斷橋殘雪」就因此得名。還有，斷橋又是白堤的終點，從平湖秋月而來的白堤到此中斷。講到這裡，或許大家已經明白，原來是「堤斷橋不斷」。

大家再看斷橋後面那座山叫寶石山，海拔78米。這座山的岩石和西湖群山不同，主要由流紋岩和凝灰岩構成，其中有一種名叫碧玉的「寶石」，嵌在紫灰石中，在陽光照射下，分外耀眼，這就是寶石山得名的由來。山上那座秀麗挺拔，高高聳立的塔，就是保俶塔。保俶塔初建為九級舍利塔，現在的塔是1933　年重建的。它是用磚砌成的實心建築，塔身呈八菱型，高45.3米，上下匀稱，線條柔和優美，在湖上諸塔中，保俶塔的造型最為俏麗，體態最為窈窕。歷史上與保俶塔相對應的還有一座雷峰塔，在西湖風景布局中，同位於一條中軸線上，一南一北，隔湖相望，一個敦厚典雅，一個纖細俊俏。在雷峰塔未倒塌前，西湖上曾呈現出「南北相對峙，一湖映雙塔」的對景，所以民間有「雷峰如老衲，保俶如美人」的說法，道出了當年雷峰塔和保俶塔的不同風姿。

各位朋友，西湖沿岸的景觀就介紹到這裡，接著我們去觀賞湖中三島。首先我們來看西湖中最大的島「三潭印月」，也叫小瀛洲。這是一個「湖中有島，島中有湖」的湖上花園。全島面積7　萬平方米，其中水面占60%。全島呈「田」字形，東

華東地區

西連柳堤，南北建曲橋，曲橋兩側種植著大片紅、白各色的睡蓮。此外，歷史上三潭印月還以種植西湖蓴菜而著名。

接著我們再來看湖中那座飛檐翹角的亭，它名叫湖心亭，是西湖中最大的一座亭，也是在西湖三島中最早營建的一座島，初建於明嘉靖三十一年（公元1552年），距今已有440多年的歷史。「湖心平眺」是錢塘十景之一。站在湖心亭處眺望西湖，水光山色，盡收眼底，西湖風景，一覽無餘。

湖心亭西北的那個小島稱為阮公墩，是西湖三島中最小的一個，面積僅5561平方米。它是在清朝嘉慶年間（1800　年），浙江巡撫阮元用疏濬西湖後的淤泥堆積而成的。阮墩垂釣已成為杭州市民假日休閒的好去處，阮墩夜遊則是為各地旅遊者隆重推出的西湖夏季的一個特色旅遊項目。

遊完湖中三島，我們的船已駛向即將停靠的蘇堤。大家請看，前面這條自南而弱橫貫西湖，全長2.8公里的湖中長堤就是蘇堤。堤上共有6座石拱橋，分別是映波、鎖瀾、望山、壓堤、東浦、跨虹。堤岸種植桃柳、芙蓉，形成「西湖景緻六條橋，一枝楊柳一枝桃」的景色。說到蘇堤，人們自然會想起北宋詩人蘇東坡。蘇東坡曾兩次擔任杭州的地方官，他組織20萬民工疏濬西湖，築成了這條從南屏山下直通棲霞嶺麓的長堤，後人為了紀念他的功績，取名「蘇堤」。後來，堤的南端修建了「蘇東坡紀念館」供人們參觀，緬懷蘇東坡的功績。

各位朋友，西湖作為著名景點，接待過的世界各國元首不計其數。孫中山先生曾說西湖是世界上獨一無二的勝景，沒有任何其他的湖泊能與之媲美。瑞士日內瓦的萊蒙湖太大，看不到全景，而西湖正合適，不大也不小。因此，西湖不僅是杭州的明珠，更是東方的明珠，世界的明珠。

各位朋友，今天我們的行程就到這裡。希望西湖的山山水水永遠留給您美好的回憶！再見！

Qiandao Lake （千島湖）

Ladies and Gentlemen,

Good morning! Welcome to Qiandao Lake!

Qiandao Lake, located in Chun'an County, the west of Hangzhou, Zhejiang Province, is one of China's first-class national scenic spots and is currently its largest national forest park. The lake covers 570 square kilometers and has over a thousand differently sized islands. Besides the surrounding green hills and large numbers of animals and plants, it is also famous for its water. The average depth of the water here is more than one hundred feet and the visibility in the water is twenty two to twenty nine feet. This national first-class water is pure enough to be drunk directly from the lake.

In recent years Qiandao Lake has developed over twenty travel sites, having different features.

Meifeng Mountain

Now we are in the Meifeng Mountain. Set in the middle of the lake, this is the best part of Qiandao Lake and is named after five conjoined mountains. It resembles a plat blossom and is famed for its beautiful natural scenery and perfect environment. The sight-seeing platform in this section is by far the best place to view the surrounding area. The other one is Ostrich Island. On this island visitors can feed ostriches, take photos of them, and even ride on their backs.

Stone Forest

Now we can see the Stone Forest. This section is made up of three parts, the Xishan, Turquoise, and Hawksbill sections, covering 10 square kilometers. It is called "the first stone-forest in East China". With strange stones, cliffs, elf caves and an ancient path, it embodies both calm and beauty.

華東地區

195

Dragon Hill(Long Shan)

Then we are going to the Dragon Hill. It consists of Dragon Hill and Five-Dragon Island. The Hairui Temple was built here by the local people to commemorate Hairui, a famous official of the Qing Dynasty, who once served as head of this county. Hairui Memorial Temple is the essential structural work piece and includes wood, stone, and brick carvings. There is also over twenty pieces of poem steles in Hairui Memorial Temple. A bell tower stands on top of the Dragon Hill.

Xian Hill(Xian Shan)

Xian Hill lies in the southeast area of the lake and includes Xian Hill, Tian Chi(a pond）, Guihua Island(Guihua Dao), and Mi Hill(Mi Shan). Xian Hill has trees which bear fruit all year round. The scenery on other parts of the hill is also charming and beautiful.

Animal-Series

Animal-Series section is mainly made up of three areas: Monkey Island, which has over five hundred monkeys including Honghe monkey, Sichuan short-tail monkey, and red-face monkey;Peacock Garden, where white, blue, green and variegated peacocks are raised; and Magic Dragon Island, which actually is an island of snakes, where visitors can play with them and watch special shows.

Qiandao Lake is located in the center of tour route of "Hangzhou-Qiandao Lake-Huangshan", so it is very convenient to get there. Now there are more than thirty hotels providing over seventy-five hundred beds. What interests some people the most is the food here—the forest here produces large amount of edible plants and fresh water fish is also abundant.

Qiandao Lake is also a place of historic interest. This is the hometown of Sun

Quan, the King of Wu, during the Three Kingdoms Period. It is the ancient town of Fuyang Longmen, where Sun Quan's descendants have continually gathered up through the present day. It is reported recently that he descendants of Liu Bei, the king of Shu during Three Kingdoms Period were also found in Fuyang. Now the descendants of Sun Quan, Liu Bei, and Zhu Geliang are all in Fuyang.

Qiandao Lake is not only a place of beauty but also of historic interest. Welcome to come here again.

各位朋友早上好！歡迎來到千島湖遊覽觀光！千島湖位於浙江省淳安縣境內，毗鄰杭州市西，是國家首批公布的風景名勝區之一，也是目前國內最大的國家級森林公園。湖面約570 平方公里，內有大小島嶼1000 多個。千島湖平均水深度超過30 米，在水中能見度約6.6 ～9米，作為中國一流的純淨水，它可以直接飲用。近年來，千島湖上已經開發了20 多個旅遊景區，特色各異。

梅峰景區

現在我們所在的地方就是梅峰景區，它位於湖的中央，是千島湖最好的景區，以五座相連的島嶼而命名。它像一個茂盛的花園，以景色自然和環境優美而著稱。現在我們來到的觀景平台是迄今為止千島湖的最佳觀賞地點。另一邊是鴕鳥島，遊客可在這裡給鴕鳥餵飼料，拍照留念。

石林

現在大家可以看到石林。這個景區由三個部分組成：西山部分、黛玉部分和怪石部分，景區占地10平方公里。它被稱為「華東第一石林」。景區以「怪石、懸崖、古道、靈洞」為景觀內容，峰林造型奇特，古道深幽靜謐。

龍山

現在我們將前往龍山。它包括龍山和五龍島兩個部分，這裡有海瑞祠，是當地人為紀念清代著名的官員，曾擔任過縣官的海瑞而修建的。海瑞祠堪稱龍山島建築的精華所在，建築雕樑畫棟，有大量的木雕、石雕和磚雕，此外，還有20多塊海瑞親筆作詩的碑石。在龍山的最頂端矗立著一座鐘樓。

羨山

羨山位於千島湖東南湖區，包括天池、桂花島、蜜山島。羨山上的樹木四季常青，山上其他地方的風景同樣美麗迷人。

動物島群

動物島群主要有三個部分：猴島（餵養了500多隻猴子，包括紅河猴、四川短尾猴、紅面猴等）、孔雀園（有白的、藍的、綠的和其他混色的孔雀）和神龍島。這裡實際上是一個蛇島，遊客們可以和它們一起玩耍，並參觀專門的展覽。

千島湖地處「杭州—千島湖—黃山」旅遊線路的中心位置，交通非常便利。景區現有30 多家酒店，提供超過75100 個床位。遊客們對千島湖最感興趣的是這裡的美食——景區的森林裡有大量可食用的植物，大家還可以享用這裡獨特的淡水魚。

千島湖也是一個歷史文化名勝地，是三國時期東吳王孫權的故里，這裡的另一個城市，阜陽龍門古鎮是孫權子孫的聚居地。據報導，最近在阜陽還發現了三國時期蜀國劉備的後裔，現在孫權、劉備和諸葛亮的後裔都聚集在了阜陽。

千島湖不僅風景秀美，而且歷史悠久，歡迎大家下次還到千島湖來觀光遊覽！

Putuo Mountain （普陀山）

Ladies and Gentlemen,

Welcome to Putuo Mountain. It is my honor to be your tour guide, I'd like to take this opportunity to introduce myself to you all. [Introduce yourself to the guests.]

Putuo Mountain, one of the Four Holy Buddhist Mountains, covers an area of 12.5 square kilometers. Famous temples, monasteries, nunneries are located all over the mountain. The remaining ten ancient architec-ture complexes and historical sights were built during the Song, Yuan, Ming, and Qing dynasties. In its heyday Putuo Mountain once had 82 temples and 128 huts accommodating 4,000 monks and nuns. When you walk on the paths, you probably can come across monks in kasaya (the robe of a Buddhist monk). The glorious scenery, as well as the glamour concerned with Buddhism, makes it a sacred mountain.

Puji Temple

Now we are in front of the biggest temple on Putuo Mountain. It is the largest of its kind in Southeast China. Puji Temple was first built during the Tang Dynasty (618-907 A.D.). In the 3rdyear of the reign of Emperor Shenzong of the Song Dynasty (1080 A.D.) it was reconstructed, moved and given its present name, the Puji Temple. Repair of the temple began during the 38thyear of Qing Dynasty Kangxi Emperor's reign and this work was finished by the 9thyear of Emperor Yongzheng's reign (1731 A.D.). It was then also granted the horizontal inscribed boards, each of which had the words of "popular-saving masses of souls" and "popular-saving Buddhist temple" inscribed on them. According to legend, one day an emperor wanted to visit this temple. Because he came dressed as a normal peasant, a monk wouldn't let him in through the main door and instead let him in through the side door. Furiously, the emperor ordered that no one be allowed to enter that entrance. So now you have to enter it through a side door.

There are altogether over 200 structures, including Hall of Heavenly Kings, Hall of Yuantong, Building of Buddhist Scriptures, and Hall of Abbots. The 9 halls, 12 pavilions and 1612 houses cover an area of 14,000 square meters and makes the Puji Temple magnificent and grand in scale. The Hall of Yuantong is the main building in

華
東
地
區

Puji Temple, in which there is an 8. 8-meter-high bronze statue of Kwan-yin, the only representation of Kwan-yin constructed by native inhabitants living around. On both sides of the hall there are 32 statues of the reincarnation of Kwan-yin, as legend has it that Kwan-yin was infinitely powerful that she would grant any wish. In its main hall sits also a magnificent Buddha flanked by statues of the Eighteen Mythical Disciples. The temple can hold more than 1,000 people at the same time. In the early morning (4: 00 a.m.) you can accompany the monks in their chanting and worshipping of the goddess Kwan-yin.

Haiyin Pool

Look! The beautiful pool is named Haiyin Pool. Its literally meaning is Lotus Flower Pool because it used to be covered with lotus flowers. The Pool has been polluted and the flowers could no longer be seen. Nowadays it has been cleaned and there are already new plants growing which you can admire at the end of the summer. Haiyin Pool was built during Ming Dynasty.

It is also called the "setting-free pool", because Buddhist monks release turtles and fish in the pool. Tourists can buy little turtles and release them in the pool. The area around Haiyin Pool is a gathering place for tourists, Tai Chi practitioners, and souvenir vendors.

There are three stone bridges crossing the pool, the middle one for the emperor, the east one for nobles, and the west one for commoners. The bridge in the middle is flat and broad. In the north direction it leads to the central entrance of Puji Temple, and in the south it leads to Yubei Pavilion (Imperial Stele Pavilion). In the middle of the bridge stands a little octagonal pavilion. The bridge in the east is called Yong Shou Qiao (Bridge of Longevity) and was also built during the Ming Emperor Wanli's reign (1573-1620 A.D.). The bridge is 6 meters high, 33.3 meters long and 7.5 meters wide. Some 20 miniature lions standing, lying and sitting in different positions line both sides of the bridge. The bridge in the west is called Yao Chi Bridge.

Yubei Pavilion

This is Yubei Pavilion which means a pavilion with an imperial stele in it. It was built in 1734 during the Qing Emperor Yongzheng's reign. The square pavilion is 9 meters high, while the one to the side is 9.5 meters high. In the middle of the pavilion stands an imperial stele made in 1931 with a height of 5.2 meters, a depth of 0.32 meters, and a width of 1.32 meters. The top of the stele is decorated with Buddhist figures.

Multi-Treasure Pagoda

The Multi-Treasure Pagoda is a 5-story quadrangular pagoda completely made out of stones from Taihu Lake in Jiangsu Province. The pagoda is 18 meters high. The lower part is a huge platform encircled by stone balustrades. On the platform is the pedestal of the pagoda, also made of stone and surrounded by balustrades. The steeple is a box-shaped stupa, the four corners of which are in the shape of four banana leaves. The four sides of the pagoda have carved images of Buddha and niches. The platform below the pagoda also has carved images of Buddha, bodhisattvas and Buddhist devotees, demonstrating excellent craftsmanship.

The Multi-Treasure Pagoda is located on the east side of Haiyin Pool, southeast of Puji Temple. It was built under the supervision of the monk Yuzhong in 1333-1334 during the reign of the Yuan Dynasty's Yuantong Emperor. It was then rebuilt in 1592.

The Multi-Treasure Pagoda is regarded as a rare treasure among China's ancient pagodas because of its unique architecture form, exquisite carvings and excellent state of preservation. It is the only stone pagoda built during the Yuan Dynasty in Zhejiang Province. It is one of Putuo Mountain's three treasures.

華東地區

Fayu Temple

Now we are in the second largest temple on the island. This temple is famous for its ancient architecture, delicate wood carvings and calligraphy inscribed by ancient emperors. It is located on the left side of Baihua Hill's summit, close to 1,000-pace Beach. You can either walk up or take a cable there.

Its history reportedly goes back to 1580, during the Ming Dynasty. As the monk Da Chi prayed to Kwan-yin at the Cave of Tidal Sound, he envisioned that a large bamboo had washed ashore on the 1,000-pace Beach. Soon afterward, he built a hut on the beach and named it the "Sea Tide Nunnery" (Haichao Nunnery). Many faithful adherents helped the modest temple expand through the years. In 1699, Emperor Kangxi of the Qing Dynasty decreed that the deserted imperial palace in what is now Nanjing had to be moved to Putuo Mountain to enshrine Kwan-yin. The main hall was added and Emperor Kangxi bestowed a horizontal tablet inscribed with four characters of "Tian Hua Fa Yu" , which has been interpreted as meaning that Buddhist doctrines are like rain and flowers from heaven. Hence, the Fayu Temple got its name.

There are now 294 halls and rooms, occupying a floor space of 8,800 square meters. A miniature golden pagoda stands between the Nine-dragon wall and the first of the temple's several halls, where visitors can toss coins through windows for good luck. The main hall is called Jiulong Hall and was built during Qing Dynasty. The ceiling is concave and 9 dragons playing with pearls are craved into the middle of it.

Huiji Temple

As we can see, this temple is ideally located on the peak of the hill, commanding an excellent view of the rising sun in the morning. The temple, then third largest on the mountain, has four halls, seven palaces and six attics. Its halls are cleverly built in one line according to the geographical position. The Buddha Sakyamuni is worshipped only in Huiji Temple. Some 1,000 stones make a path down the hill from the front of the temple. You can also visit the temple using the cableway.

In the early days of the temple, it was just a pagoda made of stone. During Ming Dynasty it was made into a small temple. In 1793, during the Qing Emperor Qianlong's, this small temple was enlarged to a bigger temple and under the reign of Emperor Guangxu (1871-1908 A.D.), it became the third largest temple on the island. Currently the temple covers an area of 7,902. 93 square meters.

Fanyin Cave

The cave in front of us is Fanyin Cave, which means Sanskrit Sound Cave. The two walls of its entrance are like cliffs facing each other and are about 70 meters high and 50 meters deep inwards. There is a big natural rock spanning over the cliff like a huge stone bridge. It can be reached by walking from the cliff top down along the cliff stairs more than 200 steps.

It is foggy everywhere in the cave and the fog changes into many strange shapes under the influence of the sunlight and waves. The Buddhist believers regard these changeable phenomena as the embodiment of Kwan-yin and prostrate themselves in worship. When the sea tide enters the cave, the frightening sounds are like a lion's roar and tiger's howl. Indeed, the sounds are loud enough to make your ears tingle.

Stone of Two Tortoises

The Stone of Two Tortoises is more than just a rock at the west foot of the Meiling Peak. It's a sculpture of two tortoises made by nature. One is squatting on the top of the rock turning its head back to look down；the other is climbing up to the rock, and looking up. The legend has it that the two tortoises used to be the premiers in the Dragon Palace in the East China Sea. They were sent to listen to Kwan-yin's preaching in secret. They were so fascinated by the preaching that they forgot to go

華東地區

back down to the sea and became stones forever.

Pantuo Rock

Its name means literally a huge stone on a mountain. It looks like a cone, standing on the top of another rock. The rock appears to be hanging in the air and seems ready to fall. However, it has stayed there for thousands of years and has never moved or been shaken.

Kwan-yin of the South Sea

Now the wonderful statue in front of us is the Kwan-yin of the South Sea. It was built with bronze, limestone, marble and gold in 1998. The statue of Kwan-yin is 20 meters high and, together with the supporting base, reaches a height of 33 meters. The height of 33 meters could represent the 33 bodies of Kwan-yin or the 33 layers getting to the Buddhist Paradise in Buddhist doctrine. Since the completion of this imposing statue, it has been annually visited and worshipped by millions of pilgriMs.The statue itself is a great piece of art, visible by boat far from the island. Today, the statue has become one of Putuo Mountain's most symbolic sights. Kwan-yin of the South Sea protects the fishermen and helps them catch fish. She is holding a helm in her left hand, symbolizing her alliance with the fishermen.

Legend has it that Kwan-yin was born on February 19thof the lunar calendar, achieved enlightenment on June 19th and achieved nirvana on September 19th. On such dates, pilgrims from home and abroad congregate at Putuo Mountain to pay homage to the Goddess. Her anniversary—the opening of the statue—is celebrated on the 26thof October.

The Cave of Tidal Sound

The Cave of Tidal Sound is situated in front of the Purple Bamboo Forest, on the seaside. It is not a real cave but a big vertical gash in the cliff face. Day and night you can hear the thundering sound of the tide. During Qing Emperor Kangxi's reign (1662-1722 A.D.), its name was written on one side of the cave. Pilgrims and monks once believed that Kwan-yin would appear here in visions in response to fervent prayers.

Purple Bamboo Forest

Purple Bamboo Forest is on the topside of the Cave of Tidal Sound. Although the purple bamboo isn't as exciting as it sounds, there is a little temple worth seeing. In the earlier days it was called "listening to the tides temple". In 1928, it was renamed Zizhulin. It has been rebuilt a few times, the last time being in 1990. That reconstruction lasted 3 years. The temple has 3 main buildings, there are 128 rooms, and its total area is 4,424 square meters.

Kwan-yin Footprint

Close to the Purple Bamboo Forest and the Statue of Kwan-yin, you can find Kwan-yin's footprints. You can see the goddess' double-human size footprints on a rock by the sea. She jumped to a place about 10 km away from the Mount Luojia.

The Beaches

Apart from being a sacred buddhist mountain, Putuo Mountain is also known as a haven of blue sea, golden beaches and sun, making it an ideal place to spend a relaxing weekend. The island boasts a few excellent beaches on each of its corners ; among these, the 1,000-pace Beach and the 100-pace Beach are the most famous and are regarded as the best beaches near Shanghai.

100-pace Beach lies to the east of the Multi-Treasure Pagoda, on the northeast of the Chaoyang Pavilion, which is adjacent to the beach. It is 600 meters long, and a small cape named "Lion's Tail" is located in its middle. The beach boasts very fine sand and an excellent surf. The latter feature makes it a ideal place to surf and bath. It is also a great place for watching the sunrise. In summer, it is quite charming：the blue sky sets off the blue sea, golden sands set off white waves, and you can enjoy yourselves very much.

The 1,000-pace Sand Beach is about 1000 meters long. The sand is clean and pure and reputed to be as "soft like moss with the color as yellow as gold". You can enjoy yourselves by walking on the flat sands barefoot, accompanied by blasts of billows.

Ladies and gentlemen, because time is limited, we have to stop here today. I hope you will return to Putuo Mountain, and I will be very happy to be your guide again. OK! Good luck to all of you. Goodbye!

各位朋友大家好！歡迎來到普陀山遊玩！很榮幸成為大家的導遊，首先讓我來自我介紹一下。〔作自我介紹〕

普陀山是四大佛教名山之一，占地面積12.5平方公里。山上名寺名庵星羅棋布。遺存下來的十大古代建築群和歷史遺蹟建於宋、元、明、清各個朝代。在鼎盛時期，普陀山曾有82 座寺廟，128 間茅棚，僧尼達4000餘人。當你走在路上，隨時就有可能碰到身著袈裟的僧尼。迷人的風景和佛教的魅力使普陀山成為一座聖山。

普濟寺

現在在我們面前的就是普陀山最大的寺廟，它是中國東南部規模最大的寺廟。普濟寺起源於唐代，在宋朝神宗皇帝統治的第三年（公元1080 年）重建，並改名為現在的「普濟寺」。清康熙三十八年（公元1699年）開始對普濟寺進行修復，雍正九年（公元1731年）完工，並分別賜予了「普度眾生」和「普濟寺」的匾額懸掛於寺廟頂端。傳說當年有一位皇帝想進此寺，但由於他穿了一套普通的服飾，和尚不讓他走正門，請他從側門進。此後，被激怒的皇帝便下令，不允許任何人從正門入，所以現在我們得從側門進入。

普濟寺共有200　間建築物，包括天王寺、圓通寺、藏經閣、方丈室等，共有9個大廳、12　座樓閣和1612間房間，建築宏偉、規模龐大，占地1.4萬平方米。圓通寺是普濟寺的主體建築，其中有一個高8.8米的觀音銅像，是由普陀山當地人興建的代表觀音的唯一雕像。大廳兩旁有32座觀音轉世像。傳說觀音是法力無邊，有求必應的。宏偉壯觀的一尊佛像兩旁是十八羅漢像。廟裡能夠同時容納1000人以上，常人在清晨（凌晨4時）可以和僧侶們一起誦經和參拜觀音菩薩。

海印池

瞧！這個美麗的池子叫做海印池。它的字面意思是蓮花池，因為池子裡面曾經長滿了蓮花，後來池子被汙染，所有的花朵都凋謝了。海印池起源於明代，它又稱「放生池」，因為佛教僧侶將海龜池魚在這裡放生，遊客也可以買到小龜，在這裡將他們放生。海印池一帶還是旅行團、太極拳練習者、紀念品商販們的聚集之地。大家看，這裡有三個石橋橫跨池子，中間的橋是皇帝專行，東橋為王侯貴族們通行，西邊的橋則是普通老百姓通行的。橋的中間是廣恩樓，往北方向延伸是普濟寺的入口處，往南方向則通往御碑亭。中間的橋上有一座小八角涼亭。東大橋叫做永壽橋，建於明萬曆年間。橋高6米，長33.3米，寬7.5米，橋的兩邊各有20只小獅子立在不同位置。人們把西大橋叫做　池橋。

御碑亭

這是御碑亭，意思就是皇帝御賜碑的亭子，它始建於清朝雍正統治期間的1734年。這座方形的亭子高9米，在亭子中間豎立著一塊5.2米高、0.32米厚、約 1.32 米寬的皇碑。在碑的頂端裝飾著佛像。

多寶佛塔

多寶佛塔是一座五層高的四角佛塔，整座塔由太湖石建成。佛塔高18 米，底部是一個石欄環繞著的大平台，平台上是寶塔的基座，基座也是由石頭建成，石欄圍護。塔尖是箱形的舍利塔，舍利塔的四個角形狀猶如四片香蕉葉。四方的佛塔刻有佛龕，底部的平台也雕刻著精緻靈巧的佛像、菩薩和一些信徒。

多寶佛塔位於海印池東側，普濟寺東南邊，它始建於元朝圓通皇帝時期，高僧榆中主持的1333年至1334年期間，1592　年重建。多寶佛塔由於其獨特的形式、精美的雕刻和完好的保存被視為中國罕見的珍寶。這是浙江唯一一座始建於元代的石佛塔，也是普陀山三大鎮山法寶之一。

法雨寺

現在我們來到了島上的第二大寺廟，它以古老的建築藝術、細膩的木雕和古代帝王的書法而著稱。它位於百花山的左頂端，接近千步灘，你可以選擇坐索道或是步行上山。

法雨寺的歷史可以追溯到　1580　年。明朝時期，一名僧人在潮音洞祈求觀音時，他想像到有一根大竹子被沖上了千步灘，隨後，他在沙灘上建了一間小屋，命名為「海潮寺」。許多忠實信徒解囊捐助以擴大寺廟。1699　年，清朝康熙皇帝明令，在南京荒廢的皇宮遷至普陀山以供奉觀音，大廳增設了康熙皇帝御筆「天花法雨」的匾額，意思是佛教教義如同天上掉下來的鮮花和雨水一樣，法雨寺因此而得名。

目前法雨寺有294　個房間及廳堂，占地面積8800平方米。一個微型的黃金寶塔立於九龍壁和第一禮堂之間，在這裡，遊客們可以投擲硬幣以求好運。正殿叫做九龍殿，建於清朝。天花板上凹進去的部分是九龍戲珠。

慧濟寺

我們可以看到，這座寺廟位於最理想的山頂位置，是觀看日出的最佳地點。這座寺廟是普陀山的第三大廟，共有四個大廳、七個宮殿和六個閣樓。從地理位置來看，大廳巧妙地建在同一個中軸線上。慧濟寺是祭祀佛祖釋迦牟尼的。廟前有千級石階下山，大家也可以乘坐索道參觀寺廟。

在早期，這裡只是石頭堆積的塔，在明朝時建了一座小寺廟。1793年，清朝乾隆時朝將廟宇進行了擴建，到光緒時期，慧濟寺成了島上的第三大廟宇，如今廟占地面積7902.93平方米。

梵音洞

現在展現在我們面前的洞穴是梵音洞。入口處的兩堵岩壁相互對立，約70 米高、50 米深，龐大的天然岩石峭壁像一個巨大的橫跨石橋。步行從懸崖絕壁由上而下沿樓梯下 200 多級，就可以到達。

洞中濃霧瀰漫，在陽光和海浪的作用下，霧的形狀變化萬千。佛教信徒們把這些變幻莫測的現象看做是觀音的化身。當海潮進入洞穴時，驚恐的聲音聽起來像獅子的吼叫、老虎的咆哮，震耳欲聾。

二龜聽法石

二龜聽法石不是在西岩腳下梅嶺山頂的一塊普通石頭，它是大自然的雕刻品。一只龜蹲坐在高高的岩石上，頭轉回往下看；另一只是向上爬岩石，仰視著。傳說，兩隻龜原為東海龍宮的大臣，他們被秘密地送去聽觀音說教，他們聽得入了迷以至於忘了回到大海，結果變成了永遠的石塊。

磐陀石

磐陀的名字從字面上看就是山上的一塊巨石的意思。看起來像一個松果，立在另一個岩石的頂部。石頭似乎是懸在空中，好像隨時會掉下來，不過，它卻在那裡佇立了幾千年，從來沒有動搖過。

南海觀音

我們面前的這座優美的雕像是南海觀音。它建造於1998 年，是由青銅、石灰石、大理石和黃金組成的。觀音塑像高20 米，連同座基達33 米。33米的高度可能代表了觀音的33個化身或者是佛教教義中到達西天的33層機關。自從這一塑像落成之後，每年的朝聖遊客都有百萬人。塑像本身就是一個巨大的藝術品，坐在遊船上很遠就可以看得見。今天，它已成為普陀山塑像最風光的象徵。南海觀音保護著當地的漁民順利起航，她左手持掌舵，象徵她與漁民共患難。

潮音洞

潮音洞位於紫竹林前方，靠近海邊。它不是一個真正的大洞，而是峭壁邊的一個巨大裂縫。白天和晚上都可以聽到隆隆的浪潮聲。康熙年間，有人將「潮音洞」的名字刻在了一邊的山洞。香客和僧侶認為，觀音會在這裡回應教徒們的熱切祈禱。

紫竹林

紫竹林位於潮音洞上方，雖然紫竹並不像人們所聽到的那樣神奇，但有一個小寺廟還是值得人們去看一看。早期它被稱為「聽潮廟」，1928 年更名為紫竹林。它歷經了幾次重建，最後一次重建是在1990年，重建歷時3 年。廟宇有3 個主體建築，共128室，總面積達4424平方米。

觀音腳印

接近紫竹林和觀音塑像，大家可以找到觀音的腳印。大家可以看到觀音的腳印在靠近海邊的石頭上，是普通腳印的兩倍大小，她跳到珞珈山的附近，大約10公里以外的地方。

海灘

除了佛教聖山，普陀山還以其碧海、金色沙灘、陽光、度過理想輕鬆的週末而著稱。島上美麗的海灘遍布每一個角落，其中，百步灘及千步灘被視為上海附近最有名、最好的海灘。

百步灘，位於多寶佛塔東部，朝陽亭東北方，毗鄰千步灘。跨度達600 米，中間有些海角命名為「獅子尾巴」。這裡擁有柔軟的沙灘，是海浴、衝浪、看日出最好的地方。在夏季，這是更加迷人——藍天碧海，金沙灘掀起白色波浪，大家可以充分地享受。

千步灘大約有公里長，沙子干淨透明，被譽為「黃如金沙軟如苔」。伴隨著陣陣海浪，大家可以充分地享受赤腳走在軟綿綿的沙灘上帶來的快感。

各位朋友，由於時間有限，我們今天的遊覽就到這裡！我希望大家能再次到普陀山來遊玩，我也會非常高興再次為大家導遊。好了，祝各位好運，再見！

Jiangsu Province江蘇省

A Glimpse of the Province （本省簡介）

Su is short for Jiangsu, a province located along China's eastern coast. With Yellow Sea to its east, Jiangsu adjoins Anhui Province and Shandong Province in the west and north respectively, with Zhejiang Province and the city of Shanghai as its neighbors in the southeast. Jiangsu Province covers an area of 102.6 thousand square kilometers. The plain area of Jiangsu is 70.6 thousand square kilometers, and water surface area is 17.3 thousand square kilometers. The province has a coastline of 954 kilometers.

The province has a typical monsoon climate. It approximately takes the Huai River Irrigation Line as the demarcation, to the south of which is the subtropical monsoon climate and to the north the warm moist monsoon climate. Generally, the weather is mild with moderate rainfall and four distinct seasons with annual average temperatures ranging from $13°C$ to $16°C$.

Tourism Resources

The province is crossed by the Yangtze River from east to west and by the Grand Canal from north to south. The province is also blessed with more than 900 kilometers of coastline. With rivers, lakes, streams and seas, it is no wonder that the province is popularly famed for its towns set by the water. The history and culture of Jiangsu are inseparable from water. Ancient towns and gardens incorporate water into their structures. Seafood from the rivers, lakes and oceans highlight the famous Jiangsu-Huaiyang cuisine. Jiangsu's handicrafts, delicate music, and rich heritage of folk customs are all connected to water and express both the province's poetic qualities and the romance and warmth of its people. Jiangsu has been a tourist paradise ever since ancient times. Nanjing, Suzhou, Yangzhou, Zhenjiang, Changshu, Xuzhou and Huai'an are famous historical and cultural cities. Two cities in the province have been designated China's Excellent Tourist Cities, that is, Nanjing—the capital of six dynasties, and Suzhou—the Paradise on the Earth. There are 3 major tourist centers in Jiangsu, namely the Yangtze River Area, the Tai Lake Area and the Xuhuai(Xuzhou and Huai'an) Area. As a charming destination, Jiangsu owns a lot of wonderful attractions, of which Kun Opera and Suzhou's Classical Gardens are the representatives. Currently, China has only two world intangible heritage listings; Kun Opera is the most important one. And Suzhou's Classical Gardens are on the World Culture Heritage list. Besides the beautiful ancient towns, crumbling city walls and Buddhist sites, Jiangsu boasts delicate and attractive arts and crafts.

Local Snacks

Lianyungang oriental couple shrimp, crab meat dumplings, pumpkin and rice porridge, sticky rice balls flavored by roses or other flowers, Nanjing salty duck, Huangqiao baked biscuits, Suzhou cakes, and Confucian Temple snacks.

Local Culture

Kun Opera originated in Jiangsu's Kunshan region. It is one of China's classical operas, with a history of more than 500 years. Other Jiangsu opera include Xi Opera, Huai Opera and Yang Opera. Suzhou Pingtan, which is a form of storytelling and ballad singing in Suzhou dialect, are also famous. There are also many kinds of folk songs and local dances in Jiangsu.

Special Local Products

Suzhou silk embroidery is one of the province's most beautiful traditional crafts. Clay figurines are Wuxi's most famous folk craft. Suzhou's Biluochun tea has long been one of China's best loved teas. Nanjing Yuhua tea, Yuhua Stone, Suzhou fans, Changzhou combs, Yangzhou lacquer, Yangzhou jade carving, Nantong kites, Yixing teapots and Zhengjiang vinegar also have good reputations.

Attraction Recommendation

Suzhou has been called "the Oriental Venice" and has a history going back 2,500 years. Suzhou's Classical Gardens embody the city, while the Grand Canal runs through it from north to south. There are many famous lakes in Jiangsu, such as Tai and Hongze Lakes, Yangzhou's Slim West Lake and Nanjing Xuanwu Lake. There are also many mountains that are well worth visiting, such as Nanjing's Bell Mountain and Qinglian Mountain, as well as Beigu, Jin and Jiao Mountains in Zhenjiang City.

Tourist City

Nanjing, Suzhou, Yangzhou and Wuxi are the main tourist cities in Jiangsu.

江蘇省簡稱蘇,位於中國東部沿海,東濱黃海,西鄰安徽省,北接山東省,南連上海市和浙江省。江蘇省總面積10.26萬平方公里,其中平原占7.06萬平方公里,水域占1.73萬平方公里,擁有954公里長的海岸線。

江蘇地處典型的季風氣候帶,以淮河灌溉流域帶作為分界,此線以南屬亞熱帶季風氣候，此線以北則是暖濕季風氣候。總體而言，江蘇四季分明，降雨適中，年平均氣溫13℃～16℃。

旅遊資源

長江貫穿江蘇省東西，京杭大運河流經南北，除此之外，江蘇省還擁有900 多公里長的海岸線，加之湖泊遍布全境，難怪江蘇以她的「古鎮水鄉」而揚名中外。江蘇的歷史文化與水是密不可分的，古鎮和園林的建造就是以水為基礎的。淮陽菜系當中，河鮮海味是其最重要的組成部分。手工藝、音樂、民俗民風，都與江蘇詩情般的水淵源和浪漫熱情的江蘇人民是密不可分的。江蘇自古就是旅遊者的天堂。南京、蘇州、揚州、鎮江、常熟、徐州、淮安是國家歷史文化名城。16個國家優秀旅遊城市中的「六朝古都」——南京和「人間天堂」——蘇州在江蘇境內。長江流域旅遊帶、太湖流域旅遊帶和徐淮（徐州和淮安）旅遊帶是江蘇省三大旅遊中心。作為著名的旅遊目的地，江蘇擁有許多旅遊資源，其中最著名的有崑劇、蘇州園林作為代表。目前，崑劇是世界非物質文化遺產之一，蘇州園林是世界文化遺產之一。除此之外，美麗的水鄉古鎮，古城牆遺蹟，佛教寺廟，精美的藝術和手工藝製作都能讓你來到江蘇流連忘返！

風味美食

連雲港東方對蝦、南京板鴨、泰興黃橋鎮的「黃橋燒餅」、富春包子、蘇式糕點、夫子廟小吃等都是江蘇有名的風味食品。

地方文藝

崑劇發源於江蘇崑山地區，它是中國古老劇種之一，有五百多年的悠久歷史。除此之外，江蘇還有錫劇、淮劇、揚劇等地方戲曲表演藝術品種。其中蘇州評彈、揚州評彈影響較大。江蘇各地山歌、民謠、舞蹈數不勝數，美不勝收。

地方特產

蘇繡是江蘇最漂亮最有名的傳統手工藝品。無錫泥塑也是有名的民間手工藝品。蘇州的碧螺春茶是中國最好最受歡迎的綠茶之一。南京雨花石、蘇州扇、常州梳篦、揚州漆器、揚州玉雕、南通風箏、宜興紫砂壺、鎮江醋也是久負盛名。

主要推薦景點

已有2500多年歷史的蘇州城，享有「東方威尼斯」之美稱。蘇州園林是蘇州城的代表。京杭大運河縱貫南北，太湖煙波浩瀚，洪澤湖碧波萬頃，揚州瘦西湖清雅秀麗，南京的玄武湖、莫愁湖，徐州的雲龍湖等都是著名的遊覽湖泊。南京鐘山、清涼山，鎮江北固山、金山、焦山是江蘇省內不錯的遊覽去處。

主要旅遊城市

南京、蘇州、揚州、無錫是江蘇主要的旅遊城市。

Nanjing City （南京之旅）

Ladies and Gentlemen：

Good morning! Welcome to Nanjing City!

Nanjing has been the capital of ten dynasties in Chinese history and is famed for its rich culture, long history and beautiful landscape.

As one of the eight great ancient capitals in China, Nanjing has a long history and is awarded the title of "Famous Historic and Cultural City" by the State Council. In 472 B.C.Goujian, the king of Yue State, started to build the city at Yuhuatai and called it "Yue city". In 229 A.D.the Eastern Wu Dynasty of the Three Kingdoms moved its capital to Nanjing and started to develop "Jianye city" as it was named then. Subsequently the Eastern Jin, Song, Qi, Liang and Chen Dynasties, Southern Tang Dynasty, Ming Dynasty, Taiping Heavenly Kingdom and Republic of China all made

Nanjing their capital. In so doing, they left behind many famous attractions, including the willowed banks of Xuanwu Lake, bright lights and river scenery of Confucius Temple, ancient city wall （the best preserved in the world）, World Heritage-listed Ming Tomb, Dr.Sun Yat-sen's Mausoleum, Jinghai Temple, Presidential Palace and many other places of historical interest. Among the many protected cultural relics and sites in Nanjing, one has been inscribed on the World Heritage List, 14 enjoy national-level protection, while 135 have provincial level protection. As a result, Nanjing has three distinctive types of culture：the culture of the Six Dynasties, the culture of the Ming Dynasty, the culture of the Republic of China.

Nanjing's favorable geographical location and picturesque landscape have made it a famous tourist city. Nanjing is situated on the lower reaches of the Yangtze River where the four seasons are clearly demarcated, bringing plenty of rainfall and abundant produce. The mountains, lakes, rivers, forests and the city are beautiful all the year round. In spring, it is common to visit Niushou Mountain scenic area's misty greenness. In summer the sunlight and clouds in the eastern suburbs are famous, while in autumn people prefer to climb up the splendid Qixia Mountain, and lastly, in winter it is recommended to view the stone city wall under the white snow. Nanjing's magnificent scenery extends across the seasons and across the city's reach.

Nanjing is a modern city brimming with dynamism and confidence. Nanjing has comprehensive strengths and is one of the four national key cities for science and commerce. The city's highly developed infrastructure makes it an important transportation and communication hub in Eastern China. With dynamic trade and commerce sectors, it is also the most important commercial city in the Yangtze River delta region after Shanghai. As an ancient capital city, green city, cultural city, riverside city and city of fraternity, Nanjing has emerged as one of China's most attractive destinations for investment and living. Nanjing has been awarded several honorable titles for its outstanding achievements, including "National Advanced City for Scientific and Technological Progress", "National Excellent Tourist City",

"National Hygienic City" and "National Model City for Environmental Protection". As one of the "forty Chinese cities with best environ-ments for investment", Nanjing is also regarded as one of the Asian-Pacific Rim cities with the best development prospects in the 21st century.

Well, my friends, so much for my brief introduction to Nanjing, any questions will be welcomed! Thank you!

女士們、先生們：早上好！歡迎來南京旅遊！

南京是一個以古都聞名的城市，以其豐富的文化、悠久的歷史和旖旎的風光而著稱。

作為中國八大古都之一，南京有著悠久的歷史，被國務院授予了「歷史文化名城」的稱號。早在公元前472 年，越王勾踐開始在雨花台建立南京城，因而南京又被稱為「越城」。公元229 年，三國時的東吳遷都南京，開始建造「建鄴城」。此後，東晉、宋、齊、梁、陳、南唐、明、太平天國和中華民國都曾設都城於南京。這些朝代留下了許多著名的景點，包括：玄武湖柳堤、孔廟、古城牆、明陵、孫中山紀念堂、靜海寺、總統府及其他許多名勝古蹟。在南京眾多的文物和遺址中，被列入世界遺產名錄的有1處，屬於國家一級保護單位的有14處，屬於省一級保護單位的有135處。

南京具有有利的地理位置和優美的自然景觀，也是著名的旅遊城市。南京地處長江下游，四季分明，降水豐富，從而帶來大量的農業產值。春天，可見到牛首山風景區的濛濛綠意；夏日，東郊的陽光和雲海最負盛名；而燦爛的秋季棲霞山最受遊客青睞；冬季則可欣賞石頭城牆下的白雪。可以説南京的美景無時無處不在！

南京是一個充滿活力和自信的現代化城市。南京綜合實力很強，是四大國家重點科技商務城市之一。南京基礎設施齊全，是華東地區重要的交通通信樞紐之一，也是繼上海之後長江三角洲地區最重要的商業城市。作為古都城、綠色城、文化城、沿江城和友好城，南京已成為中國最具吸引力的投資目的地和生活地。南京獲

華東地區

得了許多榮譽稱號，主要包括：「中國科技進步先進市」、「中國優秀旅遊城市」、「國家衛生城市」、「國家環境保護模範城市」。同時，南京還被列為「中國投資環境最好的40個城市」，也被譽為亞太地區21世紀最具發展前景的大城市之一。

好的！各位朋友，我對南京的簡單講解就到這裡！如果有什麼問題歡迎大家提問！謝謝！

Dr.Sun Yat-sen's Mausoleum （中山陵）

Ladies and Gentlemen, Good morning! Now we are at the Dr.Sun Yat-sen's Mausoleum in Nanjing. I welcome you here and sincerely hope every one of you will have a good time during your visit.

When talking about the Mausoleum, we should begin by discussing the life of Sun Yat-sen, the great pioneer of Chinese democratic revolution. Dr.Sun's original name is Sun Wen and he styled himself as Yat-sen. So foreign friends would call him "Dr.Sun Yat-sen". Since he took "Woodcutter in Zhongshan" as his alias when he took part in the revolutionary activities in Japan, he was respectfully and widely called Mr.Sun Zhongshan in China. On November 12, 1866, Mr.Sun was born in a farmer's family in Cuiheng Village of Xiangshan County(the present-day Zhongshan City), Guangdong Province. When he was still young, he had great expectations. He studied medicine in Honolulu, Hong Kong and elsewhere places and after graduation, he worked as a practitioner in Guangzhou, Macao and other places. Later he gave up medicine as his profession to take part in political activities. In 1905, he set up China Alliance Organization in Japan and was elected as its president. He put forward the famous guiding principle "driving the invaders out, restoring the sovereignty of China, establishing a republic and equalizing the land ownership" and the Three People's Principles of "Nationalism, Democracy and the People's Livelihood." On October 10,1911, the Wuchang uprising broke out and Dr.Sun was elected as President of the

Republic of China by representatives from seventeen provinces. On the following New Year's Day (January 1,1912), Dr.Sun took the oath of office in Nanjing. From then on, Dr.Sun experienced Yuan Shikai's usurpation, the Second Revolution, and "Campaign Protecting the Interim Constitution." In 1921, Dr.Sun took the position of President in Unusual Times in Guang-zhou. At the first National Congress of Kuomintang held in Guangzhou in 1924, he perfected the original Three People's Principles and put forward "Three People's New Principles". He also proposed the policies of "Making an alliance with Russia and the Communist Party of China and helping the farmers and workers." In November 1924, in spite of his illness, Dr.Sun went up to Beijing to discuss state affairs with General Feng Yuxiang. Unfortunately, he broke down from constant overwork and passed away on March 12, 1925 in Beijing.

The location of the Mausoleum was chosen by Dr.Sun himself. It is the perfect place to build a mausoleum. You may wonder why, as Dr.Sun was born in Guangdong but died in Beijing, and his life was spent traveling throughout China while working for the revolution. So why did he choose Nanjing as the site for his tomb?

It is said that well before Dr.Sun took office in 1912, the abbot of Lingu Monastery had suggested to him that this place is a highly suitable mausoleum location because it faces the plain and is backed up by green mountains as its protective screen. On March 31, 1912, Dr.Sun resigned as a political compromise for the sake of the union of the North China and the South China. One day in early April, he went hunting with Hu Hanmin around the Piety Tomb of Ming Dynasty. They took a rest in the place where the Mausoleum is located now. Dr.Sun looked around and said "If possible, I would like my countrymen to allow me to have this place to bury my coffin." Surely, the fengshui(geomantic omen) of the Zijing Mountain is not the basic reason for the location of Dr.Sun's mausoleum. The basic reason is that, he said on dying "After my death, you can bury me at the foot of the Zijin Mountain in Nanjing in memory of the Revolution of 1911, because Nanjing is where the temporary government was founded. " Although Dr.Sun did not stay in Nanjing for very long, the city had a special meaning

華東地區

for him. Fundamentally speaking, the reason he chose Zijing Mountain as his permanent resting-place is to commemorate the revolution of 1911 and to encourage other revolutionaries.

To respect Dr.Sun's wish, the Preparatory Committee of Sun Yat-sen's Funeral, including his wife, Song Qingling, and his son, Sun Ke, examined the area and chose the site for the Mausoleum. They delimited 133 hectares and offered a reward in newspaper for the best mausoleum design. Among all the designs submitted, young architect L Yanzhi's design, which gave the mausoleum the shape of a bell, was highly praised and gained the first prize. L was also invited to supervise the whole project.

Work on the project began on March 12, 1926, the first anniversary of Dr.Sun's death, and was completed in the spring of 1929. It cost a total of 1.5 million Yinyuan to build.

Unfortunately, the gifted young architect, L Yanzhi, endured much hardship while supervising the project. He died at the age of 35, exhausted from his work, just before the mausoleum's completion. The completion ceremony was held on June 1, 1929 and Dr.Sun's remains were transported from Beijing to Nanjing. From then on, Mr.Sun has slept here.

The construction of Dr.Sun Yat-sen's Mausoleum was an important event in the history of Nanjing. In order to ensure that Dr.Sun' s coffin was smoothly carried to the mausoleum, the first asphalt road was built from Zhongshan Port in the west to Zhongshan Gate in the east. It is 12 kilometers in length and is also called Zhongshan Road and remains up to this day one of Nanjing's most important main roads. At the same time, the city gate Chaoyang Gate, which was built in Ming Dynasty, was renovated and changed its name to Zhongshan Gate. Between Zhongshang Gate and Dr.Sun Yat-sen's Mausoleum, a road called the Mausoleum Road was built. Just as the people of Paris take pride of their les Champs-Elysees and the people of New York boast about Fifth Avenue, Nanjing's citizens are very proud of their boulevards. And the 3-kilometer-long Mausoleum Road undoubtedly is the best representative of these boulevards. Nanjing's main trees, which Chinese people call French plane trees, but which in fact are a local variety, line both sides of this "green corridor". The trees are named French plane trees because Frenchmen took them from Yunnan Province and transplanted them in their leased territory in Shanghai.

Now, we are going out of the Zhongshan Gate and driving along the Mausoleum Road. The destination ahead is a square in shape of crescent. Now, please look to the south. There is an octagon platform structured with reinforced concrete but covered with Suzhou Jinshan stone. The platform is divided into three layers and each layer is enclosed by stone rails. The copper "ding" (an ancient cooking vessel) with two looped handles and two legs weighs 5, 000 kilograMs.It is 4. 25 meters high and its diameter is 1. 23 meters. It is one of the mausoleum's special features aimed at memorializing Dr.Sun. The "ding" was built during the autumn of 1933 with donations from Zhongshan University's students and teaching staff and Mr.Dai Jitao. One side of the "ding" is engraved with three characters "Inte-lligence, Humanity and Brevity". These three words are Zhongshan University's motto. Inside of the "ding" stands a hexagon copper tablet on which Dai Jitao's mother's handwriting of the "Filial Piety" is engraved. The "ding" is just like a pendulum for the bell-shaped mausoleum and striking it can be used to alarm the whole nation.

Stepping on the steps, we will see a soaring memorial archway with four columns. The archway was built between 1931 and 1933, and is 12 meters high and 17. 3 meters in width. While it is made out of huge granite blocks quarried in Fujian Province, its structure is in Chinese traditional wood construction style. Now, look up at the shining words inscribed on the horizontal board. The words in English mean fraternity and were written by Dr.Sun Yat-sen and taken from the Tang Dynasty poet Han Yu's poem, "Fraternity is humanity". It is said that Dr.Sun very much liked to write

華東地區

these two words as a gift to others. He devoted his whole life to bourgeois democratic revolution with great fraternity and struggled for the national independence and freedom for many years. So we can say that "fraternity" is a word that best describes his life.

Further down from the Fraternity Archway, there is a road leading to the mausoleum. The road is 480 meters long and dozens of meters wide. The whole design of the mausoleum gives prominence to the grand and solemn Chinese traditional style. In order to embody the greatness of Dr.Sun, the mausoleum followed the example of ancient mausoleums and was built against mountains and the coffin chamber was placed at the top of the mountain, which is 160 meters high. In addition, the mausoleum's plants are symmetric, which gives it a more solemn feel. Now, please look forward to the north, along the hillside, situate the Sun Yat-sen Mausoleum's Gate, Stele Pavilion, Memorial Hall and coffin chamber right behind these structures. The pines, cypresses, ginkgoes and maples on the both sides of the road represent Dr.Sun's revolutionary spirit and lofty quality. They take the place of statues and stone beasts which usually flanked ancient sacred roads. Among the trees, cedar is one of the "four kinds of trees for appreciation" and has been honored as the tree of Nanjing City.

According to L Yanzhi's design, the place of the Mausoleum is like a "duo", a big wooden bell, which was used to announce a policy, decree or a war in ancient time. The duo's sound is loud and clear, as if ringing it can make the whole world peaceful and happy. The design reminds the people of Dr.Sun Yat-sen's well-known saying, which is meant to alert later generations, "The revolution is far from success and we should continue working hard." The crescent-shaped square is the bottom of the "Bell of Freedom".

The grand archway at the end of the Mausoleum Road marks the mausoleum's formal boundary. It is 16 meters high, 27 meters wide and 8. 8 meters deep. It is also made out of granite from the Fujian Province. Dr.Sun Yat-Sen's handwriting is inscribed on the horizontal board of the middle passage. It means that the state doesn't belong to one family but belongs to the entire nation and the common people. This is the goal for which Dr.Sun struggled for his whole life and it is also the excellent explanation of the Democracy of the Three People's Principles. We have passed the gate of the Mausoleum, and the Stele Pavilion now stands in front of us. The 9-meter-high Stele in the middle of the pavilion was engraved with 24 gold-plated Yan Zhenqing characters that read, "Chinese KMT buried Premier Sun here on June 1, 18thyear of the Republic of China". These words were written by Tan Yankai, one of the KMT's founding members. While the stele was being set up, Wang Jingwei and Hu Hanmin were given the task of writing an inscription for Dr.Sun; however, after two years they had still not written anything because they thought that Dr.Sun's merits couldn't be captured by words. They thus chose to use the present form to praise Dr.Sun without engraving an inscription.

Going out of the pavilion, we'll see numerous layers of steps. The people of Nanjing often say that there are as many steps in the mausoleum as there are stone lions on the Lugou Bridge(known for Westerners as Marco Polo Bridge). Visiting tourists often ask, "How many steps on earth are there in the Mausoleum?" Well, my friends, now you know and if you are interested you can count them yourself!

Now we are coming near the top platform. Look, there are two big copper "dings". They were contributed by the then Shanghai municipal government shortly after the mausoleum was finished. Now, please look carefully. There are two holes in the bottom of the left "ding". Why? Well, when the Japanese Army attacked Nanjing in late 1937, their soldiers shot two holes through the left ding during the fighting. Now, although the circumstances have changed, the two holes always remind Chinese people not to forget their national humiliation at the hands of the Japanese imperialists. Not far away, there are two ancient style bronze dings that were presented by Dr.Sun's son, Sun Ke, and his family.

Ascending the steps, now we have reached the top of the platform. Here we can have a bird's-eye view of what is in the distance. The Memorial Hall is the half way up to the mountain and there are altogether 392 steps up to it from the archway of Fraternity. While the vertical distance is 70 meters, the plane distance is 700 meters. If you count the steps from the Stele Pavilion, the number of steps is 290. In order to vary the ascent, the architect divided the 392 steps into 10 parts and each part has a platform. Even better, if you look up from the bottom, you can see that the steps extend to the top without a stop and you can't see any platform. But if you look down from the top, you only see the platforMs.The number of the steps, 392, is not a random number; it instead represented the size of China's population at the time the mausoleum was built, which stood at 392 million people.

Now we are in front of the Memorial Hall and the coffin chamber, which are the major parts of the mausoleum. The Hall's structure is modeled on the style of ancient Chinese wooden palaces. It is 30 meters long, 25 meters wide and 29 meters high, surrounded by smaller fortress-style structures and two 12. 6-meter-high cloud columns. Its roof, with double-eaves and 9 ridges, is covered with blue glazed tiles. The outside of the wall is covered with granite from Hong Kong. The inscription on the horizontal board is engraved with seal characters cut in relief "Nation" "Democracy" and "The people's livelihood". These are the most basic and general guiding principles of Dr.Sun's revolutionary activities. Above "Democracy", there is a horizontal inscription board with Sun's handwritten words, "Fill the World with Justice".

Please follow me into the Memorial Hall. The floor is covered with white and black marble from Yunnan Province. The colors of white and black are among the traditional color for burial ceremonies in China. There are 12 black stone columns, and each has a 0. 8 meter diameter. You will see that the interiors of the walls around are inset with black marble. Now you can have a look at Dr.Sun Yat-sen's handwriting of "Programme for Founding a State", engraved on the east and west walls. The hall's main colors are black, white and blue, which are used to express filial piety in China. The inside windows are inlaid with smaltos, and they give the hall's design a western touch and let in lots of sunlight. The style of the whole structure is a blend of the East and the West, representing the well blended doctrine of Dr.Sun Yat-sen.

A statue of Dr.Sun Yat-sen sitting and wearing a robe lies in the middle of the room. It is 4.6 meters high and the bottom is 2.1 meters wide and was sculpted by the famous French sculptor, Paul Arinsky, whose native country was Poland. He was given the task of sculpting the statue by the committee of Dr.Sun Yat-sen's Funeral and used the finest Italian marble. In 1930, the sculpture was sent to the Mausoleum from Paris. Its total cost was 1. 5 million francs. The reliefs below are pictures depicting Dr.Sun's life and revolutionary activities.

Passing through the hall, we have come to the Coffin Chamber. There are two doors that you need to get through. The outer door consists of two American-made safety door leafs which are made of copper. The nails on them and the mysterious beasts on the copper loops are typical traditional Chinese door decoration. The horizontal inscription board was engraved with the words "The noble spirit will never perish", words Dr.Sun used to memorialize the 72 martyrs' tomb in Huanghua Mound of Guangzhou. The second door is a single copper leaf engraved with the seven characters for "Dr.Sun Yat-sen's Tomb", which were written by Zhang Jingjiang.

The tomb is shaped like a half globe. The design of the KMT emblem forms a mosaic in the vaulted dome. The floor of the round room is covered with marble. The room's diameter is 18 meters and the height is 11 meters. The walls are covered with pink marble. The circular marble pit is 1. 7 meters deep and 4. 33 meters in diameter and is enclosed by 1-meter-high white marble rails. A statue of Dr.Sun Yat-sen lying down and wearing a Zhongshan suit is at the center of the pit. This statue is sculpted in accordance with Dr.Sun's remains by a Czechos-lovakian sculptor. His copper coffin lies about 5 meters below the sculpture. You may ask why on earth the clothes Dr.Sun wears for the sitting statue are so different from those worn in the lying statue. In those years, the leftists and the rightists inside of the KMT had severe conflicts. The

華東地區

rightists, headed by Chang Kai-shek wanted to restore the ancient ways and opposed revolution. They insisted that Dr.Sun should wear long robe, while the leftists insisted he wear Zhongshan suit. Since they had different opinions thus the two statues have different clothes styles.

My friends, I suspect you're wondering about whether Dr.Sun's remains are in the tomb or not. In fact, his remains had an unusual experience. After his death, his remains were dealt with antiseptic and placed in Biyun Monastery in Beijing in March of 1925. When the warlord Zhang Zongchang was defeated by the North Expeditionary Army and withdrew to Beijing in 1926, he ascribed his failure to Dr.Sun's remains and decided to burn them. Fortunately, the patriotic general, Zhang Xueliang, sent troops to protect the remains. But while this ensured the safety of Dr.Sun's remains, they were once exposed to the air. On May 28, 1929, Dr.Sun's coffin was sent to Pukou from Beijing by Jinpu Railway, and on June 1stit reached the mausoleum. The bottom of the tomb is granite. Under the copper coffin, there is a specially made wooden pad and enclosing the coffin is a well-sealed crystal box. After the Resistance War Against Japan broke out, the KMT government put Dr.Sun's remains on a plane and transported them to Chongqing. At the end of the conflict Chang Kai-shek intended to transport the remains to Taiwan by aircraft. However, due to the difficulty of moving the coffin and the possible harm such action could cause to Dr.Sun's remains, this plan was heavily protested by both engineers and the KMT's left wing. Confronted by this resistance, Chang finally gave up on this plan, making it possible for Dr.Sun's remains to safely remain here up to the present day.

After passing through the door in the back wall of the square outside you will arrive at the Mausoleum Park. The back wall of the park is an "Exhibition of Construction of Dr.Sun Yat-sen's Mausoleum". The exhibition contains nearly 200 precious historic materials which show how the mausoleum was constructed and Dr.Sun's remains were transported to it.

In addition to the main structure, other structures built to honor Dr.Sun's memory surround the mausoleum. Most of them were built after 1929 with the donations made by Chinese people from all walks of life both in China and overseas. For example, the Fraternity Pavilion on top of the Plum Hill is built with the donation of a Taiwanese compatriot. It was completed on November 12, 1993, the 127thanniversary of Dr.Sun's birthday.

Ladies and gentlemen, Dr.Sun struggled for a better China for his whole life and overthrew the old dynastic feudal system which lasted for more than 2000 years. In his later days, he carried out the principal policies of "Making an alliance with Russia and the Communist Party of China and helping the farmers and workers". These great feats have earned Dr.Sun great respect and praise from people both in China and abroad. Thus after China's liberation, both its central and local governments have exerted great efforts in preserving this excellent heritage.

Now, as one of the "Top Forty Tourist Resorts in China", Dr.Sun Yat-sen's Mausoleum receives numerous Chinese and international friends every year. People come here to pay homage to Dr.Sun. Today, the unification has become the main tendency in terms of the relations between the Chinese on both sides of the Straits. I believe that most Chinese people, from both home and abroad, are expecting from the bottom of their hearts the coming of the day when their country is united and getting more prosperous. And if Dr.Sun could hear this news, I'm sure he would be smiling happily in the other world.

OK, thank you very much for your cooperation. Good bye and good luck!

各位朋友，早安！現在我們所在的地方就是南京中山陵。歡迎大家來這裡參觀，我衷心地希望大家能在這裡度過一段難忘的時光！

説起中山陵，首先我們不得不提到偉大的中國民主革命先行者——孫中山先生。孫先生本名孫文，字逸仙。因此很多外國友人都稱他為「孫逸仙博士」。因為他在日本從事革命活動時曾用過「中山樵」的化名，所以他在國內被尊稱為孫中山。孫中山先生1866年11月12日出生於廣東香山縣（今中山市）翠亨村的一個農民家庭。他從小胸懷大志，先後赴檀香山、香港等地學醫，學成後在廣州、澳門等地行醫。後來，他棄醫從政，於1905年在日本成立中國同盟會，並被推舉為總理。孫中山先生提出了「驅除韃虜，恢復中華，建立民國，平均地權」的著名綱領及「民族、民權、民生」的三民主義學說。1911年10月10日武昌起義爆發後，孫先生被十七省代表推舉為中華民國臨時大總統，並於次年元旦（1992年1月1日）在南京宣誓就職。此後，孫先生經歷了「袁世凱竊國」、「二次革命」、「護國運動」、「護法運動」等風風雨雨。1921年他在廣州就任中華民國非常大總統。在1924年1月廣州召開的中國國民黨第一次中國代表大會上，他將舊三民主義發展為新三民主義，提出了「聯俄聯共扶助農工」的三大政策。同年11月，他應馮玉祥將軍之邀抱病北上討論國家大計，終因積勞成疾，於1925年3月12日在北京逝世。

現在我們來到的地方就是孫中山先生的墓地所在。中山陵是孫先生生前選定的。這裡視野開闊，氣象雄偉，的確是建造陵墓的風水寶地。大家也許會問；孫先生出生於廣東，逝世在北京，畢生為革命奔波於各地，為什麼要選擇南京作為自己的長眠之地呢？

據說，早在1912年孫先生就任臨時大總統時，靈谷寺的住持和尚就曾向他推薦過這塊「前臨平川，後擁青嶂」的風水寶地。同年3月31日，中山先生為求南北和平統一，毅然辭去總統之職。4月初的一天，他與胡漢民等人到明孝陵一帶打獵，來到現陵墓所在地休息。孫先生環顧四周，對隨從人員說，我將來死後，想向國民求得這塊土地以安葬（原話是「待我他日辭世後，願向國民乞一抔土以安置軀殼爾」）。當然，紫金山的氣勢風水還不是孫先生作此決定的根本原因。孫先生臨終前囑咐：「吾死之後，可葬於南京紫金山麓，因南京為臨時政府成立之地，所以不忘辛亥革命也。」因此，儘管孫先生在南京停留時間並不長，但南京對於孫先生是具有特殊意義的。他選擇南京紫金山為墓址，從根本上說，是為了紀念辛亥革命，激勵革命同仁。

為尊重孫先生的遺願，由孫夫人宋慶齡、兒子孫科等人組成的孫中山葬事籌備處實地察看，選好陵址，劃地133公頃修墓，又登報懸獎，徵集陵墓設計方案。在眾多應徵者中，青年建築師呂彥直設計的鐘形圖案被一致評為首獎，他本人也被聘主持全部工程。1926年3月12日，孫先生逝世一週年之際，舉行了奠基典禮。歷時3年多，耗資150萬銀元，中山陵終於在1929年春竣工。令人惋惜的是，留學美國、才華橫溢的青年建築師呂彥直在主持建陵過程中，嘔心瀝血，鞠躬盡瘁，不幸與孫先生一樣身患肝癌，在工程臨近尾聲時病逝，年僅35歲。1929年6月1日舉行奉安大典，孫先生的遺體從北京運到南京。從此，孫先生一直長眠在這裡。

中山陵的建造可以說是南京建設史上的一件大事。當年為了迎接孫先生靈柩，南京修築了第一條柏油馬路——西起中山碼頭，東至中山門，長達12公里的中山路。直到今天，中山路依然是南京最主要的交通幹道之一。當年還改造翻修了明代城門朝陽門，並改名為中山門。在中山門到中山陵之間還修築了一條陵園路。如同巴黎人以香榭麗舍大道為驕傲，紐約人為第五大街而自豪一樣，南京人對自己城市美麗的林蔭大道最是得意。而這條長達3公里的陵園路無疑正是南京林蔭道的最佳代表。在這條「綠蔭長廊」兩側，種植著南京最主要的行道樹——梧桐。人們習慣上稱它為法國梧桐，但追根溯源起來，它可是我們中國的「土特產」。只因當年法國人將它從雲南移植到上海法租界，才得了現在這麼一個土洋結合的名字。

車出中山門，沿陵園路行駛，終點便是中山陵前的半月形廣場。大家請向南看，廣場正南面是一座八角形石台。石台由堅固的水泥澆築而成，表面覆蓋一層蘇州金山石。石台共三層，每層均有石欄圍台。台上那尊雙耳三足的紫銅寶鼎，重5000公斤，高4.25米，腹徑1.23米，是中山陵紀念性裝飾之一。此鼎鑄於1933年秋，由廣州中山大學全體師生和戴季陶捐贈。鼎一面鑄有「智、仁、勇」三個字，是中山大學校訓。鼎內豎有一塊六角形銅牌，上刻戴母手書《孝經》全文。

由廣場踏階而上，迎面是一座四楹三闕門的沖天式石牌坊。這座牌坊建於1931～1933年，高12米，寬17.3米。建坊用的都是大塊福建花崗岩，但採用的卻是中國傳統木結構形式。大家抬頭可以望見坊額正中金光閃閃的「博愛」兩字。這兩個字是孫先生的手跡，原出自唐韓愈《原道》「博愛之為仁」一語。據說孫先生生前最愛題這兩字送人。孫先生畢生以偉大的博愛精神致力於資產階級民主革命，為民族的獨立自由奮鬥不息，可以説「博愛」二字正是對他一生的高度概括和最好寫照。

由博愛坊向前走，是一段長480米，寬數10米的墓道。中山陵的整體設計，突出中國的傳統風格，莊嚴肅穆，獨具特色。為了體現孫先生的崇高偉大，中山陵沿用了古代依山為陵的慣例，將墓室築於海拔約160米的全陵最高處。此外，整個陵區的建築植被講究中軸對稱，更給人以法度莊嚴之感。請大家向前看，朝北順坡而上，依次有陵門、碑亭、祭堂和祭堂後的墓室等建築。而墓道兩邊的這些雪松、松柏、銀杏、紅楓兩兩相對，代替了古代慣用的石人石獸，象徵著孫先生的革命精神和高尚品質。雪松是世界四大觀賞樹種之一，現已成為南京市的市樹。

根據呂彥直的設計，整個陵墓平面為「木鐸」形。鐸，就是平常我們説的大鈴鐺。在古代它是用來宣布政教法令和戰爭令的。鐸的聲音洪亮，而且傳得很遠，有「使天下皆達道」的喻義。陵墓選用這樣一個圖式，讓人不禁想起孫先生「革命尚未成功，同志仍需努力」的名言，其用意也正在警示後人。這裡的平台廣場就是當年呂彥直設計的「自由之鐘」的下緣。這座宏偉的三拱門，是陵區的正式開端。它高16米，寬27米，進深8.8米，也是用福建花崗岩築成的。中門橫額上是孫中山手書「天下為公」，出自《禮記·禮運》中的「大道之行也，天下為公」，意思是説國家政權不是哪一家的天下，而是天下人的天下，老百姓的天下。這是孫先生畢生奮鬥的理想，也是他所倡導的三民主義的極好註解。

過了陵門便是碑亭。亭正中這塊9米高的巨碑上，刻有國民黨元老譚延闓手書的「中國國民黨葬總理孫先生於此中華民國十八年六月一日」24個鎏金顏體大字。當初討論立碑時，計劃由汪精衛、胡漢民等人分別撰寫銘文、墓誌銘等。可花了兩年時間也沒寫出來。大家都認為先生的思想功績是文字所無法概括的，於是索性不寫銘文，改用現在的形式。

出碑亭，迎面石階層層疊疊。南京人常説中山陵的台階像是盧溝橋的石獅子——數不清。所以來這兒遊覽的客人常常要問：中山陵究竟有多少級台階呢？各位朋友，大家不妨也來數數看，怎麼樣？

來到臨近頂端的平台，可以看見一對大銅鼎，上刻「奉安大典」字樣，是當時上海市政府捐贈的。大家仔細看，會發現在左邊那個鼎下面有兩個洞。為什麼會這樣呢？原來這是1937年年末日軍攻占南京時向中山陵炮擊造成的，這兩個洞就是當時留下的彈洞。如今雖時過境遷，但這兩個彈洞仍時時提醒我們莫忘國恥。距此不遠的前方還有一對仿古青銅鼎，那是由孫先生的兒子孫科一家敬贈的。

拾級而上，終於登上了頂台。由此既可鳥瞰，更宜遠眺。置身此間，背倚巍巍鐘山，耳聽陣陣松濤，更覺偉人的浩然正氣與大自然同存。祭堂處在鐘山半山腰，從博愛坊到祭堂總共有392 級台階，高差約70米，平面距離700米。如從碑亭數起則有290級台階。建築師為避單調，將這392 級台階分作10段，每段1個平台，總計有大小10個平台。更妙的是，從下向上看時一望到頂，石階連綿不斷，不見平台；而各位現在朝下看時，卻反而不見台階，只見平台了。這392級的數字並非巧合，而是暗喻了當時全中國3.92 億同胞。一路登行，「高山仰止，景行行止」，對中山先生敬仰之情不禁油然而生。

現在大家面對的就是祭堂和墓室，這是陵墓的主體部分。當年呂彥直督建至此，就因身患絕症而逝，常令後人發出「出師未捷身先死」之嘆。祭堂是仿木結構宮殿式建築，長30米，寬25米，高29米，四周有堡壘式的小建築物，並有兩座高12.6 米的華表拱衛。祭堂屋頂為重檐九脊，上覆藍色琉璃瓦，外牆全用香港花崗岩砌成。祭堂門額上有「民族、民生、民權」陽文篆字，這是孫先生從事革命活動最基本最概括的指導思想。居中的「民生」門楣上端，又有孫中山手書的「天地正氣」四字匾額。

請各位跟我進入祭堂。祭堂內部以雲南產白黑色大理石鋪地。堂內有直徑0.8米的黑色石柱12根，四周牆壁下嵌黑色大理石。大家可以看見東西兩壁上所刻的孫中山手書《建國大綱》全文。整個祭堂以黑白藍色為基調，均為中國傳統孝色。而鑲嵌彩色玻璃的內窗，在陽光照射下卻顯出另一番西洋色彩。如此中西合璧的風格，正與孫先生融貫中西的精神氣度相契合。祭堂正中是孫中山著長袍馬褂的石刻全身坐像。像高4.6 米，底座寬2.1米。這座雕像是當時世界著名的法籍波蘭雕刻家保羅‧阿林斯基受孫中山葬事委員會之托，用義大利白石雕刻而成的，於1930年從巴黎運至中山陵，全部造價150萬法郎。坐像下四面的6幅浮雕是截取了孫先生從事革命活動的6個片段。

經過祭堂來到墓室。墓門分兩道，第一道是兩扇美國產的紫銅保險門，門上的門釘和銅環上的神獸（椒圖）極富中國傳統特色。門楣上刻「浩氣長存」橫額，取自孫中山為黃花崗烈士墓所書手跡。第二道門為獨扇銅門，上刻張靜江所寫「孫中山先生之墓」七個篆字。

墓室是半球形封閉建築，頂呈西式穹隆狀，以馬賽克鑲成國民黨黨徽圖案。室內圓形，鋪以大理石，直徑約18米，高11米，四壁以淡紅色大理石貼面。正中的圓形大理石礦，直徑4.33米，深1.7米，四周圍是1 米高的白色大理石欄杆。墓穴上安放著孫先生穿中山裝的大理石臥像，這是捷克雕塑家高琪按孫先生的遺體形象所作。孫先生的紫銅棺就安放在臥像下5 米左右處。為什麼祭堂內的坐像身著長袍馬褂，而這裡卻改穿中山裝了呢？原來當年國民黨內左右兩派矛盾尖銳，以蔣介石為首的右派主張塑像穿長袍馬褂；而左派則主張穿中山裝。兩派意見不合，結果各搞各的，就出現了上述情況。

各位朋友，孫先生的遺體究竟是否還在中山陵，這是每一位來這裡的遊客最關心的問題。事實上，自孫先生逝世後，他的遺體的確是歷經磨難。1925年3月12日孫先生逝世時，他的遺體經過防腐處理，暫時被安置在北京香山碧雲寺。1926年，被北伐軍打敗逃到北京的軍閥張宗昌，把失敗的原因歸咎為孫先生的遺體壓住了他的風水。於是他打算要焚化遺體。後經愛國將領張學良派兵保護，遺體才得以保存，但已受到空氣侵蝕。1929年5月28日靈柩由津浦鐵路從北京運抵浦口，6月1日運達中山陵。奉安大典儀式完畢後，即用水泥將靈柩澆入壙中。墓穴用花崗岩墊底，四周建隔牆，紫銅棺下有一特製楠木墊，棺上有一層密封著的水晶透明板。當年公祭時，站在石礦邊，扶欄即可瞻仰中山先生遺容。抗戰爆發後，國民黨政府曾準備將遺體運往重慶；解放戰爭後期，蔣介石又曾想將遺體遷往臺灣，但由於爆破墓穴勢必會損壞遺體，因而受到工程界愛國人士和國民黨左派的極力勸阻，終於使遺體得以安然保存至今。

　　沿祭堂外廣場兩側後壁有一道門，通向墓堡公園。中為墓室寶頂，呈覆鐘形。墓堡後牆設有「中山陵建設史料展」，近200幅珍貴歷史資料展現了中山陵的建設和中山先生的遺體奉安全過程。

　　除了陵墓主體建築外，中山陵周圍還有一些紀念性建築設施。包括藏經樓、音樂台、光化亭、行健亭、仰止亭、流徽榭等。它們大多是1929年奉安大典後，各界人士和海外僑胞友人捐款修建而成。另外，位於梅花山頂的博愛閣，是一位臺灣同胞捐資興建的，於1993年11月12日孫先生誕辰127週年時落成。

　　各位朋友，孫中山先生一生為革命奮鬥，推翻了兩千多年的封建帝制，晚年又採取聯俄、聯共、扶助農工的三大政策，建立了偉大的功勛，也贏得了中外進步人士的廣泛擁戴和頌揚。中國共產政權成立後，中山陵受到國家高度重視，1961年被中國國務院公布為國家級文物保護單位。

　　如今，作為「中國旅遊勝地四十佳」之一的中山陵每年接待著來自世界各地的無數炎黃子孫與國際友人。人們懷著對中山先生偉大精神的崇敬與景仰來到這裡憑弔拜謁。在兩岸統一成為大勢所趨、人心所向的今天，面對目前海峽兩岸的現狀，海內外炎黃子孫都期盼著祖國統一、繁榮昌盛的那一天早日到來。彼時彼刻，倘若孫中山先生泉下有知，必會含笑長眠的。

　　謝謝大家的合作，祝各位好運，再見！

Qinhuai River （秦淮河）

Hello! My friends, There's an old Chinese saying, "What a delight to have friends from afar". On behalf of our travel agency, I warmly welcome you to a Qinhuai River sightseeing tour. I hope that all of you will enjoy your short stay here and take home pleasant memories of this journey.

The Qinhuai River is the cradle of the ancient civilization of Nanjing and is

華東地區

favored by both nature and history. In particular, this river served as the breeding ground for the special gorgeous Jinlin culture. It is said that unless you have come to the Qinhuai River, you can not say that you have ever been to Nanjing. People get used to take "Qinhuai" as the nickname of Nanjing. In ancient times Qinhuai River was called Huaishui. It is said that when the first emperor ruled China, people cut through Fangshan Mountain to get to a river named Huaishui, which flowed through the city. The river was then renamed the Qinhuai River. The Qinhuai River scenic area, is a national 4A degree scenic area located south of the ancient city of Nanjing and is one of the top 40 Chinese tour resorts. It only takes 20 minutes to take a bus from the city center. Centered around the Confucius Temple, the Qinhuai River scenic area has all of the traveling, shopping, tasty local snacks, and local specialities and features of the old city of Nanjing. No matter in the past or in the present times, thanks to the uniquely favorable geographic features and culture, the Qinhuai River scenic area is scattered with countless scenic spots and endless anecdotes exist about them. It has always been the most flourishing place in Nanjing for 1, 800 years. But it is better to actually see this place, rather than hear me talking about it. If you want to have a deep understanding of Qinhuai River, please go for a visit with me.

Gongyuan (A Place for Examination)

If you mention the Confucius Temple, both people who visited it and those who have never been to Nanjing or never have seen the temple itself will have at least some knowledge about it. The so-called Confucius Temple in people's mind actually consists of three large architectural complexes which are the Confucius Temple, Xuegong (ancient school) and Gongyuan (place for exam). It was not only Nanjing's cultural and educational center during Ming and Qing dynasties, but also ranked as the best architectural complex of culture and education in all of China's northern and southern provinces. We first will pay a visit to Gongyuan. The place where we are now is Gongyuan Street. An ancient and large examination hall, the Gongyuan of the southern Yangtze River, is located north of here. This hall was first built in the fourth year of the Southern Song Emperor Qiandao's reign, or about 1168 A.D., and now it has a history of more than 800 years. Historically, Gongyuan was a very large building, with some 20, 640 rooMs.Since it is the largest examination hall in Chinese history, many famous historical figures have taken examinations here, including Wen Tianxiang, a national hero, Yan Zhenqing, a great calligraphist, and Chen Duxiu, the first general secretary of the Communist Party. Lin Zexu, Li Hongzhang, and Zeng Guofan also once acted as the examiners here. However, it is a pity that few of the Gongyuan's older buildings remain standing. The Minyuan Tower is just one of the remains, while most of the other structures have been rebuilt into markets. So the Minyuan Tower is the only existing image of the Gongyuan's pomp and history.

Mingyuan Tower

Please go forward with me, now the three-floor ancient building in front of us is Mingyuan Tower. It is the Gongyuan's main building and was built during the 13thyear of the Ming Dynasty Emperor Jiajing's reign (1534 A.D.). Though it has existed for more than 460 years, it remains in good condition and is the oldest examination hall still standing. This building with traditional bird-like eaves takes the shape of square and it has windows on all four sides. Standing on the building, you can have a bird's-eye view of the Gongyuan. In ancient times, it was the place from which commands were issued and the entire examination hall was monitored. Following examinations, the billboard announcing the names of successful candidates would be displayed on Gongyuan Street. But later it lost its functions when the Imperial Examination System was abolished for recruiting civil servants. The Gongyuan's outside wall is inlaid with the inscription describing its vicissitudes. In 1919, with exception of the Mingyuan Tower and some rooms left to exhibit cultural relics, all of the buildings were torn down so that markets could be built in their place. But now when we stand on this building looking in the distance, we can still get a sense of the older culture, even if examinees no longer rush to the examination hall to take their tests. Now you have some time to visit it freely and appreciate more the deep culture of Imperial Examination System for

Recruiting Civil Servants left by our ancestors.

Confucius Temple

After visiting Mingyuan Tower, we will continue to appreciate Qinhuai's scenery by visiting another landmark, the Confucius Temple, which honors Confucius, the most famous philosopher and educator in China's history. It was first built in the 1styear of the Song Dynasty Emperor Jingyou's reign（ 1034 A.D.) and was then expanded on the basis of the Study Palace of Eastern Jin Dynasty. The Qinhuai River, which in ancient times was called the "Pan Pool" is in front of the Confucius Temple. On the river's south bank stands China's longest "Zhaobi", or screen wall facing the gate of a house. In the east and in the west, stand the Kuiguang Pavilion and Juxing Kiosk, which signify the prosperity of civilization. And the Lingxing Gate, Dacheng Gate, Dacheng Temple, Mingde Hall, and Zunjing Pavilion are all located on an axis line.

Now the Qinhuai River is in front of us, and this part of it has been called the "Pan Pool". It was also known since the Song Dynasty as the Confucius Temple's "crescent pool". On the opposite river bank stands part of a vermilion stone wall, which was built during the Ming Dynasty, and is 110 meters long and 8 meters high. It claims to be the best wall under heaven and it is even larger than that of the Confucius Temple located at Qufu, Shandong Province. After repair, the Confucius Temple's current "Zhaobi" has a dignified air with black tiles, and red walls, on which two golden dragons are chasing each other with a bead. Turn around, you will find an attic style building. That is Kuixing Pavilion. In legends, Kuixing was the foremost star of the Charles's Wain and controls the vicissitude of culture and protects all the scholars. This deity has been esteemed since Han Dynasty and became even more popular in Tang and Song Dynasties. During these times, all Confucius Temples were built with two Kuixing pavilions on both sides, and scholars from all dynasties dared not offend this deity. The building which is close to the street and adjacent to the river was constructed during the long reign of the Qing Dynasty Qianlong Emperor, was twice destroyed and then reconstructed in 1985.

Square

Let's continue our visit. Here we come to the front square of the Qing Dynasty Temple. On the east and west extremes of the square, there are two stone tablets, both about 3 square meters in size, engraved with Chinese characters "文武大臣至此下馬"—all the officers and officials should dismount here—written in both the Man dialect and Mandarin Chinese to show respect to the saint Confucius. The six-angle kiosk with double eaves is called the Juxing Kiosk. Despite experiencing countless cataclysms, it remained in good condition prior to the 1960s, when the Cultural Revolution broke out and it was dismantled as one of the "four stinking olds". The present one was built in 1984. It is an excellent reconstruction of a rare and beautiful ancient kiosk, with double eaves like birds ready to take off.

Now look at that magnificent memorial gateway in the center of the square. That is Wenshufang Gateway. Let's go forward. This gate, the Lingxing Gate, is the first gate of the temple. Everybody, please walk through the Lingxing Gate and we will come to the Confucius Temple's main entrance, Dacheng Gate, which is also called the Ji Gate. Dacheng Gate is built in traditional style, with three doors standing side by side. Each has 45 nails and dragon shape knockers. Each door's inner side has a stone tablet from the Nanqi, Yuan, and Song Dynasties, each of which provides an account of the life of Confucius.

Dacheng Temple

The corridors on both sides of the Dacheng Gate are directly connected with the lofty Dancheng Temple which is the core architecture of the Confucius Temple. The officials of the feudal times could get in through the main entrance while ordinary people were only allowed to get in through the side ways. Now please follow me, let's

華東地區

237

go into the main temple of the Confucius Temple, the Dacheng Temple. Here the white marble tablet you see now was written with "南京夫子廟", or the Nanjing Confucius Temple by a famous ancient calligraphist;details about the Confucius reconstruction have been engraved on the reverse side. Dacheng Temple's main temple is 16. 22 meters high, 28. 1 meters long, and 21. 7 meters deep. "Dacheng" means that Confucius' ideas embodied with all the great thoughts of all the ancient sages. The Dacheng Temple was originally used to make sacrifice to Confucius and his four great students. A dozen statues of Confucius'students sit on both sides of the temple. The Dacheng Temple has now been changed into Nanjing Local Civilization Museum. Going forward, we will reach the Confucius Temple's school. On the door, there was once a horizontal inscribed board on which the two characters "Ancient School" are written in vermilion Chinese ink, and outside the door, there is a memorial gateway which was written "The number one school in southeast. " In the back, there are four studies which were used for students to study by themselves. Just ahead is the Mingde Hall built in Nansong Dynasty and its present name was inscribed by Wen Tianxiang, who is one of China's national heroes. Mingde Hall is a major ancient architectural landmark. During the Imperial Examinations for Recruiting Civil Servants, skillful writers would come here to attend a lecture on the 1stand 15thdays of each month. Well, everybody, having visited so many scenic spots and historical sites, let's go to taste some local snacks.

Local Snacks

I assume that all of you know something about the local snacks here, which have a history as long as that of the Qinhuai River. The Confucius Temple's local snack in Qinhuai is one of the four great types of local snacks in China. This area is full of teahouses, restaurants and snack stalls which form a food concentration area with uniquely traditional Qinhuai characteristics. After many years of hard work, seven refreshment stores made eight excellent snacks which boast good techniques, attractive appearance, and well-chosen ingredients. They have been called the "Eight excellent snacks of Qinhuai" by the Qinhuai Local Snacks Institute after being appraised by independent experts in September of 1987. The number one snack is the "Egg in Tea with Five Flavours", "Five-Flavour Bean" and Yuhua Tea from the Kuiguang Pavilion. Number two is the Yongheyuan Shrimp and Yellow Sesame Seed Cake. Number three are the shredded snacks with sesame oil and the Qifang Pavilion Crisp Sesame Seed Cake. Number four is the Luifeng House bean curd and scallion cake. Number five is the Qifang Pavilion assorted stuffed bun and noodles with shredded chicken. Number six are Jiangyou Restaurant's beef soup and beef. Number seven are the Zhanyuan Noodle House's dumplings and noodles with fried fish. Number eight is the sweet dumplings with osmanthus flavor and five-color pastry. Maybe you can't wait to taste them, so let's now go and eat some of them. You'll have two hours to enjoy all the great food here, but please don't forget to come back here on time.

Qinhuai Boats

Having finished our meals, let's go boating on the Qinhuai River to appreciate the beautiful scenery. The Ming Dynasty style river boat is a gailypainted pleasure-boat which integrates a coach's ceiling with a fishing boat's body. Red colored balls and lanterns dangle from its bow. During each lantern festival, Nanjing's citizens would come here to play around. This kind of boat is also called light boat, and there is old saying that "Qinhuai Light Boats are the best under heaven". As an important carrier of water culture, the gaily-painted pleasure-boat displays cultural infor-mation and ideas and is trademark of historical cultural value. The gaily-painted pleasure-boat floats in the river with people walking in it. The water of Qinhuai River flows by our side, leaving us with beautiful sounds which make us spontaneously recall many things. Next we will take the gaily-painted pleasure-boat and the guide on the boat will introduce the scenery and the history of Qinhuai for us. Now you can go boating on the river to appreciate the culture and the traces of history. See you later!

Isn't it specially interesting to visit Qinhuai by boat? Ok everybody! Our journey is

華東地區

about to end. And I have to say goodbye to you all. Anyway I am very glad to have spent such a happy and unforgettable day with you. I just hope that the scenery and legends of Qinhuai have left you a good memory. And I hope many years later, you can still remember the water, the boat and the snacks of Qinhuai. Thank you all! I wish you a happy journey!Goodbye!

各位朋友，大家好啊！「有朋自遠方來，不亦説乎！」我代表旅行社對大家來秦淮河旅遊、觀光表示熱烈歡迎。希望大家在秦淮河逗留期間能夠玩得開心，吃得放心，同時希望大家在遊覽過程中能有較大的收穫，並留下美好的回憶。

秦淮河是南京古老文明的搖籃，是大自然和歷史的恩賜，正是這條河孕育了綺麗的金陵特色文化。沒來秦淮河就枉來南京城，人們貫於把「秦淮」當做南京的代名詞。秦淮河古稱淮水，據説秦始皇時鑿通方山引淮水，橫貫城中，故名秦淮河。秦淮河旅遊區是中國國家4A級旅遊景區，也是中國旅遊勝地四十佳之一，位於南京老城區城南，從市區出發，坐汽車約需20分鐘就能到達。它是一個以夫子廟為中心，集遊覽、購物、品嚐風味於一體，展示古城風貌和民族風情的旅遊勝地。在這「十里珠簾」的秦淮風光帶上，點綴著數不盡的名勝佳景，匯集著説不完的逸聞掌故。這裡始終是南京最繁華的地方之一。百聞不如一見，大家要想對秦淮河有一個深刻的瞭解，就請跟我一起遊覽吧。

江南貢院

提起夫子廟，無論到沒到過南京的人，總有幾分曉得。人們通常所説的夫子廟，實際包括夫子廟、學宮和貢院三大建築群，它不僅是明清時期南京的文教中心，同時也是居東南各省之冠的文教建築群。我們首先去參觀一下夫子廟的古建築群之一——江南貢院。

現在我們所站的地方便是貢院街，貢院街北面就是古代時南京規模龐大的考試場——江南貢院。江南貢院始建於南宋乾道四年（公元1168 年），迄今已有800多年的歷史。江南貢院在歷史上建築的規模十分宏大，原有號舍20644間。江南貢院在歷史上是中國最大的考場，有許多歷史名人都曾是這裡的考生，林則徐、李鴻章、曾國藩等都曾經在這裡做過考官。民族英雄文天祥、大書法家顏真卿等，中國共產黨第一任總書記陳獨秀都是這裡的考生。可惜現存貢院建築已屈指可數，明遠樓就是保存下來的貢院建築之一，而其他大部分已被闢為市場。下面我們只能透過參觀明遠樓來想像一下當時江南貢院的盛況了。

明遠樓

請大家隨我繼續往前行，現在呈現在我們眼前的這座三層古建築，就是明遠樓了。明遠樓為江南貢院的中心建築，修建於明嘉靖十三年（公元1534年），距今雖已有470 多年歷史，但仍保存完好，它是中國目前所保留的最古老的一座貢院考場建築。樓呈四方形，飛檐出甍，四面設窗，站在樓上，可以一覽貢院，它當時起著號令和指揮全考場的作用。考生考完後，「金榜」就張貼在前面的貢院街。清末廢除科舉後，貢院也隨之失去了原來的作用。外牆嵌《金陵貢院遺蹟碑》，記述了貢院的興衰歷史。1919年除留下明遠樓和一部分號舍建築用以陳列歷史文物外，其餘一併拆除，闢為市場。站在明遠樓上駐足觀望，雖然往日的繁盛趕考場景已不能再現，但還是能夠讓人感受到那個時代留下的文化氣息。現在給大家一點自由的時間登樓參觀，好好感受一下我們祖先留下的文化遺產。

夫子廟

從明遠樓出來，我們將繼續去體驗秦淮風光的另一個精華——夫子廟。夫子廟是孔廟的俗稱，是供奉和祭祀中國古代著名的思想家、教育家孔子的廟宇，其全稱是「大成至聖先師文宣王廟」，簡稱「文廟」。夫子廟始建於宋景祐元年（公元1034年），由東晉學宮擴建而成。前面以秦淮河為泮池，南岸有中國最長的照壁。東有奎光閣，西有聚星亭，象徵文風昌盛。中軸線上建有櫺星門、大成門、大成殿、明德堂、尊經閣等建築。

現在我們眼前的這段秦淮河，自宋以後就成了夫子廟（孔廟）的泮池，又稱月牙池。我們對岸有一段朱紅色石磚牆，這就是夫子廟的照壁，始建於明萬曆年間，

華東地區

長110米，高8米，規模超過山東曲阜孔廟照壁，號稱天下第一壁。經修整一新後，目前的夫子廟大成照壁黑瓦紅牆，兩條金龍戲珠，十分氣派。請大家回頭看，這座樓閣式建築叫魁星閣，魁星原是北七星中最前面的一顆星，神話傳說中則把它奉為主宰文章興衰與保護文人學士的保護神。中國從漢代即開始尊崇這位保護神，到唐宋更盛行之，大部分夫子廟前左右都有兩座魁星閣，歷朝各代文人學子也都不敢怠慢了這位尊神。這座臨街傍水的建築初建於清乾隆年間，曾兩次被毀，1985年重建。

廣場

請大家跟我繼續參觀。現在我們來到了清代開闢的廟前廣場，廣場東西兩端豎有兩塊碑，高有一丈許，上面刻有滿漢兩種文字「文武大臣至此下馬」，表示對聖人孔子的崇敬。左側的這座六角重檐亭子叫「聚星亭」。它歷盡劫難，居然保存到1960年代仍安然端立，但在「文革」期間，卻被作為「破爛的四舊」而拆除了。現在的聚星亭是1984年開始動工復建的。全亭重檐雕脊，檐角起翹飛，有鳥雀欲躍之勢，是南京罕見的精美古亭。

請看廣場正中端立著的這座巍峨壯美，十分引人注目的牌坊，它叫「天下文樞坊」。請大家隨我往前走。這座門是廟的第一道大門，叫櫺星門。各位遊客，走過櫺星門，便是孔廟的正門，叫大成門，也叫戟門。大成門為古代抬梁穿鬥式建築，翹角龍脊，三門並立，每扇門上有45　枚門釘及龍頭啣環。門內左右兩側立南齊、元、宋時期的石碑四塊，記載了孔子生平事跡。

大成殿

大成門內兩側的走廊連接著大成殿，巍峨輝煌的大成殿是夫子廟的核心建築，封建時代只有官員可以由大門出入，一般士子只能從旁邊進出。請各位遊客隨我進入孔廟主殿——大成殿。

現在映入大家眼簾的這座漢白玉臥碑，正面是古代名書法家題的「南京夫子廟」，背面鐫刻詳細記載了夫子廟重修的經過。大成殿的主殿高16.22米，寬28.1

米，深21.7 米，重檐飛翹，斗栱交錯。「大成」的意思是孔子集古聖先賢思想之大成。大成殿內原先正中供奉的是孔子和他的四位高徒，兩旁是孔家子弟塑像十二尊。現在的大成殿已被闢為「南京鄉土文化博物館」。

請大家再往前走，這裡便是夫子廟的學宮。門楣上原有朱紅墨字「學宮」匾額，門外原有柏木牌坊，上書「東南第一學」。其後原有四書齋，為學子的自修室。再後為明德堂，建於南宋（公元　1139年），現堂名為文天祥書寫。明德堂是學宮的主體建築，科舉時代秀才每月逢朔望都到這裡聽訓導宣講。各位遊客，參觀完了這麼多的名勝古蹟，已經讓我們大飽眼福，現在讓我們也去過一下嘴癮。

小吃

大家一定對秦淮風味小吃早有所聞吧，它的歷史幾乎和秦淮河一樣悠久。夫子廟秦淮風味小吃是中國四大小吃群之一。夫子廟地區茶樓飯店，街邊小吃，滿目皆是，形成獨具秦淮傳統特色的飲食集中地。經過多年的努力，夫子廟地區有七家點心製作店，因其工藝精細，造型美觀、選料考究、風味獨特而著稱。南京秦淮區風味小吃研究會於1987年9月正式命名這八套秦淮風味名點小吃為「秦淮八絕」，現推薦給廣大遊客：「一絕」為魁光閣的五香茶葉蛋、五香豆、雨花茶；「二絕」為永和園的開洋乾絲、蟹殼黃燒餅；「三絕」為奇芳閣的麻油乾絲、鴨油酥燒餅；「四絕」為六鳳居的豆腐澇、蔥油餅；「五絕」為奇芳閣的什錦菜包、雞絲麵；「六絕」為蔣有記的牛肉湯、牛肉鍋；「七絕」為瞻園麵館的薄皮包餃、紅湯爆魚面；「八絕」為蓮湖甜食店的桂花夾心小元宵、五色糕團。大家一定等不及了吧，好聽不如好吃，讓我們趕快行動吧。給大家兩個小時的時間盡情品嚐，不過別因為留戀美食忘了集合的時間地點哦。

秦淮畫舫

酒足飯飽後，讓我們泛舟秦淮河去欣賞一下兩岸旖旎的風光。現在大家所看到河中的仿照明代建築風格製造的船就是傳說中的秦淮畫舫，秦淮畫舫是將中原的馬車頂棚和江南的漁舟之身相結合而形成的，船頭掛有大紅綵球和紅燈籠。每到元宵佳節，南京人習慣來這裡遊玩賞燈。秦淮河的燈船、河船久負盛名，素有「秦淮燈船甲天下」之説。因河而生的秦淮畫舫作為一種重要的水文化載體，承載著文化訊息的傳播、文化觀念的展示，具有重要的歷史文化價值，是秦淮品牌之一，蕩一次秦淮畫舫，聽一段秦淮故事，嘗一道秦淮小吃，賞一河秦淮花燈！舫在水中走，人在舫中遊，秦淮水在耳邊輕輕吟唱，使人油然生出無盡暢想。接下來我們將乘仿古畫舫遊覽秦淮河，船上有導遊向遊客介紹十里秦淮的兩岸風光及歷史故事。全程約45 分鐘。各位朋友，我的介紹就到這裡。下面就請您根據自己的興趣，親身投入到秦淮河的懷抱裡，沿著歷史文化的足跡慢慢地遊覽，仔細地品味。我們回頭見。

　　槳聲燈影裡看秦淮是不是別有一番滋味呢？好的，各位朋友！我們的旅程馬上要結束了，我也要跟大家説再見了，今天非常高興能和大家度過愉快而難忘的一天，也許我並不是很好的導遊，但是我相信秦淮風光和傳説卻是最美的，希望多年後，您還能時常憶起秦淮的水，秦淮的船，秦淮的小吃，永遠珍藏這段美好的秦淮之旅。謝謝各位！願大家旅途平安愉快，再見！

Suzhou Classical Gardens （蘇州園林）

Hello, My dear friends coming from afar. It's my pleasure to join you while visiting this beautiful city, Suzhou, which is dubbed "the heaven on earth". Before we get the destination, I would like to introduce the Suzhou gardens to you first. Since ancient times, Suzhou has been praised as "the city of gardens", and there is an old saying which goes "gardens in the south of Yangtze River belittle those elsewhere, and Suzhou's gardens belittle those in the south of Yangtze River". Due to their beautiful scenery, Suzhou's gardens enjoy good reputation both at home and abroad. It has a history of more than 2, 000 years which earned it unique historical status and value in world gardening history. In December of 1997, UNESCO designated Suzhou's Classical Gardens as a World Heritage Site.

Our garden tour will include four destinations, namely the "four great gardens" :Canglang Kiosk, Lion Woods, Zhuozheng Garden, and Liu Garden, which respectively represent garden styles of four dynasties, which are the Song, Yuan, Ming, and Qing.

Well, now we've reached the first destination of our Golden Journey, the Liu Garden.

Liu Garden

Located outside Suzhou's Xichang Gate, which is famous for its magnificent gates and doors, the Qing style Liu Garden was first built during the Ming Dynasty Emperor Wanli's reign, more than 400 years ago. In the first few years, Liu Garden was owned by Liu Rongfeng, who called it his "Hanbi Mountain Villa". Because the surname of its owner was Liu, it was generally called "Liu Garden". In the Qing Dynasty's Xianfeng period, the Garden survived a terrible war out of the Chang Gate of Suzhou, in which all the surrounding houses and streets were destroyed. Then during the reign of Emperor Tongzhi, Sheng Kang from Changzhou bought this garden and rebuilt it, after being rewarded for curing Empress Cixi's dermatitis.

There are three kinds of sayings to explain the origin of "Liu Garden". A common way is to rename the garden by using homophonic words, so the former surname "Liu" was changed into the latter "Liu" that means remains. The second saying is that when Sheng Kang was repairing the garden, he found a stele engraved with "長留天地間" which was said to be written by Liu Bowen. Liu believed that since the garden survived the war, it was blessed and protected by the God; he also wanted the garden to remain in the hands of Sheng Kang's family for ever. Another saying derives from the sentence "但留風月伴煙夢" in which the word "留" signifies that visitors are reluctant to leave the scenery.

Thanks to the attentive care of Sheng Kang's son the Liu Garden's reputation grew and it became a famous private garden. But before the liberation, it was badly damaged

華東地區

by the Japanese army and Kuomintang. The present garden was restored after these disasters.

Now we will enter the entrance hall. Let's appreciate the panoramic painting on this large-scale carved lacquer ware screen.

The Liu Garden can be divided into four parts:central, east, west and north. The central part mainly consists of miniature mountains and rivers depicting water and mountain scenery. The east part is famous for its architecture. In the west part you can have fun in the woods and the north part embodies rural life. A corridor runs more than six hundred meters through the garden.

Now, let's go and appreciate all this beautiful scenery. Firstly, please turn back and look at the black gate we have just walked through. You must feel strange why in such an unconventional garden the gate isn't conspicuous. In fact, most gardens in Suzhou were built as private gardens by officials after they resigned from their posts. After a long period of being officials, they were exhausted and no longer wanted to deal with vexing probleMs.They just wished to pursue a life in solitude, so none of the private gardens in Suzhou have big gates. They are very simple and similar to gates at ordinary people's houses.

Going forward, we come to the central part of Liu Garden and what we see is one of the Eighteen Scenes—Old Interwound Trees（ "古木交柯" ）.

In the middle wall, there embedded a horizontal inscribed board inscribed with "古木交柯" . Beside the horizontal inscribed board there is a parterre in which there is a cypress and a Yunnan camellia. The "古木" refers to the cypress and camellia in the parterre, "交柯" refers to the crisscrossing branches of those two trees symbolizing couples love each other and remain attached for life. It is a vivid mountains-and-waters painting with a pink wall as the background and with cypress and camellia embellished on bricks.

Well, let's move forward. Now the little house L Yin （綠蔭） by the pool is famous as a good site for appreciating spring scenery.

Originally, beside the house there is an old beech tree and an old maple tree, the branches of which are like two big umbrellas over the roof. Since the house was in the shade of those old trees, it was therefore given the present name L Yin which also derives from a poem sentence by the Ming Dynasty poet, Gao Qi. And the four characters, "花步小築" are written on the L Yin house's back wall. Why did people leave these characters on the wall?The past name of the areas around Liu Garden was Huabuli （花步裡）. And "小築" means small-scale building. It is a modest way for the owner to say that his garden is just a small building on the verge of Huabuli.

After appreciating the L Yin House's spring scenery, we come to Hanbishan Hall （涵碧山房）, a Yingshan style building with a curl shed and three rooMs.It is the main hall in the central part of the garden and its name is taken from a poem which written by the Song Dynasty scholar, Zhu Xi. The building adjacent to Mingse storied building （明瑟樓） in the east was built facing the pool and was separated from the Little Penglai by the pool.

In midsummer when the surrounding mountains and woods reflected in such a green pool and all the lotus flowers in it are in full bloom, it becomes an excellent site to appreciate the latter's beauty and was therefore also called Lotus Flowers Hall. This hall's notable feature are its French windows, which take the place of walls in the south and north, and make the hall seem spacious and bright.

Go along the mountain climbing corridor on the west side of Hanbishan Hall, we will come to the highest building, the Wenmuxixiang Small Room （聞木樨香軒）, which is a kind of small room in the central part of the garden. It is in fact a kiosk

華東地區

built alongside the corridor.

"木樨" is another name of osmanthus. The surrounding places are planted with osmanthus.

Every mid-autumn, when a heady fragrance of laurel blossoms wafts through the fresh air and the bright moon in the sky is reflected in the pool agitating with waves, the Wenmuxixiang Small Room, becomes the best place to appreciate autumn scenery.

In the front of the small room, there is a couplet which means the varied lake stones set off by osmanthus trees have an exquisite and primitive simplicity, and when autumn comes the whole mountain will be bathed in the fragrance of osmanthus. Here the word "動" is used extremely good. It makes the scenery vivid.

Besides, Wenmuxixiang Small Room also contains profound Buddhist thoughts which is like the fragrance of osmanthus. It is everywhere but we can not see it or touch it. Only by （Buddhist） meditating by heart, can everybody get the implied meaning.

Walking out of the Wenmuxixiang Small Room and going along the winding stone path heading north, we will see a six-angle pavilion among these ginkgo trees. These ginkgo trees are 100 to 200 years old and are a rare species. As "亭" （pavilion） in Chinese sounds like "停" （stop）, we can say it is time to stop and have a rest here.

Please look at the little stone desk in the kiosk. It is made of Lingbi stone which has always been regarded as good stone material from Lingbi County, Anhui Province.

Around Ke kiosk people planted plum blossoms for appreciating snow scenery in winter, making the pavilion the best place in the central part of Liu Garden to appreciate winter scenery.

From Ke kiosk we can see Mingse storied building（明瑟樓） and Hanbishan Hall（涵碧山房）to the south. These three buildings are separated by the pool. Mingse storied building resembles a comfortable and gaily painted pleasure boat's bow and forecastle, while Hanbishan Hall is its cabin.

Huajie street （花街） is located north of the Ke kiosk, which is about 50 meters long, and is behind a rockery. It seems like brocade on which there are pictures of Chinese flowering crabapple made of cobblestones, bits of porcelain, stones, tiles and some other materials.

The Yuancui Pavilion is located at the end of the Huajie. Please follow me as we come to the little "little Penglai" island in the middle of the pool.

Legend has it that in the Bohai Sea, there are three mountains Penglai, Fangzhang, and Yingzhou on which celestial beings live. Since the First Qin Emperor wished to live forever, he once sent Xu Fu to ask for their elixir vitae and built three mountains modeled on those in Bohai Sea. From then on, building three celestial mountains in the middle of a pool, referred to as the method of "one pool, three islands" has been commonly used in building classical gardens. The pool in the middle of Liu Garden takes the shape of a square. Bridge island divides the pool into two parts, one seems spacious and the other tranquil. In addition to building the rockery in the middle of the pool, people built a narrow mountain stream in the west of the pool to make the source of water appear endless and vivid.

Walking through the little bridge in the east part of Little Penglai, we will find the little square Haopu Pavilion. Both Hao and Pu are names of ancient rivers.

It is said that Zhuangzi once fished on Pu River and enjoyed the sight of fishes on Hao River with Huizi. Here, fishing and enjoying the sight of fish can arouse people's interests in their quest to free themselves from the world's troubles by withdrawing

華東地區

from society and living in solitude.

Haopu Pavilion was built across the pool. Please look at the peak-like stone in front of the kiosk named "Yinyue（印月）". The eddy in the peak-like stone is just like the moon when reflected in the pool, enabling people to appreciate the moon irrespective of whether it is actually in the sky. This method of taking advantage of one scene to express another is rare and original.

OK, let's move on. Now the building with two floors in front of us is the Quxi tower （曲溪樓）. It is about ten meters in length, which is only about half of its original scale, and its depth is only about 3 meters.

Let's go into this building to pay a visit. Those holes on windows are used for sightseeing. It is a way of creating scenery and having the beautiful change as people walk alongside them. You can have a try.

Heading north further, we come to the Wufengxianguan （五峰仙館）, which is one of the major buildings in the east part of Liu Garden. Its structure is made of Nanmu and all the fitments in it are of classical beauty and in elegant taste. This building is the largest existing hall in Suzhou and is famed for being "the first hall in the south of Yangtze River". It once was used by its owner as the place for big banquets, weddings, funerals, and the like.

Well, now you have some time to visit the courts and other buildings around the hall by yourself.

Lions Grove Garden

Liu Garden really makes people reluctant to leave, but the next site we are going to visit also has its own unique characteristics. It is the Lions Grove Garden, which was built by a Buddhist monk Tian Ru in the second year of Zhizheng Period, Yuan

Dynasty. As the representative of gardens in Yuan Dynasty, this 600-year-old garden is famous for its rockeries. It has China's largest group of ancient rockeries. The lake stone and rockeries in it are superb and have led people to call it "the kingdom of rockeries".

Now we've got to the destination. Please follow me. Let's go inside to pay a visit. The big hall we see now is the Bei Family's Ancestral Temple. Its roof has statuettes of the three immortals, 福（happiness）, 祿（good fortune）, 壽（longevity）, as well as a child, which symbolize all the descendants will be blessed by these three immortals.

Walking through Bei Family's Ancestral Temple, we will come to Yanyu Hall （燕譽堂）, one of the main halls in this garden. Its name indicates good fame, high salary and bringing good honor to ancestors. In the front court, there is a parterre under the big white wall and in this parterre there are rows of peonies and yulans implying "riches and honors".

Please walk forward, then we arrive at a square hall （小方廳）. The specially made bricks under the back window are "gold bricks" for palace. On the left and right, there are big windows for sightseeing. From the window in the east you can see chimonanthus and the window in the west looks out to the Suzhou City Woods. You can observe and learn from this means of artistic expression in designing gardens. Now we are in the north court of the little square hall. Please look at the big Tai lake peak stone in the parterre. It is Nine Lions Peak （九獅峰） because if you observe carefully you can see nine different shapes of lions.

Let's go on. Here is the two-storey pavilion Zhiboxuan （指柏軒）, which was once used for Buddhist monks to handle cases and discuss ideas and thoughts. From this building, you can see the rockeries in the Lions Grove Garden. It is said that Qing Emperor Qianlong once sketched and painted here. And you are free to take photos of

華東地區

this lovely place.

We have been intoxicated with the wonderful scenery in the garden. Now we are in Zhenqu Pavilion （真趣亭）, in which there is a golden base board on which Qianlong wrote the two green characters "真趣", along with painted beams, painted rafters and beautiful decorations. All these make it entirely different from other private gardens. This place is the major sightseeing place within the garden. It is like a big landscape painting full of poetic and artistic conception with Baishi mountain （百獅山） in the east, rockeries to the south, waterfalls to the west and kiosks and bridges to the north.

Now we are climbing miniature mountains to appreciate the charming "kingdom of rockeries". After climbing these miniature mountains, we will continue our visit. Now we are at Lixue Hall （立雪堂）. The second character in this name is "snow," and there is an interesting story about how it got to be included here. During Northern Song Dynasty, one day Yangshi and Youcu went to Chengyi's to consult him. But Chengyi was taking an afternoon nap, so both of them just waited outside. Then it started to snow and when Chengyi waked up, there was about an inch of snow on the ground.

Well, that's the end of our tour of Lions Grove Garden.

Zhuozheng Garden(The Humble Administrator's Garden)

Everybody, the next site we are going to visit is a classical garden in Ming Dynasty style. It is one of China's key cultural relics, a UNESCO world cultural heritage site, and ranks among the four great gardens in the country, alongside the Summer Palace in Beijing, Chengde Summer Resort, and Liu Garden in Suzhou.

Now, we are standing in front of the Zhouzheng Garden's gate. Its first owner, Wang Xianchen, was not happy working as a government servant and quit his post. He bought land to build a garden in his hometown and named it Zhuozheng Garden quoting the passage, "拙者之為政", from an essay written by the earlier Jing Dynasty scholar, Pan Yue. The passage refers to the kind of person who derives livelihood as well as pleasure from growing vegetables and flowers and is therefore free of worldly affairs and worries. Here it denotes the humble administrator who was able to devote himself to gardening and made it his "official" duty. Let's now go inside to have a look. We are now at the east part of Zhuozheng Garden. Let's first visit Lanxue Hall（蘭雪堂）. It is the main hall in the east. It faces south and has three rooMs.Its name was taken after one of Li Bai's poeMs.Let's go inside. There is a screen in the middle of the hall and on it you can see a lacquer ware carved panorama of Zhuozheng Garden which is divided into three parts:the east part, the central part and the west part.

In the east part you can enjoy rural scenery. While the quintessence of the garden lies in the central part and it still keeps the style of Ming Dynasty. The east part was rebuilt by Zhang L qian, the owner in Qing Dynasty. So this part is partially based on Qing Dynasty architectural style.

Walking out of Lanxue Hall and through rockeries, we will reach Lotus Pavilion（芙蓉榭）, which has an elegant ancient Chinese architectural style. It is flexible because it is constituted by its surrounding scenery. As it is built over the pool, Lotus Pavilion is the best place in the east part of the garden to appreciate these flowers. And it is because of the hibiscus planted around the structure that it is given the name Lotus Pavilion. Let's move forward. The eight-angle pavilion with double eaves in front of us is the Heaven Spring Pavilion（天泉亭）and is the Zhuozheng Garden's biggest pavilion. A well is located under this pavilion, along with the Yuan Dynasty Dahong Temple's（大弘寺）remains, so it is called the "Heaven Spring Pavilion". The pavilion is surrounded by green grass and thick woods. Don't you get the feeling of being in rural scenery? After visiting Heaven Spring Pavilion, we then come to Shuxiang Court（秫香館）to enjoy the sight of rice paddy fields. Standing here, we can better realize the leisure life of the owner after he left office.

華東地區

Having walked through a long double corridor, we come to the central garden—the quintessence of this garden. The overall display is centered by a pool and all the pavilions, terraces, towers and corridors are built by this and other bodies of water. Some are even built above the water, which has the characteristics of South Yangtze River Region's rivers and lakes. Let's first pay a visit to Wuzhuyouju （梧竹幽居）, namely the square kiosk in front of us. It is the major scenic site in the central part. The pavilion is built unconventionally with four round holes or doors on the four walls. From any angle, you can get a peculiar sight of those holes overlapping one with another. "Seeing is believing and seeing is amazing, " so let's appreciate the intelligence of the old designers. Well, now look at the couplet written by the Qing Dynasty calligrapher, Zhao Zhiqian. Those 14 words express precisely the quintessence of the scenery in this garden, the ways to appreciate and the feelings about it. So we can think carefully of this classical couplet.

We need to proceed more quickly, because there are still many beautiful scenes for our visit. Please look at the boat-like building. It is Xiangzhou （香洲）, one of the typical views in Zhuozheng Garden, which is in the oft-used boat style. This architectural style has the characteristics of a small room （軒）, a pavilion or house on a terrace （榭）, and a storied building （樓） that harmonize with other buildings. Xiangzhou is a typical boat-style building that is exquisitely decorated and is well coordinated with the surrounding mountains and waters. We might as well go inside to appreciate its beauty.

Let's continue our journey. Now we come to Little Canglang Pavilion （小滄浪亭）, which is named after Suzhou Zhuozheng Garden's Canglang （滄浪） Kiosk. The four pillars are made of pine and look simple and elegant. We can have a rest on the stone desk and stools here. Looking to the north, we can see the corridor bridge reflected in the pool. When there are ripples on the pool, the reflection image of corridor bridge is just like a rainbow. So it is the best place to appreciate water scenery. When you are taking a break, don't forget the beautiful water scenery.

Coming out of Little Canglang Kiosk and continuing to head east, we will go to see Yuanxiang, or Drifting Fragrance Hall （遠香堂）, a typical four-sided hall on the central pool's south end. There are lotus flowers both in front and back of it. The Zhuozheng Garden has indivisible relations with lotus flowers, and Yuanxiang Hall is the best place to enjoy their beauty. Those who like lotus flowers should not miss this place.

Having appreciated lotus flowers, we then go to "Loquat Garden" which is planted with loquat trees. I think you cannot hide your greed when heard the name of this garden. But it is not the season for the harvest of loquat. Does it disappoint you? It doesn't matter; there are good views in it. The gate of the "loquat garden" is ingeniously designed. Now look at the white wall in front, you may think there is no way ahead, but just a few steps forward you may find a door hidden from the view of a rockery made from yellow stones. And as we move further, the door will expand gradually and when you come to the door you may find the door is like a moon inlayed in the white wall. Walking through the door and going forward, you may find the "moon" will be hidden from the view of the rockery gradually again. The owner ingeniously chose the best place for this moon-like door by aligning it with the Xuexiangyunwei, or Fragrant Snow and Abundant Clouds Pavilion （雪香雲蔚亭）, Yuedong, Moon Gate （月洞門）, and Jiashi Pavilion （嘉實亭）. And it is amazing that the moon-like door connects the sights on both sides and thus forms a new kind of scene.

Next, we will visit the western style garden or Buyuan （補園）. Most of the buildings located in the east and central part were built during the Qing Dynasty. What you now see is a Mandarin Duck Hall （鴛鴦廳） with a style of its own. It is divided into two halls.

Well, you will have a little free time to visit some small scenic spots.

華東地區

Seeing that you are not willing to leave, I really don't want to urge you for our next site. But our journey has been carefully planned, and we have to go by the schedule, so please be quick. Thanks for your cooperation.

Canglang Pavilion

The last destination we are going to visit is the oldest classical garden in the history of Suzhou, the Canglang Pavilion, which was first built by Su Shunqin as his private garden in North Song Dynasty. It is a typical Song Dynasty style garden with mountains and waters. The method used to build the Canglang Pavilion is extraordinary. Standing outside, you can see the ripples on the green water and willows weeping in the wind. How beautiful the scenery is! Let's save our praise to appreciate the charming views inside.

In the hall, you can see many stone inscriptions, so it is also known as Stone Tablet Hall. The historical information on these stone inscriptions is valuable, as they provide valuable knowledge regarding the Canglang Pavilion's former appearance and history. Go and take a look at them.

The Canglang Pavilion's principal mountain, Zhenshanlin （真山林） which is built mainly out of dirt rather than stone, is located just outside of the hall. Scholars have verified that it can be traced all the way back to the Song Dynasty about 900 years ago. Despite its age, the mountain now still looks fresh, and the old and new trees on it are thriving. Don't you think it is as real as one of the mountains outside of the garden?

Walking along the corridor, we will get to Water-Facing Room （面水軒）. This is a four sided hall with four French windows. Since it faces a clear pool, it is named Water-Facing Room; this name also derives from the poems written by two old and famous Chinese poets named Du Fu and Su Shunqin. You can go inside to look freely. It is a good place to appreciate water scenery while chatting with others. Going forward, we will come to a square kiosk named the Fish Sightseeing place （觀魚處）, which was given this name because three of its sides facing water. The water in the pool is clear, and we can have a rest here to get a feel for ancient leisure life.

Now, we start to climb the Zhenshanlin Mountain. The verdant age-old trees and the hanging vines along the road make you have a feeling of returning to nature. Unconsciously, we reach the peak of the mountain without great efforts. Please look at the square kiosk on the mountain's peak:that is Canglang Pavilion, which was originally built during the Northern Song Dynasty and was then destroyed by wars. The present one was built in the 35 th year of the Qing Emperor Kangxi's reign. A couplet is written on this kiosk saying "the breeze and bright moon are worthless, mountains nearby and waters far away are all interesting". The first line of the couplet is from Ou Yangxiu's poem, and the second line of the couplet is from Su Shunqin's poem. This couplet was composed by Liang Zhangju when he rebuilt this kiosk. You can try to look down from Canglang Kiosk then you will get a panorama of this garden.

Going down the hill, we will then go to visit Mingdao Hall （明道堂） whose former name was Hanguang Hall （寒光堂）. It is the principal hall with three rooMs.The hall's name was taken from a Su Shunqin poem. Please follow me and go inside. The hall is spacious and elegant. In the hall, there are four marble hanging panels with two couplets. Those who are interested in poems and couplets can take a careful look at them.

Walking along the corridor, we then come to Yaohua Bourn （" 華境界"）. There is a quadrangle style building group with corridors on its sides located south of Mingdao Hall. In legends, Yaohua is an immortal flower as white as jasper. People can have long life eating it.

It was once a stage for officials and scholars in Qing Dynasty. It is said that Lin

Zexu also watched Kunju opera here.

Walk along the path, we will see a cottage surrounded by green bamboo groves. Here is Cuilinglong （翠玲瓏）. We can go inside to have a look. It was once the owner's study composed of three little houses. It seems it has been separated from the outside world in such bamboo groves. Therefore, it has always been the place for men of literature and writing to chant and write poetry, as well as paint.

Let us go forward to the Memorial Hall of Five Hundred Late Sages （五百名賢祠）, which consists of a little court with five rooMs.Three of them in the middle are halls and the other two are side rooMs.In front of it, there is a corridor with decorations hanging between the eaves and pillars. Eighteen French windows stand between the pillars. It was first built by Tao Peng during the 7thyear of Qing Dynasty Emperor Daoguang's reign and was rebuilt by Zhang Shusheng during the 12thyear of Emperor Tongzhi's reign. A horizontal board is inscribed with the words "be a model for others". Three of the walls are inlayed with 549 images carved by the Qing Dynasty scholar Gu Xiangzhou. Each of these figures were vividly engraved on one stone with poems and the persons' names, posts and ranks. It includes Suzhou's historical figures over the 2500 years spanning the Spring and Autumn Period to the Qing Dynasty. It is rare to see such age-old stone inscriptions with so many carefully engraved images from the Spring and Autumn Period to the Qing Dynasty. So you can have some time to know something about the historical figures and to better understand Suzhou's history.

OK, let's move on to the Qingxiang Court （清香館）. It was given this name because of two kinds of sweet trees in the north court. When the blossom season comes, the delicate fragrance will float everywhere. All the furniture made of roots inside the room have a history of more than 100 years. They were all delicately and ingeniously made with vivid birds and animals carved on it.

The last site is Emperor Stone Tablet Pavilion （御碑亭） on which Emperor Kangxi wrote poeMs.That's why it is called Emperor Stone Tablet Pavilion. And you will have a little time to take photos.

When coming out of Canglang Pavilion, our journey in the garden also finishes. I hope the people, the streets and the classical gardens have left you a good memory and welcome to Suzhou again.

來自遠方的各位朋友：

大家好。很高興能和大家一起遊覽有著「人間天堂」美稱的蘇州。在車到景點之前，我先為大家介紹一下蘇州園林的基本情況。蘇州自古以來就被人們譽為「園林之城」，有「江南園林甲天下，蘇州園林甲江南」的説法。蘇州以園林美景久負盛名，享譽天下。蘇州古典園林歷史綿延2000 餘年，在世界造園史上有其獨特的歷史地位和價值。1997年12月，聯合國教科文組織遺產委員會將蘇州古典園林列入世界文化遺產名錄。

我們這次的園林之旅是遊覽蘇州的「四大名園」：滄浪亭、獅子林、拙政園、留園。它們分別代表了宋、元、明、清四代的古園林風格。好，現在我們到了今日黃金遊的第一站——留園。下面我們就正式開始我們的園林之旅吧。

留園

留園坐落在蘇州西閶門外，以重門疊戶、堂皇富麗稱絕，具有明顯的清代風格。留園始建於明萬曆年間，距今已經有400 多年歷史。清嘉慶初年，留園為劉蓉峰所擁有，稱為寒碧山莊，又因園主姓劉，故一般人又稱之為劉園。咸豐年間，蘇州閶門外遭兵燹，園子周圍街巷宅屋幾乎毀盡，唯獨該園倖存下來。到了同治年間，常州人盛康因用偏方治好了慈禧太后的皮炎，得到朝廷賞賜，從此發跡，於是購得此園，並重新修建一新，將它改名為「留園」。

叫留園的一個原因是「劉家花園」的「劉」與「留園」的「留」諧音，這是花園易主常用的一種改名方法。再有，盛康在整修花園時曾發現一塊「長留天地間」的石碑，據説是劉伯溫寫的，他認為這個花園歷經戰火仍然保留下來，似乎在冥冥之中有老天爺的保佑，也希望留園能永遠留在盛家手中。另外「但留風月伴煙夢」，這個「留」字也有讓客人流連忘返之意。後來，經過盛康兒子的用心經營，留園聲名大振，成了著名的私家園林。但在抗日戰爭期間，留園遭受到了日軍和國民黨很大的破壞，我們現在看到的留園是後來經過整修而成的。

現在我們進入門廳，請大家隨我一起來欣賞這大型漆雕屏風上繪的全景圖。留園可分中、東、西、北四個景區：中部是以山水奪目，東部是以建築見長，西部則是山林野趣，北部頗有田園風味。全園曲廊貫穿，長達六七百米。

下面我們就進入園中去細細品味一番吧。首先請大家回頭看一下剛剛經過的這扇黑漆大門，大家一定感到非常奇怪，為什麼這麼別緻的園林，門廳卻如此不起眼呢？其實，蘇州的園林，很多都是辭官引退後回鄉的官僚所建的私家花園。他們由於長期在朝為官，深感身心疲憊，所以不願應酬世俗煩事，只想去追求一種寄情山水的隱居生活。因此蘇州的私家園林均無氣派顯眼的高大門樓，其正門都力求淡化、簡單，以求接近普通民居。

請大家跟我往前走，現在我們到達了留園的中部，我們看到的是十八景之一的「古木交柯」，正中牆面嵌有「古木交柯」磚匾一方，磚匾旁邊是一個明式的花台，花台內種的是一棵柏樹和一棵雲南山茶樹，「古木」指花壇裡的古柏和山茶樹，「交柯」指兩樹枝幹交錯纏繞，象徵夫妻連理，百年好合。這裡以粉牆為底，翠柏山茶，上有磚額點綴，勾勒出一幅充滿生機的山水畫。

好了，我們繼續往前。現在我們看到的這臨水而築的小屋，這是賞春景的最佳去處——「綠蔭」。原來，小屋旁曾種有一棵老櫸樹，一棵老楓樹，樹枝像兩把大傘遮在屋頂上，小軒處在這古樹的綠蔭之下，借此而得名。軒名取自明代詩人高啟的「艷發朱光裡，叢依綠蔭邊」詩句。在綠蔭軒的後牆上有「花步小築」四個字，為什麼要寫上這幾個字呢？留園一帶舊名「花步裡」，「小築」就是小的建築，這是主人很謙虛的説法，意思是説我這個花園只是花步裡邊上的一處小建築而已。

在綠蔭軒欣賞完春景，現在我們來到「涵碧山房」，這三間卷棚硬山造建築，是中部花園的主廳。其名取自宋代文人朱熹的詩「一水方涵碧，千林已變紅」。建築面池而建，東臨明瑟樓，隔水與小蓬萊相望。周圍山巒林木倒映在水清如碧的池中，每當盛夏時節，池內荷花盛開，荷香陣陣，這裡便是賞荷的絕佳之處，所以又稱「荷花廳」。該廳幾乎無裝修，廳內部樸素大方，南北兩面都不設牆，是落地長窗，顯得寬敞明亮。

循著涵碧山房西側的爬山廊，我們來到中部花園中最高建築聞木樨香軒。從建築形式上看，這實際上是一個依廊而建的半亭。「木樨」就是桂花，這兒四周遍種桂花，每年中秋，丹桂飄香，晚上可以看到明月高懸，倒映水中，隨波蕩漾。因此，這兒是觀賞秋景的地方。軒前是一副對聯：「奇石盡含千古秀，桂花香動萬山秋」。這是一副狀景聯。此處千姿百態的湖石在桂花樹的掩映下，顯的玲瓏而古樸，而每到秋風送爽時，則滿山蕩漾著桂花的香氣。這裡的「動」字用得極妙，將「香味」這一園林中的虛景寫活了。不僅如此，此處的「聞木樨香軒」也包含有深刻的禪理。佛教的禪宗講究悟道，佛理就像桂花香一樣無處不在，無處不有，但卻看不見，摸不著，無影無蹤。只要用心參禪，人人都可以頓悟得道的。

出聞木樨香軒我們沿著石徑曲折向東繼續前行，大家請看這些古老的銀杏中間那個六角飛檐攢尖頂的小亭，這就是可亭。這些銀杏都有一兩百年的樹齡，是中國特有的珍稀物種之一。「亭者，停也」，也就是說可以停下來休息一下了。可亭的意思是可以供遊人停留小憩之亭。請看亭中這個小石桌，您可不要小瞧它，這是用出產於安徽靈璧縣的靈璧石製成的。靈璧石歷來被視為石中上品。可亭四周植有梅花，且宜觀賞雪景，因此，可亭也被稱為留園中部欣賞冬景之佳處。可亭與南面的明瑟樓、涵碧山房隔水相望。明瑟樓就像畫舫的前艙，涵碧山房猶如船艙，兩座建築組成了一艘形神兼備的「寫意式」畫舫，微風吹拂，波光蕩漾，這艘船就像在水中緩緩航行一般。

在可亭北面的假山後有一段長50多米的花街鋪地，用鵝卵石和碎瓷、石片、瓦片等各種材料築成海棠花紋，猶如織錦鋪地一般給人以美感。這條花街盡頭就是遠翠閣，請大家隨我往下走，現在我們來到了中部水池的小島「小蓬萊」。傳說渤海中有蓬萊、方丈、瀛洲三座仙山。秦始皇曾經派徐福前往求長生不死之仙丹，同時又在自己的宮院中仿造了三座仙山。這以後在水池中構築三座「仙山」，即所謂「一池三島」就成了古典園林造園的常用造景手法。留園中部的水池略呈方行，比較規整。橋島在劃分水面的同時，使水面造成了曠、幽不同的兩種水面效果。另外，在構築中部假山時，特意在水池西部造成一條狹窄的山澗，令人產生池水淵源不盡之感，使池水活了起來。

走過小蓬萊東側小橋，呈現在我們眼前的這個小方亭，就是濠濮亭，濠、濮都是古代河流的名字。據說，莊子曾在濮水上垂釣，也曾與惠子在濠梁上觀魚，這裡以古人的觀魚和垂釣來喚起一種超然世間煩惱的自由感，表現出歸隱田園、歸情自然的超然情趣。濠濮亭跨水而築，請看亭前水邊這一峰石，名「印月」，峰石中的渦孔倒影池中印有的一輪明月，在此不管月半中秋，有無明月當空，均能賞月。這種借景手法是比較少見的，別具匠心。

好了，我們繼續向前行，現在呈現在我們眼前的兩層建築就是曲溪樓了。曲溪樓長十餘米，因為只有半間，進深僅三米左右，其底樓實際上就是一道寬寬的廊。請大家隨我入樓觀看，這些窗框門洞都是用來觀景的，這是移步易景的造景法，每走一步都可以看到不同的秀美景色，大家可以試一試。再向北繼續前行，現在我們到達五峰仙館，此館是留園東部的主要建築之一，為楠木結構，內部裝修陳設華麗，裝修精美、陳設古雅，是蘇州現存最大的廳堂，素有「江南第一廳堂」之美譽。這裡是園主以前用於舉行重大宴飲以及婚喪壽喜的活動的場所。好了，現在給大家一點自由時間參觀廳堂周圍的院落和其他建築。

獅子林

留園實在讓人留戀，但是接下來我們將遊覽第二站——獅子林。獅子林是一座寺廟園林，元代至正二年（公元1342年），天如禪師在此築寺，距今已有600多年的歷史了，是元代園林的代表。此園以假山著稱，擁有國內尚存最大的古代假山群。湖石假山出神入化，素有「假山王國」的美稱，很多石峰形象獅子，因而得名。

　　好了，我們到達了目的地，請大家跟隨我一起進入園內參觀遊覽吧。現在我們看到的這座大廳就是貝家祠堂。在祠堂的屋頂上，有四個小雕塑，分別是福、祿、壽三位老神仙，冉加上一個小孩子，意味著子孫綿延，代代享受著福、祿、壽三位神仙的庇佑。穿過貝家祠堂，我們來到了燕譽堂，是園內主廳之一，堂名取自「式燕且譽，好爾無射」，表示名高祿重，榮宗耀祖。燕譽堂前庭內，高大的白牆下築花壇，牡丹叢植，玉蘭夾峙，寓意為「玉堂富貴」。請大家繼續往前走，現在我們來到了小方廳，此廳為正方形，廳背窗下是特別烘製後供皇宮用的「金磚」。廳的左右各有大型的空窗，是用來框景的，東窗外是素芯臘梅，西窗外卻是城市山林。大家可以好好體驗一下這種造園的藝術手法。現在我們來到小方廳北亭院內，請看花壇內這座高大的太湖石峰，這就是九獅峰，請您仔細觀察，是不是能看出九頭不同姿態的獅子呢。

　　請大家繼續往前行，現在我們看到的這座兩層的閣樓就是園內正廳——指柏軒。指柏軒原為禪僧講公案、鬥機鋒的場所。登樓南望，可見對面獅子林的假山群。傳說乾隆皇帝還在這留過影，如果大家有興趣的話，也可以攝影留個紀念。

　　我們一路陶醉在這美麗的園林中，現在來到了真趣亭，亭內懸掛金底綠字「真趣」匾是乾隆皇帝的御筆，亭內雕樑畫棟、金碧輝煌，顯示出與私家園林截然不同的皇家氣派。此處為園中主要觀景點，東品百獅山，南賞假山群，西觀山林瀑布，北見畫亭曲橋，獅子林猶如一幅徐徐展開的山水畫卷，充滿詩情畫意。如此好的觀景我們豈能錯過，給大家多一點自由時間盡情得欣賞。

　　現在我將要帶領大家一起去鑽洞爬山，好好體驗一下「假山王國」的魅力。

　　鍛鍊了一下筋骨讓我們繼續往前參觀，現在我們來到立雪堂，立雪還有一個典故：是指北宋時揚時和游酢一起去向程頤請教，程正在午睡，兩人就侍立等候，這時下雪了，等程醒來看到他們時，積雪已有一尺深了，於是就有了程門立雪這個典故。請大家跟我進入堂內，我們看這副對聯：「蒼松翠竹真佳容，明月清風是故人」。這副對聯反映了主人以松竹風月為友，脫俗超塵的情趣。從立雪堂出來，我們的行程又將告一段落。

拙政園

各位遊客，我們接下來將要遊覽的是拙政園——一座保持著明代風格的古典園林，該園為中國重點文物保護單位、中國特殊遊覽參觀點之一、世界文化遺產，與北京的頤和園、承德避暑山莊和蘇州留園合稱為中國四大名園。迄今為止同時具備這四項桂冠的中國僅拙政園一家，所以是非常值得去的地方哦。

現在我們來到了拙政園門前，該園第一位主人王獻臣晚年仕途不得意，罷官而歸，買地造園，借晉代文人潘岳《閒居賦》中「拙者之為政」句意，取名為拙政園。請大家隨我一起踏入園門。

現在我們來到了拙政園的東部，首先我們來參觀蘭雪堂吧，此堂是東部的主要廳堂，坐北朝南三開間，堂名取意於李白「獨立天地間，清風灑蘭雪」的詩句。我們進入堂內參觀吧，堂正中有屏門相隔，大家請看屏門南面這幅漆雕《拙政園全景圖》。在這幅圖上我們可以清楚地看到拙政園分成三部分：東部、中部和西部。東部以田園風光為主；中部是全園的精華所在，完好地保留了明代的風格；西部是清代主人張履謙重修的，風格上帶有明顯的清代時尚特徵。

從蘭雪堂出來，我們穿過假山，來到芙蓉榭，榭是中國古代一種很美的建築形式，憑藉周圍風景而構成，形式靈活多變。芙蓉榭是東部花園賞荷的最佳景點，一半建在岸上，一半伸向水面，秀美精巧，因周圍種植木芙蓉而得名。讓我們繼續往前走，現在呈現在我們眼前的這座重簷八角亭叫天泉亭，是拙政園中最大的亭子，亭子之所以取「天泉」這個名字，是因為它的下面有一口井，相傳為元代大弘寺遺物，終年不涸，水質甘甜，所以取名「天泉」。亭周圍綠草茵茵，林木繁盛，大家是不是也有一種回歸田園的感覺呢。過了天泉亭，我們來到了「秫香館」，這是遊人體驗稻麥飄香的地方。站在這裡，我們更能夠很好地體會園主歸隱田園的那種悠閒。

穿過一條長長的復廊，現在我們來到了全園精華所在的中部花園。其總體布局以水池為中心，亭台樓榭皆臨水而建，有的亭榭則直出水中，具有江南水鄉的特色。首先我們來觀賞「梧竹幽居」。就是我們眼前這座方亭，是中部池東的觀賞主景。亭的構思巧妙別緻，四周白牆開了四個圓形洞門，洞環洞，洞套洞，在不同的角度可看到重疊交錯的分圈、套圈、連圈的奇特景觀。「不看不知道，一看不得了」我們都親身體味古人的聰明才智了吧。好，現在請看兩旁的這副對聯「爽借清風明借月，動觀流水靜觀山」，對聯為清末名書家趙之謙撰書，簡單的十四個字把園林景觀的精髓、欣賞方式和感受都準確地表達出來了。我們也好好思索一下這經典的對聯吧。

我們要加快腳步，後面還有更多的美景等著我們呢。大家請看這座船形建築物，這就是香洲，香洲是拙政園中的標誌性景觀之一，為典型的「舫」式的結構，舫實際上是軒、榭、樓的組合建築形式，需與園中其他建築相協調呼應，一氣呵成。香洲是最為典型的舫，造型比例恰到好處，內部裝修精美，與山水環境極為協調。我們也不妨到舫中來感受這宛如畫中的感覺。

請大家隨我繼續前行，現在我們來到小滄浪亭，小滄浪是園主借蘇州拙政園滄浪亭而命名的。四柱都是原始松木建築，看起來非常淡雅古樸，富有野趣。亭內有石桌、石凳，我們在這裡稍事休息，從小滄浪亭往北看，廊橋「小飛虹」倒映在水裡，水波蕩漾，猶如彩虹。這裡是觀賞水景的最佳去處，大家在休息的時候也千萬別錯過觀賞美麗的水景。

從小滄浪亭出來，我們往東繼續前行，現在我們來到了遠香堂，典型的四面廳，其廳位於中部水池南面，四周落地長窗透空，前後水塘都種有荷花。拙政園與荷花有著不可分割的情愫，而遠香堂卻是營造賞荷的最好的地方，所以愛蓮人士們一定不要錯過。

賞完荷花，我們來到了「枇杷園」，顧名思義，這裡是種枇杷的地方。聽到這個園名，大家一定垂涎三尺了吧，但是現在不是枇杷豐收的季節，可能會讓您有一點點的失望，不過沒關係，裡面有更好的景緻等著我們呢。「枇杷園」的園門設計得很巧妙。請看前面這道雲牆，還以為沒有路了。真沒有料到，只要再往前走，就可以發現，黃石堆砌的假山遮住了旁邊的一個門洞。隨著我們一步一步走近，門洞就一點點擴大。到了門口，才發現門洞像一輪明月，鑲嵌在白色的雲牆上。過門洞後再往前走，這輪明月又被這邊的湖石假山慢慢地遮住了。園主巧妙地選擇了辟月洞門最佳位置，使「雪香雲蔚亭」「月洞門」「嘉實亭」三點同處在一條視線上，並透過月洞門聯繫前後佳景，從而組成一組對景。真是很奇妙吧！

接下來我們將遊覽西部花園。西部花園又稱「補園」。穿過別有洞天的圓洞門，我們就到了西部花園。西部園內建築大都建成於清代，其建築風格明顯有別於東部和中部。現在大家看到的是一個風格獨特的鴛鴦廳，它是一個在屋頂下面分為南北兩部分方形的獨特的建築，周圍還有一些小的景點給大家一點時間自由參觀，拍照留念。

看見大家一副戀戀不捨的樣子，我真不忍心催促大家。但是由於我們行程緊張，必須加緊時間。謝謝大家的配合。

滄浪亭

我們園林之旅的最後一站是蘇州歷史最悠久的古典園林「滄浪亭」。滄浪亭始建於北宋，為文人蘇舜欽的私人花園，具有宋代造園風格，是寫意山水園的範例。滄浪亭的造園藝術非同尋常，未入其門，就可見綠水蕩漾，垂柳依依，讓人不禁對園內的景色更加嚮往。閒話少聊，下面就讓我們趕快去領略它園內的風姿吧。

踏入門廳，廳內有很多的石刻，所以又稱碑記廳。這些石刻很有史料價值。從這些石刻可以瞭解滄浪亭的舊貌和概況，請大家自由觀看。

從門廳出來，呈現在我們眼前的這座土山就是滄浪亭的主山——真山林。這座假山土多石少，據考證是宋朝留下的，歷經900餘年仍風貌依舊。山上古木新枝，生機勃勃，宛如一座真山野林。

現在我們來到了面水軒，這是一座四面廳，因而取名「面水廳」。四面都是落地長窗，前面是一個清澈的水池，遠遠望去，就像是一艘旱船。軒名取自杜甫詩「層軒皆面水，老樹飽經霜」和蘇舜欽詩「高軒面曲水」句意。大家進去自由參觀一下，這可是一個一邊閒聊一邊觀水景的好地方。我們繼續往前行，現在呈現在我們眼前的這座三面臨水的方亭，就是「觀魚處」，亭前池水清清，我們在這裡稍停片刻，享受一下古人生活的閒情雅緻。

現在我們開始登真山林，一路走來，古樹蒼翠，藤蘿蔓掛，讓人有一種回歸大山的感覺，不知不覺我們就來到了山巔也沒感覺一絲疲倦。大家請看這座聳立在山頂的方形石亭這就是滄浪亭，北宋時建在水邊，後毀於戰火，現在的花園是康熙三十五年重修的，亭上有一副對聯：清風明月本無價，近山遠水皆有情。上聯出自歐陽修「滄浪亭」詩「清風明月本無價，可惜只賣四萬錢」；下聯出自蘇舜欽《過蘇州》詩「綠楊白鷺俱自得，近水遠山皆有情」，由梁章鉅復建滄浪亭時集成。登上滄浪亭鳥瞰園林，所有景色全收眼底，我們不妨來試一試。

接下來我們將參觀「明道堂」。此廳原名「寒光堂」，是滄浪亭的主廳，大廳共三間。廳名取蘇舜欽《滄浪亭記》中「形骸既適則神不煩，觀聽無邪則道以明」之意，請大家隨我進入廳內參觀。廳內高大寬敞，非常有氣勢，堂內懸掛大理石掛屏四幅，楹聯兩副。對詩詞楹聯感興趣的遊客可以過去參觀一下。

現在我們沿著走廊來到了「　華境界」，在明道堂正南，兩側有廊相連，組成一個四合院式的建築群。傳說「　華」是一種色白如碧玉的仙花，服之可以長壽。清代的時候這裡曾經是一個戲台，專為官吏文人而設。據說，林則徐曾在此觀賞過崑劇。

沿著小路一直往前走，有一片翠綠的竹林映入我們的眼簾，一座小屋就在這翠竹的環抱之中，叫「翠玲瓏」，我們一起進去看看吧。這裡原來是園主人的書齋，是由三間低矮的屋子組合而成，隱藏在這片竹林之中，給人一種脫離世俗的感覺。此處歷來為文人墨客雅遊靜觀，吟詠作畫之處。

繼續前行，就是著名的五百名賢祠。這是面闊五間的小院，當中三間為堂，東西為側室，前檐一界為軒廊，檐柱間設掛落，堂前步柱之間置落地長窗18扇。道光七年（公元1827　年）陶澍所創，同治十二年（公元1873年）張樹聲重建。祠內有

「作之師」的匾額，取《論語》的「作之君，作之師」的句子，這裡是為人師表的意思。南面是落地長窗，內部三麵粉牆上，嵌有549 幅歷代人物平雕石刻像，為清代名家顧湘舟所刻，每五幅刻於一方石上，每幅還刻有傳贊詩句和姓名職銜，刻像栩栩如生。百名賢畫像有一定文獻價值。收錄自春秋至清代2500年間與蘇州歷史有關的人物，人物之多，跨越年代之長，繪製之精，鐫刻之工，在清代石刻群像中尚屬罕見。給大家一點時間好好接觸一下這些歷史人物，更好地瞭解蘇州的歷史。

好了，請大家繼續往前行，現在我們來到了清香館。清香館又名木犀亭。北院中種有桂花和臘梅，每逢花開時節，清香四溢，因而得名。室內陳設的樹根家具，已有一百多年的歷史了。製作精細，都做得酷似飛禽走獸，造型奇巧，形象生動。

從清香館出來，我們來到最後一個景點「御碑亭」，因亭中石碑上刻有清康熙帝御筆題寫的詩文，所以稱御碑亭。最後給大家留點時間拍照留念。

從滄浪亭出來，我們的這次園林之旅就結束了。不知道蘇州的人，蘇州的街，還有這些古典別緻的園林是否給您留下了美好的印象，歡迎您下次再到蘇州來作客。

Shandong Province山東省

A Glimpse of the Province （本省簡介）

Geographic Location

Shandong Province is located in Eastern China, at the end of the Yellow River and between the capital city, Beijing, and the country's biggest commercial city, Shanghai. It is one of the most important coastal provinces. It borders ocean in the east and land in the west and its coastline is defined by the Shandong peninsula. This peninsula protrudes between the Bohai and Yellow Seas, and faces the Liaodong peninsula in the north across the Bohai Straits, thereby forming a maritime outpost for Beijing. The western inland part borders, from north to south, Hebei, Henan, Anhui, and Jiangsu provinces.

Climate Characteristics

Shandong has a warm-temperate monsoonal climate. It has hot and wet summers, as well as short springs and autumns, with an average annual temperature ranging from 11℃ to 14℃. The temperature ranges become more dramatic from east to west than from the south to north. Average annual rainfall ranges from 550 to 950 millimeters and the amount of rainfall gets smaller as one moves from southeast to northwest Shandong. Shandong Province has abundant sunshine, making it possible to plant two crops over the course of year.

History Evolution

Shandong was the cradle of ancient Chinese Longshan and Qilu culture and is also where Confucius spread his ideas and Sun Wu wrote about warfare. The former's ideas

華東地區

have served as the backbone of the Chinese traditional culture, while Sun Wu's, The Art of Warfare, is one of the greatest and most famous works written about war.

Tourism Resources

Shandong has rich tourism resources, including beautiful natural scenery and plenty of places of historical interest. Mt.Taishan is a World Natural and Cultural Heritage Site, while the "Sankong" in Qufu, the hometown of Confucius, is World Cultural Heritage site. Other worthy Shandong sites are Linzi, the ancient capital of Qi State, Qingdao, known as the International Beer City, the coastal resort city of Yantai, also called "the End of the Sky, " and Ji'nan, which is renowned for its natural springs. Visitors can also enjoy marvelous scenery at the Yellow River's estuary, hike the Kunyu Mountain (The Ancestor of Divine Mountain), and visit Liangshanpo, made famous over the centuries by the famous well-known novel about the Shuihu Heroes.

Ten Classic Shandong Dishes

Dezhou Braised Chicken; Prawns in Brown Sauce; Nine-turn Intestines; Pear Balls with Honey Juice; Four Happiness Meat Balls; Diced Pork in Pot; Sweet-and-Sour Carps; Supreme Bean Curd;Fried Stomach Tips and Chicken Giblets; and Edible Bird's Nest Soup.

Local Culture

Luju (Shandong Opera) is the most important opera genre; other operas include Zaobang, Yigougou, Shandong Dagu, Qinshu, Kuaishu, and the like.

Special Local Products

Millennium-old history, abundant tourism resources and the rich color of folk-custom give Shandong numerous distinctive traditional craftwork, local specialties and cultural artworks. An example is Lu Embroidery, one of China's eight great embroideries. Other examples are redwood engraved with silver, otherwise known as the treasure of Weifang, Yangjiabu's kites and New Year pictures, and Qingdao's shell sculptures and beer. There are also Qufu's three treasures—rubber from a stone inscription; Nishan ink-slab and Kai wood inscription—and Zibo pottery. And Yantai boasts delicious apples, while Laiyang is known for its sweet pears. All of them are endowed with rich Shandong color and will provide travelers with lasting memories of the province.

Recommended Tourism Cities

In 1998 Shandong began to set the first group of "China Excellent Tourist Cities". By December 2005, the cities of Jinan, Qingdao, Weihai, Yantai, Taian, Zibo, Weifang, Liaocheng, Rizhao, Linyi, Jining, Qufu, Penglai, Wendeng, Jiaonan, Qing-zhou, Zoucheng, Shouguang, Rongcheng and Rushan had all been designated "China Excellent Tourist Cities. " These cities have either beautiful natural scenery, major cultural attractions, or a combination of both. No matter what destination you visit, you will have a profound impression of Shandong.

Attractions Recommendation

Shandong abounds in tourist resources. Mt.Taishan is praised as No. 1 Mountain in China. Ancient emperors frequently came here to worship the heaven. The Confucius Temple and Kong's Mansion, with its forests, have been listed as World Cultural Heritage Sites. And the Penglai Pavilion, along with Qingdao, Yantai, Weihai, and Rizhao's waterfront scenery, are also well-known at home and abroad.

地理位置

山東省地處中國東部，黃河下游。山東半島伸入渤海與黃海之間，東與朝鮮半島、日本列島隔海相望；北與遼東半島相對，是首都北京的海上門戶；西與河北、河南省接壤；南與安徽、江蘇省毗鄰。特殊的地理位置，使山東省成為沿黃河經濟

華東地區

271

帶與環渤海經濟區的交會點，華北地區和華東地區的結合部，在中國經濟格局中占有重要地位。

氣候特點

山東的氣候屬暖溫帶季風氣候類型。降水集中，雨熱同季，春秋短暫，冬夏較長。年平均氣溫11℃～14℃。年平均降水量一般在550～950毫米之間，由東南向西北遞減。全省光照資源充足，農作物一般是一年兩作。

歷史沿革

古地山東，是中國古老的龍山文化、齊魯文化的發祥地。孔子創立的儒家學說，成為中國傳統文化的支柱。古代著名軍事家孫武的《孫子兵法》，至今仍然是中外軍界和商界推崇的經典。

旅遊資源

山東旅遊資源豐富，自然風光秀麗，文物古蹟眾多。「世界自然文化遺產」——泰山；孔子故里——曲阜；齊國故都——臨淄；國際啤酒城——青島；國際葡萄酒城——煙台；被譽為「天盡頭」的榮成；泉城濟南；自然風光原始獨特的黃河入海口；海上仙山之祖——昆　山；古典名著《水滸》故事發生地水泊梁山。所有這些都是您來山東旅遊的理想選擇。

十大經典魯菜

德州扒雞；紅燒大蝦；九轉大腸；蜜汁梨球；四喜丸子；罈子肉；糖醋鯉魚；一品豆腐；油爆雙脆；清湯燕窩。

地方文藝

呂劇是山東重要的地方戲。此外還有棗梆、一勾勾、山東大鼓、山東琴書、山東快書等。

特色旅遊商品

悠久的歷史、豐富的旅遊資源和濃郁的民俗特色，使得山東省有數不清的富有地方特色的傳統工藝品、土特產品、文化藝術品。中國「八大名繡」之一「魯繡」；濰坊的「國寶」紅木嵌銀漆器，濰坊楊家埠的風箏年畫；青島的貝雕，青島啤酒；曲阜三寶——碑帖、尼山硯、楷木雕；淄博陶瓷；煙台蘋果；萊陽梨等，無不附著著濃郁的山東特色，是您來山東旅遊，留下美好記憶的首選商品。

主要旅遊城市

山東從1998年就成為首批「中國優秀旅遊城市」的一員。到2005年12月，共有20個城市榮獲「中國優秀旅遊城市」的稱號，它們是濟南、青島、威海、煙台、淄博、濰坊、聊城、日照、臨沂、濟寧、曲阜、蓬萊、文登、膠南、青州、鄒城、壽光、榮成和乳山。這些城市或者有優美的自然風光，或者有濃厚的文化底蘊，無論您如何選擇，都會給你的山東之行留下深刻的印象。

推薦旅遊景點

山東擁有眾多旅遊資源。泰山有「天下第一山」之美譽，古代皇帝登基多來泰山祭告天地；孔廟與孔府、孔林一起已被列入《世界遺產名錄》；蓬萊閣，青島、煙台、威海、日照的海濱風光也馳名中外。

華東地區

Qingdao City （青島之旅）

Good morning, ladies and gentlemen.

Welcome to Qingdao. I will be your local guide during your stay in Qingdao. If you have any problems or special interests, please don't hesitate to let me know. I will do my best to make your visit a pleasant one. Now, I would like to give you a brief introduction to Qingdao.

Qingdao is located at the southern tip of the Shandong Peninsula. It is characterized by a unique blend of sea and mountains and a pleasant climate. Qingdao has a total coastline (including its islands) of 862.64 kilometers, 730. 64 kilometers of which are continental coastline, accounting for one fourth of the total length in Shandong Province. There are numerous capes and coves along the zigzag coastline.

Qingdao has seven urban districts and five county-level cities under its jurisdiction with a total area of 10, 654 square kilometers and a population of 7, 311, 200. The urban area measures 1, 102 square kilometers and urban residents total 2, 584, 000.

Qingdao lies in the North Temperate Zone and has the typical temperate monsoon climate. Under the direct influence of the southeastern monsoon and the sea currents and tides, the city proper features marked marine climate, humid air, mild temperature and clear-cut seasons. In spring, the weather becomes warmer slowly, usually one month later than the inland areas. Summer weather is humid and rainy, but not very hot, while autumns are cool and dry. Winter here is long and usually windy but not unbearably cold.

As the birthplace of Taoism, Qingdao has a long history. Human settlement here dates back to some 6, 000 years ago. In the Eastern Zhou Dynasty, the town of Jimo was established, which was then the second largest city in the Shandong region. After unifying China in 221 B.C., Yingzheng, the First Emperor of the Qin Dynasty, thrice climbed to the top of the Langyatai Hill in the present satellite city of Jiaonan. Xu Fu, an official of the Qin Dynasty, set sail with his fleet at the foot of the Langyatai Hill eastbound to Korea and Japan. Liu Che, one of the emperors during the Han Dynasty held sacrificial rites at the Jiaomen Palace at Mt.Buqi, which is now in Qingdao's Chengyang District. He also ordered nine temples to be constructed at Mt.N gu along the Jiaozhou Bay, to worship God and his ancestors. By the end of the Qing Dynasty, Qingdao had grown into a prosperous town and was then known as Jiao'ao. Qingdao city was first established on June 14, 1891, when the Qing government sent troops here. In November 1897, Germany occupied Qingdao by force on the pretext of the Juye Litigation over religious disputes. When the First World War broke out in 1914, Japanese invaders took over Qingdao and continued the colonial rule. Protests against the then Chinese government yielding to Japanese pressure and demands for the restoration of Chinese sovereignty over Qingdao ignited the famous May 4thMovement in 1919. On December 10, 1922, the Northern Warlord government regained control of Qingdao and established a government office for port commercial affairs. It was in July, 1929 that Qingdao was granted the status of the Special City and in 1930 was officially renamed "Qingdao". In January 1938, the Japanese troops invaded Qingdao again, but their occupation came to an end in September 1945 when the KMT government regained control of the city. On June 2, 1949, Qingdao was liberated by the Chinese People's Liberation Army under the leadership of the Communist Party of China, putting an end to the five decades of turbulence and colonial rule. In 1986 Qingdao was authorized to exercise special State plans and was given the status equivalent to provincial economic administration. In 1994, Qingdao was included in China's list of 15 vice-provincial-level cities.

Qingdao is an excellent tourist city. Qingdao has beautiful scenery and an agreeable climate. As early as in the 1920s, Qingdao became a famous tourist resort. Its zigzag seashore, undulating hills, European-style red-roofed houses, and green trees make the city unique. Historical sites and constantly improved modern facilities further enhance the city's attractiveness. Qingdao is an excellent place for sightseers, holidaymakers and for holding business talks and exhibitions.

Qingdao's old urban, known for it red houses, green trees, blue sea and azure sky lies on the west side of the city. Qingdao's east side is the new urban area dotted with modern high buildings. Both the old and new areas constitute a seaside city with both

華東地區

European and Asian landscapes. Walking along the coastal sidewalk, tourists can enjoy Qingdao's beautiful coastal sights. From west to east, the entire scenic area is divided into the following four scenic spots with their own special features.

Historical Culture and Euro-Asian Culture Area:This area contains numerous cultural landmarks and sights set within beautiful natural scenery. This valuable heritage of the century-old city stems from the combination of eastern and western culture. Historical sites, foreign-style villas and excellent beaches form a unique Euro-Asian cultural area. The western-style buildings here feature the architecture of over 20 countries. Typical ones include the former German Governor's Residence and Office Buildings, the Catholic Church, the Lutheran Church and the villa area in Badaguan, where numerous newly-weds, photographers and tourists come to visit all year round.

Tourist attractions in the East of Qingdao:Donghai Road, Hong Kong Road, Macao Road, the Sculpture Garden of Cultural Celebrities, the May 4th Square and the Music Square provide a highly scenic environment for this modern international metropolis.

Shilaoren National Holiday Resort:This part of Qingdao has unique tourist villas, hotels, excellent beaches and numerous cultural and sports facilities that no tourist will want to miss. These include the Seaside Sculpture Park, Dolphinarium, International Beer City, golf courses, an International Convention Center, Cultural Exhibition Center, Century Square, Sports Center, Qingdao Polar Sea World, a Modern Arts Center, and the Yacht Club.

Laoshan National Scenic Spot:Located on the shore of the Yellow Sea, the 1, 133-meter-high Mt.Laoshan is known as the leading religious mountain along China's coastline and birthplace of Taoism. Labelled as a national tourist attraction by the State Council, this area is composed of nine sections, five scenic spots under restoration and some surrounding scenic spots. It is a national model scenic area, which ranks a national 4A scenic area.

Mt.Laoshan has a humid temperate climate. It is an important Taoist shrine and is known as the "Second Largest Taoist Monastery in the World". Grotesque rocks in the mountain resemble all kinds of live creatures, so Mt.Laoshan has also been called a natural sculpture park. The ancient trees, rare vegetation and rich natural resources, especially mineral water and undersea jades, have made Mt.Laoshan widely known.

Qingdao enjoys an abundance of natural scenic spots and places of interest in its outskirt regions. In the famous Langyatai Tourist Resort where the Yue Emperor Goujian met his dukes and princes, history can be relived. Yingzheng, the first emperor of the Qin Dynasty, visited this place three times and it is from here that Xu Fu sailed eastward for Japan. Tianhengdao Island is a historic site recording the heroic feats of five hundred soldiers who died as martyrs in the West Han Dynasty more than two thousand years ago. The Cliff Inscriptions in Mt.Tianzhu in Pingdu are regarded as national treasures. The State-level nature reserve, the Mashan Hoodoos, and the Great Wall Relics of the Qi Kingdom in the Spring and Autumn Period (770-476 B.C.) are also located in this area.

This is my entire introduction. Thanks for your cooperation. I do hope my introduction is satisfying and enjoyable. Wish you pleasant journey and good health.

各位朋友：早上好，歡迎您來到青島旅遊。我是大家這次青島之行的導遊。如果您有什麼問題或者要求的話，請告訴我。我會盡最大的努力使您有一個舒適愉快的旅程。現在，我先簡單地給大家介紹一下青島的情況。

青島市地處山東半島南部，它的特點是獨一無二的大海、山脈及舒適氣候的融合。全市海岸線（含所屬海島岸線）總長為862.64　公里，其中大陸岸線730.64公里，占山東省海岸線的1/4。海岸線曲折，岬灣相間。

青島包含七區五市，全市總面積為10654平方公里，人口為731.12　萬。市區面積為1102 平方公里，人口258.4萬。

青島地處北溫帶季風區域，屬溫帶季風氣候。市區由於海洋環境的直接調節，受來自洋面上的東南季風及海流、水團的影響，故又具有顯著的海洋性氣候特點。空氣濕潤，雨量充沛，溫度適中，四季分明。春季氣溫回升緩慢，較內陸遲1個月；夏季濕熱多雨，但無酷暑；秋季天高氣爽，降水少，蒸發強；冬季風大溫低，持續時間較長。

青島是一座歷史文化名城，中國道教的發祥地之一。6000年以前這裡已有了人類的生存和繁衍。東周時期建立了當時山東地區第二大市鎮——即墨。秦始皇統一中國後，曾三次登臨現位於青島膠南市的琅琊台。秦代徐福曾率船隊由琅琊台起航東渡朝鮮、日本。漢武帝劉徹曾在現位於青島市城陽區的不其山「祀神人於交門宮」，並在膠州灣畔女姑山祭天拜祖設立明堂9所。清朝末年，青島已發展成為一個繁華市鎮，昔稱膠澳。1891 年6 月14日，清政府在膠澳設防，是為青島建置的開始。1897年11月，德國以「巨野教案」為藉口派兵強占青島。1914年第一次世界大戰爆發，11月，日本侵占青島，取代德國對青島進行軍事殖民統治。1919年，中國近代史上著名的「五四運動」便是以「收回青島」為起因。1922年12月10日，中國收回青島，設立膠澳商埠督辦公署，直屬北洋政府。1929年7月，設青島特別市。1930年，改稱青島市。1938 年1月，日本再次侵占青島。1945年9月，國民黨政府接收青島，仍為特別市。1949 年6 月2 日，青島解放。1986年青島市在中國國家計劃中實行單列，賦予相當省一級經濟管理權限。1994年被列為中國15個副省級城市之一。

青島是一座十分美麗的旅遊城市，擁有優美的風景和宜人的氣候。早在1920年，青島就已經是著名的旅遊勝地了。曲折的海岸，巍峨的群山，歐式的紅頂房和綠色的樹木使這座城市變得獨一無二。歷史景區和不斷完善的現代化設置更增添了青島的魅力。青島是集觀光、渡假、商務和展覽於一體的現代化城市。

青島市區，西部為「紅瓦綠樹，碧海藍天」的老風貌保護區，東部為現代化建築風貌區，新、老兩區相融相映，形成了「海上都市、歐亞風情」的城市形象。漫步在海邊，遊客能夠欣賞到城市美麗的海景。從西到東，整個風景區可以分為以下四個各具特色的部分。

歐亞風情區：這一區域包含了很多自然和文化交相輝映的景點。這個有著一個世紀歷史的老城是東西方文化相結合的產物。外國風情的別墅和優美的海灘形成了一個獨一無二的歐亞文化區域。這裡包含了超過20個國家的西式建築風格。典型的有前德國統治者的居住樓和辦公樓，天主教教會，馬丁· 路德教堂，八大關別墅區等。這些地區一年到頭都有很多新婚夫婦、攝影者和遊客參觀遊覽。

東部的旅遊景區有東海路、香港路、澳門路、文化名人雕塑園、五四廣場和音樂廣場等，洋溢著濃郁的現代氣息。

石老人國家旅遊渡假區有獨一無二的觀光別墅、飯店，優良的海灘和許多文化、運動設施，如弄海園、海上樂園、國際啤酒城、國際美食娛樂城、國際高爾夫球場、環字國際城、體育中心、海洋公園、浮山公園、現代藝術中心等，都是遊客不可錯過的地方。所有這些將隨著渡假、娛樂、展覽和運動競賽的便利條件使青島成為一個全面發展的觀光旅遊地。

嶗山國家風景區位於青島市區東部黃海之濱，主峰海拔1133米。嶗山以中國沿海第一宗教山脈和道教的發源地而聞名於世。嶗山被國務院命名為國家旅遊風景區，由9個風景遊覽區、5個風景恢復區和周圍一些風景區組成，是國家4A級旅遊示範區。嶗山氣候濕潤。是道家的重要傳播之地，被譽為「道教全真天下第二叢林」。山中奇形怪狀的岩石很像各種各樣的生物，所以嶗山以自然雕塑公園而聞名。古老的樹木，罕見的植物和豐富的自然資源，特別是礦泉水和水下的玉石已經使嶗山遠近聞名。

青島市郊也有大量自然景觀和風景勝地。在著名的琅琊台旅遊勝地，越王勾踐會見大臣和王子的遺蹟均有所保存。這裡也是秦始皇三次遊歷的地方；徐福東渡到日本也是在這裡始行的。田橫島是一個具有歷史意義的島嶼，早在兩千多年前就曾經發生過驚天動地的故事：秦末漢初，齊王田橫屬下的五百壯士，寧死不降劉邦，為赴大義，集體自刎於島上。平度天柱山的摩崖刻石，為稀有的書法石刻藝術瑰寶。這裡還有馬山國家級自然保護區、修建於春秋（公元前770～前476年）時的齊長城遺蹟等景點。

華東地區

我的介紹到此就結束了，謝謝您的合作，我希望我的介紹能夠給大家帶來收穫和樂趣。祝您一路平安，身體健康。

Qufu （曲阜三孔）

My dear friends,

Welcome to Qufu, the hometown of Confucius. Confucius had a famous remark: "What a delight to have friends from afar." Today I am very glad to have an opportunity of making new friends and to be your tour guide. I wish to thank you for your cooperation and am also ready to take your suggestions and advice regarding my service.

The Confucius Temple

What we are visiting now is the Confucius Temple. This temple is where sacrifices are offered to Confucius. Work on these structures began during the second year after Confucius's death. The Confucius Temple imitates the imperial palace's construction. The layout is as follows:there are 3 roads, 9 courtyards, 466 buildings, halls, palaces and workshops, 54 gates and pavilions, and over 1000 stone tablets and steles. It covers an area of 21. 8 hectares (equals to 327. 5 mu) and is over 1 kilometers long from north to south. It is magnificent and resplendent and irrespective of the angle from which you enjoy viewing the temple, it is commensurate with influence and fame of Confucius. As such, it is very rare world historial treasure.

The Confucius Temple's first gateway is called Golden Sound and Jade Vibration Gateway. "Golden Sound" and "Jade Vibration" symbolize the whole process of playing music. The music starts with the beating of a drum and ends with the striking of an inverted bell. This means that Confucius's thoughts are a comprehensive expression of all previous saints'ideas.

Unicorns called "avoiding evil spirits" or "growling towards the sky" are engraved on the stone gateway and lotus throne. These decorations were used only for the mansions of dukes in feudal society.

[Ling Star Gate] This gate was erected in Ming Dynasty and was rebuilt in 1754. The three characters were written by Emperor Qianlong. The legend has it that there are 28 constellations in the galaxy. The star in charge of culture has been given the three names:the "Ling Star," "Wenqu Star," and "Tianzhen Star". The ancient Chinese offered sacrifices to Ling Star before offering sacrifices to Heaven because it was believed that their reverence to Confucius was just as important as it was to Heaven.

There is one stone stele on the temple gate's eastern wall. It is written on this stele that "officials should dismount here." In the past, the civil and military officials and people in the street were required to get off from their horses or sedan chairs and walk on foot when they passed by to show their reverence for Confucius and his temple.

We are now entering the Hongdao Gate. The name is taken from a remark in Lunyu: "Man can carry forward virtues, but virtues can not carry forward man." It implies that Confucius elucidated virtues of Yao, Shun, Yu and Tang as well as Zhou Wengong and Zhou Wugong who were considered virtuous rulers. Two stone tablets lie at the foot of the gate; the one on the east side records the development of Qufu through dynasties; the one on the west side writes Grave Inscriptions for Mr.Chu Shi and has high calligraphic value.

The Great Middle Gate is Confucius Temple's Song Dynasty gate. It is also called "Middle Gate". This copies Confucius's thoughts of mediocrity. "Impartial is the kingly way, and mediocrity is the theorem of the world." Justice can not be done without being impartial and mediocre. One must be unbiased in one's words and action. "Mediocrity" is actually the highest norm of dealing with people, and it is hard for commoners to do so. It is absolutely different from modern society's "trying to mediate differences at the sacrifice of principle".

This stele is a famous one in the Temple of Confucius. It was erected during the Ming Emperor Xianzong Zhu Jianshen's reign. The stele has two characteristics:one is that the regular script is standard and exquisite; the other is the inscription singing the highest praise for Confucius. I'd like to ask you a question. There is an animal similar to a tortoise under the stele. I wonder if any one of you can tell me its exact name. All right, no one? Let me tell you then. The animal carrying the stele is not a tortoise but a dragon called Bixi. Bixi is the 8thson of the dragon and it is fond of literature and can carry heave things. Therefore, it is assigned to carry the imperial stele.

This was originally a building to preserve books given by the emperors. It was built in 1018 and has stood here for more than 900 years. This unique and grand construction is one of the famous wooden pavilions in China. It has remained intact through many earthquakes. In the 5thyear of the Qing Emperor Kangxi's reign, "nine out of ten collapsed in the earthquake", but the Kuiwen Pavilion stood rock-solid there.

This is the 6thcourtyard of the Temple of Confucius. There are 13 stele pavilions, with 8 in the south and 5 in the north. 55 stone steles were erected during the Tang, Song, Jin, Yuan, Ming and Qing dynasties. The inscriptions are all in commemoration and evaluation of Confucius, given by emperors and imperial envoys when they came to pay tribute or offered sacrifices to Confucius. The stele was made of a block of stone quarried from Beijing's Western Mountain and was carried all the way down the Grand Canal to Qufu. It weighs 65, 000 kilograMs.The ancient people transported the stone on icy road and could only move it a few meters each day. This story illustrates how much Emperor Kangxi revered Confucius and how hardworking and great the laboring people were.

[Dacheng Gate] The Temple of Confucius is divided into three layouts from here.

The middle gate is the Dacheng Gate; the two beside the Dacheng Gate are the Golden Sound Gate on the left and Jade Vibration Gate on the right. The one on farther western side is the Qisheng Gate and the one on farther eastern side is the Chengsheng Gate.

This is the main hall of the Temple of Confucius. Dacheng Hall, together with the Forbidden City's Hall of Supreme Harmony and Daimiao Temple's Tiankuang Hall in Tai'an city are called the three greatest halls in China or "the Three Greatest Halls in the East". This hall is 24. 8 meters high, 45. 78 meters wide and 24. 8 meters deep. It is surrounded by 28 dragon columns carved out of whole blocks of stone. The 10 columns in front are deep relief sculptures and the others are shallow ones. They are made with exquisite technique and are treasure of the whole world. Carved on each column are two dragons twisting and flying. They are made true to life and are completely different from each other. The birthday of Confucius is on September 28thand grand commemoration activities are held here in which people pay homage to Confucius. During the festival, music and dancing are performed and visitors from home and abroad swarm to Qufu. Various cultural and tour activities are rich and colorful and you're welcome to come to attend this festival and enjoy yourselves in this world-famous event.

This memorial temple is designed to enshrine Confucius's wife Qiguan. It is the third largest in Confucius Temple. Qiguan came to Shandong from Henan Province and married Confucius at the age of 19. Later, she gave birth to Kongli. Qiguan was a good mother and virtuous wife and died 7 years before Confucius passed away. There are also 28 stone columns outside the palace. Seventy-two phoenixes are carved on each column. The number equals that of dragons and this is so-called "the dragon and the phoenix bringing prosperity. "

My dear friends! The Temple of Confucius is not only a grand and large history museum, but a sacred culture museum. No matter from what aspect you try to appreciate it, you will always find it amazing. Well, that is all about the temple, and now let's

華東地區

move on and visit the "First Family under Heaven," the living Quarters of Kong Family.

The Living Quarters of Kong Family

The Kong Family's Living Quarters is also called the "Duke Yansheng's Mansion". Like the Confucius Temple, the Kong Family's Mansion was also divided into 3 layouts with 9 courtyards. It covers an area of 16 hectares (equals to 240 mu) and has 463 halls, buildings and houses.

Two stone lions guard the gate on both sides to show the dignity. Mounting stone and dismounting stone are in front and at the back respectively. In the middle of the gate hangs an inscribed board with "聖府"(p ny n:Sh n f) written on it. There are a pair of antithetical couplets on the two sides of the gate. All the characters are written in golden color with a blue background. This antithetical couplet eulogizes the Kong Family for it went through thick and thin with the nation and would survive to the last day of the earth. Two characters are written wrongly on purpose. One is "fu". It lacks a lot and this implies there is no end of wealth; the other is "zhang". You can see there is a vertical stroke through the character and this means that the articles reflect the universe.

Above the gate are characters "Gate of Saints". Entering the second gate, you will find a gate which does not connect the walls and has four wood columns to prop up the roof. Usually it was closed and was open only on grand occasions, including ceremonies held by the emperors, the reception of imperial edicts, and sacrifices made to honor Confucius.

[The Major Hall] This is where "Duke Yansheng" read imperial edicts, received officials, heard cases and held grand ceremonies.

The second hall is also called the "back hall". Duke Yansheng used to receive officials above 4th rank here. The stone steles and inscribed boards inside were bestowed on Dukes of Yansheng and their wives by the Qing Dynasty Emperor Guangxu and Empress Dowager Cixi. It is said that in the past when officials made obeisance to the emperors, they were only allowed to be accompanied by two servants, but Duke Yansheng could be accompanied by four servants.

The third hall is where Duke Yansheng tackled internal affairs of the family. The above-mentioned three halls demonstrate the rigid stratification and the dignity and influence of the Kong Family.

After the three halls, we now come to the "Interior Residence". In the past, people were not allowed to go inside without special permit. Dozens of guards were on watch in turns and if anyone disobeyed the order, the guards would have the right to beat him to death. The water storage in the west of the gate to the Interior Residence is called Shiliu. In the past, the water carriers were not allowed to enter either, so they poured the water into Shiliu and the water would flow into the Interior Residence.

The Qiantang building is a two-storey building with 7 rooMs.You can see the magnificence. The things set out inside are what they were at that time. Rare calligraphic works, paintings, treasure and clothes are also on display inside. The inner bedroom was for Kong Lingyi's wife, Madam Tao.

The Houtang building has three supplementary buildings. This is where Mr.Kong Decheng held his wedding ceremony. Wedding items and inscriptions and gifts given by celebrities are displayed inside.

The Back Garden was built in 1503 and was designed by Li Dongyang, Minister of the Board of Civil Office. He was also the father of Kong Wenshao's daughter-in-law. Kong Wen-shao was the 62ndgeneration descendant, by the way. During the reign of Emperor Jiajing of the Ming Dynasty, another powerful minister Yan Song helped renovate the garden. The granddaughter of Yan Song married the 64thDuke Yansheng Kong Shangxian. In the Qing Dynasty, Emperor Qianlong married his daughter to Kong Xianpei, the 72thDuke Yansheng, and much new construction was undertaken to rebuild the garden. After these three big renovations, the garden is larger than that of the Forbidden City. There are various rare flowers and plants, as well as ancient trees and famous rocks here. Please have a good look while we move on.

There are a good number of priceless cultural relics in the Kong Mansion. One particular treasure is the over ten thousand volumes of archives of the Kong Family's history.

Just now we have visited the temples where sacrifices were offered to Confucius and the Kong Family's Mansion. Next we will visit the Graveyard of the Kong Family where Confucius and his offsprings were buried.

The Graveyard of the Kong Family

After his death, Confucius was buried here, south of Sishui and north of Zhushui. During the Qin and Han dynasties, the area of the graveyard was less than one hectare, but as Confucius's fame grew, the graveyard became larger and larger. After the Han Dynasty, it underwent 13 renovations, 5 tree plantings, and 3 expansions. Now the total area is 200 hectares (equals to 3000 mu), and the circumference is 7. 5 kilometers. The Kong Family's Graveyard has the longest history and largest area of any family graveyards in China. It has been listed as a cultural relic under the state protection and is also a UNESCO world cultural heritage site. It is said that when Confucius passed away, his disciples transplanted here rare trees and plants from everywhere. Now there are some 100, 000 trees in the graveyard, including old and famous trees. Qufu's stone steles also together make up one of China's three largest stele forests in China. Among the 5, 000 steles, 3, 000 are placed in the graveyard. Stele inscriptions written by many famous calligraphers, such as Li Dongyang, Yan Song, Weng Fanggang, and He Shaoji, can be seen in this graveyard.

As we are now walking along the 5-km-long Huanlin Road, it would good for us to learn more about the graveyard. The people buried in the graveyard are all Confucius's descendants. According to the customs of the Kong Family, there were 3 kinds of family members who were not allowed to be buried in the graveyard:the first are those who died before 18; the second are those who violated the state law and were sentenced to death; the third are daughters who got married.

This is the tomb of Confucius. It is surrounded by a red enclosure. The house to the west of the tomb is where Zi Gong guarded the tomb. After Confucius's death, his disciples guarded the tomb for 3 years and left one after another except Zi Gong who stayed there for another 3 years. To the right of the Confucius's tomb is Kong Li's tomb, and the one in front of the Confucius's tomb is that of his grandson, Kong Ji. The three graves are in the shape of "carrying the son and the grandson. " These pavilions are called "Zhubiti Pavilion" and used to be the resting-place for the emperors when they came to pay homage to Confucius.

My friends, that ends my introduction. If you have any questions, please ask me, and I will try my best to give you detailed answers. At last, may you have a nice stay here and thanks for your cooperation. I hope that you can come again. See you next time!

各位嘉賓：

不知道您讀沒讀過《論語》，那上面開篇有一句話叫「有朋自遠方來，不亦樂乎」。那麼我就以孔子的這句名言，熱烈地歡迎您來孔子的故鄉曲阜參觀遊覽。下面，就由我陪同各位遊覽並進行導遊服務，非常感謝您的合作，並衷心地希望您對我的工作多提出批評意見。

孔廟

現在我們參觀孔廟。孔廟位於曲阜城中心，是中國古代封建王朝祭祀孔子的地方，始建於孔子死後第2年。孔廟仿皇宮之制，分九進院落，左右對稱排列，整個建築群共有五殿、一閣、一壇、兩廡、兩堂、17座碑亭、54座門坊，共466間，南北長約1公里，占地21.8公頃（約合327.5畝）。孔廟恢弘壯麗，面積之大，歷史之久，保存之完整，是世界建築史上的唯一範例。

孔廟的第一座石坊叫「金聲玉振坊」。「金聲」、「玉振」表示奏樂的全過程，以擊鐘開始，以擊磬告終，比喻孔子的思想集古聖先賢之大成。石坊上面蓮花寶座上各刻有一個獨角怪獸，稱「闢邪」，也叫「朝天吼」，這是封建社會王爵府第才可使用的飾物。

欞星門建於明朝，1754 年重建。「欞星門」三個字為乾隆所書。傳說天上有28 個星宿，掌管文化的星宿被稱為「欞星」或「文曲星」、「天鎮星」。中國古代官員下令在祭天之前必須先祭祀文曲星，他們認為讚頌孔子思想如同天地生育萬物。

孔廟大門東牆外面有「官員人等至此下馬」的碑刻，過去，文武官員、庶民百姓從此路過要下轎下馬徒步而行，以表示對孔子的尊敬。

我們進入的大門，稱「弘道門」，取「論語」中「人能弘道，非弘道人」之意。讚揚孔子總結了先賢先聖的經驗，尤其弘揚了堯舜禹湯，文武周公之道。弘道門下有兩塊石碑，東邊的四棱碑是「曲阜歷代沿革志」，記載了曲阜沿革變遷的歷史，史料價值很高。西邊的是「處士先生墓誌」，具有很高的書法價值。

大中門是宋代孔廟的大門，稱「中和門」，意為用孔子的思想處理問題都可以迎刃而解。此門也稱為「大中門」，贊孔子的學問是集人類知識之大成。中，取「中庸」之意，「中者天下之正道，庸者天下之定理」，中不偏，庸不易。離開中者，就不是正道。

現在大家眼前的這塊碑是石孔廟中很有名的一塊，它為明憲宗朱見深所立。這塊碑因書法精湛而著稱於世，碑文用論辯形式寫成，在極力推崇孔子方面，可以說是一最。問大家一個問題，碑下面有個很像烏龜的動物，有誰能告訴我這動物的確切的名字嗎？沒有人嗎？讓我來告訴大家吧，這碑下面的動物不是烏龜，叫贔屭，是龍的第八個兒子，特別能負重，所以用來馱碑。

我們面前的這座木結構建築名叫「奎文閣」，是收藏御賜書籍的地方，始建於1018年，有900多年的歷史了。這座唯一且龐大的建築是中國最著名大木結構宮殿之一，歷經多次地震之後仍安然無恙。康熙五年間曲阜曾有過一次大地震，「人間房屋傾者九，存者一」，而奎文閣卻傲然屹立，安然無恙，由此可見中國古代勞動人民的聰明智慧和高超的建築藝術。

我們現在進入孔廟的第六進院落，展現在大家面前的是13座碑亭，南邊8座，北邊5座。亭內保存著唐、宋、元、明、清各代石碑共55幢，碑文多為皇帝對孔子的追謚加封、拜廟親祭、整修廟宇的記錄，用漢文、八思巴文、滿文等刻成。此排中間的這座碑，重約65噸，採自北京的西山，當時人們在冰面上運送這塊石頭，一天只能移動幾米。從這可以看出康熙對孔子的尊重及勞動人們的偉大。

〔大成門〕孔廟在此被分為3道門。最西邊為啟聖門，是供奉孔子父母的地方，中路為孔廟最中心的地方，東為承聖門，原為孔子故居。

矗立在我們面前的大殿就是名揚天下的「大成殿」，它是中國的「三大殿」之一，與北京故宮的「太和殿」，泰山岱廟的「天貺殿」齊名，其雄偉壯麗有過之而無不及。殿高24.8米，寬45.78米，深24.8米，雕樑畫棟，金碧輝煌，特別是周圍28根石柱，為世界文化瑰寶，均以整石雕刻而成。前面10根為深浮雕，每柱二龍戲珠，盤繞升騰，栩栩如生，刀法剛勁有力，各具變化。兩側及後廊的龍柱為淺浮雕，每柱72條龍，總共1296條。大成殿內供奉著孔子塑像，兩側為四配，東西是復聖顏回、述聖孔及，西面是宗聖曾參和亞聖孟子。再外是12哲。每年9月26日、9月28日，我們都在這裡舉行盛大的國際孔子文化節和孔子誕辰紀念儀式，表演大型祭孔樂舞和「簫韶樂舞」，舉行豐富多彩的文化、旅遊活動，歡迎各位到時光臨。

寢殿是供奉孔子夫人齊官氏的專祠，是孔廟內的第三大殿。齊娟19歲從河南來到山東嫁給孔子，後來生下孔鯉。她是一位優秀的母親和善良的妻子，先孔子7年辭世。寢殿外還有28根石柱，每根石柱上刻有72隻鳳凰，與龍的數量相同，這就是所謂的「龍鳳呈祥」。

孔廟是一個巨大的文化博物館，我們匆匆看一次，只可窺豹一斑，不能觀其全貌，尤其是不能會其神韻，那就留待各位以後再來時細細品味吧。下面我們參觀孔府。

孔府

孔府即「衍聖公府」，是中國重點文物保護單位。與孔廟相似，孔府也分為三路布局，九進院落，有廳、堂、樓、房 463 間，占地 16 公頃（約合 240畝）。

孔府大門有一對石獅守衛，更加顯示了其尊嚴。上馬石和下馬石分別位於前後。孔府大門上方高懸藍底金字「聖府」二字。有趣的是門兩邊這副對聯：上聯是「與國鹹休安富尊榮公府第」，「富」字缺上面一「點」，寓「富不到頂」，下聯為「同天並老文章道德聖人家」，「章」字一豎直通「立字」，寓「文章通天」。「與國咸休」「同天並老」，這是多大的氣派！

孔府二門裡，這座獨具風格的門叫「恩賜重光門」，進門後你會發現一個沒有靠牆只有四根柱子支撐的門。過去這門一般都是關著的，只有盛大的場合如皇帝舉行大典或者孔府接到聖旨後者祭祀孔子的時候，此門才會打開。

孔府「大堂」，是「衍聖公」宣讀聖旨、接見官員、審理重大案件，舉行重大儀式的地方。

二堂，也叫後廳，是當年衍聖公會見四品以上官員的地方，裡面的石碑和牌匾是清朝光緒、慈禧太后等封賜給衍聖公及夫人的。據說，過去官員赴京朝拜天子，一般只允許一主兩伴，而只有「衍聖公」可以一主四伴。

三堂，也叫退廳，也是衍聖公私設公堂，處理家庭內部事務的場所。以上三個大堂，層層疊進，很是森嚴，足顯出孔府的聖威和顯赫。

二堂過後，我們進入「內宅」。在過去，內宅絕對不許擅入，有皇帝賜給的虎尾棍、燕翅鐺、金頭玉棍，由十幾人輪流把守，有不遵令入內者，「打死勿論」。內宅門西邊這個水槽叫石流，過去挑水夫不得進入內宅，只把水倒進石流，淌入內宅。

前堂樓是七間二層樓閣，富麗堂皇，室內陳設布置，全為當年原貌，內有珍奇書畫墨寶、古玩衣冠，裡套間為孔子後代孔令貽夫人陶氏臥室。

這個院子是後堂樓，各有配樓三間，後堂樓是孔德成先生當年結婚的地方，堂中陳列著當年結婚的用品和名人贈送的禮品和題字。

我們現在參觀孔府後花園，它建於明弘治16年（公元1503年），由吏部尚書太子太傅，也是孔子62代孫衍聖公孔聞韶的親家李東陽設計監工建造的，到了明嘉靖年間，太子太傅、吏部尚書、當朝權臣嚴嵩又助修建，嚴嵩的孫女嫁給了孔子64代衍聖公孔尚賢為一品夫人。到了清代，乾隆將自己的女兒嫁給了72代衍聖公孔憲培，又為修建孔府花園大動土木。經過前後三次大修，花園成了現在的規模，面積比北京故宮的花園還要大些。這裡面有各種奇花異草，古樹名石如「五柏抱槐」「太湖石假山」等，請各位隨意觀賞一下。

孔府存有大量無比珍貴的文物，尤其是十餘萬卷孔府檔案，更是稀世文物。

各位朋友，剛才我們看了祭祀孔子的廟宇，看了孔子後代居住的府第孔府，下邊我們參觀埋葬孔子以及孔子後代的基地——孔林。

孔林

孔子死後，葬在曲阜泗水之陽，洙水之陰，即現在的孔林。秦漢時期，孔林地不過一頃，隨著孔子地位的提高，孔林的規模越來越大。自漢以後，孔林先後重修13次，增植樹木5次，增地3次，圓周長7.5公里，總占地面積200公頃（約合3000

華東地區

291

畝）。孔林是世界上延時最久、面積最大的家庭墓地，為中國重點文物保護單位，世界文化遺產之一。相傳孔子死後，弟子們從各地移來奇木異草栽植。現在孔林**內**有10餘萬株樹木，其中不乏古樹名木。曲阜是中國三大碑林之一，古碑數量最多，共約五千餘塊，其中孔林占三千塊。林**內**尚有李東陽、嚴嵩、翁方鋼、何紹基等書法大家的碑刻。

現在我們沿一條約5 公里的環林路瞭解一下孔林的主要風貌。孔林**內**埋葬著孔姓後裔。按照孔家的風俗，孔林有三不埋：不滿18歲的人死後不進孔林埋葬；犯了國家王法被判死刑的人不能進孔林；雖是孔姓婦女但已嫁出去的女人不能埋進孔林。

這便是孔子墓，周圍用紅牆圍繞。墓西這座房子是子貢守墓處，孔子死後，眾弟子守墓3年，盡皆離去，只有子貢守墓6年。孔子墓右邊是孔子的兒子孔鯉墓，前邊是孫子孔及墓，三座墳墓呈「攜子抱孫」形。這座亭子，叫駐蹕亭，是當年皇帝祭孔時休息的地方。

各位朋友，「三孔」的遊覽就到這裡，如果對我的講解有什麼不懂的地方，請您提出來，我會盡最大的努力為大家講解清楚。最後，祝大家旅途愉快，謝謝大家的合作，希望您再次來曲阜參觀遊覽，我也希望再次為您提供服務。再見！

Penglai Pavilion （蓬萊閣）

Ladies and gentlemen, good morning.

Welcome you to China and Penglai, the Fairyland in the World. I will be your local guide during your stay in Penglai. If you have any problems or special interest, please don't hesitate to let me know. I will do my best to make your visit as pleasant as possible.

Today we'll visit the Penglai Pavilion. Before going there, I would like to give you a brief introdu-ction to this place.

With a long history of more than 940 years, the Penglai Pavilion was first built in the Northern Song Dynasty, rebuilt and extended in the Ming Dynasty and the Qing Dynasty. Now it covers an area of 3280 square meters, of which the building area is 1890 square meters. This magnificent complex consists of more than 100 rooms belonging to the Palaces of the Dragon King and Heavenly Empress, Penglai Pavilion, Sanqing Hall, Hall of the Immortal L   Dongbin, and the Amitabha Buddha Temple. Roofed with yellow glazed tiles and decorated with upturned eaves and scarlet doors, these structures, just like all the stars twinkling round the moon, seem at first to be randomly strewn around the Penglai Pavilion, but upon closer viewing blend into one harmonious whole. Antithetical couplets, stone tablets, calligraphies and paintings can be found everywhere in the halls, temples and corridors, such as the original handwriting of the famous Song Dynasty poet, Su Dongpo, and the portrait of L Dongbin, one of the legendary Eight Immortals. Both the handwriting and portrait are carved on the stone. Visitors can enjoy here the well-known cloudlands, such as the Immortals'Pavilion Rising High up in the Air, the Mirage, the Crystal Clear Sea Wave, and the Mists and Cloud around the Lion Cave. The complex combines excellent cultural attractions and natural landscape, where the pavilions and halls are well spaced and the temples and gardens add radiance and beauty to each other. Penglai is famed throughout the world for its red hills, blue seas and clear air.

The Archway of Danya Fairyland

We are now at the Archway of Danya Fairyland. Supported by four pillars, the wooden-structured archway was renovated in the latter half year of 1981. The four Chinese characters "丹崖仙境" (meaning Red Cliff Fairland) was written by Dong Biwu, Vice Chairman, when he visited the Penglai in 1964. The Danya Hill, where the Penglai Pavilion is located, is composed of breccias cemented by red iron oxide. Its reddish brown color and precipitous cliffs give it the name "Danya", meaning Red

Cliff. The Penglai Pavilion is a place where mirage can be seen, so it has long been known as the Fairyland.

Passing through the Archway of Danya Fairy-land, we are entering the Fairyland. Well, do you feel as if you have become immortal?

The Palace of the Dragon King

The Place of the Dragon King was first built in the Tang Dynasty. It was then rebuilt and expanded during the Song and Yuan Dynasties. It is divided into three courtyards:the Main Gate, the Front Hall and the Rear Hall.

Now here we are at the palace's Front Hall. The statue in the middle is of Ao Guang, Dragon King of the East Sea, flanked by two Buddhist Doctrine Protectors. In front of them stand on either side eight immortals in charge of wind, rain, thunder, and the like.

Here is the Rear Hall of the palace, or the Dragon King's bedroom. In ancient times when droughts occurred, people came here to pay homage to the dragon king. With willow hats on their heads, then they carried the Dragon Kings's statue while wandering about the streets. Wherever they went, the residents would sprinkle water upon them. It really worked and timely rainfall would soon occur.

The Opera Tower

Now here we are at the Opera Tower. Look ahead, please. There is an antithetical couplet written on the pillars in front of the gate. The first line means that the music played at the tower sounds like immortal's music in heavenly palace and accompanied by the tides in the morning and evening and is spread all over the Penglai Island. The second line means that just when the music and opera begins, the sound goes directly to the three immortal mountains.

On the Goddess of the Sea's birthday, the sixteenth day of the first lunar month of each year, the local fishermen act and perform local Shandong Province operas at the tower.

The Palace of the Heavenly Empress

Coastal people most admire the Heavenly Empress, as she is the protector of seamen and fishermen. According to statistics, the Palace of the Chinese Heavenly Empress can be found in more than 300 countries or cities. The Palace of the Heavenly Empress in Penglai is the largest of its kind in the North of China. It consists of the Front Hall, the Main Hall and the Rear Hall.

This is the Front Hall. There stand two statues of heavenly guards who safeguard the Heavenly Empress.

Here we are at the Main Hall. In the middle of the hall sits the Heavenly Empress, or Goddess of the Sea, flanked by four maidservants. Standing on the two sides are the dragon kings and civil officials. Compared with other Heavenly Empress Palaces, the one in Penglai is quite unusual. This is because the Dragon Kings of the East, West, South and North Seas stand in front of the Heavenly Empress. Do you know the reason? One explanation is that in different dynasties, the Goddess of Sea was conferred on the Heavenly Empress, who controlled all the immortals and monsters in the vast sea. Her jurisdiction was far beyond that of the dragon kings. As a result, the four dragon kings had to act on her order. Another saying goes that the Heavenly Empress had once subdued the East Sea Dragon King.

This is the Rear Hall, the bedroom of the Heavenly Empress. It was said that she stayed in the east room on odd days and in the west rooms on even days.

The Heavenly Empress's birthday falls on the 23rdday of the third lunar month, and on that day, people hold a grand worship ceremony honoring the Goddess of Sea. The

Qing Emperor Kangxi once prescribed the protocol and sacrificial utensils for offering sacrifices to the Heavenly Empress. The pious men and women far and near spontaneously flock to the Palace of the Heavenly Empress to kneel and worship the Heavenly Empress.

The Penglai Pavilion

Now here we are at the Penglai Pavilion, the chief building of the complex. It is one of the four famous towers in China, of which the other three ones are the Yellow Crane Tower, the Yueyang Tower and the Tengwang Pavilion.

It was first built in the Song Dynasty and then rebuilt and expanded into its present size during subsequent dynasties. Facing south, it is a wooden-structured building with upturned eaves and painted rafters, presenting a magnificent view. More than 100 pieces of stone inscriptions from three dynasties are preserved here. Three powerful Chinese characters, "蓬萊閣", meaning the Penglai Pavilion and written by the famous Qing Dynasty calligrapher, Tie Bao, are inscribed on the horizontal tablet located at the pavilion's north side. There are also stone inscriptions in the handwriting of other well-known historical figures, such as Su Dongpo of the Song Dynasty, Dong Qichang of the Ming Dynasty and Weng Fanggang of the Qing Dynasty. These stone inscriptions give a vivid record of the wonderful sights on the mountains and sing the fascinating pavilion's praises.

The first floor serves as the room for exhibiting the photographs of Party and Government leaders when they visited the Penglai Pavilion.

The second floor reproduces the scene when the Eight Immortals—Tie Guaili, Lan Caihe, He Xiangu, Han Zhongli, Zhang Guolao, L Dongbin, Han Xiangzi and Cao Guojiu—got drunk. Each immortal has a different musical instrument in hand and their expressions, moods and postures also differ. Hence it is said that when the Eight

Immortals crossed the sea, each one showed his or her special feats. It is in Penglai that the tale about the Eight Immortals Crossing the Sea took place. One day after attending the Peach Banquet held by Queen Mother of the West, the Eight Immortals came to the East Sea. Traveling on the vast blue sea, each one showed his or her special feats. They were unexpectedly seen by Prince of the Dragon King who wanted to seize the magical instruments in their hands. Then a severe fight took place. They didn't stop fighting until Avalokilesvara (Guanshiyin) came as an intermediator. The magical instruments of the Eight Immortals are all bound up with how ancient people conquered the sea. The staff used by Tie Guaili is an epitome of the canoe and the donkey ridden by Zhang Guolao should be a symbol of raft made of donkey skin. There is another local story about the Eight Immortals. Opposite the Penglai Pavilion lie the Miaodao Isles, which is the site of an ancient convict settlement. It was the rule that food was only provided for 300 persons everyday. However, on the isles there were more than 300 convicts. As a result, some convicts were thrown into the sea. On a stormy night, the convicts rose in rebellion. Only eight of them succeeded in landing on Penglai. Since the convicts used just simple and crude canoes and wooden basins to cross the sea, the people living around Penglai could not believe these eight escaped convicts were ordinary men. They instead suspected that they were immortals. This is how the legendary tale about the Eight Immortals began to spread.

Look. The table and chair over there are called Eight Immortals table and chair. You can have a seat and this way enjoy a bit of contact with the immortals.

This is also a famous place for enjoying mirages. A mirage is a natural phenomenon produced by hot air conditions, causing light to be refracted and reflected in the atmosphere. Penglai is a place where warm and cold sea currents meet. When cold current overlays warm current, the temperature of the lower atmosphere is high at the upside and low at the downside, while the air density of the lower atmosphere is low at the upside and high at the downside. This causes the ocean's surface to become very stable and smooth. Being refracted by light, the mirage is formed on the surface.

華東地區

Mirages usually occur from the beginning of Spring through the autumn after it clears up following a rainstorm, when there are clouds and mist near the water's surface along with a light breeze. A mirage can bring good luck, but can only be seen by chance, not on purpose. Indeed, many people who live around Penglai have never had the good fortune to see a mirage.

The Wind Shelter Pavilion

Originally called the Mirage Pavilion, the Wind Shelter Pavilion was built in the Ming Dynasty. Standing on the mountain peak and facing the sea, the pavilion stays absolutely still even when the wind is blowing violently.

One explanation for this stillness in the face of heavy winds is that the pavilion once saved a valuable pearl taking shelter from the wind. However, the actual reason rests with its unique architectural layout, which ingeniously combined human building techniques and the place's natural physical environment. North of the pavilion is a low tooth-like wall, whose outer wall is arc-shaped. The wind rising from the sea ascends immediately and rapidly along the arc-shaped wall, overflies the eaves and runs southward, preventing it from entering the pavilion.

Below the pavilion is an irregular natural cave, several meters above the water, 14 meters deep and 2 meters wide. The cave is named "Lion Cave" because of the huge rock shaped like a crouching lion standing at the mouth of the cave. In the rainy season, the humid and hot air which enters the cave is cooled and coagulated into mist. Then the mists float out of the cave repeatedly, now visible and now hidden, which is called the Mists and Clouds around the Lion Cave. It is one of Penglai's top ten views.

The Billows-viewing Pavilion

Standing on Danya Hill and overlooking the sea, the Billows-viewing Pavilion is the best place for viewing the sea. In particular, if you view the sea when the wind has subsided and the waves have calmed down, you will find it vast and boundless. The sea is merged into the sky in the distance and the ripples stay static, giving you a sense of relaxation and happiness. When the spring tide appears, the muddy waves almost seem to reach the sky as they crash heavily on the rugged shore.

The L Dongbin Immortal Hall

The L Dongbin Immortal Hall was the place for offering sacrifices to L Dongbin, one of the eight immortals. The fairy tale about Eight Immortals Crossing the Sea has long been widely spread. Why was there only a hall built for L Dongbin? The reason is that L Dongbin was esteemed as one of the five founders of the Complete Unity Sect of Taoism, one of the two major sects of Taoism.

The Sanqing Hall

Enshrined in the main hall are three founders of Taoism. They are the Gods of Yuqing Yuanshi, Shangqing Lingbao and Taiqing Daode. Taoism is the only major religion that came exclusively from Chinese roots and grew to maturity in Chinese soil. These three gods are therefore widely known throughout China.

The Water Fortress

There are two cities in Penglai. One is the city of Penglai. Do you know where the other one is?Well, the other one is just in front of us. It is the Water Fortress.

With an average height of 2 meters, a width of 8 meters and a perimeter of 2, 200 meters, the Water Fortress is a complete and well-knit defense system composed of a water area, city walls, water gates, forts, marinas, lighthouses and seawalls. Only two gates were opened for military purposes. One of them is the South Gate, also known as the Zhenyang Gate, which connected the Water Fortress to land roads;the other is the North Gate, also known as the Water Gate, a key point to the sea, where there is a

華東地區

sluice. The long but narrow water area divides the city into the west section and the east section. In the Ming and Qing dynasties, it was the place where the navy was stationed and underwent training. North of the fortress, the Lighthouse stands high in the air, providing a good observation post for overlooking the sea and observing any enemy warships. Two water gate forts dominate the nearby sea. It was here where Qi Jiguang, a famous Ming Dynasty national hero and an anti-Japanese general, once led his army to beat the Japanese pirates.

All right, we have finished the tour of the Penglai Pavilion. Does anyone have any questions?No? Well, then I will give you thirty minutes to look around and take some pictures. If you have any questions, please feel free to let me know.

Well, my introduction is over. I hope my service is satisfying. Thank you for your cooperation. I hope that I can become your guide next time. Have a good journey.

各位朋友：

早上好，歡迎來到人間仙境蓬萊。我是大家蓬萊之旅的導遊，如果您有任何問題或者特別的興趣，請告訴我，我會盡全力使您的旅行愉快。今天我們將要參觀的是蓬萊閣。

首先，我簡要地給大家介紹一下蓬萊閣的情況。

蓬萊閣創建於北宋嘉祐六年（公元1061 年），至今有近940 多年的歷史。經過明清兩代不斷擴建和改建，現在蓬萊閣占地面積已達約3280 平方米，建築面積約1890 平方米。這一宏偉壯麗的建築群包括龍王宮、天后宮、蓬萊閣、三清殿、呂祖殿、彌陀寺六個單元，共100 多間。這些飛檐走壁、黃瓦朱門的建築，像眾星捧月般簇擁在主閣周圍，高低錯落，渾然一體。各殿宇廊壁之間，楹聯、碑文和名人字畫比比皆是，其中有宋朝著名詩人蘇東坡的手跡、神話傳說中八仙之一呂洞賓的石刻肖像、將領馮玉祥所題「碧海丹心」等。在這裡可以觀賞到著名的「十大仙景」，那就是：仙閣凌空、海市蜃樓、萬里澄波、獅洞煙雲、魚梁歌約，萬斛珠璣、日出扶桑、晚潮新月、漏天銀雨、銅井含靈。整個古建築群，樓台殿閣分布得體，寺廟園林交相輝映，融人文景觀與自然風光於一體，山丹海碧，清風宜人，成為名揚四海的遊覽區。

丹崖仙境坊

這座四柱三間式木結構牌坊，原來叫丹崖仙境坊，清光緒年末被毀壞，民國初年修復後改為現名。後又被毀壞，這是1981年下半年修復的。「丹崖仙境」四個字，是董必武1964年來蓬萊閣時題寫的。因為蓬萊閣坐落在丹崖山上，山體由紅色氧化鐵膠結的角礫狀石英構成，呈紅褐色，又因岩壁陡峭直立，故稱「丹崖」。蓬萊閣因有海市，素有「仙境」之稱，過了這丹崖仙境坊，我們便進入仙境了，大家有沒有成仙的感覺呢？

龍王宮

龍王宮初建於唐朝，後在宋、元又有擴建。龍王宮包括山門、前殿和後殿的三重院落。

這裡是龍王宮的前殿，東西兩側各塑有海中護法一尊，東為定海將軍，西為鎮海將軍，各持法寶，護衛著正殿中的東海龍王敖廣，兩側塑有八名站官，右邊第一位是巡海夜叉，第二位是千里眼，第三位是電母，第四位是雷公，左邊第一位是趕魚郎，第二位是順風耳，第三位是風婆，第四位是雨伯。

這裡是龍王宮的後殿，也是龍王的寢殿。過去這裡有龍王的木質雕像和龍王出行的步輦、儀仗，那是人們為了求雨而設的。古時遇上大旱，人們便到這裡頂禮膜拜，然後頭戴柳條帽高呼「求大雨、求大雨」，抬著龍王雕像走街串巷，走到哪裡，兩邊住戶都要端水潑灑。人們求雨説來也十分有趣，若酷暑大旱，屢求不應，人們便把龍王爺抬到烈日下暴晒，直到龍王爺滿頭大汗時為止，不久便會普降甘霖，而且這個方法百試百靈，在當地廣為流傳。

戲樓

這裡是戲樓。請看戲樓兩側台柱上的對聯，上聯為「樂奏鈞天，潮汐聲中喧島嶼」，意思是這戲樓上演奏的音樂像天宮仙樂一樣，伴著早潮晚潮的聲音響遍蓬萊仙島；下聯為「宮開碣石，笙歌隊裡砌蓬萊」，是説戲台上的音樂戲曲一開始，演奏隊伍的樂聲便直通到三神山。

每逢正月十六海神娘娘生日，當地漁民都要在此唱戲，所演的劇均為山東地方戲。

天后宮

天后是海上生產作業的保護神，是沿海地區民間最崇拜的神。據不完全統計，中國有300多個縣市建有天后宮，蓬萊閣的天后宮是中國北方最大的天后宮之一，共分前殿、正殿、後殿。

這是天后宮的前殿，也叫馬殿。這兩尊塑像東為嘉應，西為嘉祐，是保護天后的神將。傳説他們原是莆田湄洲的妖怪，後被天后降伏，跟隨天后左右做護法神將。

這是天后宮的正殿。正中端坐的就是天后海神娘娘，旁有四名侍女，東西兩側各有四名站官。東邊四位分別是東海龍王、南海龍王、傳達天帝旨意的文官和手持萬法歸宗的文官，如果海中魚鱉蝦蟹興風作浪，他都記在上面，屬於哪個海的就交給哪個海龍王處置。西側分別為西海龍王、北海龍王、手持環海司命傳達海神娘娘旨意的文官和手持印章管理行文蓋章的文官。

這是天后宮的後殿，是天后的臥室，東西兩間設有窗幔被縟、梳洗工具。每天有專人負責打洗臉水、灑掃臥室、疊放臥具、焚香敬茶。據説海神娘娘單日住東間，雙日住西間。

人們對海神娘娘的崇拜平時尚且如此，到農曆三月二十三她生日這天更為隆重。清代康熙皇帝曾規定祭祀天后的規格和使用的祭器。在民間，善男信女自發從四面八方湧向天后宮，婦女獻上精心繡制的花鞋、幔帳，男人們則焚香燒紙、頂禮膜拜，船家或漁行也以此還所許之願，唱戲酬神。

蓬萊閣

現在大家所看到的就是蓬萊閣了。它與黃鶴樓、岳陽樓、滕王閣並稱中國四大名樓。

蓬萊閣始建於宋代，歷代均有整修，才有如今規模。你看這座坐北朝南的木結構建築，氣勢恢弘、飛檐八角，真是畫棟飛雲、竹簾卷雨。閣內布滿了三朝石刻100餘片，閣北高懸金字橫匾「蓬萊閣」三個雄渾大字，是清代書法家鐵保手書。還有為我們所熟悉的宋代蘇東坡、明代董其昌、清代翁方綱等書法家的手跡。這些碑文石刻生動地記載了海山奇觀，謳歌了仙閣勝境。

一樓現為黨和國家領導人遊覽蓬萊閣的影像資料展示。

二樓是八仙醉酒的場景再現，依次為鐵拐李、藍采和、何仙姑、漢鐘離、張果老、呂洞賓、韓湘子、曹國舅。他們形態各異，手中有不同的法器，八仙過海的傳說發源於此。傳說某年某月某日，八仙赴完王娘娘的蟠桃會後，乘著酒興來到東海，八人各顯神通，游在萬頃碧海上，不想被龍太子發現，欲奪八仙寶物，於是發生大戰。後來觀音從中調解，雙方才各自罷兵。八仙的法物和古代人征服海洋有關，拐就是獨木舟的縮影，張果老的驢應是驢皮筏子。其實八仙的傳說在當地另有說法。蓬萊閣對面是廟島群島，在古代是流放犯人的地方。這裡有一個規定，每日限供三百人口糧，但島上收容犯人卻不限於此。人多口糧不足，禁卒便將一部分犯人投入大海。傳說在一個暴雨的夜晚，犯人發生暴動，但只有八人登上蓬萊，蓬萊人發現他們所用的泅渡工具只是獨木舟、木盆等簡陋的工具，感到不可思議，疑心他們是神仙，所以能泅渡茫茫大海。自此以後，八仙的故事開始流傳開來。

旁邊的八仙桌椅大家不妨坐一坐，沾一沾仙氣。

這裡還是海市蜃樓的著名觀賞地。海市蜃樓是在一定條件下，光線在大氣中經過折射和反射形成的一種自然現象。蓬萊地處暖寒流交匯之處，當寒流覆蓋暖流之

華東地區

上時，低層空氣出現上暖下冷的逆溫現象，使空氣密度上疏下密、判別顯著，形成較為穩定的面，透過光線折射和全反射，形成海市蜃樓。海市蜃樓在春夏、夏秋之交，雨過天晴，海面上還有雲霧時，若微風颳起便有可能出現。海市蜃樓是可遇而不可求的，即使蓬萊本地人也有沒見過的。

避風亭

這座亭子叫避風亭，原名海市亭，明正德八年（公元1513年）知府嚴泰修建。亭子高踞山巔，面臨大海，但任憑室外狂風怒吼，亭內卻是燭火依舊。

過去人們傳說這裡有避風珠，但實際原因卻在於它那獨特的建築結構，可以說是人工建築與自然環境的一種巧妙結合。亭子北前方是一齒狀矮城牆，外壁呈弧形，海風由海面吹來時隨即由弧形牆壁急劇上升、飛越屋簷、向南而去，亭內便無風可進了。亭的東西南三面牆壁，恰成氣流死角，空氣不能對流，因此，儘管海風呼嘯，門窗洞開，亭內卻燭火不驚。

避風亭下有一形狀不規則的天然石洞。高出水面數米，深約14米、寬約2米。洞口有一巨石，狀如獅子伏臥，故名「獅子洞」。洞內舊有仙人像五尊，故又名「仙人洞」。岩洞處於石英岩層中斷發育，石岩層為大小不一的角礫狀，洞壁凹凸不平，係受構造積壓所致，經海水長期沖蝕成洞。雨季時濕熱空氣進入洞內，受冷凝結成霧氣，隨之對流出洞外，煙雲屢屢，縹緲虛幻，故有「獅洞煙雲」之說，被列為蓬萊十景之一。

觀瀾亭

觀瀾亭足踏丹崖，俯視大海，亭前毫無遮攔，是亭上觀海的最佳去處。風平浪靜時，在此觀海，茫茫無垠，海天一色，漣漪不動，令人心曠神怡。要是趕上大潮汛，則見濁浪排空，驚濤拍岸，大有錢塘漲潮的氣勢。

呂祖殿

呂祖殿是祭祀八仙之一呂洞賓的地方。八仙過海的故事，在這裡流傳很廣，為什麼單單建了一個呂祖殿，獨尊呂洞賓呢？據說王重陽創立全真派，並到登州等地傳道，所以蓬萊道教就是王重陽及其徒弟丘處機所傳。全真派稱呂洞賓為「北五祖」之一，元代呂洞賓曾被封為「純陽帝君」，蓬萊的道士們自然要在道教集中的蓬萊閣上給呂洞賓一席之地的特殊待遇了。

三清宮

正殿內祭祀的就是三位道家始祖。中間的一位是玉清原始天尊，手拿元珠，象徵洪元時代；東邊是上清靈寶天尊，手持太極圖，象徵混元時代；西邊是太清道德天尊，手搖扇子，象徵太初時代。道教是中國四大宗教之一，是中國唯一土生土長的宗教，所以這三位神仙可以稱得上是家喻戶曉了。

登州水城

蓬萊有兩座城，一座是蓬萊城，另一座在哪裡呢？其實它就在我們眼前。看，那就是登州水城。

水城平均高度約2米、寬8米，周長共2200米。它由小海、城牆、水門、炮台、敵台、碼頭、燈樓、平浪台、放浪壩等組成一個完整嚴密的防禦體系，攻守兼備。出於軍事需要，水城僅開兩門，南門叫振楊門，俗稱土門，與陸路相通；北門叫水門，奠基海中，是入海咽喉，並設有柵欄，控制船隻出入——平時閘門高懸，船隻出入無阻；有事時則放閘入水，切斷海上通道。小海是城北門的一片水城，呈窄長形，南北655米，將城分為東西兩半。城北燈樓凌空屹立，俯瞰大海，原有導航設備，並可在上觀察敵情。水門設有兩座炮台，分列東西，護衛犄角，控制著附近海面。明清兩代在此駐紮水師、停泊戰艦、出哨巡洋，成為邊防要塞。當年著名民族英雄、抗倭將領戚繼光，就曾率領著他的戚家軍在這裡操練水師，抗擊倭寇。

好的，蓬萊的遊覽到這裡就要結束，如果大家沒有什麼疑問的話，給大家半個小時的自由活動時間，大家可以在這裡盡情地拍照留念。

華東地區

305

各位朋友，我的講解到這裡就結束了，希望我的講解能給您帶來快樂，謝謝您的合作，希望有機會再次為您服務。祝您旅途愉快。

Mt.Taishan （泰山）

Ladies and gentlemen,

I sincerely welcome you to Mt.Taishan. It is my honor to be your tour guide during your stay in Mt.Taishan. If you have any problems or special interest, please don't hesitate to let me know. I will do my best to make your visit pleasant and enjoyable.

Today, we will climb to the summit together from the central road.

This huge and ancient mountain contains abundant natural and cultural riches and has been listed as World Natural and Cultural Heritage Site. Now, we would like to ask like the ancient people: "What shall I say of the Great Peak?" Then, let's climb up the mountain to see the charm of Mt.Taishan.

Here is Dai Temple. As we walk from this place and pass the Daizongfang and Shengxianfang, as well as the Red, Zhongtian, and South Gates, we'll be treading down the roads on which ancient emperors made sacrifices. Today this road is called "the pleasure of ascending to heaven" road. It is also called "the Central Road" and is oldest of the six roads to Mt.Tai's summit and will be our road up to the peak today.

Please look at the front of Dai Temple and you will notice a smaller temple. This is the "Yaocan Pavilion" which was the place where ancient emperors began sacrificial ceremonies at Mt.Taishan. When emperors came here to make sacrifices, they all held a simple ceremony here to pay homage to the Gods. Therefore, before Ming Dynasty, it was called "Caocan Pavilion". It was then enlarged and its name was changed to "Yaocan Pavilion". While the name may have changed, the Yaocan

Pavilion remains a place of piety and holy worship.

Dear friends, you know that China's ancient architecture occupies a unique place in world architectural history. The Yaocan Pavilion was designed to serve as starting point for sacrificial ceremonies, which would gradually climax as the Emperor visited other higher ceremonial places. This progression is very much in line with ancient Chinese thinking regarding ceremonial aesthetics.

Now, we are in the Dai Temple which is a mysterious place. The Dai Temple's charm is due to its special characteristics. Firstly, its fence differs from the usual temple fences. The fence is 1, 300 meters long, has 5 cornerstones, was built with big blue bricks, and is shaped like a trapezoid. It is 11 meters wide on the top and 17. 6 meters wide on the bottom and about 10 meters high. The Dai Temple has a total of 8 gates:Zhengyang Gate is the center gate and main entrance into the temple. Coming into the Dai Temple from Zhengyang Gate, you will see the Peitian Gate, on which is written Confucius's words, "The moral matches the heaven and earth". Flanking the two sides of Peitian Gate are the "Sanlinghou Palace" to the east and "Tai Wei" to the west. The three palaces were connected by the walls which ring the Dai Temple's first outer yard.

After crossing Ren'an Gate, we come to the grand "Song Tiankuang", which is also called Junji Palace. It is Dai Temple's main body and has 9 rooms; there are also 5 houses, each of which is 17. 18 meters long and 23. 3 meters high. Please look and notice how the Tiankuang Palace is situated on the spacious white station base, surrounded by the stone carved fence. One really notable feature is the cloud shaped row of columns.

The winding courtyards around the Tiankuang Palace merge into one big courtyard. In Chinese architecture, the porch plays an important role in building. Porches help give spaces a consistent, convergent, close and rigorous feel. The Dai Temple's winding

華東地區

corridor closely follows the palace's double-eaved roof. The contrast of straight and lofty has aroused reverence among all those who visit this place. Ancient Chinese architecture fully realized that structures are neither absolutely big nor absolutely small and the size is produced from the contrast between big and small. Besides the low winding corridor, two exquisite imperial tablets pavilions were built in the platforms standing in front of the Tiankuang Palace. These platforms both highlight the Tiankuang Palace and also provide a sense of majesty and tranquility.

Upon leaving the Tiankuang Palace's back door, you will notice that three brick roads are connected to it. Since Mt.Taishan was named "Emperor" by the Song Dynasty Emperor Zhenzong, and since the "emperor" must have a "wife", people also gave the mountain a wife whose name was "Shu Ming Hou". Looked at from this perspective, the Dai Temple is more like an imperial palace than a Taoist Temple. The Dai Temple's particular layout underscores it's dual function and utility as both a place of worship and a center of political activity.

A moment ago, we visited the Dai Temple through the main road. But the Temple's two sides originally had 4 courtyards, two of which are on the east side and two of which are on the west side. The front courtyard on the east side is the "Hanbo Yard"; this is where the Han Dynasty Wu Emperor was said to have planted six ancient cedars. The back courtyard is named the "Dong Yu Zuo" and is where emperors stayed when making sacrifices at Mt.Taishan.

Here is the famous 18 Pan. About 2. 5 billion years ago, during what geologists call the "Mt.Taishan Movement, " Mt.Taishan first rose from the sea. Mt.Taishan later rose and some more, only to be submerged again, until eventually about 30 million years ago, during the Himalaya Mountain Orogeny Movement, it assumed its present-day shape. The ancient movement has created three fault zones which rise like ladders south of Mt.Taishan. The top fault zone stretches from the Yuanbu Bridge to the peak. Here the elevation suddenly rises more than 400 meters, producing the striking contrast to the other mountains all around and making Mt.Taishan's shape resemble that of a sword on the top of a pagoda. Hence the mountain's nickname, "pillar in the east".

Here is the Path of Eighteen Bends, which is the most difficult road to climb the mountain. Let's look at the stone inscriptions carved by the ancient people. They encouraged us by saying, "climb up diligently" and "climb blue ladders together". Think about the people who carried loads up this road or worked on building this road and who did not leave their names. While no record exists about these people, their hard work and efforts can drive us and others onward. My friends, mountaineering is just like carrying out some great enterprises. Only by making great efforts and going upward, can we overcome difficulties and reach the summit of achievement.

This is the Nantian Gate. We are now near the boundary between the mountain and sky. Although we have no certainty of becoming an immortal, we understand here how "climbing Mount. Tai makes the world feel and look small".

After entering the Nantian Gate, we can see "Wei Liao Xuan". Each side of the "Wei Liao Xuan" has a gate leading north. After passing through these gates, we can see a hill called "Yueguan Hill," which has a view pavilion. It is said that in the late autumn when the sky is clear, people can see the "golden belts of the Yellow River."

Tianjie Street is located east of the Nantian Gate. Walking along the street, we can see a gateway in the central north which is inscribed "Wang Wu Sheng Ji", where Confucius and Yanyuan saw a white horse outside the Wujing Gate. The Confucius Temple lies in the north of the gateway.

The east of Tianjie Street is the Azure Cloud Temple. Now, I will tell you the story of Bi Xia Yuan Jun. The predecessor of Bi Xia Yuan Jun is the goddess of Mt.Taishan and is worshipped like the Avalokitesvara Buddhists. For many years, a great

華東地區

number of people came to Mt.Taishan to offer incense to the Supreme Lord Azure Cloud, who is worshipped widely by Chinese people, especially those living in North China.

OK, let's go into the Azure Cloud Temple. It consists of two courtyards, the front courtyard and the rear courtyard. There are five rooms in the main hall inside the entrance. The eaves and the roof tiles of the hall and the bells at the four corners are all made of bronze. The eastern and western annexed chambers and their gates are roofed with iron tiles. This group of buildings, exquisite and ingenious, is well conceived in its overall arrangement and compact in structure.

All right, everyone, it is only at the precipitous peak that we can enjoy the infinitely fine scenery. Now, the summit of Mt.Taishan meets our gaze. Follow me, please. We will go further to visit the Jade Emperor Peak, Yuhuang Peak, Mt.Taishan's highest summit. Yuhuang Temple was built on that peak. Its red ocher and green wall give Mt.Taishan a laurel crown. Enter the temple and look at the "Peak Stone" in the center of the yard. There is a tablet around it which says: "The Peak of Mt.Taishan— 1545 Meters." According to geological analysist originated in the seabed and is some 30 million years old.

Now our tour is about to end. I hope that you can come to Mt.Taishan for sightseeing once again. Thanks!

各位朋友，大家好！

熱誠歡迎你們到泰山來遊覽，很高興能成為大家這次旅行的導遊！如果您有任何問題或者特別的興趣，請告訴我，我會盡全力使您的旅行愉快。今天我將和大家一起從泰山中路登上山頂。

這座高大、古老的泰山蘊涵了豐富的自然與文化的積澱，已被聯合國教科文組織列入世界自然與文化遺產名錄。現在，我們仍要像古人那樣問一句「岱宗夫如何」，然後，跟我一起步入大山，去領略泰山的神韻。

這裡是岱廟。從岱廟開始，經岱宗坊、一天門、紅門、中天門、升仙坊至南天門，是古代皇帝封禪泰山所走過的路，現在被人們稱為「登天景區」，也稱中路，是如今泰山登山6條路中最古老的一條。我們將從這條路登上極頂。

大家注意到了巍峨的岱廟前，還有一座較小的廟宇，這就是「遙參亭」，是當年皇帝封禪泰山的起始點。當年帝王來泰山舉行封禪祭典時，都先要在這裡舉行簡單的參拜儀式，因此明朝之前，稱此為「草參亭」。明代加以擴建時，改名為「遙參亭」。雖是一字之易，虔誠卻盡含其中了。

朋友們，中國的古代建築在世界建築史上有著獨特的地位，這座遙參亭的建築構思既出於封禪大典將由此為前奏而步步進入高潮的需要，也是中國古代先抑後揚的美學思想的體現。

正陽門內就是岱廟了，這是一個神奇的地方。岱廟有著如此的魅力，取決於它自身的特徵。首先，它的圍牆便與一般廟宇不同，圍牆周長為1300米，5層基石，上砌大青磚，呈梯形，下寬17.6米，上寬11米，高約10米，共有8座門：正中為正陽門，是岱廟的正門。由正陽門進得岱廟來，迎面是配天門，取孔子說的「德配天地」之意。配天門兩側，東為三靈侯殿，西為太尉，三殿之間以牆相連，構成岱廟中間第一進院落。

過了仁安門，便是雄偉高大的宋天貺，它又叫峻極殿，是這座廟宇的主體。天貺殿面闊9　間，進深5間，17.18米，通高23.3米。大家看，天貺殿坐落在寬敞的白色台基之上，周圍石雕欄楯環繞，雲形望柱齊列，使天貺殿與四周的環境產生了奇妙的效果。

天貺殿周圍有迴廊，形成了一個大院落。在中國的建築中，廊是起著使空間有連貫、斂氣、緊密、嚴謹而又富於變化的作用，這在世界建築史上都被稱道的。岱廟的迴廊把一座重檐廡殿的大建築物緊緊地環抱著，平直與崇高的對比更激起了人們對天貺殿的景仰。中國古代建築家深知世上沒有絕對大或絕對小，大小是從對比中產生的，除了四周低平的迴廊外，天貺殿前平台上還修了兩個精巧的御碑亭，既突出了天貺殿，又於雄偉中寓含著恬靜閒適，因此天貺殿並不是雄偉兩個字可以概括得了的。

從天貺殿後門出，有磚石甬道與後寢宮相連。宋真宗封泰山時，因將泰山封為「帝」，帝則應當有「后」，於是便為之配了個夫人「淑明后」。從這一點看來，岱廟與其說是道教神府，還不如說更像皇家宮廷，這種布局進一步透露了封建統治者利用岱廟進行政治活動的功利目的。

剛才，我們是沿著岱廟的主軸線遊覽，而主軸線兩側，原另有4 個別院，東面前後兩院，前為「漢柏院」。相傳漢武帝所植的6 株古柏就在此院內；後為「東御座」，是皇帝祭泰山下榻的地方。

這裡就是泰山有名的十八盤了。大約25億年前，在一次被地質學家稱作「泰山運動」的造山運動中，古泰山第一次從一片汪洋中崛起，以後幾度滄桑，泰山升起又沉沒，沉沒又升起，終於在3000 萬年前的「喜馬拉雅山造山運動」中，泰山最後形成了今天的模樣。古老的造山運動造就了泰山南麓階梯式上升的三個斷裂帶，最上一層從雲步橋斷裂帶到極頂，海拔陡然上升400 多米，使得這一層地帶與四周群峰產生強烈對比，猶如寶塔之剎，形成了「東天一柱」的氣勢。

這裡是緊十八盤，也是整個登山路中最為艱難的地段了。大家看，石壁上有古人的題刻：「努力登高」、「首出萬山」、「共攀青雲梯」……那是在勉勵我們。大家再看，那負荷百斤的挑山工，再想想當年無名無姓的鑿石修路人……大山無言，但它們能激勵人們向上。朋友，登山猶如幹任何事業，只有義無反顧地向上，才能戰勝險阻，才能到達最高的境界！

南天門到了，我們現在已置身「天界」了，雖然我們並沒有成仙，但我們在這裡能領略到「登泰山而小天下」的豪邁。

進了南天門，與之相對的是大殿取名為「未了軒」，未了軒兩側各有一門可以北去。出門往西有一山峰叫「月觀峰」，山上有亭，名月觀亭。據說，天高氣爽的深秋時節，在這裡還可以一覽「黃河金帶」的奇異景觀：在夕陽映照的天幕下，大地變暗了，只有一曲黃河水，反射出了太陽的光輝，像一條閃光的金帶，將天和地連在一起。入夜，在皎潔的月色下，由此北望可見濟南的萬家燈火，因此「月觀峰」又稱「望府山」。

出南天門院落東拐即為天街。天街，天上的街市，多富詩意的地方。沿天街東行，中北有一坊，匾額上題有「望吳聖蹟」，這就是相傳孔子與顏淵看到吳國閶門外一匹白馬的地方。坊北有孔子廟。

天街最東端就是碧霞祠了，我給大家講講碧霞元君的故事。碧霞元君的前身是泰山女神，在民間被稱做「天仙玉女碧霞元君」，是百姓心目中的泰山主神，並被稱做「泰山奶奶」、「泰山老母」。民眾對泰山老母的信仰與喜愛，是一種歷史積澱下來的埋藏在人們心靈深層的對母親的愛。多少年來，碧霞元君贏得了百姓的愛戴，至今仍高踞泰山之巔，接受著善男信女的香火，召喚著去鄉離國的遊子。

好，讓我們進到碧霞祠來。2500平方米的地方，建起了山門，正殿，配殿，3座神門，鐘樓、鼓樓、香亭、萬歲樓、千斤鼎、火池，還有照壁、歌舞樓、御碑亭，殿為銅瓦、碑為銅鑄，金光閃閃，儼然天上宮闕。泰山碧霞祠的高度建築技巧被認為是中國古代高山建設的典範，人們到這裡來進香並不感其小，反而覺其高大，神聖感油然而生。如今，泰山碧霞祠是建築群中獨具一格的神品。

朋友們！無限風光在險峰啊！現在泰山的頂峰就在我們眼前了！請大家跟我一起去遊覽泰山的最高峰——玉皇峰吧！玉皇廟建在極頂上，紅牆碧瓦像是給泰山戴上了一頂桂冠。由山門進廟，最先看到的是院中央的「極頂石」。極頂石臥在一圈石欄中，高不盈米，表面粗糙，如果在別處，將是一塊最普通不過的石頭了。但是在這裡，它的旁邊有碑恭恭地寫著：「泰山極頂1545米」。根據地質學分析，就是它，根植於1萬米的地殼深處，在3000萬年前從海槽中率先拱起；就是它，有著數百平方公里的基座。整座大山在托舉著它，使它高聳雲天，以至玉皇廟中的玉皇大帝簡直就成了它的守護神。

朋友們，一天的行程已經結束。希望你們能再度到泰山來遊玩。謝謝大家！

Jiangxi Province江西省

A Glimpse of the Province （本省簡介）

Jiangxi Province has been described as "a land endowed with rich natural resources and outstanding intelligent people". It lies on the southern bank of the. Yangtze River's middle and lower reaches and borders Zhejiang, Fujian, Guangdong, Hunan, Hubei, and Anhui provinces. Jiangxi covers an area of 166, 900 square kilometers. Its northern territory is relatively flat, while the southern, western and eastern parts of the province are mountainous. Jiangxi Province's Poyang Lake is not only China's largest freshwater lake, but also the world's largest habitat for migratory birds. Jiangxi is located near the Tropic of Cancer and has a mild and humid subtropical climate with abundant rainfall and sunshine. Some 59% of Jiangxi province is thus covered by forests, ranking it first among Chinese provinces with respect to forest coverage.

Tourism Resources

Jiangxi has picturesque scenery and historical sites, making it a perfect tourist destination. There are many beautiful places here, such as Mount Lushan, Dragon-Tiger Mountain, Sanqing Mountain, Jinggang Mountain and the Tengwang Pavilion, which ranked as one of the top three pavilions in all of southern China. The UN has placed Mount Lushan on its list of world cultural heritage sites. In addition to beautiful scenery, Jiangxi is filled with history. It has been the seat of glorious ancient civilizations and also served as cradle of the Chinese Revolution. Mao Zedong and Liu Shaoqi first organized and mobilized workers in Anyuan, Pingxiang city, while the celebrated August 1stUprising took place in Nanchang. Mao Zedong set up the rural revolutionary base at Jiangxi's Jinggang Mountain and Ruijin became famous as "The

Red City" because it served as the main seat of the worker-peasant democratic government during the second revolutionary civil war time. And last but not least, the celebrated Long March started in Jiangxi Province.

Local Snacks

Nanchang Stone Street's Mahua; Xingguo's cowskin candy; Nan'an salted duck; Ganzhou confection; Nanfeng bean curd skin; Pingxiang cake; Xiajiang rice noodles; Jiujiang sweet-scented osmanthus teacake.

Special Local Products

Jiangxi's most famous local product is Jingdezhen porcelain. Other notable specialties include agarics, yulan slices, Lushan yunwu tea, Wuyuan ink, Longwei ink stones, De'an jade carvings, Jinggangshan bamboo carvings and root carvings.

Local Culture

Jiangxi is noted for its wide variety of operas, including Gan, Ninghe, Donghe, Yihuang, and Yuhe Opera.

Tourism City

Nanchang is the capital of Jiangxi Province and is also its political, economic and cultural center. Nanchang's name means "Jiangnan prosperity," and the city has a long and colorful history. For example, Wang Bo of Tang Dynasty praised Jiangxi as "the birthplace of heroes who bring glory to China". More recently, Zhou Enlai and Zhu De led the famous August 1stNanchang Uprising, during which the People's Liberation Army was born. Hence Nanchang's reputation as the "Hero City".

Jingdezhen is a beautiful city in northeast Jiangxi Province. Jingdezhen chinaware

華東地區

kiln fires have burned continuously over the past 1, 700 years, making a valuable contribution to human civilization in the form of rare ceramic relics and art and superbly crafted porcelain which embody the full flavor of local custoMs.

Jiangxi Province's four classic tour routes

1. Cultural tour—famous mountains, rivers and China's porcelain capital.

Nanchang—Jiujiang（Mt.Lushan）—Jingde-zhen town—Wuyuan.

2. The tour of seeking for the trace of Taoist culture—famous mountains and towns.

Nanchang —Yingtan（Mt.Dragon-Tiger）—Guifeng—Shangrao (Mt.Sanqing).

3. Cultural eco-tour—famous mountains, rivers, towns.

Nanchang—Jiujiang（Mt.Lushan）—Jing-dezhen—Wuyuan—Shangrao（Mt.Sanqing）—Yingtan(Mt.Dragon-Tiger）— Nanchang.

4. The "Chinese Red Culture" tour.

Nanchang—Mt.Jinggang—Ganzhou—Ruijin.

江西省有「物華天寶，人傑地靈」的盛譽。它地處中國東南偏中部長江中下游南岸，東鄰浙江、福建，南連廣東，西靠湖南，北毗湖北、安徽而共接長江。全省土地總面積16.69萬平方公里，境內除北部較為平坦外，東西南部三面環山。境內的鄱陽湖為中國最大的淡水湖，同時也是世界上最大的候鳥棲息地。江西處北迴歸線附近，全省氣候溫和，雨量充沛，日照充足，為亞熱帶濕潤氣候。全省生態環境良好，森林覆蓋率達59.7%，居中國前列。

旅遊資源

　　江西自然風光秀美，山清水碧，景色誘人，是觀光旅遊和進行愛國主義教育、革命傳統教育的理想佳地。著名風景名勝有廬山、龍虎山、三清山、井岡山以及被譽為江南三大名樓之一的滕王閣等。其中，廬山已被聯合國作為「世界文化景觀」列入世界遺產名錄。江西還是舉世聞名的革命根據地，境內革命遺址眾多。如八一起義的英雄城市南昌、中國第一個農村革命根據地井岡山、第二次國內革命戰爭時期中央革命根據地中心瑞金和中國工人運動發源地之一的安源等地。南昌被稱為「紅色城市」，震驚世界的長征就是從這裡邁出了第一步。

風味小吃

　　南昌石頭街麻花，興國牛皮糖薯乾，南安板鴨，贛州蜜餞，南豐豆腐皮，萍鄉花果糕，峽江米粉，九江桂花茶餅。

地方特產

　　景德鎮陶瓷，國之瑰寶，素以「薄如紙、明如鏡、白如玉、聲如磬」等獨有的特色享譽中外；此外，木耳、玉蘭片、廬山雲霧茶、婺墨、龍尾硯、德安玉雕、井岡山竹雕、根雕也是江西有名的特產。

地方文藝

　　贛劇、九江的寧河戲、贛州的東河戲、宜黃的宜黃戲、廣昌的盯河戲等。

主要旅遊城市

　　南昌是江西省省會，全省政治、經濟、文化的中心。南昌，取「江南昌盛」之意而得名，它歷史悠久，一九八六年被國務院列入第二批國家歷史文化名城。南昌風景秀麗、人文薈萃、經濟繁榮、名人輩出，唐代王勃贊之為「物華天寶」、「人傑地靈」。在現代史上，周恩來、朱德領導的「八一」南昌起義舉世聞名，人民軍隊由此誕生。故此，南昌又有「英雄城」之美稱。

華東地區

景德鎮市位於江西省的東北部，是江南一座秀麗的古城。在長達1700　多年的漫長歲月裡，景德鎮燒瓷窯火不斷，為人類文明做出了寶貴的貢獻，留下了豐富的陶瓷歷史遺蹟、珍貴的陶瓷藝術、精湛的制瓷器技藝和瓷味十足的地方風情。這些構成了獨具特色的陶瓷旅遊項目。

推薦旅遊路線

1.文化之旅——名山、名河和瓷都

南昌—九江（廬山）—景德鎮—婺源。

2.探尋道教文化之旅——名山和小鎮

南昌—鷹潭（龍虎山）—圭峰—上饒（三清山）。

3.文化生態之旅——名山，河流和小鎮

南昌—九江（廬山）—景德鎮—婺源—上饒（三清山）—鷹潭（龍虎山）—南昌。

4.紅色之旅

南昌—井岡山—贛州—瑞金。

Beautiful Valley Scenic Area in Mt.Lushan （廬山錦繡谷景區）

Ladies and gentlemen,

Welcome to the Mt.Lushan Beautiful Valley Scenic Area. The Beautiful Valley is in the northwest part of Mt.Lushan, beside the Flower-Path Lake. It is located where the Dalin Ridge and the Tianchi Mountain meet. In the fourth ice age, the valley, which used to be a concave with its mouth opening to the southwest, was changed by glaciers into a steep, isolated valley.

The valley is named "Beautiful Valley" because it abounds in all kinds of flowers that bloom year round, displaying a splendid and beautiful picture. The Song Dynasty poet, Wang Anshi, wrote a poem when he visited the valley: "It is already a bewitching morning when I return home, happily, I feel like a host of this great mountain. Cheerfully, I set out to meet my friends from afar, inviting them to share this wonderful springtime in this Beautiful Valley." We will start our journey today with this poem.

In the Beautiful Valley spring and summer are the best seasons to appreciate the flowers and clouds, while autumn and winter are best for viewing the rocks and trees. In spring we mostly watch light or peach red azaleas. When climate starts to get warm and flowers are in full bloom, a multi-colored brocade overspreads the whole valley. A phrase quoted from a poem written by another great Song Dynasty poet, Huang Tingjian, best describes this charming picture: "to embroider a brocade." The most romantic flower in the valley is the "Rui (Auspicious) Fragrance". The famous Ming Dynasty pharmacologist, Li Shizhen, made particular note of it in his "Compendium of Medical Materials". Legend has it that long ago, a monk sleeping close to a rock during the daytime smelt something strongly fragrant in his dream, he woke up and looked for it around and found the flower, so he named it "The Sleeping Fragrance". Later generations thought that it was an auspicious sign and changed its name to "Rui (Auspicious) Fragrance".

Heavenly Bridge

Now we've arrived at the first scenic spot of the valley. Look forward to the left; we see a steep, huge rock that looks like a bridge suspended in mid air. That is the Heavenly Bridge, formed by huge rock fault. The towering cliffs, standing opposite to

華東地區

each other, were created by glacial erosion. In ancient times it was called "the Tray of the Immortals" and was the place where the monks of Dalin Temple in Mt.Lushan used to meditate.

Legend has it that, late in the Yuan Dynasty, the army of Zhu Yuanzhang and Chen Youliang fought at Poyang Lake. The former was defeated and fled to this place. With a deep ravine in front and an army in hot pursuit, his situation was desperate. Suddenly there were golden lights shining with every hue and a golden dragon descended from the sky and turned into a bridge. On seeing this, Zhu Yuangzhang raced over it on horseback. Chen Youliang came flying close behind, nearly bumping into the tail of Zhu's horse. Then a bolt of lightning came out of the blue sky, thunder rumbled and the day turned into night. Immediately a ray of brilliant blue light appeared and broke the bridge. In an instant the bridge disappeared, the clouds melted away and the sun came out again. What left behind was this unique valley with its cliffs opposite to each other. Chen Youliang had to take another way. This place was also called "the Tray of the Immortals". Try to find the hoof prints here, for it is said that the man who finds them will have a good fortune!

Dangerous Ridge

Now we are at the "Dangerous Ridge". Mao Zedong once described it as having Mt.Lushan's most beautiful view. From it we can view Tianchi Mountain to the left and Hawk's Mouth Precipice to the right. Hawk's Mouth Precipice is one of the best places from which people can appreciate the clouds and mists of Mt.Lushan. Far away is the Yangtze River and to the north there is Lion Peak's apex, which has also been named, "Two Lions Playing with a Ball". "Broken Bow" often presents itself here and the most interesting moment comes while cloud and mist rise. Taking a short break here, we can smell the fragrance of the clouds and mist and hear their whispers. If we are really fortunate, we may personally see "upward rain" rising from the bottom of the valley.

Now we are at the bottom of the Dangerous Ridge, please look back:the rock strata in the cliff look just like books on a bookshelf. So, in ancient times, it was called Book Cliff. It is easy to understand why men of letters of every generation loved to discuss literature in Mt.Lushan. This is because there are so many books on the top of Mt.Lushan!

The three characters, "錦繡谷" (p　ny　n:J　nxi　　; literally means "The Beautiful Valley"), are engraved on the cliff to the west of the Dangerous Ridge. The cliff was the ideal place for Buddhist disciples to sacrifice themselves for nirvana, so it is called "Petty Sacrifice Cliff". Yet it looks like a pig's head from another angle, so it is also jokingly called "Pig's Head Peak".

The famous Ming Dynasty pharmacologist, Li Shizhen, often collected herbal medicines here with his sons and prentices. The "Herbal Medicine Collecting Rock" was the place where they collected and sorted herbal medicines. Dozens of herbs from "Beautiful Valley" were recorded in "Compendium of Medical Materials". Above the "Herbal Medicine Collecting Rock" there is another rock pointing toward the sky and it resembles the huge head of an old man. So it is named "The Head's Rock", as it really appears to be a vivid, clear, true-to-life picture of an old, weary-looking man.

Immortals-Seeking Path

After leaving the Jinxiu Gate, we will begin to walk down the so-called Immortals-Seeking Path. It got this name because it was said that Ming Dynasty's first emperor sent his men to seek celestial beings down this path. Along the path we first see the Celestial Being-Seeking Pavilion, which was built in 1930 with funds donated by Jiang Jieshi, the former leader of the Guomindang. When staying in Mt.Lushan, Jiang Jieshi often watched the evening glow here. Many times, he was enchanted by the beautiful scene and reluctant to leave. In 1946, when the envoy George C. Marshal sought to mediate the military conflict between the Guomindang and the Chinese Communist Party, he held negotiations here with Jiang Jieshi. So it is also called "the Negotiation Platform".

The Bamboo Temple

Shaolin Temple is on the earth while the Bamboo Temple is in the heaven. Shaolin Temple can be seen, but Bamboo Temple was in the Valley and people could not see it. However, when there was a change in weather, people could hear the striking of bells and drums from the Bamboo Temple, and maybe catch a glimpse of the temple's shadow high in the clouds. It was said that Zhu Yuanzhang, the first emperor of the Ming Dynasty, ran into problems when his army fought against the army of Chen Youliang. Zhu turned danger into safety with the help of Zhou Dianxian, the celestial monk of the Bamboo Temple. In order to requite Zhou, Zhu sent his men to look for the Bamboo Temple in Mt.Lushan after he became emperor. They found nothing except the three characters, "竹林寺" (p ny n:Zh l ns ;literally means "the Bamboo Temple"), engraved high on a cliff. So the later generations called the Bamboo Temple "The Temple of Heaven".

Wonder-Appreciating Pavilion

The older pavilion was damaged for lack of protection and maintenance, so a newer one, the one you see now, was built on the original site. It is a hexagonal, concrete and stone structure. It is said that Jiang Jieshi used to view the scenery here, and once he shouted out "wonderful" three times:the Xilin Temple's bell tolls were wonderful; the sunglow in the valley was wonderful; the fairyland-like scenery was wonderful. So the pavilion is also called "Three-wonder Pavilion".

The Cave of the Immortals

Millions of years'weathering gradually created a natural cave here upon the grit stone. Rocks stretch out and green pines overhang from the top of the cave entrance. This makes the cave look like a Buddha's hand, so it is also called the "Rock of Buddha's Hand Cave".

The cave is 7 meters high, 12 meters wide and 14 meters long. There is a room made of stones in the Cave called Chunyang Palace in which there is a white jade statue of L   Dongbin. Most of the inscriptions on the walls are ruined and only a few poems inscriptions are well preserved. Within the cave, there are two springs named "springs in the heaven". They were recorded in "The History of the Latter Han Dynasty" and reputed to be "The splendiferous Liquid". Because of the high mineral specific gravity, the water will rise up above the rim of a glass, but still won't spill out. You can see this happen by putting a coin into a cupful of water. The Cave of the Immortals is a tranquil and secluded place.

On the left flank of the cave stands a Taoist temple for Laojun, the legendary founder of Taoism. This Taoist temple is a typical palace-like Chinese structure. A couplet written on the temple pillar says:westward a black buffalo wades; eastward some purple air blows. Enshrined inside the temple is a sculpture of Laojun sitting on a buffalo's back. Many Taoists pray and worship here. Going on from the chapel of Laojun, a huge rock standing aloof comes into our sight. It is called the Toad Rock and a famous pine tree grows out of the rock crack! Eight big Chinese characters in calligraphic style are inscribed in its front and upper surface: "縱覽雲飛" and "豁然貫通", meaning "the clouds in motion falls all into our sight" and "a feeling of instant thoroughfare hits upon our minds". In 1960, Mao Zedong wrote a poem of four lines with seven characters to a line: "the hardy pine in boundless darkness stands self-possessed, the cave was born a cave of the celestial being; the most beautiful scenery is in the summit." The "hardy pine" and "a cave of celestial being" mentioned in this poem are the pine and cave here.

Now we are at the Cave of Immortals arch entrance, and the inscriptions of its

Chinese name are written on the mid-upper part of the gate. A couplet on the left and right side of the gate says: "The Taoist immortals have left with a yellow crane;the Buddhist stories still here with the white lotus." Chairman Mao Zedong once sat and took a picture here when he visited Mt.Lushan. Now, our Beautiful Valley tour comes to an end. Thank you all!

各位朋友：

大家好！歡迎來到廬山錦繡谷景區參觀遊覽。錦繡谷位於廬山西北部花徑湖畔，由大林峰與天池山交匯而成。因第四紀冰川的作用，錦繡谷這塊面向西南的山間凹地，經過冰川的反覆切割，形成了一個底平壁陡的幽谷。

錦繡谷四時紅紫匝地，花團錦簇，故名錦繡。王安石詩雲：「還家一笑即芳晨，好與名山做主人。避逅五湖乘興往，相邀錦繡谷中春。」這首詩據説是他遊覽錦繡谷即興之作，讓我們也借古人的雅興開始我們的行程吧！

錦繡谷春夏看花和雲，秋冬觀石和樹。春季正好是看花的好季節，大家看到的大多數是雲錦杜鵑，花呈淡紅色、桃紅色等，春暖花開時，花開巧舞，燦爛若錦。錦繡谷取宋代詩人黃庭堅的詩句「錦上添花」之意，亦稱「雲錦花」。錦繡谷中還有一款最富傳奇色彩的花——瑞香，明李時珍在《本草綱目》中記載：「瑞香產廬山，原名『睡香　　』，傳説古代有一僧侶，晝寢岩下，夢中但聞異香撲鼻，醒而尋之，故名。」後人驚奇，認為是瑞祥之照，改名「瑞香」。

天橋

我們來到的谷中第一景。朝左前方看，一塊峭立橫空而出的巨石，有如懸在半空中一座橋，所謂「天橋」是由巨型岩石斷層所組成的，兩崖拱峙。這裡古稱「仙人盤」，曾經是廬山大林寺歷代的大和尚們悟道參禪的好地方。

相傳朱元璋與陳友諒大戰鄱陽湖時，一次朱元璋被打得無處安身，率領殘兵敗將逃至廬山，由於慌不擇路，單騎策馬逃命至此，前臨深壑，後有追兵，朱元璋仰天長嘆「天滅我也」。忽然霞光閃耀，從天上降下一條金龍，橫臥在深壑之上，化為一石橋，待朱元璋縱馬過橋後，頓時烏雲滾滾，雷聲隆隆，天昏地暗，只見一道灼眼的藍光將石橋擊斷。橋斷後，雲散日出，一切又恢復了原來的面貌，仍然是雙崖對峙的絕澗。陳友諒只好另尋他路追趕。我們不妨試著找找岩石上的馬蹄印，聽說找到能交好運呢！

險峰

這裡就是毛澤東同志讚許的「無限風光在險峰」中的險峰，現在於此，不知大家有無這種感慨呀！站在此處，往左看到的山是天池山，往右可望鷹嘴石。鷹嘴石是觀賞廬山雲霧最佳地點之一，遠可眺望長江，北可觀賞對面獅子峰頂「雙獅戲球」，廬山「佛光」經常在這裡出現，最有趣的莫過於雲霧上來的時候。此處只要您在這小憩片刻，您即可以嗅到廬山霧的芬芳，聽到廬山霧的私語，機會巧的話，您還能親眼看到那由山谷底朝天上「下」的「上雨」。

我們走下險峰後，再請大家回頭看看剛剛離開的險峰，那形成峰林的崖層，像不像堆在書桌上的一堆書呢？古人曾叫做「書經崖」這就不難理解為什麼自古以來，中國曆代文人有「南墜廬山當書案」的習慣，原來這裡藏了這麼多的天書啊！

險峰西邊的崖壁上刻有「錦繡谷」三個大字，傳說是佛教信徒們捨身成佛的理想之地——「小捨身崖」，其實你從另一個角度看，它又似豬頭，所以被打趣地稱為「豬頭峰」。

明代藥物學家李時珍曾多次帶著徒弟、兒子上廬山錦繡谷採藥，採藥石是他們採藥和分揀藥材的故地，在《本草綱目》裡就收錄了十幾種采自錦繡谷中的藥物。大家現在看到的採藥石上方的那塊巨石，叫「人頭石」，因為它酷似一個巨大的老人頭，不知你是否感覺維妙維肖呢？

訪仙路

走出錦繡門，踏上的小路是訪仙路，據說因為明代開國皇帝讓部下沿著這條山路遍訪神仙而得名。進入訪仙路，迎接我們的是訪仙亭，訪仙亭是原國民黨領袖蔣介石在1930　年出資修建的。蔣介石在廬山時，常在這裡欣賞晚霞，美好景色讓他流連。1946年美國特使馬歇爾為調解國共之間的軍事衝突，曾在此與蔣介石談判，故又叫「談判台」。

竹林寺

天上有竹林，地下有少林，地上的少林寺我們可以見到，可天上的竹林寺有誰見過——真是有心難見竹林寺，無意常遇仙客來。大家現在看到的這塊石壁上有「竹林寺」三個字，為什麼只見其字，不見其寺，這還有一個傳説呢——相傳竹林寺就隱藏在這山谷中，每當風雲變幻的時候，還能聽到竹林寺中傳出的鐘鼓聲，也有機會看到雲端寺院的影子。據説，明代開國皇帝朱元璋大戰陳友諒和身患疾病時都曾得到廬山竹林寺的神仙、和尚周顛仙的幫助，多次化險為夷。為感謝救命恩人，朱元璋得天下後，派人到廬山來找尋竹林寺，可每次來人除了找到這崖壁上高高鐫刻的「竹林寺」三個大字外，別無所獲。為此，後人就把「竹林寺」稱為天上的寺院。

觀妙亭

原亭由於年久失修，早已毀壞，現亭乃在原址上重建，水泥塊石結構，呈六角形，簡樸大方。據説蔣介石曾在亭中觀賞廬山風景時，連喊三聲「妙妙妙」：一「妙」山下西林寺的鐘聲；二「妙」谷中晚霞之美；三「妙」景緻如仙人境地，所以觀妙亭也叫「三妙亭」。

仙人洞

仙人洞是由於砂石崖經過大自然長期風化，逐步形成的天然石洞，洞頂上緣翠松懸掛，石向外參差，宛如巨大佛掌覆蓋，故原名佛手崖。

洞高約7米，寬12米，深14米，洞內有石鑿神龕稱「純陽殿」，洞內有一漢白玉雕像正是呂洞賓。原來滿壁石刻遭毀，現在僅有「仙人洞」，「洞天玉液」等少數詩詞。洞後兩處有微細滴泉，稱「天泉」，早在《後漢書》中便有記載，譽為「瓊漿」，由於水含礦物質比重大，凸出杯口不溢，大家也可以丟硬幣試試，看是否會溢出。仙人洞清幽雅然，有一對聯稱讚道：「仙崖翠壁逢萊勝地，池中玉液閬苑洞天」。

仙人洞的左側是一座道觀——老君殿，殿為單檐歇山式建築，門柱有楹聯：青牛西渡，紫氣東來。內供太上老君李聃騎牛雕像，香火頗為旺盛。由老君殿往上行，有一巨石凌空兀立，這就是蟾蜍石，石隙中的那棵松樹便是有名的廬山石松！巨石前方與巨石上方分別刻有「縱覽雲飛」、「豁然貫通」八個大字。1960年，毛澤東同志「七絕」裡「暮色蒼茫看勁松，亂雲飛渡仍從容，天生一個仙人洞，無限風光在險峰」，講的就是這裡的「勁松」、「飛雲」、「仙人洞」。

朋友們，我們現在來到仙人洞的進口處一圓形石門，門上方正中鐫刻著「仙人洞」三個大字，左右刻有對聯「仙蹤渺黃鶴，人事憶白蓮」。毛澤東同志登廬山時曾坐在這裡留下了光輝形象。遊覽至此，錦繡谷的景點便全部結束。謝謝大家！

Revolutionary Martyrs' Mausoleum in Jinggang Mountains （井岡山革命烈士陵園）

Ladies and Gentlemen,

Today we are going to visit the Revolutionary Martyrs'Mausoleum in Jinggang Mountains.

The Revolutionary Martyrs' Mausoleum in Jinggang Mountains was built to cherish the memory of the great contributions made by Mao Zedong, Zhu De and other veteran proletarian revolutionists in creating the Jinggang Mountains revolutionary base area and developing the Jinggang Mountains spirit. Work on this project began in 1985 and it was completed and opened to visitors in October of 1987 to commemorate the 60thanniversary of the founding of the Jinggang Mountains revolutionary base area.

The 27-hectare mausoleum facing the south includes a memorial hall, a forest of the steles, a monument and a park of great men's statues. The road to the mausoleum consists of two groups of steps. The first group of 49 steps symbolizes the founding of the New China in 1949 and the second group of 60 steps means that its construction was finished on the 60th anniversary of the establishment of the Jinggang Mountains base area in October, 1987.

Now, we are in the memorial hall. The horizontal scroll of calligraphy: "Eternal Glory to the Revolutionary Martyrs of Jinggang Mountains Base Area!" above the gate was written by Peng Zhen, the ex-chairman of the National Planning Commission in 1987. The memorial hall is divided into the Display Room and Respects-Paying, Condolence and Martyrs'Halls.

Facing the door is a white marble wall inserted with the six-Chinese-character inscr-iption written by Mao Zedong in 1946 meaning: "Long Live the Martyrs!" The Jinggang Mountains revolutionary martyrs'rolls are displayed in the glass cabinets. The floral wreaths and flower baskets to honor their memory contributed by the Party and top government officials visiting the mausoleum are laid in this hall.

The display room on the right houses 48 portraits of some of the main leaders during the Jinggang Mountains struggle who died after the founding of the New China. The front 4 are main founders of the Jinggang Mountains revolutionary base area. In 1927 Mao Zedong led the Autumn Harvest Uprising troops to the mountains and initiated the first Chinese rural revolutionary base area. Then, Zhu De, Chen Yi, Peng Dehuai and other revolutionary leaders brought more troops to the mountains. From then on, the Chinese revolution walked on the road of building up bases in the countryside and seizing the cities by force by gradually encircling them. After the founding of the New China, the Chinese People's Liberation Army conferred military ranks among the military officers in 1955 for the first time and five of its ten newly named marshals once fought in the Jinggang Mountains. The portraits of Zhu De, Chen Yi, Peng Dehuai and Luo Ronghuan are displayed in this room. The other person in this group is Lin Biao. The other portraits include 3 senior generals, 10 generals, 16 lieutenant generals, 4 major generals, and 10 leading comrades in the Party and governmental organs.

Portraits of the revolutionary forerunners who died before the founding of the republic are displayed in the left exhibition room. They were veteran Red Army men and cadres who experienced the struggle of the Jinggang Mountains. There are 47 portraits of martyrs in all.

The names of the revolutionary martyrs who died in the struggle of the Jinggang Mountains were carved and inserted on the four walls of the Condolence Hall. The 15, 744 martyrs recorded on these walls were from one county of the base area and many left nothing behind. Therefore, we built a monument to the unknown martyrs, cherishing the memory of the revolutionary forerunners.

The ashes of the 5 veteran Red Army men, Zhang Lingbin, He Changgong, Wen Yucheng, He Minxue and Chen Yunzhong, have been placed in the Martyrs'Hall. Their relatives and teenagers from all parts of the country come here to enshrine and worship them in order to cherish the memory of the revolutionary forerunners.

Walking upward along this path through the sweet-scented osmanthus tree wood and bamboo grove, we come to the Jinggang Mountains' Stele Forest. The Stele Forest was designed by the Jiangxi Province Architecture Designing Institute and construction of it began in July of 1987. The project consisted of two phases. The first phase of the Stele Forest was completed in 1989 and the second was finished in 1992. The garden-like style of the south of the Yangtze was adopted in the Stele Forest. It is divided into the shapes of stele corridors, kiosks and walls and all the kiosks, platforms, buildings and pavilions are linked together.

Walking upward, we can see 139 calligraphy perfectly crafted stele carvings. They mainly cover the contents of the inscriptions written by top Party and state officials during their inspections in the Jinggang Mountains; Red Army veterans who experienced the struggle of the Jinggang Mountains, and famous calligraphers, pain-ters, writers and celebrities across the country to sing the praises of the Jinggang Mountains.

Walking upward along the stone steps, we will get to the Monument to the Jinggang Mountains'Revolutionary Martyrs.

The monument project was started in 1993 and completed and opened to visitors in October of 1997, the 70thanniversary of the founding of the Jinggang Mountains revolutionary base area.

The monument consists of the foundation, the monument basement and the main monument, with an area of 1, 200 square kilometers. The main monument is made of titanium-plated stainless steel. The 27-meter-high monument means that it was in 1927 that Mao Zedong and other veteran proletarian revolutionists initiated the first country revolutionary base area in China. The shape of the main monument highlights the image of the mountains. It also has several other meanings. When viewed from the distance, it looks like a fire and hence is in line with the well-known statement, "A single spark in the Jinggang Mountains can start a prairie fire". It also resembles a gun, implying Chairman Mao's famous saying, "Political power grows out of the barrel of a gun. " The basement of the main monument is laid with red marble. The 9. 7-meter-high basement symbolizes that the monument was built in 1997 at the 70thanniversary of the founding of the Jinggang Mountains revolutionary base area. The 10 Chinese characters, meaning "Monument to Revolutionary Martyrs in the Jinggang Mountains", were written by Deng Xiaoping in 1984. There are three white marble relief sculptures of groups of people, reflecting the hardship of the Jinggang Mountains struggle on the monument basement. The theme of the front one is "Gathering Together in the Jinggang Mountains", displaying the joining of the two Red Army forces in the mountains; the theme of the eastern one is "Red Independent Regime"; and the theme of the western one is "Fighting Bloody Battles in the Luoxiao Mountains".

Before the monument a "Mother" sculp-ture is placed, implying that the Jinggang Mountains is the cradle of the Chinese Revolution.

Now, we will go to the mountains' Sculpture Park.

It is the first sculpture park of revolutionary historical figures in the country. Nineteen sculptures of revolutionary martyrs and forerunners stand in the park. They were important members of the Chinese Communist Party's Front, Military and the Special Committees during the struggles waged in the Jinggang Mountains. The bronze, white marble and granite sculptures were all created by nationally well-known Chinese sculptors. They are extremely lifelike and have different styles, showing the graceful and heroic bearing of the great men during the Jinggang Mountains struggle period.

Dear friends, that's the end of the tour to the Northern Peak Revolutionary Martyrs' Mausoleum. I hope the mausoleum has left a deep impression on you. Thank you!

各位遊客：

上午好！今天我們要參觀的是井岡山革命烈士陵園。

為了緬懷毛澤東、朱德等老一輩無產階級革命家創建井岡山革命根據地的豐功偉績，弘揚井岡山精神，1985年，在茨坪北山興建了「井岡山革命烈士陵園」。1987年10月，即井岡山革命根據地創建六十週年之際，烈士陵園建成並對外開放。

陵園占地27公頃（約合400畝），坐北朝南，分紀念堂、碑林、紀念碑、雕塑園四個部分。順山有兩組台階，第一組有49級，象徵著1949年新中國成立，第二組有60級，寓意著烈士陵園是在井岡山根據地創建六十週年的1987年10月建成。

現在請大家參觀第一部分——紀念堂。紀念堂大門上的橫幅「井岡山根據地革命先烈永垂不朽」，是彭真委員長1987年為烈士陵園題寫的。紀念堂內設有瞻仰大廳、陳列室、弔唁大廳、忠魂堂。

瞻仰大廳正面漢白玉牆上嵌刻著毛澤東1946年為烈士們題寫的「死難烈士萬歲」六個大字，正面玻璃櫃中存放的是井岡山革命烈士名冊。這裡還擺放了黨和國家領導人來井岡山時向烈士敬獻的花圈、花籃。

右側陳列室陳列的是新中國成立以後逝世的參加過井岡山鬥爭的主要領導人的肖像，共有48位。最前面的四位是井岡山革命根據地的主要創始人。1927年，毛澤東同志率領秋收起義的部隊來到井岡山，創建了中國第一個農村革命根據地，隨後朱德、陳毅、彭德懷等人率領部隊上井岡山。從此，中國革命走上了一條農村包圍城市、武裝奪取政權的道路。1955年，中國人民解放軍第一次授軍銜時，解放軍的十大元帥中有5位參加過井岡山鬥爭，這裡陳列了四位，他們是朱德、彭德懷、陳毅、羅榮桓，還有一位是林彪。同時陳列的還有3位大將，10位上將，16位中將，4位少將和10位擔任黨政部門領導工作的同志。

左側陳列室陳列的是新中國成立前犧牲的革命先烈，他們都是井岡山鬥爭時期的老紅軍、老幹部，這裡的烈士掛像有47位。

弔唁大廳的四周牆上嵌刻著在井岡山鬥爭時期壯烈犧牲的烈士英名錄，這是當年井岡山革命根據地一個縣市的烈士，共有15744位，還有許許多多沒有留下姓名的革命烈士。我們特地在這裡位他們立了一塊無名碑，表示對無名先烈的深切懷念。

忠魂堂內安放有5位老紅軍戰士的骨灰，他們是張令彬、何長工、溫玉成、賀敏學、陳雲中。每年清明節他們的親屬和各地的青少年都會來到這裡弔唁他們，寄託後人對他們的哀思。

沿著這條桂花、翠竹相擁的小道往上走，我們就到了井岡山碑林。井岡山碑林是由江西建築設計院設計的，1987年7 月破土動工，分兩期工程完成。第一期碑林建成於 1989 年，第二期碑林是1992年建成的。整個碑林採用江南園林建築風格，分為碑廊、碑亭、碑牆三種建築造型，亭、台、樓、閣相結合。

順山而上一共陳列有139塊精湛的書法碑刻，主要有二部分內容：一是黨和國家領導人上井岡山視察工作時的題詞；二是參加過井岡山鬥爭的老紅軍題詞；三是中國著名書法家、畫家、作家和知名人士熱心讚頌井岡山的題詞。

沿著腳下的台階繼續前行，就到了井岡山革命烈士紀念碑。

井岡山革命烈士紀念碑是 1993 年籌建，於1997年10月，也就是井岡山革命根據地創建七十週年之際建成對外開放的。

紀念碑由基座、碑座和主碑三部分組成，占地1200平方米。主碑是用鍍钛的不鏽鋼製作的，它高達27米，表示1927年毛澤東等老一輩無產階級革命家在井岡山創建了中國第一個農村革命根據地。主碑的造型突出「山」的形象，並且有幾層含義：遠看像一團火焰，寓意井岡山的「星星之火，可以燎原」；近觀如林立的鋼槍，寓意「槍桿子裡面出政權」。主碑的基座部分採用「將軍紅」大理石砌成，高9.7米，表示紀念碑1997 年即井岡山革命根據地創建七十週年建成，碑座上「井岡山革命烈士紀念碑」幾個大字是鄧小平同志1984 年題寫的。碑座有三組反映井岡山艱苦卓絕鬥爭的漢白玉浮雕。正面這組浮雕的主題是「薈萃井岡」，展示了井岡山紅軍兩軍會師的情形，東面這組浮雕的主題是「紅色割據」，西面的這組浮雕主題是「浴血羅霄」。

紀念碑的前沿還有一尊「母親」塑像，寓意井岡山是中國革命的搖籃。

參觀完紀念碑後，請大家往下走，可以到達井岡山雕塑園。井岡山雕塑園是中國第一座以革命歷史人物群像為題材的雕塑園。園內共安放有19尊革命烈士和革命先輩的雕像。這19位革命烈士和革命先輩主要是井岡山鬥爭時期共產黨的前委、軍委、特委的代表。這些用青銅、漢白玉、花崗岩鑄造的銅像，都是由中國著名的雕塑大師創作，風格各異，栩栩如生，展現了這些偉人在井岡山時期的風采英姿。

各位遊客，整個北山革命烈士陵園我們就參觀完了，希望陵園豐富的內涵能給

華東地區

大家留下一個深刻的印象。謝謝。

Tengwang Pavilion （滕王閣）

Ladies and Gentlemen,

This is the Tengwang Pavilion, one of Jiangxi's best-known scenic spots. It has been ranked the "No. 1 Pavilion in the West River" and also ranked first among the three famous pavilions located south of the Yangtze River. It has been experienced a lot of history over the past 1300 years and was rebuilt 28 times. This magnificent pavilion standing before us is the result of the latest 29threbuilding effort and was designed by the famous architect Liang Sicheng, who imitated the Song-Dynasty style. The pavilion is 57. 5 meters high and covers an area of 53 hectares. Its construction area is called "The 9thLevel Heaven". The Tengwang Pavilion, with all of its primitive magnificence, is taking on a remarkable and wonderful look.

The Tengwang Pavilion was first built in 653 by Li Yuanying, Li Shimin's younger brother and the 22ndson of the emperor Li Yuan. He didn't achieve his political ambition in his life, but nurtured in a literary imperial family, he was very interested in music, dance and painting. He was well-known as the King of Lechers. When he was the commander-in-chief of Hongzhou (the former Nanchang City), he always indulged himself in pleasure and made merry among music and dances in his mansion. Then, he got tired of the life in his mansion and decided to build a pavilion for amusement. It has been given his name, "Tengwang". It is located at the confluence between the Gan River and the Fuhe River. Not only was this a good place to enjoy music and dances, but also the best site to enjoy the beautiful view of the Gan River and the distant stretch of mountains. The pavilion was destroyed and rebuilt 28 times. It has been renowned because of Wang Bo's "Preface to Tengwang Pavilion". This literary masterpiece made the pavilion famous.

When approaching the pavilion, we may see that the 12-meter 2-storey basement symbolizes the ancient city wall. In the front of the basement are the foundation stone and Han Yu's notes on the rebuilding of the pavilion. The 89 steps signify that the Pavilion was last rebuilt, for the 29thtime, in 1989. After the steps, we see the first floor. The couplet, "The single wild duck is flying along with the setting sun; one can not tell the color of the autumn waters from that of the sky" is written on the front pillars of the white marble relief sculpture. It tells the story about Wang Bo and his "Preface to Tengwang Pavilion". It is said that in 675, Wang Bo was on his way to visit his father. At Madang his ship was blocked by a great head wind. He stopped to visit the place. In front of a temple, he encountered an old man who was the Water God of the Central Plains. He said to him: "Tomorrow will be the Double Ninth Festival. There will be a get-together in the Tengwang Pavilion of Hongzhou. If you go there and write a composition, you will surely be crowned with eternal glory." Wang Bo asked: "How can I get there in a night since I am 350 kilometers away from Hongzhou?" The god answered, "I'll help you with a favorable wind and you will get there in time". In response to the old man's advice, he got on board. Suddenly, the wind changed its direction and sent him to Hongzhou in one night. In Hongzhou, the commander-in-chief was holding a celebration to mark the completion of the Tengwang Pavilion. At the celebration banquet, Wang Bo created the outstanding "Preface to Tengwang Pavilion". The relief sculpture depicts the meeting between the Water God and Wang Bo.

Now, let's visit the "Outstanding Figures'Hall" on the 2ndfloor. The front horizontal inscribed board says: "Talented Figures Com-ing Forth in Large Numbers." Throughout its early history, Jiangxi has had more than its share of talented figures. The hall mural portrays 80 of Jiangxi's major figures from the early Qin Dynasty to the late Ming Dynasty. Some of them were not from Jiangxi, but they nonetheless served as officials in the province. The first portrait is of Zhang Daoling, from Zhangshu, who established a Taoist sect on the Dragon and Tiger Mountain. The next portrait is of the pastoral poet, Tao Yuanming. We can then gaze at Wang Anshi, Ouyang Xiu and Zeng

Gong. They are among the 8 great men of letters in the Tang and the Song Dynasties. Then comes Tang Xianzu, "the Oriental Shakespeare", and the national hero, Wen Tianxiang.

The hall on the 3rdfloor is the ancient banquet hall. It is said that after Ming Emperor Zhu Yuanzhang defeated Chen Youliang at Poyang Lake, he held a great banquet here to celebrate his victory. In the hall, we may see the mural "Tang Xianzu is Dreaming of Performing the Peony Palace". It tells the story about Du Liniang and Liu Mengmei. They battled the feudal conventions and sought their true love. The characters in the painting close their eyes with the blue background, which means they are in the dream. On the back of the mural, there is a bronze relief sculpture, "Tang Kabuki Performance", reflecting the thriving culture in the Tang Dynasty.

Well, this is the "Rich Land Hall" on the 4th floor. It displays Jiangxi's rich landscape and history. The large mural in the hall is entitled "The Rich Land", and it describes the province's beautiful mountains and streaMs.From left to right, the mountains include Duyu Mountain, which has Mei Pass, the first pass leading to Guangdong Province, grand Sanqing Mountain, magn-ificent Guifeng Mountain, picturesque Poyang Lake, and the Stone Bell Hill. Besides being the birthplace of the Taoism, the Dragon and Tiger Mountain is famous for its monstrous hills and rocks, precipitous cliffs and valleys. Both the Dragon and Tiger Mountain and Sanqing Mountain were put on the list of nationallevel scenic spots in 1988. The Jinggang Mountain, the cradle of the Chinese Revolution, consists of several different mountains with dense trees, bamboo and plants, as well as magnificent waterfalls, streams and springs. Mt.Lushan is famous not only for its beautiful scenery, but also for the famous poems written by many famous men about it. Li Bai wrote the famous poem: "Down the waterfall cascades a sheer three thousand feet; As if the Silver River were falling from Heaven!" Poyang Lake is China's largest freshwater lake and covers an area of 4000 square kilometers. And Stone Bell Hill is famed for the celebrated poem written by Su Shi about it. Its precipitous cliffs also made it become an important ancient military defense post.

Now, we are on the 5thfloor. From this hall we can look far and wide. In the front of the hall, there is the model of the whole Tengwang Pavilion. If we have a bird's-eye view at it from this angle, it looks like a big rock flying westward. On the front wall there are 16 bronze boards recording Wang Bo's "Preface to Tengwang Pavilion". It covers three parts. The first part describes the geographical features and scenic spots in Yuzhang, the second part the banquet and the guests and host, and the last part is his complaint about the bad luck encountered in his official career. Many of its epigrams were collected in the nation's language treasure storehouse and became idioMs.There are many ornaments in the composition with outstanding diction. Its back is the lacquer painting "One Hundred Flowers and One Hundred Butterflies" done to honor the memory of Li Yuanying. Though he was a King of Lechers, he was good at painting butterflies and established the "Teng School of Butterfly Painting". This is an imitation of his work of "Butterflies".

Here we are on the 9thfloor. We may enjoy the performance in the style of the ancients by Nanchang Song and Dance Troupe here. The dragon wall and the phoenix wall on both sides, together with the dance and music, show the prosperous look of the Tang Dynasty.

Well, you may go and enjoy it yourselves. Thank you for your cooperation.

　　各位朋友：大家好！我們現在所在的就是江西省著名的旅遊風景點——滕王閣。滕王閣被譽為「西江第一樓」，也是江南三大名樓之首。它歷盡一千三百多年滄桑，曾遭廢興28次。矗立在我們眼前的這座四重飛檐、雕樑畫棟、碧瓦丹柱的樓閣是第29次重建的，是由中國著名建築學家梁思成先生仿宋代滕王閣設計的。它高57.5米，占地53公頃，建築面積15 000平方米，屬明三暗七格局，再加上兩層基座共有九層，所以滕王閣的最高層次又稱為「九重天」。滕王閣背城臨江，坐落在贛江和撫河交匯口上。整個建築華麗而古樸，呈現出一種「瑰瑋絕特」的氣勢。

　　滕王閣始建於唐永徽四年（公元653年），建造者李元嬰是唐高祖李淵的第22個兒子，也是唐太宗李世民的弟弟。他在政治上一生都不得志，但生長在帝王之家的他從小受到宮廷藝術的熏陶，酷愛音樂、舞蹈、繪畫，是個出名的花花太歲。在他被調任洪州都督時，帶一班歌舞樂伎，終日在都督府中吹彈歌舞，尋歡作樂。後來他膩煩了在都督府中聽歌賞舞，於是在南昌城西贛江與撫河交匯口上，建一樓閣作為聽歌賞舞的別居，並且以他的封號「滕王」命名。滕王閣背城臨江，地方開闊，風景優美，不僅是一處觀歌賞舞的好地方，更是覽山峰秀色的好去處。滕王閣因初唐四傑之一的王勃所作的《滕王閣序》而聲名遠颺，可以說是「文以閣名，閣以文傳」。

　　走進滕王閣，我們可以看到在它的下面有兩層台基，高12米，象徵古城牆，基座正面有奠基石和韓愈為重修滕王閣做的標記。在基座上有89級登閣台階，這是為紀念1989年第29次重建而設計的。上完台階我們來到的便是滕王閣的第一層，第一層正面柱上用不鏽鋼製的，「落霞」「秋水」聯為毛澤東手跡，送給兒媳邵華的。好，我們現在進到第一層序廳，迎面看到大廳裡名為「時來風送滕王閣」的漢白玉浮雕，描繪的是王勃當年遇中原水神和他寫《滕王閣序》的一段神話故事。傳說675年，王勃往交趾看望其父，經過馬當，船遇逆風三日不得行。於是泊船登岸遊覽。在一座廟宇前見一老者（中原水神），老者對他說：「明日重陽，洪州滕王閣有廟會。若你前去參加，並寫篇文章，一定能名垂千古。」王勃說：「這裡距洪州六七百里，一夜怎麼能趕得到？」中原水神說：「我助你一帆順風，你只管上路就是了。」果然王勃登船後，風向改變，帆如展翅，一夜工夫，王勃就到了洪州，趕上了洪州都督為重修滕王閣的落成之宴。並在宴會上留下了千古名篇《滕王閣序》。這幅浮雕表現的就是中原水神與王勃會面的場景。

　　好，我們現在來到的是二樓「人傑廳」。正面匾額為「俊彩星馳」。江西歷史上人才輩出，在廳中的這幅壁畫中描繪了從先秦到明末江西的八十位名人。這80位名人中並不是每位都出生於江西，有些是在江西為官的。首先我們看到的是張道陵，他是江西樟樹人。東漢末年在龍虎山煉丹修道，創「五鬥米」道教，人們尊他為張天師。此處還有東晉田園詩人陶淵明，唐宋八大家中的王安石，歐陽修，曾鞏以及有「東方莎士比亞」之稱的湯顯祖，民族英雄文天祥等。

來到三樓，這個大廳叫古宴會廳，相傳明太祖朱元璋在鄱陽湖打敗陳友諒後在此大擺酒席慶功。在大廳裡我們看到的這幅壁畫叫《湯顯祖夢演牡丹亭》。它所描繪的是杜麗娘與柳夢梅反抗封建禮教，追求愛情自由的故事。大家可以仔細看一下，在這幅畫中人物的眼睛都是閉著的，整個畫面也呈藍色的冷色調，這些都表現了一種夢的意境。在壁畫的反面牆壁上是一幅銅板浮雕《唐伎樂圖》表現盛唐文化藝術的繁榮景象。

現在我們來到了四樓的地靈廳，這個廳與二樓的人傑廳相呼應，表現江西物華天寶，人傑地靈。在廳裡的這幅大型壁畫叫《地靈圖》，它所描繪的是江西省「鍾靈毓秀」的山川景色，從左至右分為——大庾嶺梅關，被譽為「嶺南第一關」。這裡山勢峻險，峰巒對峙，為歷代兵家必爭之地。逾關而過的梅嶺古道為古代中原通往嶺南交通要衝。雄奇的三清山，它有玉京、玉虛、玉華三峰，峻峭挺拔，如道教所尊玉清、上清、太清三神列座其巔而得名。呈丹霞地貌的弋陽圭峰和貴溪龍虎山，圭峰瑰麗多姿引人入勝，千姿百態猶如天然盤景。龍虎山是道教發源地，整個景區奇形怪石，峰谷旋回，景色十分優美。它和三清山1988年同被列為國家重點風景名勝區。井岡山，革命搖籃，峰巒峻拔挺美，飛瀑流泉，茂林修竹。廬山，景色奇美，是一座神仙之廬，歷代文人墨客在這裡留下了名篇絕句，使廬山增色不少。如在廬山山南秀峰的瀑前，李白就寫了「飛流直下三千尺，疑是銀河落九天」的名句。再過來就是中國第一大淡水湖——鄱陽湖。鄱陽湖古稱「彭澤」，面積有4000平方公里。再過來就是因蘇軾《石鐘山記》而聞名的石鐘山，全山分上下兩部分，山雖不高，卻懸崖峻拔，有江湖鎖鑰之勢，古往今來均為兵家必爭之地。

現在我們登上了五樓縱覽廳。這一層是縱目遠眺的最佳層次，也是登高抒懷的好去處。廳的前部是滕王閣的整個景區的模型，在這裡大家可以俯瞰一下滕王閣，看它像不像一支展翅西飛的鯤鵬呢？在廳正面牆壁上，這十六塊銅碑就是王勃的《滕王閣序》，是按《晚香堂帖》中所刻小行書放大製作的。整個序分三部分，第一部分寫豫章地理、風光；第二部分寫宴會場面和賓主；第三部分感嘆自己懷才不遇，報國無門。文中的很多佳句已收進民族語文寶庫，成為成語，如「老當益壯，窮且益堅」，「萍水相逢，高朋滿座」等。全序辭藻華美，對仗工整，首尾照應。反面是磨漆畫「百花百蝶圖」，是為紀念藝術家李元嬰而製作的。李元嬰雖是位花花太歲，但卻擅長畫蝴蝶，被畫界奉為「滕派蝶畫」，這幅畫是仿其《蝴蝶圖》而作。

現在我們來到了滕王閣的最高層九重天古戲台，在這裡我們可以觀賞到南昌歌舞團仿古展演。在這一層兩旁牆壁上的龍牆和鳳壁，以《霓裳羽衣舞》和《破陣樂》為主題表現出大唐盛世歌舞昇平、國泰民安的繁榮景象。

好，有關滕王閣的講解就告此一段落，接下來大家可以自由參觀。謝謝大家合作！

August 1st Nanchang Uprising Museum （八一南昌起義紀念館）

Ladies and Gentlemen,

You are welcome to the August 1stNanchang Uprising Museum. The grey building in front of us is the August 1stNanchang Uprising Museum we will visit today. The museum is located at the juncture of the Zhongshan Road and the Shengli Road. It formerly was the Jiangxi Grand Hotel with 4 storeys and 96 guest rooMs.Its design was the combination of Western and Chinese styles. At that time, the building was the tallest structure in Nanchang City. After arriving in Nanchang during the late ten days of July, 1927, in disguise of the headquarters of 20th National Revolutionary Army's 1stDivision, the revolutionary soldiers rented the building and used it as the headquarter for the August 1stNanchang Uprising. In 1957, to commemorate the 30th anniversary of the victory of Nanchang Uprising, the Central Military Commission decided to establish a museum here. The museum's name, the "August 1st Nanchang Uprising Museum," was inscribed by Marshal Chen Yi.

Now, let's get in. On the right of the grey building we can see 5 statues of the uprising's leaders. From left to right, these men are Liu Bocheng, Ye Ting, Zhou Enlai, He Long and Zhu De. Well, we'll enter the first floor. The big gilded Chinese characters

"This Is the Sacred Place Where the People's Liberation Army Was Born" on the stone tablet was inscribed in Jiang Zemin's handwriting to mark the 70thanniversary of the victory of the August 1stNanchang Uprising. The central part of the floor is a courtyard with four big vats. It is said that because of the shortage of drinking water at that time, workers of the hotel and some neighboring civilians voluntarily carried drinking water to the four vats for the revolutionary soldiers. On both sides of the courtyard are rooms where the guards and medical workers worked and lodged. Now, they are the display rooms to show the weapons and medical gear used by the revolutionary soldiers. The southern hall of the first floor served as the uprising headquarter's main meeting room. Prior to the uprising, it was the place where wealthy people held celebrations in the hotel. During the uprising preparations, many meetings of the commanders and officers of the uprising troops were held here and orders were issued from this hall. Among the articles on display, the 4 old-fashioned wooden armchairs, 2 tea tables on the left and the mirror in front of us are original. The rest are reproductions. Now, please pay attention to the old-fashioned desk clock on the desk before us. Its hour hand is pointing at two. It means 2 o'clock in the morning, which is when the uprising was scheduled to start. With regard to the uprising time, there is a story. From July 27thto July 30ththe uprising front committee headed by Zhou Enlai was busy preparing for the uprising. But on the morning of July 30th, Zhang Guotao, the representative of the CPC Central Committee arrived in Nanchang. He openly fought with the CPC and insisted on winning Zhang Fakui's support in order to stop the uprising. Because of Zhang Guotao's objection, the uprising was delayed until 4 a. m. on August 1st, 1927. However, because a traitor gave the secret away one day before the uprising, the decision was made to begin the uprising two hours ahead of its scheduled time. Therefore, on the early morning of August 1st, 1927, the uprising troops led by the CPC fired the first shot against the Kuomintang Reactionaries. To the left of the celebration hall was the No. 10 Guest Room where the leading comrades and workers of the uprising troops lodged. To the right of the celebration hall was the No. 9 Guest Room where the staff officers for Liu Bocheng, chief of staff of the uprising, worked.

華東地區

Now, let's go to the exhibition hall on the second floor. This is the antechamber of the hall. The exhibits here are mainly the bronze busts of the 5 leading leaders of the uprising. On both sides of the busts are the relief sculptures of the background of the uprising. Behind the busts is a large map photo of Nanchang City in 1927. Now, let's visit the No. 1 Display Room on the second floor. This room mainly introduces the Nanchang Uprising's historical background. After the Revolution of 1911, conflict between rival warlords erupted throughout China. The revolutionary situation dictated that the CPC initially cooperate with the Kuomintang in 1924. To bring an end to the Northern Warlords' rule and continued imperialist oppression, the two Parties organized the Northern Expedition Army in July, 1926 and launched the Northern Expedition War to secure these objectives. At the beginning of 1927, when the vigorous revolution was rolling on with full force and winning one victory after another, the Kuomintang right-wingers, who represented the interests of the big landlords and bourgeoisie, betrayed the revolution and cruelly butchered the communists and revolutionary masses. They staged the "April 12th" and the "July 15th" counterrevolutionary coups. At this critical moment, the CPC realized the importance of armed struggle from these bitter lessons and began preparing for an uprising. The first part of this hall is to show background documents and slogans and caricatures against Chiang Kaishek put on the walls of streets by the revolutionary masses. Facing the failure of the great revolution, Chen Duxiu followed the Right-deviationist and capitulationist route and announced the joint communique with Wang Jingwei to argue for the counterrevolutionary activities of the Kuomintang Right-wingers. To save the revolution, the CPC Central Committee restructured the political bureau of the Central Committee in the first ten days of July, 1927 and the temporary committee, whose core members were Zhou Enlai, Li Lisan, Zhang Tailei and Zhang Guotao, was established. What's more, the overall policy of armed struggle and land reform was approved. At that time, all revolutionary forces were gathering in Nanchang, and this map depicts their concentration in the city. This oil painting, "Greeting the Iron Army", reflects the revolutionary masses'sincere love for the revolutionary troops. On July 21, 1927, Li Lisan and some other suggested that an uprising be held in Nanchang and organized the front committee with Zhou Enlai serving as its secretary. On July 25, 1927, Zhou Enlai secretly came to Nanchang from Wuhan and planned the uprising. After full preparations, on August 1st, 1927, three signal shots from the Nanchang City Wall started the uprising. After 5 hours' fierce fighting, the uprising troops killed over 3, 000 enemy soldiers and seized over 5, 000 guns and over 700, 000 bullets. The uprising won a great victory. The No. 25 Guest Room to the left of the No. 2 Display Room on the second floor used to be Zhou Enlai's office. The No. 20 Guest Room to the right of it was the place where Comrade Lin Boqu, chairman of the Financial Department of the Revolutionary Committee, worked and lodged. There is a sand model to depicting the uprising.

The third floor display hall records the uprising and the fighting that occurred during it with photos and documents. On the first day of the victory, the Chinese Kuomintang Revolutionary Committee was established and on August 3rd, 1927, the troops involved in the uprising evacuated Nanchang and made for Guangdong province for further struggle. On the way, they won further battles and gathered more popular support. However, because the uprising troops were outnumbered by the enemy, they suffered great setbacks in Chaoshan area. Some of the surviving soldiers entered the Hailufeng area to join forces with the local peasant troops. The rest, led by Zhu De and Chen Yi, went to the mountainous areas of Jiangxi, Guangdong and Hunan to wage guerilla war. In late April of 1928, these men, together with the soldiers Mao Zedong led in the Autumn Harvest Uprising, joined forces in the Jinggang Mountains. This fusion is historically referred to as the famous "Convergency of Zhu-Mao Forces" . The two forces merged to form the 4thArmy of the Chinese Worker-peasant Revolutionary Army with Zhu De as the commander of the army, Mao Zedong the Party representative and Chen Yi the director of the Army's Political Education Department. Thus the people's army led by the CPC was born. Then the army became the 4thArmy of the Red Army. In the November of 1931, the Soviet Temporary Central Government was founded in Ruijin. In the July of 1933, the temporary government agreed to form a Worker-peasant Red Army based on the Nanchang Uprising and decided to celebrate the

華東地區

Army Day on August 1stevery year from then on.

Now, we'll go to the last part, the Inscription Room. In this room there are many inscriptions and photos left by the Central Party and Government officials when they visited the museum. Among them are President Jiang Zemin's inscription, "This Is the Sacred Place Where the People's Liberation Army Was Born", written in 1997 when he came to celebrate the 70thanniversary of the founding of the army and Li Peng's "Heroic Nanchang City" written in 1990.

The introduction to the display rooms is now finished. The Nanchang Uprising led by the CPC fired the first shot against the Kuomintang reactionaries and marked the new stage of the armed struggle of the Chinese revolution. The revolutionary forerunners devoted themselves to the revolution. We'll never forget them!

Now, please have a 30 minutes' free visit and then we'll meet at the parking lot. Thank you for your cooperation!

各位遊客：

大家好！我們現在看到的這幢銀灰色建築就是我們今天要參觀的八一南昌起義紀念館。紀念館位於南昌市中山路和勝利路的交界處，其前身是「江西大旅社」。該建築共四層，有96間房間，造型為中西結合，呈回字形，是當時南昌首屈一指的高樓大廈。1927年7月下旬，起義部隊到達南昌後，以國民革命軍第20軍第1師司令部的名義包租下了整幢建築，作為起義的總指揮部。現在大家看到館門上的館名為「八一南昌起義紀念館」，是1957年為紀念南昌起義勝利30週年，設立紀念館時由陳毅元帥題寫的。

好，現在請大家隨我進館參觀。我們在樓前庭院的右邊可以看到的五尊塑像，就是當時起義的五位主要領導人，從左至右分別是劉伯承、葉挺、周恩來、賀龍、朱德。我們現在是在紀念館的第一層，迎面看到石碑上刻的幾個鎏金大字「軍旗升起的地方」是江澤民主席於八一南昌起義勝利七十週年前夕所題寫的。中間這塊空地叫天井（天井中間有四口大缸，據說當時用水困難，大旅社的職工和附近的老百姓就義務為起義部隊提供的生活用水就裝在這四口缸裡）。天井兩側的房間是當時警衛人員和醫務人員工作和休息的地方。現在裡面陳列的是起義部隊使用過的武器和醫療器械。南面的這個大廳是當時起義總指揮部的會議大廳，這裡原是江西大旅社的喜慶禮堂，也叫喜慶廳，是供有錢人辦喜事的地方。起義前，起義部隊曾在這裡舉行過多次部隊負責人會議。當時起義的命令就是從這裡發出的。大廳裡的擺設中，靠右邊的那四張太師椅，兩張茶几以及我們前面的那面鏡子是原物，其餘都是複製品。大家請看，我們前面桌子的那台舊式座鐘的時針剛好指向兩點整。這代表什麼意思呢？對，這就是八一南昌起義的時間，凌晨兩點。1927年7月30日，正當以周恩來為書記的前敵委員會在加緊進行起義的準備工作時，中共中央代表張國燾到達南昌，他在張發奎已經反共的情況下仍然要爭取張，否則就不發動起義。後來張聽說汪精衛由於張國燾的干涉，要來南昌，才勉強答應起義並要求將起義推遲到8月1日凌晨四點，但是起義前一天，有叛徒告密，於是起義被迫提前兩小時舉行。於是8月1日凌晨兩點，起義部隊打響了中國共產黨武裝反抗國民黨反動派的第一槍。喜慶廳左邊是原江西大旅行社的10 號房間，是當時起義部隊領導同志和工作人員休息的地方，右邊的是9號房間，這裡曾是劉伯承任參謀長的起義部隊參謀團辦公的地方。

好，一樓我們就參觀到這，現在請大家隨我上二樓參觀。大家首先來到的是二樓展廳的序廳，這裡陳列著剛才我們介紹過的五位起義的主要領導人的半身銅像。銅像兩側是以起義為背景的浮雕，銅像後面的巨型照片是1927年南昌老城區圖。下面我們繼續參觀設在二樓的第一陳列室。這裡主要介紹的是南昌起義的歷史背景。辛亥革命後，中國又陷入軍閥混戰，迫於革命形勢的需要，1924年，國共兩黨實現了第一次合作，共同反抗北洋軍閥統治和帝國主義的壓迫。1926年7月，國共兩黨組成北伐軍開始了推翻北洋軍閥統治的北伐戰爭。1927年年初，正當大革命風起雲湧，北伐戰爭節節勝利的時候，代表大地主、大資產階級的國民黨右派集團背叛了革命，他們血腥屠殺共產黨人和革命群眾，先後發動了「四‧一二」和「七‧一五」反革命政變。在這生死關頭，中國共產黨人從血的教訓中認識到武裝鬥爭的極端重要性，開始醞釀南昌起義。這個展廳的第一部分就展列了當時的一些歷史背景資料以及群眾在大街上張貼的反蔣標語和漫畫。展廳的第二部分展示的是起義的醞釀和決定。面對大革命的失敗，陳獨秀錯誤地執行右傾投降主義線路，與汪精衛發表聯合宣言，為國民黨右派反革命活動進行辯護。為了挽救革命，中共中央於1927年7月上旬改組了中央政治局，成立了以周恩來、李立三、張太雷、張國燾為首的臨時委員會，並確定了武裝鬥爭和土地革命的總方針。當時，各種革命力量雲集南昌。7月25日，周恩來從武漢秘密來到南昌，研究和部署起義的準備工作。1927年8月1日凌晨2點，南昌城頭傳來了三聲信號槍聲，起義開始了。經過四五個小時的英勇搏鬥，全殲敵軍3千餘人，繳獲槍支5千餘支，子彈70餘萬發，起義取得了勝利。第二陳列室左邊的二十五號房，曾是周恩來辦公的地方，右邊的二十號房是當時革命委員會財政委員會主席林伯渠同志居住和辦公的地方。在第二陳列室的右邊還有一個沙盤模型，演示的是起義的經過。

參觀完二樓陳列室，我們現在來到了三樓陳列室。這裡陳列了大量起義部隊轉戰的圖片資料。起義勝利當天，成立了「中國國民黨革命委員會」。8月3日，按原定計劃起義部隊撤離南昌，南下廣東，繼續開展鬥爭。轉移時受到沿途各地群眾的熱烈歡迎，並取得了一些戰役的勝利。後在潮汕地區由於敵強我弱，遭受嚴重打擊，保存下來的部隊一部分轉移到海陸豐地區與當地農民武裝會合，而另一部分在朱德、陳毅率領下轉入贛閩粵湘山區開展游擊戰爭，並於1928年4月底與毛澤東率領的秋收起義部隊在井岡山勝利會師。這就是歷史上有名的「朱毛會師」，會師後成立了中國工農革命軍第四軍，毛澤東任黨代表，朱德任軍長，陳毅任政治部主任。後來，改稱為紅軍第四軍。1931 年11 月在瑞金成立了蘇維埃臨時中央政府。從此，一支在中國共產黨領導下的人民軍隊誕生了。

接下來我們要繼續參觀的是最後一部分——題詞紀念室。這裡存放了大量黨和國家領導人參觀後留下的照片和親筆題詞，其中有江總書記於1997年在南昌起義70週年紀念前題的「軍旗升起的地方」以及李鵬總理於1990年題的「英雄城南昌」等。

八一南昌起義紀念館的樓層概況就介紹到這裡。南昌起義作為中國共產黨領導人民武裝向國民黨反動派打響了第一槍，標誌著中國革命進入了武裝鬥爭的新時期。星移鬥轉首義業，立業建功垂青史。革命烈士用他們的生命捍衛了正義，他們的豐功偉績，我們永遠銘記在心。

　　各位朋友，紀念館的講解就此告一段落，下面大家自由參觀。三十分鐘後我們在停車場集合。謝謝大家的合作！

華東地區

Wuyuan （婺源）

Ladies and gentlemen，

Welcome to the beautiful county, Wuyuan. Wuyuan lies on China's Mt.Huangshan-Jingdezhen-Mt.Lushan golden tour line and is a bright pearl reflecting the area's green ecosystem and the ancient civilization. Wuyuan County, facing Quzhou to the east, neighboring Mt.Sanqing to the south, connecting Jingdezhen to the south, backing Mt.Huangshan to the north, covers an area of 2, 947 square kilometers and its population is 337, 000. The county's central town is Ziyang Town.

In the ancient times Wuyuan was in the central part of Zhejiang and on the edge of Hunan. It formally became a county in the 28thyear of Tang Dynasty Emperor Kaiyuan's reign（740 A.D.). Since the ancient times, Wuyuan, with deep deposits of culture, has been honored "the South's Qufu" and "Scholars'Hometown". Since the Song Dynasty, the cultural atmosphere has become even livelier. Some 2, 665 officials have lived here and 3, 100 books have been published in the town. Of these books, 172 have been collected into Volumes of Siku. An area's water and soil raise its own people. The deposits of culture in Wuyuan have brought forward many famous historical persons. They include the Literator, Zhu Mou, Philosopher and Master of Li Theory, Zhu Xi, the Ming Dynasty seal cutter, He Zhen, the Qing Dynasty economist, Jiang Yong, the Father of China's railway Zhan Tianyou, and the modern medical expert, Cheng Menxue.

Wuyuan is rich in eco-tourism resources. The forest covers 81. 5% of its total area. It is one of the 16 advanced Chinese counties that have effectively pioneered eco-agriculture. Indeed, the entire county seems to be one big park and many people claim it to have the "most beautiful countryside in China" and is the country's "Last Shangri-la". Mt.Wengong, Lake of Mandarin Ducks, and the National Forest Park with Rock Caves are rightly called "Ecological Wonders". At Jiangwan, Likeng, Wangkou, Sixi, and Likeng, visitors can enjoy well preserved ancient villages featuring white-walled buildings with black tiles and hanging eaves set against the backdrop of green mountains and clear rivers.

The National Forest Park of Lingyan Caves

Approved by the State Forestry Department, the park covers an area of 30 square kilometers. It is a province-level scenic area which contains natural landscape and man-made scenes. The park consists of three parts: "Group of Lingyan Caves", "Group of Ancient Trees at Shicheng", and "Wonders of Stone Forest".

The Group of Lingyan Caves consists of 36 caves, such as Qingyun, Penghua, Hanxu, Qiongzhi, and Cuiling. The big caves are magnificent and the small ones are exquisite. The spring in the cave is clear and clean, with the pebbles and flowing water contrasting with each other. Different shapes and poses of stone shoots, flowers, bolts, and stone curtains can be found here. The most precious features in the caves are the 2, 000 handwritings left by tourists since the Tang Dynasty. These include "Yue Fei Touring Here", "Zhu Xi Living between Zhejiang and Anhui", and the like.

The Group of Ancient Trees at Shicheng shades the ground. The trees are over 100 years old and include ginkgo, Chinese torreya, and nanmu. The most striking feature is a group of 17 ancient trees, which are 1, 000 years old. The biggest breast diameter reaches 4. 8 meters and the tallest tree is 26 meters high, which may make it the tallest in all of China.

The Wonders of the Stone Forest are spectacular. A large area of stones stand in the small basin. Some stand alone, some are braced against each other, and some mix together to form a group. The stone forest's different shapes and poses are so attractive that the national hero Yue Fei couldn't help but carve the words, "nothing more to be seen", on one of the crags with the long spear.

華東地區

Little Bridge over Flowing Water at Likeng

Originally named "Litian", Likeng was built by the Northern Song Dynasty official, Li Dong, after he resigned from office. Later, because the residents were those whose surname was Li, it was named Likeng. The villagers live on the either side of the stream, so there has been a saying: "Families live by the little bridge over flowing water". The stream flows through the village from the east to the west. The ancient houses on either side of the stream are all white-walled with black tile roofs. The striking contrast between white and black produces a plain and austere aesthetic style. In the ancient village there were 12 big or small ancestral halls, 17 temples, 17 pavilions on bridges or by the road, as well as academies of classical learning, private schools, and the Wenfeng Tower and Shuilou Park. The most important sites are the Zhongshu Bridge, Li Yigao's and Li Shulin's Old Houses, the Official's House, Shenming Pavilion, Tongjin Bridge, Coin Mint, and House by the Fishing Pond. Likeng is honored as the "First Village in Eastern Wuyuan".

The Old Rainbow Bridge at Qinghua

Qinghua town was the location of Wuyuan's government and was also an important transportation center connecting north Wuyuan to Anhui Province. Some poems were written to describe the prosperity in the old days: "The upper street and the lower street connected are as long as 2, 500 meters long, by the Flower Bridge the blue curtain of the wine house is flying". The Rainbow Bridge, also called the Corridor Bridge because of its long corridor, spans the Qinghua River. The bridge was originally built in the Song Dynasty. Its name came from the poem written in the Tang Dynasty: "Between two rivers is a pond likes a mirror, the rainbow connects the bridges over the two rivers". The bridge, which is 140 meters long, 3. 1 meters wide, with four piles and five arches, consists of 11 pavilions within the corridor. The design is excellent and the style is unique. This bridge is honored as "No. 1 Corridor Bridge in China".

Baizhu Ancestral Hall at Huang Village

In Huang Village of Gutan Township stands Baizhu Ancestral Hall, where the families named Huang studied classical learning. Because there were more than 100 poles in the hall, it was called 100-pole hall. The ancestral hall was originally built in Kangxi's period, Qing Dynasty. Its structure is of brick and wood, consisting of yards, gates, and a main hall, rear hall, and back hall. The photos of the ancestral hall were displayed in Paris, France in 1982, as the representative of China's ancient artistic architecture.

Hongguan Ancient Village Known for Producing the Ink of Anhui Province

Hongguan Ancient Village is located on the border connecting Jiangxi Province and Anhui Province. Zhan's family established it during the reign of the Southern Song Dynasty Jianyan Emperor. It was named Hongguan for two reasons:Hong means the rainbow, which brings auspicious fortune into the village, and Guan means the pass connecting Jiangxi Province and Anhui Province. Hongguan was also where most of Anhui Province's ink was produced. There were 80 mills at the climax of its prosperity. This kind of ink was famous far and wide among Chinese people. The main scenic spots are:Tongjin Bridge, L de, Liugeng, and Yuying Halls. the Yongji Pavilion for Drinking Tea, and the Ancient Camphor Tree at Hongguan.

Likeng Village of Officials

Likeng, surrounded by mountains, is located north of Wuyuan. The scenery is very beautiful. The village was built in the latter years of the northern Song Dynasty. Because the stream named Liyuan flows by the village, it has been called Likeng. Likeng is a "Learning Center", where people like learning and follow slogans like "Study the books written by Zhu Xi", "Believe in Zhu Xi's theory", and "Practice Zhu Xi's ideas". A bridge with a pavilion crossing the stream is at the village's entrance. The words "Home of Academy" and "Origin of Li Theory" are written on the post of this pavilion. Two other bridges are also located at the village's entrance. The upper one is called Tianxin Bridge, which is shaped like a heart, implying the villagers are rich, safe and fit. The lower bridge is called "Baizi Bridge" and is shaped like the tablet held by officials when they were received by the Emperor, implying high officials lived in this village. In fact, many high officials had houses here during the Ming and the Qing dynasties. Their houses and those of ordinary citizens are good examples of Ming and Qing Dynasty architecture. The officials' houses gates consist of stone lintel and water-polished bricks. The arch and the eaves are overlapped with as many as five layers. On one side of the gate is inlaid a square stone post, which means the owner of the house was an important supporter of the feudal dynasty. The main scenic spots include the Liyuan Bridge, Xixiantou, Governor's House, Minister's House, House of the Official in Capital, Yunxi Village, and the Guan and Flower Halls. Finally, Wuyuan has various kinds of folk arts. They include elegant Anhui opera, as well as more exotic performances, such as the art of "Lifting Child Performers at Jialu", which has been named "one of China's superb arts", and the fantastic tea dropping performance.

各位朋友：

大家好，歡迎來到美麗的婺源參觀。婺源是鑲嵌在黃山—景德鎮—廬山中國旅遊黃金線上的一顆綠色生態與古文化相輝映的明珠。她東連浙江衢州，南通上饒三清山，西接景德鎮，北臨黃山。全縣面積2947萬平方公里，人口32萬，下轄的紫陽鎮為千年古鎮。

婺源古屬吳中楚尾，正式建制於唐開元28 年（公元740年）。有著深厚文化底蘊的婺源，自古以來就被譽為「江南曲阜」和「書鄉」。由宋而下，文風愈是強勁，有仕宦2665 人，著作3100 多部，其中選入《四庫全書》有172部。一方鄉土養一方人，百代文風造傳世名流，文學家朱牟、哲學家和理學大師朱熹、明篆刻家何震、清經濟學家江永、中國鐵路之父詹天佑、現代醫學家程門雪都從這裡走向中國、走向世界。

　　婺源的生態旅遊資源十分豐富，全縣森林覆蓋率達81.5%，是中國十六個生態農業先進縣之一。境內處處為景，猶如一個大公園，有人説她是「中國最美的農村」，也有人説她是「最後的香格里拉」。文公山、鴛鴦湖、靈岩洞「國家森林公園」堪稱「生態奇觀」，江灣、李坑、汪口、思溪、理坑等許多保存良好的古村與青山綠水、粉牆黛瓦、飛檐戧角構成一幅幅恬靜自如、天人合一的畫卷。

靈岩洞國家森林公園

　　1993年被國家林業部批准的靈岩洞國家森林公園，面積約30平方公里，是一個自然與人文景觀為一體的省級風景名勝區，內分「靈岩洞群」、「石城樹群」和「石林奇觀」三個景區。

　　靈岩洞群由卿雲、蓬華、涵虛、瓊芝、萃靈等36個洞組成。洞體大者雄渾壯闊，小者玲瓏秀麗。洞內泉流澄清皎潔，水石相映成趣，石筍、石花、石栓、石幔琳瑯滿目、千姿百態，特別稱絕的是洞群間保留有「岳飛遊止」、「吳徽朱熹」等唐代以來的遊人題墨2000餘處。

　　石城古樹綠蔭蔽日，有百年樹齡的銀杏、香榧、楠木、青栲等；尤其引人注目的是17棵群生一處的古玉南，樹齡已癒千年，其最大的胸徑為4.8米，高26米，堪稱中華之最。

　　石林奇觀尤為壯觀，千畝石林從小盆地拔地而起，有的偉岸獨立、有的相抱依偎、有的堆疊成群……石林的千姿百態竟引南宋著名民族英雄岳飛也情不自禁用長矛在高壁刻下「觀止」兩個大字。

李坑小橋流水

　　李坑原名「裡田」，北宋時退隱官宦李洞在此建村，因李姓人家聚居，故名李坑。李坑村民夾溪而居，故有「小橋流水人家」之謂。小溪由東向西穿村而過，溪邊古宅，黛瓦粉牆，黑白相間的格調，調出一種素淡的美感。古村原有大小宗祠12座，觀廟樓閣17座，橋亭路亭17座，以及書院、私塾、文峰塔、水樓公園等，重要景觀有中書橋、李翼高故居、大夫第、申明亭、通濟橋、銅綠坊、李書麟故居、魚塘屋等，被譽為「婺東第一村」。

清華千年彩虹橋

清華鎮為婺源古縣治，是婺北至徽州府的交通要道。「上下街連五里遙，青簾酒肆接花橋」形容其昔日繁華。彩虹橋為長廊式人行橋，也叫廊橋，橫跨清華河，始建於宋代，因唐詩「兩水夾明鏡，雙橋落彩虹」得名。橋長140米，寬3.1米，橋4墩5洞，由11座廊亭構成，設計巧妙，風格獨特，素有「中國第一廊橋」之譽。

黃村百柱宗祠

百柱宗祠位於古坦鄉黃村，為黃氏宗祠——經義堂，因內置木柱百餘根而得名。宗祠建於清康熙年間，為磚木結構，由庭院、門樓、正堂、後堂、後寢組成。其照片曾於1982年作為中國古建築藝術代表在法國巴黎展出。

徽墨名村虹關

虹關古村位於皖贛交界處，南宋建炎年間由詹姓建村，因「仰虹瑞紫氣聚於關裡」，又地處皖贛關隘，故取名「虹關」。虹關還是明清時期徽墨的主要產地，極盛時墨鋪有80餘家，所產徽墨聞名遐邇，享譽天下。主要景觀有：通津橋、慮得堂、留耕堂、玉映堂、玉堂仙吏、永濟茶亭、虹關古樟等。

官宦故宅理坑

理坑地處婺源北部，群山環抱，景色優美，北宋末年建村，因理源小溪繞村而過，取名理坑。理坑為「耕讀書鄉」，村人好讀成風，崇尚「讀朱子之書，服朱子之教，秉朱子之禮」。村口橋亭，跨河而立，上書「山中鄒魯」，「理學淵源」。村口有雙橋，上游「天心橋」，形似元寶，示意村人富足安康；其下游「百子

橋」，寓意權貴仕宦之村。理坑的明清官邸數量之多，款式之精，國內少見，是
「中國明清官邸、民宅最集中的典型古建築村落」。官宅大門多為石庫門枋，水磨
青磚打造。門樓飛檐，重疊五層，門側嵌　方形石柱，有中流砥柱、國家棟樑之
意。主要景觀有：理源橋、溪弦頭、司馬第、尚書第、天官上卿、雲溪別墅、官
廳、花廳等。

另外，婺源的民間藝術也十分豐富，如典雅的徽劇、享有「中華一絕」美名的
甲路抬閣藝術、獨具韻致的茶藝表演等

Fujian Province福建省

A Glimpse of the Province （本省簡介）

Lying in the southeastern coast of China and bordering Zhejiang, Jiangxi and
Guangdong Provin-ces, Fujian faces Taiwan across the Taiwan Straits and is one of the
closest mainland provinces to Southeast Asia and Oceania. This location makes it an
important window to the outside world and base for China's interaction with the rest of
the world. Boasting a long history, Fujian was called the Region of Minyue during the
Spring and Autumn Period and the Prefecture of Min-Zhong during Qing Dynasty. In the
middle of Tang Dynasty, the post of Fujian Military Commissioner was established, and
the province was hereafter called Fujian. The brief name of Fujian, "Min", comes
from the Min River, the greatest river in the province.

Covering a land area of 121, 400 square kilometers and a sea area of 136, 000
square kilometers, Fujian has nine municipal cities, including Fuzhou, Xiamen,
Quanzhou, Zhangzhou, Putian, Longyan, Sanming, Nanping and Ningde. The province
also has 85 subordinated counties, cities and districts(including Jinmen County). As
one of the earliest provinces opening to the outside world, Fujian has been a leader in
China's "opening up" process by launching 12 national development and special
economic zones. The people of Fujian are famed for their diligence, courage, industry

華東地區

and hospitality. This mountainous province is also renowned for the tradition of starting a career in overseas countries, which makes it a famous hometown for overseas Chinese.

Geography and Climate

Located in the subtropical zone, Fujian has a moderate climate with abundant rainfall. The annual mean temperature is 15. 3℃ -21. 9℃, and the average rainfall totals 930 to 1, 843 millimeters, making it one of China's wettest provinces. Fujian can be divided into Central Asia tropical zone and South Asia tropical zone demarcated by the line connecting Fuzhou, Fuqing, Yongchuan, Zhangping and Shang-hang. The province's climate has six primary characteristics. The first is a monsoon climate, in which climate changes and the four seasons follow the monsoon circulation. The second is short winters and long summers, with abundant thermal resources. The third characteristic are relatively warm winters and hot summers, and a significant temperature difference between south and north and small temperature difference between south and north. The fourth is a clearly demarcated rainy season and dry season, with sufficient water resources. The fifth characteristic is a diversified climate, due to complicated landforMs.And the final feature is frequent natural disasters such as flood, drought, windstorms and frost.

Customs and Habits

Fujian's multicultural and confluent folk customs mainly originated from pre-Han and pre-Qing aboriginal, Han Chinese, minority nationality, and foreign folk custoMs.Fujian folk customs are represented by the folk customs of different nationalities and different regions of the Han nationality, as well as the combination of Chinese customs and foreign custoMs.Fujian is also the principal habitat of She nationality, whose customs feature a strong national style and have become an important part of Fujian's folk custoMs.Furthermore, some customs of Mongolian (Yuan

Dynasty) and Manchurian (Qing Dynasty) have also been integrated into Fujian folk customs, while the costume of Hui'an Women, Hakka Tulou (building constructed with clay) and the tradition of snake worship and carp protection are all Fujian special folk custoMs.

Tourism Resource

Fujian's distinctive features include "mountain and sea as an integrative whole; close relationship with Taiwan; distinctive folk customs; multiple religions". Wuyi Mountain has been listed as UNESCO world natural cultural heritage site, while Taining is known as the world's geology park. Fujian has developed ten major tourism brands:the charming wonderland of Wuyi Mount, the romantic piano island of Gulang, the holy pilgrimage to Mazu, the unique Danxia (Red Grit Stone) landform on water, the charm of appealing Hui'an women, the mystical Hakka Tulou, the site of glorious Gutian Meeting, the centuries-old Tanshishan Culture, the marvelous spectacle of the mysterious Baishuiyang and the magnificent Zhangzhou Coastal Volcano. The province boasts 4 national historic and cultural cities, 7 China excellent tourism cities, 13 national key scenic zones, 10 national nature reserves, 19 national forest parks, 8 national geology parks, 2 national tourism and holiday zones and 85 national key cultural relics protection departments. The total area of natural reserves, forest parks and scenic zones accounts for 8% of Fujian's total land area. The excellent environment set aside in these places helps maintain harmony between human beings and nature.

Native Specialties

Xiamen has various local specialties like subtropical fruits, pie, fish-skin peanut, Bodhi ball, thirst-easing olive, Xiamen bead embroider, lacquer thread sculpture, Xiamen painted sculpture, Xiamen porcelain carving, black mushroom and meat paste, Xiamen medicated wine and dried marine products, plums, jasmine tea, bodiless lacquerware, Shoushan Stone sculpture, wood paintings and sculptures, paper umbrellas, shell carvings, and porcelain.

Attraction Recommendations

These include the world natural cultural heritage site of Mount Wuyi, as well as the Garden on the sea, Gulangyu, the world's geology park, Taining, the holy Mazu temple; the mystical Hakka Tulou, the site of glorious Gutian Meeting, the centuries-old Tanshishan Culture, the marvelous spectacle of the mysterious Baishuiyang, and the magnificent Zhangzhou Coastal Volcano.

福建地處中國東南沿海，與浙江、江西和廣東毗鄰，並隔臺灣海峽與臺灣相望，它是離東南亞和大洋洲最近的一個大陸省份，也是中國全球貿易中一個重要窗口和基地。有著悠久歷史的福建在春秋時代被稱作「閩粵」，在秦朝則被稱為「閩中」。在唐朝中期，成立了福建軍事局，此後就被稱為「福建」。福建簡稱「閩」，是源於該省境內最長的「閩河」。

福建有12.14萬平方公里的土地面積和13.6萬平方公里的海域，福建包括福州、廈門、泉州、漳州、莆田、龍岩、三明、南平和寧德（九個市政城市），以及85個居次要地位的縣、市和區（包括津門縣）。作為最早期對外開放的省份之一，福建開發了12個國家級發展區和特別經濟區。福建人以努力、勇氣、勤勞和好客聞名。這個多山的省份也因為有在國外創業的傳統而有名，這使它盛名為海外華僑的故鄉。

氣候特徵：福建地處在亞熱帶區域，有著適宜的氣候和豐富的降雨。年平均氣溫是15.3℃ ～21.9℃，平均降雨量是930～1843mm，是降雨量最多的省份之一。福建可劃分為中亞熱帶區域和南亞熱帶區域，區分線連接福州、福慶、永川、章平和上航。主要特徵有：1）氣候和季節的變動跟隨季風循環；2）冬短夏長，有豐富的熱量資源；3）冬季南部和北部之間有著巨大溫差；夏季南部和北部之間只有細小溫差；4）雨季、旱季分明；5）複雜的地形帶來多樣化的氣候。

民俗風情

福建有多文化匯合的民俗特徵，主要起源於秦朝和漢朝之前的原始風俗，漢族風俗，少數民族風俗和外國風俗。福建民俗的特點是由不同民族的風俗和不同地區的漢族風俗集匯而成，其中也有中國風俗和外國風俗的匯合。福建還是　族的主要居住地，有著突出的民族風格，並成為福建風俗的一個重要組成部分。此外，蒙古語（元朝）和滿族語（清朝）的一些風俗也融入了福建民俗中，惠安女裝、客家土樓（用黏土修建的建築）和崇拜蛇、保護鯉魚的習俗是福建所特有的。

旅遊資源

「山海一體，閩台同根，民俗奇異，宗教多元」是福建旅遊的鮮明特色。武夷山是世界文化與自然遺產，泰寧是世界地質公園，迷人的武夷仙境、浪漫的鼓浪琴島、神聖的媽祖朝覲、奇特的水上丹霞、動人的惠安女風采、神奇的客家土樓、光輝的古田會址、悠久的曇石山文化、神秘的白水洋奇觀、壯美的漳州濱海火山構成了福建獨具特色的十大旅遊品牌。全省有4座國家歷史文化名城、7座中國優秀旅遊城市、13個國家重點風景名勝區、10個國家級自然保護區、19　個國家森林公園、8個國家地質公園、2個國家旅遊渡假區、85　　個中國重點文物保護單位。自然保護區、森林公園、風景名勝區的面積占全省土地面積的8%，形成了人與自然和諧共處的良好環境。

地方特產

有各種亞熱帶瓜果、餡餅、魚皮花生、菩提丸、青津果、廈門珠繡、漆線雕、廈門彩塑、廈門瓷塑、香菇肉醬、廈門藥酒、海產乾貨、茉莉花茶、脫胎漆器、壽山石雕、木畫、木雕、紙傘、貝雕、瓷器等。

主要推薦旅遊景點

世界文化與自然遺產——武夷山；海上花園——鼓浪嶼；世界地質公園——泰寧；神聖的媽祖廟、光輝的古田會址、悠久的曇石山、神秘的白水洋、壯美的濱海火山等。

華東地區

Mount Wuyi （武夷山）

Hello! My friends.

On behalf of the travel agency I warmly welcome you to have a sightseeing of Mount Wuyi. I hope all of you will enjoy your short stay here.

Now we are going to visit Mount Wuyi. The beautiful Mount Wuyi, which is located in northern Fujian Province and along the southeast slope of the northern Wuyi Mountain Range, is praised as the most attractive mountain in southeast China. The cliffs and waters of Mount Wuyi are exceptionally attractive. This is the area where southeastern plants are best preserved and is home to many animals near extinction. With a long history of human activity, it is a place where people live in harmony with the nature influenced by the tradition of Chinese Confucianism. In 1988, Mount Wuyi was protected under World Preservation Zone of Biosphere Protection Act. In 1999 it was added by UNESCO to its list of the World Cultural Heritage sites.

Mount Wuyi is southeast China's best area for biodiversity conservation, forming refuge for a large number of ancient and rare species. It contains large numbers of reptiles, amphibians and insect species, many of which are peculiar to China. The Nine Bend River's serene beauty and dramatic gorges, which are dotted with its numerous temples and monasteries, many now in ruins, provided the setting for the development and spread of neo-Confucianism. This doctrine, in turn, played a dominant role in the countries of East and South-East Asia for many centuries and influenced philosophy and politics over mant parts of the world since the 11thcentury.

One Line Sky Scenic Spot

All my friends, the cliff which we are seeing, which is hundreds of zhang (a Chinese measure-ment) long and thousands of feet high, is called the "Ling Cliff" .

This cliff consists of three adjoining cliffs and holes:the Ling Cliff is over to the left, the Wind hole is located in the middle, and the Fuxi hole is over on the right. Now, please follow me inside through Fuxi hole. It is very dark, so please take care. Now, we have reached the bottom of the rock, so please raise your heads. There is a crack on the top, just like a split axe. It is less than one foot wide and over one hundred meters long, from which one light is leaking into the cliff, just like the rainbow bridging in the blue sky. That is the miracle of uncanny workmanship and hence the name, "One Line Sky".

As for its origin, there are so many folklore. Some have said it is pictured by a peach blossom maid using embroidery needles; others have said it is cut by Fuxi using Jade axe. However, according to the scientific analysis, the red rock of Wuyi is layered by Sandston, Conglomerate and Shale. The nature of the stone is relatively loose and fragile. In the process of crust rising, the layer will become slightly split, owing to the influence of uneven pressure, which forms the so-called "Veins". These vertical veins will begin to dissolve and erode as the water flows over the rock through time, only to expand and enlarge gradually. And the loose Shale in the bottom of the layer will also be eroded into shallow stone holes. Thus, three holes in one line, leading to the creation of the "One Line Sky's" natural scenery.

After appreciating the "One Line Sky" in the Fuxi Cave, we will take a few steps and enter the Wind Cave, where we can feel the cool wind blowing from the stone crack. Even though it is mid-summer, you will find this place cool and pleasant. The words, "Wind Cave", were written on the cliff by Xu Ziqiang, who was born during the Song Dynasty. After leaving it, we will go across one stone corridor named the "Ling Grotto". It is said that an immortal person surnamed Ge conquered monsters here. So it is also named "Immortal Ge Grotto". Inside there is an old well called "Holy Water Well".

After leaving the Ling Grotto and walking several hundred meters, we can see a

華東地區

vertical rock stone like a wall that has many small holes resembling the windows of a large building. According to the legend, this is the so-called "Immortal Attic", as well as Attic Crag. The left side is the "Rock Lan". The cliff sculptures are arranged in a crisscross pattern. You can see that one stone leans against the cliff, and there is a stone path into it, just like a path named "Gate in the Heaven". The cave in front of the rock is called "Luo Shi Cave". It takes a few miles to get from Attic to the valley, and then you can see steep stones standing alone in a highly noticeable way on the left. That is "Tiger Screaming Cave". According to a well-known legend, an immortal rode a screaming tiger. Actually, the sound of the tiger comes from one stone cave, as the wind blowing through the cave sounds just like a screaming tiger.

All my friends, I wonder whether you find any similarity between the "Tiger Screaming Cave" and the "Dawang Peak". "Dawang Peak" is elegant, all-round steep and towering aloft. The path of mountain-climbing is winding, just like a ladder leading to the sky. A half crag hovers over the cliff and there is a small platform at the foot of the rock. Do you think it looks like a deck of a small boat?That is one of the eight tigers screaming scenes, or "Bu Lang Zhou". Next to it, there is a grotto which is covered by steep cliff, overlooking valleys, or the "Zhuzhen Grotto". It can take dozens of people here. During Qing Emperor Kangxi's reign, a county magistrate named Wang Zi visited here. After seeing the cave next to a brook, he changed the name into "Huxi Cave", carving the words, "Huxi Ling Cave", on the stone cliff. If we step away, we will see the old site, the "Tiancheng Xiangyuan", which is a famous yard on Mount Wuyi. The cliff here is slanted, the brook is against the current, and the terrain is deep and serene, as well as spacious. The houses built here only have four-sided earth walls without any tiles, in case of erosion. At night, you can look up at the stars and moon and listen to the sound of the flowing water, which places yourself in the midst of moon and stars, while being immersed in the mix of water and sky. The stone gate in front of Xiangyuan Yard is named "Pumendou", meaning that Guanyin delivers all living creatures from torment. The rock sculpture of Guanyin holding "ruyi" is made of jade, a symbol of good luck. and was built in 1994. It is ten meters high, leans against the cliff, and is dignified and sedate. This spring on the right side of Buddhist is named "Yu'er Spring". It winds between the stone cracks, and the sound of its flowing water swashing against the rocks is just like baby babbling. That is the origin of its name. According to the statement in "Miscellany of Wuyi", written by the Ming Dynasty author, Wu Shi, the spring is as strong as paste and is so clear that we can recognize each hair clearly when put it in a cup. It also tastes sweet and rich, and makes people comfortable and soft. So when people began drinking tea, they made a point of fetching this pure and natural water when boiling their tea. After tasting "Wuyi Rock Tea" made from "Yu'er Spring" by the Xiangyuan Yard's monks, the Qing Dynasty poet, Yuan Mei, wrote: "Smell comes first, and then its flavor, I chew it slowly and the delicate fragrance comes out. Even the sweet smells linger around my tongue. Cup by cup, it makes people free from anxiety and feel relaxed. Then we will find Longjing is insipid despite clean, Yangxian is good but its lingering charm is weaker, that is just like the difference between jade and crystal." Ok, there is a tea-booth ahead, and you can have a rest and taste some tea. As we proceed from here, I wonder whether you can feel the drops of water drip on your heads. That is "Yanliu" dropping from the top cliff. Sometimes, a whole line of drips pour down constantly, a "Fayu Xuanhe", which is one of eight tigers screaming scenes.

Tianyou Peak Scenic Spot in Wuyi Mountain

Ladies and gentlemen, the wall we see now is the relics of Wuyi Academy. It was designed and built by Zhu Xi, the great Song Dynasty geologist, during the eleventh year of the Song Dynasty Chunxi Emperor's reign. In this academy, Zhu Xi engaged himself in writing and preaching for as long as ten years, thus cultivating a large number of talents. At the same time, feudal rulers across various dynasties attached great importance to the academy's work. The Wuyi Academy's remains have now been maintained by the governors of Fujian and Zhejiang Province for over 200 years. After walking along the Wuyi Academy for several hundred meters, we can see more than ten grottos of different sizes at the Joint-Bamboo Peak's foot. These caves came into being

華東地區

when rocks collapsed. During spring or winter clouds and mist arise out of the caves and float around the rocks. Theses clouds constantly change by merging and drifting apart; hence this spot has been named as "Cloud Nest".

Now the stone gate in front of us is the relics of Shugui Academy. And the four Chinese characters "Shugui Jingshe" can be clearly seen written on the gate, right? Shugui, whose full name is Jiang Zhi, was recommended to assume official commission for his filial and impartiality in the Northern Song Dynasty. There has been a fastidious monu-ment in memory of him, built in the early Qing Dynasty. It is a pity that there is only a stone gate left. Through the gate, we can find another scene, grandiose and bright. On the left beside the Nine Bend Brook is the Shizhao Lotus Pavilion; on the right is the Hidden Screen Peak. This peak is connected to the Joint-bamboo Peak, whose three horizontal hillside traits are actually joints.

The Water Moon Pavilion is located below the Hidden Screen Peak. It is said that in a bright evening with a full moon and few stars, people who drink there can see four moons. Can you guess, my friends, which are they? Of course, they are the one in the sky, the one in the water, the one in the cup and the one in your heart.

Look! The giant black stone amidst the Cloud Nest seems to be a crouched elephant. It is known as Iron-elephant Rock. A fissure lies in the middle of the rock, and when walking through it we can only see a thin thread of light. Thus we call it "Little One Line Sky" to distinguish it from the One Line Sky in Xinan.

Iron Elephant Rock divides the Cloud Nest into an upper and lower part. Its superior location has made many a scholar yearn to work here. For example, during the 11thyear of Ming Dynasty Emperor Wanli's reign（1583）, Chen Sheng, the Minister of the Ministry of War in feudal China, built the Youxi Hut between the upper and lower Cloud Nest. It consisted of ten beautiful building, including Binyun Hall, Chaoyun Tower, Shengyun Terrace, and Qiyun and Chiyun Pavilions. These names all refer to places for clouds to gather and scatter. However, it is said that those buildings have been deserted. Only the stone inscriptions remind people of their prosperity in bygone days.

Now please look at the two Chinese characters "Hidden Tiger" on the front rock. They were carved by Youxi Hut's master, Chen Sheng. In 1583 Chen Sheng relieved of his duties in the government, due to his conflicts with the Prime Minister, Zhang Juzheng. Although urged to stay by the emperor, he still resigned and returned to his hometown Fujian Province. Depressed for not being able to realize his political ambitions, he decided to retire to Wuyi Mountain. After seeing this sleeping-tiger-like rock, he then carved on it, implicating that he wished he could regain his status and serve the emperor.

On the right side of Hidden Tiger Rock are bamboos, you see? They are square bamboo mentioned by Mr.Guo Moruo in his poem, Touring Mount Wuyi . This kind of bamboo seems round but really is square, which is very strange. If you do not believe that, come to have a touch.

At the end of the stone path in front of the rock, a stone gate will come into your sight, with the words, "Lofty and Steep Ignorance" on its porch. Inside the gate is another view sight, and the cave is called Tea Cave. The quality of tea produced there is even better than that in Wuyi Mountain. Standing in the cave, we can look down at the Joint-Bamboo, Tianyou, Immortal's Palm and Hidden-Screen Peaks, the Qingyin Rock, as well as Xianyou Rock at the Third Bend. And this cave is surrounded by wall-like barriers; the only path is the aperture on the west side. As this cave covers merely 0. 4 hectares, our view looking up is limited, much like that of a frog in a well. The famous Chinese geographer, Xu Xiake, left detailed records of the Tea Cave's scenery in his prose Travelling Notes on Mount Wuyi.

Going through the Stone Gate, the Rooster's Breast and the Dragon's Back, one can

華
東
地
區

see "Boundary Between Mortals and Immortals" written on the cliff, which means only those who dare to complete the dangerous path in Wuyi Mountain, the Rooster's Breast and the Dragon's Back, have chance to get to the top of the peak, the fairyland.

Yilan terrace, located in the center of Wuyi, is a tiptop terrace for sightseeing. Here we can enjoy the five tiptop sceneries as time goes by. They are the sun-rising, the clouds and mists, the halation of Buddha, the sun-setting and the moon. If we have an overlook from the Yilan Terrace, we'll find clusters of peaks. The west peak is called Tri-religion and the east one is called King. Looking down at the Nine Blend Brooks on which floats the bamboo rafts, the mountains and rivers are all in our view. This will make us feel open-minded and be taken by the scenery. We'll never think of going back.

Keeping going ahead from the Yilan Terrace, we'll see the Tianyou Cloister, a building of palace style. On the Miaogao Terrace behind the cloister, there's the rare-seen red berry with the ancient name panel. When they are in mature time, the bean-pods drop to the earth. Then the blackish red beans, blinking and lovely get out of the bean-pods. Wang Wei, a poet in Tang Dynasty once wrote a poem, saying: "When those red berries come in springtime, flushing on your southland branches;Take home an armful, for my sake, as a symbol of our love. " I hope you can bring several red berries home as the best remembrances.

My friends, that's all about Tianyou Peak. Now please take a break and then we'll go to the next scenic spot, the Jiuqu Stream.

Jiuqu (Nine-Turns) Stream

Jiuqu (Nine-Turns) Stream takes its source in the southeast of Huanggang Peak of Wuyi Mountain Nature Reserve and is 60 kilometers long. Thanks to the conservation and purification of more than 50, 000 hectares of green forest around, it is rich in water resources and its runoff amounts to 700 million cubic meters every year.

Moreover, the water is very clear and its quality is excellent. It twists through the Wuyi Mountain scenic spot from west to east, and its course has nine turns. These nine turns are why it is called Jiuqu Stream. The stream flows for about 10 kilometers through the scenic areas mountains. Every turn of the stream presents visitors with a charming landscape painting. Traveling downstream on a bamboo-boat, we can view and admire the mountains, enjoy the pure and transparent water, feel the splashing waves and appreciate the songs of the various birds. It is really too pleasant and wonderful for words. If Mount Wuyi is compared to a symphony, Jiuqu Stream is a recurring theme; if Mount Wuyi is compared to the art museum, Jiuqu Stream is the most spectacular landscape promenade.

Rivers and streams must meet rigorous international standards to qualify as scenic rivers and streaMs.Water must flow through them all the year round, the water must be clear, not muddy, the river's course should be bended, not straight, the width of the river must change, and the scenery surrounding the stream or river should be mountainous. These mountains should be varied and beautiful in appearance and the ratio and distance between them and the river or stream should vary. Finally, the mountains and the surrounding in general must have a good ecological environment with varied flora and fauna. According to those standards, what do you think of the Jiuqu Stream? Give a mark to it after your appreciation.

Honorable guests, since you have toured the Jiuqu Stream, how do you like it? Is it really very singular and splendid? The 9. 5-kilometer Jiuqu Stream winds its way through the whole area, but the river's straight-line distance is only about 5 kilometers. That is to say, due to so many turns in the river, Jiuqu Stream is 4. 5 kilometers longer. The bending coefficient of the river together with the gradient of the river bed gives rise to the fast water flow and the severe erosion. As a consequence, water flows slowly and splashes over the convexes while water flies over concave banks, where there are green pits to produce one vortex after another. Jiuqu Stream with nine turns is full of alternating shoals and pits.

華東地區

Jiuqu Stream mainly flows from west to east, and this course is obviously determined by the east-to-west fracture. However, the bend channel segments flow in a south to north direction, and this course is obviously determined by the south-to-north fracture. The impact of fractures in different directions, as well as erosion and accumulation effect by water flow acts on all nine turns of this stream. As a result, the Nine Turns stream landscape comes into being.

This stream lies between two steep cliffs and is very narrow. This is a typical feature of river valley landscapes, which are formed by the combined action of powerful uplift by the crust and strong downward erosion caused by flowing water. Jiuqu Stream and the hills and mountains around it fit beautifully together. This landscape is changing constantly, and rafting on the bamboo-boat along the stream is a popular way of touring Wuyi. Moreover, there are lots of scenic spots and rich historical and cultural landscape around the stream. Are they all very attractive?

Honorable guests, have you ever fully appreciated the beautiful scenery of Wuyi Mountain? I hope that the Jiuqu Stream water has made an incredible impression on you. OK, our tour to Jiuqu Stream is over now. Thank you all for your cooperation!

各位朋友，大家好！

我代表旅行社對大家來武夷山旅遊、觀光表示熱烈歡迎。希望大家在武夷山逗留期間能夠玩得開心，吃得放心，同時希望大家在遊覽當中能夠得到一個較大的收穫，留下一個美好的回憶。

我們現在要去參觀遊覽武夷山。武夷山位於福建省北部、武夷山脈北段東南麓，素有「奇秀甲東南之譽」，以丹山取勝和秀水稱奇。武夷山是中國雨林植物保存最好的地方，許多瀕臨滅絕的動物都在這裡安家。在中國儒家傳統思想的影響下，人類在這個地方活動已經有了很長的歷史，它是人與自然和諧共處的典型例證。早在1988 年，武夷山就加入了聯合國「人與生物保留地網組織」，1999 年被聯合國教科文組織列入世界遺產名錄。

武夷山是中國東南部生物多樣性保護最好的地方，保存了大量古老和珍惜的植物物種，包括大量的爬行類、兩棲類遺蹟，其中很多都是中國獨有的。武夷山九曲溪奇特的峽谷風光秀美，有數量眾多的寺廟，為朱子理學的發展和傳播提供了很好的環境。作為一種學說，自11世紀以來，朱子理學曾在東亞和東南亞國家中占據統治地位很長時間，並在哲學和政治方面影響了世界很大一部分地區。

一線天景區

各位朋友，現在我們看到的這座山岩，長數百丈，高千仞，名靈岩。岩端傾斜而出，覆蓋著三個毗鄰的岩洞：左邊是靈岩洞，中間是風洞，右邊是伏羲洞。現在請隨我從伏羲洞進入岩內。由於岩洞內較黑暗，請大家注意走好。現在我們已到達岩洞內的深處，請大家抬頭看，岩頂有一裂罅，就像利斧劈開一樣，相去不滿一尺，長約一百多米，從中漏進天光一線，宛若跨空碧虹。這就是令人嘆為「鬼斧神工之奇」的一線天。

關於一線天的由來，民間傳說很多。有的説這是桃花女用繡花針劃出的；有的説這是伏羲大神用玉斧所劈。但據科學分析，武夷山的紅色岩層，是由砂岩、礫岩和頁岩交間成層的，岩性比較鬆脆。在地殼抬升的過程中，岩層由於受到不均勻的應壓力的影響，就會產生輕微的斷裂，形成所謂的「節理」。這種垂直的節理，在流水長年累月的溶解和侵蝕下逐漸地擴大、延長。而岩層底部質地鬆軟的頁岩，也就逐漸侵蝕而去，成為扁淺的岩洞。於是，三洞並列，一線天的自然景觀就出現了。

從伏羲洞觀賞完一線天，沿石罅前行數十步，就可折入風洞。進入風洞，大家會感覺到涼風從石罅中習習吹來，即便是盛夏酷暑時節到此，只要稍坐片刻，就會感到肌骨透涼。洞口石壁上的「風洞」二字，系宋景定元年建安郡人徐自強所書。出了風洞，再繞過一道石廊，就是靈岩洞。相傳先前有個姓葛的仙人曾在此降妖，故此洞又稱葛仙洞。洞內這口古井，叫聖水井。

出靈岩洞，往前行約百餘米，可見一座壁立如屏的石岩，岩壁石洞較多，似高樓窗戶，相傳這就是所謂的神仙樓閣，故此岩名為閣岩。岩的左邊這一石岩，名蘭岩。岩壁石刻縱橫。岩下可見一石倚於崖壁，石徑伸入其間，如同一道關隘，號稱天門。岩前亂石堆中的這個洞，叫螺螄洞。從樓閣岩入山谷數里，可見路左有山岩峻峭，巍然獨立，這就是虎嘯岩。相傳虎嘯岩是因為有仙人騎虎吼嘯其上而得名。其實「虎嘯」之聲，是來自岩上的一個石洞，山風穿過洞口，有如虎吼，聲傳空谷，震撼群山。

各位朋友，大家是否發覺虎嘯岩與我們遊覽過的大王峰很相似，四壁陡峭，屹然獨聳。其登山的路徑，宛轉曲折，彷彿是登天的天梯。從岩度盤折而上，到了半壁，岩下向前伸出這塊小平台，大家看像不像一條小船的艙面甲板，這就是虎嘯八景之一的「不浪舟」。緊鄰「不浪舟」的這個上覆危崖，下臨絕壑的岩洞，就是駐真洞。此洞可容數十人，清康熙年間崇安縣令王梓遊此，見其洞前臨西溪，便改名虎溪洞，刻「虎溪靈洞」四字於石壁。從虎溪洞再往上，大家看到的這處舊址，就是武夷山久負盛名的天成祥院遺址。這裡岩壁斜覆，山溪回流，地勢既高敞，又幽深。所建房屋，僅有四堵土牆，不施片瓦，風雨不侵。夜晚身居屋內，抬頭可見星月，側耳可聞水聲，彷彿「置身星月上，濯魄水雲中」。祥院前的石門，即虎嘯八景之一的「普門兜」，意為觀世音普度眾生之門。這尊手托如意的觀世音菩薩岩雕建於1994 年，雕像高十餘米，依岩傾俯，端莊慈祥。禪院右側這道泉水，即虎嘯八景之一的「語兒泉」。它進出於石隙，循崖而流，因其水流相激之聲，若小兒牙牙學語得名。據明吳拭《武夷雜記》記述，這道泉水「濃若停膏，瀉杯中鑒毛髮，味甘而博，啜之有軟順意」。故以往有飲茶嗜好的，每每攜帶茶具來此，取泉烹茶，有天然真味。清代著名詩人袁枚品味了祥院僧人用語兒泉水沖泡的武夷岩茶後，生動地論述道：「先聞其香，再味其味，徐徐咀嚼而體貼之，果然清芳撲鼻，舌有餘甘。一杯之後，再試一杯，令人釋躁解矜，怡情悅性，始覺龍井雖清而味薄矣，陽羨雖佳而韻遜矣，頗有玉與水晶不同之致。」前面有個茶亭，請大家在此品茗歇息一會兒。從語兒泉前行，大家是否有感覺水珠不時滴落頭頂，這就是崖頂落下來的「岩溜」。有時一整排嘀嗒不停，這就是虎嘯八景之一的「法雨懸河」。

天遊峰景區

各位朋友，現在我們看到的這堵牆就是武夷精舍遺址。武夷精舍是宋淳熙十一年時，理學家朱熹親自設計、建造的書院。朱熹在武夷精舍著書立說，倡道講學達十年之久，培養了大批理學人才。歷代封建統治者也非常重視武夷精舍，對其加以擴增。至今殘留的精舍遺址，是閩浙總督捐俸修建的，距今已有200多年的歷史。

從武夷精舍前行數百米，在接筍峰下，有因峰岩崩塌而形成的岩洞10餘處。冬春兩季時，從洞穴裡常常會冒出一縷縷淡淡的雲霧，在峰石之間輕輕遊蕩，變幻莫測，時而聚集一團，時而又飄散開來，故此地名為「雲窩」。

過了問樵台，大家看見的這個石門，就是叔圭精舍舊址。門額上「叔圭精舍」四字清晰可見。叔圭姓江名贄，北宋人，官舉孝廉。這裡原有一座考究的古建築，是清初為紀念江贄而建造的，現僅存這道石門。穿過叔圭精舍石門，就會發現另外一番豁然開朗的景象。

左邊這個瀕臨九曲溪的亭子叫石沼青蓮，右邊這座山峰是隱屏峰，而依附於隱屏峰，峰腰橫列三痕，彷彿折斷又連接在一起的，叫接筍峰。

隱屏峰下的這座亭叫水月亭。據說月明星稀的夜晚在亭中把酒賞月，可見到四個月亮。請各位朋友猜猜看，有哪四個月亮？那就是天上一個，水中一個，杯中一個，還有心中一個。

雲窩中間這塊漆黑巨石，大家看像不像一頭伏臥的大象，它俗稱鐵象岩。鐵象岩中間裂開一罅，人穿行於其中，但覺天光如線，人稱「小一線天」。

雲窩以鐵象岩為界，分上、下雲窩，以其地理優勢而出名，是古代文人墨客隱居養心之所。明萬曆十一年（公元1583年），兵部侍郎陳省曾在上下雲窩間興建「幼溪草廬」。它包括十處富麗堂皇的建築，如賓雲堂、棲雲閣、巢雲樓、生雲台、遲雲亭等。可惜這些建築早已廢棄，岩壁間留下的些許摩崖題刻，還能讓人依稀記起昔日的繁華。

請大家注意看，前面這塊壁上刻有「伏虎」二字。題刻的作者系幼溪草廬的主人陳省。明萬曆十一年，陳省因與宰相張居正政見不一而受到排擠。皇上雖數賜，但他仍然辭職歸閩。深感懷才不遇，他決定隱居於武夷山中。當他看到這塊如蹲虎狀的岩石時，便刻下「伏虎」二字，意在於他企盼有朝一日東山再起，再為皇上效力。

伏虎岩右邊這一竹叢，就是郭沫若先生在《遊武夷》詩中提到的方竹。這種竹看似圓，摸上去卻是四方的，十分奇特。不信，大家可以來摸摸。

登上伏虎岩前的石徑，便可看到一道石門，門額上刻有「　嶸深鎖」四字。進石門則眼前豁然開朗，別有洞天。這就是素有產茶「甲於武夷」之稱的茶洞。從洞中可放眼眺望接筍峰、隱屏峰、清隱岩、天遊峰、仙掌峰，以及遠在三曲的仙遊岩。峭壁聳立的危崖，就像一堵堵高大的城牆，把它團團圍住，唯一的通道，就是西邊的一條岩罅。人在這個面積不過0.4公頃的洞中，有如陷入井底一樣，抬頭仰視，僅見青天一圍，恰如徐霞客在《武夷山遊記》中描寫的那樣。

穿石門，過「雞胸」、「龍脊」，可見岩壁上有「仙凡界」題刻，意為這裡是人間與仙境的分界線，只有有膽有識敢過武夷山險徑——「雞胸」、「龍脊」的人，才能步入頂峰仙境。

各位朋友，請大家做好登山準備，現在我們開始攀登天遊峰。從茶洞到天遊峰一覽台共有八百多級石階，有興趣的朋友，不妨邊登邊數，看誰數的數字最精確。

現在我們終於登上了天遊峰一覽台，大家一路辛苦了。根據剛才大家報來的數字看，張先生、李先生數得最為精確，共有石階826　級，謝謝大家的合作。天遊峰東接仙遊岩，西連仙掌峰，高聳群峰之上。每當雨後初晴，晨曦微露之時，白茫茫的煙雲彌山漫谷；風吹雲蕩，起伏不定，猶如大海的波濤，洶湧澎湃。站在一覽台上望雲海，變幻莫測，宛如置身於蓬萊仙境，遨遊於天宮瓊閣，故名「天遊」。

一覽台位於景區中心，是一處絕好的武夷山水觀賞台。隨著時序流轉，在這裡可以觀賞到被稱為「天遊五絕」的日出、雲霧、佛光、夕陽和明月。從一覽台上憑欄遠眺，但見群峰點點，西望那座山峰就是八曲的三教峰，東望這座山峰是一曲的大王峰。俯瞰九曲蜿蜒，竹筏輕蕩，武夷山水盡收眼底，令人心胸開闊，陶然忘歸。

從一覽台前行，眼前這座宮觀式的建築，就是天遊觀。觀後的妙高台上，大家看到的這棵掛有古樹名木牌子的樹，就是罕見的紅豆樹。每當成熟季節，山風輕拂，豆莢就紛紛撒落在地，滾出殷紅的豆粒，晶瑩閃亮，鮮艷可愛。唐朝詩人王維有詩道：「紅豆生南國，春來發幾枝？願君多採擷，此物最相思。」但願大家能在樹下多找出幾粒帶回家中，作為武夷山之旅的美好紀念。

各位朋友，天遊峰遊覽到此結束。請大家歇息一下，下一站是九曲溪。

九曲溪景區

九曲溪發源於武夷山自然保護區主峰黃崗山西南，全長60公里，有豐富的水源、優良的水質，年徑流量達7億立方米，是5萬多公頃綠色森林涵養、淨化的結晶，溪水的色度在5度以下。它由西向東穿過武夷山景區，盈盈一水，折為九曲，因此得名。九曲溪在景區全長約10公里，山挾水轉，水繞山行，每一曲都是一幅動人的山水畫卷。遊人乘坐竹筏順流而下，抬頭可觀山景，俯首能賞水色，伸手能觸飛泉，側耳可聞百鳥之鳴，真是怡然自得，妙不可言！如果把武夷山比作一部交響樂，九曲溪就是反覆出現的主旋律；如果把武夷山比為一座藝術館，九曲溪則是最精彩的山水畫長廊。國際上衡量河川風景的標準是非常苛刻的，主要有這幾個方面：水是終年持續的還是季節性的，是流動的還是靜止的，是清澈的還是混濁的；河道是曲的還是直的；河床的寬度是變化的還是單一的；兩岸有沒有山，那些山美的程度、變的程度；還有河寬、山高的比例和距離；山上得有植被，擁有生物，形成鳥語花香的良好生態環境……如果從這些方面看，大家對九曲溪會有什麼想法呢？那麼，今天就請諸位給九曲溪考評打分吧！

各位嘉賓，遊覽了九曲溪，一定感到這條溪非常奇特、非常美妙吧！九曲溪蜿蜒9.5公里，然而河道頭尾直線距離只有5公里。這就是説，由於河道彎曲，延長了4.5公里。河道的彎曲係數大，加上河床坡度大，水流速度快，侵蝕作用強，所以凸岸水速減緩，水流翻滾嘩嘩響，如同噴雪濺玉；凹岸則急流飛越，常有碧綠的深潭，產生一個個漩渦。九個大彎曲，實際上是一個淺灘連接一個深潭，灘潭交錯。九曲溪主流由西向東，顯然受到近東西向的斷裂控制；所有轉折河段都是近南北向的，顯然受到近南北向的斷裂影響。九曲溪各段分別受到不同方向的斷裂構造控制，在流水的侵蝕和堆積作用下，才成為如今曲折的九曲溪景觀。九曲溪兩岸丹岩峭壁夾峙，溪水緊束，這是由於地殼強烈抬升、流水強烈下切侵蝕，因而形成深邃的典型的深切河曲，構成河谷地貌的主要特徵。九曲清波繞武夷，山回水轉，水貫山行，山水景色變幻無窮，輕筏凌波終於成了遊武夷的一大特色；更何況兩岸可供觀賞的景點不少，歷史文化景觀豐富多彩呢？

各位嘉賓，您是否也充分領略了武夷山秀麗風光的幾分韻味呢？願九曲溪水在您心中流淌！願諸位人生、事業如今天乘舟一樣——一帆風順！九曲溪遊覽到此結束。謝謝大家的合作！

Gulangyu （鼓浪嶼）

Hello! My friends,

On behalf of the travel agency I warmly welcome you to have a sightseeing of Gulangyu. I hope that all of you will enjoy your short stay here.

Gulangyu, separated from Xiamen by the 500-metre-wide Egret River, with an area of 1. 77 square kilometers, enjoys a laudatory title "Garden on the Sea". The original name of the islet was Yuan Zhou Zi. In the Ming Dynasty it was renamed Gulang, meaning "drum waves", because the holes in the southwestern reefs hit by the waves make a sound that is like hearing a bunch of drums being beaten.

The roar of the waves breaks on the rocks. Impressive melodies surrounding and lingering on this island make it famous for its piano-laden past. As a place of residence for Westerners during Xiamen's colonial past, Gulangyu is famous for its architecture and for being home to China's largest piano museum. It is known as the piano island because the people living here love the piano. As early as 1913, students in schools run by foreigners started learning the piano. The enthusiasm for music later spread to more ordinary people on the island. Many families then bought pianos and their sons and daughters became accomplished musicians. There are more pianos here than in any other places in China, even though the population of the island numbers just 20, 000 people.

No tourist can afford to miss one attraction located on the island, namely China's biggest piano museum. Divided into two exhibition halls, the museum guides visitors through a vivid history of the instrument with displays and illustrations. All different types of pianos such as miniature pianos, automatic pianos, accordion pianos and round-shaped pianos are on display.

The architecture in the islet varies greatly in style with respect to both Chinese and foreign buildings. Thus the islet has a laudatory title "the World Architecture Museum". Covered in green all the year round, it is charming, elegant, secluded and serene. A great variety of villas stand shrouded by lush wood resembling numerous jadeites embellished upon a piece of verdant silk brocade. Hundreds of flowers grown on the Riguang Rock (Sunlight Rock) vie with one another for beauty. With the caressing sea breeze, it's a quite cool place in hot summer. At the foot of the rock, there's the Memorial Hall to honor the national Hero, Zheng Chenggong.

Today, Gulangyu is listed as one of the nation's major scenic spots. The main sites of interest here include the Sunlight Rock, Shuzhuang Park, Gangzihou Bathing Beach and Memorial Hall to Zheng Chenggong, which are visited annually by millions of people from all parts of the country and the world. For people living in the hustle and bustle of today's metropolis, citizens on this island seem to live in a paradise with a relaxing, healthy and placid lifestyle.

華東地區

Sunlight Rock

The rock is also called Huang Rock (Dazzling Bright Rock), which is located on the top of Dragon Head Mountain slightly south of the islet's center. It is 92. 68 meters above sea level and is the highest point on the whole islet. On the top, there is a sightseeing platform, where tourists can have a panoramic view of Xiamen and the Gulang islet.

On the mountain, huge and precipitous rocks form many caves and gullies. Pavilions are hidden among green trees. If you go up the steps, you will come to the Lotus Flower Convent first, where a huge rock named "A Piece of Tile", sitting on the top, forms a hall below. On the large rocks beside the convent are inscribed "Wonderland of Gulang", "Heavenly Wind and Sea Billows", and "Number One along the Egret River".

Close to the convent is the historical site of Zheng Chenggong's Dragon Head Mountain Fastness and the platform for directing and training of his seamen. In addition, plenty of caves, ancient walls and stone carvings can be seen indistinctly among the trees. They would stir up people's feelings and lead them to contemplate the present and recall the past. It takes only about 10 minutes to walk from the ferry to the rock.

Shuzhuang Garden

Built in 1931, the garden is located in the south of the islet, facing the sea and against the Sunlight Rock, with tourist village in the east and the Gangzihou Bathing Beach in the west. Originally it was the private villa of the local well-known figure, Lin Erjia, and was transformed into a garden and open to the public in 1955.

The whole garden can be divided into two parts:Canghai Garden for sea views and Bushan Garden for hill views. Each part has five sightseeing spots. Walking on the meandering "Fifty-four Bridge", tourists would feel as if they were walking on water. And "Twelve-Cave Paradise", the tortuous, interlinked and spiraled rockeries built on the hill are especially interesting. The scenic spots in the garden are well proportioned and harmonious. The garden is on the sea and the sea is included in the garden. It combines the beauty of exquisite garden with vigorous sea view of splashing waves and hovering seagulls. Activity and inertia contrast and complement each other. Visitors are always attracted and enchanted by the beautiful scenery.

Bright Moon Garden

The garden is located southeast of the islet, facing the Lujiang harbor. The garden occupies an area of nearly 30, 000 square meters. It was established in August 1985. The Zheng Chenggong Statue, standing between the sky and the earth, is the main structure of the garden. It is 15. 7 meters high and is the biggest Chinese historical figure statue. On the plaza in the garden, a group of bonze statues depict Chinese people driving the Dutch invaders out of Taiwan under the leadership of Zheng Chenggong.

The garden forms a wonderful view combining buildings of Ming Dynasty style with natural beauty, like gulls, trees, sea view and mountain sight. Altogether they constitute a picture of natural beauty. It takes only five minutes' walk from the ferry to the garden. Every main crossing has clear direction signs. With them, you can never get lost on the islet.

Yu Garden

Going along the Zhangzhou Road or Fuxing Road by the side of Bright Moon Garden, we reach the Yu Garden. This beautiful and peaceful garden was built in 1984 in memory of Professor Lin Qiaozhi, a medical scientist and expert in gynecology and obstetrics. The garden is well proportioned. There is a statue of Professor Lin, made of

華東地區

white marble in the garden. The two hoop pines standing beside the Exhibition Room for Lin Qiaozhi's Life Story, were planted by the famous revolutionary, Deng Yingchao, and represent the noble character of Professor Lin.

Piano Garden

Piano Garden is a tourist attraction, and a deep cultural atmosphere pervades it. It is located on Hero Mountain opposite to the Sunlight Rock. It consists of several different parts, the names of which are related to music, particularly the piano, such as Melody Square, Thinking-of-piano Square, Harmoni-ous Music Building, Flowing Music Building, Lingering Sound Gate, and the like.

The islet is also famous for its ownership of pianos. In fact, it is ranked No. 1 in China with respect to per capita piano ownership, and so many talented musicians and pianists have come from here. It is often referred to as the "islet of Pianos and Cradle of Musicians". On pleasant days, if you walk on the islet, the peaceful streets, the piano and violin music from the houses and gardens will surely bring you great happiness and relaxation.

Sea-view Garden

Sea-view Garden is a holiday villa with unique natural scenes in the southeast part of Gulang islet. With an area of 100, 000 square meters, it combines the delightful serenity of traditional Chinese gardens and the lively openness of the western-style villas. Under the management of Xiamen Gulang Islet Sea-view Garden Holiday Villa Company, the garden not only boasts a sea and mountain landscape, but also possesses a villa hotel to serve guests, conference needs and tour groups both home and abroad. Equipped with luxury and general suites, standard rooms, a sea-food restaurant, karaoke and dancing halls, a market place, yachts and a special dock, the hotel can also provide other services like dining and lodging, entertainment and one day sightseeing on the sea package tour.

Xiamen Museum (Eight Diagrams Building)

Standing in a high place anywhere in Xiamen, you can easily find the two landmarks of Gulang islet:Sunlight Rock on the highest peak by Lujiang Harbor and the Eight Diagrams Building overlooking Xiamen and Gulang islet. The original owner of the building, Lin Heshou, is a cousin of Lin Erjia, original owner of Shuzhuang Garden, set up the building in 1907. Now it is Xiamen Museum. Because of its special red dome and the Eight Diagrams, people call it Eight Diagrams Building. Within the museum, there are records of Xiamen's history and developments, the construction process of the SEZ, its sports accomplishments and develop-ment of its relationships with other cities and countries. There are also collection of porcelain, jade, and weapons through the ages.

OK, my friends! Our journey is about to end. And I should say goodbye to you all. Anyway I am very glad to have spent such a happy and unforgettable day with you. I just hope that the Gulangyu have left you a good memory. Thank you all! Wish you a happy journey! Good-bye!

各位朋友大家好！

我代表旅行社對大家來鼓浪嶼旅遊、觀光表示熱烈歡迎。希望大家在鼓浪嶼逗留期間能夠玩得開心，吃得放心，同時希望大家在遊覽當中能夠有較大的收穫，留下美好的回憶。

鼓浪嶼與廈門市區相隔著500米寬的白鷺河，鼓浪嶼面積有1.77平方公里，素有「海上花園」之美譽。鼓浪嶼原名「園州子」，明朝時改稱為「鼓浪」，這是因為在小島的西南隅海邊，當波濤撞擊著岩石上的洞時，能發出如鼓的浪聲。

洶湧的波浪擊打著岩石，周圍瀰漫的是醉人的曲調，鼓浪嶼以它的鋼琴歷史而

華東地區

出名。在殖民時期，作為一個西方人聚集的地方，鼓浪嶼因建築和中國最大的鋼琴博物館而聞名世界。這裡的人們很喜歡鋼琴，因而被稱為鋼琴之島。早在1913年，在外國人開設的學校裡，學生就開始學習鋼琴。之後，對音樂的狂熱又蔓延到更多的普通居民。儘管鼓浪嶼只有2萬居民，但那裡鋼琴的擁有量在中國居於前列。

沒有旅遊者會錯過鼓浪嶼的一大景觀——中國最大的鋼琴博物館。博物館分為兩個廳，向遊客用表演和圖解的方式生動展示了樂器的演變歷史，展示了各種各樣的鋼琴，例如鋼琴縮影，自動演奏鋼琴，手搖鋼琴，四角鋼琴等。

小島上薈萃了上千座風格各異、中西合璧的中外建築。鼓浪嶼被譽為常年掩映在綠樹之下的「世界建築博物館」，它魅力四射、雄偉壯觀、與世隔絕、安詳寧靜。數量眾多的別墅掩映在茂密的樹林旁邊，就像成千上萬的翡翠鑲嵌在一塊青翠的絲綢錦緞之上。成百上千的鮮花盛開在日光岩上，爭奇鬥艷。夏天，伴隨海上微風的輕撫，這裡會讓人感到無比的清涼與舒適。在日光岩的腳下，是民族英雄鄭成功的紀念館。

如今，鼓浪嶼是中國主要的風景名勝之一。主要觀光點有：日光岩、菽莊花園、港仔後浴場、鄭成功紀念館等。每年都有超過十萬的海內外遊客前來參觀。相對於生活在繁忙之中的居民和現代繁忙的都市生活來說，這裡的居民生活在一個輕鬆、健康和寧靜的天堂裡。

日光岩

日光岩俗稱「晃者」，位於龍頭山脈的最頂端，島中央稍偏南的地方。日光岩海拔92.68米，是鼓浪嶼的最高峰。在日光岩頂築有圓台，站立其間，憑欄遠眺，廈門和鼓浪嶼風光就盡收眼底了。

在山上，眾多巨大險峻的岩石形成了許多岩洞和溝壑。很多亭子掩映在綠樹之間。沿著天梯而上，首先來到荷花修道院，這裡有一塊名為「一片瓦」的大石頭，矗立於其上，下面就形成一個大廳。在修道院旁邊的岩石上刻著「鼓浪之極地」、「大風巨浪處」和「白鷺河第一」。

緊靠著修道院是一處歷史遺址——鄭成功龍頭山寨和指揮訓練水軍的觀望台。另外，在樹叢中數量眾多的岩洞、古城牆和石刻在這可一目瞭然。這些會激發人們的情感，引起他們思考現在和回憶過去。

菽莊花園

菽莊花園建於1931年，位於島的南部，面向大海，背靠日光岩。它的東部是遊客村，西面是港仔後浴場。起初菽莊花園是當地名人林爾嘉的私人別墅。1955年被改成一座花園而對外開放。

整個花園可以分為為觀海而建的藏海園和為觀山而建的補山園兩個部分。每個部分都有五個觀光點。行走在蜿蜒的「五十四橋」上，遊客彷彿感覺到自己在水上行走。修建於山上的十二洞天、蜿蜒小道、頑石山房都特別有趣。花園中的這些風景點都非常協調、完整和統一。園在海上，海中有園。菽莊花園兼具可觀賞海浪飛濺的美景和翱翔盤旋的海鷗的雅緻花園之美，動靜相襯，彼此協調。遊客經常被這些美景所吸引而流連忘返。

皓月園

皓月園位於鼓浪嶼的東南隅，正對盧江港口。全園占地面積約為3萬平方米，是1985年8月修建的。矗立於天地之間的鄭成功雕像，是全園的主要組成部分。鄭成功雕像高15.7 米，是中國最大的歷史英雄人物的雕像。園區廣場上的青銅群雕向我們展示了鄭成功率領部下把荷蘭侵略者趕出中國的場景。

皓月園風景秀麗，明代建築樣式與自然美和諧共存，例如海鷗、樹、海景和山脈風光。所有這一切組成一幅美麗的圖畫。從籬笆到園區走路僅需五分鐘。在主要幹道，有明顯的指示牌。有了它們，你絕對不會在島上走失。

毓園

穿過皓月園一側的漳州路或復興路即可到達毓園。美麗寧靜的毓園是為了紀念醫學家、婦產科醫學專家林巧稚教授而在1984年修建的。毓園布局合理。園中樹立著林巧稚大夫的漢白玉雕像。在「林巧稚大夫生平事跡展覽室」旁邊，是兩株南洋杉，由革命家鄧穎超親手種植，象徵著林大夫高尚的品格。

鋼琴園

鋼琴園是一個文化氛圍濃厚的旅遊景點。它位於鼓浪嶼的英雄山上，正對日光岩石。它由幾個不同的部分組成，而且所有的組成部分的名字與音樂都有一定的關係，特別是與鋼琴有關係，例如，旋律廣場、思想鋼琴廣場、和諧音樂樓、流動音樂摟、回聲大門等。

鼓浪嶼也因為其鋼琴的擁有量而出名，這裡的人均鋼琴擁有量為中國第一。很多天才音樂家和鋼琴家都來自這裡。這裡經常被認為是「鋼琴之島」和「音樂家的搖籃」。在天氣晴朗的日子裡，如果你步行在島上或平靜的街道上，從房間裡傳出來的鋼琴演奏聲和笛聲，會讓你感到非常快樂和放鬆。

觀海園

觀海園位於鼓浪嶼東南隅，自然風光獨特，是休閒渡假的好地方。它占地面積約10　萬平方米，既有中華民族傳統園林的建築風格，又有西洋建築明快開朗之特點。在廈門鼓浪嶼觀海園假日別墅有限公司的管理下，花園不僅提升了海洋和山石的風景質量，也擁有一家別墅酒店以滿足渡假者、商務會議需求以及來自國內外的旅遊團隊。觀海別墅擁有豪華套間、經濟套間、標準房、海鮮餐廳、卡拉OK廳、舞廳、商店、快艇和一個特別的碼頭。這家渡假別墅同樣也提供諸如食宿、娛樂和海上一日遊等其他服務。

廈門博物館（八卦樓）

在廈門市區內任何一個居高的地方，都可見到鼓浪嶼兩個突出的標誌：屹立鷺江第一峰的日光岩和傲視廈門、鼓浪嶼的八卦樓。八卦樓的原主人林鶴壽，是菽莊花園原主人林爾嘉的堂兄弟。該樓始建於1907　年，現已作為廈門博物館。該樓圓圓的紅頂樓蓋獨具特色，有八卦形狀，被人們稱為「八卦樓」。廈門博物館內記載著廈門的歷史變遷、特區的建設歷程、廈門體育事業的發展、與其他國家和城市的友好往來、歷代瓷玉和兵器等。

　　好了，各位遊客，鼓浪嶼的參觀活動就要結束了，我不得不跟大家説再見了，很高興和大家共度了美好、難忘的一天。希望鼓浪嶼能給你們留下美好的回憶，謝謝！祝你們旅行愉快！再見！

Anhui Province安徽省

A Glimpse of the Province （本省簡介）

Anhui Province is called "Wan" for short and is located in southern China. The province covers an area of 139, 600 square kilometers and its capital is Hefei. Anhui Province has an extremely varied topography:it is hilly and mountainous in the southwest and is low and flat in the northeast. Major rivers include the Huaihe River in the north and the Yangtze River in the south. One of China's largest freshwater lakes, Lake Chaohu, is located at the center of the province; there are also many lakes in southeastern Anhui near the Yangtze River. Anhui Province has humid monsoon climate with four distinct seasons. It is also rich in resources and is one of China's most important grain-producing provinces. Tea is the province's main cash crop; the famous varieties are Huangshan Maofeng, Lu'an Guapian, and Qimen Black Tea, all of which are listed among China's top ten well-known tea varieties.

Tourism Resources

Anhui Province is rich in tourism resources. Mount Huang or Huangshan is famous for its unique pines, grotesque rocks, fantastic clouds, and hot springs and has been designated by UNESCO as a World Natural and Cultural Heritage site. Other well-known Anhui mountains include Mount Jiuhua, one of China's four well-known Buddhist

華東地區

mountains;Mount Tianzhu, which has been called "The South Peak" for hundreds of years; Mount Langya, famed for a thousand years because of the "Note on the Old Tippler's Tower"; and Mount Qiyun, one of the four famous Taoist mountains in China. Southern Anhui's Yixian County is widely admired as "A Living Ancient Residential Museum". And there are also many historic sites in Northern Anhui Province. For example, Bozhou and Fengyang were the childhood homes of Caocao, one of the central figures of the Three Kingdoms Period and Zhu Yuanzhang, the founding Emperor of the Ming Dynasty, while Shouxian County is the former capital of the Chu State. The important festivals include Bengbu Huagu Lantern Festival, Ma'anshan International Poem-Reciting Party, and Huangshan International Tourism Festival.

Local Snacks

Anhui cuisine is one of China's eight great cuisine. The traditional courses are soy braised mandarin fish, stewed soft shell turtle with ham, fried flocky bean curd, and steamed stone frog. The local snacks are Huangshan-braised pigeon, Bagongshan bean curd, Wucheng saut ed dried Tofu, Huizhou steamed dumplings, and saut ed pork with rice flour.

Special local Products

The special local products are famous tea varieties, such as Huangshan Maofeng, and Qimen Black Tea, wild mushrooms, like the Yixian Torreya seeds and Huangshan ferns, and fresh fruit, particularly Dangshan Pears and Huaiyuan Megranates. Anhui Province is also famed for its calligraphy products. The best known are Xuan ink brushes, Hui ink, Xuan paper, and She ink slab, all of which are regarded as China's best "Four Treasures of Study". Other notable local products are Huizhou lacquer wares and Wuhu iron-made picture.

Local Culture

Anhui Province is regarded as the birthplace of many opera forms, such as Nuo Opera, one oldest Chinese opera forms still being performed today and traditional Mulian Opera. Hui Opera is one of the major precursors of Beijing Opera. Other local operas include Huangmei, Fengyang Huagu, and Lu Operas.

Tourism City

Anhui's capital, Hefei, is situated between the Yangtze and Huaihe Rivers. It is famous for its scenic beauty and abundant products. Its scenic spots and historic sites include the Leisure Ford, the site of a famous battle fought during the Three Kingdoms Period; the Mingjiao Temple, which was built in the Tang Dynasty; the Memorial Temple and statue of Bao Zheng, an upright official of the Song Dynasty; and the Honest Spring Pavilion.

Huangshan City is located in southern Anhui Province and has rich tourism resources. The Huangshan Scenic Area is a national treasure and is known throughout the world as the prime representative of traditional Chinese mountain scenery. The Huizhou area's unique culture is marked by a variety of forms, such as Huizhou merchant culture, engraving, and architecture, as well as Xin'an Painting, all of which occupy an important position in Chinese history and culture.

Classical Tour Routes in Anhui Province

1. Ancient Anhui cities tour.

Bozhou—Shouxian—Fengyan—Heifei—Tongcheng—Anqing.

2. Natural beauty tour.

Anqing (Mt.Tianzhu)—Chizhou (Mt.Jiu-hua)—Huangshan.

華東地區

3. "Chinese Red Culture" tour.

Huangshan—Jixi—Jingde—Jingxian—Xuan-cheng—Wuhu

安徽省簡稱「皖」，地處中國東部，總面積13.96萬平方公里，省會合肥。安徽地形複雜，山川壯麗，地勢西南高，東北低。長江和淮河自西向東橫貫全境，中國五大淡水湖之一——巢湖和其他眾多湖泊分布於中部。安徽屬季風氣候類型，氣候溫和濕潤，四季分明。美麗富饒的安徽大地，資源豐富，是中國重要的產糧省之一。經濟作物以茶葉最為著名，其中黃山毛峰、六安瓜片和祁門紅茶被列入中國十大名茶，享譽海內外。

旅遊資源

安徽山河秀麗，風光優美，旅遊資源豐富。以「奇松、怪石、雲海、溫泉」聞名天下的黃山被聯合國教科文組織列入世界自然和文化遺產目錄。九華山是中國四大佛教名山之一，天柱山曾以「南嶽」封號數百年，琅琊山因《醉翁亭記》享譽千年，齊雲山則是中國的四大道教名山之一。皖南黟縣等被稱為「中國古民居博物館」。皖北多古蹟，如亳州、鳳陽分別為曹操、朱元璋的故里，壽縣為楚國故都。蚌埠的花鼓燈會、馬鞍山國際吟詩會、黃山國際旅遊節都是重要的旅遊節會。

風味食品

安徽的徽菜是中國的八大菜系之一，傳統名菜有紅燒臭鱖魚、火腿燉甲魚、油煎毛豆腐、清蒸石雞等。地方風味小吃主要有：黃山燉鴿、八公山豆腐、五城茶干、徽州蒸餃、粉蒸肉等。

地方特產

安徽有不少名特產品，如黃山毛峰、祁門紅茶等名茶，黟縣香榧、黃山蕨菜等山珍、碭山酥梨、懷遠石榴等鮮果。宣筆、徽墨、宣紙、歙硯是中國文房四寶中的珍品。徽州漆器、蕪湖鐵畫也是安徽的特產。

地方文藝

安徽是戲曲之鄉，保存有「戲曲活化石」之稱的儺戲和古老的目連戲。徽劇則是京劇的前身之一。另外還有家喻戶曉的黃梅戲、鳳陽花鼓、廬劇等地方劇種。

主要旅遊城市

合肥作為安徽省的省會，位於江淮之間，風景優美，物產豐富。名勝古蹟有：三國時的古戰場逍遙津，是曹操名將張遼大戰孫權的地方；有唐代所建的明教寺；有坐落在包河的包公祠，是紀念宋代著名清官包拯的祠堂，祠內有包拯的塑像，祠邊有廉泉亭。

黃山市地處安徽省南部，山靈水秀，旅遊資源非常豐富。其間有被譽為國之瑰寶、世界奇觀的黃山風景區，是中國山嶽風光的傑出代表。古老的徽州山水，孕育出獨特的徽州文化，其徽商、徽雕、新安畫派、徽派建築、徽墨、徽劇等經濟、文化流派無不博大精深，在中華民族歷史文化中占有重要一席。

推薦旅遊路線

1.安徽古都名城之旅

亳州─壽縣─鳳陽─合肥─桐城─安慶。

2.青山秀水遊

安慶（天柱山）─池州（九華山）─黃山。

3.紅色之旅

黃山─績溪─旌德─涇縣─宣城─蕪湖。

華東地區

North Sea Scenic Area in Mt.Huangshan （黃山北海景區）

Ladies and gentlemen,

Welcome to Mt.Huangshan's North Sea Scenic Area. The North Sea Scenic Area（including the West Sea）is located in the center of Mt.Huangshan. It is a 1, 600-meter-high open mountainous area. It consists of high peaks, stone and rock formations, picturesque pines, temples, terraces, and clouds. These features combine to form a fantastic landscape with ever-changing colors that presents a charming natural picture and is well-known as the Mount Huangshan's scenic window. The "North Sea Scenic Area" is the most important scenic area in Mt.Huangshan and contains all of its "Four Wonders".

Beginning-to-Believe Peak

Now, please look ahead. This famous peak is named the Beginning-to-Believe Peak. It is one of Mt.Huangshan's 36 small peaks and its name has a peculiar origin. In ancient times, a tourist came from the Cloudy Valley Monastery to this spot and believed that he had entered a wonderland of picturesque scenery. It was at this spot that the tourist began to believe that Mt.Huangshan was a uniquely beautiful place.

Mt.Huangshan has unique pines, grotesque rocks, fantastic clouds, and soothing hot springs. While rare pine species can be seen on all of the peaks, the pines at this peak are spectacular. It is said that "It is only at the Beginning-to-Believe Peak that you can see the pines of Huangshan". Their characteristics include short bent branches, flat crowns, short, thick and dark green conifer leaves, and vine-like roots among the rock fissures. The pine trees stand upright and are majestic in their appearance. This pine tree in front of us is called Black Tiger Pine. It is 15 meters high and its trunk is 65 centimeters at its widest point. The tree has gone through many years of strenuous growth and is one of Huangshan's famous pines.

And this is the Dragon-Claw Pine, a rare sight in Mt.Huangshan. As you can see its main root is deep underground, while the other five thick sub roots are all exposed and shaped like a giant dragon claw.

Now please look at the pine on this side. It spreads itself with two branches close to the cliffs of the peak, so the local people call it Sleeping Dragon Pine. Somewhere further down, there is another pine tree, with one of its branches twice as long as the whole tree. This branch reaches into the cloudy valley. When the mist and cloud fill the valley, the branch looks like it is exploring in the sea, so it is called the Sea-Exploring Pine.

Please watch your steps, as we are now crossing 4 meter long and 1 meter wide stone bridge crossing the cliffs. It is called Heaven-Crossing Bridge, meaning that anyone who crosses the bridge will enter Heaven and become a heavenly being. We are now on the top of the Beginning-to-Believe Peak, which is 1668 meters high, and enjoying a thrilling view of the landscape.

Not far away, is a famous sight of Mt.Huangshan. On top of the slender rock column with sharp tip separated from the top stands a small pine. People call it the Peak of Pen and it is also called the Tip of a Magic Writing Brush. On its left side, there is a peak revealing its five branches in the shape of a writing brush stand—the best match made by Nature.

Refreshing Terrace

We are now on Mt.Huangshan's No. 1 terrace, the Refreshing Terrace, which is the best spot to watch the sunrise in the early morning. From here, we may get lucky and see the Buddhist brilliance—a unique natural phenomenon. At drawn or at dusk, when the sun is at a lower horizontal position, clouds and mists gather before your eyes and make a natural screen catching the sunshine from behind to form a spectacular scene of rainbow.

Looking westward, we can see a flat-topped peak, with a monkey-shaped rock sitting on the summit and watching the cloud sea. This rock is called "The Monkey Gazing at the Sea" or "The Monkey Looking at Taiping"; the latter name stems from the fact that Taiping County can be seen from there off in the distance. Near us is a pine tree with tough roots and a bundle of 56 branches closely joined, symbolizing China's 56 nationalities, so people call it the Union Pine Tree.

Red Cloud Peak

Following this path up, we will arrive at Red Cloud Peak, where we can often see red clouds hanging round the peak. It is a nice spot for watching both sunrise and sunset.

Cloud-Dispelling Pavilion

Cloud-Dispelling Pavilion is now in front of us. This is the best place to view Mt.Huangshan's oddly shaped and interesting rocks. Near us is a huge rock at the base of the cliff that is shaped like an inverted boot and is called "An Immortal Drying His Boot in the sun".

On our left is a smooth peak like a bed, with a small pine tree slanting from a rock on the right of the "bed". The tree makes a smooth embroidered frame and is called "A Fairy Maiden Doing Embroidery." On the right of the peak, a rock in the shape of human figure is sitting at a flat rock resembling a clavichord. These two rocks are called "A Fairy Maiden Playing the Clavichord".

Flying-over Rock

This giant rock is the famous Flying-over Rock. It is 12 meters high, 7. 5 meters long, and 1. 5-2. 5 meters wide; it weighs about 360 tons. According to one story, the ancient Goddess, N wa, made some rocks to fix a leak from heaven and had two unused rocks left over after finishing this job. One of them turned into a crystal jade— the very jade in the mouth of the newly born Jia Baoyu, the hero of the classic 18thCentury Chinese novel, "Dream of Red Mansions" —while the other stone flew to Mt.Huangshan and landed on this spot.

Bright Top Peak

Now, we are on the top of Bright Top Peak. It is 1, 860 meters high and is Mt.Huangshan's second highest peak. It is said that in the Ming Dynasty's Wanli period, a monk called Zhi Kong set up a Mass Mercy Temple on Immortality-Pill-Cultivation Peak. The temple is no longer on the spot now, but the name Bright Top has been remained till now.

Looking far away, we can see Mt.Huangshan's most spectacular peak, Tiandu Peak (Heavenly Capital Peak), rising 1, 810 meters into the sky. People in ancient times regarded it as the abode of Immortals and other heavenly beings. The peak is also known as the "Pyramid of Mt.Huangshan".

Nearby another peak towers above the sky, and it and the many surrounding peaks resemble a lotus in full bloom. This peak is thus named Lotus Peak and with an elevation of 1, 864 meters, it is Mt.Huangshan's highest peak.

Between the Tiandu Peak and Lotus Peak, we can see a group of red roofed buildings with yellow walls—the Jade Screen Mansion. The peak nearby is called Jade Screen Peak and is famed for being Mt.Huangshan's wonderland. Here visitors can see the Welcoming Guest, Seeing-off Guest, and Escorting Guest Pine Trees, as well as the Lying Buddha.

Crocodile Peak

華東地區

Just in front of us, creeps the Crocodile Peak, and on its back sits a rock like a golden turtle moving slowly forward. The sight is popularly known as "Crocodile Carrying Golden Turtle on its Back". Now our North Sea Scenic Area tour comes to an end. Thank you all!

各位朋友：

大家好！歡迎來到黃山北海景區參觀遊覽。北海景區（包括西海）位於黃山中部，是一片海拔在1600米左右的高山開闊區域，北海景區，匯集了石、松、塢、台、雲等奇景，色彩變幻莫測，構成一幅幅偉、奇、幻、險的天然畫卷，是黃山的風景窗。北海景區是黃山最重要的景區，這裡集合了黃山的四絕勝景，大家是絕對不能錯過的。

始信峰

大家請看前方，這裡是黃山著名的始信峰，位列黃山三十六小峰第十五。峰名得來十分獨特：相傳古時有人從雲谷寺遊山至此，如入畫境，似幻而真，始信黃山風景奇絕。

黃山以奇松、怪石、雲海、溫泉「四絕」而聞名天下。奇松遍布黃山峰谷，但是尤以始信峰的松樹最為獨特，因而有「不到始信峰，不見黃山松」的說法。黃山松的主要形態特徵為：枝葉短粗而稠密，葉色濃綠，枝幹曲生，樹冠扁平，盤根於石，傲然挺立。我們現在看到的是黃山名松之一的黑虎松。松高15米，胸徑達65釐米。這邊這棵松樹叫龍爪松。從樹形、樹齡看並無突出之處，但卻成為黃山一景。大家仔細看，此松主根深扎地下，另有五根粗壯的支根全部裸露在外，狀似蒼龍之爪，所以人們給它取名為龍爪松。

請大家再看山峰頂側的這株松樹，它橫於懸崖石壁之中，在樹幹20釐米處分兩支盤曲生長，伏臥昂首，人們給它取名為臥龍松。再請順著臥龍松往下看，這株松樹冠平整，極像迎客松，最下一側枝的長度幾乎是樹高的一倍。此枝向谷中伸出，當雲霧在山壑間瀰漫飛騰時，伸出的側枝猶如凌波探海，所以人稱探海松。

請大家小心腳下。我們正在經過的這座長4米、寬1米的橋名為仙人橋，又名渡仙橋，意為渡過此橋，即入仙境。過了這淨土門，就真正登上了始信峰絕頂了。古詩有「山登絕頂我為峰」之説，此時我們已站在了海拔1668米的始信峰山頂了。

臨近我們的是一著名景觀。這一石柱修長，頂端尖銳，柱與頂被一道裂縫分開的山峰叫筆峰。人們把這松石天合的奇景命名為「夢筆生花」。請大家向「夢筆生花」的左邊看，這座頂分五岔，形似筆架的山峰為筆架峰，筆架峰相稱相配，奇景天生。

清涼台

現在我們到達的是被稱為黃山第一台的「清涼台」。這裡是觀看日出的最佳地點之一。在清涼台上，還有機會見到「佛光」。佛光是一種非常奇特的自然現象，在傍晚或清晨，有時雲霧會構成一道天然「屏幕」。當太陽光由身後投射到這塊屏幕上時，即可看見五彩繽紛的光環。

從清涼台往西看，有座山峰，峰頂平坦，上面的一塊巨石形似猴子，這就是著名的「猴子觀海」，也稱為「猴子望太平」。名為「望太平」，是因為猴子的雙目似在向下凝望古老的太平縣城。大家請看這邊的一棵松樹，鐵根盤結，團團簇擁，與其他松樹相比，很是奇特。人們把它稱為「團結松」。為什麼呢？因為這棵松樹不多不少正好56根枝枒，而中華民族大家庭也正好由56 個民族組成，緊緊團結在一起，這棵松樹體現了中華民族的團結精神。

丹霞峰

沿著這條路上去便是丹霞峰。此峰因常有紅色的霞光籠罩而得名，這裡是觀賞晚霞的最佳地點，也是朝觀日出的理想之地。

排雲亭

朋友們，排雲亭到了。這兒是觀賞黃山奇石最理想的地方，有「黃山奇石博物館」之稱。離我們較近的這塊奇石，像一只半高筒的雨靴放在懸崖上，這叫「仙人曬靴」。

在左邊山頂平坦如床的石床峰右邊，有一塊獨立的石頭，在它的胸部還有一棵松樹斜刺生長，構成「仙女繡花」的景觀。而在「仙女繡花」的右側高峰上，有一塊人形模樣的石頭，微伏而坐，前有一塊石頭像平放的古琴，這就是「仙女彈琴」。

飛來石

這塊巨大的巧石就是「飛來石」。石頭高約12米，長7.5米，寬1.5～2.5米，重約360噸。相傳女媧煉石補天，剩下兩塊石頭，一塊變成晶瑩的美玉，也就是《紅樓夢》裡賈寶玉出生時嘴裡所銜的那塊「通靈寶玉」；另一塊後來飛到了黃山，變成了我們現在看到的這塊巧石。

光明頂

遊客們，我們現在所在的地方就是海拔1860米的光明頂。光明頂是黃山的第二高峰，明萬曆年間，有位智空和尚原在煉丹峰頂創建大悲院，又名大悲頂。如今，光明頂上的大悲院早已蕩然無存，但光明頂這個名稱卻流傳至今。

從這裡向左邊遠眺，最遠的那個高峰就是黃山最險的峰——天都峰。海拔1810米，因拔地摩天，險峻雄奇，古人視為「群仙之都會」，所以取名天都峰。它也被稱為黃山的「金字塔」。

距天都峰較近的這座山峰峻峭高聳，氣勢雄偉，主峰突兀，群峰簇擁，峰頂好像片片荷瓣簇擁荷心，似一朵盛開的新蓮。這就是黃山的第一高峰——蓮花峰，海拔1864米。

在天都峰與蓮花峰之間，可以看到一片黃牆紅頂的房子，那就是「玉屏樓」，其所在的山峰名為玉屏峰。玉屏峰被稱為「黃山絕勝處」，有「人間玉屏，天上人家」之稱。著名的迎客松、送客松、陪客松以及黃山臥佛等都在這兒。

鰲魚峰

在我們面前的這座山峰是鰲魚峰。你看，整個山峰猶如一條巨大的鰲魚，頭向左，尾向右。在鰲魚的嘴前有三塊小巧石，像三個螺螄，因此組成「鰲魚吃螺螄」景觀。在鰲魚背上，有石如龜，向前探首，峰石結合，構成「鰲魚馱金龜」的奇景。遊覽至此，黃山北海景區的景點便全部結束。謝謝大家！

Mount Jiuhua （九華山）

Ladies and gentlemen,

Today, accompanied by the sunshine in early morning, we are going to pay a visit to Mount Jiuhua. First allow me to briefly introduce Mount Jiuhua. Mount Jiuhua is located in southwestern Qingyang County, Anhui Province. It combines Buddhist culture with beautiful scenery and ancient temples, and it is one of the four sacred Buddhist mountains in China.

Mount Jiuhau has 99 peaks surrounding its summit, Shiwang Peak, which is 1, 342 meters high. Mount Jiuhua has a long history of religious culture, with Taoism preceding Buddhism. Among the more than eighty temples still standing today, Huacheng, Ganlu, Tiantai, and Qiyuan Temples, Roushen Hall, and Zhantan Forest are the best preserved. The architectural style is distinguished by its free and vivid design mixing Buddhist temples and local residences in the mountain region. There are not only big temples of a grand scale and strict style, but also small quiet temples made up of one room and one hall.

Mount Jiuhua is a special place of Buddhist worship where religious rites are held for the worship of Ksitigarbha, known in Chinese as D z ng (地藏), who is a

Bodhisattva and protector of souls in hell in the Mahayana Buddhist tradition. It is recorded that during the Tang Dynasty, Jin Qiaojue, the near clan of the King of Koyro Kingdom, or present day Korea, came to China and practiced Buddhism in Mt.Jiuhua until he died at the age of 99, much like the famous Buddhist sage, Ksitigarbha, so he is regarded as the Ksitigarbha Bodhisattva. Since a grave tower was built to bury him on Shenguang Ridge, it became the place for worshiping Ksitigarbha. The tower is always filled with incense smoke and every year, a temple fair is held lasting 10 days. The fair has been included in nation-wide touring programs and welcomes many domestic and foreign pilgriMs.Today, due to limited time, we are just going to visit Jiuhua Street and Tiantai Scenic Area.

Jiuhua Street Scenic Area

Now we are walking on the Jiuhua Street. It is located in a spacious area at the foot of Furong Peak 600 meters, above sea level and surrounded by mountains, which serves as Mount Jiuhua's reception center. Temples, local residences, and shops are mixed together on Jiuhua Street, and monks, nuns, pilgrims, visitors and the local inhabitants wander around here all day.

Qiyuan Temple

What we see now is Qiyuan Temple, which is also called Qiyuan Buddhist Temple. It was originally built in the Ming Dynasty. The structure of the buildings resembles those of a palace complex;however, unlike the buildings in a palace complex, they are not symmetrically laid out. Indeed, even the gate is slanting to one side. Please look at the aisle in front of the temple; it has a relief sculpture of lotus with the pattern of ancient coins engraved on it, symbolizing the holy trace of Sakyamuni. Entering the gate, you can see two Buddhist warriors on the two sides with frightening facial expressions. In the middle is the statue of Linguan, the judge, with a wide-open eye on his forehead and a long whip in his hand. Linguan was originally a god of

Taoism, but why did he come into a Buddhist temple? It is said that one day, when Vitasoka, the protector of Ksitigarbha went out to inspect the mountain, a scholar who was a non-believer of Buddhism thrust an iron needle at the leg of Ksitigarbha to see if he was real. Seeing the blood oozing from the leg of Ksitigarbha, the scholar was scared and hurried down the mountain. When Vitasoka came back and was told about it, he chased the scholar in spite of Ksitigarbha's stopping, and beat the scholar to death with one whip at Wuxi Bridge. Ksitigarbha was rather angry, for the monks should be merciful, so he dismissed Vitasoka and asked Lingguan to take his place. Today, the relics of the scholar's tomb at Wuxi Bridge can be the proof for the legend.

Roushen Hall

We are now in the famous Roushen Hall. More than 1, 200 years ago, the eminent monk Jin Qiaojue used to chant sutra and sit in meditation on Shenguang Ridge. When he died, he sat in a vat and was placed in Nantai. As the ground shone magically, it was renamed Shenguang (Magic Shine) Ridge. Three years later, the vat was opened. His body was still soft, his face was still lively and his bones sounded clearly when shaken. As the Buddhist sutra showed, he was the reincarnation of Buddha, so he was honored Ksitigarbha and a high hall and a wooden pagoda were built to protect him, which was named Roushen (incarnation) Hall. The structure of a pagoda inside a hall, a vat inside the pagoda, and an incarnated body inside the vat is unique.

Tiantai Scenic Area

We've arrived at Tiantai Scenic Area. Tiantai Scenic Area is situated southeast of Mount Jiuhua where most of the high peaks gather. Tiantai Peak is 1, 325 meters high, making it a little lower than Shiwang Peak. But it is always been regarded as the center of the high peaks because of its many scenic sights and ancient temples. Starting from Minyuan to Tiantai, you'll enjoy various magnificent views one by one as you climb higher and higher.

華東地區

Tiantai Temple

Tiantai Temple now is in our sights. It is also called Wanfo Building and Ksitigarbha Buddhist Temple and has three parts. First you'll enter the Maitreya Buddha Hall, then the Hall of the Three Sages in the western world, at last the Grand Hall. Now, please look up, you can see on the wooden ceiling, thousands of small Buddhist figurines are lined with various vivid expressions. The temple has no outside yards, but is still spacious and bright, due to its special design. On the rock at the corner of the hall is a big footprint which is paired with one on another peak, the East Cliff. They were the holy prints left by Jin Qiaojue when he took off striding over the two peaks. The big drum was presented in 1982 by the pious Buddhist believers in Kowloon, Hong Kong.

Well, the tour of Mount Jiuhua now comes to an end. I thank you all and wish you a happy journey home!

各位朋友，大家好！

沐浴著清晨的陽光，我們將前往九華山風景區遊覽。我先簡單介紹一下九華山風景區的概況。九華山位於安徽省青陽縣西南，景色秀奇，古剎林立，是以佛教文化為特色的山嶽風景區，中國四大佛教名山之一。

九華山群峰林立，高高低低的山峰圍繞著海拔1342米的主峰十王峰，猶如兒孫繞膝，老少歡聚。九華山宗教活動歷史悠久，其道教在先，佛教更盛。現存寺廟80多座，其中被列為國家重點保護的有化成寺、祇園寺、肉身寶殿、旃檀林、甘露寺、天台寺等。其建築形式很有特色，大部分以佛教殿堂與皖南民居相結合，依山傍勢，布局靈巧，既有規模宏大的殿宇，也有一舍一佛堂的清淨小庵。

大家可能都知道，九華山佛教以地藏道場而聞名。據古蹟記載，唐代開元年間，古新羅國（今朝鮮半島）王族近屬金喬覺渡海來華，在九華山苦修，於貞元十年（公元764年）夏99歲時圓寂。佛教界以他生前苦行，寂後形跡與經典所載地藏菩薩相合，尊為地藏菩薩應化，在神光嶺上建墓安葬，九華山自此被闢為地藏應化道場，香火日盛。這裡每年定期舉行廟會，一般都要持續10天，已經成為了中國性的旅遊項目，為海內外遊人香客所歡迎。因為時間的關係，我們主要遊覽九華街和天台景區。

九華街景區

現在我們正走在九華街上。九華街位於芙蓉峰下海拔600米的開闊地帶，四面環山，是九華山的接待中心。這裡是佛國，也是街市，寺廟、民宅、商店交錯分布，一條環形小街，終日人來人往，有僧尼，有香客，有遊人，還有當地的普通居民，他們各行其是，既清靜又熱鬧。

祇園寺

大家現在看到的這座寺院是祇園寺，又名祇園禪寺，初建於明代，是九華山唯一的宮殿式完整寺廟，但整個建築並不像宮殿那樣取中軸線對稱形式，而是曲曲折折，連寺門也偏向一邊。大家先請看寺前的浮雕蓮花甬道，上面刻有古錢幣圖案，表現了僧人對虛無縹緲的「七寶蓮池」琉璃世界的憧憬，象徵著釋迦牟尼的聖蹟。進入寺門後，請看兩邊：兩尊金剛居於左右，一哼一哈，令人生畏。中間是靈官護法，他額生豎眼，手執長鞭，顯示出他的職責和佛法不可侵犯。靈官本是道教的神仙，為什麼來到了九華山呢？傳說有一天地藏的護法神韋馱外出巡山，來了個不信佛的狀元，用鋼針朝地藏的腿上扎去，看看是不是真身。一紮果然流出血水，那狀元便急忙下山去了。待韋馱回來問明情由後，不顧地藏的勸阻，偷偷下山追到五溪橋，一鞭打死了狀元。地藏為此十分生氣，逐走了韋馱，請來了靈官。至今，五溪橋頭仍有「狀元墳」遺蹟作為這個傳說的佐證。

肉身寶殿

大家現在來到的是著名的肉身寶殿。1200多年前，高僧金喬覺常到神光嶺上誦經，晏坐。唐貞元十年（公元794年），金喬覺圓寂，依浮屠之法，坐殮缸內，安置於南台（西嶺）。因當時地發神光，此地便改名為神光嶺了。三年後開缸，其遺體綿軟，顏貌如生，撼其骨節有金鎖般響聲，依佛經所示，乃菩薩應世，遂立三級小浮屠供奉，尊為地藏王菩薩，以後又外築高殿，木塔寵護。肉身殿在九華山的廟宇中，可謂是最具特色的建築了，這「殿中有塔，塔中有缸，缸中有肉身」的結構實屬罕見。

天台景區

我們現在已進入天台景區。天台景區位於九華山的東南方，以登高覽盛為特色，九華高峰多匯於此。天台峰海拔1325米，略低於十王峰，但這裡景觀薈萃，古寺重重，歷來被視作九華高峰的中心。我們由閔園上天台，一步一景，越上越奇。

天台寺

現在映入我們眼簾的是天台寺，俗稱萬佛樓，又名地藏禪林。於明代初年興建，清代光緒年間重修。天台寺第一進是彌勒殿，第二進是西方三聖殿，第三進是大雄寶殿即萬佛樓。大家請抬頭看，殿宇的木樑上密密麻麻地排列著萬尊小佛像，千姿百態，栩栩如生。該寺一無院落，二無天井，卻寬敞明亮，足見設計者頗費匠心。殿角小門的崗頭上有一巨大腳印，與東崖上的正好是一對，那是金喬覺騰空跨兩峰時留下的聖蹟。1982年，香港九龍的信士向天台寺捐獻了一只大鼓，天台的鐘聲鼓聲便傳遍了九華山的峰峰嶺嶺。

到此，今天的行程就全部結束。非常感謝大家，祝願大家旅途愉快！

Ancient Villages in Southern Anhui Province （皖南古村落）

Ladies and gentlemen,

Today, we are going to pay a visit to Xidi and Hongcun Villages. Now, I'd like to briefly introduce these two well-known scenic attractions. Xidi and Hongcun Villages are good examples of Southern Anhui Province's culture and its unique ancient villages. They and other such ancient villages have their regional and cultural origins in the region south of the Yangtze River and possess special Huizhou cultural features. Xidi village has been reputed as "A Living Ancient Residential Museum", while Hongcun village is described as "China's Picturesque Village". Both were added to UNESCO's list of World Cultural Heritage sites in 2000.

Xidi Village

Xidi Village is in southeast Yixian County, Anhui Province, with 300 ancient houses built in the Ming and Qing Dynasties, 124 of which are in perfect condition. The design of the streets and lanes and other houses follows the older pattern, maintaining the village's ancient style of life and architecture. Foreign experts have declared that "they are the finest examples of ancient residences under best protection and preservation" and are among the most beautiful villages in the world. "

華東地區

Xidi Village extends 700 meters from east to west and 300 meters from north to south, giving it the shape of a large boat. The village first became prominent during the Ming Dynasty Jingtai Emperor's reign and became highly prosperous from the reign of the Ming Dynasty Jiajing Emperor to the Qing Dynasty Qianlong Emperor's reign. This prosperity was due to the efforts of high-ranking officials and successful merchants. Yet, the strict hierarchy of feudal society was also shown in the construction of residence. The merchants could only choose the best materials and plan most sophisticated workmanship to show off their wealth and position. In Xidi Village, we can see many examples of fine stone, brick, and wood carvings.

The Archway of Hu Wenguang the Prefectural Governor

The first sight that appears before us when we approach Xidi Village is a high archway—the Archway of Hu Wenguang the Prefectural Governor. It is the archway to the honor of Hu Wenguang's merits and virtues. In Southern Anhui Province archways are built for different purposes, including loyalty, merits and virtues, benevolence and filial piety, and chastity. Hu Wenguang, a native of Xidi Village, won his position of candidate in the provincial examination in 1555 and was appointed the County Governor of Wanzai County. During his time in office, he ordered that the city walls be built, set up schools, and contributed much to the benefit of the local people. Later, the Provincial Governor recommended that he be appointed Jiaozhou's Prefectural Governor in charge of oceanic shipping service. Later, he was promoted for several times. In the 6thyear of Ming Dynasty Wanli Emperor's reign, the emperor approved of the establishment of this archway in his hometown to reward his devoted service and efforts for the public interest.

Mansion of the Senior Official

We are now visiting the Mansion where the senior official, Hu Wenzhao once lived in. It was built in 1619 during the early Qing Dynasty and has a unique feature—a delicate and elegant pavilion extends from the upright wall close to the street. The pavilion hangs there, with a flying-up roof and up-turned eaves and has rails and windows along three sides. Originally, it was used for landscape-appreciation. But later, people used it for silk-ball-throwing, a local practice for matching-making between young man and young woman. Such practice is often described in dramas and novels, as those young ladies of rich and decent families could only arbitrarily decide their marriage by throwing silk-ball to anyone who caught it. This was done because it was hard for such ladies to choose among so many suitors. You can now also take part in this activity

and have a bit of fun doing so.

Hongcun Village

Now we are in Hongcun village. Hongcun Village was designed and constructed in the shape of a buffalo. If seen on a higher place, the whole village is like a buffalo lying beside the stream. A hillock in the west stands like a buffalo's head; with two big trees as tow horns; four stone bridges across Jiyang River are like the four legs of the buffalo; the blocks of ancient houses in the village make up the body; while a 1, 000 meter long stream winding among the houses is just like the bowel of the buffalo; a pond in the shape of a half-moon is the stomach, and a larger pool in the south of the village is the belly of the buffalo. The local people used their intelligence and diligence to design and construct such a buffalo-shape village.

Chengzhi Tang (Ambition Hall)

Please look at the building. It is called Cheng-zhi Tang and was built in 1855. It served as the residence of the well-known Qing Dynasty salt merchant, Wang Dinggui. According to an old local saying, "There is no town but with Huizhou-style buildings and there is no business but with merchants from Yixian County." It is obvious that Yixian County men played a very important role in the Huizhou business community. Wang Dinggui was a shrewd salt trader and made large profits from it. In order to honor his ancestry, Wang constructed magnificent residence in his hometown.

Now we are in the center of the courtyard, and here Chengzhi Tang's main hall. The door frame and porch are decorated with wood and brick carvings of vases, ancient plum flowers, the Eight Immortals, and the like. On the two sides of the gate there are the carvings of "Carp Jumping over the Dragon Gate", symbolizing the owner's political ambitions after his success in the business world.

The tour of Xidi and Hongcun villages now has come to an end. Thank you all. I hope you can remember the beauty of the ancient villages in Southern Anhui Province and expect you will come back to visit here again.

華東地區

各位朋友，大家好！我們將前往西遞和宏村景區遊覽。先簡單介紹一下這兩個著名的古村落。西遞和宏村是皖南古村落中最具有代表性的兩座古村落，是皖南地域文化的典型代表。現在我們所指的皖南古村落是指安徽省長江以南山區地域範圍內，具有共同地域文化背景的歷史傳統村落，具有強烈的徽州文化特色。西遞有「中國古民居博物館」之稱，宏村則有「中國畫裡的鄉村」之譽。2000年，它們被聯合國教科文組織列入世界文化遺產名錄。

西遞村

西遞村位於安徽省黟縣東南，村中300幢民居絕大多數是明清時修建，保存完好的有124 幢，街巷布局依然如故，風貌古樸，被國外一些建築專家譽為「世界上保護最完好的古民居建築群」、「世界上最美的村鎮」。

西遞村東西長700米，南北寬300米，平面呈船形。它發展於明朝景泰年間，明嘉靖至清乾隆時期達到鼎盛。西遞之所以興旺，主要是因為村中屢出高官和富商，聚集了大量的財富，有了較雄厚的經濟基礎。但是在封建社會，建築府第宅院是有嚴格的等級規範的，徽商只能儘可能地選用上好的石頭、木材，在精雕細刻上下工夫，並以此作為炫耀財富和地位的手段。所以在西遞，精美的石雕、磚雕、木雕隨處可見。

胡文光刺史坊

大家看，前面就是西遞村，村頭迎面矗立的一座高大的石牌坊，叫胡文光刺史坊。這是一座功德牌坊。順便介紹一下，在徽州，牌坊分為忠義、功德、慈孝、貞節四類。胡文光，西遞村人，於明代嘉靖三十四年（公元1555年）中舉，擔任過萬載縣縣令，築城牆、修學校，做了不少利國利民的好事。後經巡撫推薦，擔任了膠州刺史兼理海運。後來又被多次提升。明萬曆年間，皇帝批准胡文光的鄉親在此建立了這座功德牌坊，以表達胡文光在任期間對民眾做的好事。

大夫第

大家現在參觀的是大夫第。它建於清康熙三十年（公元1619年），為朝列大夫胡文照故居。大夫第有個突出的特點，就是在臨街牆的平面，懸空挑出一座小巧玲瓏、古樸典雅的亭閣式建築。閣頂飛檐翹角,三面有欄杆、排窗,顯得突兀別緻。這座懸閣危樓原本是用於觀景的,但後來人們便把它作為**拋綵球**的繡樓了。**拋**繡球這種事,大家在小說和戲劇中都看到過的。人多是這些待守閨中的小姐,或者因求婚者多,且多有權勢,如何抉擇左右為難,或者是因待守少女擇婚主張與父母意見不合,愛女也許早有意中人,於是便出現了**拋**綵球選婿這種戲劇性做法。現在有興趣的朋友也可以參與一下,看看自己的運氣如何。

宏村

不知不覺,我們已經步入了宏村。宏村是一座「牛形村」,整個村莊從高處看,宛若一頭斜臥山前溪邊的青牛。西邊的雷崗巍巍而立,宛如「牛首」;村口的兩棵參天古樹恰似「牛角」;前後四座橫跨吉陽水的橋樑正如「牛腿」;村中數百幢明清古建築,猶如臥牛盤踞;一條公里之長的水渠環繞全村,盤曲流經各家各戶,這是「牛腸」;村中一半月形池塘,那就是「牛胃」;村南有一較大水面南湖,那是「牛肚」。宏村人用自己的智慧和辛勤的汗水,做活、做絕了牛形村,創造了絕妙的田園風光。

承志堂

大家請看這座建築,這是承志堂,是清代大鹽商汪定貴的住宅,建於清咸豐五年(公元1855年)。有句古語叫「無徽不成鎮,無黟不成商」,可見「黟縣幫」當年在徽商中的重要位置。據說汪定貴為人精明,經營鹽業發了大財,為了光宗耀祖,便在家鄉大興土木,建造豪華住宅。

現在我們到了院**內**正中,是承志堂正堂。先讓我們看看它的門罩,門樓上的雕刻,同別的庭院一樣,有磚雕花瓶、古梅、八仙等。八字門樓的兩邊,刻有「鯉魚跳龍門」,反映了房主在占有大量財富後企求政治上飛黃騰達的願望。

西遞和宏村之旅到此就要結束了,感謝大家,希望大家能記住皖南古村落的秀美,有空再來看看。

華東地區

Part III Mid-South China中南地區

Henan Province河南省

A Glimpse of the Province （本省簡介）

Henan Province is located in eastern central China, on the plain between the Yellow and Huaihe rivers. Since most of Henan is south of the Yellow River, which runs for over 700 km through the province, it was given the name Henan (South of the River). Neighboring Hebei, Shaanxi, Hubei, Anhui and Shandong provinces, Henan covers an area of 167, 000 square kilometers.

Located between the northern sub-tropical zone and warm temperate zone, Henan has four distinctive seasons with complicated weather conditions characterized by hot and rainy summers. Southern Henan is in the northern sub-tropical zone. The province's average yearly temperature is 13℃ -15℃, the average annual rainfall is 570-1, 120 milimeters, and has on average 275 to 308 frost-free days a year. Henan Province is in

中南地區

the transitional area between the second and third steps of China's four-step terrain rising from east to west, with rolling mountains over 1, 000 meters above sea level in its western part and plain area that is no more than 100 meters above sea level in its east. The 2, 413. 8-meter-high Laoyacha Peak, which is located near Lingbao City, is Henan's highest mountain. The province's lowest point, 23. 2 meters, is located at the place where the Huaihe River leaves the province.

High in the west and low in the east, even in the north and concave in the south, Henan is surrounded by four mountain ranges, the Taihang, Funiu, Tongbai and Dabie, which stand in its north, west and south, leaving subsidence basins here and there. In its middle and eastern parts there is a vast fluvial plain created by the Yellow, Huaihe and Haihe rivers. Mountainous regions comprise 44. 3%of its total area, and the plains, 55. 7%. Four rivers run across Henan, the Yellow River, Huaihe River, Weihe River and Hanshui River, with the Huaihe River valley covering up 53% of the province.

Tourism Resources

As one of the major birthplaces of the Chinese civilization, several epoch-making archeological discoveries have been made in Henan, including the Peiligang Culture Site dating back 7, 000 years, the 6, 000-year-old Yangshao Culture Site, and the 5, 000-year-old Dahe Culture Site. More than 20 ancient Chinese dynasties have established their capitals in Henan. Three of China's seven great ancient capitals are located in Henan:Anyang, the Shang Dynasty's capital, Luoyang, the capital of nine dynasties, and Kaifeng, the capital of seven dynasties. Three of ancient China's four great inventions, the compass, paper-making and gunpowder, were made in Henan. More underground cultural relics are located in Henan than in any other places in China and the province ranks second highest with respect to the number of cultural relics on the ground. The Yellow River, with numerous ancient relics and scenic attractions, provides Henan another rich tourist resource.

Local Snacks

Notable local snacks and dishes include Liyu Beimian (carp covered with baked noodles in sweet and sour sauce), Luoyang Shuixi (feast highlighted by Luoyang style soup), Songgong Miangao (pastry originating from the Song Dynasty Imperial Palace).

Local Culture

Yuju (Henan Opera) is the most important opera genre; other operas include Quju, Yue Diao, and the Henan bangzi.

Special Local Products

The traditional specialties are Bianjing roast duck, Kaifeng Henan embroidery, Xinyang Maojian Tea, and Ruyang Dukang Wine. There are also many famous specialties produced in Henan Province, such as Yuanyang rice, Xinzheng Chinese date, Kaifeng water-melon, Qixian and Zhongmou garlic, Xinyang pale coloured tips and chestnut, Xixia Chinese gooseberry, Lingbao apple, Jiaozuo yam and Luoyang peony flowers. Among these specialties, the Luoyang peony flowers are famous not only in China, but across the world as well.

中南地區

Tourism City

Zhengzhou is the capital of Henan province. It is of great strategic importance in China as the "Hinterland of nine divisions and thoroughfare of ten provinces" . With the Yellow River to the north and the Songshan Mountain to the west, Zhengzhou sits astride the Huanghuai Plain. Luoyang is renowned for its history and served as the capital of 13 dynasties. It is recognized as the Capital of Poems for its numerous literati and the Capital of Flowers for its peony flowers. During the Song Dynasty (960-1279 A.D.), Kaifeng was not only China's political, economic and cultural center, but also one of the most prosperous international capitals. As you walk about its ancient streets today, you can still see many traces of this earlier prosperity.

Attraction Recommendation

Due to its central position in Chinese history, Henan has an abundance of tourist sites and attractions. The places of interest include Songshan and Jigong Mountains, the Eastern Zhou Dynasty (770-256 B.C.) Imperial Mausoleum, White Horse Temple in Luoyang, Longmen Grottoes, Chancellor Temple in Kaifeng, Shaolin Temple in Dengfeng, Zhongyue Temple, Songyang and Yingtian Academies of Classical Learning, and Dufu and Xuan Zang former residences.

河南省位於中國的中東部，處於黃河與淮河之間的平原上。黃河貫穿河南達700公里，因為大部分地區位於黃河之南，所以稱為河南。河南占地167000平方公里，近鄰河北、陝西、湖北、安徽以及山東。

河南省屬北亞熱帶與暖溫帶過渡區氣候，具有四季分明、雨熱同期、複雜多樣的特點。南部屬北亞熱帶，全省年平均氣溫為13℃　～15℃，年平均降水量570～1120 毫米。全年無霜期275 ～308 天。河南地處中國地勢第二階梯向第三階梯的過渡帶，西部山地綿延起伏，海拔高公里以上，東部為平原，海拔在百米之下。靈寶市的老鴉岔為全省最高峰，海拔高度為2413.8米，海拔最低處為淮河出省處，僅23.2米。

河南省地勢西高東低、北坦南凹，北、西、南三面有太行山、伏牛山、桐柏山、大別山四大山脈環繞，間有陷落盆地，中部和東部為遼闊的黃淮海沖積大平原。山區丘陵面積占44.3%，平原面積占55.7%。境內有黃河、淮河、衛河、漢水四大水系，其中淮河流域面積占53%。

旅遊資源

河南是華夏文明的主要發祥地之一。在河南已經發現的7000　年前的裴李崗文化遺址、6000 年前的仰韶文化遺址和5000 年前的大河文化遺址，在中華民族的發展史上均有劃時代的意義。在中華民族數千年的文明史中，先後有20多個朝代在此建都或遷都。中國已確定的七大古都河南有其三，即殷商古都安陽、九朝古都洛陽和七朝古都開封。中國古代四大發明中的指南針、造紙、火藥三大技術均發明於河南。河南地下文物居中國第一位，地上文物居中國第二位。眾多的文物古蹟和著名的黃河等自然風光構成了河南豐富的旅遊資源。

風味食品

糖醋　鯉魚焙麵，洛陽「水席」，宋宮麵，小籠灌湯包子，「套四寶」。

地方文藝

豫劇是河南最大劇種。此外還有曲劇、越調、河南梆子。

地方特產

河南特產名食有汴京烤鴨，名酒有汝陽杜康酒，其他農特產有碧綠清香、中國十大名茶之一的信陽毛尖等。此外，河南有很多名優特產品，如原陽大米、新鄭大棗、開封西瓜、杞縣及中牟大蒜和板栗、西峽奇異果、靈寶蘋果、焦作四大懷藥等。洛陽牡丹馳名中外。

主要旅遊城市

鄭州為河南省會，地處中華腹地，九州之中，十省通衢，北臨黃河，西依嵩山，東、南接黃淮平原。河南洛陽是一座歷史悠久的文化名城，從夏朝以來，有13個王朝在此建都。洛陽因文人雲集而得名「詩都」，又因牡丹花香氣四溢而被名為「花都」。開封曾為宋都，直到今天，走在舊時的宋都御街上，仍能想像當時店鋪林立，車水馬龍的熱鬧景象。

主要推薦景點

中南地區

河南省具有豐富的旅遊資源，包括上古文化遺址、太昊陵、東周王陵、北宋皇陵，還有蘇秦故里、玄奘故里、杜甫故里、白馬寺、少林寺、相國寺、龍門石窟等古蹟值得一遊，洛陽太學、嵩陽書院、應天府書院等古代學府墨香猶存。

Longmen Grottoes （龍門石窟）

Ladies and gentlemen,

Welcome to Longmen Grottoes. They are located in the south of Luoyang City. They are between Mount Xiang and Mount Longmen and face Yi River. Longmen Grottoes, Yungang Caves and Mogao Caves are regarded as the three most famous treasure houses of stone inscriptions in China. The grottoes were started around the year 494 when Emperor Xiaowen of the Northern Wei Dynasty (386-534 A.D.) moved the capital to Luoyang. Work on them continued for another 400 years until the Northern Song Dynasty (960-1127 A.D.). The first caves of Longmen were excavated in 494, the 12th year of the Northern Wei Dynasty Xiaowen Emperor's reign. The grottoes extend for some 1, 000 metres (about 1, 094 yards) from north to south. They contain over 2, 300 holes and niches, 2, 800 steles, 40 stupas, 1, 300 caves and 97, 000 sculptured figures that have survived the test of time. Most of these works date from the Northern Wei Dynasty and the flourishing age of the Tang Dynasty (618-907 A.D.). Lots of historical materials concerning art, music, religion, calligraphy, medicine, costume and architecture are stored in the Longmen Grottoes.

Fengxian Temple

Fengxian Temple was built in the Tang Dynasty and it is the largest grotto in Longmen Grottoes with a width of 36 metres (about 118 feet) and a length of 41 metres (about 136 feet). There are nine major figures of various facial appearances and temperaments in the temple that were built in accordance with Buddhist rites by the artists. The most impressive figure is the statue of Vairocana Buddha sitting cross-legged on the eight-square lotus throne. It is 17. 14 metres (about 56 feet) high; the head alone is four meters (about 13 feet) high, and the ears are nearly 2 metres (about 6 feet) long. Vairocana means illuminating all things in the sutra. The Buddha has a well-filled figure, a sacred and kindly expression and an elegant smile. According to the record on the epigraph, the Empress Wu Zetian together with her subjects took part in the ceremony of Introducing the Light (a Buddhist blessing that the Buddha opens the spiritual light of himself and shares it with others). At the sides of Vairocana there are two statues of Vairocana Buddha's disciples, Kasyapa and Ananda, wearing prudent and devout expressions. The figures of Bodhisattvas and Devas can also be found in the temple. Some have dignified and genial expressions, while others are majestic and fiery. The various appearances and delicate designs are the representations of the Tang Empire's powerful material and spiritual strength and the wisdom of its people.

Wanfo Cave

The Wanfo Cave which was completed in 680, is a typical cave of the Tang Dynasty of two rooms and square flat roofs. Its name is due to the 15, 000 small statues of Buddha chiseled in the southern and northern walls of the cave. The main Buddha Amida sits on the lotus throne, having a composed and solemn face. The wall behind Amida is carved with 54 lotuses, upon which there are 54 Bodhisattvas in different shapes and with various expressions. In addition, very pretty and charming lifelike singers and dancers are also chiseled on the wall. The singers are accompanied by various kinds of instruments and the dancers dance lightly and gracefully to the music, giving the cave a lively and cheerful atmosphere. A 85 centimeter high statue of Kwan-yin holding a pure bottle in his left hand and a deer's tail—a symbol of brushing off the dust in spirit—in right hand is on cave's southern outside wall. This figure is well designed and is regarded as the Longmen Grottoes' best example of a Tang Dynasty Bodhisattva statue.

Guyang Cave

中南地區

Guyang Cave is the oldest cave in Longmen Grottoes. There are three tiers of niches on the northern and southern wall of the cave, in which are hundreds of statues, and most of the statues are engraved with the names of the artists, the dates and the reasons for carving them. The sculptures are of diverse shapes and patterns that are representations of the Gandhara Art style after the grotto art transmitted to Luoyang. A statue of Sakyamuni is situated in the middle and is nearly 8 meters (about 26 feet) high. Nineteen of the most famous Twenty Calligraphies are found in Guyang Cave. The Twenty Calligraphies represent the Wei style steles, which are the Longmen Grottoes'basic stele calligraphies.

Binyang Cave

After constructing the Guyang Cave, the royalty of the Northern Wei Dynasty carved out a series of lager scale caves, which are the northern, southern, and middle Binyang Caves. The middle cave took the longest time to complete (from 500 to 523) and is the only one of the three finished during Northern Wei period. There are 11 big statues in the cave. Sakyamuni is of dignified and serene appearance, while his disciple and Bodhisattva are of slender figure and elegant look, which are the typical style of the late Northern Wei Dynasty. The floor is engraved with lotus patterns and on the rooftop is a flourishing lotus flower relief.

Lotus Cave (Lianhua Cave)

Chiseled grottoes on the base of the natural limestone caves are also seen in Longmen, and the Lotus Cave is one of them. Unlike the sitting statues, Sakyamuni is of standing figure, showing that he has trudged a long distance to develop Buddhism from India to China. A huge relief of a well sculpted lotus flower is engraved on the dome, with a seed bud in the center and petals of honeysuckle patters circling around. Around the lotus are six flying musicians with vivid gestures, as if they are dancing along with the melodies of the music.

Xiangshan Temple

Xiangshan Temple, which is ranked the first among Longmen Grottoes'ten temples, is situated in the middle mountainside of the East Hill. The East Longmen Hill is teeming with spices and is therefore very fragrant smelling. It's name, Xiangshan, means "Fragrant Hill" in Mandarin. The temple was also named Xiangshan Temple. The present Xianshan Temple was reconstructed during the Qing Dynasty in 1707 and this work was based on the old Temple's design. In 2002, Xiangshan Temple was expanded on the basis of the Qing Xiangshan Temple by Longmen Grottoes Administration, with a newly constructed Bell and Drum Tower, Wing Room, as well as Halls of Mahavira and Nine Persons. In addition, the belfry, Hall of Arhats, Emperor Qianlong's stele and palace, Wing-room, Jiang Jieshi and Song Meiling's Villa, along with the stairs, plank roads and temple walls have all been rebuilt and restored. A new gate was constructed south of the temple. The temple takes on a new look today, and it is really a rare scenic world cultural landmark.

Bai Garden

The Bai Garden is located on Pipa Peak north of East Longmen Hill (Xiangshan Hill) and was reconstructed by Tang Youzeng of the Qing Dynasty in 1709. The temple is surrounded by green pine trees and cypress, looking solemn and serene. It was designated a key site for protection at the state level by the State Council in 1961. The tomb of Bai Juyi is a round mound of earth, 4 meters high, with a circumference of 52 meters. In front of the tomb stands 2. 8-meter-high tombstone, which reads, "The Tomb of Bai Juyi" . Bai Juyi's family was originally from Taiyuan in Shanxi Province and then moved to neighboring Shaanxi Province. He lived from 772 to 846 A.D., and his style name was Letian. Bai Juyi was one of the Tang Dynasty's most outstanding poets and enjoyed great literary fame both in and outside of China. He held a number of high government posts and instructed a prince during his later years. After retiring, he came to Luoyang and made good friends with "Nine Persons of Xiangshan Hill" , who

中
南
地
區

often composed and sang poems at the Longmen Grottoes. Meanwhile, he donated money for the construction of Xiangshan Temple. When Bai Juyi died, he was buried, in accordance to his will, in the present Bai Garden. The important scenic spots in the Bai Garden are the Tingyi, Cuiyue, Bai, and Songfeng Pavilions, Letian Hall, Bird's Head Gate, Pipa Peak, Bai Juyi's Tomb, Wogu Tablet, Poem Corridor, and Daoshi Reading Room. As a garden constructed according to style of the Tang Dynasty, it is both a tourist resort and a good place to pay homage to the great poet.

In addition, there is Prescription Cave that has about 140 prescriptions engraved on the walls, showing the achievements of ancient Chinese medicine. Some of the prescriptions are still used today. Other caves and temples like Xiangshan Temple, Huangfu Cave, and Qianxi Temple can also be found at the Longmen Grottoes.

Well, my friends, Longmen Grottoes's visit nearly come to an end, and I have to say goodbye to you all. Anyway I am very glad to have spent such a happy and unforgettable day with you. Welcome you to come here again for sightseeing. Thank you all!Have a happy journey! Goodbye!

　　各位朋友大家好！我們現在要去參觀遊覽龍門石窟。龍門石窟位於河南省洛陽市南郊，處於香山（東）、龍門山（西）兩山之間，面朝伊水。它同甘肅的敦煌石窟、山西大同的雲岡石窟並稱中國古代佛教石窟藝術的三大寶庫。龍門石窟開鑿於北魏孝文帝遷都洛陽（公元494年），直至北宋前後延續四百多年。龍門石窟南北長約1000米，現存洞和窟共2300個，窟龕2800個，佛塔40餘座，石窟1300多個，佛像97000餘尊。絕大部分是北魏和盛唐時期的作品。大量涉及藝術、音樂、宗教、雕刻、醫藥、服飾和建築的歷史材料被保存在龍門石窟中。

　　奉先寺

　　奉先寺是龍門唐代石窟中最大的一個石窟，長為41米，寬為36米。在寺中，藝術家塑造了9個相貌、氣質各異的佛教神像。最能給人留下印象的是正中盧舍那佛的叉腿坐像。這個佛像身高17.14米，頭高4米，耳朵長1.9 米。盧舍那意即光明遍照。這尊佛像豐頤秀目，嘴角微翹，呈微笑狀。據造像銘載，女皇武則天曾親率朝臣參加了盧舍那佛的「開光」儀式。在盧舍那佛兩側有兩尊佛像，他們是迦葉和阿難。這兩位菩薩衣飾華麗，端莊而矜持。天王和力士也能從寺中找到，有的嚴肅威武而碩壯有力，有的堅毅勇猛而無所畏懼。這些形神兼備、維妙維肖的佛像，反映了唐帝國強大的物質和精神力量，也反映了唐代人民高超的技藝和智慧。

萬佛洞

萬佛洞完工於公元680 年，前後兩室，有一平頂廣場，是典型的唐代建築。它因洞內南北兩壁雕刻的一萬五千多尊小佛像而得名。正壁主尊阿彌陀佛高約4米，頭飾波狀髮髻，面相豐滿圓潤，結跏趺坐於八角形束腰須彌蓮花座上，神情安詳肅穆。後壁刻著五十四枝蓮花，每枝蓮花上各坐一尊菩薩或供養人，構思新穎奇特。南北兩壁壁基雕有多尊伎樂人和舞者。伎樂人手持各種樂器，形象生動傳神，似乎已陶醉在自己奏出的天籟之聲中。舞者婀娜多姿，衣袂飄飄，彷彿正在精心演繹最曼妙的舞蹈。整個洞窟營造了一種西天極樂世界裡歌舞昇平，萬人成佛的場景。洞外南壁雕有觀世音菩薩像，勻稱適度，右手執塵尾，左手提淨瓶，表現了「萬法皆空歸南海，一塵不染靜禪心」的佛家至高境界。這個佛像設計精美，是唐石刻觀音菩薩的傑作。

古陽洞

古陽洞是龍門石窟中開鑿最早的一座洞窟。古陽洞北側牆壁上排列了三層大型佛龕，裡面很多佛龕造像，這些佛龕造像多有題記，記錄了當時造像者的姓名、造像年月及緣由，這些都是研究北魏書法和雕刻藝術的珍貴資料。這些題記的式樣和風格代表了隨後傳至洛陽的魏碑體。一尊高7.82米的釋迦牟尼像安坐在洞窟中央。舉世聞名的「龍門二十品」中古陽洞獨占十九品。「龍門二十品」代表北魏「秀骨清像」造像風格，是龍門石窟的精髓所在。

賓陽洞

中南地區

興建古陽洞之後，北魏王室又建造了一系列大型洞窟，那就是賓陽北洞、賓陽南洞和賓陽中洞。賓陽中洞從公元500年開鑿直到523年停工，是三洞中唯一在北魏時期完成的。洞中有11尊大佛像，主佛釋迦牟尼表情溫和，神采飄逸，體態修長，面容清瘦，造像手法是典型的北魏後期的風格。賓陽中洞的地面雕刻著大型蓮花，周邊是蓮花花瓣、水波紋和其他裝飾圖案，如同鮮艷美麗的地毯式樣子。

蓮花洞

龍門石窟中也有基於自然洞穴而雕刻成的石窟，蓮花洞便是其中典型一例。與一般的坐像不同，這裡的釋迦牟尼是站像，體現了他長途跋涉從印度往中國宣傳佛法之艱辛。穹隆頂上雕有一朵碩大精美的蓮花，花瓣朝外，每片都有不同的風格。圍繞蓮花，還有6 個手捧果品、迎風飛翔的大型飛天浮雕，婀娜多姿，生動傳神，而天衣、雲彩隨著天女的舞動在翩飛飄揚。

香山寺

號稱「龍門十寺」之首的千年古剎香山寺位於龍門東山山腰。東龍門山因其香味而被稱為「香閣」，也稱香山，其寺便稱為香山寺。現有的香山寺是於清朝年間（公元 1707 年）在舊址上重建的。2002年，龍門管理局在清代香山寺的基礎上進行了擴建，包括興建了鐘鼓樓、大雄寶殿、廂房、門樓、觀景廊、蓮花池、南北山上步遊道等仿古建築；改建、維修了天王殿、羅漢殿、御碑亭、蔣宋別墅、衣鉢塔等舊有建築。景區管理部門還對香山寺及龍門東、西兩山石窟群周邊環境進行了清理。現在的香山寺已經恢復「危樓切漢，飛閣凌霄，石像七龕，浮屠八角」的風貌，確實是不可多得的美景。

白園

白園位於龍門東山（香山）琵琶峰，為清代唐友曾重建（公元1709年）。園內松柏蔥鬱，景色清麗。1961年與龍門石窟一起被列為國家級重點文物保護單位。園內的白居易墓高4米，四周有52米長的圍牆。在墓前有一高2.8 米的墓碑，上刻有「白居易之墓」。白居易，字樂天，祖籍山西太原後遷至陝西，生於公元772年，卒於公元846年。作為中國唐代著名詩人之一，白居易在國內外文學界都有較高聲譽。他在朝廷擔任多個職務，晚年曾為太師，告退後來到洛陽，與經常在龍門賦詩作曲的香山九老結為好友，並捐贈修建香山寺。他死後，人們按其意願將他葬於白園。白園建有清谷、聽伊亭、樂天堂、白亭、烏頭門、道時書屋、詩廊、翠樾亭等仿唐建築，是一個緬懷偉大詩人的優美景點。

這裡還有藥王洞，牆壁上刻有140 個藥方，體現了中國古代的醫學成就。有些藥方沿用至今。其他的洞和寺廟如皇甫洞和潛溪寺等也在龍門石窟中。

好了，各位遊客，龍門石窟參觀活動就要結束了，歡迎大家有機會再到這裡參觀旅遊，謝謝！再見！

Songshan Shaolin Temple （嵩山少林寺）

Ladies and Gentlemen,

Welcome to the world-famous Songshan Shaolin Temple in Henan province. It is my honor to be your tour guide. Now we are going to visit the birth place of Chinese Zen, the Shaolin Temple. The construction of Shaolin Temple began during the 19th year of the Northern Wei Dynasty Xiaowen (Yuan Hong) Emperor's reign (495 A.D.) to settle the Indian Buddhist priest Batuo. It is named "Shaolin Temple" because it is located in the midst of Shaoshi Mountain's forests. In 527, the 3rdyear of the Northern Wei Dynasty Taihe Emperor's reign, Bodhi Dharma, a 28thGeneration Buddha, arrived at Shaolin after three years' long journey. His arrival sparked the rapid growth of Zen Buddhism's influence and popularity. Hence, Shaolin Temple is known as "the imperial sacrifices courtyard" throughout the Buddhist world and developed rapidly, especially after the thirteen sticks monks rescued Li Shimin, a very famous and able emperor in Chinese history. The temple won an important place in the Tang dynasty and was reputed to be the "Number One ancient temple in the world".

中南地區

For present Shaolin Temple, the ancient and mystical Buddhism has brought its name far in the world. However, Shaolin is most renowned in China and elsewhere for its exquisite Shaolin Kung Fu. As an old saying goes, "the Chinese Kung Fu crowns the world and its source is the Shaolin Temple". The temple is the cradle of Shaolin martial arts, which are universally acknowledged as the orthodox martial arts school in China.

The Shaolin Temple scenic area is one of the most famous tourist attractions in China. In 2000 the Shaolin Temple scenic area was designated a first batch 4A level traveling area and recognized by the national travel agency as the highest-level Chinese tourist attraction.

The Shaolin Temple scenic area consists of the Shaolin Temple, Pagoda Forest, Anc-estor's and Second Ancestor's Monasteries, Dharma Cave, Yongtai Temple and Shaoshi Tower and other main scenic sites.

Shaolin Temple

Ladies and gentlemen, we are now approaching the Shaolin Temple. Shaolin Temple is at the core of Shaolin Temple scenic area and is the place where the deacon monks and priests carry out Buddhist religious ceremonies. It has 7 rows of rooms, covering more than 30, 000 square meters.

Now we are standing in front of Shanmen, or mountain gate. The Shanmen is Shaolin Temple's front gate and was first built during the Qing Dynasty and was rebuilt in 1975. The Chinese characters, Shaolin Temple, were handwritten by the Qing Emperor Kangxi. Its seal, the "treasure of the Kangxi Emperor brush", is off to the side.

The two lions beside the entrance were made in the Ming Dynasty. They are vertically engraved in Buddhist style to symbolize good fortune. There are also two stone tortoises outside, and they were constructed during the Ming Dynasty.

Pay attention here, please. The figure in the palace entrance with the big stomach is Maitreya, who is the Buddha that welcomes guests. His benign smiling countenance greets you as you arrive. It is said of the Maitreya Buddha that the "the solemn grave entrance happy to look the glory illuminating, smiles welcome the coming person to pray for heavenly blessing and infinite happiness".

Behind the entrance palace niche is a statue consecrating the Bodhisattva, the person who protects Buddhist Jin'gang law. He grasps the Jin'gang valuable pestle and protects the temple's three treasures:the temple Buddha, Buddhist law, and the monks'security.

Please look around. There are many stele carvings along the entrance road's two sides. This is the Shaolin Temple stele forest. The Shaolin Temple tablet porch is located east of the Stele forest. It not only records the temple's rises and declines, but also provides a valuable historical record for research on the Temple and its carving is a valuable work of art. Shaolin Temple's stele forest and the tablet porch have a total of 108 pieces of stele carvings.

Chuipu Hall is located on the west side of Stele Forest. It has 42 blocks around the corridor. It uses the clay sculpture and the woodcarving to vividly demonstrate the Shaolin Temple martial arts. These carvings illustrate Kongfu's origins, development, repertoire, and role in national defense. They all show monk soldiers using martial arts during combat. There are 14 groups of 216 hammers spectra pictures depicting fighting techniques, such as running circles around Buddha, the eight different brocade sections, small red, scarlet, arm passing, Luo-Han, and illustrious positive fists. The actual fighting scenes shown include the 13 sticks monk rescuing Qin Wang, Xiaoshan Buddhist priest as commander-in-chief preparing to go to battle, and Yuekong master battling Japanese pirates. It is said that "After spending five minutes in Chuipu Hall, one can practice Shaolin Kung Fu. " And in fact, everybody may practice the Shaolin Kung Fu by studying and following these cast postures.

Now, we are entering an entirely rebuilt structure, the Hall of Heavenly God. The original hall was burned down in 1928 and was repaired in 1982. These two big Jingang outside palace gate are "generals Heng and Ha" . Their responsibility is to protect the Buddhist doctrine. The main hall inside has four great heavenly gods, which are also called the four big Jin'gang. Their responsibilities include monitoring the good and evil behavior of all the living creatures, helping the distressed, and bestowing blessings upon the world.

Shaolin's central temple is Mahavira Hall and is where ceremonial Buddhist activities take place. It and the Hall of Heavenly God were both burned down in 1928 by the warlord Shi Yousan. Mahavira Hall was reconstructed in 1985. The middle statuary in the hall is the present world Buddha, the Buddha Sakyamuni, while the one on the left is the past world Buddha, represented by the colored glazed world pharmacist Buddha in the east. Over to the right is the future world Buddha, the extremely happy world Amitabha Buddha in the west. Figures of Kingnaro, the Shaolin Cudgel's founder, and Dharma, the founder of Chinese Zen Buddhism, stand beside those three Buddhas. This placement is very different from that of other Mahavira Halls. At the feet of the pillars in this Mahavira Hall are stone lions that are more than one meter (a little over 3 feet) high.

On both sides in front of the Mahavira Hall stand the Bell and Drum Towers. The original towers were also destroyed in 1928. They were rebuilt in 1994 and the bell is rung every hour during the moring, while a drum is beaten every hour during the afternoon. Hence, the saying "morning bell and afternoon drum" .

In front of the Bell Tower is the stele "Emperor Songshan Shaolin Temple Tablet" , also called "the Stele of Li Shimin" . It was engraved in 16thyear (728

A.D.) of the Tang Dynasty Emperor Xuanzong's reign. The frontpiece is a story written by Li Shimin describing Shaolin monks rescued Prince Li Shimin from Wang Shichong. Li Shimin later became a Tang Dynasty Emperor and personally wrote the stele inscriptions. His signature is on the fifth column to the right of the stele. The seven large brush-written Chinese characters, "the Second Emperor Wen Imperial Handwriting", on the stele carving is the handwriting of the Tang Dynasty Xuanzong Li Longji Emperor. The backpiece is "Li Shimin Bestows Shaolin Temple the Bai Guzhuang Imperial Book". This book records the story of how the 13 sticks monks rescued Qin Wang and also served the historical basis for the celebrated martial arts movie, "Shaolin Temple".

Just north of the "Li Shimin Tablet" is the "Xiaoshan Master's Merits Tablet". It records the exploits of the Shaolin Temple's Cao Dongzong, or the 24thgeneration Chuanfa master and how his merits have inspired the Shaolin monks. At its back is the "All Sorts of People Tablet"; its top quarter is a pictorial depiction of Buddhism, Daoism and Confucianism. The tablet reflects Mt.Songshan's importance as a common meeting place for Buddhism, Daoism, and Confucianism and underscores the confluence between the three major religions. Now look north and you will see the "Qianlong Imperial Tablet", which was engraved during the 15thyear (1750 A.D.) of the Qing Dynasty Qianlong Emperor's rule.

The palace on the east side is Kingnaro hall, which was reconstructed in 1982. Here you can see three different images of Kingnaro, the God who protects the Shaolin Temple.

On the west side of Kingnaro hall is the sixth ancestor palace. It was reconstructed in 1982. It consecrates the Situation, Puvirtuous, and Manjusri Bodhisattvas, as well as the Goddess of Mercy. Two sides consecrate the first ancestor of the Zen Dharma, second ancestor Huike, third ancestor Sengcan, the fourth ancestor Daoxin, the fifth ancestor Hongren, and the sixth ancestor Huineng. People esteem them

中南地區

as six ancestors trans-formed by the Goddess of Mercy. On the west wall is the large-scale painted sculpture "Dharma turns over to the west with one shoe" .

This structure is known as Depositary of Buddhist Sutras and was built during the Ming Dynasty. It was destroyed in 1928 and rebuilt in 1994. Rare books concerning secrets of martial arts are also safely kept here.

The Depositary of Buddhist Sutras' east wing is the East Meditation Room, while the west wing is the West Reception Room. The former is used by Buddhist priests for meditation, while the latter is used for receiving guests.

This is the Shaolin Temple abbot/abbess court and is where the abbots live. Emperor Qianlong once stayed here when traveling to Mt.Songshan. A Yuan Dynasty clock is on the east side and its purpose is to sound the alarm during emergencies.

This pavilion is named Dharma's Pavilion or Lixue Pavilion, which means "Standing in the snow" in English. It says:After Buddha Dharma came to China, many Chinese Buddhists wanted to be his followers, and Shengguang was the most prominent of them. He always followed him whenever and wherever he went and whole-heartedly served Buddha Dharma. But Dharma didn't want to accept Shengguang as a disciple. Shengguang didn't lose heart and became even more steadfast. On a snowy night, he begged as usual with Bodhidharma outside, standing in the knee-high snow. The master set forward a prerequisite:he would not meet his demand unless it would snow in red flakes. Shengguang drew out the sword and cut off his left arm and stained the snowy ground. Bodhidharma was so moved that he passed his mantle, alms bowl and musical instruments on to Shengguang and gave him a Buddhist name of Huike. He was regarded as the second founder of the Zen sect. Emperor Qianlong wrote a phrase on a plaque in commendation.

The Manjusri Palace is located on Dharma Pavilion's east side and consecrates the

Manjusri Bodhisattva. Everyone please follow me to visit the highest most holy Shaolin Temple hall.

All right, everyone, now we are in the last hall, Pilu Hall, also called the Thousand Buddha Hall. It's also Shaolin Temple's main highlight and was built during the Ming Dynasty. The hall is 20 meters high and covers over 300 square meters, making it Shaolin Temple's largest Buddhist hall. It consecra-tes the Pilu Buddha in the center of the palace. Look at the floor. There are 48 pits in 4 rows on the hall's brick floor; that's where Shaolin monks used to stand and practice Kung Fu. Those pits are called "Zhanzhuangkeng" in Chinese. It is said that they are the footprints left by monks when they practiced Shaolin Martial Arts. We can know how wonderful they were from these foot pits.

So until now, the visit of the Shaolin Temple is almost over. I think you may have some questions about the temple, or you want to take some photos. So, please do remember, you have half an hour. After half an hour we will gather at the Front Gate Hall, and make sure you'll be there on time. And then we are going to the Pagoda Forest.

Pagoda Forest

Now, we come to the Pagoda Forest, the Temple's graveyard for Buddhist dignitaries through the ages. Its total area is 14, 000 square meters. In 1996, the State Council included it in China's national cultural relic preservation program. There are 240 towers made in bricks and stones in the Pagoda Forest dating back to the Tang, Song, Jin, Yuan, and Ming Dynasties. The Shaolin Temple's Pagoda Forest is the oldest and largest one in China. On average, the pagodas are less than 15 meters (about 49 feet) high. The layer and the shape of a pagoda depend on many factors, such as one's Buddhist status, attainment and prestige.

中南地區

The Ancestor's and Second Ancestor's Monasteries

Outside the temple we continue walking to northwest, and then we will take a look at two monasteries, named the Ancestor's and Second Ancestor's Monasteries. The first monastery is built by a Dharma disciple to commemorate the Dharma's nine years of meditation in a cave. It has a big hall supported by 16 stone pillars on whose shafts are exquisitely carved warriors, dancing dragons and phoenixes. The second monastery is a nursing home of the second ancestor Huike who cut his left arm in order to show his sincerity to study Buddhism from Dharma. Four springs created by Dharma to make it possible for Huike to easily fetch his water are in front of the monastery. They are called "Spring Zhouxi" and each has its own distinctive flavor.

Dharma Cave

The cave we see next is the Dharma Cave. In this cave Dharma patiently faced the wall and meditated for 9 years. Finally, he reached the immortal spiritual state and created the Buddhist Zen. The cave is seven meters deep (about 23 feet), three meters high (about 9. 8 feet) and 3. 5 meters wide (about 11. 5 feet). Many stone inscriptions are carved on both of its sides. There is a Meditating Stone in the cave. It is said Dharma's shadow was reflected upon the stone and embedded on it, due to his long period of meditating in the cave. Unfortunately the stone was ruined during wars.

Shifang Chanyuan

After passing the Dharma Cave, we come to the Buddhist Living Quarters for transient monks, which were called "Shifang Chanyuan" . It is on the south bank of the Shaoxi River opposite the temple. First built in 1512 of the Ming Dynasty, it was renovated during the Qing Dynasty. The quarters are noted for the simple and distinctive design. It collapsed in 1958 and then was repaired in 1993.

Shaolin Temple Wushu Training Center

Now we are going to visit the Shaolin Temple Wushu (Martial Arts) Training Center. Its beautiful environ ment provides a perfect backdrop practicing the Chinese Shaolin Kung Fu. Shaolin monks have been practicing Kung Fu for over 1, 500 years. The system was invented by Dharma who taught the monks basic methods by which they could improve their health and defend themselves. These martial art performances show the true Chinese Shaolin Kung Fu. For example, Tong Zi Gong, performed by teenagers, is a kind of martial art to train one's flexibility and strength.

Ladies and gentlemen, this is the end of our visit to the Shaolin Temple. Thank you for your cooperation. Hope to see you again here. Thank you. Goodbye!

尊敬的各位來賓：

大家好！歡迎來河南嵩山遊覽，很榮幸能成為你們的導遊。我們現在要去參觀遊覽中國禪宗的發源地——少林寺。少林寺始建於北魏太和十九年（公元495年），由孝文帝元宏為安頓印度僧人跋陀，依山辟基而創建，因其坐落於少室山密林之中，故名「少林寺」。北魏孝昌三年（公元527 年）釋迦牟尼的第二十八代佛徒菩提達摩歷時三年到達少林寺，首傳禪宗，影響極大。因此，少林寺被世界佛教統稱為「禪宗祖庭」，並在此基礎上迅速發展，特別是唐初十三棍僧救駕李世民後得到了唐王朝的高度重視，博得了「天下第一名剎」的美譽。

現在的少林寺不僅因其古老神秘的佛教文化名揚天下，更因其精湛的少林功夫而馳名中外。「中國功夫冠天下，天下武功出少林」，這裡是少林武術的發源地，少林武術也是舉世公認的中國武術正宗流派。

少林寺景區還是中國著名的旅遊勝地之一。2000年，少林寺景區被國家旅遊局首批認定為4A級旅遊區。

少林寺景區包括少林寺常住院、塔林、初祖庵、二祖庵、達摩洞、十方禪院、武術館等主要旅遊景點。

中南地區

少林寺常住院

現在我們看到的是少林寺常住院。

少林寺常住院是少林寺的核心，是住持和尚和執事僧進行佛事活動的地方，總面積3萬多平方米，為七進建築。

山門就是少林寺的大門，這是清代建築，1975年翻修，門額上的「少林寺」三字是清康熙皇帝親書，上有「康熙御筆之寶」方印一枚。

山門殿台階下兩側的石獅是明代刻立的，既顯示了佛門的氣派，又像徵著鎮邪與吉祥，山門外兩側還有明代嘉靖年間建造的東西石坊各一座。

大家看，山門殿佛龕中供奉的是大肚彌勒佛，又稱迎賓佛，他慈眉善目，笑迎大家的到來。人們稱讚彌勒佛「端莊莊重山門喜看世間光輝照，笑哈哈迎來人祝福極樂永無窮」。

山門殿佛龕後面供奉的是韋馱菩薩，人稱護法金剛，他手持金剛寶杵，保護寺院佛、法、僧三寶的安全。

山門通道兩側有很多碑刻，人稱少林寺碑林。碑林東側為少林寺碑廊，它記載著寺院的榮辱興衰，在歷史、書法、雕刻等方面有很高的研究價值。少林寺碑林和碑廊共計有碑刻108通。

碑林的西面是錘譜堂，這裡迴廊一週42間，它用泥塑和木雕等形象地展示了少林寺武術的緣起、發展、練功、精華套路、國防功能、僧兵戰跡、武術活動等內容，共陳展14組216個錘譜像。有坐禪、跑經繞佛、八段錦、小紅拳、大紅拳、六合拳、通臂拳、羅漢拳、昭陽拳、練基本功、十三棍僧救秦王、小山和尚持帥出征、月空法師平倭寇以及俗家弟子習拳練武等。俗話稱：錘譜堂裡五分鐘，出來一身少林功，大家比照這些塑像姿勢就可以練習少林功。

　　我們現在看到是第二進建築天王殿，天王殿的原建築於1928年被石友三燒燬。這是1982年重修的，殿門外的兩大金剛，傳為「哼」、「哈」二將，職責是守護佛法。大殿內側塑的是四大大土，又稱四大金剛，他們的職責是視察眾生的善惡行為，扶危濟困、降福人間。

　　大雄寶殿是全寺的中心建築，是僧人進行佛事活動的重要場所，該殿和天王殿一樣在1928　年被軍閥石友三燒燬。這是1985年重建的。殿內正中供奉的為現世佛——釋迦牟尼如來佛，左為過去佛——東方淨琉璃世界的藥師佛，右為未來佛——西方極樂世界的阿彌陀佛，殿內東西山牆懸塑的是十八羅漢，屏牆後壁懸塑的是觀世音。少林寺大雄寶殿與其他寺院大雄寶殿的不同之處在於這裡的三世佛左右各塑有緊那羅王（少林寺棍術創始人）和達摩祖師（少林禪宗創始人）站像。另外，在該殿中間的兩根大柱下還有麒麟雕像，有一米多高（約為3.33英呎）。

　　大雄寶殿前兩側的建築為鐘、鼓二樓，東南為鐘樓，西南為鼓樓，原建築毀於1928年的兵火，1994年進行了重修，它們是寺院用來報時的。這也就是我們常說的「晨鐘暮鼓」。

　　鐘樓前這塊碑刻為《皇帝嵩岳少林寺碑》俗稱《李世民碑》，它刻立於唐玄宗開元十六年（公元728年）。正面是李世民告諭少林寺上座寺主等人的教文，表彰了少林寺僧助唐平定王世充的戰功，右起第五行有李世民親筆草簽的「世民」二字，碑刻「太宗文皇帝御書」七個大字系唐玄宗李隆基御書。背面刻的是李世民《賜少林寺柏谷莊御書碑記》，記述了十三棍僧救秦王的故事，也是影片《少林寺》拍攝的歷史依據。

　　《李世民碑》的北邊是《小山禪師行實碑》，記述了少林寺曹洞宗第24代傳法禪師的經歷和重振少林禪宗的功德。它的背面是《混元三教九流圖贊碑》，上面刻有佛、道、儒三教混元圖像，此碑反映了嵩山是佛、道、儒三教薈萃之地，體現了三教合流的重要思想。再往北我們看到的是清乾隆15　　年（公元1750年）刻立的《乾隆御碑》。

中南地區

大雄寶殿東側的殿宇是緊那羅殿，重建於1982年，內塑的緊那羅王是少林寺特有的護法神。這裡展示了緊那羅王的報身、法身、應身三種不同的形象。

大雄寶殿西側與緊那羅殿相對的六祖堂是1982年重建的，殿內正面供奉的是大勢至菩薩、文殊菩薩、觀音菩薩、普賢菩薩、地藏菩薩，兩側供奉的是禪宗初祖達摩、二祖慧可、三祖僧燦、四祖道信、五祖弘忍、六祖慧能，人稱六祖拜觀音。六祖堂的西壁是大型彩塑「達摩只履西歸圖」。

眼前的這個建築便是藏經閣，為明代所建，毀於1928年，1994年重建。珍貴的書籍包括大量寶貴的藝術作品都被保存在這裡。

藏經閣東西兩廂分別是東禪堂、西客堂，東禪堂是供僧人坐禪的地方，西客堂現為接待賓客的場所。

方丈室是少林寺住持僧（也就是方丈）起居生活和理事的地方。乾隆十五年九月二十九日，乾隆遊歷嵩山時曾在此住宿。方丈室門口東側的鐘為元代鑄造，此鐘只能在遇到緊急情況下方可擊之，起報警作用。

達摩亭又稱立雪亭。說起達摩亭還有一個動人的故事。據佛教經典記載：達摩來到少林寺後，有很多中國的信徒想跟隨他，其中最突出的是一中國高僧神光。他不論何時何地，都全心全意地追隨和服侍達摩。但是，為了考驗神光，達摩拒絕了他。神光並不灰心，甚至更加堅定。在冬天的一個夜晚，達摩在達摩亭坐禪入定，神光如往常一樣侍立在亭外。這時天上下起了大雪，大雪淹沒了神光的雙膝，神光仍雙手合十，一動也不動，第二天早上達摩開定後，見神光站在雪地裡，就問他：「你站在雪地裡幹什麼？」神光回答說：「求師傅傳授真法。」達摩說：「要我傳法給你，除非天降紅雪。」神光解意，抽出戒刀，砍去了自己的左臂，鮮血頓時染紅了白雪，達摩心動，遂把衣鉢法器傳給了神光，作為傳法的憑證，並為其取名為「慧可」。他因此被稱為禪宗二祖。乾隆皇帝曾御筆題匾以為紀念。

達摩亭東側的為文殊殿，殿內供奉的是文殊菩薩，下面請大家跟隨我去參觀少林寺最高的大殿，當然也是最珍貴的殿堂。

大家請注意，現在我們要進入最後一個大殿毗盧閣，也稱千佛殿。這是少林寺中最大的建築。這裡是最精彩的觀光之處。千佛殿是明朝建造的，殿高20餘米，面積300餘平方米，是寺內最大的佛殿，殿內神龕中供奉的是毗盧佛（釋迦牟尼佛的法身）。我們往地上看，殿內磚鋪底面上有4排48個站樁坑，它們是少林寺僧練拳習武的腳坑遺址，這些腳坑見證了少林功夫非同一般。

塔林

現在，我們來到了塔林。少林寺塔林是歷代少林寺高僧的墳塋，總面積14 000餘平方米，1996年被國務院公布為國家級重點文物保護單位。塔林現存唐、宋、金、元、明、清各代磚石墓塔240餘座，其中唐塔2座、宋塔2座、金塔10座、元塔46座、明塔148座，其餘為清塔和年代不詳的塔。少林寺塔林是中國現存古塔群中規模最大、數量最多的古塔群，這裡的塔高一般在15米以下。塔的高低、大小、層級、形制是根據和尚生前在佛教的地位、佛學造詣、佛徒數量、威望高低、經濟狀況及歷史條件而定的。

初祖庵和二祖庵

出寺後朝東北走，我們去看看兩座庵，即初祖庵和二祖庵。初祖庵是達摩的後代弟子為紀念達摩在洞中面壁所建。它的大廳被16根石柱支撐著。石柱上有雕刻精美的武士及龍鳳圖案。二祖庵是二祖慧可為示求法誠心斷左臂後靜養之所。在庵前有四汪泉水是達摩為方便慧可取水而掘，它們被稱為周溪泉，四泉其味各不相同。

達摩洞

我們接著參觀的洞為達摩洞。就是在這個洞裡，達摩面壁冥思達九年，終成正果，首傳禪宗。達摩洞位於少林寺西北的五乳峰上，石洞深約7米（約為23英呎），高3米（約為9.8英呎），寬3.5米（約為11.5英呎）。洞兩旁山岩上有歷代名人留下的多處石刻。洞中有一塊冥思石。據稱由於達摩長時間面壁沉思，其背影反射並被鐫刻在石頭上。可惜，這塊石頭已毀於戰火。

中南地區

十方禪院

穿過達摩洞，我們來參觀行腳僧人住宿的十方禪院。十方禪院位於少林寺對面少溪河南岸，始建於明朝的1512 年，清時得到重修。十方禪院設計精巧，古樸典雅。原院已於1958年倒塌，於1993年得到重修。新建的十方禪院與過去不同，是一組新的佛教禪景——五百羅漢堂。

少林武術訓練中心

我們馬上要進入的是少林武術訓練中心，優美的環境使得這裡成為修煉中國功夫的理想場所。少林和尚練習武藝有1500多年的歷史。武術體係為達摩所創，並授之僧人以強身健體和自衛。這些武術表演體現了真正的中國功夫。如童子功便由十來歲的小孩表演，主要訓練其柔韌性和力度。

好了，各位遊客，少林寺的參觀活動就要結束了，歡迎大家有機會再到少林寺參觀旅遊，學拳習武，謝謝！再見！

Hunan Province湖南省

A Glimpse of the Province （本省簡介）

With the Xiangjiang River zigzagging through it, the word Hunan refers to the province's location on the southern side of Dongting Lake. This lake is a huge basin surrounded on three sides by mountains and hundreds of small lakes and ponds dotted everywhere along its east side. With a population of 66 million, Hunan, traditionally called "Xiang" for short, covers a total area of over 210, 000 square kilometers. Hunan has a humid subtropical monsoon climate, with wet summers, cold winters and abundant rainfall. It is a land of rice and fish with an average temperature of 16℃ -18℃ and rainfall 1250- 1750 millimeters. The province's major ethnic groups include Han Chinese as well as the Tujia, Miao, Dong, Yao, Hui, Uygur and Zhuang ethnic minorities. Noted for its famed mountains, rivers and great historical and contemporary figures, Hunan boasts a large number of tourism attractions and resources. Six major national railway lines run through the province, which is also criss-crossed by roads, making it easily accessible. And there are four airports in the province (They are Changsha Airport, Zhangjiajie Airport, Changde Airport and Yongzhou Airport).

Historical Figures of Hunan

A large number of outstanding figures have historically come from Hunan Province, so the province enjoys the reputation of "The Kingdom of Chu, the unique home of talented people". For example, Cai Lun, who hails from Leiyang in Hunan, improved papermaking technology and introduced the first piece of paper from multiple plant fibers in 105 B.C.This invention has been honored as one of ancient China's "Four Great Inventions". The founder of the Confucian school of idealist philosophy in the Song and Ming Dynasties, Zhou Dunyi, came from Yongzhou in Hunan Province. Wang Fuzhi, an outstanding 17thCentury Chinese philosopher, was from the Hunan city of Hengyang. During the 79 years from the Opium War to the May Fourth Movement, Hunan Province witnessed the appearance of many important figures in Modern Chinese history. These include Wei Yuan, Zeng Guofan, He Shaoji, Zuo Zongtang, Tan Sitong, Chen Tianhua, Huang Xing and Song Jiaoren. During this period, some 83 people from Hunan are listed in the Dictionary of Major Chinese Historical Figures, or nearly 11% of total number of figures listed in the book. From the May Fourth Movement to the New Democratic Revolution or even to the socialist revolution and construction period, a great number of Party leaders, government officials and military figures emerged from this province. The most outstanding representatives are Mao Zedong, Cai Hesen, Ren Bishi, Liu Shaoqi, Peng Dehuai, He Long, and Luo Ron-ghuan. Meanwhile, a large group of talented writers, artists, scientists and educators have hailed from Hunan Province. These figures include Qi Baishi, the great master of Chinese painting, the noted playwright, Tian Han, the famous playwright, and the well-known writers Shen Congwen and Zhou Libo.

中南地區

Hunan Cuisine

Hunan cuisine, one of the eight regional cuisine of China, is famous for its use of chilli and spicy flavor. It is sometimes called Xiang cuisine. Hunan's chili-rich cuisine is similar to that of western China's Sichuan province. Chili, garlic, along with the unusual so-called "strange sauce" enliven many dishes. Chairman Mao, who was Hunanese, once claimed that the more chilies one eats the more revolutionary one becomes. It was meant as a joke (most probably) but the statement is in accordance with the Chinese belief that diet makes a great difference to a person's well being.

Special Local Products

Xiang embroidery, Liuyang chrysanthemum stone, Liuyang fireworks, Junshan green tea, Huogongdian snacks, white lotus sects, Tujia preserved ham, Yiyang, Shaoyang bamboo weavings and Liling porcelain.

Recommended Attractions

Yuelu Mountain Scenic Resorts and Historic Sites, Hunan Provincial Museum, Emperor Yan's Mausoleum, Chairman Mao Zedong's former residence, Nanyue Hengyang Mountain, Langshan Scenic Area, Yueyang Tower, Peach Blossom Garden, Suxian Mountain, Wanhua Rock, Xiangxi Mengdong River, South Great Wall of China, Fenghuang Old Town, Wulingyuan Scenic Area.

　　湖南因位於洞庭湖之南而得名，因湘江縱貫簡稱「湘」，面積約21　萬平方公里，人口約6600　萬。境內呈東、南、西三面環山的馬蹄形盆地，東北部的洞庭湖平原湖塘密布，素有「魚米之鄉」之稱。湖南屬於濕潤的亞熱帶季風性氣候，夏熱冬冷，全年雨水充沛，年平均氣溫 16℃～18℃，年平均降水量1250～1750毫米。主要民族有漢族、土家族、苗族、侗族、　族、回族、維吾爾族和壯族。湖南省是個旅遊大省，旅遊資源十分豐富，素有「旅遊勝地」之稱。著稱於世的古蹟遍布三湘四水。湖南交通便利，六條鐵路線縱橫貫穿於境內，有長沙黃花機場、張家界機場、常德機場、永州機場四個機場。

湖南省歷史名人

湖南因人才輩出而享有「唯楚有才，於斯為盛」的美譽。公元前105年，蔡倫，湖南耒陽人，發明的造紙術被譽為中國古代「四大發明」之一；周敦頤，湖南永州人，宋明時期儒家理學思想的奠基人；王夫之，湖南衡陽人，17世紀中國著名的思想家。從鴉片戰爭到五四運動的79 年間，中國近代史上出現了很多湖南名人，如魏源、曾國藩、何紹基、左宗棠、譚嗣同、陳天華、黃興、宋教仁等。他們都被收錄到《中國名人辭典》，占據了全書總人數的10.9%。從五四運動到新民主主義革命和社會主義革命和建設時期，有許多國家領導人都是湖南人，具有代表性的有毛澤東、蔡和森、劉少奇、任弼時、彭德懷、賀龍、羅榮桓等。同時，湖南也出現了大量文學、藝術、科技和教育方面的人才，如著名國畫大師齊白石；著名劇作家田漢；著名作家周立波等。

湘菜介紹

湘菜是中國的八大菜系之一，因辛辣而出名。湘菜多放辣椒，和四川菜有相似之處，主要特色表現在辣味和熏臘製品上，具有濃郁的山鄉水鄉風味。毛主席曾經說過：「吃不得辣椒就幹不得革命！」這當然是個笑話，但也說明了大家普遍認為的飲食決定一個人性格的說法。

特色產品

湘繡、瀏陽菊花石、瀏陽花炮、岳陽君山綠茶、火宮殿小吃、湘蓮、土家臘肉、益陽邵陽竹器、醴陵陶瓷等。

主要景點推薦

岳麓山風景名勝區、湖南省博物館、炎帝陵、毛澤東故居、南嶽衡山、莨山風景區、岳陽樓、桃花源、蘇仙嶺、萬花岩、湘西猛洞河、南長城、鳳凰古城、武陵

中南地區

源。

Former Residence of Mao Zedong （毛澤東故居）

Good morning, ladies and gentlemen,

Welcome to the Former Residence of Mao Zedong. Shaoshan is the birthplace of the Late Chairman Mao. The quaint farmhouse you see now is locally known as the Upper Cottage. It was here on December 26, 1893, that comrade Mao Zedong, the great leader of the Chinese people, was born. As early as March, 1963, the State Council pronounced this place to be one of the early Chinese Revolutionary History's National Heritage sites. For its cultural and natural sights, Shaoshan has since been a major tourist destination. It is estimated that nearly 40 million tourists, Chinese and foreign, have visited comrade Mao Zedong's former residence since the founding of the People's Republic of China. Among the distinguished guests are over 100 Chinese party leaders or state leaders, 14 foreign heads of state, 30 foreign governmental leaders, and visitors from over 150 countries.

The farmhouse stands in front of two water ponds:Lotus Pond and Southern Bank Pond. In his lifetime, comrade Mao Zedong was mad about swimming. He used to swim a lot in Southern Bank Pond in his boyhood. In November of 1963, Guo Moruo, on his visit to Shaoshan, pointed to the pond, and emotionally declared, "Mao Zedong swam in a water pond in his boyhood and did so in the Yangtze River in his old age."

With a northern exposure, Comrade Mao Zedong's boyhood home is typical Southern Chinese mud brick farmhouse. Down in a hollow, it is situated at the foot of a green hill and beside a clear stream. To borrow a locally used term, it is shaped like "a load of firewood". In the old days, the farmhouse was shared by two families. The Maos lived on the eastern end of 13 blue-tile rooms and their neighbor on the western end of 4 thatched rooMs.The entrance hall was shared by two families.

The present building is modeled after its prototype of 1918, showing the Maos in the prime of economic life, in possession of 13 tiled rooms, a half of the entrance hall and about 1. 47 hectares of farmland. Mao Zedong didn't commit himself to inheriting his family property. He left Shaoshan and walked onto the stage of Chinese politics instead. Mao Zedong, a son of a peasant's family, became a great revolutionary, strategist and theorist of the proletariat.

A horizontal board of rosewood with comrade Deng Xiaoping's inscription in golden characters "Comrade Mao Zedong's Former Residence, " which personally written by him on April 2, 1983, hangs from the front entrance's lintel.

Entrance Hall

Please step into the entrance hall. As mentioned earlier, this is the entrance hall that was shared by the two families. In Southern China, the entrance hall also serves as a banquet hall for entertaining guests on festive occasions. The square table and benches are originals. This is a shrine for worshipping Buddha or ancestors.

A small door at the back of the hall leads to a back room. This big pot was used for cooking pig fodder. The basin on the right was used for taking a bath or washing cloths. Mao Zedong used to help his parents with housework, carrying water with buckets for example. This big bucket is an original. This skylight, common in south China, is used for ventilation and lighting.

Hearth

This is a hearth. In wintertime, southern farmers warm themselves around the hearth with firewood burning inside. Dangling over it is a hook, on which a kettle is hung for boiling water; there were no thermos bottles in the farmhouse at the time. A guest was served a cup of boiled water poured from the kettle. A cooking pot could be suspended from the hook for cooking food so the whole families were sitting around

中南地區

the hearth, chatting over a meal. What a cozy home! Mao returned home in the Spring of 1921, when he was busy preparing the establishment of the Chinese Communist Party. Both his parents had died. His mother's birthday fell on February 15th. That evening, he asked his brothers, sister-in-laws and sisters to sit around the hearth for a family chat. His younger brother Mao Zeming told him about disasters the family had suffered over years. "That's true," Mao Zedong said, "The suffering not only affects our family but the most other Chinese families as well. A single family cannot expect to live an easy life in a time of nationwide chaos. So we should sacrifice a smaller family to serve a bigger family in the interests of general public." Under Mao Zedong's cheering guidance, his family members left Shaoshan one after the other to embark on a revolutionary road. In the protracted revolutionary struggle, he would ask his family members to work in the hardest places or to fight in the most dangerous places. His six family members laid down their lives for the revolutionary cause successively. His family clearly is an illustrious revolutionary family. You may get detailed information about this in a special section of the Exhibition Hall of Comrade Mao Zedong.

Bedroom of Mao Zedong's Parents

This is the bedroom of Mao Zedong's parents. Comrade Mao Zedong was born in this room on December 26, 1893. This is the late parents'portrait. Mao Shunsheng（Mao Zedong's father）, was an industrial, thrifty, intelligent and capable peasant. He died at the age of 50 in 1920 from acute typhoid fever. Thanks to his father's savings, Mao Zedong had a chance to further his studies outside Shaoshan in his early life. Mao Zedong's mother, born in 1867, was a peasant woman, hardworking, kind-hearted, clever and virtuous. She was gentle and loving and often helped out her neighbors. The fine qualities of the working people his parents maintained exerted a great influence on his formative years.

Gazing at the portrait of his mother in 1959, Mao Zedong said, "I bear a close resemblance to my mother." After a long gaze, he continued, "If only it had been today. She would not have died if it had been today. " The timeworn wooden bed you are looking at is an original.

Mao Zedong's Bedroom

This is Mao Zedong's bedroom. The picture hanging on the wall is a group photo of Mao Zedong, his mother and his two younger brothers, taken in Changsha in the spring of 1919. At the time Mao Zedong worked in Changsha and his second younger brother Mao Zetan studied there. And his first younger brother Mao Zeming took his mother, who was terminally ill, to Changsha for medical treat-ment. That's why the family of four had a chance to have their group photo taken, which is the only such photo that exists of the family. His mother passed away in October of that year. This valuable photo had been left in the care of Mao Zedong's grandmother, and we are fortunate that this early record of Mao and his family survived.

This is the place where Mao Zedong read and studied. It is by this oil lamp that Mao Zedong read his books at night. He was bright and talented and was an avid reader. His room was infested with mosquitoes on summer nights. He would lie in bed and poke his head out of a closed mosquito net, reading by an oil lamp on a bedside bench. On winter nights he would lie beneath a quilt and read late into the night. Aged 13 to 15, he had to quit school to help his parents with farm work. Even during this period, he devoted his spare time to studies.

Mao Zetan's Bedroom

This is the bedroom of Mao Zedong's second younger brother Mao Zetan. Mao Zetan was born in 1905. He followed his elder brother to Changsha for schooling at the age of 13. In 1923 he joined the Chinese Communist Party and participated in the party's political and military activities for many years. After the main force of the Red Army went on the Long March in October, 1934, he remained in the Soviet Area of the

中南地區

CPC Central Committee of Jiangxi and carried out guerrilla warfare. He once served as commander of the Independent Division of the Red Army. He died a hero at the age of 29 in April, 1935 in a battle east of Ruijin. Gazing at the portrait of Mao Zetan, Deng Xiaoping, on his trip to Mao Zedong's birthplace in 1983, recalled the days when they stuck together in Jiangxi through thick and thin and heartily praised Mao Zetan, "He was indeed a good comrade."

Mao Zemin's Bedroom

This is the bedroom of Mao Zemin. Born in 1895, he was Mao Zedong's first younger brother. When Mao Zedong returned to Shaoshan in spring, 1921, Mao Zemin had been married. He spent much time persuading his married brother and his family members to throw themselves into the revolution at the time. Mao Zedong pointed that one should think not only of his own family, but should think of the whole society and the suffering borne by the majority of people. Under his elder brother's careful instruction, Mao Zemin resolutely gave up an easy life at home and went out in pursuit of the revolutionary cause. He joined the Chinese Communist Party in 1922 and worked in the financial and logistics departments of the party. In 1943, at the age of 43, he was killed by Sheng Shicai, a Xinjiang warlord. Hearing this on his 1991 Shaoshan visit, Jiang Zemin, the then party Secretary-general of CPC said affectionately, "Mao Zedong's family is an outstanding one, making great contributions to the revolutionary cause." Four more of Mao's family members, besides Mao Zemin and Mao Zetan, all laid down their lives for the Chinese revolution.

各位遊客：

大家好！歡迎來到毛澤東故居遊覽。現在呈現在大家面前的這棟古樸的農舍叫「上屋場」。1893年12月26日，中國人民的偉大領袖毛澤東同志就誕生在這裡。早在1961年3月，國務院就將其列為中國重點文物保護單位，成為中國重要的革命紀念地之一。自新中國成立以來，毛澤東同志故居共接待中外客人近4000萬，其中包括100多位中國黨和國家的領導人、14位外國國家元首、30多位外國政府首腦及150多個國家和地區的來賓。

故居的前面是荷花塘和南岸塘。毛澤東同志一生酷愛游泳，南岸塘就是他少時「習武練藝」的最好地方。1963年11月，郭沫若參觀韶山時，曾指著這口塘感嘆地說：「毛主席是少時游池塘，老年游長江啊！」

我們來看毛澤東同志故居。這是一棟坐南朝北、土木結構的典型南方農舍，它門臨綠水，背依青山，成凹字形結構，這裡老百姓稱為「一擔柴」。當年這裡居住著兩戶人家，東邊13間小青瓦房為毛澤東家，西邊四間茅草屋為鄰居家，中間堂屋為兩家共用。

大家今天看到的房子是按1918年的原狀恢復的。這個時候是毛澤東家庭經濟狀況最好的時期，當時家裡擁有這13間半瓦房和約1.47公頃田土。但是身為毛家長子的毛澤東並未繼承父業，而是走出韶山，登上了中國政治的大舞台，由一個農民的兒子成長為偉大的無產階級革命家、戰略家、理論家。

大門頂端掛著的「毛澤東同志故居」金字紅木匾，是鄧小平同志1983年4月2日親筆題寫的。

堂屋

現在請大家隨我進堂屋參觀。這裡是堂屋，前面提到的兩家共用的堂屋指的就是這一間。它在南方是擺酒席、宴請客人的地方，這裡的方桌和板凳都是原物，這是神龕，是供奉神佛、祖宗用的。

穿過堂屋這扇小門往後走，我們便來到了「退堂屋」。這個大鍋是煮豬食用的。右邊的腳盆是用來洗澡和洗衣服的。毛澤東小時候經常在此幫父母幹活，用水桶挑水。這個大水桶是原物。這是南方農舍一般都有的天窗，它用來通風、透氣、採光，天窗下有暗溝，用來排水。

中
南
地
區

441

火堂

這裡是火堂。南方農家在冬天一般都架柴燒火取暖，這上面有個掛鉤，俗稱「爐膛鉤」，是用來掛壺燒水的。過去農家沒有熱水瓶，客人來了，馬上打水燒起來。當然這裡也可掛吊鍋，用來煮飯，冬天全家圍坐一團邊吃邊聊，那可是熱氣騰騰的呢！1921年春，毛澤東在籌建共產黨的過程中回到韶山。當時他的父母已經去世。2 月15 日是毛澤東母親的生日，那天晚上，他邀弟弟、弟妹及妹妹圍爐烤火、拉家常。弟弟毛澤民一口氣講了這幾年遭受到的災難，毛澤東説，這些不只是我們一家發生的事，天下大多數人都這樣，國亂民不得安生，所以我們要捨小家為大家，出去做一些有利於大多數人的工作。在毛澤東的諄諄教導下，全家人相繼離開家鄉走上革命道路。在長期的革命鬥爭中，毛澤東又總是教育自己的親人到艱苦的地方去工作，到最危險的崗位上去戰鬥，一家先後有六位親人英勇獻身，毛澤東的家庭成為革命家庭。關於這部分內容，毛澤東同志紀念館有專題陳列，歡迎參觀。1991年，江總書記在此參觀後説：「這個地方很有意義。」

毛澤東父母的臥室

1893年12月26日，中國人民的偉大領袖毛澤東同志就誕生在這裡。這是毛澤東同志父母的遺照。毛澤東同志的父親毛順生是一位非常勤勞節儉、精明能幹的農民，1920年他因患急性傷寒病去世，享年50歲。父親的勤勞節儉和善於持家理財為早年毛澤東外出讀書提供了一定的經濟基礎。毛澤東的母親生於1867年，是一位勤勞善良、聰明賢惠的農家婦女。她性情溫和，富有愛心，經常接濟周圍貧困的鄉親。父母親勞動人民的優良品德對少年時代的毛澤東影響很大。1959 年毛澤東看到母親這張照片時説：「我還是挺像我母親的。」他凝視良久，然後又説：「要是現在就好了，要是現在就死不了。」大家看到的這張陳舊木床是原物。

毛澤東的臥室

這裡是毛澤東的臥室。牆上的照片是毛澤東和母親及兩個弟弟1919年春在長沙的合影。當時毛澤東同志在長沙工作，小弟毛澤覃在長沙讀書。因母親病重，大弟毛澤民送母親去長沙治病，所以他們母子四人才有機會留下這唯一的一張合影，毛澤東的母親就是這年10月去世的。這張珍貴的照片由於毛澤東外婆家的珍藏而倖存下來。

這裡是毛澤東小時候學習的地方。當年，毛澤東晚上讀書就是用的這盞小油燈。毛澤東天資聰穎，又酷愛讀書，夏天的晚上蚊子多，他就在床邊放一張條凳，凳上放一盞燈，人躲到蚊帳裡面，將頭伸到帳子外看書。冬天，他常常躺在被子裡讀書到深夜。甚至在他13歲至15歲停學在家勞動的時候，他也往往白天下田勞動，晚上讀書讀得很晚。

毛澤覃的臥室

這間是毛澤東小弟弟毛澤覃的臥室。毛澤覃生於1905年，13歲就跟隨哥哥毛澤東到長沙讀書，1923年加入中國共產黨，長期從事黨的政治和軍事工作。1934年10月紅軍主力長征後，他留在江西中央蘇區堅持游擊戰爭，曾任紅軍獨立師師長。1935年4月，在瑞金東部的一次戰鬥中，不幸中彈，壯烈犧牲，時年29歲。1983年鄧小平同志來到毛澤東故居參觀，當他看到與自己在江西同生死共患難的戰友的遺像時，久久凝視著，深情地讚歎道：「毛澤覃是個好同志！」

毛澤民的臥室

我們現在來到的是毛澤民的臥室。毛澤東的大弟弟毛澤民生於1895年。1921年春，毛澤東回家動員親人幹革命，重點是做毛澤民的工作。因為毛澤民當時已成家。毛澤東教育他，不能只看到自己這個小家，應該看到大家，想到大多數人的痛苦。毛澤民在兄長的耐心開導下，毅然捨棄小家，走上了革命道路。1922年，他加入中國共產黨。參加革命後他一直從事黨的財經和後勤工作。1943年被新疆軍軍閥盛世才殺害，時年47歲。1991年江總書記參觀到這裡深情地說：「毛主席一家很了不起，為革命做出了巨大的貢獻！」的確，除了毛澤民、毛澤覃，主席一家還有四位親人先後為革命獻出了生命。

Ancient Town of Fenghuang （鳳凰古城）

Ladies and gentlemen,

Good morning. Welcome to the ancient town of Fenghuang. The ancient town of Fenghuang you are visiting now was rated as one of the two most beautiful small towns in China by the eminent New Zealand writer, Rewi Alley. Bordering on the scenic areas of Mengdong River in Northwest Hunan and Fanjing Mountain in Guizhou, the town provides access roads to Huaihua, Jishou of Hunan and Tongren of Guizhou. It is the birthplace of the illustrious Chinese writer, Shen Congwen. Picturesque in scenery, abounding with historical sites, the town of Fenghuang makes an ideal sightseeing destination. The town boasts eight notable tourist sights:Sunrise at Dongling, Nanhua's Wooded Hills, the Playful Fish Dragon Pool, the Mountain Temples' Bell Tolls, the Dazzling Peaks, Moonlit Bridges on Streams, Lanjing Woodcutters'Folk Songs, and Fange's Rolling Waves. Ancient towers, quaint compounds dating back to the Ming and Qing dynasties, and flagstone-paved street remain a common sight in the town. In the town's vicinity, there are such striking sights such as the National Forest Park of Nanhua Mountain, the well-preserved Ancient Tang Dynasty town of Huangsiqiao, the Underground Qiliang Cavern Arts Palace, miraculous, rocky, and wind-driven Jianduoduo Waterfall, mysterious Gaodabu Gorge, General-like Three-gate Cave Rock, and scenic Tunliang, Fenghuang, Elephant Trunk, Tianxing and Lale Hills.

The town is not only a scenic area but also the birthplace of great men. Zheng Guohong, commanding officer of Chuzhou of Zhejiang, Tian Xingshu, provincial military commander of Guizhou, Xiong Xiling, the first Prime Minister of the Republic of China, Shen Congwen, an illustrious Chinese writer and Huang Yongyu, an outstanding Chinese painter are Fenghuang natives.

The Former Residence of Shen Congwen

Walk down a flagstone-paved road, you will get to No. 10 Zhongying Street. The house was the former residence of Mr.Shen Cong-wen, an illustrious Chinese writer and archeo-logist. The house was built by his grandfather, Shen Hongfu, in the first year of the Qing Dynasty Tongzhi Emperor's reign (1886). Shen Congwen was born on December 28, 1902 in this combination Ming and Qing style quadrangle like house. He spent his boyhood and formative years here. His family's financial situation declined when he was young. In 1917 Mr.Shen left his hometown and joined the local army at the age of 15 and then spent years roaming around along Yuan River, and You River, witnessing war-torn areas. From these experiences, he developed a great interest in writing. In 1919 Mr.Shen went to Beijing and started his writing career with great difficulties. His literary works like Border Town and Northwest Hunan made him well-known in Chinese literary circles, and he became almost as famous as Lu Xun, who was 20 years older than him. Following the 1950s, Mr.Shen devoted himself to the study of traditional Chinese garments, writing The Study of Traditional Chinese Garments, a remarkable acade-mic work in the field.

Mr.Shen's works and his personality share the following qualities:natural, honest, diligent, profound, and dignified. Mr.Shen wrote literary works of five million words in his lifetime, a great contribution to the treasure house of world literature, leaving behind him priceless historical resources in the study of Old China and Old Northwest Hunan.

中
南
地
區

The Former Residence of Xiong Xiling

As we pass through Fenghuang's Hall of Fame, which is a side arm of the Confucius Temple, a flagstone path takes us to No. 10 Wenxing Street. This is the former residence of Mr.Xiong Xiling, the first prime minister of the Republic of China.

Xiong Xiling, who styled himself as Bingsan, was born in the small bungalow on July 23, 1870. Even in his boyhood, he earned a name of Hunan Prodigy. He was a successful candidate in the imperial examina-tions at the county level at the age of 15, at the provincial level at the age of 21, and to crown it all, a palace graduate and awarded a title of a great scholar in the Imperial Academy at the age of 24.

Having made a name in the world, he vigo-rously campaigned for constitutional reform and modernization. He started the reformist periodical, the so-called Hunan Newspaper, and founded the School of Current Political Affairs and the Changdexilu Normal School. As famous as Tan Sitong in Hunan, he was one of leading forces in the 1898 Constitutional Reform and Modernization Movement. Some of his students became outstanding revolutionaries such as Xiang Jingyu, Lin Boqu, Teng Daiyuan, Song Jiaoren (a leftist in the Nationalist Party) and Jiang Yiwu (Commander-in-chief in the Wuchang Uprising). He served as fin-ancial inspector of three northeastern pro-vinces, governor of Rehe province and finance minister of the republic. In 1913 he became as first prime minister of the Republic of China. The government he worked in was eulogized as 'Cabinet of Talents'. Yuan Shikai dissolved the cabinet and removed Xiong from premiership for his criticism of Yuan's dictatorial rule. After leaving the government, Xiong Xiling started a number of businesses and undertook charity work. He ran the Xiangshan Orphanage and when Fenghuang County was struck by a severe drought in 1925, ruining the rice harvest, Mr.Xiong raised 100, 000 silver dollars, 40, 000 of which were donated by Mr.Mei Lanfang, an eminent Peking Opera actor, for relief efforts. In his late life, Mr.Xiong served as president of the Chinese Red Cross and threw himself into field rescue work in the War against Japanese Aggression, making outstanding contributions in fighting Japanese invaders. Mr.Xiong Xiling died of a disease at the age of 67 in Hong Kong on December 5, 1937.

The Gate Tower and Old City Wall

Fenghuang County includes an historic landmark that was formerly known as "Zhen Gan". It was the government seat of five stockade villages during the Ming and Qing dynasties. The city wall consists of mud that was revamped with bricks in

1556. During the reign of Emperor Kangxi, the town acted as the government seat first of the directly affiliated district, then as the district deputy governor seat, and finally as the military headquarters for the River Chen and Yuan's local forces. The city wall was rebuilt with stone in 1715 during Qing Emperor Kangxi's reign, It is 2, 000 meters in circumference. Four gates to the town were built on four sides, each with a tall gate tower:the Eastern Gate (the Gate of Sheng Heng), the Southern Gate (The Gate of Jing Lan), the Western Gate (the Gate of Fu Cheng) and the North Gate (The Gate of Bi Hui). Xue Yue, the commander-in-chief of the Ninth Theater of Operations and then governor of the Nationalist Party Hunan Provincial Government, argued in 1940 that the walled towns were sitting ducks for air strikes and were difficult to evacuate. He further argued that once walled towns fell to enemies, it was hard to retake them. He therefore ordered that all the city walls in Hunan's counties be pulled down. As a result, all the walls and gates were dismantled, save for the Eastern Gate and Northern Gate. These two gates were kept in place to guard the town against floods, but their battlements and forts were removed. The ruins of the broken walls remain visible between the Eastern and Northern Gates.

A road along the ruins of broken walls passing through the Northern Gate takes you to a souvenirs shopping street. Six-hue Store there offers tourists a great variety of Miao national minority folk arts and handicrafts. You may find rare masterpieces of folk arts and handicraft there:tie-dyed products made by Mrs. Wu Jinglian, a UN-certified master artist of folk arts and handicrafts, and Mr.Xiong's batik printed Chinese paintings of water colour, rated as first class by the eminent Chinese painter, Zhang Ding.

The Bridge of Rainbow and the Scenic Area of Sha wan

This is the Rainbow Bridge, built during Ming Dynasty Hongwu Emperor's reign and then renovated in 1670. There used to be a storied pavilion on stilts on the bridge housing a dozen shops in it. Unfortunately, the pavilion and its archways were torn down in 1956 owing to a road expansion project.

中
南
地
區

Standing under the bridge there are a row of century-old stilted houses. Down below, dragon boat races, a traditional Fenghuang sports event, are regularly held. During the Moon Cake Festival, local people turn two freight boats into a racing boat and compete in a boat race in this small river.

Walking down the bridge, one comes in sight of three scenic spots in Shawan:the Moonlit Bridges over Streams, the playful Fish in Dragon Pool, and the Dazzling Peaks. There used to be eight scenic wonders here, but only three remain now.

This is the Palace of Longevity, also known as the Water Palace Temple. It was built by businessmen from Jiangxi. Therefore, it is customarily called the Lodge of Jiangxi. The Palace of Longevity is the biggest human structure in Fenghuang, covering an area of over 4, 000 square meters.

各位朋友：

大家好！歡迎來鳳凰古城遊覽。現在大家所在的地方，是被新西蘭著名作家路易‧艾黎先生稱讚為中國兩座最美麗的小城之一的湖南鳳凰古城。這裡與風景名勝區湘西猛洞河、貴州梵淨山毗鄰，位於湖南懷化、吉首和貴州銅仁三地之間，是著名作家沈從文的故鄉。鳳凰風景秀麗，名勝古蹟很多，歷來是人們遊覽的勝地，自古就有東嶺迎輝、南華疊翠、龍潭漁火、山寺晨鐘、奇峰挺秀、溪橋夜月、蘭徑樵歌和梵閣回濤八大景觀。城內，古代城樓、明清古院和石板小街現在仍是風采依然；城外，南華山國家森林公園、唐代修建的至今仍保存完好的黃絲橋古城、地下藝術宮殿奇梁洞和神奇的風動岩、壯觀的尖多朵瀑布、神秘的高達不峽、三門洞將軍岩以及如畫的屯糧山、鳳凰山、象鼻山、天星山、臘樂山都在向您招手。

鳳凰不但風景秀美，而且人傑地靈。浙江總兵鄭國鴻、貴州提督田興恕等民族英雄和中華民國第一任內閣總理熊希齡、著名作家沈從文和著名畫家黃永玉都是鳳凰人。

沈從文故居

沿著石板小路，我們來到中營街10號，這裡就是中國著名作家和考古學家沈從文先生的故居。

這所建築是沈從文的祖父沈洪富於清同治元年（公元1866年）所建。1902年12 月28 日，沈從文先生就誕生在這座具有明清建築風格的四合院裡，並在這裡度過了他的童年和少年時期。1917年，沈先生15歲時，因家道中落，參加湘西土軍，離開了家鄉，輾轉於沅、澧、酉水流域，親歷了如火如荼的戰爭，從而激發了創作慾望。1919 年，沈先生隻身來到北京，開始了他的從文生涯，創作了《邊城》、《湘西》等一系列文學作品，不久就蜚聲中國文壇，幾乎與年長他20 歲的魯迅先生齊名。20 世紀50年代之後，沈先生潛心於中國古代服飾的研究，寫出了驚世之作——《中國古代服飾研究》。

沈先生的作品與人品表現出了強烈的一致：自然、厚樸、謙虛、勤奮、博大而凝重。沈先生一生所創作的500多萬字的作品，是世界的文學瑰寶，給後人研究舊中國和舊湘西留下了寶貴的遺產。

熊希齡故居

順著小巷的砂石板小道，從大成殿——即孔子廟的挑檐下經過，我們來到了文星街10號，這裡是中華民國第一任內閣總理熊希齡先生的故居。熊希齡，號秉三，1870年7月23日出生在這間小平房裡。熊先生少年時就有湖南神童之稱，15 歲中秀才，21歲中舉人，24 歲中進士，被授予翰林院庶吉士（俗稱點翰林）。

熊先生成名後，積極主張維新變法，曾創辦《湘報》、時務學堂和常德西路師範學校，是湖南與譚嗣同齊名的維新派中堅。中國的一些著名革命家如向警予、林伯渠、滕代遠、國民黨左派宋教仁、武昌起義總指揮蔣翊武等都是熊先生的學生。後來，熊先生出任東三省財政監理官、熱河都統、財政總長等職，民國三年（公元1913 年）就任中華民國第一任政府總理，當時的這一任政府被輿論界稱為「才子內閣」。後來，因熊先生反對袁世凱獨裁，被袁世凱逼迫解散內閣，辭去總理職務。從此，熊先生轉而獻身實業和慈善事業，並開辦香山慈幼院，收養了一大批孤

中南地區

兒。民國十四年（公元1925　年），鳳凰縣遭大旱，絕大部分田土無收，熊先生知道消息之後，送來賑災款大洋10萬（其中著名京劇表演藝術家梅蘭芳先生捐大洋4萬元），救助了很多災民。晚年，熊先生就任中華民國紅十字會會長，積極投身抗日戰場戰地救護，其功德可昭日月。1937年12月5日，熊希齡先生病故於香港，享年67歲。

城樓及古城牆

鳳凰縣城所在地原名鎮竿，元明兩朝為五寨長官司所在地，當時建有土城，明嘉靖三十五年（公元1556年）改土城為磚城。清康熙年間，鳳凰直隸廳通判、總兵和辰沅水靖兵備道衙門設在這裡。康熙五十四年（公元1715　年）建石城。石城周長2000米有餘。開設四座城門，東門叫升恆門，南門叫靜谰門，西門叫阜城門，北門叫碧輝門。各有巍峨的城樓。1940年，國民黨第九戰區司令兼湖南政府主席薛岳以「城堡一旦落於敵手，反攻不易，而不利於空襲疏散」為由，通令所屬各縣將所有城牆拆除。鳳凰東、北二門因防水需要，僅拆除城堆碉樓，其他城門全部拆除。所以，現在只能看到東、北二門連接其間的半壁城牆。

沿著半壁舊城牆，出東門，是旅遊商品一條街。這裡的六色坊有很多苗族的民間工藝品供大家選購和參觀，獲得聯合國頒證的民間工藝美術大師吳景蓮（吳花花）女士的扎染工藝品和東門內熊氏蠟染國畫更是別具一格，受到廣大遊客的好評。

虹橋及沙灣風景區

現在來到虹橋，這座橋始建於明洪武年間，清康熙九年（公元1670　年）加修，橋面上原有吊腳樓亭，亭內設有12 家店鋪，1956 年因修公路，原樓亭和兩側牌坊均被拆除，就成了現在這個樣子。

橋下是一排有百年歷史的舊吊腳樓。吊腳樓下是鳳凰傳統體育節目——賽龍舟的地方。每到端午節，人們就將兩只運貨的木船捆紮起來，在這小河裡一爭高下。

下了橋，步入沙灣，可以看到鳳凰縣舊時八大景中的「溪橋夜月」、「龍潭漁火」、「奇峰挺秀」三大景。

現在看到的是萬壽宮，又叫水府廟，因為是江西商人所建，大家習慣叫它江西會館。萬壽宮占地4000多平方米，是鳳凰最大的民間建築物。

Han Tombs of Mawangdui （馬王堆漢墓）

Hello, friends.

Welcome to the exhibition for unearthed artifacts from the Mawangdui Han Tombs in Changsha. The Han Tombs of Mawangdui are located at the former Mawangdui Township in the eastern part of Changsha City, about four kilometers outside of the city's downtown. On the even ground, there are two earth tombs connected in the middle, protruding abruptly, with a shape similar to a saddle. Legend goes that here was the burial ground of Ma Yin, king of Chu State of Five Dynasties period, hence the name "Mawangdui", or the Tomb of King Ma. But as was written in the Records of a Peaceful World—Changsha County, during the Northern Song Dynasty, this place was called "Two Ladies' Tomb (Shuangn zhong)", where King Liu Fa of Changsha State of the early Western Han Dynasty buried his mother Cheng and consort Tang. Who on earth is the true occupant of his mysterious ancient tomb of Mawangdui? It had been an enigma for a thousand years before the tomb was unearthed.

At the end of 1971, 366 Hospital of Hunan Province Military Command decided to build its underground warehouses and wards here. This construction necessitated an archeological dig, which unearthed this mysterious thousand year-old underground palace.

Model of Tomb Pits of the Han Tombs of Mawangdui

There are three tombs in Mawangdui, which are coded in No. 1, No. 2, and No. 3 respectively in accordance with their unearthing sequence. Among them, Tombs No. 1 and No. 2 are in parallel with each other from east to west, while Tomb No. 3 is to the south side of Tomb No. 1. The mouth of the Tomb No. 1 is square, and under it is the tomb pit in the shape of a square filter, which is the typical tomb shape of Western Han Dynasty. The tomb mouth is 19. 5 meters long from south to north and 17. 8 meters wide from east to west. It is 20. 5 meters deep. Four steps and a ramp path north of the tomb from its mouth lead directly down from the ground to the tomb bottom. Over 1, 800 cultural relics have been unearthed from this tomb, including lacquered wood works, textiles and silk paintings, and a well-preserved woman's corpse. Tomb No. 2's mouth and middle are round while it is square 3 meters downward. Owing to repeated robbery of the tomb and poor sealing of the white seal clay, the whole tomb greatly collapsed and only 200 culture relics remained. Tomb No. 3 is the same with Tomb No. 1 in shape and well preserved. More than 1000 culture relics were unearthed here, including silk books and paintings, bamboo slips, lacquer wares, and textiles. Unfortunately, the corpse in it was totally rotten and only a skeleton remained. An examination determined that the person buried here was a 1. 85 meter tall, 30 year old male.

Jade Seal of "Li Cang"

Through archaeological excavation, we discovered that Mawangdui was the burial ground of an early Western Han Dynasty Marquis family. Judging from the Li Cang jade seal and the Seals of Marquis Dai (bronze seal) and the "Changsha Chancellor" (bronze seal), which were unearthed from Tomb No. 2, the occupant of Tomb No. 2 should be a first generation member of the Marquis Dai's family. The Marquis Dai, also named Li Cang, served as Changsha State's Chancellor. He was born in the late years of Warring States Period and died in the second year of the reign of Empress Dowager Gao (186 B.C.). In his youth, Li Cang followed Liu Bang, the first Emperor of the Han Dynasty, in the peasant uprising and in the battle between Chu and Han States, and made an outstanding contribution to the founding of the Western Han Dynasty Kingdom. In early Han Dynasty, he was promoted to chancellor of Changsha State. He did his best to consolidate the central power and maintain the unification of the country. As recorded in Shi Ji (History Records) and Han Shu (History of Han Dynasty), he was again promoted to Marquis Dai in April of the second year of the reign of the Han Emperor Hui. Due to his merits, the name Dai was given to a place between present-day Luoshan and Guangshan Counties in Henan Province. His fief town contained 700 households and compares poorly with Cheng Ping and Zhang Liang, who were marquises with fiefs of ten thousand households. But Li Cang had a special position in Changsha State, and so his family enjoyed all the comforts of luxury and pomp, including extravagant funerals after their deaths.

Seal of "Marquise Xinzhui"

Li Cang's wife was buried in Tomb No. 1. We know from the unearthed "Marquise Xinzhui" seal. Though as noble as a mar-quise, she experienced great sorrow over the loss of husband when she was relatively young and her son in her late years. She passed away in 163 B.C.at the age of about 50. In accordance with the corpse and the image of Xinzhui on the silk painting, we asked the Xi'an Great Historical Figures Sculpture Research Academy to make a wax statue to restore a middle-age marquise Dai, thus reproducing her original glory and grace.

White-yarn Full Front and Back of a Gown

The white yarn is the undyed yarn, and a gown is a dress without liner. These two dresses weigh 48 and 49 grams, rather than 1 liang, or 50 graMs.If the heavier edges on the collar and sleeves are not counted, its weight was only a little over half a liang. It was really as light as the smoke and mist, and as thin as cicada's wings. Of course, the quality of superior yarn materials is not evaluated by the number of voids, but by the fiber size of natural silk, which should be uniform and long. In textiles there is a

中
南
地
區

453

measurement unit for fiber size, denier, which is equivalent to a single 90, 000 meter long silk thread weighing 1 gram. So the smaller the denier, the finer the natural silk. The natural silk size of the white yarn gown was only 10. 5 to 11. 3, while that of the superior silk fabrics produced now is 14. This demonstrates how fine, light and thin the white yarn is. How did the women in the Han Dynasty wear such a thin dress? They wore such gowns on the bright and beautiful embroidered robes, to make the magnificent decorative patterns on the robes partly hidden and partly visible, thereby displaying a dim beauty.

T-shape Silk Painting of Tomb No. 1

This painting had the shape of English character "T", so we call it T-shape silk painting. As recorded in the inventory of funeral furnishings, it was like a dress but not a dress. When unearthed, it was covering, upside down, the cover of the inner coffin in Tomb No. 1. A bamboo rod traversed the top of the painting, and at every drooping angle were tied silk ribbons or bust-fiber belts. According to textual research, this was an article belonging to flags and streamers. In funeral rites, it was raised high in the head of the funeral procession to guide the spirit to heaven, much like a funeral streamer.

The whole painting was 205 cm long, and could be divided into three parts from up to down, namely the heaven, the human world, and the nether world.

Heaven is over the aureole. In the upper part of the painting, is a god with man's head and snake's body, sitting there with his hair hanging loosely. As recorded in the ancient Chinese geography book Book of Mountains and Seas, the god was the almighty "Zhu Long", who was in charge of the changes of day and night and fine and bad weather. On the right are drawn nine red suns half hidden in the blue mulberry tree. The legend goes that the mulberry tree grew in the East Sea. It was about ten thousand meters tall, and amidst it, the ten suns rested and took turns to be on duty. But in the painting, there were only nine suns, and the other one might be on duty and had not yet returned. In the biggest sun was drawn a black bird called "Jin Wu (gold crow)" in ancient times. This drawing was in fact based on the ancient people's observation of a sunspot. On the left was a crescent moon, under which, a beautiful girl dances graciously. Some regard her as the moon goddess, who was holding the moon to rise slowly. Some regard her as Chang'e, who was flying to the moon after stealing an elixir from her husband and swallowing it. In the moon, a big, flat toad is holding a glossy ganoderma in its mouth; the Jade Hare is beside it, whose elegance forms a striking contrast with the fat toad. Two janitors are respectfully bowing and scraping by the gate to the Heavenly palace, welcoming the Marchioness into Heaven.

The Human World part took the aureole as the roof, and decorated it with rose finches. Under the aureole, the plump Marchioness in extravagant dresses with jade pendants jingling, slowly steps forward with a stick in her hand. Three personal maids closely follow her. Two alchemists present their elixir to her. Two dragons pass through the wall on both sides of the picture, symbolizing nobility and good luck. The painting below might be the scene in which the servants made sacrifices after the Marchioness' death. They are serious and silent, with their faces grey, showing their excessive distress.

In the nether world, the naked Earth God Gun supports the flat earth with his hands, and his feet press down on two huge evil sea turtles intent of causing problems on earth, such as earthquakes. The nether world also has strange dogs with repulsive appear-ances and owls with their eyes wide open, who are quelling the spirits and ghosts to disturb the old Marchioness.

This is a masterpiece integrating mythology, imagination and real life. Every part of it reflects the ancient conception of heaven and desire for immortality. Thus the "T-shaped" silk painting is a rare and outstanding masterpiece of ancient Chinese art.

中南地區

The Female Corpse

The 2, 100-year-old female corpse was unear-thed from Tomb No 1. She is the wife of Li Cang, the first-generation Marquis Dai, and chancellor of Changsha State in the early Western Han Dynasty. Her name was Xin Zhui. When unearthed, she was 1. 54 meters tall and weighed 34. 3 kilograms and had type A blood. Her head, neck, trunk and limbs all maintained their intact forMs.Her skin was wet and covered her whole body. It was light-yellow-brown and felt oily. Her hair, eyelash and hair in her nostril remained in their original places. Parts of her joints were still movable. Her subcutaneous fat was rich, and tissues were still elastic, which, after being pressed by hand, could rapidly recover the original form. When injected with a preservative fluid, the tissue swelled and the fluid could be diffused and be absorbed rather quickly. X-ray examination showed that all her skeleton was intact, her two sides were symmetrical, small bones as nasal bone and phalanx could still be distinguished, and their outward forms were no different from the skeletons of modern human beings. The corpse did have early signs of decay, such as the eye ball getting out, mouth opening, tongue slightly protruding, and rectum prolapsing. But owing to the excellent sealing of Tomb No. 1, this decay ceased shortly after the corpse was buried.

This kind of well-preserved female corpse is a very rare archeological find. It is obviously different from mummies, which look shriveled and dry, and "corpse wax", making them resemble a body model made with wax. It is also different from peat-tanned cadavers, which are easily broken, due to the skeleton softening from calcium loss. So, it is now internationally admitted that in the classification of corpses, such "wet corpses" as the one unearthed from Mawangdui should be named "Mawangdui Corpses", which are characterized by long preservation time, elastic tissue, and presence of internal organs.

　　各位朋友，大家好！歡迎參觀長沙馬王堆漢墓出土文物陳列館。馬王堆漢墓位於長沙市東部地區原馬王堆鄉，距市中心約4 公里。這裡地勢平坦，地面有土塚兩個，它們大小相仿，平地兀起，中間相連，形狀頗似馬鞍。相傳這裡是五代時楚王馬殷的墓地，故名「馬王堆」。但根據北宋《太平寰宇記‧長沙縣》的記載，這裡是西漢初年長沙王劉發葬其母程、唐二姬的墓地，號曰「雙女塚」。究竟馬王堆這座神奇古墓的墓主人是誰呢？在未發掘之前，實為千古之謎。

1971年年底，湖南省軍區366醫院決定在此修建地下病房和倉庫。為了配合基建，我們對此進行了考古發掘，這才揭開了這座千年地宮的神秘面紗。

馬王堆漢墓墓坑模型

馬王堆共有三座墓，按發現秩序的先後，分別編為一號、二號、三號。其中一號、二號墓東西方向平行並列，三號墓在一號墓南側。一號墓墓口呈方形，下面為鬥形墓坑，是典型的西漢墓葬形式。墓口南北長19.5米，東西寬17.8米，從封土算有20.5米深。自墓口向下有4級台階，墓室北面有一條由地面幾乎直達墓底的斜坡墓道。墓中共出土漆木器、紡織品、帛畫等各類文物1800餘件及一具保存十分完整的女屍。二號墓墓口和中部為圓形，下面3米處為方形，由於曾經多次被盜，且白膏泥密封較差，故整個墓葬已嚴重坍塌，僅殘餘200餘件文物。三號墓與一號墓形制相同，因該墓保存得較好，出土了帛書、帛畫、簡牘、漆木器、紡織品等1000多件文物。遺憾的是，該墓屍體已經腐爛，僅殘存一具骨架。經鑑定，墓主人是一個身高約1.85米，年齡在30歲左右的男性。

「利蒼」玉印

經過考古發掘，我們發現馬王堆是西漢初期軑侯家族的墓地。從二號墓出土的「利蒼」玉印、「軑侯之印」（銅印）和「長沙丞相」（銅印）來看，二號墓墓主人應該是第一代軑侯、長沙國丞相利蒼。他生於戰國末年，死於西漢高後二年（公元前186 年）。早年利蒼曾跟隨漢高祖劉邦參加過秦末農民起義、楚漢之爭，為西漢王朝的建立立下了汗馬功勞。漢初他升任長沙國丞相，極力鞏固中央政權，維護祖國統一大業，據《史記》和《漢書》記載，惠帝二年四月（公元前193 年），利蒼因功再封軑侯。軑，是地名，在現在的河南省羅山縣和光山縣之間。食邑為七百

中南地區

戶，與陳平、張良等萬戶侯相比，是個不太大的侯。但是由於利蒼所在的長沙國位置獨特，所以家族成員生前甘食美服，享盡人間的榮華富貴，死後也得到厚葬。

「妾辛追」印

利蒼的夫人葬於一號墓，根據墓中出土的一枚「妾辛追」的印章可以得知她的姓名叫辛追。雖然貴為侯爵夫人，她卻經歷了早年喪夫、晚年喪子的錐心之痛，於漢文帝后元一年（公元前163年）左右撒手人寰，死時大約50 歲。根據女屍和 T形帛畫上辛追的形象，我們請西安超人雕塑研究院復原了一個中年軑侯夫人的蠟像，再現了辛追當年的風采。

素紗直裾襌衣

素紗是指沒有染色的紗，襌衣就是沒有襯裡的衣服。這兩件衣服，重量分別為48克和49克，還不到1兩，如果除去袖口和領口較重的緣邊，重量就只有半兩多一點點，可謂「輕若煙霧，薄如蟬翼」。當然，高級的紗料並不以空隙多就算好，而主要是以蠶絲的纖度勻細見長。紡織學上有個對纖度的專門計量單位叫緊，每9000米長的單絲重1克，就是1緊。因此，緊數越小，說明蠶絲越細。素紗襌衣的蠶絲纖度竟然只有10.5 至11.3，而現在生產的高級絲織物其紗纖度卻是14，足見素紗的纖細輕薄。這樣輕薄的衣物，漢代的婦女又是怎樣穿著的呢？當時人們是罩在色澤艷麗的錦袍上穿，使錦袍上華麗的紋飾若隱若現，給人一種朦朧的美感。

一號墓T形帛畫

此畫因其形狀呈英文字母「T」形，為了便於稱呼，就稱之為「T」形帛畫。史料中則記載為「非衣」，可能有「似衣非衣」之意。它出土時反蓋在一號墓內棺棺蓋上，頂部橫裹一根竹竿在每個垂角下並都繫著絲帶或麻質帶子。據考證這是旌旗畫幡一類的物品，出葬時，由人高舉著走在儀仗的最前面，用以「引魂升天」，相當於「招魂旛」。

整幅畫全長205釐米，內容從上至下可分為天上、人間、地獄三個部分。

華蓋以上為天上部分。正上方有一人首蛇身、披髮而坐的神。根據「山海經」記載，它是威力巨大的燭龍神，主管著天氣的陰晴和晝夜的變幻。右邊繪有九個紅色的太陽半隱半藏在藍色的扶桑樹中。傳說扶桑生長在東海，有幾千丈高，十個太陽在此棲息並輪流出去值班。而畫中卻只有九日盤旋其中，另外一個太陽可能正在值班尚未歸來。最大的太陽中繪著一只黑色的鳥，古人稱之為「金烏」，這大概是古人對太陽黑子的觀測結果。左邊則是一輪彎月，月下一個美麗的女子輕舒廣袖翩跹而舞。有人說她是月神正托舉月亮緩緩升起，也有人說是偷取了不老丹藥的嫦娥向月宮飛去。月中一只肥胖碩大的蟾蜍口銜一株靈芝草，而體態輕盈的玉兔與之形成了鮮明的對比。天門兩旁兩位守門神一司閣正躬手而立，恭敬作揖，歡迎升天的老夫人。

人間部分以華蓋做屋頂，上有朱雀鳥作為裝飾。華蓋以下體態豐腴的軚侯夫人錦衣華服、環珮叮噹，正手持拐杖踽踽前行。三個貼身的奴婢緊跟其後，兩位煉丹的方士正向她獻上長生不老的丹藥。人像兩側是交蟠穿璧的雙龍，象徵尊貴和吉祥。下面的圖畫可能是老夫人去世後家人守靈祭祀的場景。他們面色青藍，神色肅穆，盡顯哀傷之態。

地獄裡赤身裸體的地神——鯀正平托著白色的大地，腳下踩踏著兩條意欲興風作浪的鼇魚，制止地震山崩的發生。地府中更有面目猙獰的怪狗和雙目圓睜的貓頭鷹，鎮壓鬼怪妖魔不去侵擾老太太的亡靈。

這是一幅把神話、想像和現實生活完美統一的傑作，它無處不體現了古人對天國的想像和追求永生的幻想。因而，「T」形帛畫是中國古代繪畫史上難得一見的傑作，具有難以估量的藝術價值，堪稱中華民族的藝術瑰寶。

女屍

女屍出土於長沙馬王堆一號漢墓，距今2100多年。她是西漢初年長沙國丞相、第一代軚侯利蒼的夫人，名叫「辛追」。出土時身長有1.54米，體重為34.3 千克，血型為A型，頭、頸、軀幹、四肢均保存了完整的外形，皮膚濕潤且覆蓋完整，呈

中南地區

淡黃褐色，手摸有油膩感。頭髮、眼睫毛、鼻毛等毛髮附在原位。部分關節仍然可以活動。皮下脂肪豐富，軟組織豐滿而有彈性，用手按壓後，能很快恢復原位。在注射防腐劑時，軟組織鼓起，能較快擴散、吸收。經Ｘ射線檢查，全身骨骼完整，兩側對稱，小至鼻骨及趾骨依然能分辨，外形與現代人骨沒有任何差別。屍體有眼球脫出、口張開、舌頭稍微挺出、直腸脫垂等死後早期腐敗現象。但因一號墓密封良好，屍體的腐敗現像在下葬後不久就停止了。

這具女屍保存的年代之久、保存程度之好，在世界屍體保存記錄中都是十分罕見的。由於它明顯不同於呈乾癟狀的「木乃伊」和表面似蠟制模型軀殼的「屍蠟」，也不同於骨骼脫鈣軟化而易於折斷的「泥炭鞣屍」，因此國際上已認同，在屍體的分類上，應該把馬王堆這類歷史悠久、軟組織仍有彈性、內臟俱在的「濕屍」，命名為「馬王堆屍」。

Mt.Hengshan （南嶽衡山）

Ladies and Gentlemen, dear friends,

Good morning. Welcome to Mt.Hengshan, lying in the central south of Hunan Province; Mt.Hengshan is one of the five sacred mountains of China. It has been placed on the Official List of the First Key Chinese Scenic Areas and has also been designated a First 4A Chinese Sightseeing Destination. Finally, it is the only place in Hunan to be ranked among China's Pilot Civilized Scenic Areas—the only representative from Hunan in this regard. Picturesque in scenery, Mt.Hengshan abounds with cultural sites and tops the other four sacred mountains in scenic beauty, thereby earning itself a title of Chinese Mountain of Longevity.

Mt.Hengshan leads the rest of sacred mountains in fame. Its outstanding qualities are attributable to its enchanting scenes, varied species, and imposing appearance.

Billed as the leader of the five sacred mountains, Mt.Hengshan boasts charming and beautiful natural scenery. While exploring Mt.Hengshan, you will see wooded hills, vying with one another for beauty, hovering clouds and bubbling streaMs.No wonder it is popularly said of this mountain that "At every turn, a tourist comes in view of a different picture, experiencing a kaleidoscope of sights". Mt.Hengshan has more beautiful views than the eye can take in. The most famous is the "Four Grand Sights of Mt.Hengshan", consisting of the Hall of Scriptures, known for its beauty, the Fangguang Temple, known for its depth, Zhurong Peak, known for its height, and Water Beads Cavern, known for its quaintness.

Mt.Hengshan has a subtropical monsoon climate with high humidity. With a long frost-free season, a short freezing season and heavy precipitation, it has cool summers and cold winters. Usually foggy and windy, it features periodic changes in temperature. A green landscape of wooded hills is attributable to its ideal natural condition. Four-fifths of Mt.Hengshan is covered with forests and some 1, 700 tree species can be found growing on its slopes. The mountain covers an area of 20, 000 hectares 3, 800 hectares of which are secondary virgin forests. It is a heavenly sanctuary for rare wild animals such as golden pheasants, bamboo partridges, and flat-breast turtles with big heads and pangolins.

Towering over the surrounding plains, Mt.Hengshan soars into the air straight from the South Hunan Basin, thereby forming a number of spectacular sights. Its scenery features four seas:a sea of flowers in spring, clouds in summer, sunrise in autumn and snow in winter. The clouds over Mt.Hengshan are especially worth mentioning. Like Mt.Huangshan's pines, the clouds over Mt.Hengshan have been viewed and talked about with great relish since ancient times. The mountain's enchanting clouds have the following characteristics. Firstly, they vary in shape from season to season:during spring the clouds are like quilts; during summer they resemble feathers, during the autumn they resemble waterfalls, and during the winter they are as dark as ink. Secondly, the gathering clouds sometimes spring up or hang low like mushrooms after the rain, taking on a peculiar look. Thirdly, the wind mixes with the scudding clouds, rising from

中
南
地
區

461

mountains in early morning or at dusk, blowing through the pine forests over tourists'faces. A deep rumbling sound of pine trees sounds frightening in the distance. Coming nearer, it gets fainter and fainter, removing tourists'fears. No wonder ancient Chinese eulogized them, saying "a sea of clouds reverberates in our hearts".

Mt.Hengshan not only has beautiful scenic sights but also abounds with cultural sites. It is the treasure house of Chinese culture, renowned as the "Civilized Museum of Great Learning". Throughout all Chinese dynasties, emperor, princes, and celebrities paid their tributes to the mountain; men of letters, poets, scholars paid their visits to it, leaving behind them steles, temples, and poems at Mt.Hengshan; they made great contributions to turning it into the priceless treasure house of Chinese culture and making it a famed mountain of Hunan culture.

In line with famous saying, "Monks take up their abode in most of famed mountains", Mt.Hengshan is not only a mountain of scenic beauty, but also a sacred religious mountain. Unlike other famous religious mountains, it embraces both Buddhism and Taoism which exist side-by-side and complement each other here.

The Ancient Town of Nanyue

A little further from the Archway of Mount Hengshan and we arrive at the ancient town of Nanyue. No one knows for sure when the town came into existence. We do know that it was a boom town as early as the Tang Dynasty. The millennia-old flagstone road you are traveling on is well trodden, looking polished and glossy. Leather shoes clank on it as if a robed monk beats his wooden block chanting scriptures, striking a deep chord in pilgrims'hearts.

The streets in the town are all paved with stone slabs. They are lined with two-storied protruding houses of equal size. Whitewashed and glazed in red, the houses have upturned eaves, roofs carved with dragons and painted with phoenixes. The houses are kept as they were, lending a primitive simplicity to the town. A joss stick bought in a store or a cup of tea sipped in a roadhouse can provide tourists with either a new experience, such as imbibing a bit of profound Buddhism, or give them an aftertaste of traditional Chinese culture. More interestingly, there is an endless arcade on either side of a street. Therefore, you may roam along street without carrying an umbrella in rainy days.

Though small in size, Nanyue ancient town is self-sufficient with restaurants, hotels, incense and general stores, temples and studies smelling of ink. It is worth mentioning the restaurants here, offering local specialties such delicious wild mushrooms, the unique tasting Mt.Hengshan bean curd, and nutritious mountain bamboo shoots. The local specialties are mouth watering in taste. To make your trip here perfect, you should have a taste of the special dishes in Mt.Hengshan, which are as famous as Xi'an bread filled with lamb, Tianjin fried dough sticks, and Chongqing chafing dishes.

Walking past the flagstone streets of long duration, living quarters with a long history, and soul-purifying temples and incense altars, aren't you enlightened? After a visit here, don't you have a special feeling for Nanyue? Much more thought for life? Therein lies the beauty of this ancient town.

The Grand Temple of Nanyue

Beyond the North Street, the landscape opens up to a wide vista. In sight is a magnificent ancient building complex. Standing before us is the largest ancient palace complex in Southern China. The Grand Temple is an ancient building complex of pagan, Buddhist, and Taoist temples and residential palaces. It is the largest religious building complex in Southern China and the country's five sacred mountains. The present temple complex, which is nine sections deep, has four courtyards, eight Buddhist temples, and eight Taoist temples. It covers an area of 98, 500 square meters, and is 375 meters

中南地區

deep, 139 meters wide in the outer section, and 174 meters wide in the inner section. It is partitioned off in the Confucian style of architecture:eight Taoist temples on the eastern side and eight Buddhist temples on the western side. This is the only temple in the world, embracing Confucianism, Taoism and Buddhism in one place of worship.

The Temple to Martyrs

Located at the foot of the Fragrant Incense Peak, the Nanyue Temple to Martyrs is billed as one of the earliest and largest historical sites in China commemorating the War of Resistance Against Japanese Aggression. It is the only big mausoleum left behind on the mainland by the Guomindang Nationalist Government honoring revolutionary fighters during this conflict. Planning for the mausoleum's construction began in 1938 and it was completed in 1943. Modeled on Dr.Sun Yat-sen's Mausoleum in Nanjing, it was built on a hillside, facing north with a symmetrical layout. It has five component parts:the archway, the monument, the memorial hall, the stone tablet of tributes and the tomb site. Some of commanders and soldiers of the Ninth and sixth Theaters of Operation are buried here. The site is now placed on the official list of Chinese National Heritage Sites.

The Temple to Martyrs' front gate is a marble archway of three arches and a single tier of eaves. A horizontal beam hangs over the archway, inscribed with the title, "The Nanyue Temple to Martyrs". These glistening words were handwritten by Xue Yue, the then governor of Hunan Provincial Government of the Nationalist Party and commander in chief of the Ninth Theater of Operations.

Upon entering the archway, you find yourselves in a flat open square. Some of the tourists may ask out of curiosity why Mt.Hengshan was chosen for burying martyrs out of such a big country as China. We need to give some background information concerning the burial site. Soon after the War of Resistance Against Japanese Aggression broke out, northern China, eastern China and southern China mostly fell into enemy 's hands. As a result, the central government of the Nation-alist Party moved to Chongqing and Mt.Hengshan became one of the fighting fronts against the Japanese imperialist forces. In November, 1938, Jiang Kaishek, called a top-level military conference in Mt.Hengshan. Zhou Enlai and Ye Jianying attended the conference as representatives of the Chinese Communist Party. After hearing the war reports given by military commanders of various theaters of operations, Jiang Kai shek, realizing so many officers and soldiers had died and were unburied in battlefields, ordered their immediate burial. After a discussion, it was agreed at the conference that the Temple to Martyrs and the Cemetery of Martyrs should be built in Nanyue. The central government contributed the largest sum of money for this project, with other funds coming from the Ninth and Sixth Theaters of Operations and contributions made by people from all walks of life. The remains of dead officers and soldiers, therefore, were buried and their bodies were laid to rest here. That is how the Temple to martyrs originated.

At the center of the square stands an odd-looking statue. It is the Monument of Lugou Bridge Incident of July 7, 1937. It is composed of five upside-down stone shells (four big shells and one small one). They stand for the five Chinese nationalities:the Hans, the Mans, the Mongolians, the Huis and the Tibetans. Inscribed on three sides of the marble statue (front, left and right), were two bold words 『July 7', symbolic of Lugou Bridge Incident which brought in united resistance against Japanese aggression. The shells in an upside-down position, pointing to the blue sky and the sun, symbolize Chinese resistance against Japanese aggression.

After a visit to the Monument in Comme-moration of Lugou Bridge Incident, you are taken to the Memorial Hall, the third section of the Temple to Martyrs. The present horizontal board was inscribed with bold words handwr-itten by Qu Wu, ex-chairman of the Revolutionary Committee of the Chinese Nationalist Party. In the center of the memorial hall stands a marble stele, 6 meters high, inscribed with "the History of the Memorial Hall in the Nanyue Temple to Martyrs", written by General Xue Yue, giving an account of the historical background and construction of the hall. Exhibition

中南地區

displays are on each side of the hall devoted to photographs, paintings, and historical literature regarding Nanyue and the War of Resistance Against Japanese Aggression.

The back door of the hall leads to two rows of stone steps upward on the mountainside. Its 276 steps represent the 276 officers and soldiers who died in the War Resisting Japanese Aggression. A patch of wooded land between two rows of steps was set aside for displaying touching words, "Eternal Glory to National Martyrs", "Nation, the Rights of People, the Livelihood of People". There are nine flights of steps.

Walking up the steps, we arrive at the tomb site, the last but certainly not the least important building in the Temple to the Martyrs. Over the front door hangs a big horizontal board inscribed with bold words, "Temple to Martyrs", handwritten by Jiang Kaishek. Please have a close examination of the words on the board. Have you found anything special about the words?

Walking out of the tomb site, you come in view of mounds on either side of the tomb site. This is a cemetery for the martyrs who died in the War of Resistance Against Japanese Aggression. Covering an area of over 13 hectares, the cemetery has seven group tombs burying the dead of the 60thdivision of 37thArmy and 19thdivision of 70thArmy, as well as ten personal tombs burying generals such as Hu Heyun and Zheng Zuomin. The tombs lie hidden from sight under pine and cypress trees, some stately, others standing tall and erect, still others arranged in lines and the rest looking up into the sky. Veiled in respectful silence for the dead, the cemetery looks solemn and grave.

The Zhurong Peak

The Zhurong Peak is the highest peak of the seventy two peaks in Mt.Hengshan, 1,290 meters above sea level. The lofty Zhurong Peak is in marked contrast to the low-lying South Hunan Basin and seems to reach into the clouds. The peak commands a bird's eye view of South Hunan. The Zhurong Temple stands atop the Zhurong peak. Built on a giant rock, the temple is broken down into two component sections. The temple is roofed with tin-plated tiles, each 0. 6 meter long, 0. 3 meter wide and 15 kilograms in weight. Dozens of the tiles were cast in the Song Dynasty Imperial Foundry. The tiles are not rusty and look shiny after a thousand years of use. You may ask out of curiosity why were tin-plated tiles used for roofing? The building architecture shows great originality and distinctive features of its own. Look around and you find only a few low trees growing sparsely at the peak. Category 4 and 5 storms blowing over the peak all year round are to blame for this. If the temple had not been roofed with tin-plated tiles, its roof would have been blown away by these typhoon force winds.

Walking out of a small stone door on the right side of the temple, one finds a stone terrace with such inscriptions as "A Skyline View of the World" and "Beating Anyone in Height". This is the Moon-viewing Terrace, the highest point in Mt.Hengshan. Looking over railings at the hanging moon, one may feel like standing high above clouds, getting closer to the moon, having entered the heavenly gate, being instantly relaxed and happy.

中南地區

各位女士、各位先生,各位朋友,你們好!歡迎大家來到南嶽衡山做客!衡山位於湖南省中南部,是中國著名的五嶽之一,首批國家重點風景名勝區、首批國家4A級旅遊區和湖南省唯一的「中國文明風景旅遊區示範點」。衡山風光秀美,人文薈萃,素有「五嶽獨秀」、「中華壽岳」之稱。

南嶽衡山之所以能夠在中國眾多名山中脫穎而出,首先應歸功於它那旖旎多姿的風光、豐富多樣的物種和瑰麗無比的氣象。

南嶽號稱「五嶽獨秀」,以「秀」為主要景觀特色。這裡群巒疊翠,萬木爭榮,雲霧繚繞,溪泉叮咚,真是「五里不同景,十里兩重天」呀!衡山的風景美不勝收、數不勝數,其中最著名的當屬「衡山四絕」:藏經殿之秀,方廣寺之深,祝融峰之高和水簾洞之奇。

衡山屬中亞熱帶季風性濕潤氣候，無霜期長，冰凍期短，具有夏涼冬寒、雨量充沛、霧多風大、氣溫垂直變化明顯等特點。良好的自然條件造就了衡山無山不樹、無處不綠的特色景觀。南嶽衡山共擁有600 多科、1700 多種樹木，風景林面積達2 萬公頃，原始次生林面積達3 800公頃，森林覆蓋率高達80%以上，與之相伴的還有珍稀的野生動物錦雞、竹雞、大頭平胸龜、穿山甲等，可以稱得上是一座天然的生物資源寶庫。

衡山自湘南盆地中拔地而起，突兀聳立，與周邊地區形成了鮮明的反差，也促成了許多美妙奇特的氣候景觀。衡山風景有「四海」之稱，即花海、林海、雲海和雪海。春觀花、夏看雲、秋望日、冬賞雪是觀賞衡山四季風光特色所在。在這其中，衡山的雲尤其值得一提。「衡山雲、黃山松」，自古就為人們所津津樂道。衡山的雲一奇在四時變幻，春雲同被，夏雲如羽，秋雲像瀑，冬雲似墨；二奇在雲嘯，有時雨後，衡山的雲聚集起來，拔地而起，在半空中擴展成蘑菇狀，十分罕見；三奇在響雲，清晨或傍晚山風吹過松林，挾著層層雲塊向遊人撲來，其中隱隱帶有松濤之聲，令人膽顫心驚，但一到身邊便化作無數輕紗，飄然散去，使人頓覺心中鬱悶一掃而光，難怪古人曾長嘆「雲海蕩吾心胸」呀！

衡山之秀，外秀於林，**內秀於文**。南嶽是中華文化的寶庫，以「文明奧區」享譽天下。歷朝歷代的帝王天子、達官貴人來此祭拜的歷史記載屢見不鮮，而文人騷客、鴻儒巨學的來訪更是不計其數。他們立碑建祠、訪古探幽、吟詩作賦，給衡山留下了寶貴的物質和精神財富，也使衡山成為湖湘文化名山。

常言道：「天下名山僧占多。」衡山不僅是風景名山，也是宗教聖山。但衡山與其他宗教名山相比，其獨特之處是山上佛道並存，互彰互顯，同尊共榮。

南嶽古鎮

經過南嶽衡山牌坊，向前一拐，便踏入了南嶽古鎮。古鎮的具體形成年代已不可考，但至少在唐代時，這裡就已經形成了非常興旺的香市。大家請看腳下這條青石路面，歷經千年歲月，已經被磨得光可鑒人，鞋跟踩在上面發出清脆的響聲，宛若禪鐘木魚，敲擊著每一位香客的魂魄！

南嶽古鎮的街道都是用麻石板鋪成的，兩側是高矮一致的兩層挑樓，清一色朱瓦白牆、高高挑起的飛簷和雕龍畫鳳的犀脊，全部保持著舊時的風貌，處處體現出南嶽古鎮的古樸之美。在這裡的攤鋪裡買一炷香，在茶樓上品一盞茶，都會感覺受益匪淺。古鎮的街道還有一奇，那就是兩側房屋下都有一條長廊，連成一線。這樣即使是在下雨天，不用打傘就可以悠然地漫步長街。

古鎮雖小，但飯館、客棧、香肆、商店、佛堂，甚至是墨香猶存的書屋應有盡有。尤其是這裡的飯館，供應的都是本地特色菜餚，像鮮嫩美味的野生蘑菇、口感獨特的衡山豆腐和營養豐富的山中竹筍，無不令人垂涎三尺。到了衡山不嘗嘗當地的風味菜餚，就像去了西安不吃羊肉泡饃、去了天津不吃狗不理包子、去了重慶不吃麻辣火鍋一樣，總是有些美中不足！

走過了寫滿滄桑的青石板路，走過了印滿歷史的古棧民居，走過了蕩滌心靈的佛堂香肆，大家的心中是否也點亮了一盞明燈呢？大家是否對南嶽又產生了一種異樣的情愫呢？大家是否對人生又多了一份思考呢？這就是古鎮真正的美之所在！

南嶽大廟

穿過北街，前面豁然開朗，一座巍峨宏大的古建築群展現在我們面前，這就是中國南方最大的宮殿式古建築群——南嶽大廟。

南嶽大廟是一組集民間祠廟、佛教寺院、道教宮觀和皇宮殿宇於一體的古建築群，也是中國南方及五嶽之中規模最大的廟宇。大廟現存建築共有九進、四院、八寺和八觀，前後縱深375　　米，左右橫寬前半段139米，後半段174米，總計占地98500平方米。它的中軸線上為儒家建築風格，東邊為八個道觀，西邊為八個佛寺，像這樣儒、道、佛三教共存一廟，在中國乃至全世界都是絕無僅有的。

忠烈祠

中南地區

南嶽忠烈祠坐落在香爐峰下，是中國建築時間最早、規模最大的抗日戰爭紀念地之一，也是國民政府在大陸唯一一處保留下來的紀念抗戰烈士的大型陵園。忠烈祠籌建於1938 年，1943 年落成。陵園仿南京中山陵樣式建造，坐南朝北，依山而築，左右對稱，層次分明。它沿中軸線共分為牌坊、紀念碑、紀念堂、致敬碑和享堂五部分。在這裡，長眠著國民黨第九戰區和第六戰區的部分抗日陣亡戰士，是國家重點文物保護單位。

朋友們，眼前的這座三拱橋單檐牌坊就是忠烈祠的正門。它是由花崗岩石砌成的，正上方的漢白玉石匾上鑲嵌著原國民黨湖南省政府主席兼第九戰區司令長官薛岳題寫的「南嶽忠烈祠」五個鎏金大字。

步入牌坊，便來到一個平坦而又開闊的廣場上。有的朋友也許會覺得奇怪：中國如此之大，為什麼要選擇在南嶽衡山修建忠烈祠呢？要說明這個問題，就不得不談一談當時的時代背景了。抗日戰爭爆發後，華北、華東和華南大部分地區相繼淪陷，國民黨政府遷都重慶，衡山成了抗日前線大本營之一。1938年11 月，蔣介石在衡山主持召開了高級軍事會議，中共代表周恩來、葉劍英等也參加了這次會議。在會上，蔣介石聽取了各戰區指揮官的匯報後，鑒於「陣亡將士，多暴屍戰場」，指示要盡快將烈士遺體設法掩埋。經過討論，會議決定由中央下撥巨款，第九戰區、第六戰區和湖南省政府出資並接受社會各界捐款，在南嶽名山修建忠烈祠和烈士公墓，安葬陣亡將士的遺骸，以告慰烈士在天英靈。這便是修建忠烈祠的由來。

來到廣場的中心，大家肯定會被這個造型奇特的雕塑所吸引，這便是「七·七紀念塔」。它是由五顆倒立的石製砲彈組成，砲彈四大一小，代表著中國的五大民族——漢、滿、蒙、回、藏。雕塑的正面和左右兩側，都嵌有漢白玉砌的「七七」兩個字，象徵著從1937年7月7日盧溝橋事變爆發後，中國人民同仇敵忾，共禦外侮，掀起的全民抗日的民族怒潮。這些砲彈倒立在地上、直指藍天、直指太陽，寓意著「抗日」。

參觀了「七·七紀念塔」，便來到了忠烈祠的第三進建築——紀念堂。匾額是前民革中央副主席屈武題寫的。紀念堂的正中豎著一塊高達6 米的漢白玉石碑，上面刻有薛岳將軍撰寫的《南嶽忠烈祠紀念堂碑記》，記述了建祠的歷史背景和經過。堂的兩側現在開闢為展覽室，陳列著關於南嶽與抗戰的一些圖片文字資料。

從紀念堂的後門走出，大家可以看到兩排石階依山勢而上。石階共有276級，代表著抗戰時期犧牲的276位將官。兩排石階的中間為精心設計的綠地，其中用大理石片鑲嵌著「民族忠烈千古」和「民族、民權、民生」的大字。

拾級而上，就來到了忠烈祠最後也是最主要的建築——享堂。在享堂正門上方懸掛著鎏金巨匾「忠烈祠」，是蔣介石的手跡。

從享堂出來，大家請看兩側的山坡，這是抗日英烈的公墓區。整個墓區占地約13 公頃，共有37軍60師、70軍19師等集體墓葬7座，胡鶴雲、鄭作民等將軍個人墓葬10 座。這些公墓，都掩映在蒼松翠柏之間，有的華表相望，墓闕凌空；有的碑碣成行，塔尖插雲。其氣象肅穆，隱現英烈忠魂，令人景仰，讓人欽佩！

祝融峰

祝融峰是衡山七十二峰的最高峰，海拔1290米。由於它獨立於地勢相對低窪的湘南盆地之中，更顯得峻極天穹，因此登高一望，湘南風景盡收眼底。祝融峰頂建有祝融殿。殿宇完全修建在一座絕頂巨石之上，分為兩進，在殿頂上蓋有二尺長、一尺寬，重達30多斤的加錫鐵瓦。在這些鐵瓦中，有數十塊由宋朝報國寺鑄造，至今歷經千年而不鏽，光潔如新。有的朋友可能覺得奇怪，為什麼這裡要用鐵瓦呢？其實這裡也體現了建築師的匠心獨具。大家看一下祝融峰頂的四周，樹木稀少而且低矮，這是由於這裡終年不斷的四五級大風造成的。要保持殿頂不被颶風掀起，非鐵瓦不足以勝任。

從祝融殿右側小石門走出，外面還有一個石台，上刻「乾坤勝覽」和「唯我最高」。這是望月台，也是南嶽衡山真正的最高點。站在這裡憑欄望月，會覺得雲低月近，如登天門一般，令登臨者心曠神怡，魂遊物外！

Naturally Picturesque Huangshizhai （ Yellow Stone Stockade ） （如詩如畫黃石寨）

Hello, dear friends,

Welcome to Zhangjiajie. I am very glad to be your tour guide. Today we will visit Zhangjiajie's biggest sightseeing terrace soaring into the air, the Huangshizhai, or Yellow Stone Stockade. People often say that "You can't be said to have been to Zhangjiajie if you have not reached Huangshizhai" . So we can see that Huangshizhai is the quintessence of Zhangjiajie scenic area. The mountain, seen from afar, resembles an almighty lion. Since the Chinese words "lion" and "stone" are the same in sound. namely "shi" , hence the name "Yellow (『Huang』 in Chinese) Lion Stockade" , or Huangshi Stockade.

Huangshizhai is located in the center of the Zhangjiajie National Forest Park, rising about 1, 200 meters above sea level. The stockade area covers over 133 hectares. It is a magnificent, strange and beautiful terrace, with numerous sheer precipices and overhanging rocks. Overlooking the periphery from the top of the stockade, you can see numerous valleys covered by clouds, many of peaks clustering together, with green trees poking into the sky and floating thin mist. A renowned poet once praised Huangshizhai with the following poem:

Advancing five steps, you praise it "Mar-velous" ,

Advancing seven steps, you praise it "Mat-chless" ,

Advancing ten steps beyond, you will become speechless.

Secluded Path in the Fir Forest

Before us first we see a line of steep and winding stone steps, half-hidden in the thick and tranquil fir forest. That is the "secluded path in the fir forest". In the ancient times there was only one path up to Huangshizhai, and it was located at the back of the mountain. The path we are using was finished and opened a decade ago. Scenic views abound alongside this secluded path and provide a visual feast for your eyes.

The Arhat is Welcoming the Guests

The scenic spot before us is called "The arhat is welcoming the guests". Please look at the stone wall on the upper left. A big-bellied arhat is sitting by a pine tree with his legs crossed. He is wearing a monk cap, and with his mouth and eyes slanting, he is all smiles as he overlooks the mountains.

Big Stone House

Now let us go on our visit. This is a stone cover where we are. It is about 3 meters high and about 20 meters long. Over it is a suspending stone cover called "big stone house". It is not only a fit place for visitors to have a short rest, but also a wonderful terrace for sightseeing. The views looking to the east include Huaxiyu (The Flower Stream Valley), the Seed Garden, and Luoguta (The Tower of Gongs and Drums). They constitute a fairyland with range upon range of mountains, dozens of peaks towering into the clouds and mist.

Half-Mountain

Over the "big stone house" there is a peak protruding out from the mountainside. It takes on a golden and brilliant color when the sun is shining. Seen from below, it resembles a big hand with its five fingers stretching out and its palm slightly contracted. People call it "half-mountain" because it resembles the half of a mountain that has been cut open by an axe.

中
南
地
區

Terrace for Singing

Please listen to the singing like sounds coming from in front of us. These are melodious Tujia national minority folk or mountain songs. The place we see in the front is a terrace on which stand Tujia girls wearing beautiful dresses singing and dancing to greet you. Will their pleasant melodies make you yearn to learn more about Tujia national minority morals and customs? Will their hospitality, simplicity, and kindness bring you relaxation and happiness you have never experienced? Right here and at this time, have you sensed the true meaning of "beautiful mountains, beautiful rivers and even more beautiful people" of Zhangjiajie?

Terrace for Mustering Officers

Now we have reached the middle of the mountain, already half way to the top of the stockade. Please look at the huge stone protruding into the sky in front of us. Under it is a forest of firs, with its vast greenness rising and falling. This scenic spot is "Terrace for Mustering Officers". Tradition has it that Zhang Liang, Marquis Liu of Han Dynasty, came here to live and study in seclusion. But he was suspected by the powerful and tyrannical Empress Dowager L . In order to be ready for any eventuality, Zhang Liang trained his men here day and night. It is said that this is the right place where Zhang Liang once mustered his officers and assigned them tasks.

Recreation Terrace

Now we have passed the "Terrace for Mustering Officers". Please go up along the steps on the right, and you will arrive at a concave precipice sightseeing terrace arched by natural stone walls, called "Recreation Terrace". From here, you can see "Treasure Case for Heavenly Books" right in your front. In the distance, you can see Huaxiyu (The Flower Stream Valley). Looking up, you can see numerous peaks unevenly towering into the sky and vivid green forests. Now please look at the mountain opposite to us on the right. There stands a 20 meter high stone column. On its top is a platform, on which there is a stone case about 3 meters long and 1. 5 meters wide. A stone cover is on the case, half of it protruding into the air, and the other covering the case. Around the case are five jade-green pines and cypresses. Legend has it that Zhang Liang once hid the three volumes of the Heavenly Books of his teacher, Master Huangshi, in this case. After the war stopped, he took out the books to put them in another place. But he forgot to put on the drawing cover, leaving the stone case half covered to this day. For the Heavenly Books were once hidden in this stone case, it was honored the name "Treasure Case of Heavenly Books".

South Gate to the Heavenly Palace

Now let us go on climbing up. Please look forward. Two mountains are huddled together, leaving only a small path between them, in the shape of a gate. It is said of this gate that if one man guards it, then ten thousand men cannot break it open. This is "Nantianmen" —South Gate to the Heavenly Palace. Please look at the two peaks on both sides. They tower there, one on each side, powerful and almighty, like the ancient palace guards, guarding the gate all the time. People call them the "Door-guarding Generals". They wear armors, with fine swords and feather arrows, stout as giants, really life-like. It is said that they are also the mountain gods guarding Huangshizhai.

Coin Willow

Have you noticed this ancient tree soaring into the sky? It is over a hundred years old. People call it the "Qingqian Willow" or "Coin Willow", for its fruits are just like ancient coins in strings, with a golden-yellow color when they are ripe, with a kernel in the center of each, and patterns around it. From the bottom, its root splits into big forks. In spring and summer, its crown is just like an open big umbrella, with its dense branches and luxuriant leaves giving us cool shade from the hot sun. In autumn and winter, its leaves turn yellow and its fruits are ripe. As the wind blows, strings of

中南地區

the fruit fall on the ground, just like strings of golden copper-coins. No wonder it is called "the coin tree".

Magical Needle Stabilizing the Sea and Sole Pillar of South Sky

Now, this way, please. Not far from the "Coin Tree" in front of it is the "Magical Needle Stabilizing the Sea". It towers tall and erect, as if it were supporting the whole mountain with its firm trunk. The "Magical Needle Stabilizing the Sea" and "Golden Whip Rock" echo each other at a distance, forming a most magnificent "Natural Grand Spect-acle". Now what scenic spot is this isolated column peak in front? It protrudes abruptly from the earth and, with a height of over 300 meters, it soars into the clouds. With its roots firmly planted in the earth, it truly resembles a stone pillar in the sky. This is the renowned "Sole Pillar of South Sky"; it has this name because it is standing under the South Gate to the Heavenly World. The sole pillar of the south sky echoes with "the Sole Pillar of West Sky". Legend has it that they were changed from two macaques, each with only one leg. Long ago, in their attempt to save the Monkey Sun Wukong (the famous Monkey King in the Chinese novel Journey to the West), they were transformed, by magic, by Erlangshen, a god with a third and vertical eye in his forehead. They had no choice but to just stand here.

The "Sole Pillar of South Sky" is the feature of the whole "Wulingyuan" scene. It towers straight from the ground, embodying a stubbornly resistant spirit in the face of constant change. As the miniature of the geomorphology scene of quartzes sandstone peak forest of the whole "Wulingyuan", it is the festival medal and symbol of "Zhangjiajie International Forest Protection Festival".

Star-picking Terrace

Now, we have smoothly climbed up to Huangshizhai. The round stone peak, whose summit is flat and lower slope is terraced, is Star-Picking Terrace. Standing on the terrace you cannot help but feel that "all peaks are dwarfs under my feet". From here, you can enjoy many major scenic spots in the distance, such as "Two Doors Open to Welcome Guests", "Natural Wall-Paining", "Yupingfeng (Jade Vase Peak)", and "Rabbit Watching the Moon". Especially in the evening, you will feel extremely near to the stars, as if you could pick them down when stretching out your hands.

Pavilion of Six Strangenesses

This artificial scenic spot is the "Liuqige", or "Pavilion of Six Strangenesses". By "six strangenesses", we mean the strange mountains, waters, clouds, stones, and plants. This is the only artificial scenic spot in the park. It was constructed with marble stones and reinforced concrete. The four-story building, with various corners on its roof and protruding eaves, is a special pavilion integrating the folk customs, calligraphy and natural scenes. Standing on the third floor, you can feast your eyes on the Zhangjiajie's magnificent scenery. On the top of the pavilion, you can see Yuanjiajie, Yangjiajie, Tianzishan, Chaotianguan, and the Peak of Three Sisters.

Now let us go along the 2, 200 meter mountain-top loop-route to visit scenic spots, such as Wuzhifeng (Five-finger peak), the Front Garden, and the Piers of a Ruined Heavenly Bridge. Every rock peak here is an ancient work of art, and in every rock peak are hidden limitless mysteries of nature. Several years ago, a woman writer from northeast China stood on the sightseeing terrace of Five-finger Peak, sighing: "I feel no regret to die now since I have seen the scenes of Zhangjiajie!" And then she continued to say: "I feel that I have more reasons to live well since I have seen the scenes of the Zhangjiajie!" These words seemed paradoxical. But actually the first sentence expresses that, having seen such wonderful scenes as those in Zhangjiajie, she felt satisfied in her life, while the second sentence expresses that life was so beautiful that she should better treasure her life.

Back Mountain Gate

中南地區

477

Now we have arrived at the Back Mountain Gate. It is like a stone gate, steep in the middle and narrow on both sides, very difficult to approach. In the past, this was the only access to Huangshizhai. It was from here that Ex-General Secretary Jiang Zemin ascended and descended Huangshizhai in March of 1995. During a break in the trip up the mountain, he jubilantly played the erhu—the two-stringed Chinese fiddle—to accompany the local Tujia national minority girl singers. On the stockade top, he couldn't help but sing the Beijing Opera "Taking Weihu Mountain" aria, "Killing a Tiger in the Up-mountain Trip".

So much for Huangshizhai, hopefully, you have had a pleasant and unforgettable memories of the mountain. Welcome back to Huangshizhai for another sightseeing tour at your convenience.

各位朋友：

大家好！歡迎來到張家界，非常高興能同大家一起遊覽張家界最大的凌空觀景台——黃石寨。人們常説「不到黃石寨，枉來張家界」，可見黃石寨是整個張家界風景的精華。從遠處眺望，此山像一頭威猛的雄師，所以稱為「黃獅寨」。又因「石」音同「獅」，故又稱「黃石寨」。

黃石寨位於張家界國家森林公園的中部，海拔約1200米，寨頂面積達200多畝，是由無數懸崖峭壁共同托起的一塊雄偉、奇特而又美麗的台地。從寨頂眺望四周，只見雲漫萬壑，千峰攢聚，綠樹凌空，薄霧飄舞。黃石寨是張家界風景的精華，一位著名詩人這樣評價黃石寨：「五步稱奇，七步叫絕，十步之外，目瞪口呆。」

杉林幽徑

首先呈現在我們面前的是一排陡峭而又曲折的石級，隱隱約約躺在茂密寧靜的杉林裡，那就是「杉林幽徑」。自古登黃石寨只有後山一條路，今天走的這條路，是十多年前人工開鑿的。從杉林幽徑上山，兩邊的風景，讓人目不暇接。

羅漢迎賓

前面這個景點叫做「羅漢迎賓」。請大家注意左上側的石壁上，一個大肚羅漢正靠近一棵松樹盤腿而坐，他頭戴僧帽，歪嘴斜眼，滿臉堆笑地凝望著山下。大家若仔細看就會發現，他特別像民間傳說中的「濟公」和尚。

大岩屋

離開「羅漢迎賓」，請繼續往上走。現在所在的地方是一座岩罩，它高約3米，長約20米，上面有一個2米多寬的岩石懸罩，它叫做「大岩屋」。這裡既是遊客們小憩的好地方，也是一處絕妙的觀景台，往東可以看到花溪峪、種子園與鑼鼓塔一大片風光，其間重巒疊嶂，萬峰聳立，雲霧繚繞，恍如仙境。

半壁江山

在大岩屋的上面，有一座突兀在山腰上的山峰，顏色金黃，在陽光下灼灼閃光，人們稱它為「半壁江山」。從下面看，它猶如一扇巨大的手掌，五指伸開，而且手掌略收。它聳立在那裡，正如同大斧劈開的半邊山一樣，真是鬼斧神工！

點歌台

人家請注意聽，前面傳來了陣陣歌聲。這是悅耳動聽的土家山歌，前面便是土家姑娘的點歌台。看，一個個衣著秀麗的土家姑娘正在載歌載舞地歡迎著各位來賓，她們優美的歌聲是否會喚起您對土家民風的無限嚮往呢？她們的熱情好客、淳樸善良是否帶給您一種從未有過的輕鬆和快樂？此時此刻，您是否感悟到了張家界「山美、水美、人更美」呢？

點將台

大家現在已經到半山腰了，離寨頂只差一半的路程了。大家請看，前面有一塊巨石凌空突出，崖下一片杉林連綿起伏，綠濤洶湧，這個景點就是「點將台」。相

中南地區

479

傳漢留侯張良當年為了尋找師傅的蹤跡，來到此地，卻遭到大權在握、專橫一世的呂后的猜忌。為了對付呂后的大軍圍攻，張良在此日夜操練人馬，以防不測。據說，這裡就是張良當年登台「點將」的地方。

娛樂台

過了「點將台」，大家往右邊台階向上走，上面是一處天然石壁拱成的凹形崖壁觀景台，這便是「娛樂台」。這裡可以近看「天書寶匣」，遠觀花溪峪，上眺千峰錯列，下瞰林木蒼翠。大家請看右邊對面的山上，有一個約20米高的圓形石柱，兀自獨立，頂端為一平台，上面有一塊長約3米，寬約1.5米的石匣，匣上有一個石蓋，一半凌空，一半蓋於匣上，周圍環繞著五棵翠綠的松柏。傳說張良曾將黃石公的三卷天書藏於匣內，後因戰事平息，張良又取出天書放置在其他地方，但他卻忘記合上抽蓋，至今留下一只半掩半開的石匣。由於石匣內曾藏過天書，因而被人譽為「天書寶匣」。

南天門

看過天書之後，繼續攀登。大家請看前方，兩山相擠，中間僅有一條通道，其形如門，大有「一夫當關，萬夫莫開」的氣勢，這裡就是「南天門」。大家請注意旁邊的兩座山峰，排列整齊，威武雄壯，酷似古代的武士，一左一右，常年守候在南天門旁邊，人們稱他們為「把門將軍」。他們身穿鎧甲，腰懸寶刀，背插羽箭，身材偉岸，形態逼真。據說這是把守黃石寨的山神。

搖錢樹

不知大家注意到身邊這一棵參天古木沒有，其樹齡在百歲以上，叫「青錢柳」。它結籽成串，形狀如錢，成熟時色呈金黃，中間有仁，周圍還有花紋，與古代的銅錢一模一樣。它的樹根從底部分成大丫，春夏季節，樹冠就像是一把撐開的巨傘，枝繁葉茂，給我們一片清涼；秋冬時分，樹葉泛黃，果實成熟，風一吹動，串串果實灑落在地上，就像是一串串金黃的銅錢，由此得名「搖錢樹」。

定海神針與南天一柱

大家請看這邊，過了「搖錢樹」不遠，前面便是「定海神針」。它高大挺拔，巍然屹立，似乎在用強硬的身軀支撐著整座大山。「定海神針」與「金鞭岩」遙遙相對，形成了一幅十分壯觀的「天然壯景」。那前面這座孤立的柱峰又是什麼景點呢？它拔地而起，直插雲霄，高達300 餘米，根部穩紮大地，真像一根擎天石柱！這就是張家界有名的「南天一柱」了，因立在南天門下面而得名。它與「西天一柱」遙相呼應，傳說二者是兩只獨腳獼猴所變，當年它們為救孫悟空，被二郎神點化，只得永遠立在這裡了。

「南天一柱」是整個「武陵源」風景的特寫，它拔地而起，上大下小。在它身上有一種歷經萬年滄桑卻仍然堅忍不拔的精神，是整個「武陵源」石英岩峰林地貌景觀的縮影，也是「張家界國際森林保護節」的節徽和標誌。

摘星台

大家現在已順利登上黃石寨了。前面這座上平下懸的圓形石峰就是「摘星台」。站在台上，使人油然產生「一覽眾山小」的感慨！這裡可眺望「雙門迎賓」、「天然壁畫」、「玉瓶峰」、「兔兒望月」等主要景點。特別是到了晚上，有一種與星星近在咫尺的感覺，似乎一伸手，就能將天上的星星「摘下來」。

六奇閣

前面這個人工景點就是「六奇閣」。「六奇」準確地說是指山奇、水奇、雲奇、石奇、動物奇、植物奇。這是公園內唯一的人造景觀，它採用大理石和鋼筋混凝土等材料建成，高四層，攢尖飛頂，重檐突出，是一座集民俗、書法、自然景觀於一體的特殊樓閣。站在三樓，可以盡情飽覽張家界的壯麗風光。站在閣頂，可以看到袁家界、楊家界、天子山、朝天觀、三姐妹峰……

接下來沿著長2200米的山頂環繞線遊覽五指峰、前花園、天橋遺墩等景點。這裡的每一座岩峰都是一件古老的藝術品，每一座岩峰都隱藏著大自然的無窮奧秘。

中南地區

幾年前，一位來自東北的女作家，就站在五指峰觀景台感嘆道：「看了張家界的風光，覺得真可以死了！」接下來她又說：「看了張家界的風光，覺得更有理由好好活了！」兩句話看起來前後矛盾，其實不然：前一句是說能見到像張家界這樣奇美的風光，此生足矣；後一句是說人生是如此美好，理應更加珍愛生命。

後山門

現在來到後山門，它猶如一道石門，中間陡峭，兩邊狹窄，地勢十分險要。過去這裡是登黃石寨的唯一通道。1995年3月，江澤民總書記就是從這裡上下黃石寨的。上山途中，江總書記在休息時興致勃勃地拉起二胡，為當地的土家族女歌手伴奏；登上寨頂後，又情不自禁地唱起京劇《智取威虎山》中的「打虎上山」唱段，與遊客們同樂。

我的講解就到這裡，希望張家界的美景留給大家的是永遠美好的回憶，希望大家下次再來黃石寨觀光旅遊。

Hubei Province湖北省

A Glimpse of the Province （本省簡介）

Located on the middle lower reaches of the Yangtze River, Hubei means, "North of Lake," due to its location on the northern side of the Dongting Lake. In ancient times, it was simply call "E", as it was part of the old state of E'zhou. It is about 740 kilometers long from the east to the west, 470 kilometers wide from the north to the south, and covers 185, 900 square kilometers, accounting for 1. 94% of China's total territory. It is the 16thlargest province in China in terms of size. Hubei's terrain mainly consists of mountains surrounding its east, west and the north sides, while the middle of the province consists of incompletely formed and southward facing open-basin. The Yangtze River flows through Hubei for some 1, 061 kilometers, while its largest tributary, the Han River, also flows across the province for some 878 kilometers.

The Han River joins the Yangtze River at Wuhan, the capital of Hubei. There are about 300 lakes that are larger than 3 square kilometers in Hubei, and most of them are scattered across the Jianghan Plain. Parts of Hubei have a subtropical monsoon climate, while parts of it lies in the transitional zone between the subtropical and temperate climate zones. The entire province is marked by abundant sunshine and warmth, long frost-free periods, and lots of rain. This climate mix makes Hubei a rich agricultural region. Average annual temperatures are 15℃ -17℃ during the winter and range from 27℃ -29℃ during July. The maximum temperature in Jianghan Plain is above 40℃, making it one of the hottest areas in China.

Hubei belonged to Chu State in ancient times. Chu culture was cultivated here. Along with the Yellow River plain, Hubei is one of the two major sources of the Chinese civilization. It was first named Hubei during the 6thyear of Qing Emperor Kangxi 's reign (1776 A.D.). Hubei has a long history. Ancient human remains dating back more than 100, 000 years have been found in areas such as Yunxi and Changyang. Four-thousand-year-old eggshell pottery has been unearthed in Qujialing City in Jingshan County. And the ancient Shang Dynasty "Panlongcheng" city and relics dating back 3, 500 years have been discovered in Huangpi County. Finally, Jiangling and Xiangfan are the famous national historic and cultural cities.

Transportation and communication are co-nvenient in Hubei. Wuhan, Jingzhou, Yichang, Xiangfan, Enshi and Laohekou have airports, and Wuhan's Tianhe International Airport receives domestic and international flights. There are many railway lines running through Hubei province, including the Jingguang, Xiangyu, Handan, Jiaozhi, Zhiliu and Wuda lines. Wuhan has direct rail access to all parts of the province and is also linked directly to Beijing, Zhengzhou, Tianjin, Luoyang, Chongqing, Xi'an, Kunming, Guiyang, Changsha, Liuzhou, Guangzhou, Nanchang, Shijiazhuang and other major Chinese cities. Hubei has a complete network of roads extending to both its major cities and mountains. Finally, the Yangtze River provides convenient shipping and boat transportation and also links Hubei to the sea.

中南地區

Hubei's Famous Historical Figures

Many famous and gifted people have hailed from Hubei Province. They include statesman, poets, artists and other great individuals. Some of Hubei's notable political figures are the renowned general Wu Zixu, the "No. 1 loyal officer," Sun Shuao, the noted Han Dynasty statesman, Chen Youliang, the ancient Chinese Prime Minister, Zhang Juzheng, and the beautiful princess, Wang Zhaojun, who married a distant prince and helped bring peace to her kingdom. Hubei was also the home of the proletarian revolutionary pioneers, Li Xiannian and Dong Biwu. Famous Hubei poets and artists include the famous calligrapher, Mi Fu, the pastoral poet, Meng Haoran, the great patriotic poet, Qu Yuan, as well as three leading representatives of the "Gong'an" poetry school, Yuan Zongdao, Yuan Hongdao, and Yuan Zhongdao. Hubei also boasts several leading thinkers, such as the tea sage, Lu Yu, and Taoist philosopher, Laolaizi. Finally, a number of outstanding scientists have come from Hubei, including the famous ancient physician, Li Shizhen, the great geologist, Li Siguang, and the inventor of moveable type, Bi Sheng.

Special Local Products

There are many special local products in Hubei, such as brick tea, Wuchang fish, Xiaogan sesame chips, day-lily buds, mandarin fish, Zigui oval oranges, and baked sesame cakes.

Hubei Famous Dishes

Hubei has many well-known dishes. Examples include sliced pork with cream sauce, Huangpi three（fish and pork meat balls and rice balls mixed together）, Mianyang steamed three（meat and vegetables steamed together）, steamed Wuchang fish, Xiaotaoyuan simmered soup, Yunxian leaf lard wrapped red bean paste, eight-diagram-shaped appetizer soup, braised pullet with ginkgo nuts in clay pot, fried wild ducks, chickens and fish with peach blossoms, Jingzhou rice field eel, and Jingzhou fish balls.

Hubei Snacks

The province also boasts many special snacks. Examples are packet noodles, cool cakes, fried gingko, Liangxiang chestnuts, red-glutinous rice powder, Ding Ding cake, stewed lotus seeds, Ezhou "Dongpo cake", Huangshi harbor cake, Huangzhou Shaomei, alkali pastries for dessert (Wuhan), and orange flap Yuyuan, baked bread, lotus root glutinous rice gruel, cool noodles, cold shrimp, radish dumplings, Macheng meat puddings, Wuhan fruit meat, dry noodles, red dates, and bean curd. Attraction Recommendation

The province has a total of 1, 500 tourist spots. Major natural scenic sites include Wuhan's East Lake, Wudang Mountain, the Shennongjia Forest Nature Reserve, Jiugong Mountain, and Yangtze River's world famous Three Gorges. Some major historical places are the Yellow Crane Tower, Guiyuan Temple, Xiangfan Gulongzhong, Puqi Cliff and Zigui Qu Yuan Temple, Qu Yuan Residence, Ji'nan Old City, Zhaojun Hometown, Wuhan Guqin Pavilion, Former Site of the Wuchang Insurgent Army Government, and Jing-Han Railroad Labor Movement "Twenty-seven" Memorial Hall.

中南地區

湖北因位於長江中游,洞庭湖之北而得名,又因古屬鄂州,簡稱鄂,省會武漢。湖北東西長約740公里,南北寬約470公里。全省總面積18.59 萬平方公里,居中國第16 位,占中國總面積的1.94%。湖北地形大致為東、西、北三面環山,中間低平,略呈向南敞開的不完整盆地狀。長江自西向東,流貫省內的長度為1061 公里。漢水是長江最大支流,到武漢進入長江,境內流長878公里。湖北面積在3平方公里以上的湖泊目前有300個左右,大部分集中於江漢平原。湖北省屬北亞熱帶季風氣候,具有從亞熱帶向暖溫帶過渡的特徵。全省光照充足,熱量豐富,無霜期長,降水豐沛,雨熱同季,利於農業生產。年均溫15℃ ～17℃,7 月均溫為27℃～29℃,江漢平原最高溫在40℃以上,為中國酷熱地區之一。

湖北古屬楚國領域，楚文化誕生於此，與中原文化並列為華夏文明二大源頭。康熙六年（ 1776年），這裡歷史上第一次定名湖北，沿用至今。湖北省歷史悠久，在鄖西、長陽等地發現古人類化石，證明幾十萬年前這裡就有人類生息。京山縣屈家嶺出土的蛋殼彩陶，距今已有4000 多年；黃陂區發掘出土的商代古城「盤龍城」遺址，距今也有3500多年。省內江陵、襄樊等是中國歷史文化名城之一。

湖北省交通發達，武漢、荊州、宜昌、襄樊、恩施、老河口都有民用機場，其中武漢天河國際機場開闢有多條國內和國際航線。湖北境內的鐵路線有京廣線、襄渝線、漢丹線、焦枝線、枝柳線及武大線等，省會武漢有直達省內各地的列車，此外還有直達北京、鄭州、天津、洛陽、重慶、西安、昆明、貴陽、長沙、柳州、廣州、南昌、石家莊等市的列車。湖北省有一個較為完整的公路網，以大城市為中心的公路四通八達，可一直延伸到深山之中，同時也將鐵路和水路運輸連接起來。湖北省內正在建設多條高速公路，目前已經建成通車的有從黃梅縣經黃石至武漢的武黃高速公路和從武漢經荊州至宜昌的漢宜高速公路。此外還有武漢—襄樊—十堰、武漢—信陽（河南）、荊州—荊門—襄樊、宜昌—利川、武漢—赤壁等高速公路正在建設中。湖北省境內的長江總長達1000 多公里，因而湖北省的長江航運也非常發達。

湖北省歷史名人

湖北省在歷史上人才輩出，如炎帝神農氏，偉大的愛國主義詩人屈原，中原霸主楚莊王，一夜白頭名將伍子胥，第一循吏良臣孫叔敖，道家人物代表老萊子，大漢政權的建立者陳友諒，著名書法家米芾，山水田園詩人孟浩然，茶聖陸羽，民族和親的使者王昭君，宰相之傑張居正，「公安派」領袖袁宗道、袁宏道、袁中道，活字印刷術的發明人畢昇，醫學家李時珍，地質泰李四光，無產階級革命家李先念，董必武等。

湖北特產

湖北特產眾多。如青磚茶、武昌魚、孝感麻糖、黃花菜、鱖魚、秭歸鵝蛋柑、麻烘糕等。

湖北著名的特色菜

湖北有很多特色菜。如廣水滑肉、黃陂三合、沔陽三蒸、清蒸武昌魚、小桃園煨湯、鄖縣網油砂、八卦湯、白果燒雞、紅燒野鴨、雞泥桃花魚、荊州皮條鱔魚、荊州魚糕丸子等。

湖北特色小吃

湖北有許多的特色小吃。如包麵、冰涼糕、炒白果、炒良鄉栗子、沖糯米粉、頂頂糕、燉蓮子、鄂州「東坡餅」、黃石港餅、黃州燒梅、鹼酥餅（武漢）、橘瓣魚圓、烤麵包、蓮藕糯米粥、涼麵、涼蝦、蘿蔔餃子、麻城肉糕、武漢果子肉、武漢熱乾麵、武漢肉棗、武漢三鮮豆皮、武漢酸白菜等。

主要景點推薦

據普查，全省旅遊景區（點）共1500 餘處。主要風景有：武漢東湖、黃鶴樓、歸元寺、襄樊古隆中、武當山、神農架、江漢古城、蒲圻赤壁、秭歸屈原祠、秭歸屈原故里、長江三峽、九宮山、紀南故城、昭君故里、武漢古琴台、武漢起義軍政府舊址、京漢鐵路工人運動「二七」紀念館等。

中南地區

Yellow-Crane Tower （黃鶴樓）

Ladies and gentlemen,

We'll now begin our tour of the Yellow-Crane Tower.

Hubei Province's Yellow-Crane Tower of Wuhan is one of the three most famous towers in southern China. Along with Dongting Lake's Yueyang Tower and Tengwang Pavilion alongside the Ganjiang River in Nanchang city, it is world-renowned for its grand scale, complex architectural structure, and peculiar roof style. However, the Yellow Crane has the longest history and most majestic appearance of all these ancient towers.

Do you know what Yellow-Crane Tower was at first made out of? Initially it was not used for viewing scenery. During the Three Kingdoms Period (223 A.D.), Sun Quan sought the "prosperity of the country by force" and thus built a tower on the edge of the Yangtze River for military observation. Later when the war was over, the Yellow-Crane Tower became a good place for people to enjoy the beauty of nature. Many famous writers went there to be inspired and left many essays, poems and the like here. In particular, several Tang Dynasty writers and poets had a very peculiar relationship with the Yellow-Crane Tower. You can guess who they are?Yeah, they are Li Bai and Cui Hao. It is said that the two poets competed to write poems here. Cui Hao's best known lines are "the immortal person departed from Yellow Crane long ago, only the Tower is left here. " It was said that after Li Bai entered this tower, he was excited with versification, but when he found Cui Hao's poem, he said it is perfect and did not believe that he could write better than Cui Hao. Thus in order to protect his reputation, he refrained from writing a poem during this visit to the Yellow-Crane Tower. He instead wrote a doggerel consisting of four lines: "a hammer breaks the Yellow-Crane Tower, a foot kicks over Parrots Islet, beautiful scenery are not expressed, for Cui Hao wrote poem first. " Afterwards, a person drew upon this legend to build a "pavilion of signing off" in the east of the Yellow Crane-Tower. There was still a wall on which Cui Hao ever wrote in Yellow-Crane Tower Park. However, sometime later, the poet, Li Bai, bid farewell to the poet, Meng Haoran, by writing in the Yellow-Crane Tower a poem entitled, "Farewell Meng Haoran. " Several lines read, "My friend has left the Yellow Crane Tower, to go to Yangzhou in March. The only boat has disappeared in the blue sky; however see the Yangtze River flow from the sky line. "

The Yellow-Crane Tower has become a major tourist spot not only due to its magnificent appearance, but because of its location on the summit of She Mountain alongside the mighty Yangtze River. Many notable figures such as Bai Juyi, Jia Dao, Lu You, Yang Shen, and Zhang Juzheng have visited this place and written many outstanding poems here. One such masterpiece is Cui Hao's poem "Yellow-Crane Tower". In fact, this poem is such a famous and old masterpiece that many Chinese people can recite it from memory. And because of this poem, many people have a yearn to visit the Yellow-Crane Tower. In February of 1927, the great Chinese leader Mao Zedong came to Wuchang after inspecting the Peasant Movement in Hunan, and wrote the famous poem, Pu Sa Man—Climb Yellow Crane-Tower.

Do you know the origin of the name about Yellow-Crane Tower? There are two stories about this. One concerns the immortal person, or "Shen Xian" in China while the other concerns a mountain.

Regarding the first story, a long time ago, a person surnamed Xin sold wine in an inn at Huanghu Hill. One day, an old man stumbled to his place and asked for wine to drink. Xin pitied on him and generously agreed and continued to give him wine for an entire year. One day, after seeing the old man go to the inn, Xin quickly prepared food and wine. The old man refused and said: "I don't want to drink, I'm just coming to say goodbye to you". Then he painted a picture of yellow crane on the wall. The old man said, "If you clap your hands, the Yellow Crane will be down to dance for the guest." The next day the guests came to the hotel and he thought of the old man's words. After clapping hands for a test, the crane really catapulted down, singing loudly and dancing before then going back into the wall. Guests found this performance to be very interesting. The news spread widely, and the people from three towns of Wuhan and the visitors from far and near were attracted to the hotel to see the crane dancing. With all this new business, Xin quickly made a fortune. A decade later, one day, the old man appeared again in the hotel, Xin desired to appreciate him, but the old man refused and then played his flute, causing the Yellow Crane to come down. After that, he sat on the Yellow Crane and flew away on it. To commemorate the old man and his yellow crane, Xin built a high tower on the inn and named it the Yellow-Crane Tower. This story

中
南
地
區

about the immortal person, Shen Xian, has spread widely across China for thousands of years and is a very influential legend explaining the origins of the Yellow Crane Tower. Another similar legend is that a person called Fei Wei successfully attained immortality on the Yellow Crane Hill and, like Shen Xian, used the crane to go to heaven. Later to commemorate Fei Wei, people constructed Yellow-Crane Tower on top of the Yellow Crane Hill.

But modern research tells a different story regarding the origins of Yellow-Crane Tower's name. This explanation points to the place the Tower was built on top of, namely Yellow-Crane Hill. So, it is named Yellow-Crane Tower.

My dear friends, we have arrived at Yellow-Crane Tower. In fact, Yellow-Crane Tower we see now is rebuilt after the founding of New China. Due to wars and other events, Yellow-Crane Tower has been repeatedly destroyed and rebuilt. The last Qing tower was built in 7thyear of the Qing Tongzhi Emperor's reign（1868）and then was destroyed again during the 10thyear of Emperor Guangxu's reign (1884). Nearly a century passed before further rebuilding work was done on the Tower. The latest reconstruction of the tower began in October of 1981 and was finished in June of 1985. The main building took the Qing Dynasty tower as its blueprint, but the use of modern technology and construction techniques has given the Yellow-Crane Tower a more unique shape and enhanced its ancient magnificence.

The original ancient Yellow-Crane Tower was three-storey structures and 33 meters high, which in traditional Chinese measure system was 9 zhang and 2 chi high, plus a 7-chi copper roof, thus there were 2 nines (The number "9" was an auspicious one in traditional Chinese). We are now viewing the new 5 storey Yellow-Crane Tower and its gourd shaped roof. The roof is 5 meters high and the entire tower is altogether 51. 4 meters high, making it nearly 20 meters higher than the old Yellow Crane Tower. The base of the new Tower is also twice as wide—30 meters vs. 15 meters—as that of the old Tower. Thus the Yellow Crane Tower has been reconstructed, rather than restored. While some features of the old design have been preserved, it has been rebuilt to better fit people's needs and modern aesthetic perspectives.

It was also necessary to move the Yellow-Crane Tower during its reconstruction to make way for new Wuhan Yangtze River Bridge. Fortunately, the structure has been made even more majestic than the former tower. The present Yellow-Crane Tower consists of main buildings, matched pavilions, corridors and memorial archways, all spreading over a three story terrace along a central axis that becomes higher and higher. The west entrance of the Yellow-Crane Tower Park is located on the first terrace. The second terrace has a memorial archway flanked by pavilions and a bending corridor. The newly built Yellow-Crane Tower stands on the third and central terrace.

We can see the new complex is an attractive mix of different and unique architectural styles. This is particularly true of the Yellow-Crane Tower, which consists of several different layers. The bottom layer is a tall spacious hall, whose kelp well is as high as 10 meters. On frontispiece wall there are huge ceramic murals named "Cloud Yellow Cranes". There are seven meter long poetic couplets along both sides of the columns. On the marble wall of the hall on the second floor is engraved in the Yan Bojin's "Yellow-Crane Tower", recording the tower's history and all of the major figures who visited here and drew inspiration from this place. There are two murals on both sides of these inscriptions. One mural is of the "Sun Quan Fortification" and concretely illustrates the Tower's original purpose and its first setting, Wuchang City. The other mural depicts "Zhou Yu's Banquet", which celebrates the famous historical figures who visited the Tower and their activities in it during the Three Kingdom's period. The murals in the hall of third floor are "Embroidered Portrait Painting" of Tang and Song Dynasty poets such as Cui Hao, Li Bai and Bai Juyi and also contains famous lines from the celebrated poems they wrote in the Yellow-Crane Tower. The fourth floor's hall is divided into several rooms by screens, displaying the photos of many contemporary famous Chinese people for visitors to enjoy and purchase. The top hall has scrolls and wall paintings, such as the "Yangtze Wanli Map".

中南地區

Well, you can visit freely. Two hours later we will gather here. I hope all of you have a good time.

My friends, our journey is about to end. And I should say goodbye to you all. Anyway I am very glad to have spent such a happy and unforgettable day with you. Thank you very much for your support and cooperation. I hope today's visit will leave you with many pleasant memories. Thank you!

各位朋友，

大家好！現在我們要開始向今天遊覽的目的地——黃鶴樓出發了。

大家都知道黃鶴樓是江南三大名樓之一，它位於湖北武漢市。它和洞庭湖邊的岳陽樓、南昌贛江之濱的滕王閣，都因為宏偉的規模、複雜的建築結構和奇特的屋頂造型而著稱於世。那麼黃鶴樓在其中又排列第幾呢？對！黃鶴樓又以其歷史之悠久，樓姿雄偉而居三樓之首。大家知道最初修建黃鶴樓是做什麼用的嗎？當初並不是為了觀賞風光用的。三國時期的吳黃武二年，也就是公元223年，孫權為了實現「以武治國而昌」，就在長江邊上的蛇山上建了一座樓用來瞭望軍情，這是黃鶴樓的前身。後來戰爭過去了，黃鶴樓也逐漸成為了人們遊山玩水的好地方，也為歷代文人騷客登臨吟詠之地。留傳至今的詩詞過千，文賦逾百。尤其是唐朝時的幾位文人，更是在黃鶴樓的歷史留下了非常特別的痕跡。大家可以猜猜是哪幾個人？對，是李白和崔顥。相傳李白和崔顥曾在此鬥詩。其中以崔顥的「昔人已乘黃鶴去，此地空餘黃鶴樓」詩句為最。據說李白登臨此樓後，也是詩興盎然，當他發現崔顥的這首詩後，連稱「絕妙」，怕自己寫的沒崔顥好，毀了一世英名，便擱筆不寫。於是寫了四句打油詩：一拳捶碎黃鶴樓，一腳踢翻鸚鵡洲，眼前有景道不得，崔顥題詩在上頭。後來有好事之人據此在黃鶴樓東側修建了一座李白「擱筆亭」。現在黃鶴樓公園內有崔顥的題詩壁，對面就是李白的擱筆亭了。不過，後來李白在黃鶴樓送別友人孟浩然時，寫下了一首《送孟浩然之廣陵》：「故人西辭黃鶴樓，煙花三月下揚州。孤帆遠影碧空盡，唯見長江天際流。」這首詩也成為詠誦黃鶴樓的絕句。

黃鶴樓因瀕臨萬里長江，雄踞蛇山（又稱「黃鵠山」）之巔，挺拔獨秀，輝煌瑰麗而成為名傳四海的遊覽勝地。歷代名士如白居易、賈島、陸游、楊慎、張居正等，都先後到這裡遊樂，吟詩作賦。尤其是崔顥的《黃鶴樓》詩，一直被認為是千古佳作，很多人都能背誦。因這首詩，使很多人產生了對黃鶴樓的嚮往。1927年2月，毛澤東考察完湖南農民運動後來到武昌，曾在此寫下了著名的《菩薩蠻‧登黃鶴樓》。

大家有誰知道黃鶴樓名字的由來嗎？

很久以前，有位姓辛的人在黃鵠山頭賣酒度日。有一天，有位衣衫破爛的老道蹣跚而來，向他討酒喝。辛氏看見老道很可憐，就慷慨地答應了。這樣的情況持續了一年。有一天，老道又來到酒店，辛氏一見，急忙準備酒菜款待老道，老道攔住說：今天我不喝酒，我是來向你告別的。並在客棧的牆壁上畫了一只黃鶴。老道對辛氏說：只要你拍手相招，黃鶴便會下來，為酒客跳舞助興。第二天酒店來了客人，他想起了老道的話，拍手一試，黃鶴竟然真的一躍而下，引頸高鳴，翩翩起舞，舞畢又跳回到牆上。客人看了非常驚訝。消息傳開後，吸引了武漢三鎮的老百姓和遠近的遊人，都來店中看黃鶴起舞。從此酒店生意興隆。辛氏因此而發了財。十年後的一天，老道又出現在酒店，辛氏想感謝老道。老道拒絕了，用鐵笛吹了一首曲子，引下黃鶴，跨上黃鶴飛走了。辛氏為了紀念老道和他的黃鶴，在酒店旁蓋起了一座高樓，起名黃鶴樓。千百年來，這個故事在中國廣為傳播，成為黃鶴樓因仙得名最有影響的傳說。另一個傳說是有一位名叫費偉的人，在黃鶴山中修煉成仙，然後乘黃鶴升天。後來人們為懷念費偉，便在這黃鶴山上建造了一座黃鶴樓。

但是經過考證，黃鶴樓因山得名的真實性是最大的。黃鶴樓建在黃鵠山山頂。古漢語中，鵠和鶴兩個字是通用的，所以又叫黃鶴山，黃鶴山上的樓閣，當然就取名為黃鶴樓。

各位遊客，我們已經來到黃鶴樓。我們現在看到的黃鶴樓其實是新中國成立後重修的。之前，由於戰亂等原因，黃鶴樓屢建屢廢。最後一座「清樓」修建於同治七年（公元1868年），毀於光緒十年（公元1884年），在這之後近百年沒有再重修

中南地區

過。一直到1981年10月，黃鶴樓重修工程才破土開工，1985年6月落成。主樓以清同治樓為藍本，但是運用了現代的建築技術施工，既不失黃鶴樓的獨特造型，又比歷代的舊樓更加雄偉。

古黃鶴樓高三層，高9丈2尺，加銅頂7尺，共成九九之數（總高約合33米）。我們現在所看到的是新建的黃鶴樓，高5層，加5米高的葫蘆形寶頂，共高51.4米，比古樓高出將近20米。古樓底層各寬15米，而新樓底層則是各寬30米。因此，黃鶴樓不是修復，而是重建。它保留了古樓的某些特色，但更多的是根據現在的需要和人們審美觀點的變化來設計的。

重建的黃鶴樓因為修建武漢長江大橋所以離開了故址，氣勢上更勝於舊樓。黃鶴樓建築群由主樓、配亭、軒廊、牌坊等組成，分布在三層平台上，沿中心軸線逐層升高。第一層平台是黃鶴樓公園的西大門。第二層平台上有牌坊，兩側是曲廊和南北配亭。第三層平台的中央聳立著黃鶴樓。

我們可以看到整個建築具有獨特的民族風格。尤其是黃鶴樓內部，層層風格不相同。底層為一高大寬敞的大廳，其正中藻井高達10多米，正面壁上為一幅巨大的「白雲黃鶴」陶瓷壁畫，兩旁立柱上懸掛著長達7米的楹聯：爽氣西來，雲霧掃開天地撼；大江東去，波濤洗淨古今愁。二樓大廳正面牆上，有用大理石鐫刻的唐代閻伯瑾撰寫的《黃鶴樓記》，它記述了黃鶴樓興廢沿革和名人軼事。樓記兩側為兩幅壁畫，一幅是「孫權築城」，形象地說明黃鶴樓和武昌城相繼誕生的歷史；另一幅是「周瑜設宴」，反映三國名人去黃鶴樓的活動。三樓大廳的壁畫為唐宋名人的「繡像畫」，如崔顥、李白、白居易等，也摘錄了他們吟詠黃鶴樓的名句。四樓大廳用屏風分割幾個小廳，內置當代名人字畫，供遊客欣賞、選購。頂層大廳有《長江萬里圖》等長卷、壁畫。

好了，現在大家可以自由參觀，去感受一下古人的情懷。兩個小時後還在這裡集合。希望大家玩得開心。謝謝！

Shennongjia （神農架）

Ladies and Gentlemen,

Welcome to the Shennongjia. I am pleased to serve as your guide today. Now we're going to pay a visit to Shennongjia. Shennongjia is located in the junction of Sichuan and Hubei. An administrative division was established here in 1970, covering a total area of over 3, 253 square kilometers, two-thirds of which is covered by forests. About 79, 000 people live here and the major ethnic groups living in the area are Han Chinese and the Tujia and Hui national minorities.

Do you know the origin about Shennongjia?What kind of stories are there? Now let me tell you. In ancient times, the Shennongjia region was covered by a vast ocean. Then the Orogeny Uplift of the Yan and Himalayan mountains occurred, and the Ba mountains extended eastward from the Tibet-Qinghai Plateau. The Ba Mountains are highest in the north and lowest in the south. Their average elevation is 1, 500 meters, and over 20 peaks are more than 2, 500 meters above sea level. The tallest peak is 3, 105 meters high and is called "the first peak in central China". At an elevation of 398 meters, the Southwest Pillar River is Shennongjia's lowest point, so elevation difference between the area's high and low points is 2, 707 meters.

Shennongjia has a long history going to the Paleolithic period, when early man first settled this area. It is said Emperor Yan or Shennong taught the first people living here how to build houses, find herbs, and farm the land, so the area called Shennongjia. "jia" means "a peak of a mountain" in Chinese. Shennongjia initially referred to a particular peak, but now is the name for the entire Shennongjia forest areas. Shennongjia is also one of the birthplaces of Bachu culture. In the 1980s the folk songbook and mythic epic tale, "Darkness", was discovered in Shennongjia. This landmark archeological find helped explain ancient Chinese views on the universe, along with the origins of human society in China.

Do you know about any names regarding the Shennongjia area? It is a very prestigious title. Right! That's it, the Central Roof. This is because at 3, 105 meters above sea level, Shennongjia's highest peak is the tallest point in Central China. Hence it is called the Middle Kingdom's Central Roof.

We all know that Shennongjia is a primitive forest, which has variety of insects, fish, animals and birds, as well as lots of endangered flora and fauna. Why? It is because Shennongjia has both geographical advantages and a fine natural environment. In particular, it has maintained its primitive and pristine state, enabling many very rare animals and plants to live here. In addition, Shennongjia contains many plants and herbs used in producing many kinds of medicine. Finally, Shennongjia has the world's only intact mid-latitude subtropical forest ecosystem, making a unique global tourist attraction. The area thus richly deserves to be named the "Green Pearl", "Natural Botanical and Animal Gardens", "Biological Haven", "Species Gene Pool", "Natural History Museum", and "Cool Kingdom".

Shennongjia is currently seeking to fully exploit its rich tourist resources by building a sauna, constructing hiking and bike paths, encouraging rock climbing, rafting, fishing and other popular tourist activities.

Shennong Altar

Well, my friends, we are now at the Shennong Altar located in the southern Shennongjia scenic tourism area. Although it occupies less than 1 square kilometer, the Altar is an attractive structure and is surrounded by beautiful natural scenery. And the Shennong Altar is at the core of the Shennongjia scenic area and is a place where the Chinese people can commemorate ancestors and worship God.

Do you know why we commemorate Emperor Yan? Because he was the first person who domesticated cattle and also found many herbs able to cure people of life-threatening diseases.

The stage on both sides and the lawn we now see are modeled on those at the royal palace. The middle path was reserved for the emperor, while the side-paths were used by his officials. The number nine in ancient times was considered to be the largest number, so the number of the stages on both sides is a multiple of that number. Below step is the sacrificial altar where Chinese people can worship their ancestors.

Shennong Peak

After leaving the Shennong Altar, we will go to the top of Shennongjia peak. It is located in west Shennongjia scenic area and is called the "central roof", as it is the highest point in central China standing 3, 105 meters above sea level.

Fengjingya

We have now arrived at the Fengjingya, which was originally named Badongya, and is known as "Shennong's perfect scenic spot". Standing at an altitude of 2, 800 meters, Fengjingya is full of special and beautiful scenery, and this visual feast is accentuated by the area's abrupt weather changes. You can look around now and see for yourself.

The Banbi Rock

Well, we have arrived at the Banbi Rock, which attract visitors with its primitive appearance and stone forests. Thick stands of arrow bamboo surround Banbi Rock and form a natural barrier. Legend has it that Shennongjia "wild men" often make fleeting appearances in these bamboo groves. Traces of these "wild men", such as hair, excrement, and bamboo nests, are often found there. Study of their hair cell structure indicates that these creatures are an evolutionary step above advanced primates. In addition to being the home of the "wild men", this area is notable for the picturesque boulder on Fengjingya's northern slope. This boulder hugs the slope, much like a mother hugging a child or lovers whispering to one another. Painters and

中
南
地
區

photographers often spend a few hours to creating works around the boulder.

Now we are going to the Banbi Rock and stone forest and have a walk. If we have good luck we may even see one of its "wild men".

Well, after touring the Banbi Rock and stone forest, our journey is about to end today. Thank you very much for your cooperation. Welcome to the Shennongjia again. Good luck!

各位朋友，大家好！

很高興能成為大家這次旅行的導遊。下面請大家和我一起去遊覽神農架。神農架地處川鄂交界地帶，1970年建立行政區劃，面積約為3253平方公里，其中森林覆蓋率達67%，區內居住有漢、土家、回等民族，人口約7.9萬。

大家知道神農架的來歷嗎？又有些什麼樣的故事流傳其中呢？現在就讓我為大家介紹一下。遠古時期，神農架地區還是一片汪洋大海，是燕山和喜馬拉雅造山運動將其抬升為多級陸地，成為大巴山東延的餘脈。山脈呈東西走向，山體由南向北逐漸降低。山峰多在海拔1500　米以上，其中海拔2500米以上的山峰有20多座。最高峰神農頂海拔3105.4米，為「華中第一峰」。西南部石柱河海拔398米，是神農架的最低點，最高點與最低點的相對高差為2707.4米。

神農架的歷史十分悠久，早在舊石器時代就開始有原始人類在此活動，相傳炎帝神農氏曾率眾在此搭架採藥，教人們耕種，故將這裡稱作神農架。神農架最初只是指一座山峰，到現在則指整個神農架林區。神農架也是巴楚文化的發祥地之一。20世紀80年代，在神農架發現了一部民間唱本《黑暗傳》，以解釋宇宙和人類社會的起源、敘說中國古代歷史為主要內容，其特徵近似神話史詩，受到學術界的重視，也填補了華中地區沒有發現過長篇神話史詩的空白。

大家知道神農架還有別的稱呼嗎？對，有一個十分氣派的稱號——華中屋脊，這是因為神農架中的最高峰——神農頂海拔高達3105.4　米，為華中第一高峰，故而有此稱號。

大家都知道神農架是一片原始森林，其中有種類繁多的烏獸蟲魚，而在別的地方見不到的物種在神農架卻可以見到，這是為什麼呢？

因為神農架憑藉其優越的地理位置以及自然環境，至今尚較好的保存著原始森林的特有風貌，所以有多種極為珍稀的動物在此繁衍。此外，神農架也是一座規模很大的天然藥材庫，有中草藥兩千多種。目前，神農架是中國內陸保存完好的唯一一片綠洲和世界中緯度地區唯一的一塊綠色寶地。它所擁有的在當今世界中緯度地區唯一保持完好的亞熱帶森林生態系統，是最富特色的壟斷性的世界級旅遊資源。因而神農架也享有了「綠色明珠」、「天然動植物園」、「生物避難所」、「物種基因庫」、「自然博物館」和「清涼王國」等眾多美譽。

現在神農架憑藉其豐富的自然資源及旅遊資源，在作為觀光渡假旅遊區的基礎上，還開展了森林沐浴行和自行車、攀岩、漂流、垂釣等頗受旅遊者喜愛的旅遊活動。

神農壇

好，各位遊客朋友，現在我們已經進入了神農壇景區，請大家稍做準備，我們馬上就要下車去遊覽。

現在我們所在的神農壇風景區位於神農架旅遊區的南部，是神農架旅遊的南大門。雖然面積很小，只有0.7平方公里，但整個景區層次分明，自然風光十分優美。

好了，現在我們就來到了神農壇。神農壇是神農架風景區的核心部分，是專供炎黃子孫在此緬懷先祖，祭祀神靈的場所。

大家知道為什麼炎帝神農氏受到我們的紀念嗎，因為他首創牛耕，採藥救民，為子孫後代繁榮昌盛、持續發展與進步作出了巨大的貢獻。

中南地區

499

我們現在所看到的草坪和兩邊的台階也是根據過去皇宮的格局所布置，中間為天子所走，左右則是大臣的通道。因為9　在古時候被人們認為是最大的數字，故兩邊的台階全是9的倍數。台階下面是祭壇，每一位炎黃子孫都可以在此祭拜先祖。

神農頂

離開神農壇，我們現在就要去神農架的制高點——神農頂風景區。神農頂風景區位於神農架的西部，被稱作「華中屋脊」，是華中第一高峰，海拔達3105.4米。

風景埡

走過了神農頂，現在我們就到達了風景埡。風景埡原名巴東埡，號稱「神農第一絕」，海拔2800米。風景埡風景奇異，氣象瞬變，將這風景埡的風光齊聚一體，大家可四處看看。

板壁岩

好了，現在我們已經來到了板壁岩，這裡因為有野人出沒和奇妙的石林而備受遊人注目。板壁岩上下箭竹林漫山遍野，是天然的屏障，據說這一帶經常有神農架野人出沒，箭竹林中經常發現野人的蹤跡，如毛髮、糞便和竹窩之類，經研究，這種毛髮的細胞結構要優於高等靈長目動物。此外，箭竹林間，最惹人注目的是北坡的一尊巨石，如母子相偎又如戀人細語……畫家和攝影家們往往要在這尊巨石周圍花上幾個小時來進行創作。

那麼現在我們就下車去板壁岩的石林和樹叢中走走，運氣好的話說不定還能看到野人呢。

好了，遊覽完板壁岩以後，我們今天的旅途也就到此結束了，感謝大家的合作，歡迎以後再來遊覽神農架！祝大家好運！

Wudang Mountain （武當山）

Ladies and gentlemen,

Welcome to Wudang Mountain. I'd like to take this opportunity to introduce myself to you all. (Introduce yourself to the guests.) I am happy to have this opportunity to show you round the Wudang Mountain. Your cooperation will be very much appreciated. Thank you.

First of all, please let me give you a brief introduction to the Wudang Mountain. Wudang Mountain is also called Taihe Mountain and Xianshi Mountain; it is located near Danjiangkou City, Hubei Province, which is China's famous Taoist resort. It is also one of the first state-level key scenic spots and a world cultural heritage site.

We know that Wudang Mountain is famous for its grand scale of construction. While the ancient architecture here was built all through the Tang, Song, Yuan, Ming and Qing Dynasties, it reached its zenith during the Ming Dynasty. It had 33 buildings, covering an area of more than 100 million square meters; after hundreds years of vicissitudes, it still covers nearly 50, 000 square meters.

Today let us go there to enjoy the beautiful natural scenery and rich Taoism culture.

There is a common saying that "Buddha occupies all of the world's famous mountains", but in Wudang Mountain, Taoism is the dominant religion. It is said that Immeasurable Buddha originally occupied the Wudang Golden Peak. When Emperor Zhenwu became an Immortal and wandered about here, he was very taken by this land and its beauty and went to seek out at the Immortal Buddha at Tianzhu Peak to discuss borrowing eight steps of this land. The Immortal Buddha was surprised that another Immortal like Emperor Zhenwu would want so little land, particularly in view of the Emperor's unlimited supernatural power. So the Immortal Buddha walked eight steps away from Tianzhu peak, and since each step covered 50 kilometers, Emperor Zhenwu

中
南
地
區

became Wudong Mountain's new permanent resident and the mountain became a Taoist shrine.

Some 72 peaks, 36 rocky cliffs, 24 streams, 10 lakes, 3 pools, and 9 springs are clustered around Tianzhu peak. Wudang Mountain also has dense forests with many varieties of plants, including 600 of the 1, 800 medicinal herbs recorded in Compendium of Materia compiled by the Ming Dynasty pharmacist Li Shizhen. Therefore the mountain is also known as a "natural herb farm".

Wudang Taoism Monastry

Who knows when Wudang Taoism Monastry was first built? Legend has it that as early as the Zhou Dynasty people began to build thatched huts here to practice Taoism. A Five-Dragon Temple was built during the Tang Dynasty Emperor's Zhenguan reign (627-649 A.D.) and renovations were done in later dynasties. So we can say that Wudang Taoism Monastry was first built during the Tang Emperor Zhenguan's reign. Taoism was further strengthened during the reign of the Ming Dynasty Chengzu Emperor. In 1412 construction work began on 33 halls and monasteries and these buildings were finally finished in 1423. This large complex consists of 9 halls, 9 monasteries, 72 temples, and 36 nunneries occupying a total floor space of 1. 6 million square meters. The Taoist Wudang Mountain still is a major Taoist center and place of pilgrimage for Taoist believers throughout China. Its buildings are splendid examples of traditional Chinese architecture and the Mountain was named a World Heritage Cultural Site in 1994.

Wudang Boxing

Wudang Mountain not only boasts a rich Taoist culture, but also can claim to be the birthplace of Wudang boxing, which is also called Neijia boxing. Wudang boxing has a long and profound history. It was pioneered by the Wudang Taoist Master Zhang

Sanfeng during late Yuan and early Ming dynasty. Wudang boxing has undergone constant development and evolution and, next to Shaolin martial arts, is the most famous Chinese hand-to-hand fighting technique. Indeed, the two schools are known as "Northern Shaolin, Southern Wudang". Wudang boxing has now spread not only across China, but outside the country as well.

Zixiao Palace

Well, after some climbing, the Zixiao Palace now stands before us. Its differently shaped and sized statues are a Ming Dynasty artistic treasure. The Zixiao Palace was built in 1413, or the 11thyear of the Emperor Yongle's reign. The original buildings include more than 860 palaces, galleries, verandas, halls and pavilions. Zixiao Palace is at the back of Zhanqi Peak, and faces Zhaobi Peak, Santai Peak, Wulao Peak, Candles Peak, Luomao Peak, and Xianglu Peak. On its right is Leishen Cave, and on its left is Yuji Pool and Baozhu Peak. Since the surrounding hills form a natural chair with two dragons playing with a pearl, Emperor Yongle called it the "blessed Zixiao land".

Nanyan

Do you know where we are now? Yes, now we are on the beautiful Nanyan in Wudang, in which the magnificent architecture of the buildings blends in with natural landscape's beauty. There is a temple on the cliff, which was built in the Yuan Dynasty. If you are interested in it, you can go and have a look.

Tianzhu Peak and Golden Palace

Now, we are finally at the Tianzhu Peak. Tianzhu Peak is 1, 612 meters high and is also called "Yizhuqingtian. " From its summit, we have a spectacular view of the "72 peaks to the big top". The splendid hall located on the peak's summit was built during the 14thyear of Emperor Yongle's reign and is China's largest golden temple. Well, dear friends, it is said that these lights never go out. Let's ask ourselves, "Why

中
南
地
區

do they continually glow?" The answer is that they are all very exquisite and precise, so their light can change according to the direction of the wind. This feature underscores the wisdom and superb artistic skills of China's ancient craftsmen.

Wudang Taoism Music

Wudang Taoism Mountain is also famous for its music. It is an important element of Wudang Taoism culture and key part of China's musical heritage. Taoist music is a unique combination of royal, folk, and religious music. It is mysterious, solemn and elegant.

Ever since the Tang Dynasty Emperor Taizong built the "Five Dragons Temple, " Wudang Mountain has become an important Taoist shrine for emperors, statesmen, generals, and ordinary people to come and pray for happiness.

Well, now you can visit freely. You can enjoy the unique culture, exquisite architecture and beautiful natural scenery here. We will get together here in two hours.

Our journey is about to end and I have to say goodbye to you all. Thank you for your cooperation. Have a happy journey! Goodbye!

各位遊客，大家好！

歡迎大家來武當山遊覽！首先讓我來簡單地自我介紹一下（自我介紹）。很榮幸能有這次機會和大家一起遊覽武當山。我先在這裡感謝大家的友好合作！

現在讓我來介紹一下武當山的基本情況。武當山舊稱太和山、仙石山，位於湖北省丹江口境內，是中國著名的道教聖地，是首批國家級重點風景名勝區，又是世界文化遺產。

我們知道，武當山以宏偉的建築規模著稱於世。其古建築始建於唐、宋、元、明、清的均有，在明代達到鼎盛。武當山共建有33 個建築群，總面積100餘萬平方米；歷經數百年滄桑，現仍存有近5萬平方米的面積。

今天我們一起去領略那裡秀麗的自然風光和濃郁的道教文化。

有一句俗話説「天下名山佛占盡」，而武當山卻是道教一統天下。傳説武當山金頂原來被無量佛占據著，後來真武大帝修仙得道，出外雲遊到此，相中了這塊寶地，便到天柱峰找無量佛商量借地，並提出只借八步即可。無量佛見他所要不多就答應了，沒想到真武大帝法力無邊，他從天柱峰頂走了八步，一步100里，八步竟占走了整個武當，從而贏得了永久居住權，武當山也因此成為道家的地盤。

武當山有七十二峰、三十六岩、二十四澗、三潭、九井、十池等勝境。眾多奇峰異景環繞天柱峰，形成「萬山來朝」的獨特風格。武當山植被完整，植物資源豐富。明代藥學家李時珍所著《本草綱目》中記載的1800 種草藥有600 種以上選自武當山。故武當山有「天然藥庫」之稱。

武當道觀

有誰知道武當道觀是什麼時候修建的嗎？據傳周代已有人開始在此結茅修煉，唐貞觀年間（公元627～649年）建五龍祠，後歷代均有修建。所以説武當道觀是從唐貞觀年間開始修建的。明朝時大力推崇武當道教，明成祖朱棣崇奉道教，於永樂十年（公元1412年）敕建宮觀達33處，至永樂二十年（公元1423 年）最後完工，從而形成了九宮、九觀、七十二岩廟、三十六庵堂的大型建築群，總面積達160萬平方米的規模。皇家的大力推崇使武當山名聲大振，成為中國的道教名山，吸引著各地的遊人觀光朝拜。這裡的建築集中體現了中國古代建築藝術的優秀傳統，於1994 年被列入世界遺產之列，成為全世界的文化瑰寶。

武當拳

武當山不僅是道教的香火聖地，還是武當拳的故鄉。我們知道武當武術歷史悠久，博大精深。武當拳亦名**內**家拳，元末明初武當道士張三豐集其大成。後經歷代武術家不斷創新、充實、積累，形成中華武術一大流派，素有「北宗少林，南尊武當」之稱。目前，武當武術已遍傳天下，並成為人們養身保健、袪病延年的體育活動。

紫霄宮

好了，經過一番跋涉，現在我們眼前的就是紫霄宮。殿內塑像形態各異，栩栩如生，是中國明代的藝術珍品。紫霄宮建於明永樂十一年（公元1413年），原建宮殿、廊廡、齋堂、亭台等860多間，賜額「太元紫霄宮」。紫霄宮背依展旗峰；面對照壁、三台、五老、蠟燭、落帽、香爐諸峰；右為雷神洞；左為禹跡池、寶珠峰。周圍山巒天然形成一把二龍戲珠的寶椅，明永樂皇帝封之為「紫霄福地」。

南岩

大家知道我們現在到了哪裡嗎？對，是武當山最美的南岩。武當山的自然景觀與精美的建築是融為一體的，在這裡可以得到充分的體現。這座雄居於懸崖上的石殿建於元朝，有興趣的朋友可以進去看一下。

天柱峰

現在，我們終於登上了天柱峰。天柱峰海拔1612米，素稱「一柱擎天」。站在這裡，可以清楚地看到「七十二峰朝大頂」的壯觀景象。而天柱峰之巔的這座金碧輝煌的殿堂就是金殿了。金殿是中國最大的銅鑄金鎏大殿，修建於永樂十四年。大家看，這邊的長明燈相傳是從來不滅的，為什麼它不會被風吹滅呢？原因是因為殿門的各個鑄件都非常嚴密精確，可以改變風吹來的方向，由此可見中國古代勞動人民智慧和技藝的高超。

武當道教音樂

武當道教音樂素負盛名，是武當道教文化的一個重要組成部分，是中華音樂的活化石。別具神韻的道教音樂，融宮廷、民間、宗教音樂於一體，具有莊嚴肅穆，神秘飄逸的獨特風格。自唐太宗始建「五龍祠」以後，武當山一直是帝王將相、云云眾生祈福禳災的重要道場。

好了，接下來的時間就讓大家自由參觀，您可以細細品味這裡獨特的文化、絕妙的建築和美麗的自然風光。

愉快的時光總是讓人覺得短暫，我們的武當山之旅到此就要結束了，我也要和大家說再見了。非常感謝大家對我工作的支持與配合。最後祝大家旅途愉快！再見。

中南地區

Yangtze River's Three Gorges （長江三峽）

Ladies and gentlemen,

I am very glad to be your tour guide here!Before we start visiting the major scenic spots, I'd like to briefly introduce the Yangtze River's Three Gorges.

Three Gorges comprise the most famous part of the Yangtze River. The Three Gorges stretch from Nanjinguan of Yichang in Hubei Province in the east to a village called "Baidicheng" of the Fengjie County in Chongqing Municipality. The Three Gorges are named Xiling, Wu and Qutang Gorge and are altogether 193 kilometers long. The Three Gorges are not only the highlight of the Yangtze River's scenery, but one of China's scenic treasures as well. The gorges are as famous as America's renowned Grand Canyon and have been designated as a "global landscape gallery. " They have been appreciated by countless numbers of visitors, both from China and outside of China. The Three Gorges have also provided the setting for many poetic masterpieces written during all Chinese dynasties. Well, my friends, now let's begin a journey to the spectacular Three Gorges!

Qutang Gorge

The first gorge of the Three Gorges is called Qutang Gorge, which is also named the Kui Gorge. The Yangtze River suddenly narrows here and is only 100 meters wide in one place. There is Kui Gate (the entrance to the Qutang Gorge) at the Gorge;people said that the world's most majestic place is Kui Gate. The Qutang Gorge is only 8 km long and is the most dangerous of the Three Gorges. The current velocity of the river here is 8 meters per second, 20 kilometers per hour. Navigation in the canyon lane is very tricky and people are usually astonished as the boat threads its way through the gorge. The Qutang Gorge has many scenic spots, including the Mengliang Staircase,

Armor Hole, and Wind Gorge. Although Qutang Gorge is the shortest gorge of the three gorges, its great beauty makes for a superb natural painting.

Fengjie

Fengjie is in the north bank of the Qutang Gorge and has a history of more than 1, 000 years. Fengjie has been the political, military, economic and cultural center of East Sichuan. Here are the first territories of the ancient Ba and Yong KingdoMs.Yufu County was established here some 2, 300 years ago during the Zhou Dynasty, making it one of the first counties established in China. In 222 Liu Bei retreated from Yiling (now Yichang) to Baidicheng, where he renamed Yufu County as Yongan County. In the 32ndyear of the Tang Emperor Zhenguan's reign (649 A.D.), the emperor in order to commend Zhuge Liang for his patriotism and loyalty, gave this place its current name "Fengjie". The distinguished poets, Li Bai, Du Fu, Su Shi, Lu You, and Liu Yuxi have all written lots of famous poems here. Thus Fengjie County is also known as "The city of poetry". On a Mid-Autumn night, as the moon gradually rises from the Gap, you can also enjoy the famous scenery of the Three Gorges and the poetic tribute to it, "The Autumn Moon of Kui Gate".

Baidicheng

Well, we are now arriving at Baidicheng. It is said the warlord Gongsun Shu built it in order to resist Eastern Han Dynasty Emperor Guangwu Liu Xiu. Baidicheng is surrounded on three sides by water and on one side by a steep hill. It is the best place to see Qutang Gorge. A winding trail passes through the hill gate, and the color statues of Liu Bei, Zhuge Liang, Guan Yu and Zhang Fei are displayed in the temple. More than 80 pieces of stone tablets showcase a variety of written art. The poets Li Bai, Du Fu and Bai Juyi, Liu Yuxi, Su Shi, Lu You, and Fan Chengda paid visits here, and left many well-known poems, making Baidicheng also known as the "Poetry City". The Qutang Gorge gap originally had a huge reef in the middle of the Yangtze River by Baidicheng,

中南地區

which was called the Yanyu heap. Navigating this part of the gorge was especially difficult, as the slightest deviation from course could cause the boat to run over the reef and sink. Hence, according to one old song, "Yanyu is as large as a horse, you can't get down Qutang;Yanyu is as large as an elephant, you can't go up Qutang". This obstacle was blown up by workers in 1958, making the gorge a much safer place for boats to pass through.

Daxi Cultural Sites

Now we are getting to the Daxi cultural sites, which are the junction of the Qutang Gorge in the East bank of the Yangtze and Daxi Rivers, about 15 kilometers from Fengjie County. National cultural relics department excavated this 570-square-meter area three times, in 1958, 1975 and 1976. Some 208 burial graves were found and more than 1, 200 pieces of precious relics were unearthed. The history of these graves and objects stretches back about five thousand years and provide an invaluable record of the social and economic development of upper reaches of the Yangtze River during Neolithic period.

Wu Gorge

Well, now we are at Wu Gorge. It is also known as the Grand Canyon Gorge, for both its relatively long length (40 kilometers long) and beautiful tranquil scenery. During the boat trip, the mountains sometimes suddenly appear and block your view. And the winding river and its beautiful scenery constantly make you as if you were in a coiling gallery.

Wushan Ancient City

Wushan ancient city is located in the mouth of Daning river in the Wu Gorge and has a long history. As early as the Qin and Han dynasties, Wushan County was named Wu County, and this name was permanently adopted from Sui Dynasty onward. It is said that in ancient Yao Shun period, there is a royal doctor called Wu who died here, afterward this place was named Wushan. There was another saying:the Nanling Hill faced Wushan and took a shape like the Chinese character "巫" (pinyin:w   ), so it got the name Wushan(Wu Hill). The most special feature of this town is that all of its streets, both big and small, are are named after Wushan's twelve peaks. Finally and most importantly, in addition to its history, Wushan ancient city is surrounded by beautiful scenery everywhere.

Daning River Small Three Gorges

Daning River was called Wizard Water in ancient times. It begins from the Daba Mountains at the junction of Sichuan, Hubei, and Shaanxi, and has a total length of nearly 300 km. It is the first tributary among Three Gorges tributaries. The Daning River has three small gorges along a 60-kilometer stretch running from Wu Hill to Dachang. These gorges are the Longmen, Bawu, and Dicui Gorges. This section of canyon is narrower and steeper than the Three Gorges of Yangtze River. It also boasts unique scenery, such as strangely shaped rocks, clear water, and many beaches. Tourists can hear the sound of boat trackers'trumpets here.

Longmen Gorge

The Longmen gorge is only about three kilometers long. The narrow gap between two mountains here makes it seem as if they are facing each other. The cliffs are very steep and the terrain is so dangerous that some people say it is more dangerous than the Kui Gate. To visit the three small gorges, tourists generally travel from Wushan County's Daning river mouth by boat against the current. They go into Longmen Gorge, pass through the Bawu to the Dicui, and then return. On the way you can glimpse peculiar and beautiful scenes before going to the next destination, Xiling Gorge.

Xiling Gorge

中南地區

Now we are in the beautiful Xiling Gorge. Since the Gezhou Dam and Three Gorges Dam were completed, it has been known for its beautiful mountain and river scenery. Xiling Gorge stretches 76 kilometers, from Xiangxi River in west Zigui County to Nanjinguan, which is located east of Yichang. It is the longest among the Yangtze River's Three Gorges. East of Nanjinguan, the Yangtze River suddenly becomes wider, going from 400 to 2, 000 meters, and its currents slow conside-rably. Xiling Gorge contains three Beaches—Xie, Green, and Kongling Beach—and four gorges—Lantern Shadow, Cattle, Buffalo and Horse's Lung, and War Book and Sword Gorge. The Gorge contains small gorges, and the beach contains small beaches. With the completion of the Gezhou Dam Project, the water level rose, causing the rapid water and beaches to disappear. But today we can still appreciate the mighty and beautiful scenery of Three Gorges Project and Xiling Gorge on both sides.

Nanjinguan

This is Nanjinguan, the starting point of the Yangtze River Three Gorges, the dividing line between upper reaches of the Yangtze River. There is a famous scenic spot at the mouth of the Xiling Gorge, which is national level scenic area and the provincial level tourist resort. Its main attractions are the Leizu Temple, Peach Blossom Village, White Horse and Three Swimming Caves, the Stream to Prison, Dragon Fountain Cave, Immortal River and Wuzhou Leisure Park. When passing through Nanjinguan, the width of the river suddenly narrows from more than 2, 000 to about 300 meters.

The Lantern Shadow Gorge

After cruising about 10 kilometers west from Nanjinguan, we arrive at the Lantern Shadow Gorge. The Lantern Shadow Gorge is also known as the Moon Gorge. It is not long, but the landscape is remarkable. The gorge wall looks luminous, pleasant, and it is as pure as carefully polished geMs.If you pass by this place in the evening, the moonlit western hill creates a special kind of scenery, too beautiful to express in words. Hence, the name "Moon Gorge". The Lantern Shadow Gorge is famous for its Horse Tooth Mountain in the south bank. It has four bizarre rocks, which look like pictures of the main characters in the early Chinese literary classic, Journey to the West. One rock is the Sun Wukong—the monkey, with one hand in front of his forehead to shade light; another rock, resembling a man touching his belly is Zhu Bajie—the pig; The other two rocks represent respectively Sha Wujing—the monk who is carrying the load, and Tang Sanzang—the master who folds his palMs.All four are vivid, lifelike and wonderful. And in the setting sun, when viewed from a distance, the gorge really resembles a shadow play game the locals call the Lantern Shadow game. Hence, its name, Lantern Shadow Gorge.

Zhongbao Island—The Three Gorges Dam Site

When we pass Xiling Yangtze River Bridge by ship, we arrive at the Three Gorges dam site. Initially rectangular in shape, the island became Zhongbao Island and was personally selected the Three Gorges Dam site by Zhou Enlai. Zhongbao Island is a magical island, and it has never been inundated by the Yangtze River's great floods. The flood in 1870 submerged Huangling Temple whose position is even higher than Zhongbao Island, but Zhongbao Island was not submerged. No convincing scientific explanation currently exists for this strange mystery. Now Zhongbao Island has disappeared for the construction of the Three Gorges Project and on this site stands the magnificent Three Gorges Dam.

Kongling Gorge

After we pass through the Three Gorges Dam and then cruise another 10 kilometers west, our ship will enter a precipitous gorge that is approximately 2. 5 kilometers long. This is the famous Kongling Gorge, which is renowned for its sheer cliffs. It is also known as the Air-cooling Gorge and originally had a reef rising above the water level, with the words, "come to me," inscribed on it. In 1900 a foreign vessel entered the

中
南
地
區

gorge and its captain could not read the sign and also ignored his crew's warnings. As a result, his ship sank on this reef. After the founding of New China and several changes in the river channel, the reef was blown up. The Gezhou Dam's completion has caused the water level to rise, so the beach no longer poses any danger. Tourists can get here safely by ship, but it is not as exciting as before.

The Home of Famous Figures along the Fragrant Brook

After passing through Xiling Gorge, we come to Fragrant Brook and a wide valley. Fragrant Brook is full of water. Two well-known historical figures hail from here, one is the great patriotic poet Qu Yuan, and the other is the Han Dynasty heroine, Wang Zhaojun. A legend exists about the latter and goes like this. One day Zhaojun was washing at the stream and intentionally scattered a necklace of pearls in the river. Because of this, the stream became clear, and water smells fragrant, so it is called Fragrant Brook. Fragrant Brook is like a stream of ribbon, which serves as a bridge to magical forests of Shennongjia. With the completion of the Three Gorges Project, tourist can directly reach Zhaojun village by ship and may then visit the poet Qu Yuan's hometown of Lepingli

Three Gorges Project

Finally, let me introduce the famous Three Gorges Project. We Chinese people all feel proud of this. The construction of the Three Gorges Project was not a smooth sailing. As early as in 1919, the great revolutionary forerunner Mr.Sun Yat-sen had brought forward the plan for construction of the Three Gorges Project. However it was not until 1994, nearly 80 years after this idea was first proposed that construction work on it began.

The building of the Three Gorges Project can be divided into four phases. The years 1992-1994 marked the initial preparatory phase, during which the 28-kilometer highway to the dedicated dam area was built. The second phase was from 1994 to 1997, when the river closure took place (this event and the spectacular scenes occurring during it was recorded by television). The third phase, from 1997-2003, was marked by the installation of the first power generation unit; the depth of the water behind the dam also rose up to 135 meters over this period. The four phase, from 2003 to 2009, saw 26 generating units coming on line. When the dam's construction is completely finished, the depth of the water behind the dam will be 175 meters.

The Three Gorges Project is currently the world's largest water hydro-electric and water conservation project and is aimed at controlling flood along the middle and lower reaches of the Yangtze River. The project's numerous benefits include power generation, navigation, irrigation and the development of the economy in the reservoir area, which plays an important role in the China's socialist modernization and development of its overall economic strength.

When completed, the Three Gorges Dam will be 1, 983 meters long and 185 meters high, with a maximum reservoir depth of 175 meters and a total storage capacity of 39. 3 billion cubic meters. The dam's total installed power capacity will be 1, 820 kw and its annual generating capacity will be 84. 7 billion degrees, or the equivalent of 10 nuclear power plants. This will enable every Chinese person with 70 degrees of extra electricity every year.

Sadly, due to the Three Gorges reservoir, lots of scenic spots attractions, such as Baidicheng, the Zhang Fei and Qu Yuan temples, Shibaozhai, the Three Gorges Famous Hill Ghost Town, ancient paths, Wang Zhaojun's hometown, and the Daning River's Three Gorges will be partially or completely inundated due to rising water levels. Some have been relocated and reconstructed.

The water storage of the Three Gorges reservoir has now reached a depth of 156 meters. Many ancient legends of Three Gorges are submerged under the water, but there

中南地區

will be some new ones.

Well, the tour of the Three Gorges is over here. Thank you very much for your support and cooperation. I've enjoyed myself being with you. I hope we will get together again. Have a nice trip. Goodbye!

各位遊客朋友，大家好！

很高興成為大家這次遊覽的嚮導！在遊覽主要景點之前先讓我來介紹一下長江三峽的基本情況。

三峽是長江上的一段河道。長江三峽東起湖北宜昌南津關，西至重慶市奉節縣白帝城，由西陵峽、巫峽、瞿塘峽組成，全長193公里。它是長江風光的精華，神州山水中的瑰寶，古往今來，閃耀著迷人的光彩，無數中外遊客為之傾倒。三峽留下了歷代騷人墨客暢遊的千古絕唱，三峽旅遊一直是萬里長江不變的主題。三峽因長江而存在，長江以三峽而驕傲。因為三峽是世界上著名的大峽谷，被譽為山水畫廊，是國家重點風景名勝區。

好的，遊客朋友們，現在就讓我們開始神奇壯麗的三峽之旅吧。

瞿塘峽

三峽的第一個峽叫瞿塘峽，又叫夔峽。長江到了這裡驟然變窄，最窄的地方只有100多米。峽口有夔門，人們稱天下最雄偉的地方莫過於夔門了。瞿塘峽全長只有8 公里。這8 公里是三峽最險峻的地方，江水的最大流速達到每秒8米，每小時20多公里。在這樣的峽谷裡航行，使人驚心動魄。峽中值得觀賞的風景名勝比比皆是，如孟良梯、盔甲洞、風箱峽等。瞿塘峽雖然最短，卻是一幅神奇的自然畫卷和文化藝術走廊。

奉節

奉節位於瞿塘峽西口的長江北岸，在近1000多年的歷史中，一直是川東政治、軍事、經濟和文化中心。這裡最早是巴、庸兩國的領地，並曾建立過夔子國，周朝時建立魚復縣，是中國最早建立的縣邑，已有2300多年的歷史。公元222 年，劉備從夷陵（今宜昌）敗退白帝城，改魚復縣為永安縣。唐貞觀三十二年（公元649年），皇帝為旌表諸葛亮的忠君愛國思想將其改名為奉節並沿用至今。歷史上著名的詩人李白、杜甫、蘇軾、陸游、劉禹錫等都在此留下了著名的詩篇。因此，奉節縣又享有「詩誠」的美譽。中秋之夜，皎潔明月從峽口冉冉升起，還能欣賞到三峽著名景緻「夔門秋月」。

白帝城

好了，現在我們到了白帝城。據說白帝城系公孫述為拒東漢光武帝劉秀軍而築。白帝城三面環水，一面靠山，是觀賞瞿塘峽的最佳地方。蜿蜒的石級小道直通山門，廟內陳列有劉備、諸葛亮、關羽、張飛等彩色塑像。80多塊石碑展現了多種書法藝術。李白、杜甫、白居易、劉禹錫、蘇軾、陸游、范成大等人均登臨此地，留下了不少膾炙人口的詩篇，因此白帝城又有「詩城」之稱。白帝城下，瞿塘峽口原有一巨大礁石橫亘江心，這就是灩澦堆。船行至此如離弦之箭，稍有不慎就會觸礁沉船，故有「灩澦大如馬，瞿塘不可下；灩澦大如象，瞿塘不可上」的古謠。1958 年，這塊阻塞巷道的巨石被航道工人炸掉。

大溪文化遺址

遊客朋友們，我們現在來到了大溪文化遺址，它位於瞿塘峽東口長江南岸與大溪河交匯處，距奉節縣城15公里。國家文物部門於1958年、1975年和1976年進行過三次發掘，發掘面積達570平方米，清理墓葬208座，出土珍貴文物1200多件，該文化遺址距今約五六千年，它對於研究新石器時代長江上游地帶的社會、經濟發展提供了極珍貴的史料。

巫峽

好的，現在我們到了巫峽。巫峽又稱大峽，全長40公里，以幽深秀麗著稱。舟

中南地區

行其間，一會兒大山橫前，石塞疑無路，一會兒峰迴路轉，風光無限，猶如一條迂迴曲折的畫廊。

巫山古城

巫山古城位於巫峽大寧河口上，古城歷史悠久。早在秦漢時，巫山稱巫縣，隋朝始用今名。據說在遠古堯舜時，有一御醫巫死於此，因而得名巫山。又有一說法：巫山對岸南陵山形如巫字而得名。最為特別的是，巫山縣城中的大小街道均用巫山十二峰的名字命名。巫山古城景色美麗，大家可以盡情欣賞一下。

大寧河小三峽

大寧河古稱巫水，發源於川，鄂、陝交界的大巴山南麓，全長近300 公里，是三峽中的第一支流。大寧河小三峽從巫山至大昌，長約60公里，由龍門峽、巴霧峽、滴翠峽組成。這一段峽谷比長江三峽更為狹窄陡峭，石怪、水清、灘多和縴夫號子成了大寧河的獨特風光。

龍門峽

龍門峽長約3公里，峽口兩山對峙，峭壁如削，狀若一門，形勢甚為險要，因此有人說它「不是夔門，勝似夔門」。遊覽小三峽，一般是從巫山縣城邊的大寧河口乘船逆水而上，進龍門峽，經巴霧峽，至滴翠峽，然後折回。沿途可以欣賞到奇特美麗的景象。接著就到了西陵峽。

西陵峽

現在我們到了風光綺麗的西陵峽。兩壩建成後，又以山靈水秀著稱。西陵峽西起秭歸縣香溪河口，東至宜昌市南津關，全長76 公里，是長江三峽中最長的峽谷。長江東出南津關後，江面驟然展寬，由400米增至2000 米左右，流速由急變緩。西陵峽中有三灘（泄灘、青灘、崆嶺灘）、四峽（燈影峽、黃牛峽、牛肝馬肺峽和兵書寶劍峽），峽中有峽，灘中有灘，大灘含小灘，灘多水急。隨著葛洲壩工程的建成，西陵峽中灘多水急的奇觀不復存在了。今天我們沿途可欣賞博大恢弘的三峽工程及西陵峽兩岸的美妙景色。

南津關

這就是南津關，長江三峽的起始點，長江上游的分界線。這裡有著名的西陵峽口風景區，是國家級風景名勝區，省級旅遊渡假區。主要景點有嫘祖廟、桃花村、白馬洞、三游洞、下牢溪、龍泉洞、仙人溪和五洲休閒樂園等景點。穿過南津關後，江面由2000多米驟然左右變窄到300米，展現在你眼前的便是色彩斑斕、氣象萬千的壯麗畫卷。

燈影峽

過南津關西行約10公里，就到了燈影峽。燈影峽又名明月峽，峽雖不長，但景緻不凡。峽壁明淨可人，純無雜色，如天工細心打磨而出。若晚間過此，月懸西山，月光之下形成的奇特景色難以言喻，這就是「明月峽」的由來。燈影峽得以以形取景，南岸的馬牙山上有四塊奇石，酷似《西遊記》唐僧師徒四人西天取經高興歸來的生動形象：手搭涼篷的孫悟空；捧著肚皮、一步三晃的豬八戒；肩挑重擔的沙和尚；合掌緩行的唐僧，形象逼真、維妙維肖，栩栩如生，妙不可言。每當夕霞晚照，從峽中遠望，極似皮影戲（當地人叫燈影戲），故名燈影峽。

中堡島——三峽大壩壩址

船過西陵長江大橋，就到了三峽大壩壩址。這裡原來是個長方形的小島，稱為中堡島，是周恩來總理親自選定的大壩壩址。中堡島是個神奇的島，歷史上不論發生多大的洪水，都淹不了這個小島。1870年的特大洪水淹了位置比中堡島高得多的黃陵廟，卻沒能淹沒中堡島，這裡的奧秘，至今還沒有令人信服的科學解釋。現在中堡島為了三峽工程的建設從地球上消失了。現在展現在大家面前的是雄偉壯麗的三峽大壩。

崆嶺峽

船駛過三峽大壩後，再西行約10公里，便進入了一個險峻的峽谷之中，這就是三峽中著名的崆嶺峽。崆嶺峽峭壁聳立。此峽又稱空冷峽，全長約2.5公里。峽中原有一塊凸出水面的礁石，上刻三個大字「對我來」。1900 年，有一艘外國輪船開進峽江，船長不知其中奧妙，又不聽峽江水手告誡，結果被礁石撞沉。新中國成立後，經過多次航道整治，炸掉了這塊礁石。葛洲壩建成後，水位抬高，險灘也不復存在。航船到這裡安然無恙，只是少了一處夠刺激的景觀。

香溪名人故里

船行出西陵峽不久就到了香溪寬谷。在這綠水悠悠的香溪之濱，歷史上曾出現過兩位著名人物：一位是偉大的愛國詩人屈原，一位是漢代的王昭君。傳說有一天，昭君在溪邊洗臉，無意中把頸上項鍊的珍珠散落溪中，從此溪水清澈，水中含香，故名香溪。香溪似一條流香溢美的綵帶，架起了一座通向充滿神奇的神農架原始森林的橋樑。三峽工程蓄水後，遊船可從長江直到昭君村，中途也可達到屈原故里——樂平里。

三峽工程

最後，讓我為大家介紹一下舉世矚目的三峽工程。我們每個中國人都會為三峽工程感到驕傲和自豪，然而工程的建設並不是一帆風順的。早在1919年，偉大的革命先驅孫中山先生就提出了建設三峽工程的構想，到1994年才破土動工，距構想有近80年的時間。

三峽工程共分為三期，嚴格說是四期，1992 年到1994年為籌建期，修築了28公里的三峽壩區專用公路。第一期是從1994 年到1997 年，以大江截流為標誌，相信大江截流時的壯觀場面大家已經從電視上看過。第二期是從1997 年到2003 年，以第一台發電機組安裝完成為標誌，水位將抬升到135米。第三期工程從2003 年到2009 年，以二十六台機組全部發電，大壩建成為標誌，水位抬升到175米。

三峽工程是目前世界上最大的水利工程，它是綜合治理長江中下游地區防洪問題的關鍵，工程還有發電、航運、灌溉和發展庫區經濟等多項綜合效益，對中國發展社會主義現代化建設及提高中國的綜合國力起著重要的作用。

三峽大壩建成後全長1983 米，壩高為185 米，最高運行水位175米，總蓄水量393億立方米，總裝機容量1820千瓦，年發電量847億度，相當於十座廣東大亞灣核電站。三峽大壩建成後，中國每年每人將可以增加用電70度。

三峽工程建成蓄水後，峽外的主要景點白帝城、張飛廟、石寶寨、名山鬼城；峽內的古棧道、屈原祠、昭君故里、大寧河小三峽等多處景點，有的將因水位升高而部分或全部被永久淹沒，有的將整體搬遷新址重建。

如今三峽庫區蓄水已達156米高程，有許多曾伴隨我們成長的古老的三峽傳奇，已永埋水下，而一些嶄新的三峽傳奇正應運而生。

好了，我們的三峽之旅到此就結束了。非常感謝大家對我工作的支持和配合。希望以後能有緣和大家再次相逢。最後祝大家旅途愉快！再見。

Guangdong Province廣東省

A Glimpse of the Province （本省簡介）

Guangdong Province, whose shortened name is "Yue", is a coastal province in southeast Mainland China, which borders Fujian Province in the east and Guizhou Province in the west. It is located on the 20° 12′ to 25° 31′ northern latitude, while its eastern longitude is between 109° 45′ to 117° 20′. The whole province contains 21 municipalities, including 2 vice-provincial cities（Guangzhou and Shenzhen), and 19 locally administered ones.

Tourism Resources

Guangdong's advantageous geography and superior scenery attracts large numbers of

中南地區

tourists. The Zhaoqing Seven Star Crag combines the beauty of Guilin's karst hills and Hangzhou's West Lake. Guangdong's four most famous mountains are Danxia Mountain in the northern part of the province, Xiqiao Mountain in Nanhai City, Luofu Mountain in Boluo county, and Dinghu Mountain in Zhaoqing.

Visitors to Guangzhou's Grand World Scenic Park can appreciate and see the world in miniature. Those who step into the Folk Culture Village will learn about the colorful customs of the different Chinese people. Guangdong's long coastline boasts many outstanding beaches and places to bathe and swim. Finally, the province has hot springs and resorts where people can relax and engage in leisure activities.

Visitors can go to inner city and suburban Cantonese restaurants and teahouses to taste authentic Cantonese cuisine. They can go also to street corner stalls and fill up on tasty snacks to get an even better appreciation of Guangdong food. And visitors to the villages and towns on the Pearl River Delta (also called "Zhusanjiao") will appreciate this area's unique "bridge, flowing water and resident" culture and directly experience Lingnan culture.

Other distinctive folk customs and landmarks display the Lingnan life style. These include the Chaoshan area's "Tower Burning" tradition, Puzhai's "Fire Dragon Dance" in Fengshun County, and the famous Southern Lion Dance. All of these things express the Cantonese people's deep love of life.

Food Specialties

Guangdong cuisine is called as Cantonese cuisine. It gradually absorbed the ingredients and cooking techniques of the Ming and Qing Dynasties, as well as Jing, Chuan and Lu cuisine. It is now one of the four most famous Chinese cuisines and people in Guangdong commonly say, "Eat in Guangzhou, taste in Chaozhou". According to local regions and their different tastes, Cantonese cuisine consists of

Guangzhou, Chaozhou, and Dongjiang, or Hakka-style food. Guangzhou cuisine is famous for its wide range of fine ingredients, excellent cooking techniques, and diversity and change. Chaozhou cuisine has a delicate elegance, while Hakka food (Dongjiang cuisine) is known for original taste and flavors. Classic Cantonese dishes include braised pigeon, roast-suckling pig, plain chicken, marinated meat combinations, honey-stewed barbecued pork, burned goose, stewed mixed vegetables, and various country dishes.

Guangdong's snacks mainly originated in the Lingnan culture and became famous after being handed down for many years as part of this culture's traditional flavor. Four different methods—steaming, pan-frying, frying, and boiling—are used to cook Guangdong snacks. Moreover, these snacks are divided into six categories. One is fried food made with rice, noodles and other grains that is full of different flavors. The second category consists of steamed foods mainly using rice and noodles, but sometimes other grains, and this material can be either fermented or non-fermented. Rice noodles, which are made using both rice and flour, are mainly boiled. There are also many varieties of gruel, which is usually named after its ingredients and flavor. The third category consists of sweets, or different sorts of sweet snacks. These snacks do not include millet cakes and pudding and mainly use plant roots, stems and stalks, flowers and fruit, as well as eggs and milk. The final category might be called "omnivorous", as it uses a variety of ingredients, is cooked in diverse styles, and is very cheap. Particularly famous examples of this cuisine include the Tortilla lotus-paste steamed stuffed bun, Water Chestnut Cake, Run Jiau Rice Cake, Honeycomb Dried Taro Chip, Crab Spawn Flattery Dumplings, Pellicle Steamed Fresh Shrimp Dumplings, Steamed dumplings with the dough gathered at the top, Rice noodles, Lotus Leaf Rice, Luxurious Pork Congee, and Tingzai Porridge.

Recommended Attractions

Danxia Mountain is located in the 54 kilometers northeast of Shaoguan, 9

中南地區

kilometers from Renhua County. It is one of Guangdong's four famous mountains—the other three are Luofu, Xiqiao and Dinghu Mountains—and is 408 meters high. This scenic spot has three layers or zones. The upper zone provides visitors with views of Zhanglao, Hailuo and Baozhu peaks. The middle layer is mainly known for Biechuan Temple, while the mountain's lower zone has the Conch, Daming, Snow, Wanxiu, Fanzhao as well as Caoxuan Grottos.

The Former Residence of Dr.Sun Yat-sen is a brick timberwork building with two stories and is a fusion of Chinese and Western architectural styles. Its main structure was built with funds provided by Sun Yat-sen's older brother and its construction was overseen by Sun in 1892. It uses different valuable cultural objects and displays pictures to systemati-cally describe Mr.Sun's life experiences. Following 1996-1997, the residence has served as a national middle and primary school patriotic educational demonstration base. It has also been listed as a key protected cultural site by the State Council.

Splendid China is one of China's richest, most vivid and complete miniature scenic and historical images site. Splendid China covers an area of 330, 000 square meters and its displays cover Chinese history, culture, art, ancient architecture and folk custoMs.Nearly 100 displays are arranged here according to a Chinese regional map. These depict famous scenery from China and its history in miniature. The Chinese Folk Culture Village, which covers an area of more than 200, 000 square meters, is located next to Splendid China. It is China's first large-scale cultural tourist attraction and displays different folk art, customs and folk architectures, including 25 villages of 22 nationalities built according to 1:1 proportion. Some 25 villages and 56 different ethnological customs are showcased here, so the village has been honored as the "China Folk Museum".

廣東省，簡稱粵，是中華人民共和國大陸南端沿海的一個省份，陸域東起饒平縣大埔鎮的閩粵省界，西至廉江市高橋鎮的粵桂省界，南自雷州半島徐聞縣的最南端，北達樂昌縣上旗頭村的最北省界；介於北緯 20°12´ ～ 25°31´、東經 109°45´～117°20´之間。全省轄21 個省轄市，其中副省級城市2個（廣州、深圳），地級市19個。

旅遊資源

由於地理位置上的優勢，廣東省的山水風光吸引著眾人的目光。肇慶七星岩，擁有桂林山之美，杭州水之秀；粵北的丹霞山、南海的西樵山、博羅的羅浮山和肇慶的鼎湖山是廣東的四大名山。

遊覽廣州的「世界大觀」，則在有限的空間領略世界風貌；移步「民俗文化村」，又可以領略到中國各個民族多姿多彩的風土人情；連綿數千公里的海岸線，不乏出色的海濱浴場，還有溫泉、渡假村，都是人們休閒放鬆的場所。

到遍布城鄉的粵式茶樓酒家品嚐正宗的粵菜，到街頭排檔去「漫吃」風味小食，體會「食在廣東」的內涵；到珠江三角洲的鄉村小鎮去體味「小橋流水人家」的水鄉風情，都能體驗到嶺南的風俗。

別具特色的民俗更是展現了嶺南人的生活風貌。潮汕地區的燒塔，豐順的埔寨火龍，還有那著名的南派舞獅，無不表達了廣東人對生活的熱愛。

特色餐飲

廣東菜稱為「粵菜」，明清時期粵菜逐步吸取了京、川、魯、蘇等菜系的烹飪原料和技術，一躍成為中國四大名菜系之一，正所謂「食在廣州，味在潮州」。按照地區和口味的不同，粵菜分為廣州菜、潮州菜和東江菜（即客家菜）三大類。廣州菜用料廣博，選料精細，技藝精良，善於變化，品種多樣。潮州菜以精緻典雅著稱，客家菜則以原汁原味見長。粵菜中的經典有紅燒乳鴿、燒乳豬、白切雞、鹵水拼盤、護國菜、蜜汁叉燒、深井燒鵝、羅漢齋等。

廣東的小吃來源於民間，大都被流傳下來而成為傳統名食。廣東小吃的成熟方

中南地區

法多為蒸、煎、煮、炸4種，可分為6類：油品，即油炸小吃，以米、麵和雜糧為原料，風味各異；糕品，以米、面為主，雜糧次之，都是蒸炊至熟的，可分為發酵和不發酵的兩大類；粉、麵食品，以米、麵為原料，大都是煮熟而成的；粥品，名目繁多，其名大都以用料而定，也有以粥的風味特色而稱的；甜品，指各種甜味小吃品種，不包括麵點、糕團在內，用料除蛋、奶以外，多為植物的根、莖、梗、花、果、仁等；雜食，凡不屬上述各類者皆是，因其用料雜而得名，以價格低廉，風味多樣而著稱，其中尤以酥皮蓮蓉包、馬蹄糕、倫教糕、蜂巢芋角、蟹黃灌湯餃、薄皮鮮蝦餃、干蒸燒賣、沙河粉、荷葉飯、及第粥、艇仔粥著名。

主要推薦景點

丹霞山位於韶關市東北54　　公里處，距仁化縣城9公里，是廣東四大名山之一（其餘三座名山是羅浮山、西樵山、鼎湖山），海拔408米，風景區可劃分為上中下三層。上層景區有長老峰、海螺峰、寶珠峰；中層景區以別傳寺為主要景點；下有海螺岩、大明岩、雪岩、晚秀岩、返照岩、草懸岩等岩洞。

孫中山故居是一座融合中、西方建築特點的兩層磚木結構樓房，其主體建築是1892年由孫中山的大哥孫眉出資、孫中山主持修建的。孫中山故居以各種珍貴的文物、圖片等系統地介紹了孫中山先生的生平事跡，於1996年至1997年先後被公布為中國中小學愛國主義教育基地、中國愛國主義教育示範基地，並被國務院列為中國重點文物保護單位。

錦繡中華是一座中國歷史、文化、藝術、古代建築和民族風情的最豐富、最生動、最全面的實景微縮景區，面積33萬平方米。景區中，近百處景緻按照中國區域版圖分布，是中國自然風光與人文歷史精粹的縮影。

與錦繡中華僅一牆之隔的是中國民俗文化村，它占地20多萬平方米，是中國第一個薈萃各民族民間藝術、民俗風情和民居建築於一園的大型文化旅遊景區。內含22個民族的25個村寨，均按1∶1比例建成。中國民俗文化村以「二十五個村寨五十族風情」的豐厚意蘊贏得了「中國民俗博物館」的美譽。

Danxia Mountain （丹霞山）

Ladies and gentlemen, good morning! It is my pleasure to be your guide as you visit one of Guang-dong's most famous scenic spots, Danxia Mountain. I will begin by giving you a brief introduction to Danxia Mountain.

Danxia Mountain, which is located approx-imately 9 kilometers south of Renhua County, is 56 kilometers away from the Shaoguan urban district. It is the most famous of Guangdong's four well-known mountains and was designated a national scenic area by the State Council in 1988. This prominent peak's elevation is 409 meters, so compared to other famous mountains, it is not very high or very big. However, Danxia Mountain combines Mt.Huang's fantasy, Mt.Hua's steepness and ruggedness, and the beauty of Guilin's karst hills. It is thus wonderful, dangerous and beautiful. The mountain's scenery differs at its upper, middle and lower elevations. At the summit, there are three peaks towering aloft. The area below the summit but above the base of the peak boasts the Biechuan temple. And at the base of the peak lies the Jinshi rock. Some 300 hundred years ago, when the zen master Dangui built the Biechuan temple, he designated a dozen places as Danxia Mountain's twelve senic spots. They are Jinshui Tansheng, Yutai Shuangqi, Jiege Chenzhong, Songjian Taofeng, Zhupo Yanyu, Shuangzhao Bihe, Danti Tiesuo, Ruquan Chunliu, Luoding Futu, Hongqiao Yongcui, Pianlin Qiuyue, and Duoshi Zhaoxi.

Regardless of whether it's morning and evening, sunny or raining, there are many different views that make it possible for visitors to appreciate Danxia Mountain's beauty during the Spring, Summer, Fall, and Winter. In the morning, we can enjoy either the marvelous light of the sunrise or the thick clouds shrouding Danxia Mountain. In the evening, we are treated to the gorgeous sunset glow and the tranquil dim light of the night. On rainy days, looking out to the distance can cause our minds to open up and all of our sadness to disappear. And during every season, these marvelous scenes can only be exper-ienced in person.

中南地區

The first thing we notice upon entering the Danxia Mountain scenic spot is its gate tower in front of us. The tower is resplendent and magnificent. The three large Chinese characters "丹霞山"（pényǐ níd nxi shēn）, written using a brush by the vice-Chairman of National People's Congress, Xi Zhongxun, can be seen on the tower. Climbing along the track up to the pavilion mid-way up the Mountain and turning left to the direction of the Jinshi Rock, we arrive at the "Mengjue Pass" Crag. Although it is only ten feet wide, it has a recognizable form resembling a statue of Buddha. From this vantage point, we can enjoy the beauty of Jinjiang River below and the cloud and stone above.

Shortly after leaving Mengjue Pass, we see a grotto weathered by wind with the four brush-written characters "You Dong Tong Tian" written on it. Of all the numerous grottos of Danxia Mountain, Jinshi rock is the most attractive for tourists. It is well-known for the contrasts in its rock wall color throughout the four seasons. It is the first area that was developed at Danxia Mountain. Up to the Ming Dynasty Chenghua Era, the Buddhist priests planted pines and built the garden halls with winding corridors and temples. Standing at Jinshi Rock Gate, we may see what looks like a spring falling from the sky and having the likeness of a dancing rainbow under the sunshine. This is one of the twelve spots "Jinyan Feipu". The spring was called Horse's Tail Spring and Dragon's Tail Spring in ancient times.

After getting mid-way up the mountain, we come of one of this scenic spot's most famous places, the Biechuan temple at Lingnan. It was originally built by the Zen Master Dangui at the end of Ming and in the beginning of Qing Dynasty. It was originally a refuge for the former ministers of Ming Dynasty from the troubled times during the beginning of Qing Dynasty. After being expanded several times by Li Yongmao's descendants, the magnificent temple was finally completed. It is named as Biechuan Temple under the meaning that Buddhism being not dependent on words and letters and being a special transmission apart from the teachings".

Initially no path existed up to the summit of Danxia Mountain. Li Yongmao's descendants cut the stone steps in the cliff behind two passes, and installed iron chains alongside the path, which then became the way up to the mountain's summit. The southern end of the summit has the Sun-view pavilion. This pavilion sits on Danxian Mountain's Zhanglao Peak and is split into two levels. It is said that viewing the sunlight from the top of Danxia Peak is much like seeing it from Mt.Huang's Lotus Peak. It is also said that "after visiting every scenic place with beautiful sunrises, the sunrise at Danxia Mountain is the most beautiful."

Some friends once sighed with regret that they could not see the sunrise after going to Danxia Mountain several times. Since weather here is quite changeable, one has to be lucky to see a really splendid sunrise on Danxia Mountain. Generally speaking, the end of summer, as well as the fall and winter, are the best times to appreciate sunrise at Danxia Mountain, especially when it rains the day before and then turns sunny. On the day after it rains, there will be a very thin veil of mist around the mountain, providing a rare chance to enjoy the magnificent sunrise.

Now, everyone, we finish the visit to Danxia Mountian. I hope you have a good day.

各位遊客朋友,大家好!

很高興能有幸陪同大家一起遊覽我們廣東著名的風景名勝區——丹霞山。首先,我先把丹霞山的概況簡要地給大家介紹一下。

丹霞山坐落於仁化縣城南約9公里處,距韶關市區56公里,為廣東四大名山之首,1988年被國務院定為國家級風景名勝區。丹霞山主峰海拔409米,它與眾多名山相比遠不算高,也不算大,但它集黃山之奇、華山之險、桂林之秀於一身,具有一險、二奇、三美的特點。風景區劃分為上、中、下三層。上層是三峰聳峙;中層以別傳寺為主體;下層以錦石岩為中心。三百多年前,澹歸禪師在丹霞山開闢別傳

中南地區

寺時，曾挑出 12 處風景，命名為丹霞十二景，即錦水灘聲、玉台爽氣、傑閣晨鐘、松澗濤風、竹坡煙雨、雙沼碧荷、丹梯鐵索、乳泉春溜、螺頂浮屠、虹橋擁翠、片鱗秋月和舵石朝曦。

丹霞山一年四季無論晴雨早晚，都有不同的景色供遊人觀賞。早上，可以在丹霞山看到日出的奇觀和滔滔雲海。晚上，可以看到絢麗的晚霞和恬靜的夜色。雨天，極目遠眺，使人胸懷開闊，萬慮頓消。至於春夏秋冬，四時景色的奇妙，則只有身臨其境者，才能體會到。

一進入丹霞山風景區，迎面是丹霞門樓，門樓金碧輝煌，牌坊上刻有中國人大副委員長習仲勳所題的「丹霞山」三個大字。沿上山小道至半山亭前，左轉往錦石岩方向，先見一石岩，這就是「夢覺關」。這石岩雖僅丈把寬，但極端整，形狀猶如佛龕。踞其上可一睹腳下錦江、頭上雲石之風采。

過夢覺關不遠即見一處風化的岩洞，上面刻有「幽洞通天」四個大字。在丹霞山眾多的岩洞中，錦石岩最為吸引遊人，它因石壁五色間錯，四時變化而得名。錦石岩是丹霞山開發最早的地方，至明成化年間，此處僧人遍植松杉，並建構起伽藍堂廊房和寺庵。站在錦石岩洞口，向外可以看到一道飛泉從天而落，在陽光折射下猶如彩虹飛舞，這就是丹霞新十二景之一的「錦岩飛瀑」，瀑布名叫馬尾泉，古稱「龍尾泉」。

步入中層風景區首先到達的就是嶺南有名的別傳寺。別傳寺原由澹歸禪師闢建於明末清初，原是南明遺民們避難的地方。幾經輾轉，在後人的苦心經營下，終於建成了一座頗具規模的寺院，取「不立文字，教外別傳」之意，名「別傳寺」。

由丹霞山的中層到上層，本無道可通，後人在二關門後的懸崖峭壁上開鑿石階，並在旁邊安上鐵索鏈，才成為通道。在上層風景區最南端的長老峰之頂，有丹霞山的觀日亭，觀日亭分上下兩層。有人說過，在丹霞山觀日出絕不亞於在黃山蓮花峰觀日出。有人盛讚：「遊盡日出風景地，獨有丹霞日出美」。

有的朋友曾慨嘆，幾次上丹霞山都看不到日出，這是因晴雨無常，要靠機緣。

即使有日出，壯觀與否也要取決於季節及天氣。一般來說，夏末和秋冬季節較為適宜，最好是前一天下午下了點小雨，接著天晴，第二天薄霧繚繞，那可是觀賞日出的難得機會。

各位遊客，丹霞山的遊覽就到此結束了，希望大家玩得愉快，遊得開心。

The Former Residence of Dr.Sun Yat-sen （孫中山故居）

Ladies and gentlemen,

Good morning! Speaking of Cuiheng Village, Chinese citizens will have a familiar and friendly feeling. It is because this village is the home town and birth place of the man behind China's first democratic revolution, Sun Yat-sen. It is located southeast of Nanlang Town, Zhongshan City. It is near the Pearl River to the east, while Qi'ao Island, Zhuhai City is directly opposite the village, across the South China Sea. Finally, Wugui Hill is directly west of Cuiheng Village. The village is now home not only to Sun Yat-sen's former residence, but to a Sun Yat-sen monumental middle school and movie city as well, all of which are related to or named after the father of modern and democratic China .

Besides being rich in history, Cuiheng village is next to mountains and the sea. This good geographical setting and its exquisite natural environment make the village's inhabitants carefree and happy. While walking in the village or stepping onto the Cuishan road, one will feel like he/she is in a forest "paradise" of trees, flowers and birds. Even within the village, you can gaze at the distant hills and cliffs. The vegetation here is well protected, so the forest is verdant and luxuriantly green. Along the two sides of the Cuishan road, the dark green umbrage helps cool the air and provides Cuiheng village with a natural air-conditioner. Even during the sultry summers, you can enjoy the mountain's cool breezes and green shade.

中南地區

531

Sun Yat-sen's former residence is located at the Cuiheng Village and faces west. The residence sits on a 500 square meter area site and is itself 340 square meters. Sun Yat-sen built it with the money sent from Honolulu by his elder brother Sun Mei in 1892. We are now standing in front of Sun Yat-sen's former residence. The building is a half-timber house and combines Western and Chinese architectural styles with a wall surrounding the courtyard. Its outward appearance imitates a Western building and its upper floor has seven ember ornamental arches. The middle of the house's penthouse is decorated with aureole under which there is an annotated hawk with a silver ring in its mouth. Going inside, we can see that the building's interior is designed in traditional Chinese architectural style. The parquet is in the middle, while separate penthouses are off to two of the parquet's sides. The four brick walls are grey with white line outlining every brick, and the windows each with two leaves open under the main roof beam. There are doors at all the four sides of the house that lead out to the street. A well is off to the right side of the courtyard, and the area of about 32 square meters surrounding the well is the place where San Yat-Sen was born on November 12, 1866.

Now we are in the parquet of the former residence. The ornaments of the hall were decorated by Sun Yat-sen himself. Please look at the two kerosene burners put on the abutment; Sun Yat-sen brought them here from Honolulu in 1883. The penthouse off to the right is Sun Yat-sen's bedroom. The bedroom still contains his big wooden bed, dresser table and the wooden bench. Sun Yat-sen lived here from 1892 to 1895 and in 1912. Stepping up to the second floor, the south part of the floor has Sun Yat-sen's study. Sun Yat-sen's photo, taken when he was 17 years old, hangs on the wall. This study also has some of the things Sun Yat-sen used everyday, such as his desk, chair and iron bed.

Let's return to the courtyard. There is a wild jujube tree off to the left. It was brought by Sun from Honolulu in 1883 and he planted it himself. It grows well. Off to the right, there is a brick raised flowerbed.

There is a big banyan tree in front of the former residence. There Sun Yat-sen used to listen to the stories of the Taiping generals against Qing told by the old farmers who had fought in the Taiping army.

Everyone, that is all. Thank you for visiting Sun Yat-sen's former residence!

各位遊客，

大家好！提起翠亨村，國人都有一種熟悉而親切的感覺，因為它是中國民主革命先行者孫中山先生的故鄉。它地處中山市南朗鎮東南部，東臨珠江口伶仃洋，與珠海市淇澳島隔海相望，西靠五桂山。至今，翠亨村和國父有關的，或者以國父命名的地方有孫中山故居、中山紀念中學、中山影視城。到這裡，可以踏尋偉人足跡，緬懷　嶸歲月。

除了豐富的人文歷史內涵，翠亨村傍山濱海，氣候宜人，優越的地理位置和優美的自然環境也令遊人心曠神怡。在村裡漫步，或者走上翠山公路，就如同置身於林木蔥茏、鳥語花香的世外桃源中。不用出村，你就可以看到遠處峰巒疊嶂，這裡的植被保護得很好，滿眼蒼翠，林木蔥茏。在翠山公路兩側，濃綠的樹蔭帶來一陣清涼，這裡是翠亨村天然的空調，即便是酷暑時節，在這裡你也可以享受山風和綠蔭帶來的涼意。

孫中山故居位於南朗鎮翠亨村，坐東向西，占地面積500平方米，建築面積340平方米，是孫中山長兄孫眉於1892　年從檀香山匯款回來，由孫中山主持建成的。故居是一幢磚木結構、中西結合的兩層樓房，並有一道圍牆環繞著庭院。它的外表仿照西方建築，樓房上層各有七個赭紅色裝飾性的拱門。屋簷正中飾有光環，環下雕繪一只口銜錢環的飛鷹。走進樓內，我們可以看到內部設計採用中國傳統的建築形式，中間是正廳，左右分兩個耳房，四壁磚牆呈磚灰色，勾出白色間線，窗戶在正樑下對開。居屋內前後左右均有門通向街外，左旋右轉，均可回到原來的起步點。在庭院右邊有一口水井，水井的周圍（約32平方米）是孫中山誕生時的舊房所在地。1866 年11 月12 日，孫中山誕生於此。

　　現在我們來到了故居的正廳，廳內擺設是孫中山親自布置的。請看放置在橋台上的兩盞煤油燈，這是1883　年，孫中山從檀香山帶回來的。右邊的耳房是孫中山臥室，當年所用的大木床、梳妝台和凳子等，仍舊擺放著。1892～1895年、1912年，孫中山都曾在此住過。走上二樓，南邊是孫中山的書房，牆上掛著孫中山十七歲時的照片，室內有孫中山日常使用過的書桌、台椅、鐵床。

　　回到故居庭院，庭院左邊栽植一株酸棗樹，那是孫中山1883　年從檀香山帶回來種子親手栽種的，生勢茁壯茂盛，右邊是磚砌的花台。

　　故居庭院前的大榕樹，是孫中山童年時代聽參加過太平軍的老人講述太平天國將領反清故事的地方。

　　各位遊客，孫中山故居就為大家講解到這兒，謝謝各位的支持！

Splendid China & China Folk Culture Village（錦繡中華和中國民俗文化村）

Ladies and gentlemen,

Good morning! Welcome to the mysterious and beautiful Splendid China and China Folk Culture Village. First, please allow me to briefly introduce Splendid China.

Splendid China is a tourist area in Shenzhen's Chinese Overseas Town and is located at the scenic Shenzhen bay. Splendid China is the biggest and richest live-micro scenery tourist site in the world today. It takes up an area of 300, 000 square meters.

The scenic spots of "Splendid China" are organized according to their geographical position in China. The entire garden looks like a giant map of China. These spots may be divided into three main groups:ancient architecture, folk customs, and landscapes. Over 50, 000 little ceramic men are placed in the various scenic spots.

Over here are miniature displays of two of the world's eight wonders, the Great Wall of China and the Qin Mausoleum's soldiers and horses. Other unique and first of their kind places in China exhibited in miniature include the world's oldest stone arch bridge (Zhaozhou Bridge), the astrono-mical observatory (the ancient observatory), the wooden tower (Yingxian Wooden Tower), the world's biggest palace (the Forbidden City). Visitors can also see miniatures of the world's largest stone Buddha statue, the Leshan Giant Buddha, the biggest royal garden, Yuanmingyuan, the longest grotto galley, Dunhuang's Mogao Grottoes, the highest and grandest palace, the Potala Palace, the most unique landscape, Guangxi's stone forest, the most exquisitely beautiful mountain peak, Anhui's Mt.Huang, and one of the biggest waterfalls, the Yellow River's Huangguoshu Waterfall. There are solemn and serene Chinese imperial mausoleums, including those of Genghis khan and the Ming Tombs, as well as Dr.Sun Yat-sen's Mausoleum. Other famous sites on display include the magnificent Confucian Temple and Temple of Heaven, majestic Mount Tai, the deep and rugged Yangtze Gorges, and the picturesque scenery around Yunnan's Lijiang Village. Finally, one can also view West Lake Hangzhou and Suzhou's gardens and other sights in Southern China.

In addition to all of this, visitors can also view the ceremonies presided over by Ancient Chinese Emperors to worship heaven, their weddings, and a Confucian memorial ceremony. In the hall of chimes, you can also enjoy hearing these ancient instruments played by people wearing authentic period costumes. You'll also be able to take in 5, 000 years of Chinese history in one day, as well as appreciate Northern and Southern China's beautiful scenery.

"Splendid China" touring route is thoughtfully designed with respect to both its green gardens and business, conservancy, and sanitation settings and facilities. Miniature displays of art treasures are everywhere as you walk along the garden track with green trees and flowers. In addition, you can appreciate the folk dance performed on the small stage in the garden. And while strolling through the white- and grey-tiled Suzhou Street, you can taste different local snacks and buy the arts and crafts made by

中
南
地
區

local artists and other local products.

The integrated service area, which is located on Suzhou Street, incorporates the best features of Suzhou's architecture and landscape art while retaining the feel of a traditional Chinese business neighborhood. Pedestrians can enjoy several different regional Chinese cooking styles, including Beijing, Sichuan, Suzhou, and Guangdong cuisine. They will also be able to observe folk handcrafted products being made. Visitors can not only buy handicrafts, antiques, but other famous local products as well, including well-known and highly effective herbal medicines.

In the course of a just single day's visit to Splendid China, tourists can step into history. Splendid China provides a fascinating window into Chinese history. Since it opened some 30 million Chinese and Western visitors have come to see Splendid China. These guests include Deng Xiaoping, Jiang Zemin, the elder former US President Bush, Henry Kissinger, Fidel Castro, and many other famous statesmen.

Splendid China turns out to be not only a window onto Chinese history, culture and tourism, but is also a world of greenery, flowers and beauty.

Then we come to the Chinese Folk Culture Village, which is separated by a wall from and stands beside Splendid China. The China Folk Culture Village covers an area of more than 200, 000 square meters. It is China's first large-scale cultural tourist attraction consisting of different folk art, customs, and architecture, including 25 villages of 22 ethnic nationalities built according to a 1:1 proportion. The Chinese Folk Culture Village takes as its building motto, "from every day life, higher than every day life; gather the quintessence with careful selection". This reflects China's varied and colorful folk culture from several different perspectives.

The Village will hold different large-scale folk community festivals every month, such as the Torch Festival, Water-Sprinkling Festival, and the like. In this Grand View

Garden with folk houses, the ship-shaped house of Li ethnic group and the railed building of Wa ethnic group form a delightful contrast and mirror ancient architectural styles. The elabora-tely carved Bai "three rooms with one screen wall" and the Han "quadrangle" showcase two different kinds of traditional Chinese residential architectural designs. Moreover, along with these residential areas are flaky Hainan coconuts, towering Xishuangbanna old banyan trees, and peacocks spreading their tails and elephants rambling about. The Village can be toured by car, boat, or on foot.

Aside from appreciating the different architec-tural styles, we also can enjoy and participate in performances from all ethnic groups along with their arts and crafts. Visitors can sample ethnic food, watch an ethnic art parade, enjoy various professional parties, visit the folk exhibition hall, and enjoy their favorite folk prograMs.All of this enables visitors to appreciate the 56 colorful kinds of ethnic culture and art on display at the Folk Village. The Folk Culture Village has more than 10 workshops and over 20 folk handicrafts and performances, including ones dealing with making snack food, Uygur hand embroidery, the Miao wax printing, and the Dai cooked rice in a bamboo tube. When night falls, the wonderful folk dancing-singing parade starts. The bold drum band, cherry dragon team, humorous folk "shehuo", and elegant folk fashion team slowly march through the Village's streets. The five-colored water column spouting out from the folk fountain combined with the music and the light beams over the night sky, provides a joyful climax to the Folk Village's splendid poem about Chinese ethnic life.

In addition to watching different folk perfor-mances in the various folk villages, visitors can enjoy larger scale theatrical shows. These include the Golden Spear Dynasty, Oriental Costume, Chinese Dragon and Phoenix Dance, and the like.

The Golden Spear Dynasty is a special drama based on actual historical events. The true story behind the drama occurred more than 400 years ago, when the Qing Dynasty Nurhachi (Nurhaci) defeated a much larger Ming Army—Nurhachi had just 40, 000 troops, while the Ming army had 200, 000. We can not only witness this savage

中南地區

battle, but also enjoy exciting horse-riding performances. Nurhachi is the Qing (China's last feudal dynasty) emperor's ancestor. His eighth son, Huang Taiji destroyed the Ming Dynasty and established Qing Dynasty. Manchu is the royal family of the Qing Dynasty which originally ruled over and was based on the Manchu people, a national minority living in northeast of China. The Qing Dynasty ruled China for nearly 300 years.

An oriental costume event will take place at 17:00 p. m. in the central exhibition hall. Here we can enjoy beautiful Chinese folk dances and the bright colorful costumes.

Big Chinese dragon and phoenix dances take place at the Phoenix Plaza every night. Nearly 500 folk performers dance on the same stage. They showcase China's ethnic folk dance, music, acroba-tics, magic, and the like. This show reflects China's colorful and splendid ethnic culture that goes with its 5, 000-year history.

Ladies and gentlemen, due to the limited time, our journey is over now. You are welcome to come again.

I hope you all enjoyed yourselves. Bye!

各位遊客，大家好！歡迎來到神奇而美麗的錦繡中華和中國民俗文化村。首先請允許我簡單介紹一下錦繡中華。

錦繡中華是深圳華僑城的一個旅遊區，坐落在風光綺麗的深圳灣畔。是目前世界上面積最大、內容最豐富的實景微縮景區，占地30萬平方米，分為景點區和綜合服務區兩部分。

錦繡中華的景點均是按它在中國版圖上的位置擺布的，全園面積有如一幅巨大的中國地圖。這些景點可以分為三大類：古建築類、山水名勝類、民居民俗類。安置在各景點上的陶藝小人達五萬多個。

這裡有名列世界八大奇蹟的萬里長城、秦陵兵馬俑；有最古老的石拱橋（趙州橋）、天文台（古觀星台）、木塔（應縣木塔）；有最大的宮殿（故宮）、最大的佛像（樂山大佛）、最大的皇家園林（圓明園）、最長的石窟畫廊（敦煌莫高窟）、海拔最高的建築（布達拉宮）、最奇景觀（石林）、最奇山峰（黃山）、最大瀑布之一（黃果樹瀑布）；有肅穆莊嚴的黃帝陵、成吉思汗陵、明十三陵、中山陵；有金碧輝煌的孔廟、天壇；有雄偉壯觀的泰山、險峻挺拔的長江三峽，如詩似畫的灕江山水；有杭州西湖、蘇州園林等江南勝景。

此外，皇帝祭天、皇帝大婚、孔廟祭典的場面與民間的婚喪嫁娶風俗盡呈眼前。在編鐘館，你還能欣賞到古裝樂隊為您演奏千古絕唱。您可以在一天之內領略中華五千年歷史風雲，暢遊大江南北的錦繡河山。

錦繡中華在遊覽路線的設計、園林的綠化、商業區的設置以及衛生管理等方面都做了精心的安排。漫步在綠樹掩映、花團錦簇的園林小徑中，可以欣賞微縮景點；還可以在園中的小舞台旁欣賞傳統的民間舞蹈；在那白牆青瓦的蘇州街上，還可以品嚐各地風味小吃，購買富有特色的工藝和土特產品。

綜合服務區（蘇州街）吸取蘇州建築及園林藝術精華，並保留中國傳統商業街坊之特色。在這裡，有京川蘇粵幾大菜系及各地風味小吃，有民間手工藝製作表演，更有琳瑯滿目的手工藝品、古董、滋補藥品、名優特產以及富有錦繡中華特色的旅遊紀念品可供選購。

「一步邁進歷史，一天遊遍中華」，錦繡中華是中華歷史文化、旅遊文化之窗。開業至今，已接待中外遊客三千多萬人次，其中包括鄧小平、江澤民，美國前總統布希、前國務卿季辛吉，古巴總統卡斯特羅等首腦政要。

錦繡中華不愧是綠的世界、花的世界、美的世界；更是中國的歷史之窗、文化之窗、旅遊之窗。

接著我們來到了與錦繡中華一牆之隔的中國民俗文化村。中國民俗文化村占地20多萬平方米，是中國第一個薈萃各民族民間藝術、民俗風情和民居建築於一園的大型文化旅遊景區，內含22個民族的25個村寨，按1：1比例建成。中國民俗文化村

中南地區

以「源於生活，高於生活，匯集精華，有所取捨」作為建村的指導原則，從不同的角度，多側面地反映了中國豐富多彩的民俗文化。

在這個民居薈萃的大觀園中，黎族的船形屋和佤族的桿欄式草樓相映成趣，再現了人類古老的建築文化；白族雕刻精美的「三房一照壁」和漢族的「四合院」，則表現了高水準的中國傳統民居建築設計工藝。而伴隨著這些民居的，則是成片的海南椰林、參天的西雙版納古榕、開屏的孔雀和漫步的大象。我們在「村」中可以乘車，步行，也可以乘船漫遊。

在這裡，除可瞭解各民族的建築風特別，還可以欣賞和參與各民族的歌舞表演、民族工藝品製作，品嚐民族風味食品，觀賞民族藝術大遊行、專業水平的演出歌舞晚會、民俗陳列館、民間喜愛節目等各種場景。民俗村內有十多個手工作坊，有20多項民間手工藝和民間小吃製作表演，如維族手繡、苗族蠟染、傣族竹筒飯等。每當夜幕降臨，氣勢恢弘的民族歌舞藝術大遊行開始，豪放的鼓樂隊、快樂的龍燈隊、詼諧的民間社火、端莊典雅的民族時裝隊，在民俗村內緩緩前行；民俗村內的民族音樂噴泉隨著音樂噴出五色水柱，景區夜空的游光光束，會把我們帶進歡樂的高潮，帶進中華民族生活的美妙詩篇之中。

到民俗村參觀除了在各民俗村寨觀看各民族演員表演的小節目之外，還可以欣賞到一些大型的文藝演出。例如，金戈王朝、東方霓裳及龍鳳舞中華等。

金戈王朝是一場別開生面的歷史實景劇，表現的是400多年前清太祖努爾哈赤用四萬兵力打敗明朝20萬大軍的歷史故事。大家不但可以目睹當年驚心動魄的戰爭情景，還可以觀賞到他們精彩的馬術表演。努爾哈赤是清朝（中國最後一個封建王朝）皇帝的先祖，他的第8個兒子皇太極消滅了明王朝，建立了清王朝。清朝的皇族是滿族人，其祖先生活在中國東北地區的少數民族；滿族人建立的清王朝統治中國近300年。

東方霓裳於下午五點在中心劇場演出，我們可觀賞到中國各民族優美多姿的舞蹈和絢麗多彩的民族服飾。

龍鳳舞中華是每天晚上在鳳凰廣場的一場大型文藝演出。近500民族演員同台獻藝，向我們表演中國各民族的民間舞蹈、音樂、雜技、魔術等，展示出中華民族五千多年歷史的燦爛無比的民族文化。

各位遊客，由於時間關係，我們今天遊覽，就到此告一段落。歡迎大家有機會再來。

祝各位身體健康，再見！

Guangxi Zhuang Autonomous Region廣西壯族自治區

A Glimpse of the Autonomous Region （本自治區簡介）

China's Guangxi Zhuang Autonomous Region is located in the southern part of the country. It covers an area of 236, 000 square kilometers and has a population of 48, 000, 000. Guangxi has very rich tourism resources. These include an abundance of highly scenic natural landscapes and a diverse and interesting cultural life. The landscape includes coastline and quintessential Karst formations. Several of the province's nationalities live in compact communities. Guangxi's tourism has the following four characteristics. The first is that nature has endowed it with unique scenic attractions, the most famous of which are the Karst formations around Guilin. Indeed, a saying about Guilin's landscape states that "The mountains and waters are the most beautiful in the world. " This unique Karst landscape features green mountains, clear water, odd caves, and interesting and attractive stone formations. The second characteristic is Guangxi's unique sub-tropical coastal landscape. Indeed, Guangxi's Silver Beach has been acclaimed as China's "No. 1 beach" . This spot's blue water, silver sand beach, and beautiful sunshine make it an ideal tourism resort. The third notable feature of Guangxi's tourism is China-Vietnam border area's mysterious landscape. The interaction between the Chinese people and Vietnam people have helped give the border region a unique flavor. Lastly Guangxi has a profound and

中南地區

541

ancient cultural life and heritage, as well as special folk custoMs.Han Chinese people and Guangxi's Zhuang, Yao, Miao, Dong, and Jing ethnic minori-ties live harmoniously together in the province. Together they have created splendid civilization which can be described as unique, charming, and colorful.

Tourism Resources

Guangxi's charming waters and mountains, subtropical seaside scenery, unique Sino-Vietnamese border areas, and ancient ethnic culture and customs make it an ideal place to take a vacation. Guangxi is lovely throughout the year, with each season offering its own distinctive flavor. The traditional customs that have been maintained by Guangxi's many ethnic communities are a magnet for both Chinese and foreign tourists. More than 40 scenic spots are scattered throughout the region. These spots form five travel divisions centered on Guilin, Nanning, Liuzhou, southeastern Guangxi, and the province's seaside. National level scenic spots include Nanning's Qingxiu Mountain, Guilin's Lijiang River, Guiping's West Hill, Ningming's Huashan, and Bei-hai's Silver Beach. Regional level resorts include Guilin's Peach Blossom River, Fangcheng's Jiang-shan Peninsula, Lingshan's Qingshi Pond, the Longsheng Hot Spring, Yulin's Fozi Mountain, Hepu's Xingdao Lake, and Lipu's Fengyu Rock.

Food Specialties

You can taste many different kinds of food while visiting Guangxi Province. The most famous dishes here include Laoyou Noodles, Juantong and Bazhen Rice Noodles, dumplings, Duck Blood, Fried River Snails, Sweetened Mung Bean Paste, Glutinous Rice Cake, and some traditional folk snacks. All the latter are extremely tasty, unique, fresh, and attractive. They will not only fill you up, but make you want to extend your visit here.

Laoyou Noodles is Guangxi's most well-known snack and its history goes back several hundred years. There is an interesting story behind this dish. At one time there was an old man who frequently went to a teahouse run by a person surnamed Zhou. One day, this old man did not go to this teahouse because he came down with a bad cold. When the boss of the teahouse got this news, he cooked a bowl of noodles using garlic powder, fermented soybeans, pepper, sour bamboo shoots, beef powder, and the like. The old man recovered quickly after having this bowl of noodles, making them instantly famous. The most notable characteristic of these noodles and their main claim to fame is that they make one's stomach feel warmer.

Bazhen Rice Noodles is also very famous Guangxi dish. It is said that during the Qing Dyna-sty, the ingredients used in Bazhen Rice Noodles included dried fruit, seafood, fresh vegetables, and the like.

Nanning people long ago developed a special affection for ducks and raising ducks. This behavior is closely related to Nanning's climate. Nanning is well-known for its hot climate and it's also said that duck meat can mitigate the heat inside one's body. By contrast, goose meat can introduce viruses into the body and cause internal swelling and inflam-mation. It is said that roast duck first became a dish during the early Qing Dynasty. The ducks used for this dish are called Sesame Ducks, which have a fragrant and tender flavor. The ingredients for dishes, their preparation, and eating styles differ widely across China's regions. That's why Nanning's roast duck and Beijing roast duck are the most distinctive representatives of northern and southern cooking styles.

中南地區

廣西位於中國的南疆，面積 23.6 萬平方公里，人口4800 萬，擁有極為豐富的旅遊資源和眾多高品位的自然景觀、文化景觀。典型的喀斯特地貌、沿海的地理位置和多民族聚居使廣西的旅遊資源豐富獨特、多姿多彩，構成了廣西旅遊的四大特色：一是自然山水風光，以「山水甲天下」的桂林為代表的，遍及廣西各地的喀斯特地貌自然景觀，「山青、水秀、洞奇、石美」聞名於世；二是亞熱帶濱海風韻，以被譽為「中國第一灘」的北海銀灘為代表的環北部灣的亞熱帶濱海風光，湛藍的海水、銀白細柔的沙灘、和煦的陽光成為濱海休閒渡假勝地；三是瑰麗神秘的中越邊關風貌，中國和越南一衣帶水，兩國風物交流融合，形成了中越邊境獨特的風情；四是古樸濃郁的民族風情和悠久的歷史文化，廣西境內聚居著漢、壯、　、苗、侗、京等12個民族，各民族世代和睦相處，共同創造了燦爛的歷史文化，造就了獨具魅力、多姿多彩的民族風情。

旅遊資源

廣西是渡假者的理想去處，因為它擁有秀美的山水、亞熱帶的海濱，古老的民族風俗以及獨特的中越邊境。廣西四季秀美，每個季節都展現著獨特的風姿。廣西各民族一直保留著傳統習俗，這一點如磁石般吸引著中外遊客。廣西區內遍布四十多個風景點，形成了分別以桂林、南寧、柳州、廣西東南部及沿海為中心的五個旅遊地區。國家級的景點包括南寧青秀山、桂林灘江、桂平西山、寧明花山以及北海銀灘。地區級勝地包括桂林桃花江、防城江山半島、靈山青獅潭、龍勝溫泉、玉林佛子山、合浦星島湖以及荔浦豐魚岩。

特色餐飲

在廣西，你不僅能品嚐桂菜、粵菜的經典佳餚和中外各國各派美食，還可以在街頭巷尾品嚐老友麵（粉）、捲筒粉、八珍粉、粉餃、鴨紅、炒田螺、綠豆沙、糍粑等樣多味美的傳統民間小吃。珍、奇、精、鮮的美食加上濃郁的民族風情，讓人胃口大開，樂不思歸。

老友麵是南寧最著名的特色小吃，擁有百年的歷史。傳說有一老翁每天都光顧周記茶館，有一天因為感冒沒有去，周記老闆便以精製麵條，佐以爆香的蒜末、豆豉、辣椒、酸筍、牛肉末等，煮成一碗熱麵條，送給這位老友吃。老翁吃後出了一身汗，病狀減輕，故得「老友麵」之名。老友麵食之開胃趨寒，此後深受食客歡迎而經久不衰。

八珍粉是南寧百年老店仙池粉店的招牌。在美食街中山路最北邊，每天從早上賣到下午一點左右，據傳是清宮食譜之一，因其配有山珍、海味、時鮮八味以上，味道相異相輔而得名。

南寧人自古喜歡吃鴨，這和南寧的氣候有極大關係。南寧天氣炎熱，居住於此的南寧先民認為鴨肉清熱祛火。據說，南寧最早出現燒鴨是在清初康熙年間。南寧燒鴨的原料多選用南寧本地的芝麻鴨，皮香肉嫩，骨頭帶香。

Lijiang River in Guilin （桂林灕江）

Hello! Ladies and gentlemen! Now, we reach Guangxi's most famous scenic spot and hottest tourist destination. I hope you'll enjoy it and have a chance to relax here.

Now, let me introduce Guilin's water system to you. It consists of two rivers and four lakes. Two rivers are the Lijiang and Taohua rivers, while the four lakes are Ronghu, Shanhu, Guihu, and Mulong Lakes. Together these bodies of water form the Guilin Water System's Dream Tour. This tour and construction of the water system began during the Tang Dynasty and was popular in Song Dynasty. During these periods, there were many lakes and ponds scattered throughout Guilin. The city's water system was thus highly developed. People could get to and enjoy all the well-known scenic spots by a small boat.

However, with the passage of time, the "two rivers and four lakes" were cut off from one another and Guilin's Water System became fragmented and the water quality worsened. In 1998, the Municipal Party Committee and the Municipal Administration carried out the "Two Rivers and Four Lakes" project. This involved connecting the rivers and lakes, cleaning out their water, particularly removing the silt and dirt, drawing water into lakes, making the hills and surrounding landscape greener, building the roads and bridges, and improving the cultural attractions. This project has not only rebuilt and expanded Guilin's old water system, but also improved the ecological environment of the central city and boosted its appearance and quality of life. For example, pleasure boats can once again be seen sailing on the waters within the city. This recreational landscape is one of the best in China and can be compared with other famous so-called "water cities", including Venice and Amsterdam with their canals

中南地區

and Paris with its Seine River. As you can see, Lijiang River is Guilin's quintessential landscape. Its water quality is also better than that of most Chinese rivers that flow through major cities. It is part of the Pearl River system and originates from "the first peaks of southern China", the Mao'er Mountain. The 83-kilometer waterway from Guilin to Yangshuo is known as the "golden waterway" and is a must see for Chinese and foreign tourists visiting Guilin. Throughout human history numerous men of letters from very different countries have written memorable prose regarding the Lijiang River and its surrounding scenery's enchanting beauty. The Tang Dynasty poet, Han Yu, once praised the picturesque and poetic Lijiang River by writing that "the river is like a blue silk ribbon and the hills are like green jade hairpins".

From Guilin to Yangshuo, the prominent landforms are karst hoodoo peak clusters. The river flows around these mountains to form valleys. The scenery is the best in Caoping, Yangdi and Xingping. There are beautiful scenes of Nine Horses Fresco Hill, Yellow Cloth Reflection, and Half Side Ferry. The Lijiang landscape's appearance varies at different times of the year, from different viewpoints, and during different climates. On sunny days, the sky and river are a vast bright green world with no bounds between them; the thousand peaks and hills will provide a visual feast for your eyes. And on foggy days, the water is wreathed in mist, with the fog constantly disappearing and reappearing. On moonlit nights, the hills are clear as if they've been washed, while the river and its ripples are so green.

In the river section in Guilin, the valley is open, famous hills like Wave-Taming, Piled Silk, Elephant, Tunnel, and Pagoda Hills stand erect from the ground, and the cliffs are so steep that they seem to have been cut by a sword. So one of Lijiang's major features is indeed "green hills, clear water, fantastic caves and charming rocks". Every scene of the hundred-mile Lijiang River is a typical Chinese ink painting.

女士們、先生們，大家好！現在我們來到了最負盛名的灕江風景區。灕江是時下一個很熱門的旅遊目的地，我希望大家能喜歡這裡的風景，在這裡能夠得到充分的放鬆。

首先，讓我介紹一下桂林的水系。桂林水系由兩江四湖組成。兩江四湖是指由灕江、桃花江與溶湖、杉湖、桂湖、木龍湖所構成的環城水系。桂林的水上遊覽興於唐，盛於宋，當時的桂林城湖塘密布，水系發達，乘一葉小舟就可以盡覽城中諸多的風景名勝。

但是隨著時代變遷，兩江四湖水道隔斷，環城水系支離破碎，水質惡化。1998年，廣西市委、市政府實施了兩江四湖工程，透過連江接湖、顯山露水、清淤截汙、引水入湖、修路架橋、綠化美化、文化建設等工程，不僅恢復、拓展了桂林的古環城水系，改善了市中心的生態環境，提高了城市的檔次與品位，而且遊船重新進入了市區水域，形成了能與威尼斯水城、巴黎塞納河以及阿姆斯特丹運河相媲美的獨特的市區水上遊景觀，堪稱中國一絕。

大家都知道，灕江是桂林山水的精華，是中國流經城市水質最好的河流之一，屬珠江水系，發源於「華南第一峰」貓兒山。從桂林到陽朔約83公里的水程，被稱為「黃金水道」，是中外遊客必遊的桂林景區。古今中外，不知多少文人騷客為灕江的綺麗風光寫下了膾炙人口的優美詩文。唐代大詩人韓愈曾以「江作青羅帶，山如碧玉簪」的詩句來讚美這條如詩似畫的灕江。

桂林至陽朔，是岩溶峰林峰叢地貌，河流依山而轉，形成峽谷，尤以草坪、楊堤、興坪為佳，有九馬畫山、黃布倒影、半邊渡等美景。灕江景觀因時、因角度、因氣候不同而變化。晴朗天時，上下天光一碧萬頃，千巒百嶂盡收眼底。煙雨之日，嵐霧繚繞若隱若現，若斷若續。明月之夜，群峰如洗，江波如練。

灕江桂林段，河谷開闊，兩岸名山如伏波山、疊彩山、象山、穿山、塔山平地拔起，四壁如削。灕江的一大特點是「山青、水秀、洞奇、石美」。百里灕江的每一處景緻，都是一幅典型的中國水墨畫。

Yangshuo （陽朔）

中南地區

Ladies and gentlemen!

Now, we come to an-other beautiful scenic spot, namely Yangshuo. And I sincerely hope that you can enjoy yourselves and relax in Yangshuo. Now, please follow me.

Yangshuo lies in northeast Guangxi Province and is southeast of Guilin City. Yangshuo's special geography makes it breathtakingly beautiful, while over 1, 400 years of history blesses the town with a deep traditional culture. Yangshuo is one of the most famous tourist destinations around Guilin. It boasts gorgeous natural scenery, mysterious ancient local dwellings, and a diverse culture and custoMs.Several places in the surrounding area offer different kinds of entertainment and other enjoyable activities. One such place, located in the center of the region, the West Street (Xi Jie) attracts so many tourists from all over the world that it is called the "Global Village". People from different countries manage stores, cafes and restaurants, giving the street an exotic flavor.

Yangshuo was one of the first places to be designated and developed as a tourist resort by the Chinese Government and its scenery is far more beautiful than that of Guilin. More than twenty thousand hills and seventeen rivers are located in and around Yangshuo. We can see picturesque landscapes and various cultural heritages here. During your visit, you may also see a great variety of ancient buildings and bridges, as well as calligraphy or scripts written by famous people. To sum up, during your visit to Yangshuo, you can enjoy beautiful landscape, green trees, beautiful farmland, interesting and strangely shaped caves, and the intriguing "Foreign West Street". A trip to Yang-shuo is thus certain to provide you with many pleasant surprises!

After decades of development, Yangshuo has built lots of hotels, restaurants, and holiday inns, most of which are at least three-star establishments. Typical Yangshuo dishes include rice noodles, beer fish, beer duck, fish soup, dog meat, and dog and lamb meat hot pot.

女士們，先生們，

現在我們來到了另一個風景名勝區——陽朔。我真誠地希望大家能在陽朔玩得開心，請大家跟我來。

陽朔位於廣西壯族自治區東北部、桂林市東南方向。得天獨厚的地理位置賦予了它特別的美，1400多年的悠久歷史賦予了它更深的文化內涵。陽朔是桂林最著名的旅遊景點，它以奇特的自然景觀，神秘的古代居民建築，以及豐富的歷史文化而聞名於世。在陽朔，你可以親身體驗到不同的樂趣。在陽朔的中心地帶，西街吸引了來自世界各地的遊客，因此得名「地球村」。他們在這經營著咖啡廳和餐廳，因此，西街也成為極富國外風情的街道。

陽朔是最早的「國家級風景旅遊名勝區」之一，其山水景色更勝桂林。境內還有挺拔俊秀的奇峰2萬多座，蜿蜒於萬山叢中的河流17條。田園風光如詩如畫，文化遺產也十分豐富，古建築、古橋樑、名人紀念地、摩崖石刻等，點綴於山水間。總之，處處是景的自然風光，古樸清秀的田園景緻，驚絕天下的熔岩奇觀，難以忘懷的「洋人」西街，陽朔之行絕對讓你別有一番驚喜！

陽朔縣經過近幾十年來的發展建設，已建起了大小幾十家各具特色的住宿賓館、酒店、飯店和招待所，多家新裝修的酒店具有三星級的條件。陽朔當地的風味除米粉外，主要有啤酒魚、啤酒鴨、清水魚、水煮狗肉、乾鍋狗（羊）肉等。

中南地區

Elephant Trunk Hill （象鼻山）

Ladies and gentlemen, welcome to the Elephant Trunk Hill scenic spot. Now, let me introduce it to you. Please follow me. Elephant Trunk Hill, which is also just called Elephant Hill, is located at the confluence of Peach Blossom and Lijiang Rivers. This place is Guilin's emblem. The hill's summit is 220 meters above sea level and it rises 55 meters above the river's water surface. The hill is made up of pure limestone deposited in the bottom of the sea 360 million years ago. Its shape is solitary, straight and steep, while its rock is old. There is a water moon cave between the elephant trunk and the legs resembling a bright moon floating on the water. This is the famous scene "Water Moon of Elephant Hill" integrating the clear hill, beautiful water, fantastic cave, charming rocks and reflection into one beautiful image. For a thousand years and through many dynasties it has inspired famous poets to write verses and is now a must-see spot for tourists visiting Guilin. It it is said that in ancient times, a divine being traveled to Guilin with his subordinates. One of their elephants became ill because the load he had to carry was too heavy. When this animal was left to die near the Lijiang River, the kind-hearted local people took good care of it and it recovered soon. The elephant was delighted with the place's beautiful scenery and kind people and naturally decided to stay there to help the farmers harvest their crops. As soon as the divine being heard about this, he sent his soldiers to take the elephant back. These troops and the local villagers fought against each other for three days and nights, with neither side securing a clear victory. So the divine being stealthily stabbed the elephant to death in the heart while it was drinking water near the river. From then on, the image of the elephant was left in the river.

女士們，先生們，歡迎來到象鼻山風景區。現在讓我介紹一下象鼻山，請跟我來。象鼻山簡稱象山，位於桃花江與灘江的交匯處。桂林的城徽即以象山為標誌。象山海拔220米，高出水面55米，由3億6千萬年前海底沉積的純石灰岩組成。山形孤拔陡峭，岩石古蒼。在象鼻與象腿之間有一水月洞，有如一輪明月靜浮水上，形成著名的「象山水月」。此景集清山、秀水、奇洞、美石、倒影於一體，成為歷代詩人吟詠不絕的對象，是遊人至桂的必遊之地。相傳遠古時候，天帝帶了天臣神獸南巡到桂林，天象因馱運過重病倒，被遺棄在灘江邊。後來，它被灘江人醫治康復，見這裡山美水美人更美，不願重返天堂，便留下來為民耕作。天帝得知，馬上派出天兵天將來捉拿。他們大戰三天三夜，不分勝負。天將趁雙方歇戰，大象到江邊喝水之時，偷偷抽出利劍，從象背插入象心，把它刺死在水邊。從此，天象的英姿就長留人間。

Beihai Silver Beach （北海銀灘）

Hello! My dear friends! Now, we have come to another scenic spot, Silver Beach. I am very glad that I have this opportunity to be your tour guide in your trip. I do hope we can have a wonderful trip here in Beihai. Silver Beach is situated south of Beihai City. It is famous for its long beach, white sand, clean water, soft waves, and unpolluted air. In 1992, Silver Beach was designated a National Tourism Resort and one of China's top 35 scenic spots. The Silver Beach is also known as China's "most beautiful beach" because of its natural attributes, including its length, abundant and gorgeous sunshine, fresh air, and clean water. Silver Beach's mild year round climate makes it an ideal tourist resort. And its fresh air contains 50 to 100 times as many negative oxygen ions as that in the non-coastal cities. The temperature at the beach also averages a comfortable 22. 6 degrees Centigrade. The air is quite good for sunbathing as it contains lots of iodine, magnesium chloride, and sodium chloride. All of this makes Silver Beach an excellent conv-alescent spot for older people and those recovering from illness.

朋友們，大家好！現在，我們來到了另一個著名的旅遊勝地——北海銀灘。我很高興能有這個機會給大家做導遊，我真誠地祝大家在北海玩得盡興。北海銀灘位於北海市南端，面臨浩瀚的藍色大海，東西綿延24 公里，以灘長平、沙細白、水溫淨、浪柔軟、無鯊魚、無汙染的特點著稱於世。1992年被列為國家級旅遊渡假區，為中國的35個「王牌景點」之一，享有「天下第一灘」的美譽。銀灘集陽光、空氣、沙灘、海水等優勢於一體，夏無酷暑，冬無嚴寒，是避暑防寒，旅遊渡假勝地。這裡空氣清新自然，負氧離子含量是內陸城市的50 ～100倍，年平均氣溫22.6℃。空氣含有較多的碘、氯化鎂、氯化鈉等，很適合於日光浴，是休閒療養的好去處。

Hainan Province （海南省）

A Glimpse of the Province （本省簡介）

Hainan Province is called Qiong for short. This shortened name derives from the Chinese word Qiongzhou in the Tang Dynasty some one thousand years ago. It is China's southernmost province, with the Qiongzhou Strait to its north. There it directly faces the Leizhou Peninsula across the Beibu Gulf. While it is China's smallest province with respect to land area, it has a longer coastline and is surrounded by more sea than any other province. It consists of the primary island of Hainan, along with Xisha, Zhongsha, Nansha islands and their coastal areas. It is between latitude 18° 10′ -20° 10′ to north and longitude 108° 37′ -111° 05′ to east.

Hainan province is China's only province with a tropical ocean. It also covers 42. 5 percent of the country's tropical land area. The average temperature on the island is 23. 8 degrees centigrade. The high monthly average temperature is 25-29 degrees centigrade in July and August, while the January and February low temperatures are between 10-24 degrees centigrade. And the sun shines 12 hours of the day. It is a real paradise for northerners to spend their holidays away from the cold winter.

Culture and Customs

Hainan has a long history. It has been called Immigration Island because its inhabitants come mainly from the mainland and everyone living here belongs to different ethnic groups that settled down here at different times. Indeed, some 30 ethnic groups live in harmony on the island. Han Chinese people form the most numerous group and they and the Li, Miao, and Hui ethnic minorities, have been living on the island for several generations.

Among the ethnic minorities, the Li people are the earliest and most numerous of Hainan's migrants. The Wuzhishan Mountain area is the main area inhabited by the Li nationality aborigines, and they have been living there and developing their culture and customs for more than 3000 years. They also have their own spoken language but use Chinese characters as their written script. The Li people are hard workers and have mainly supported themselves through farming; however, starting in the Tang and Song dynasties, they also established a family handicraft industry. Their most notable product is "Li cloth", which is famous both at home and abroad. Now their villages and way of life have become distinctive tourist attractions.

The Miao people form Hainan's second largest ethnic minority. Their numbers total 60, 000 and they mainly live in the mountainous parts of Qiongzhong and Baoting autonomous counties. The Miao people are said to have originally lived in the mountainous areas of Guangxi, Guizhou and Hunan Provinces. The Miao people have kept their rich traditions in attire and enjoy their traditional five-color glutinous rice. The Miao people are also accomplished singers and dancers.

The Hui people are one of the other major ethic groups in Hainan province. They settled on the island some time ago and have long history living here. They are concentrated mainly in Sanya Fenghuang Town and the very southern end of the island. Their numbers total more than 7, 000. The Hui people have retained their Islamic faith and customs and gather together every year on September 28thto celebrate their traditional Islamic Guerbang festival.

Hainan is not only a place of immigrants, but of emigrants as well. In fact, Hainan has become one of the three famous sources of Chinese emigration, with some 3 million overseas Chinese hailing from the island, a figure exceeded only by Guangdong and Fujian Provinces. People from Hainan can be found in 59 countries and regions throughout the world;half of them have migrated to Thailand, Singapore, Malaysia and other Southeast Asian countries.

Hainan's blend of regional cultures and cus-toms, along with the island's special local festivals, has created a truly unique and unforgettable experie-nce for anyone visiting here.

中南地區

Local Festivals

The different ethnic groups on Hainan Island live together in harmony. The ethnic minorities not only enjoy the major traditional Chinese festivals like the Spring Festival, Dragon Boat Festival and Mid-autumn Festival, but also have their own festivals as well. For example, the Sanyuesan Festival is the local Li and Miao festival. It is celebrated in the spring, on March 3rd(the lunar calendar) and provides unmarried young people an opportunity to find their loved ones. On that day the young boys and girls from nearby settlements get together in bright and attractive clothing. They hold hands and sing songs, do bamboo pole dancing, and have their dates in houses that are shaped like boats. The ladies wear "canister skirts" and both they and the men eat rice cooked in a bamboo pipe and drink Shanlan wine. Other festivals include the Flower Exchange Festival in Fucheng Town and Folk Song Competition Festival in Danzhou during the Mid-autumn Festival.

Several modern festivals aimed solely at tourists have been established since Hainan became a province in 1988. These include the Nanshan Longevity Culture Festival, Sanya International Wedding Ceremony, and Hainan Island Carnival. The last festival is an annual comprehensive international public festival held by the government and Hainan Tourism Bureau every November. It originated in 2000 as part of nationwide effort to promote "China's Tourism Island". The Hainan Carnival has become one of the biggest and most enjoyable festivals, not only for people in Hainan, but for Chinese and foreign tourists visiting the island as well. During the many festivals staged on Hainan, such as the Miss World/Universe beauty pageant, the participants, including internationally famous film stars, share their happiness with the local people and tourists.

Finally, even some foreign holidays such as the Valentine's Day, the April Fool's Day and Christmas are now celebrated by the local people.

Tourism Resources

Hainan Island is shaped like a pyramid. High mountain peaks dominate the center of the island. The central mountains include the famous 1876 meter high Wuzhishan Mountain, which is 300 meters higher than Shandong's better known Mount Tai. Wuzhishan is surrounded by more than 600 other tall peaks with valleys, plains, rivers and lakes inter-spersed among them. Hainan's topography is so complicated that supernatural and peculiar tropical physiognomy exists in its rain forests. The island has a wide variety of ecosystems, including forests, grass-lands, estuaries, mangrove swamps, coral reefs, bottomland, everglades, and lagoons. More than 50% of the island is covered by forests. Thus when viewed from outer space, the whole land looks like a jungle-covered mountain with rivers and valleys here and there.

Situated at the same latitude as Hawaii, Hainan Island has the heaviest rainfall of any place located at this latitude in the world. The island is blessed with abundant sunshine and warmth, giving a spring-like climate year-around. Tropical crops such as rice, sugarcane, palm oil, cinnamon, sisal, betel nuts, coffee, tea, sweet potatoes, groundnuts and tobacco can flourish all year round. At all times and in all places, the flowers are in full bloom and the birds are singing from the trees. Hainan Island is rich in biological resources, such as pleasant seas, attrac-tive beaches, rivers, mountains, and virgin forests. It has long been called the "Natural Greenhouse", "Hot Spring Island", "Tropical Orchard", and "Ever-blooming Garden". Hainan is well known for the sheer variety of its tropical fruit which include coconut, jackfruit, pineapple, mango, lychee, longan, banana, rambutan, naseberrie, durian, papaw, olive, guava fruit, wampee, and Chinese gooseberry. The virgin tropical rain forests are also home to more than 4, 600 kinds of fascicular plants, of which more than 600 are local species found only on Hainan Island. The island boasts some 560 vertebrate animal species, many of which are endangered or on the verge of extinction elsewhere in the world. Some 37 are amphibians, and 11 of them are found only on Hainan Island. Altogether there are 134 rare animal species and 344 rare bird species on Hainan Island that are under state

中南地區

protection. Thus Hainan can also be seen as a key storage house for rare animal species and their genes. Only in Hainan can you have the kind of feeling that time flies backward and really appreciate just how broad and mysterious nature can be. With its tropical ocean climate, many beaches, rare living creatures and clean fresh air, Hainan is becoming a popular resort site both at home and abroad.

Hainan Cuisine and Local Snacks

Hainan is also famous for four particular dishes—Wenchang Chicken, Jiaji Duck, Dongshan Mutton, and Hele Crab. Both the chicken and duck dishes are popular because their meat is tender, skin is crisp, and bones are soft. And neither dish is particularly fatty or greasy. Dongshan sheep are fed natural local tea giving both the steamed and stewed mutton a tea-like flavor. Hele crab is notable for its big body, fresh meat and red cream, which gives its meat more fat and a better flavor. Local snacks include Qiongzhou Coconut Pot, Coconut Milk Chicken, Lin'gao Roast Porket, Qukou Seafood, Plum Blossom Trepang, Sea-ears, Lobster, Wan-quan Carp, Mountain Beef, Salt Red Fish, Nada-flavor Meat, Li People Sweet Ale, Bamboo Shaft Rice, Five-color Glutinous Rice, Hainan Ver-micelli, Hainan Chicken Rice, Hainan Glutinous Rice Dumplings, Hainan Chaffy Dish, and Coconut Sticky Rice Cake.

Recommended Attractions

Hainan Island is a green island and every part of it has natural scenic beauty. The capital city of Haikou is located on the north side of the island. Many famous scenic spots, including several large tropical ecological gardens, are located in this area. The major sites include the Evergreen Garden, Haikou Western Coastal Park, Guilingyang Seaside Tourism Zone, Dongzhaigang National Mango Forest Nature Reserve, Wild Pineapple Island, Benthonic Villages, and the Hainan Tropical Oceanic World. Southern Hainan Island boasts the province's most famous tourism city, Sanya. It also boasts beautiful attractions such as the Tianyahaijiao (the end of the earth), Dadong Sea,

Yalong Bay, Butterfly Valley, Nanshan Temple, Wonders of the Mountain and Sea, Paradise Caves for Celestial Beings, and Luhuitou Park. There are many other famous attractions in Hainan Island such as the Xinglong Tropical Botani-cal Garden, Bo'ao Aquapolis, Nanwan Monkey Peninsula, Wenchang City's Dongjiao Coconut Grove, Juding Zoo's Rare Birds and Animals, Wuzhizhou Island, Wuzhishan Mountain, Wanquan River, six famous hot springs and many famous waterfalls.

海南省簡稱「瓊」（源於一千多年前唐朝的瓊州），位於中國內地的最南方，北隔瓊州海峽，穿越北部灣與雷州半島相望。海南省是中國陸地面積最小的省份，但卻是海洋面積最大的省份，其主要組成部分為海南島、西沙群島、中沙群島、南沙群島及其海域，介於北緯 18°10′～20°10′，東經108°37′～111°05′之間。

海南省是中國唯一的熱帶海洋島嶼省份，占中國熱帶土地面積的42.5%。海南島的年平均氣溫23.8度；氣溫最高月份為7～8月，平均氣溫為25℃～29℃；最冷的月份為1～2月，平均氣溫10℃～24℃，每天日照時間為12小時，可謂北方人在寒冬時節避寒渡假的天堂。

民族風情

海南歷史悠久，是一個移民島，其居民於不同的年代，在不同的背景下來自內陸的各個地方。海南省是一個多民族省份，海南島上居住著30多個民族，其中漢、黎、苗、回族是歷代常住居民，漢族的人口最多。

海南省少數民族中黎族人口最多，他們是最早的居民，五指山地區就是黎族同胞最早聚居的地方，他們有著自己的文化習俗。他們移居到這裡已有三千多年的歷史，有自己的語言，沿用漢文書寫。黎族是一個勤勞的民族，以農耕為主，他們的面錦工藝始於唐宋時期，著名的黎錦在海內外享有盛名，黎族自然村更有獨特的旅遊觀光價值。

苗族是海南第二大少數民族，現有人口大約六萬，居住在海南的瓊中和保亭自治縣，主要居住在山區。據說苗族是從廣西壯族自治區、貴州省和湖南省等地區遷移而來。苗族服飾還保留著濃厚的民族傳統特色，五色飯是苗族的特色飲食，苗族同胞能歌善舞。

回族也是海南省的主要少數民族之一，在海南有著悠久的居住史。他們主要居住在海南島最南端的三亞市鳳凰鎮，共有人口七千多人。在生活方面他們還仍保持著伊斯蘭教習俗，於每年9月28日聚會慶祝自己的伊斯蘭教傳統節日——古爾邦節。

海南島不僅是移民之鄉，也是中國著名的僑鄉之一，其華僑的數量僅次於廣東、福建兩省，居中國第三位。海南旅居或定居的海外瓊籍華僑、華人和港澳同胞300多萬人，分布於世界59個國家和地區，其中50%聚居在泰國、新加坡、馬來西亞等東南亞國家。

海南島上的各種地方節日和異樣的習俗令過往遊客流連忘返。

節慶活動

海南島上各民族同胞和諧相處，他們不僅分享著中國的重要傳統節日，如春節、端午節、中秋節等，還享有自己的節日，如「三月三」，即農曆的三月初三，是黎族和苗族的傳統節日。這一天是黎族和苗族未婚青年男女相互傳送鍾情，追求美好愛情的日子。在這一天，居住在附近的青年男女們身著艷麗的服裝，手牽著手一邊唱歌，一邊跳竹竿舞。有情的男女們相約在船形屋裡談情說愛，女人們身著別緻的筒裙，他們吃的是竹筒燜的米飯，喝的是自家釀的山蘭酒。島上的民族節日還有府城換花節、儋州中秋賽歌會等。

自從1988年海南建省以來，還有一些專為促進旅遊業而新興的地方節慶，如南山長壽文化節、三亞天涯國際婚禮節以及中國海南島歡樂節等。其中，海南島歡樂節的來歷源於海南要打造成中國的旅遊島，必須有一個為旅遊聚人氣、為遊客添歡樂的全省性旅遊節慶。為了挖掘和提升海南的旅遊文化，由海南省政府和國家旅遊局主辦，每年11月舉行。年復一年，海南島歡樂節已經聞名遐邇，成為全省、中國乃至全世界享有盛名的狂歡節之一，節日期間，人們可以和世界著名的影星、世界小姐等一起共享快樂。

近年來，國外的一些節日，如情人節、愚人節、聖誕節等，在當地也很盛行。

旅遊資源

海南島的地勢酷似金字塔，中部的山脈是著名的五指山，海拔為1876米，比中國內地的泰山高出300米，周圍六百多座高高矮矮的山峰猶如寶島的脊樑，偉岸挺拔；四周環繞著台地，還有寬窄不等的平原。大自然的神奇威力在這裡雕刻出壯觀的山川、湖泊，撒播無數物種，形成氣象萬千的熱帶雨林自然景觀，如森林、草原、田野、入海口、紅樹林、岩礁、盆地、濕地和潟湖等。海南島的森林覆蓋率達50%以上，從空中俯瞰，整個島嶼酷似一座山川相間、叢林覆蓋的山峰。

海南島和美國的夏威夷地處同一緯度，但其降雨量在世界的同一緯度堪稱之最。別樣的氣候使海南島四季如春，充足的光和熱量適宜熱帶植物四季生長，如水稻、甘蔗、棕櫚、肉桂、劍麻、檳榔、咖啡、茶葉、地瓜、花生和煙草等。綠色的海南島上處處鳥語花香，有著豐富的自然資源：宜人的海水、迷人的沙灘、高聳的崇山峻嶺，茂密的叢林植被。傳統上享有「綠色寶庫」、「溫泉之島」、「熱帶果園」及「四季花園」之美譽。

海南島不僅盛產熱帶農作物，還盛產熱帶水果，諸如椰子、波羅蜜、菠蘿、芒果、荔枝、龍眼、香蕉、紅毛丹、人心果、榴蓮、木瓜、橄欖、番石榴、黃皮、奇異果等熱帶水果。此外，在這原始熱帶雨林裡生存著4600多種野生植物，其中有600多種是海南特有的物種。這裡還生活著560　多種野生的陸棲脊椎動物，有許多是世界上瀕臨滅絕的物種，其中兩棲類37種，僅見於海南的有11種。列入國家重點保護的野生動物有134種，鳥類有344種。生態學家們認為，海南是世界上目前少有的生物基因庫。置身其中，你會產生時光倒流的感覺，也許你會感嘆大自然的博大精深神秘莫測。

風味小吃

海南有遠近聞名的「四大名菜」——文昌雞、嘉積鴨、東山羊、和樂蟹。文昌雞和嘉積鴨之所以聞名，主要是因為肉嫩色美、皮脆味香、骨酥而鮮，食之不膩。東山羊以當地天然茶為食，因此無論是燜，還是清燉，都是肉肥而不膩，湯濃而不膻。和樂蟹的獨到之處就是膏滿、肉肥、黃鮮，真是令人垂涎三尺。此外就是著名的地方風味，有瓊州椰子煲、椰奶雞、臨高乳豬、曲口海鮮、三亞梅花參、三亞鮑魚、海南龍蝦、萬泉鯉、海南山牛肉、海南紅魚粽、那大香肉、黎族甜糟、竹筒飯、黎家酸菜、五色飯、海南粉、海南雞飯、海南粽、海南火鍋、椰絲糯米粑等。

推薦景點

海南島四季常青，景色宜人。在海南島北部的省城海口，有許多著名的遊覽景區，如最大的熱帶生態園——萬綠園、海口黃金西海岸帶狀公園、桂林洋濱海旅遊區、東寨港紅樹林自然保護區、野菠蘿島和海底村莊、海南熱帶海洋世界。在海南島的南部有著名的旅遊城——三亞，那裡有景色宜人，堪稱世界之最的天涯海角、大東海、亞龍灣、蝴蝶谷、南山寺、大小洞天、鹿回頭公園等。此外，海南島還有許多其他著名的景區，如興隆熱帶植物園、博鰲水城、南灣猴島、文昌東郊椰林風景區、居丁珍稀動物園、蜈支州島、五指山、萬泉河漂流、六大溫泉以及許多著名的瀑布。

Sanya City （三亞之旅）

Good morning, ladies and gentlemen!

Welcome to our beautiful coastal city of Sanya. Firstly, I'd like to briefly introduce Sanya.

Sanya is located in the southernmost part of Hainan Island at the 18° north latitude, or the same latitude as the southern end of Hawaii, America's world famous tropical resort. Sanya has a tropical ocean climate. Temperatures average 25. 4℃ throug-hout the year. June is the hottest month with average temperature of 28℃, while

January is the coldest, with average temperatures of 21. 6℃. There are 2476. 9 hours of sunshine each year, while annual rainfall averages 1392. 2 mm. Flowers, trees and other plants are in full blossom throughout the year, so Sanya is known throughout China as a "natural greenhouse". It is especially suitable for growing crops during the winter. Indeed, Sanya has now become famous as a production base for winter melons and other fruit and is also a key nursery area for different plants. Due to its unique tropical coastal city, Sanya has become not only one of China's key tourist resorts, but an important international tropical beachfront tourist destination as well. It can be seen as a resplendent pearl adorning Hainan Island's jade-green land.

Sanya has a long history and lots of places of interest. However, in ancient times Sanya was called Yazhou and because it was inaccessible and wild, the city and surrounding area were seen as dangerous places to travel to. Indeed, the Qin Dynasty banished exiled officials to Sanya. During the Tang, Song and Yuan Dynasties alone, more than 50 officials were exiled here, including some outstanding and high-ranking ones. They were sent thousands of miles away from civilization and could never return. Thus Yazhou was known as "the gate of hell". However the unique natural landscape, rich local products and the simple Sanya life-style changed the psychology of some people.

Every part of Sanya is adorned with coconut groves. These groves and the trees that cover 60% of the city and its downtown landscape—green plants cover 40% of the central city—make for a close harmony between Sanya and the natural environment. In fact, Sanya is China's most beautiful tropical garden and was included among the country's first group of eco-demonstration cities. Its tourism resources are unique in China, even the world, making the city a choice destination for vacationers. Sanya's mountains, rivers, sea and harbors are harmoniously united and the city has the ten key tourism resources of "sunshine, seawater, sandy beaches, climate, forests, hot springs, ethnic culture, idyllic fields and grottoes". Sanya has two 5A-rated tourism districts, the Nanshan Cultural Tourism Zone and Wonders of the Mountain and Sea, or Paradise

中
南
地
區

Caves for Celestial Beings. The city also boasts three 4A-rated districts, the Yalong Bay National Resort, Tianya-Haijiao Park（the End of the Earth）, and Wu Zhi Zhou Island Resort. In addition to these attractions, the island has many other different scenic sports with unique characteristics. Indeed, Sanya has gained the reputation of "Not Hawaii, but overshadows Hawaii", for its jade-like azure waters, silky beaches, rainbow-shaped bays and picturesque scenes.

Look ahead, please! These flowers are called bougainvillea and are Sanya's official flower. Behind them lies an 18-km long coconut landscaping belt. It is famous both at home and abroad. Sanya is an inspiring land of longevity and is highlighted by its unparalleled bays with crystal-clear sea water, unspoiled sandy beaches, diversified coral clusters, shells and tropical fish. Sanya has recently refurbished its river and ocean sides with view platforms and built gala squares, staircase berths and viewing over walk bridges, as well as other recrea-tional and entertaining facilities. This construction emphasizes the city's eco-culture and the mangrove views of "egrets perching on mangrove branches while fish and crabs swim under the roots". All these efforts have led to emergence of a series of landsca-ping belts incorporating sightseeing, recreational and commercial activities as a whole. All of this had made Sanya into a city with stronger tropical atmosp-here in comparison to other tourist metropolises. It really is an international tropical beachfront tourist destination and the paradise for tourists.

Friends, here we are. Let's be at ease and melt into the international sightseeing destination.

尊敬的各位女士們、先生們，大家好！

歡迎你們來到美麗的海濱城——三亞。首先，我先向諸位介紹有關三亞的一些概況。

三亞位於海南島的最南端，地處北緯18°，和美國著名的熱帶旅遊景區夏威夷處同一緯度，屬於熱帶海洋性氣候，年平均溫度25.4℃，氣溫最高為6月，平均28.8℃；氣溫最低為 1 月，平均氣溫21.6℃；全年平均日照時間約2476.9 小時，年平均降雨量達1392.2毫米。這裡四季鮮花盛開，素有「天然溫室」之稱，尤其適宜熱帶作物的生長，是著名的冬季瓜果生產基地和南繁育種基地。三亞不僅是中國唯一的熱帶濱海旅遊城市，也是國際性熱帶海濱風景旅遊城市，猶如一顆璀璨的明珠鑲嵌在海南這塊綠翡翠上。

三亞歷史悠久，名勝古蹟眾多。然而，古時候人們稱三亞為崖州，並把它看成是「不歸之地」。遠在秦朝時期，由於三亞遠離內陸、孤僻而荒涼，人們認為到了這裡就等於進了地獄之門，故此成為封建統治者們流放貶官之地。僅在唐、宋、元朝時期，包括一些傑出的高級官員在內的被貶官員先後就有50多名被流放到這裡。然而，這裡獨特的自然風光，豐富的物產，卻改變了他們壓抑的心態，為他們提供了得天獨厚的世外桃源。

三亞椰林成蔭，與自然相互輝映，森林覆蓋率高達60%，市區綠化覆蓋率40%以上，是中國美麗的熱帶花園，中國第一批國家生態示範城市。三亞旅遊資源得天獨厚，是人們首選的旅遊勝地。這裡有山、河、海、城、港自然結合的獨特景觀，匯集了十大旅遊資源：陽光、海水、沙灘、氣候、森林、動物、溫泉、風情、田園和岩洞。區內棋布著兩個國家5A級旅遊景區：南山文化旅遊區、大小洞天旅遊區；三個國家4A級旅遊景區：亞龍灣國家旅遊渡假區、天涯海角遊覽區、蜈支洲島旅遊渡假區。此外還有許多別具特色的旅遊景點。這裡的海如玉，沙若脂，灣似虹，景如畫，使三亞贏得了「不是夏威夷，勝過夏威夷」的美譽。

請看這邊！這些美麗的花是三亞市花，叫三角梅。花的那邊就是舉世聞名的長達18公里的椰夢長廊。三亞是令人神往的長壽之鄉，有著中國無與倫比的優美的海灣，純淨的海水，潔白的沙灘，種類繁多的珊瑚、海貝和熱帶魚。近年來，三亞市沿河建設的觀景平台、節日廣場、階梯式泊岸、景觀步行橋等娛樂休閒設施，強調生態文化主題，突出「白鷺落枝頭，魚蟹棲根底」的紅樹林景觀，使城市中心出現了一系列融觀光、休閒與城市商業活動於一體的景觀帶，與其他國際旅遊休閒都市

中南地區

相比更加突出了濃郁的熱帶風情，是真正的國際性熱帶濱海風景旅遊城市，是旅遊者的天堂。

朋友們，我們要遊覽的目的地已經到了，請盡情的享受國際旅遊城的美麗風光吧！

Greater East Sea & Yalong Bay （大東海和亞龍灣）

Dadong Sea

Good morning, ladies and gentlemen!

According to the schedule, we'll visit the Greater East sea, or the Dadong Sea and Yalong Bay. As we are approaching Dadong Sea, I'd like to introduce Dadong Sea Tourist Resort. This resort is located along the bay between Yulin Port and Luhuitou Park and is about 2 kilometers away from east of Sanya. Some first-class vacation hotels have been built along the coastal vocation zone. This area has a crescent shaped bay, shining sea, sea waves, clear water, warm sunshine, coconut trees, rainbows, blue sky, sails, and sand throughout the year. This combination of a pristine and scenic environment and first class hotels with excellent customer service provides visitors with an outstanding and integrated modern vacationing and touring experience and make Yalong Bay and the Dadong Sea an irresistible tourist attraction. The peculiar coastal scenery of the tropical region makes the bay even more beautiful. Words cannot begin to describe the satisfaction and comfort you get from a leisurely swim in the sea, picking shells, digging for crabs, and sunbathing and building sand castles on the beach. It's no wonder that vast numbers of tourists every year are attracted by the Dadong Sea's natural beauty.

Even during the winter, the water temperature of Dadong Sea is between 18℃ -22℃. With warm water and flat white sand, the Dadong Sea Tourist Resort has become famous both at home and abroad. This beautiful resort is an ideal spot for winter swimming and scuba diving, as well as sunbathing. The beautiful beach began to catch the world's attention in the middle of 20thCentury. After Hainan province was set up and became a special economic zone in 1988, luxury hotels were built and marine leisure activities such as scuba diving, swimming, and sightseeing in submarines and boats became available to tourists. In 1992, the Dadong Sea Tourist Resort was listed as one of China's "40 Best National Tourist Attractions" by the State Tourism Administration. If you need stimulation, please go to the "Water Playing Paradise". Here you can jump into the pool directly from the diving platform. A more stimulating and scary but interesting experience is driving a motorboat on the sea. You can also dive or take a sightseeing submarine called "Mermaid" to see firsthand the wonders of tropical marine life. The "Mermaid" remains the world's most advanced sightseeing submarine. It can dive 75 meters deep under the sea and carry up to 46 passengers. The strong power lights between portholes for sightseeing illuminate the surrounding marine environment for the sightseers' pleasure. And the video provided by the submarine's under-water camera makes it possible for the remote views under the sea to unfold right before your eyes.

Now let me tell you about a local legend. Many, many years ago, the local folks around the Bay of Dadong Sea lived a quiet and peaceful life based mainly on fishing. The black dragon from Luobi Cave in Sanya was deeply attracted by the sunny beach, the blue water, and the calm sea there. He pleaded with the Dragon King of the South China Sea to turn the Dadong Sea into his own private playground. The Dragon King agreed. But nobody realized that the black dragon would bring him a typhoon, which had creased high waves and swift currents in Dadong Sea. That greatly affected the fishing and normal life of the local folks. Thus the Dragon King of the South China Sea only allowed the black dragon to venture into the Dadong Sea every once in a while to exercise and play in its waters.

Thank you for your attention. If there is anyone who wants to join the above activities, please let me know.

Yalong Bay

Hello everyone! Look at the beautiful scenery ahead. This spot is the Yalong Bay National Holiday area and we'll be visiting it shortly.

Yalong Bay is crescent-shaped and is located 25 kilometers from downtown Sanya. As recently as 16 years ago, Yalong Bay was a wild and unknown place in China. This natural wonder's unparalleled beauty inspired the Chinese Government to create the world's first and only national tropical tourism site. Thus construction of the Yalong Bay resort began in 1992 following approval from the State Council. And now it has become an extremely charming and picturesque national tropic tourism site. The site, including its beach, covers some 16. 8 square kilometers.

The bay was originally named "Long Ya Bay". The word "Long" in Chinese stands for dragon, while "Ya" stands for Asia. Thus Yalong Bay was considered to be the bay of the dragon both in Sanya and the rest of Asia. Due to its naturally attractive setting, Yalong Bay has been celebrated as "The first bay under the heaven". In 1992, Yalong Bay, along with its neighboring Dadong Sea attraction, was designated one of China's top forty tourist attractions. In 1994, Antonio Enriquez Savignac, the secretary general of the UN World Tourism Organization, visited Yalong Bay. He was deeply taken by its beautiful landscape and wrote, "Yalong Bay is a genuine heaven with the advantageous natural conditions, the silver sand beach, the limpid sea water, the lengthy and exquisite seashore, and unpolluted mountains with their primitive rough vegetation. "

Yalong Bay is surrounded on three sides by mountains covered with their original old growth trees and plants. The other side of the bay opens wide to the calm sea like a new moon. The sea beach is even and wide, extending over 7 kilometers with shallow water along the coast which extends 50-60 meters to the sea. The sand is white, fine and soft, the sun shines more than 300 days every year, and moun-tains with strange and interesting rock formations loom over the bay. The seawater is blue, clear, and transparent to 7. 9 meters. The sea is calm and its bottom is flat. In the layered clear waters, tourists can do all kinds of aquatic sports all year round, including swimming, diving, touring Yalong Bay in a submarine, watching coral reefs and different colored tropical fish. Visitors can also do rock-climbing at Jinmu and Yalong Capes. In addition to enjoying the sunshine and sandy beach, visitors can take advantage of the comfort and convenience provided by other nearby tourist spots, including Yalong Bay's Central Square, the Seashell Exhibition Hall, Butterfly Valley, a tennis club and golf course and some luxurious hotels.

Yalong Bay is such a charming picturesque setting that no other places in the country could compare with it. People who have traveled here are deeply attracted by its natural beauty. Comfortable tourist facilities and services, wide range of sight-seeing and recreational activities have made it a real paradise for Chinese and foreign tourists.

中南地區

大東海

女士們、先生們，大家好！首先我介紹一下大東海旅遊景區的情況。大東海景區位於三亞市東的榆林港和鹿回頭之間的海灣沿岸，距市區2　公里。月牙形的海灣、遼闊晶瑩的海面、陽光明媚的海濱、椰樹嫵媚、海浪滔滔、彩虹絢麗、碧水藍天、船帆飄飄、白沙融融；清潔的環境、酒店熱情周到的服務，營造出大東海海灣舉世無雙的魅力。獨特的熱帶海濱風光使得大東海灣特別的美麗。遨遊海中，我們無法用語言來描述從中得到的舒適和愜意：休閒游泳、享受光浴、挑選貝殼、挖掘螃蟹、壘築沙塔等等。大東海美麗的自然風光每年都吸引著眾多的遊客。

大東海冬季水溫介於18℃　～22℃，這裡「水暖沙白灘平」使大東海渡假區的風光早已蜚聲海內外，它不僅是一個美麗的冬泳避寒的渡假勝地，更是進行潛水和陽光浴的最佳首選。大東海海灘的美麗早在20世紀中期就引起了世人的矚目。1988年，海南建省成為經濟特區後，豪華的海濱渡假酒店拔地而起，一些海上休閒項目，如潛水、觀光潛艇和摩托艇等更是新穎別緻。1992年，大東海渡假區被國家旅遊局評為「中國旅遊景區四十佳」之一。如果想玩水過把癮，你就去「戲水樂園」，那裡有高高的入水台，可以直接跳入游泳池，更加驚險而又有趣的戲水是駕駛海上摩托艇。此外，你既可以潛水戲水，也可以乘坐「美人魚號」觀光潛艇去體驗熱帶海洋世界的奇觀。「美人魚號」是當今世界上性能最先進的水下觀光潛艇，可載46名乘客，最深能潛入海下75米，展現在你眼前便是那遙遠而絢麗多姿的海洋世界，你可以將海洋裡的風光一覽無餘。

我來給大家講一個來自民間，有關大東海的傳說：很久很久以前，大東海灣附近的百姓過著安靜祥和的生活，他們主要靠打魚為生。大東海灣的晴空麗日、碧波萬頃、風平浪靜深深地吸引了身居三亞落筆洞的黑龍，他央求南海龍王把大東海借給他戲水解悶，南海龍王答應了，沒想到黑龍把颱風也一同帶來了，弄得大東海浪高流急，給百姓的生活和打魚帶來了影響，於是，南海龍王只准黑龍偶爾來光顧此地，活動筋骨。

這就是大東海遊覽區，謝謝大家！

亞龍灣

諸位朋友們！請看前面這美麗的景色，這就是我們要遊覽的亞龍灣國家旅遊渡假區。

亞龍灣酷似半月形，據三亞市25　公里。就在16年前，亞龍灣還是一處鮮為人知的荒僻海灘。這一自然奇觀以其無與倫比的美景促使國家政府開闢建設第一國家景觀。亞龍灣經國務院批准於1992年開始興建。現在的亞龍灣已今非昔比，成為一個風光如畫、景色迷人、具有熱帶風情的旅遊渡假區。渡假區規劃面積包括海灘在內為16.8平方公里。

亞龍灣原名為「琅琊灣」，是黎族的地名，1996年根據該地名音譯而得。漢語的「Long」即「龍」，「Ya」即「亞」。亞龍灣既是三亞的龍灣，又是亞洲的龍灣。亞龍灣是自然形成的灣，風情萬種，美麗宜人，享有「天下第一灣」的美譽。1992　年，亞龍灣與其近鄰大東海一道被評為中國最佳40個景點之一。聯合國世界旅遊組織秘書長薩維尼亞克對亞龍灣考察後，興奮地揮筆寫道：「亞龍灣自然風光得天獨厚，沙灘潔白如銀，海水清澈透明，海濱綿延嫵媚，崖懸壁陡山疊，植被原始粗獷，這才是真正的人間天堂。」

亞龍灣三面依山，一面傍海，這裡的山布滿了原始植被，這裡的灣風平浪靜，恰似一輪明月。亞龍灣沙灘平緩寬闊，沙粒潔白細軟，綿延7公里，淺海區寬達五六十米；陽光明媚，光照日年達300　多天；灣北群山疊嶂，崖懸壁陡；海水清澈見底，能見度在7.9米以上，海底平坦無礁岩。一年四季，遊客們可以從事各種各樣的水上運動，如游泳、潛水、遨遊亞龍灣海底世界、欣賞那些千姿百態五顏六色的珊瑚礁、觀賞成千上萬種的熱帶魚，還可以在海灣的錦母角、亞龍角攀岩探險；還可以享受到陽光、沙灘帶給我們的快樂；更可以享受那些觀光及休閒場所帶給我們的方便，如亞龍灣中心廣場、貝殼館、蝴蝶谷、網球俱樂部、高爾夫球場和高檔豪華酒店等。

亞龍灣如詩如畫，自然風光國內絕無僅有，凡到過亞龍灣的人無不被這裡的美景所陶醉，舒適完善的旅遊渡假設施和獨具特色的旅遊項目，真正成為國內外旅遊者嚮往的渡假天堂！

Tianya-Haijiao （ End of the Earth ） （天涯海角）

Good morning, ladies and gentlemen! Please allow me on behalf of our Sanya International Travel Service to extend our sincere welcome to you. I hope that your visit to this ancient place will be a happy and memorable experience.

Now, in a few minutes we will be leaving for Tianya-Haijiao which is one of China's most famous scenic spots. Tianya-Haijiao is situated at the southern most tip of the Hainan Island. It is about 23 kilometers west of Sanya and faces the South China

中南地區

Sea, while Tianya Town's Mount Maling provides a stunning backdrop. The beach here is strewn with all kinds of rare stones. Two which stand out are a pair of large green-grey stones overlooking the beach. Both of them are more than 10 meters high and 60 meters long and have inscriptions carved on them. One is carved with two Chinese characters "Tianya" by a local prefect named Cheng Zhe from Yazhou (today's Sanya) during Qing Dynasty (1644-1911). The other has the characters for "Haijiao" written by a local prefect named Wang Yi from Qiongya in 1938. Tianya means Sky Limit and Haijiao means the End of the sea. From these dates onward, Tianya-Haijiao become a place of interest. Standing in the midst of the big stones, visitors can see that a vast billowy sea is surging up and seemingly engulfing the sky; at the same time, the sky is hanging low, as if to deliberately provoke the sea. No matter how hard you try to look, you can see nothing but a boundless haze before you. All that makes you feel like you have reached the end of the earth. So only when you get here can you get the feeling that you are really on an island; only when you get here do you have an exotic and romantic feeling.

Seeing only some groups of rare rocks standing at the center of the spot, you would be puzzled and wonder "Aren't there merely some big stones in Tianya-Haijiao? Why do so many visitors come here everyday?" Yes it is true, but the stones are rare and fantastic, especially the big stones that rise up into the vast and limitless skies. The stones with inscriptions carved by famous notables reflect traditional culture both from ancient and more recent times.

Now let's go to enjoy the rock "Pillar Under Southern Sky". It was said the characters, "Pillar Under Southern Sky", were written by Fan Yunti, a famous Qing Dynasty scholar. There is a moving story about it. In ancient times, the sea near Li'an, in Lingshui County, Hainan Province was very rough and turbulent. People could not travel on its surface and had hard and poverty-stricken lives. Hearing this, two fairy maidens made up their mind to do something helpful to them. They left heaven and stayed in the sea. All of a sudden, the wind died down and the waves subsided. Then the fishermen could peacefully go fishing. On hearing about this, the Lady Queen Mother got very angry. She insisted that the fairy maidens were not allowed to interfere in human affairs. So Thunder God was sent to arrest them and take them back for punishment in heaven. The maidens refused and were willing to turn themselves into double-sail shaped rocks for the fishermen's navigation. When the rock was split in two by the lightning, one half flew onto the beach of the End of the Earth. People admired the fairy maidens for being upright and above flattery and called the rock "Pillar under Southern Sky". The other remained in the sea of Li'an. So the rare stones are famous not only because they have a history of several thousand-year-old. They are also precious because they contain traces of traditional Chinese culture. These cultural traces are precious and are the reason why people have never passed up an opportunity to come to the End of the Earth when touring Hainan Island. Today the End of the Earth is not only full of historical sites, but is also a place where the International Marriage Celebrations are held once every year. The year 2009 will mark the 13thanniversary of these celebrations.

Now look ahead, this is the vast South China Sea. There are East and West Island, which can be reached by boat. You can enjoy all kinds of marine recreational activities there. To the left appears the sculpture area of notables in Tianya. All of these statues are of famous people who have played an important role in Sanya's history. Every statue has a touching story to tell from ancient times. To the right appears the coconut tree-fringed soft-sand beach. There the sunshine and blue sky are joined with the green sea forming an unmatched picturesque natural setting.

Why don't you take some pictures here? It's high time to enjoy the gentle sea breeze and admire these big rare and beautiful stones. Have you noticed that there are masses of pits on the stones? Those are the creation of typical sea wave erosion. We can imagine how the seaside stones were shaped. Can you tell who were the real artists having created these beautiful rare stones? Of course they couldn't be human beings, but were the sea waves. This provides a scientific explanation for the heap of rare stones

中
南
地
區

in the End of the Earth.

Look everybody! There along the rocky road on the seashore, a great variety of souvenirs at Tanya shopping center are waiting for us! Let's go!

女士們，先生們，大家好！

請允許我代表我們三亞國際旅行社向諸位的到來表示熱烈的歡迎，真心希望你們的旅遊將成為幸福之旅，永生難忘。

我們馬上就要起程去遊覽地天涯海角。天涯海角風景區是中國最著名的遊覽區之一，位於海南島的最南方，從三亞沿海岸向西23公里的天涯鎮下馬嶺山。前海後山，風景獨特。遊覽區內，奇石林立，被一對矗立在其中的青灰色巨石俯瞰著，這一對高10多米，長60多米的巨石赫然入目。兩石分別刻有「天涯」和「海角」字樣，意為天之邊緣，海之盡頭。「天涯」二字是由清代雍正年間，崖州（今天的三亞）知府程哲題寫；「海角」二字是由瓊崖守備司令王毅於1938年題寫，從此，這裡就成為天下聞名的一道風景線。置身於奇石間，只見茫茫大海波濤洶湧，融碧水、藍天於一色煙波浩瀚，這一切似乎使你感覺來到了天的邊際、海的盡頭。只有身臨其境的人才會有這種感受，也只有身臨其境的人才會體會到浪漫和別樣的風情。

當看到景區中心地帶有一些石頭時，你也許會感到有些不解：「天涯海角景區不就是這些石頭嗎？為什麼每天的遊客卻絡繹不絕呢？」的確不假，但這裡的岩礁巨石各個千姿百態、婀娜多姿，雄偉的巨石高聳入雲、直指蒼穹，無與倫比。學者們揮筆灑墨刻畫在巨石上的文字象徵著從古到今不同時代的傳統文化。

接下來，讓我們一起欣賞美景「南天一柱」吧。「南天一柱」據說是清代宣統年間崖州知州範雲梯所書。有一個非常動人的故事，據說很久以前，在海南省陵水縣黎安海域，海風狂怒，大浪滔天，人們無法出海打魚，只能過貧窮艱苦的日子。兩個仙女得知後偷偷下凡，立身於南海中，剎那間，海面上風平浪靜，漁民們可以平安地出海了。王母娘娘聽說後惱羞成怒，派雷公電母捉她們回去受懲。仙女們不從，化為雙峰石，繼續為漁家指航打魚。後來，雙峰石被劈成了兩截，其中一截飛到天涯之旁，成為今天的「南天一柱」，而另一截在黎安附近的海中。奇石之所以能吸引這麼多遊客，不是因為它們有多麼的古老，而是因為它們有著豐富的文化內涵。今天的天涯海角不僅是遊覽勝地，每年一度的三亞天涯海角國際婚慶節，都會在這裡舉行，2009年已經是第十三屆了。

請看前方，這就是浩瀚的南海，這邊是東島，那邊是西島，乘坐小船即可到達，島上有各種各樣的海上娛樂活動。左側是天涯歷史名人雕塑園，數十個雕塑人物都和三亞的歷史有著千絲萬縷的關聯。每個人物都在人生旅途中都有著扣人心弦的經歷。右側是椰樹環繞的沙灘，和煦的陽光，蔚藍的天空和綠色的海洋交織相融。好一幅風景如畫的自然景觀，真是令人陶醉，舉世無雙。

拍些照片吧！海上望去，陣陣微風拂面，讓我們盡情地享受。那些美麗的奇石外觀各異，讓我們盡情地欣賞。大家注意到石頭上的凹凸點了嗎？這就是海浪長年累月沖刷拍打的傑作。由此，我們不難想像出海岸上那些千姿百態的磊磊奇石是怎樣形成的。雕塑這些美麗石頭的真正藝術家們不是人類，而是海浪。巍然屹立在天海之間的奇石就是滄海桑田變遷的見證。

諸位往這邊看！沿海岸順著天涯路走，那裡就是天涯購物中心，有各種各樣的紀念品，我們去觀賞購物吧。

Bo'ao （博鰲）

Hello, everyone! According to the schedule, we will visit Bo'ao today.

For most of you, I suppose this is the first trip here. While you are here, you will learn about the culture and history, as well as the reality of modern Bo'ao. Since it is home to the Asian Forum, this place is well known both at home and abroad. It is a small water town, which is situated in Qionghai City. It only covers an area of 41. 8 square kilometers, including an aquatic area of 8. 5 square km. It is about 20

中南地區

kilometers from here to Jiaji town, 110 kilometers to Haikou city and 100 kilometers to Meilan Airport. There are 9 functional touring areas, including the City of Sun, Dongyu Islet, Wanquan River, Jade-belt Beach, Jiuqu River, and Longtan Ridge. It also now boasts Asia's only Links style golf course, the 18 hole Shapo Islet golf course. And Dongyu Islet now boasts a Hotel Sofitel which is a cultural center and meeting place of the Asian Forum. And another five first class golf courses will be completed soon.

Bo'ao Water Town is located at the mouth of Wanquan River. It has all the ingredients needed for a romantic getaway:tree-fringed rivers and lakes, green mountains, and islets with rivers and tropical plants. There are soft-sandy beaches with coconut trees, blue skies with white clouds, hot springs with rare stones, bushes with flowers, and a harbor with sand dykes. The Wanquan, Jiuqu, and Longgun Rivers and Yuanyang, Shapo and Dongyu islets, as well as three mountains wind their way toward the east. The three rivers glide gently on their way to the South China Sea and down to the Pacific Ocean. The harmony between nature and human development here makes the mouth of Wanquan River a real charming, picturesque setting. It is one of the finest examples of nature conservation in the world and is why Bo'ao was selected to be the location of the Asian Forum.

Visitors are attracted to the Bo'ao Water Town not only by its downtown view, but by the surrounding countryside's natural landscape and the area's cultural resources. The landscape and topography here are unique. It is a place where rivers, lakes, seas, mountains and islets are connected together. On both sides of the newly built roads are vegetable gardens, orchards, villages, paddyfield, small eucalyptus forest, coconut trees and sisal hemps. In the distance, tourists can see the smoke rising up from villages, farmers working in the fields, and fishermen casting and drawing their nets.

Bo'ao Water Town started attracting visitors only in 1992. By 2003 the first and second stages of the town's construction had been completed. The town now has convenient transportation, good communication and conference facilities, Golden Coast Hotel, Jinjiang Spa Hotel, Blue Coast Villa, resorts, golf courses, and hot springs. The Bo'ao Water Town of today has become not only a major tourist attraction, but is also the only regular Chinese location for the International Convention Organization Headquarter in Asia. The first session of Bo'ao Forum for Asia was held on April 12, 2002, and nearly 2000 representatives and journalists from 48 countries and areas participated in it. Bo'ao has become the focus of Asia and the world. On seeing the beauty of the location for the Asian Forum, the former chairman of China, Jiang Zemin praised Bo'ao in his poem: "There is a new look at Wanquan;Night breeze rises from the broad waters; Outs-tanding people from all over the world get together here; and it makes Bo'ao more beautiful. "

If the upper reaches of the Wanquan River are developed, you could have a full view of the beauty of the Bo'ao Water Town and Wangquan River.

各位朋友，大家好！按照旅遊計劃，我們今天的遊覽地是博鰲。

多數朋友是第一次來博鰲吧！希望本次旅遊使你們可以瞭解一些關於博鰲的歷史、文化，親自目睹現代化的博鰲。今天的博鰲以亞洲論壇的會址而聞名。博鰲是一座水上小城，位於瓊海市。包括水上面積8.5平方公里在內，其總面積僅有41.8平方公里，距嘉積鎮約20公里，距海口市110公里，距美蘭機場約100公里，內設九個功能區：太陽城、東嶼島、萬泉河、玉帶灘、九曲江、龍潭嶺等。沙坡島的18洞高爾夫球場在亞洲別具一格。亞洲論壇會展中心——索菲特酒店巍然屹立在東嶼島上。另外5個獨具匠心的高爾夫球場與星級酒店、亞洲論壇會議中心系列設施遙相呼應。

博鰲水城坐落於萬泉河口，擁有一切吸引浪漫主義的景觀：叢林環抱的河湖、四季碧綠的青山、擁有河流和熱帶植物的島嶼，還有椰樹下柔軟的沙灘、藍天白雲、奇石溫泉、花朵草叢及沙壩海港。三江：萬泉河、九曲江、龍滾河，三島：東嶼島、沙坡島、鴛鴦島，還有三山皆蜿蜒向東。三江交匯緩緩流入中國南海，匯入

中南地區

太平洋。自然與和諧在萬泉河口處打造出一幅真正迷人而景色秀麗的圖畫，是世界上自然資源保護的最佳典範，故而被選為博鰲亞洲論壇的永久性會址。

在博鰲水城，最吸引人的風景區不只是水城內，水城鄉村的自然景色和文化資源更獨具特色。融江、河、湖、海、山麓、島嶼於一體，新建的公路兩旁融田園、果園、椰林、村莊、稻田、劍麻、小桉樹林等風光令人目不暇接。遙遠望去，只見村莊炊煙裊裊，農民在地裡勞作，漁民在水裡撒網捕魚。

博鰲水城於1992 年規劃建設，到2003 年第一期和第二期工程竣工。完善了交通、通信和會議設施，興建了金海岸、錦江溫泉大酒店、藍色海岸別墅、渡假村、高爾夫球場、溫泉等。今天的博鰲水城不僅是遊客們嚮往的遊覽勝地，也是作為亞洲地區唯一定期定址的國際會議組織總部所在地。2002年4月12日召開了博鰲亞洲論壇首屆年會，來自48個國家和地區的近2000名代表與新聞記者參加會議，博鰲成為亞洲乃至世界的關注點。

中南地區

國家圖書館出版品預行編目（CIP）資料

中國著名旅遊景區導遊詞精選：英漢對照（大中原地區） /
王浪主編 . -- 第一版 . -- 臺北市：崧博出版：崧燁文化

　面；　公分
POD 版
ISBN 978-957-735-672-7(平裝)

1. 旅遊 2. 導遊 3. 中國

690　　　　　　　　　　　　　　　　　　108001895

書　　名：中國著名旅遊景區導遊詞精選：英漢對照（大中原地區）
作　　者：王浪 主編
發 行 人：黃振庭
出 版 者：崧博出版事業有限公司
發 行 者：崧燁文化事業有限公司
E-m a i l：sonbookservice@gmail.com
粉 絲 頁：　　　　　　　網 址：
地　　址：台北市中正區重慶南路一段六十一號八樓 815 室
8F.-815, No.61, Sec. 1, Chongqing S. Rd., Zhongzheng
Dist., Taipei City 100, Taiwan (R.O.C.)
電　　話：(02)2370-3310 傳　真：(02) 2370-3210
總 經 銷：紅螞蟻圖書有限公司
地　　址: 台北市內湖區舊宗路二段 121 巷 19 號
電　　話:02-2795-3656 傳真 :02-2795-4100　　網址：
印　　刷：京峯彩色印刷有限公司（京峰數位）

定　　價：800 元
發行日期：2019 年 02 月第一版
◎ 本書以 POD 印製發行